W9-ADL-442

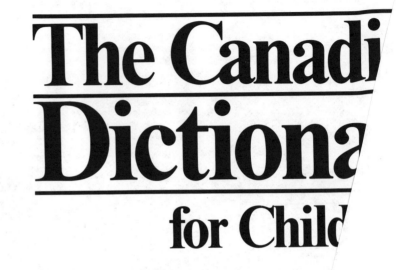

The Canadi

Dictiona

for Child

The Canadian Dictionary

for Children

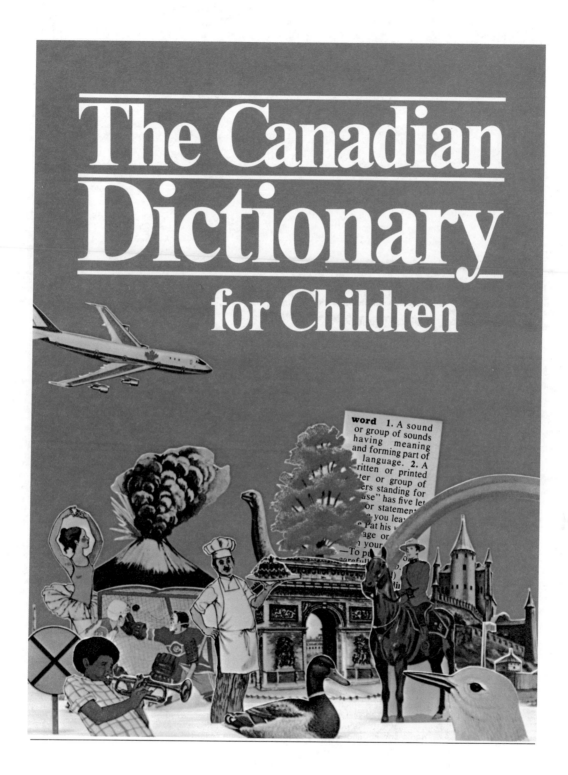

word 1. A sound or group of sounds having meaning and forming part of language. 2. A ...ritten or printed ...ter or group of ...ers standing for ...se" has five let... or statement... ...you lea... ...Pat his ... ...age or ... ...your ... —To p... ...reful...

Collier Macmillan Canada, Inc.

Canadian Cataloguing in Publication Data

Main entry under title:
The Canadian dictionary for children

ISBN 0-02-991210-5

1. English language—Dictionaries, Juvenile.

PE1628.5.C35 1979   j423   C80-2050-2

Printed and bound in Canada
ISBN 02.991210.5

3   4   5   87 86 85 84

CONTENTS

Supervising Editor   Lawrence Haskett

Editors   David Friend, Fiona Woodward Lamer, Carolyne
Lederer, Cas Pindel, Barbara Sack, Mary Willmot

Pronunciation Editor   Jack Chambers, Department of Linguistics, University
of Toronto

Consultants   Thomas Paikeday, Paikeday Publishing
Robert Strain, Assistant Co-ordinator, Curricular
Services, Prince George, British Columbia
Ronald Wardhaugh, Chairman, Department of
Linguistics, University of Toronto

Preface

The Canadian Dictionary for Children is a book prepared especially for use by young students. It is intended to be the first real dictionary that students use in the classroom. *The Canadian Dictionary for Children* is part of a complete series of school dictionaries planned by Collier Macmillan Canada, Inc. This series is designed to cover the entire range of student dictionary needs up through Grade 9.

Natural Language In planning *The Canadian Dictionary for Children,* the goal of the editors was to produce a book that would successfully answer the questions students have about language. We began by asking ourselves a question: If students in their early school years have great potential for learning language, what can we do to encourage and to develop that potential? Our answer to this question was to make a dictionary of natural language, the language that students themselves write and speak.

When a student looks up a word in *The Canadian Dictionary for Children,* the first thing he or she will see is the entry word printed solid, exactly as it would appear in a book, magazine, or newspaper. There are no dots, dashes, or spaces between syllables to create confusion. The entry word is immediately followed by the definitions. Thus the most frequently used parts of the entry appear first—spelling and meaning. Specialized language information, such as syllabication, pronunciation, parts of speech, and inflections, is set off separately at the end of the entry. Students can easily locate the information, yet it will not interfere with their reading of the definition.

Complete Sentences The basic unit of the English language is the sentence. *The Canadian Dictionary for Children* therefore consists entirely of complete sentences, with the exception of a short identifying phrase at the beginning of a definition. Following this phrase, the remainder of the definition is entirely in sentence form. There are no abbreviations, symbols, or artificial phrases. Because the natural way to learn the meaning of a word is from its context, *The Canadian Dictionary for Children* makes a practice of defining through context, by the use of one or more sentences showing the entry word in use. These example sentences enable students to learn new words just as they learn them in their own language experience.

Informative Illustrations Just as the definitions in *The Canadian Dictionary for Children* reflect actual language, its illustrations depict things as they appear in the real world. Through the use of colour, it is possible to convey much more information about an animal, bird, reptile, flower, tree, or the like than can be given by a black-and-white drawing or photograph, or even by a verbal definition. And just as the dictionary's definitions show words in context, its illustrations show objects in context—tools are shown in use, musical instruments are shown being played, and abstract concepts are explained by familiar situations.

Vocabulary Selection The vocabulary selection in *The Canadian Dictionary for Children* is based on a careful and systematic study of the words actually encountered by students, both in and out of the classroom. The editors have made a special examination of the vocabulary used in the current reading series of all major publishers. In addition, all standard word lists for this grade level have been examined, as well as many popular fiction and nonfiction books. The result of this research is a word list of nearly 30 000 entries.

Readability Control In writing a dictionary for students in the early grades, one of the most difficult problems is making sure that the definitions are simple enough to be understood. This means that the reading level must be strictly controlled. The ideal readability formula for a dictionary would be to have every definition written at least one grade level below its entry, but it became evident that this would not be possible. No meaningful definitions could be written for certain simple words without using vocabulary from a higher grade level. After a trial-and-error period to establish the lowest possible level at which definitions could be written, the following formula was established.

READING LEVEL OF ENTRY WORD	Ungraded	8	7	6	5	4	3	2	1
READING LEVEL OF DEFINITION	5	5	5	5	4	4	3	3	3

The working procedure for the readability control was as follows: First, the normal grade level of the entry word was established. Then the vocabulary of the word's definition was measured, and all words that ranked above the acceptable grade level were identified on a print out. The editors were then responsible for altering the text as necessary to bring the reading level down to the desired grade. This was never a completely mechanical process. In some cases, "unacceptable" words could not be taken out of the definition because they were essential to the word's meaning. In addition to this, a separate operation measured the overall readability of the manuscript, according to both the Harris-Jacobson and the Dale-Chall formulas.

Language Notes To encourage students to browse through *The Canadian Dictionary for Children* on their own, we have included a special feature called *language notes*. These are short essays about interesting facets of our language. Language notes can be found throughout the dictionary, and they are identified by colour.

Our goal in making *The Canadian Dictionary for Children* was to produce a book that young students would find easy to use, and also one that they would enjoy using. Every element of the dictionary is part of our effort to achieve this goal. We feel that *The Canadian Dictionary for Children* will show students just how fascinating the English language can be.

Sample Column

ENTRY WORD
See page G11

motorboat A boat that is run by a motor. Some motorboats have outboard motors. Others have larger inboard engines.
mo·tor·boat (mō′tər bōt′) *noun*, *plural* **motorboats.**

motorcycle A two-wheeled vehicle that looks like a bicycle but is bigger and heavier and is run by an engine.
mo·tor·cy·cle (mō′tər sī′kəl) *noun*, *plural* **motorcycles.**

DEFINITION
See page G17

mound A hill or heap of earth, stones, or other material. *Noun.*
—To pile in a hill or heap. Bill likes to *mound* ice cream on top of his pie. *Verb.*
mound (mound) *noun*, *plural* **mounds;** *verb,* **mounded, mounding.**

EXAMPLE SENTENCE
See page G22

mountain **1.** A mass of land that rises very high above the land around it. **2.** A very large pile or amount of something. There was a *mountain* of trash at the dump.
moun·tain (mount′ən) *noun, plural* **mountains.**

ENTRY LINE
See page G24

mountain lion A large wild cat that lives in the mountains of North and South America. This animal is usually called a **cougar.** Look up **cougar** for more information.

mountainous **1.** Having many mountains. There is good skiing in that *mountainous* area. **2.** Very big; huge. The storm piled up *mountainous* drifts of snow.
moun·tain·ous (mount′ən əs) *adjective.*

PRONUNCIATION
See page G25

Mountie *Canadian.* A member of the Royal Canadian Mounted Police. This word is also spelled **mountie.**
Mountie (mount′ē) *noun, plural* **Mounties.**

ILLUSTRATION
See page G38

Mountie

LANGUAGE NOTE
See page G39

▲ The word **Mountie** refers to the fact that, when the Mounties were first organized as the North West Mounted Police, each officer rode a horse.

G9

Guide to the Dictionary

A dictionary is a very special kind of book. Everyone in the world who knows how to read uses a dictionary, and most people use it very often. *The Canadian Dictionary for Children* is even more special than most, because it has been written and organized especially for *you*. It has all the things that other dictionaries have, but we have put them together in a way that will help you to use the book.

Turn to any page in the dictionary. Probably the first thing you will notice are the pictures. Everyone knows that often it is much easier and clearer to describe something with a picture than it is with words. We have used pictures as well as words. The next thing you will notice are the words in heavy black type. Pick out one of these words on any page and then read what the dictionary says about it. Are you surprised that it is easy to read and understand? You shouldn't be. We planned the book that way. It uses words you know to describe the words that will interest you.

Do you want to find out about new words? This book will help you. But first you must learn how to use it. This *Guide* will show you how to use the dictionary to find out many things about words. Read it carefully. Do the exercises called "Try This." Then use the dictionary as often as you can. You will learn new words that will tell you about many exciting new things. And you will find out more and more about the words you already know.

Some people read dictionaries for fun. Try to find out why!

How to Find a Word

THE ENTRY

You can think of your dictionary as a long list of words. Each word in the list is called an *entry word.* These words are printed in heavy black letters—**like this.** They are placed at the left-hand side of each column. This makes it easier for you to find the word you are looking for. The word *entry* means "a way to go into a place." The way that you go into your dictionary is by looking up one of these entry words.

All the information about an entry word comes right after the word itself. It is printed in lighter letters than the entry word. This information makes up what we call an *entry.*

braid   A strip made by weaving together three or more long pieces of hair, straw, or cloth. Carol wears her hair in *braids.* Henry's band uniform is decorated with gold *braid. Noun.*
—To weave together long pieces of hair, straw, or cloth. Ralph tried to *braid* a belt from strips of leather. *Verb.*

ALPHABETICAL ORDER

There are thousands of entry words in *The Canadian Dictionary for Children.* But when you use your dictionary, you will be looking for just *one* word at a time. Just imagine how hard it would be to use this book if all the entry words were put in just any old way. How long do you think it would take to find the word you wanted?

The detective in this picture is looking for just one person the same way you would look for just one word in the dictionary. He has to look at every picture in the book, because the pictures aren't arranged in any kind of order. But in *The Canadian Dictionary for Children* the words are arranged in a special way, so that they will be easy for you to find. The special way of arranging words in your dictionary is called *alphabetical order.*

You can think of your dictionary as a long list of words. This list follows the order of the letters of the alphabet. All the words that start with **a** come at the beginning of the list. Those that start with **b** come next, and so on through **z.**

If you think about this, you can see that it isn't enough just to put all the **a** words first, the **b** words second, and so forth. There are many different words that begin with each letter. For example, there are so many **a** words in your dictionary that it takes 46 pages to list them all!

All the words that start with the same letter are put into alphabetical order by using the second letter. Since all the words in the **a** part of the book start with the same letter, the second letter decides the order.

1. **also**   3. **apple**
2. **anyone**   4. **ashamed**

Sometimes the second, or even the third, letters of different words are the same. Then you have to look even farther along to find the word.

1	2	3
accident	**allegiance**	**article**
acorn	**alligator**	**artificial**
across	**allow**	**artist**

GUIDE WORDS

Suppose you wanted to look up the word **whisky-jack.** First you would turn to the part of the book where the **w** words are. If you do this, you will find that the **w** words begin on page 693 and end on page 718. But you do not have to hunt through every page of **w** words to find **whisky-jack.** Instead, you can look at the top outside corner of each page. There you will see pairs of words like these:

whereabouts/whirl   **whirlpool/whiz**   **who/widen**

These are called *guide words. Guide* means "show the way," and *guide words* show you the way to the word you are looking for. The first guide word tells you the first entry word on the page, and the second guide word tells you the last.

If you look at the first pair of guide words, **whereabouts** and **whirl,** you can see that your word **whisky-jack** can't be on that page. **Whisky-jack** comes after **whirl** in alphabetical order. You will have to look farther on. If you turn to the page that has **who** and **widen** as guide words, you will see that you've gone too far. **Who** comes after **whisky-jack** in

G13

alphabetical order. The right place to find **whisky-jack** is on the page with **whirlpool** and **whiz** as guide words. **Whisky-jack** comes between these two words in alphabetical order.

whirlpool   **whiz**

TRY THIS

Look up each of the following entry words in your dictionary. Write each word. Then next to it write the guide words that are on the page with that word.

enormous	machine	join
history	measure	order

How to Spell a Word

SPELLING WORDS CORRECTLY ⸻

The student in this picture is correcting a spelling mistake. It is very easy to spell words correctly when you use *The Canadian Dictionary for Children.* That is because the entry words in your dictionary look exactly the way they do in a book, magazine, or newspaper.

To spell a word correctly, spell it exactly as it appears in heavy type in your dictionary.

half	**postage**
half-mast	**postage stamp**
halfway	**post card**
Hallowe'en	**postmaster**

USING THE SPELLING TABLE ───────────────

The first section in this Guide was called "How to Find A Word." In that section you learned how to look up words in your dictionary by the way they are spelled. But what happens when you hear a new word and you are not sure how it is spelled? How can you look up a word that you do not know how to spell? The answer is: by using the *Table of English Spellings* on pages G42 and G43 of this Guide.

This spelling table shows how the different sounds of our language are spelled when they are written as parts of words. In English many words are not spelled the way they sound. As you can see from the table, one particular sound, the short **e** as in **met,** is spelled eleven different ways!

Let's take a tricky word and see if we can use the Table of English Spellings to spell it. Suppose your class has a pet mouse. One day your teacher tells you that the mouse is trying to **gnaw** through its box. Remember, we are assuming that you have only heard this word and have never seen it in writing. You want to look it up in your dictionary to learn what it is that the mouse is trying to do. Because the first sound of **gnaw** is **n,** you would probably turn first to the **n** words in your dictionary to find the word. You might look up the spelling **nau, naugh,** or **naw.** Even if you tried all the spellings you could think of, you would never find the word in the **n**'s.

If you look at the spelling table, you can see that there is an example for each different spelling of the **n** sound. If you look up each of these spellings for the **n** sound, you will find the correct spelling under **gn.**

If you are not sure of the spelling of the rest of the word, you can look at the *Example* column. When you do this, you find that one group of words has the sound you are looking for:

fall, author, caught, jaw, George, order, broad, bought

One of these sets of letters can be added to the **gn** to spell your word correctly.

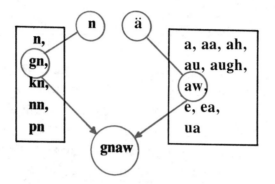

English words can sometimes be spelled in strange ways. If you keep trying the different sound spellings in the table, you are bound to find the one that fits your word. Remember to use the table, and you won't have to say: "I can't look up a word if I don't know how to spell it."

What a Word Means

THE DEFINITION

You can learn many things about a word from your dictionary. But the question that you will ask most often is, "What does it mean?" That is why we put the meaning right after the entry word itself. The meaning of a word is called its *definition*. When something is *definite*, it is very clear. The *definition* is what makes a word clear to you.

After you find the word you want, you can learn what it means right away. You will not have to read any other information first.

gavel A small wooden hammer. It is used by the person in charge of a meeting or trial to call for order or attention. **gav·el** (gav′əl) *noun, plural* **gavels.**

As you can see from the example for **gavel,** the first part of a definition in your dictionary is short and simple. It is made up of a few words that tell you quickly what you want to know—a **gavel** is "a small wooden hammer."

G17

If you read farther in a definition, you will see that other information is given. This information is always explained in sentences. Except for the short phrase at the beginning of a definition, all information in *The Canadian Dictionary for Children* is in complete sentences.

If you look at the example below, you will see that the definition for **iguana** is short—an **iguana** is "a large greenish-brown lizard." You will also see that the sentences following answer the questions, "Where is it found?" and "Where does an iguana live?"

iguana A large greenish-brown lizard. It is found in the very warm parts of North and South America. The iguana lives in trees.
i·gua·na (i gwä′nə) *noun, plural* **iguanas.**

SYNONYMS

Sometimes you will find that the second part of a definition is just one word.

wriggle **1.** To twist or turn from side to side with short, quick moves; squirm.

When you see a single word like this in a definition, it means that this word is a *synonym*. A synonym is a word that has the same meaning—or almost the same meaning—as another word. In the example above, **squirm** means the same as **wriggle.** The two words are *synonyms*.

Often when you look up a word, you will find that its synonym is a word that you already know. That will help you to understand the word. Synonyms can also help you in your writing, because you can use them to say things in a different way.

> **sociable** Liking to be with other people; friendly. Sarah is a very *sociable* girl and loves to give parties.

By using a synonym, you can say "He is a very *friendly* person" instead of "He is a very *sociable* person" without changing the meaning of what you are saying.

WORDS WITH MORE THAN ONE MEANING _____

Sometimes one word can mean many different things. Some of the words in your dictionary have five, ten, or even twenty different meanings. When a word does have more than one meaning, the different definitions are numbered.

stiff **1.** Not easily bent. The new leather belt was very *stiff*. **2.** Not able to move easily. My back was *stiff* after working in the garden all morning. **3.** Not natural or easy in manner; formal. The guard made a *stiff* bow as the king and queen passed. **4.** Hard to deal with or bear up under. There was *stiff* competition for the position of quarterback on the football team. The judge gave the thief a *stiff* sentence. **5.** Greater, stronger, or larger than usual. They're asking a *stiff* price for their house.
   stiff (stif) *adjective,* **stiffer, stiffest.**

The first meaning listed for a word is the one that is used most often. This is followed by the second most common meaning, and so on. This way, the meaning that you are most likely to be looking for comes first.

member **1.** A person, animal, or thing that belongs to a group. The *members* of the club elected Ruth president. The lion is a *member* of the cat family. **2.** A part of the body of a person or an animal. A leg or arm is a member.
   mem·ber (mem′bər) *noun, plural* **members.**

TRY THIS
Some of the words in the list below have only one meaning. Some have several meanings, and some have many different meanings. Read the words and try to guess how many meanings each one has.

apple   go
run   quit
heavy   icicle
giraffe   set
leave   rice

Now look the words up in your dictionary. Did you guess right? Can you tell anything about what kind of words have many different meanings?

G20

Suppose a friend tells you that she is "pulling your leg." You know she does not really mean that she has a hold on your leg and is pulling on it. Rather "to pull a person's leg" means "to trick or tease."

> **leg** **1.** One of the parts of the body that a person or animal stands and walks on. **2.** Something like a leg. The *leg* of the chair is broken.
> **to pull one's leg.** To trick or tease. Gail was only *pulling your leg* when she told you she was going to run away from home.

The phrase "to pull one's leg" means something quite different from what each of the words usually means. Phrases like this are called *idioms.* The word *idiom* comes from a word that means "something peculiar in language." The meaning of an idiom certainly seems peculiar when you compare it to the ordinary meanings of the words in it.

An idiom can be found in your dictionary under its most important word. Each idiom has its own definition and a sentence showing how it is used. Sometimes an explanation of where an idiom came from is given.

> **feather** One of the light growths that cover a bird's skin. Feathers protect the bird's skin from injury and help keep the bird warm.
> **feather in one's cap.** An act to be proud of. Winning the spelling contest was a *feather in his cap.*
>
> ▲ Long ago when a soldier was very brave in battle, he was awarded a feather to wear in his cap or helmet. Wearing **a feather in one's cap** was a great honour. After a while, people began to use *a feather in one's cap* for anything that a person should be proud of.

TRY THIS

Look up each of these entry words. Read all the idioms listed. Choose one idiom for each entry word and use it in a sentence.

hand   look   make   run

How a Word Is Used

sickle

A farmer uses a sickle to cut grass.

Look at the two pictures. If you did not know what a *sickle* was, you could not tell much about it from the top picture. But the picture on the bottom, which shows how a sickle is used, tells you quite a bit.

It is the same way with words. When you see how a word is used in a sentence, you can tell a lot about it. In *The Canadian Dictionary for Children,* nearly every definition has at least one example sentence — except for words whose meaning does not depend on the way they are used, like **five, Nova Scotia,** or **Saturday.**

You may not know what **abridge** means, but if you read the example sentence in your dictionary—"Because time was running out, Mr. Green had to *abridge* his speech"—you could probably guess that its meaning is "to shorten by using fewer words." In the same way, **diminutive** may be a strange word to you, but the sentence "A baby has *diminutive* hands and feet" gives you a clue. Babies have very small hands and feet, and **diminutive** means "very small."

If you think about it, you will see that these example sentences teach you about the words in the same way that you learn new words on your own, without using a dictionary. You already knew many words before you ever knew what a dictionary was. You learned about these words from hearing them used in sentences.

You can see for yourself how important the example sentences are. Try reading these definitions without the example sentences.

> **heavy** . . .   **3.** Large in size or amount. . . .
>
> **milestone** . . .   **2.** An important event. . . .
>
> **pledge** . . .   **2.** Something given as security. . . .

Are you sure of what these words mean? If you are not, try reading them again in the examples below. This time the sentences have been put in where they belong. Do you have a better idea of what these words mean now that you have read these sentences?

> **heavy** . . .   **3.** Large in size or amount. We were late because we got stuck in *heavy* traffic. We had a *heavy* rainfall last night.
>
> **milestone** . . .   **2.** An important event. Getting her first good marks was a *milestone* for Anne at elementary school. The invention of the airplane was a *milestone* in the history of travel. My sister's eighteenth birthday was a *milestone* in her life.
>
> **pledge** . . .   **2.** Something given as security. He gave the storekeeper his watch as a *pledge* that he would pay what he owed.

Sometimes you will find a word that is defined by example sentences only. This is because some very simple words can only be explained clearly by the way that they are used.

> **so**   Don't talk *so* fast; I can't understand you. It was *so* cold out that we had to come in. Susan likes to read, and *so* does her brother. Please turn out the light *so* that I can sleep. It will take an hour or *so* to finish dinner.

As you can see, all the examples in *The Canadian Dictionary for Children* are complete sentences. That's because we want your dictionary to be as much like real language as possible. Think of the way you talk with your friends, and you will see that in real language, words are almost always used in sentences.

G23

How a Word Is Spoken

THE ENTRY LINE

Following the definitions of a word, the entry word is printed again in smaller black letters. This marks the beginning of the *entry line*.

> **ac·ci·dent** (ak′sə dənt) *noun, plural* **accidents.**
> **bad·ly** (bad′lē) *adverb.*
> **car·a·van** (kar′ə van′) *noun, plural* **caravans.**
> **hurl** (hurl) *verb,* **hurled, hurling.**
> **I·nu·it** (in′oo it′) *noun, plural* **Inuit** or **Inuits;** *adjective.*
> **mar·vel·lous** (mär′və ləs) *adjective.*

The entry line tells you many useful and important things about the word.

SYLLABLE DIVISION

The first thing on the entry line is the entry word itself. This time, it is divided into smaller parts by black dots.

> **char·ac·ter**
> **Man·i·to·ba**
> **ski·doo**

These parts of a word are called *syllables.* When you want to say or spell a word, it helps to think of it as being divided in this way. Dividing a word into parts also shows you how to break up the word when you are writing. Sometimes you find that the whole word will not fit at the end of a line. Suppose you are writing the word **Manitoba,** and you have to carry over part of it to the next line. You could break it wherever there is a black dot. Put a dash at the place where you break the word to show that there is more to come on the next line.

> **My aunt lived in Mani-**
> **toba all her life.**

G24

THE PRONUNCIATION

The way a word is spoken is called its *pronunciation.* In *The Canadian Dictionary for Children,* the pronunciation is on the entry line, right after the syllable division. The pronunciation is the only thing in your dictionary that is not written in the same way as the words you see in books, magazines, and newspapers.

cat (kat)

The pronunciation has its own special alphabet. As you can see, some of the letters in this alphabet look just like ordinary letters. Others have marks above or below them, and there is one special letter, called the schwa. This is because there are only 26 letters in the regular alphabet we use to write with. But we use more than 40 different sounds when we speak.

Because this is a Canadian dictionary, the pronunciations shown are characteristic of Canadians. For example, all the following words are shown with the sound (ä):

G25

father (fä<u>th</u>′ər)   **author** (äth′ər)
call (käl)   **claw** (klä)

The words in the right-hand column usually have a differ-ent vowel sound than those in the left-hand column, but in Canada they are pronounced with the same vowel sound. This is also true of these words:

bone (bōn)   **bore** (bōr)
road (rōd)   **roar** (rōr)

These all have the same vowel sound (ō) although in other countries, where English is spoken, the words on the right usually are pronounced with a different vowel sound. You can hear that the sounds are the same in *your* own speech by saying the words out loud.

THE PRONUNCIATION KEY

If you look on page G44 of this Guide, you will see the *Pronunciation Key.* Think about how a key can open a door, and you will see why this is called a key, too. In the *Pronunciation Key,* each different sound of our language is shown on the left side. So that you will not have to turn back to this key whenever you are using your dictionary, a key showing the most common sounds appears at the bottom of the right-hand pages of your book. This key is inside a blue box.

> at; āpe; cär; end; mē; it; īce; hot; ōld;
> wood; fo͞ol; oil; out; up; turn; sing;
> thin; <u>th</u>is; **hw** in white; **zh** in treasure.
> ə stands for **a** in about, **e** in taken,
> **i** in pencil, **o** in lemon, and **u** in circus.

SPEAKING YOUR OWN WAY

It is very important for you to remember one thing— your dictionary does *not* tell you how to speak.

It tells you how to say a word in your own way. Let's take an example to explain this. The first sound in the key is "**a** as in **at**." When you see the **a** symbol in a word such as **capsize** (kap′sīz), you know you should say that sound the same way you would say the **a** in **at**. Your dictionary does not tell you how to say the **a** sound—that is up to you. People who live in different parts of Canada speak in different ways. Your dictionary will not try to change the way you speak, but it will help you to pronounce words you do not know.

THE SCHWA(ə)

There is one special letter in the alphabet used for pronunciation. It is an unusual letter—it looks like an upside down e (ə). And it has an unusual name—it is called a *schwa*. The schwa sound can be in any word that has the letters **a, e, i, o,** or **u.** When you see the ə in place of any of these letters, this means that this letter is spoken softly without any force.

Say the following words out loud: **about, taken, pencil, lemon,** and **circus.** Think about the way you said the **a** in **about,** the **e** in **taken,** the **i** in **pencil,** the **o** in **lemon,** and the **u** in **circus.** This is what the *schwa* sounds like.

ACCENT MARKS

When we say a long word, we speak some parts of it more loudly than we do others. We say the first part of the word **breakfast** more loudly than the second part. We say the second part of **tonight** more loudly than the first.

Your dictionary shows you which part of a word is spoken more loudly. To show this it uses black marks called *accent marks.* The mark comes after the part of the word that is spoken more loudly.

> **con·test** (kon′test)
> **be·gin·ning** (bē gin′ing)

Some longer words have more than one part that is spoken loudly. For these words, a lighter mark is used to show a part of a word that is spoken loudly, but not quite so loudly as the part with a heavy black mark.

bath·tub (bath′tub′)
con·grat·u·la·tions (kən grach′ə lā′shənz)

USING THE KEY

Now that you have read about the Pronunciation Key in this dictionary, let's try an example to show how it works. Suppose you were reading a story, and you saw the word **mosaic.** If this was a word you did not know before, you would probably wonder how to say it. You would look up the pronunciation in your dictionary:

mo·sa·ic (mō zā′ik)

Now check the Pronunciation Key on page G44. The first sound is easy—**m** as in **man.** Next is **ō** as in **old.** Put these two sounds together, and you have the first part of the word. Then comes the sound of **z** as in **zoo** and **ā** as in **ape.** These two sounds are the second part. The black mark tells you that this part of the word is spoken most loudly. The third part is **i** as in **it** and **k** as in **kit.** Now take all three parts and say them together, stopping for just a tiny bit of time between each part. What you have just said, whether you know it or not, is (mō zā′ik). Don't these letters seem a little less strange now that you know how they work?

WORDS THAT SOUND ALIKE _____

One of the things that makes our language tricky is that some words that sound the same are spelled differently. For example, **know** and **no, ate** and **eight,** or **sun** and **son.** These words are called *homophones,* from the Greek words *homo,* meaning "same," and *phone,* meaning "sound." (Think of *telephone* as another word made from *phone.*)

bare   bear

Suppose a friend told you he had been to the zoo and had seen an animal you had never heard of. He said its name like this: "n͞oo." If you looked up the word that seems to go

G29

best with this sound, **new,** you certainly would not learn anything about any kind of animal. It would be the same if you looked up another common word with the same sound, **knew.** But your dictionary has a way to get you to the right place. At the end of the definitions for **new** you will read this sentence. "Other words that sound like this are **knew** and **gnu.**" The **gnu** is what you're hunting for!

> **gnu** A large animal that lives in Africa. A gnu is a kind of antelope. ▲ Other words that sound like this are **knew** and **new.**
> **gnu** (n$\overline{oo}$ *or* ny$\overline{oo}$) *noun, plural* **gnus** or **gnu.**

You should watch for a black triangle like this ▲ at the end of an entry. When you see that, it means that there are other words that sound just like this one. The sentence after the triangle will tell you what they are.

> **isle** An island. Isles are usually small islands. ▲ Other words that sound like this are **aisle** and **I'll.**
> **isle** (īl) *noun, plural* **isles.**

WORDS THAT ARE SPELLED ALIKE _____

Just as two different words can sound the same, two different words can also be spelled the same way. Suppose you read that "Many baseball bats are made of **ash.**" This might seem a bit strange to you. It would be hard to hit a baseball very far with something made from the kind of ash that comes from burning something. If you look in your dictionary, you will see that there are two different entries for **ash.**

ash¹ A greyish-white powder left after something has been burned. An *ash* from Father's cigar fell on the floor.
ash (ash) *noun, plural* **ashes.**

ash² A tree that has a strong wood. It is used in building. Some baseball bats are made from the wood of the ash.
ash (ash) *noun, plural* **ashes.**

Words like these are called *homographs,* from the Greek words *homo,* meaning "same," and *graph,* meaning "writing." The entry words are marked by a small number. These pairs of words are in our language because many other languages have given words to English. Sometimes two different words, with different meanings, came into the English language with the same spelling. We list those words separately because it would be confusing to have very different meanings all listed together. Some homographs are spelled and pronounced the same:

bombardier¹ **1.** The person who drops the bombs from a bomber. **2.** *Canadian.* A corporal in the artillery.
bom·bar·dier (bom′bə dēr′) *noun, plural* **bombardiers.**

bombardier² *Canadian.* A vehicle used for travelling over snow and ice. It looks like a tank with skis on the front. It was invented by a Canadian named Armand Bombardier.
bom·bar·dier (bom′bə dēr′) *noun, plural* **bombardiers.**

Other homographs are spelled the same but pronounced differently:

entrance¹ **1.** A place through which one enters. The *entrance* to the building is in the middle of the block. Only one *entrance* to the park was open. **2.** The act of entering. Everyone stood up at the judge's *entrance.* **3.** The power, right, or permission to enter. Students were given free *entrance* to the game.
en·trance (en′trəns) *noun, plural* **entrances.**

entrance² To fill with delight or wonder. The children were *entranced* by the clown and his trick dog.
en·trance (en trans′) *verb,* **entranced, entrancing.**

G31

How Words Are Classified

The words we use are divided into different groups. These groups are called *parts of speech.* The part of speech of a word is determined by the way it is used in a sentence. The parts of speech are *noun, verb, adjective, adverb, pronoun, preposition, conjunction,* and *interjection.* The part of speech is listed right after the pronunciation.

oc·to·pus (ok′tə pəs) *noun.*
hap·pen (hap′ən) *verb.*
hap·py (hap′ē) *adjective.*
near·ly (nēr′lē) *adverb.*
it (it) *pronoun.*
at (at) *preposition.*
and (and *or* ənd) *conjunction.*
oh (ō) *interjection.*

Sometimes a word is used as more than one part of speech. Then the different parts have separate definitions, and the part of speech is shown at the end of each definition. The way the word is used most often comes first, then the second, and so on.

crease **1.** A line or mark made by folding or wrinkling something. **2.** *Canadian.* In hockey and lacrosse, the area in front of the goal. *Noun.*
—To make or get a line or mark in by folding or wrinkling. I *creased* my shirt badly when I packed it. *Verb.*
crease (krēs) *noun, plural* **creases;** *verb,* **creased, creasing.**

If you had a lot of things of the same kind—like stamps, records, or books—it would be much easier for you to take care of them if you arranged them according to a system. For example, you could arrange stamps according to what country they are from. In the same way, it is easier to understand words when they are arranged according to a system. That is where the parts of speech come in. They can help you understand more clearly what a word means and how to use it in a sentence.

How a Word Changes

Following the word that tells what part of speech a word is, there is more information about how the word can change. These word changes are shown in heavy black type:

> **al·li·ga·tor** (al′ə gā′tər) *noun, plural* **alligators.**
> **fas·ten** (fas′ən) *verb,* **fastened, fastening.**
> **broad** (brod) *adjective,* **broader, broadest.**

If the part of speech is a **NOUN,** it is followed by the word *plural. Plural* means "more than one." Most plurals are formed by adding **-s:**

ladder	**home**	**cat**	**tree**
ladders	**homes**	**cats**	**trees**

However, in some cases, the spelling is changed:

woman	**ox**	**child**	**mouse**
women	**oxen**	**children**	**mice**

TRY THIS

Write the plurals of these nouns. Check with your dictionary.

tomato	book	knife	face
box	church	fish	moose
house	goose	library	man

VERBS can be changed to show the time at which something happened.

> **change** (chānj) *verb,* **changed, changing.**
> **grow** (grō) *verb,* **grew, grown, growing.**

The first word or words in heavy black type show how the word is used to tell something that happened in the past. "Last summer I *grew* tomatoes in the back yard." "She has *grown* four centimetres this year." The last word shows that something is going on at the present. "It is *growing* dark outside."

Most of the time, the past is shown by adding the letters **-ed**, and the present is shown by adding **-ing**:

> **walk**
> **walked**
> **walked**
> **walking**

Some words have different forms:

throw	**go**
threw	**went**
thrown	**gone**
throwing	**going**

TRY THIS
Complete the following sentences using the correct form of these verbs:

run	go
skip	hop
race	jump
drive	swim
ride	skate

1. Yesterday I _____ home.
2. I have _____ home every day this week.
3. I am _____ home now.

G34

ADJECTIVES and **ADVERBS** may be changed to show the idea of *more* or *most*. We usually add the letters **-er** to mean *more* and **-est** to mean *most*. "Sue is *taller* (*more* tall) than Jane." "Ed ran *fastest* (*most* fast) in the race."

Some words, especially long ones, would sound funny if we added **-er** or **-est** at the end. For these words, we leave the word as it is and just say *more* or *most* in front of it. We would say "more beautiful" and "most ambitious."

fast	**hilarious**
faster	more hilarious
fastest	most hilarious
sad	**peaceful**
sadder	more peaceful
saddest	most peaceful

TRY THIS
Write the *more* and *most* forms of each of the following words. Then check them with your dictionary. Correct them if necessary.

awful	new
few	old
funny	regular
many	swift

G35

How a Word Is Made

Many of the words we use are made by adding parts to other words. For example, **coldness** is made by adding the word part **-ness** at the end of **cold. Unhappy** is made by adding the word part **un-** to **happy.** A word part, such as **-ness,** that is added to the end of a word is called a *suffix.* A word part, such as **un-,** that is added to the beginning of a word is called a *prefix.*

It will help you remember these words if you know that *suffix* comes from a word that means "to fasten at the back," and *prefix* comes from a word that means "to fasten at the front."

unbroken
government
unemploy**ment**

We use prefixes and suffixes all the time to put words together. But it also helps to know how to take a word

d the sentence "The builder had to
of the house because the price of
up." If you try to look up **recompute** in
u will not find it. (In fact, even the
do not have this word.) Try breaking
d **compute.** Your dictionary has entries

at means "again." *Rewrite* means "to

d out or calculate by using mathemat-
computed the cost of a new house.

r what you learned from these entries,
your sentence means, "The builder had
f the house *again* because the price of
up."

ds below the suffixes **-ly**, **-ment**,
d the suffix to the words to make

ment	-er
easure	build
ppoint	teach
xcite	speak

prefixes **un-**, **re-**, and **pre-** to the
ow each one. What new words do

	pre-
y	historic
ild	view
ver	school

How to Learn About a Word From a Picture

"A picture is worth a thousand words." That is an old saying. Even in a dictionary, which is a book of words, a picture can be very important. There are about 30 000 entry words in this book, and more than 1000 pictures—that is one picture for every 30 words.

Why does a book about words need pictures? Many times a picture can tell you more about something than a definition in words can. Prove this to yourself. Read the following definitions.

> **metamorphosis**   The series of changes in shape and function that certain animals go through as they develop from an immature form to an adult. Caterpillars become butterflies and tadpoles become frogs through metamorphosis.
> **met·a·mor·pho·sis** (met′ə mȯr′fə sis)   *noun, plural* **metamorphoses.**
>
> **bagpipe**   A musical instrument made of a leather bag and pipes. A person makes music by blowing air into the bag and then pressing the bag so that the air is forced out through the pipes. The bagpipe is often played in Scotland.
> **bag·pipe** (bag′pīp′) *noun, plural* **bagpipes.**
>
> **balance**   **1.** The condition of having all the parts of something exactly the same in weight, amount, or force. The two children kept the seesaw in *balance.* **2.** A steady position. He lost his *balance* and fell down the stairs. **3.** An instrument for weighing things. The chemist weighed some powder on the *balance.* **4.** The part that is left over. He still has the *balance* of his homework to do after supper. *Noun.*
> —To put or keep in a steady position. The girl *balanced* a book on her head. *Verb.*
> **bal·ance** (bal′əns) *noun, plural* **balances;** *verb,* **balanced, balancing.**

What happens in *metamorphosis?* How do you play the *bagpipe?* What is *balancing?*

Now look at the pictures on page G41. Do you have a better idea now of how to answer the questions?

How to Learn More About Words

By now you know how your dictionary can tell you what words mean and how they are used, how to say and spell them, and many other things. You have learned how to answer many questions about words. But you may have other questions that have not been answered:

—Where do words come from?

—Why do we have the words we do in our language?

—How do words change over the years?

To answer these questions, we have added a special feature to your dictionary. This feature is called *language notes*. Language notes are interesting stories about words. You can spot these notes easily. They begin with a blue triangle and have blue lines above and below.

> **tuque** *Canadian*. **1.** A knitted woollen cap that looks like a long stocking. One end is usually knotted. **2.** A tight, knitted cap that usually has a round tassel on top. This word is also spelled **toque.**
> **tuque** (to͞ok) *noun, plural* **tuques.**
>
> ▲ **Tuque** is a Canadian French word. It comes from the French word *toque*, which means "a cap." English Canadians have been using tuque for nearly a hundred years.

Many words in *The Canadian Dictionary for Children* are marked with the label *Canadian* following the entry word. **Tuque** is one example of such a word. What do you think it means when a word is marked *Canadian?* Other words are **anorak** and **mukluk.** If you look them up, you will find that they, like **tuque,** are words for articles of clothing that are worn mainly in Canada. Other words are **crease** and **deke.** These are different from the others because they are used in Canadian sports and recreation. All of the words in the dictionary are Canadian. But the ones that are labelled *Canadian* are Canadian in a special sense, because they began in Canada or they are more widely used here than anywhere else.

You may want to know where the letters of the alphabet come from. Your dictionary tells the history of each letter. Try looking up the letter your name begins with.

Have you ever wondered how the province you live in got its name? Your dictionary has a word story for every province.

Prince Edward Island   An island province in the Gulf of St. Lawrence. Its capital is Charlottetown.

▲ **Prince Edward Island** was named after Queen Victoria's father, Prince Edward, who was interested in the island, particularly the fort at Charlottetown.

You can learn many other interesting things from language notes. Whenever you use your dictionary, look to see if there is a language note on the same page. If there is, read it. You will be surprised to see how much you will learn.

TRY THIS

Find the answer to each of these questions by reading the language notes in this dictionary. The word in heavy black type in the question shows you which entry to look up.

1. Where did **Canada** get its name?
2. What does a **honeymoon** have to do with the moon?
3. Why was the first **sandwich** made?
4. Who was the month of **July** named after?
5. How did the **Mounties** get their nickname?
6. What did Roman soldiers use their **salary** for?
7. Where does the word **Wednesday** come from?
8. How did the **Saint Bernard** get its name?
9. What was the first meaning of **garbage?**

Your Dictionary Is Your Friend

Now that you have finished reading this Guide, you have learned how to find out just about anything you want to know about words. We hope you have also learned something else—your dictionary is a friend that can really help you when you need it. Use your dictionary whenever you have a question about words.

Here are the pictures of the words you read about on page G38.

Egg   Larva

Changing to Pupa   Pupa

Butterfly

This table shows the more common spellings for the different sounds in Canadian English. It is meant to be used as a guide to help find words you know how to pronounce but don't know how to spell.

SOUND	SPELLING	EXAMPLE
a	a, ai, au	hand, plaid, aunt
ā	a, ai, aigh, au, ay, ea, ee, ei, eigh, et, ey	rate, rain, straight, gauge, pay, steak, matinee, veil, eight, bouquet, obey
ä	a, aa, ah, au, augh, aw, e, ea, ua	art, bazaar, hurrah, author, caught, jaw, sergeant, heart, guard
b	b, bb	bit, rabbit
ch	c, ch, t, tch, ti	cello, chin, nature, batch, question
d	d, dd, ed	dive, ladder, failed
e	a, ae, ai, ay, e, ea, ei, eo, ie, u, ue	many, aesthetic, said, says, met, weather, heifer, leopard, friend, bury, guess
ē	ae, ay, e, ea, ee, ei, eo, ey, i, ie, oe, y	algae, quay, he, beach, bee, deceive, people, key, machine, field, amoeba, city
f	f, ff, gh, ph	fine, off, laugh, physical
g	g, gg, gh, gue	go, stagger, ghost, catalogue
h	h, wh	he, whom
hw	wh	wheel
i	a, e, ee, ei, i, ia, ie, o, u, ui, y	damage, pretty, been, counterfeit, bit, carriage, sieve, women, busy, build, myth
ī	ai, aye, ei, eigh, ey, eye, i, ie, igh, uy, y, ye	aisle, aye, either, height, geyser, eye, rice, tie, high, buy, try, dye
j	d, dg, dge, di, g, gg, j	graduate, ledger, judge, soldier, magic, exaggerate, jump
k	c, cc, ch, ck, cq, cqu, cu, k, kh, q, qu, que	cat, account, chord, tack, acquaint, lacquer, biscuit, key, khaki, quit, liquor, antique
l	l, ll	line, hall
m	m, mb, mm, mn	mine, climb, hammer, hymn
n	n, gn, kn, nn, pn	nice, gnu, knee, funny, pneumonia
ng	n, ng, ngue	link, sing, tongue

G42

SOUND	SPELLING	EXAMPLE
o	a, o, oa, ough	watch, lock, broad, bought
ō	ew, o, oa, oe, oh, oo, ou, ough, ow, owe	sew, so, boat, foe, oh, brooch, soul, though, know, owe
oi	aw, oi, oy, uoy	lawyer, foil, toy, buoy
oo	o, oo, ou, u	wolf, look, should, full
o̅o̅	eu, ew, o, oe, oeu, oo, ou, ough, u, ue, ui	neutral, jewel, prove, canoe, manoeuver, tool, soup, through, luminous, true, fruit
ou	ou, ough, ow	out, bough, now
p	p, pp	pill, happy
r	r, rh, rr, wr	ray, rhyme, parrot, wrong
s	c, ps, s, sc, ss	city, psychology, song, scene, mess
sh	ce, ch, ci, s, sch, sci, sh, si, ss, ssi, ti	ocean, machine, special, sugar, schwa conscience, shin, expansion, tissue, mission, nation
t	tt, bt, ed, th	ten, bitter, debt, topped, thyme
th	th	thin
t̲h̲	th, the	them, bathe
u	o, oe, oo, ou, u	come, does, flood, touch, sun
ur	ear, er, eur, ir, or, our, ur, urr, yr	earth, fern, amateur, thirst, worst, courage, turn, burr, myrtle
v	f, v	of, vine
w	o, u, w	choir, queen, we
y	i, y	onion, yes
yo̅o̅	eau, eu, ew, ieu, iew, ou, u, ue	beautiful, feud, few, adieu, view, you, use, cue
z	s, ss, x, z, zz	has, scissors, xylophone, zoo, fuzz
zh	ge, s, si, z	garage, treasure, division, azure
ə	a, ai, e, i, o, ou, u	ago, bargain, taken, pencil, lemon, furious, circus

Pronunciation Key

a	a as in **at, bad**
$\bar{a}$	a as in **ape**, ai as in **pain**, ay as in **day**
ä	a as in **all, father, car**, au as in **author**, aw as in **law**
e	e as in **end, pet**
$\bar{e}$	e as in **me**, ee as in **feet**, ea as in **meat**, ie as in **piece**, y as in **finally**
i	i as in **it, pig**
$\bar{i}$	i as in **ice, fine**, ie as in **lie**, y as in **my**
o	o as in **odd, hot**
$\bar{o}$	o as in **old, fork**, oa as in **oat**, oe as in **toe**, ow as in **low**
oo	oo as in **wood**, u as in **put**
$\overline{oo}$	oo as in **fool**, ue as in **true**
oi	oi as in **oil**, oy as in **boy**
ou	ou as in **out**, ow as in **cow**
u	u as in **up, mud**, o as in **oven, love**
ur	ur as in **turn**, er as in **term**, ir as in **bird**, or as in **word**
y$\overline{oo}$	u as in **use**, ue as in **cue**, ew as in **few**, eu as in **feud**
ə	a as in **ago**, e as in **taken**, i as in **pencil**, o as in **lemon**, u as in **helpful**
b	b as in **bat, above, job**
ch	ch as in **chin, such**, tch as in **hatch**
d	d as in **dear, soda, bad**
f	f as in **five, defend, leaf**, ff as in **off**
g	g as in **game, ago, fog**
h	h as in **hit, ahead**
j	j as in **joke, enjoy**, g as in **gem**, dge as in **edge**
k	k as in **kit, baking, seek**, ck as in **tack**, c as in **cat**
l	l as in **lid, sailor, feel**, ll as in **ball, allow**
m	m as in **man, family, dream**
n	n as in **not, final, on**
ng	ng as in **singer, long**, n as in **sink**
p	p as in **pail, repair, soap**
r	r as in **ride, parent, four**
s	s as in **sat, aside, cats**, c as in **cent**, ss as in **pass**
sh	sh as in **shoe, wishing, fish**
t	t as in **tag, pretend, hat**
th	th as in **thin, ether, both**
<u>th</u>	th as in **this, mother, smooth**
v	v as in **very, favour, salve**
w	w as in **wet, reward**
y	y as in **yes**
z	z as in **zoo, gazing**, zz as in **jazz**, s as in **rose, dogs**
zh	s as in **treasure**, z as in **azure**, ge as in **garage**

G44

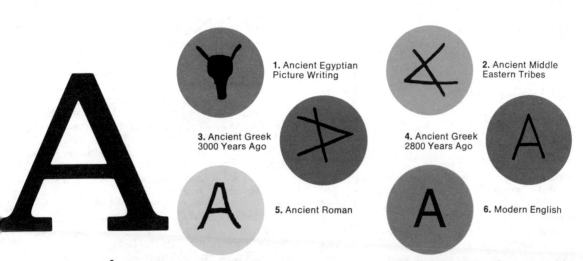

1. Ancient Egyptian Picture Writing
2. Ancient Middle Eastern Tribes
3. Ancient Greek 3000 Years Ago
4. Ancient Greek 2800 Years Ago
5. Ancient Roman
6. Modern English

A is the first letter of the alphabet. The oldest form of the letter **A** was a drawing that the ancient Egyptians (**1**) used in their picture writing nearly 5000 years ago. This drawing was borrowed by several ancient tribes (**2**) in the Middle East. They called it *aleph*, which meant "ox." If you turn the letter **A** upside-down, you will see a design that looks like the head and horns of an ox. The ancient Greeks (**3**) borrowed a form of this letter about 3000 years ago. At first they wrote it like an upside-down capital letter **A**. Several hundred years later, the Greeks turned their letter **A** around (**4**). This made it look like a modern capital letter **A**. The Romans (**5**) borrowed this letter from the Greeks about 2400 years ago. They wrote it almost the same way that we write the capital letter **A** today (**6**).

a, A   The first letter of the alphabet.
a, A (ā) *noun, plural* **a's, A's.**

a   *A* dog would love that bone. She has *a* bicycle. He washes his car once *a* week. The orange is *a* fruit.
a (ə *or* ā) *indefinite article.*

abacus   A frame with beads that move along wires or rods. A person can add, subtract, multiply, or divide with an abacus. The abacus was first used thousands of years ago. It is used today in China, Japan, and some other countries.
ab·a·cus (ab′ə kəs) *noun, plural* **abacuses.**

▲ Long ago in Greece and Rome, abacuses were made of a board covered with dust or sand. Marks could be made in the dust and then wiped away. The word **abacus** comes from a word that meant "dust."

abandon   To give up completely; leave. The captain ordered the sailors to *abandon* the sinking ship.
a·ban·don (ə ban′dən) *verb,* **abandoned, abandoning.**

abbey   **1.** A building or buildings where monks or nuns live a religious life. **2.** A group of monks or nuns who live in an abbey.
ab·bey (ab′ē) *noun, plural* **abbeys.**

abbreviate   To make something shorter. We *abbreviate* the words "Member of Parliament" as "MP."
ab·bre·vi·ate (ə brē′vē āt′) *verb,* **abbreviated, abbreviating.**

abbreviation   A letter or group of letters that stands for a longer word or phrase. *Jan.* is the abbreviation for *January, Fri.* is the abbreviation for *Friday,* and *Man.* is the abbreviation for *Manitoba.*
ab·bre·vi·a·tion (ə brē′vē ā′shən) *noun, plural* **abbreviations.**

▲ People use **abbreviations** in writing when they do not want to write out the full word that the abbreviation stands for. Most abbreviations have a period at the end. For example, *Can.* is the abbreviation for the word *Canada.* This is so that a person who reads the abbreviation will know it is not a real word. Sometimes, though, an abbreviation looks so different from a real word that it does not need to have a period. For example, *UN* is the abbreviation for *United Nations.*

abdicate   To give up power. The old king *abdicated,* and his son became king.
ab·di·cate (ab′də kāt′) *verb,* **abdicated, abdicating.**

1

abdomen 1. The part of the body that holds the stomach. It is below the chest. The abdomen has many organs that are important in digestion, including the stomach, the intestines, the kidneys, and the liver. 2. The rear part of the body of an insect.

Abdomen

ab·do·men (ab′də mən *or* ab dō′mən) *noun, plural* **abdomens.**

abide To put up with a person or thing. Tom could not *abide* his sister's messy room.
a·bide (ə bīd′) *verb,* **abode** or **abided, abiding.**
to abide by. To obey. Jim always *abides by* the law.

ability The power or skill to do something. Man is the only animal that has the *ability* to speak. Ruth has great *ability* as a singer.
a·bil·i·ty (ə bil′ə tē) *noun, plural* **abilities.**

able Having the power or skill to do something. A deer is *able* to run very fast. Joan was *able* to read at an early age.
a·ble (ā′bəl) *adjective,* **abler, ablest.**

abolish To put an end to; do away with. Parliament voted to *abolish* capital punishment.
a·bol·ish (ə bol′ish) *verb,* **abolished, abolishing.**

abolition The act of abolishing; doing away with. The town's goal was the *abolition* of water pollution.
ab·o·li·tion (ab′ə lish′ən) *noun.*

abominable 1. Hateful, disgusting. A crime is an *abominable* act. 2. Very unpleasant; offensive. The salesperson said that my sister's behaviour was *abominable* when she had a tantrum in the toy store.
a·bom·i·na·ble (ə bom′ə nə bəl) *adjective.*

aborigine One of the first people to live in a place. The Indians are the *aborigines* of North America.
ab·o·rig·i·ne (ab′ə rij′ə nē) *noun, plural* **aborigines.**

abound To be plentiful. Corn and wheat *abound* on that farm. Buffalo used to *abound* in North America.
a·bound (ə bound′) *verb,* **abounded, abounding.**

about That book is *about* Mackenzie King. Tim was *about* to leave for home. There were *about* twenty people waiting for the bus.
a·bout (ə bout′) *preposition; adverb.*

above The kite flew *above* the trees. The stars glittered *above.*
a·bove (ə buv′) *preposition; adverb.*

aboveboard Honest. He is open and *aboveboard* in his business dealings.
a·bove·board (ə buv′bōrd′) *adjective.*

▲ The word **aboveboard** comes from an old saying—"above the board." This expression was used in card games. If your hands were above the board (the card table was then called a *board*) you were thought to be honest. The idea was that if your hands were above the table, you could not cheat by hiding cards under the table.

abreast Side by side. The students walked down the hall two *abreast.* The apple trees stood four *abreast* in the field.
a·breast (ə brest′) *adverb.*

The drummers are marching **abreast.**

abridge To shorten by using fewer words. Because time was running out, Mr. Green had to *abridge* his speech.
a·bridge (ə brij′) *verb,* **abridged, abridging.**

abroad Outside of one's country. Her parents went *abroad* to France for their vacation.
a·broad (ə brod′) *adverb.*

abrupt 1. Without warning; sudden; unexpected. The bus made an *abrupt* stop at the corner. 2. Not polite or gentle; blunt. The waiter gave her an *abrupt* answer.
a·brupt (ə brupt′) *adjective.*

abscess A collection of pus in some part of the body. It usually comes from an infection.
ab·scess (ab′ses) *noun, plural* **abscesses.**

absence 1. A being away. In the teacher's *absence,* a substitute teacher took over the class. 2. A lack; being without. *Absence* of rain caused the plants to die.
ab·sence (ab′səns) *noun, plural* **absences.**

absent 1. Not present; away. When he caught a cold, he was *absent* from school for two days. 2. Lacking. Leaves are *absent* on trees in winter.
ab·sent (ab′sənt) *adjective.*

absent-minded Forgetful; not paying attention to what is going on. She stared out the window in an *absent-minded* way.
ab·sent-mind·ed (ab′sənt mīn′dəd) *adjective.*

absolute 1. Complete; entire. She believes in telling the *absolute* truth. 2. Having unlimited power. Long ago, kings were *absolute* rulers. 3. Positive; sure. The family had *absolute* proof that the land belonged to them.
ab·so·lute (ab′sə lo͞ot′ *or* ab′sə lo͞ot′) *adjective.*

absolutely 1. Completely. He is *absolutely* right about that. 2. Positively. He was *absolutely* sure that he wanted to buy a dog.
ab·so·lute·ly (ab′sə lo͞ot′lē *or* ab′sə lo͞ot′ lē) *adverb.*

absorb 1. To soak up or take in. A sponge *absorbs* water. Susan *absorbs* any new knowledge very quickly. 2. To hold the interest of. The book about animals *absorbed* Jim.
ab·sorb (ab zôrb′ *or* ab sôrb′) *verb,* absorbed, absorbing.

absorption The ability to soak up or take in. A sponge is used in cleaning because it has great *absorption*.
ab·sorp·tion (ab zôrp′shən *or* ab sôrp′shən) *noun.*

abstain To keep oneself from doing something. Her mother asked her to *abstain* from eating candy.
ab·stain (ab stān′) *verb,* abstained, abstaining.

abstract Expressing a quality without naming the person or thing that has the quality. "Beauty" is an *abstract* word because it does not refer to a particular person or thing. "Butterfly" is not an *abstract* word because it does refer to a particular thing.
ab·stract (ab′strakt *or* ab strakt′) *adjective.*

absurd Definitely not true; silly; foolish. It is *absurd* to believe that the moon is made of green cheese.
ab·surd (ab surd′ *or* ab zurd′) *adjective.*

abundance A very large amount; a quantity that is more than enough. Because the farmer had an *abundance* of food, he gave some to a poor family that did not have enough.
a·bun·dance (ə bun′dəns) *noun.*

abundant More than enough; plentiful. Rockets need an *abundant* amount of fuel when they fly into space.
a·bun·dant (ə bun′dənt) *adjective.*

abuse 1. To make bad or wrong use of. The children *abused* their free time by making a mess of the classroom. 2. To treat cruelly or badly. The dog was *abused* by its owner. 3. To put too much strain on. We *abuse* our health when we do not eat properly. *Verb.*
—1. Bad or wrong use. The ruler's *abuse* of power caused the people to hate him. 2. Bad treatment. During the trip on the old, bumpy road our car took much *abuse*. 3. Rude speech; insulting language. The girl suffered *abuse* from her friends after she got them in trouble. *Noun.*
a·buse (ə byo͞oz′ *for verb;* ə byo͞os′ *for noun*) *verb,* abused, abusing; *noun, plural* abuses.

abyss A large, deep hole in the earth; a bottomless hole.
a·byss (ə bis′) *noun, plural* abysses.

acacia A small tree or bush with leaves like ferns, found in warm areas.
a·ca·cia (ə kā′shə) *noun, plural* acacias.

academy 1. A private high school. 2. A school that trains people for a special field of study. My sister takes violin lessons at the music *academy*.
a·cad·e·my (ə kad′ə mē) *noun, plural* academies.

Acadia *Canadian.* A former French colony made up of the Maritime Provinces and parts of Quebec.
A·ca·di·a (ə kā′dē ə) *noun.*

Acadian *Canadian.* A person born in Acadia or descended from the French who settled in the Maritime Provinces. *Noun.*
—Of Acadia. *Adjective.*
A·ca·di·an (ə kā′dē ən) *noun, plural* Acadians; *adjective.*

Acadian French *Canadian.* The French spoken in the Maritimes. Acadian French is different from the French spoken in Quebec.

accelerate To speed up; move faster. The car *accelerated* as it went down the hill.
ac·cel·er·ate (ak sel′ə rāt′) *verb,* accelerated, accelerating.

acceleration A moving faster or speeding up. Tom's *acceleration* of the car frightened the passengers.
ac·cel·er·a·tion (ak sel′ə rā′shən) *noun, plural* accelerations.

accelerator A pedal on an automobile or

at; āpe; cär; end; mē; it; īce; hot; ōld;
wood; fo͞ol; oil; out; up; turn; sing;
thin; this; hw in white; zh in treasure.
ə stands for a in about, e in taken,
i in pencil, o in lemon, and u in circus.

other machine that speeds up the motor. Nancy wanted the car to go faster, so she pressed down on the *accelerator*.

ac·cel·er·a·tor (ak sel′ə rā′tər) *noun, plural* **accelerators.**

accent **1.** A stronger tone of voice given to a word or part of a word. In the word "happy," the *accent* is on the first syllable. In "forget," the *accent* is on the second syllable. **2.** A mark used on a word to show which syllable is spoken with an accent. In this dictionary, the mark ′ is used to show the syllable in the word spoken with the most force. The mark ′ is used to show a syllable with a weaker accent. In the word "abbreviate," we place the accents like this: ə brē′vē āt′. **3.** A certain way of saying words that is used by people in one part of a country. She has a Newfoundland *accent* because she grew up in St. John's. **4.** A mixing of a foreign way of speaking with the language of another country. Her grandmother speaks English with a German *accent. Noun.*
—To pronounce a word or syllable in a stronger way. You *accent* the first syllable of the word "apple." *Verb.*

ac·cent (ak′sent *for noun;* ak′sent *or* ak sent′ *for verb*) *noun, plural* **accents;** *verb,* **accented, accenting.**

accept **1.** To take or receive something that is given. She *accepted* the birthday gift from her aunt. **2.** To agree to; answer "yes" to. The speaker *accepted* the club's invitation to talk about his new book. **3.** To believe to be true. His mother *accepted* his reason for being late.

ac·cept (ak sept′) *verb,* **accepted, accepting.**

acceptable Good enough to be accepted; satisfactory. Her book report was *acceptable.* The bank said that his cheque was not *acceptable* because he did not sign it.

ac·cept·a·ble (ak sep′tə bəl) *adjective.*

acceptance **1.** A taking of something given or offered. Sarah's *acceptance* of the present pleased her mother. **2.** A being accepted; approval. The idea gained *acceptance.*

ac·cept·ance (ak sep′təns) *noun, plural* **acceptances.**

access **1.** An entrance or approach. We had easy *access* into the deserted house. **2.** A way or means of approach. The campers had *access* to the lake through the woods.

ac·cess (ak′ses′) *noun, plural* **accesses.**

accessory **1.** Something that is added to help a more important thing. The green necklace was a pretty *accessory* to the woman's blue dress. **2.** A person who helps another person commit a crime. He was an *accessory* to the bank robbery because he drove the car that the robbers used to escape. *Noun.*
—Useful but not necessary; additional. The listing of street addresses is an *accessory* feature of a telephone book. *Adjective.*

ac·ces·so·ry (ak ses′ər ē) *noun, plural* **accessories;** *adjective.*

accident **1.** Something that happens for no apparent reason and is not expected. The discovery of an oil well on the farm was a happy *accident.* **2.** An unhappy event that is not expected. During the snowstorm there were many *accidents* on the highways. **3.** Chance; fortune. I found the missing watch by *accident* while I was looking for my comb.

ac·ci·dent (ak′sə dənt) *noun, plural* **accidents.**

accidental Happening by chance; not meant to happen. While the children were digging in the park, they made an *accidental* discovery of some old coins.

ac·ci·den·tal (ak′sə dent′əl) *adjective.*

accidentally By accident. I met her *accidentally* on the bus.

ac·ci·den·tal·ly (ak′sə den′təl ē *or* ak′sə dent′lē) *adverb.*

acclaim To welcome with strong approval; applaud. The crowd *acclaimed* the astronauts. *Verb.*
—Great praise. The boxing champion was greeted with *acclaim* by his fans. *Noun.*

ac·claim (ə klām′) *verb,* **acclaimed, acclaiming;** *noun, plural* **acclaims.**

acclamation A show of approval.

ac·cla·ma·tion (ak′lə mā′shən) *noun.*

by acclamation. *Canadian.* Unopposed in an election. Since no one opposed her, Mrs. Brisbois won the election *by acclamation.*

acclimate To adjust or become adjusted to a new place or situation. John quickly *acclimated* himself to the new school.

ac·cli·mate (ak′lə māt′) *verb,* **acclimated, acclimating.**

accommodate **1.** To have room for; hold. That movie theatre *accommodates* 600 people. **2.** To do a favour for; help out. The policeman *accommodated* us when we asked him for directions. **3.** To supply a place to stay or sleep. That motel *accommodates* 200 people each night.

ac·com·mo·date (ə kom′ə dāt′) *verb,* **accommodated, accommodating.**

accommodation **1.** A convenience or a help. Giving me a ride to school was a big *accommodation.* **2. accommodations.** A place to stay or sleep. When we were travelling, we always found good *accommodations.*

ac·com·mo·da·tion (ə kom′ə dā′shən) *noun,* *plural* **accommodations.**

accompaniment   **1.** A thing that goes along with something else. Cranberry sauce is a delicious *accompaniment* to turkey. **2.** A musical part that is played as background for the main part. The girl sang with a piano *accompaniment.*

ac·com·pa·ni·ment (ə kum′pə ni mənt) *noun,* *plural* **accompaniments.**

accompany   **1.** To go along with. I'll *accompany* you to the movies. **2.** To happen at the same time as. Wind often *accompanies* rain. **3.** To play an accompaniment for another musical instrument.

ac·com·pa·ny (ə kum′pə nē) *verb,* **accompanied, accompanying.**

accomplice   A person who helps another person commit a crime. Because he supplied the guns the robbers used, the man was an *accomplice* to the robbery.

ac·com·plice (ə kom′plis *or* a kom′plis) *noun, plural* **accomplices.**

accomplish   To carry out or complete; perform. The pilot *accomplished* his mission and returned to the base.

ac·com·plish (ə kom′plish) *verb,* **accomplished, accomplishing.**

accomplishment   **1.** The act of accomplishing; completion. The *accomplishment* of our goal will be very difficult. **2.** Something done successfully; achievement. The construction of the CPR was a great *accomplishment.* **3.** A special skill or ability that is usually gained by training. Playing the piano well is his greatest *accomplishment.*

ac·com·plish·ment (ə kom′plish mənt) *noun,* *plural* **accomplishments.**

accord   Agreement; harmony. A longer holiday period is in *accord* with the demands of the workers. *Noun.*
—To agree or be in harmony with. His opinions on politics *accord* with hers. *Verb.*

ac·cord (ə kôrd′) *noun, plural* **accords;** *verb,* **accorded, according.**

of one's own accord. By a person's own choice; voluntarily.

accordance   Agreement. John acted in *accordance* with our wish that he take care of our dog while we were away.

ac·cord·ance (ə kôrd′əns) *noun.*

according   **According to. 1.** In agreement with. Everything went *according to* our plan. **2.** On the authority of. *According to* the weather forecast, it will rain tomorrow.

ac·cord·ing (ə kôr′ding) *adjective.*

accordion   A musical instrument with keys, metal reeds, and a bellows. The bellows pushes air through the reeds to make a note.

Accordion

ac·cor·di·on (ə kôr′dē ən) *noun,* *plural* **accordions.**

account   **1.** A spoken or written statement; report. There was an *account* of the baseball game in the newspaper. **2.** A record of money spent or received. My mother takes care of the household *accounts.* Joan has five hundred dollars in her bank *account.* **3.** Importance; worth. The lonely old man felt he was of little *account. Noun.*
—To consider to be. I *account* him an honest man. *Verb.*

ac·count (ə kount′) *noun, plural* **accounts;** *verb,* **accounted, accounting.**

on account of. Because of. The game was delayed *on account of* rain.

to account for. To give an explanation or reason for. How do you *account for* your lateness? The heavy snowfall *accounts for* the closing of school today.

accountant   Someone who is trained to take care of the money records of a person or a business.

ac·count·ant (ə kount′ənt) *noun, plural* **accountants.**

accumulate   To gather or pile up; collect. He *accumulated* a large number of books while he was at college. A large pile of mail had *accumulated* while we were away on vacation.

ac·cu·mu·late (ə kyōō′myə lāt′) *verb,* **accumulated, accumulating.**

accumulation   **1.** The act of accumulating; piling up. The *accumulation* of evidence against the defendant led to her being found guilty. **2.** Something accumulated; collection. There was an *accumulation* of dust in the corner of the room.

at; āpe; cär; end; mē; it; īce; hot; ōld;
wood; fōōl; oil; out; up; turn; sing;
thin; this; hw in white; zh in treasure.
ə stands for **a** in about, **e** in taken,
i in pencil, **o** in lemon, and **u** in circus.

ac·cu·mu·la·tion (ə kyoo′myə lā′shən) *noun,* *plural* **accumulations.**

accuracy The condition of being without errors or mistakes. She checked the *accuracy* of her arithmetic answers.
ac·cu·ra·cy (ak′yər ə sē) *noun.*

accurate 1. Making few or no errors or mistakes; exact. His new watch is very *accurate.* 2. Without errors or mistakes; correct. The newspaper stories about the accident were not *accurate.*
ac·cu·rate (ak′yər ət) *adjective.*

accusation A statement that a person has committed a crime; charge of doing something wrong.
ac·cu·sa·tion (ak′yoo zā′shən) *noun,* *plural* **accusations.**

accuse To state that a person has committed a crime or has done something bad. The storekeeper *accused* the boy of stealing a watch.
ac·cuse (ə kyooz′) *verb,* **accused, accusing.**

accustom To make familiar by use, custom, or habit. She had to *accustom* herself to a new school when her family moved.
ac·cus·tom (ə kus′təm) *verb,* **accustomed, accustoming.**

accustomed Usual. The dog lay in his *accustomed* place by the fire.
ac·cus·tomed (ə kus′təmd) *adjective.*
accustomed to. Used to; in the habit of. The policeman was *accustomed to* the noisy traffic.

ace 1. A playing card having one mark in the centre. 2. A person who is an expert at something. Karen is an *ace* at tennis. *Noun.*
—Of the highest quality; expert. Bob is an *ace* goalie. *Adjective.*
ace (ās) *noun,* *plural* **aces;** *adjective.*

ache 1. To be in pain. His whole body *ached* after the rough hockey game. 2. To be eager; long for. After a month away, he *ached* to get back home. *Verb.*
—A pain. After throwing the ball so much, he had an *ache* in his arm. *Noun.*
ache (āk) *verb,* **ached, aching;** *noun,* *plural* **aches.**

Ace of Hearts

achieve 1. To accomplish or succeed. She *achieved* her goal of winning the prize for the best essay. 2. To gain or to reach by effort. Emily Carr *achieved* fame as a painter.
a·chieve (ə chēv′) *verb,* **achieved, achieving.**

achievement 1. Something accomplished or achieved. The invention of the telephone was a great *achievement.* 2. Something gained by effort. The *achievement* of the right to vote for women took a long time.
a·chieve·ment (ə chēv′mənt) *noun,* *plural* **achievements.**

acid 1. Sour, sharp, or biting to the taste. A lemon has an *acid* taste. 2. Sharp or biting in actions or speech. The man's *acid* remark hurt Jim's feelings. *Adjective.*
—A chemical that joins with a base to make a salt. Acids have a sour taste when dissolved in water. An acid will cause blue litmus paper to turn red. *Noun.*
ac·id (as′id) *adjective;* *noun,* *plural* **acids.**

acknowledge 1. To admit that something is true. She *acknowledged* that she had made a mistake. 2. To recognize the ability or authority of. The class *acknowledged* that Ann was the best speller. 3. To say that something has been received. She *acknowledged* all her birthday gifts.
ac·knowl·edge (ak nol′ij) *verb,* **acknowledged, acknowledging.**

acknowledgement The act of acknowledging. Her *acknowledgement* that she had made a mistake made her feel better. This word is also spelled **acknowledgment.**
ac·knowl·edge·ment (ak nol′ij mənt) *noun,* *plural* **acknowledgements.**

acne A kind of skin disease in which a person has pimples, especially on the face. It is caused by infection in the oil glands under the skin. People most often get acne during their teenage years, when these glands are very active.
ac·ne (ak′nē) *noun.*

acorn The nut of the oak tree.
a·corn (ā′kōrn) *noun,* *plural* **acorns.**

acquaint To make familiar. New swimmers must *acquaint* themselves with the rules of the swimming pool. I am *acquainted* with most of the people who live on our street.
ac·quaint (ə kwānt′) *verb,* **acquainted, acquainting.**

Acorns

acquaintance 1. A person one knows only slightly. Helen met some *acquaintances* during her trip into town. 2. Knowledge of something gained from experience. Betty had some *acquaintance* with the game of chess because she had played it before.

ac·quaint·ance (ə kwānt′əns) *noun, plural* **acquaintances.**

acquire To get as one's own; obtain. When she went to the farm, she *acquired* a liking for horseback riding. He *acquired* the ability to speak Spanish while he lived in Mexico.

ac·quire (ə kwīr′) *verb,* **acquired, acquiring.**

acquit To free from a charge of a crime; declare not guilty. The jury *acquitted* him because they believed that the evidence did not prove him guilty.

ac·quit (ə kwit′) *verb,* **acquitted, acquitting.**

acre A way of measuring land. It is equal to 43,560 square feet in the Imperial System of Measure. An acre of land is slightly smaller in size than a football field.

a·cre (ā′kər) *noun, plural* **acres.**

acreage An area of land measured in acres; number of acres.

a·cre·age (ā′kər ij) *noun.*

acrobat A person who performs stunts that require great physical ability. An acrobat most often works in a circus walking on a tightrope or swinging on a trapeze.

ac·ro·bat (ak′rə bat′) *noun, plural* **acrobats.**

▲ The word **acrobat** comes from an old Greek word that meant "to walk on tiptoe" or "to climb up high."

across We came *across* in a rowboat. She lives *across* the street from me.

a·cross (ə krôs′) *adverb; preposition.*

act **1.** Something that is done; a deed. Saving the child's life was an *act* of bravery. **2.** The doing of something. The thief was caught in the *act* of opening the safe. **3.** A law. Federal taxes can be raised only by an *act* of Parliament. **4.** One of the parts of a play. *Hamlet* has five *acts. Noun.*
—1. To do something or move. After the accident she *acted* quickly to help the others. **2.** To perform before an audience or in a movie. The hero of the play *acted* so well that he got the main role in the next show. *Verb.*

act (akt) *noun, plural* **acts;** *verb,* **acted, acting.**

action **1.** The doing of something. Throwing a ball, jumping over a fence, and running down a hill are all *actions.* **2.** Something that is done; an act. Helping the blind man across the busy street was a kind *action.* **3.** A battle. My uncle was wounded in *action* during the war.

ac·tion (ak′shən) *noun, plural* **actions.**

activate To put into action; cause to work or operate. Pushing the button *activates* the machine.

ac·ti·vate (ak′tə vāt′) *verb,* **activated, activating.**

active **1.** Full of action; moving around much of the time. Leyla is *active* and always seems busy. **2.** In action; working. Hawaii has several *active* volcanoes.

ac·tive (ak′tiv) *adjective.*

activity **1.** The state of being active; movement. Building a house involves much *activity.* **2.** A thing to do or to be done. Jane takes part in many school *activities.*

ac·tiv·i·ty (ak tiv′ə tē) *noun, plural* **activities.**

actor A person who plays a part in a play, movie, or television program.

ac·tor (ak′tər) *noun, plural* **actors.**

actress A girl or woman who plays a part in a play, movie, or television program.

ac·tress (ak′trəs) *noun, plural* **actresses.**

actual Real; existing. That book is about *actual* people, not imaginary ones. The *actual* cause of the accident is not known.

ac·tu·al (ak′chōō əl) *adjective.*

actually In fact; really. He said that he stayed home because he was sick, but *actually* he wanted to watch the baseball game on television.

ac·tu·al·ly (ak′chōō ə lē *or* ak′chə lē) *adverb.*

acute **1.** Sharp and severe. Mary had an *acute* pain in her side after running so far. **2.** Quick in seeing and understanding. The bright girl had an *acute* mind, so she learned things easily. **3.** Very bad; serious; critical. **4.** An accent marker used in French and other languages.

a·cute (ə kyōōt′) *adjective.*

acute angle An angle that has less than ninety degrees.

ad A short word for **advertisement.** A picture or message that tries to sell something is an ad. ▲ Another word that sounds like this is **add.**

ad (ad) *noun, plural* **ads.**

A.D. An abbreviation meaning "in the year of the Lord." It is used in giving dates since the birth of Christ. 1000 *A.D.* means 1000 years after the birth of Christ.

at; āpe; cär; end; mē; it; īce; hot; ōld;
wood; fōōl; oil; out; up; turn; sing;
thin; this; hw in white; zh in treasure.
ə stands for a in about, e in taken,
i in pencil, o in lemon, and u in circus.

adage An old and familiar saying that is believed to be true; proverb. "The early bird catches the worm" is an adage.
ad·age (ad′əj) *noun, plural* **adages.**

adamant Refusing to change one's mind or position; firm. He was *adamant* in his support of equal rights for native peoples.
ad·a·mant (ad′ə mənt) *adjective.*

Adam's apple A lump in the throat just below the chin. It is made up of a kind of tissue called cartilage. All people have an Adam's apple, although it is easier to notice in men than in women.
Ad·am's apple (ad′əmz).

adapt To adjust to new conditions or surroundings. When the family moved to Victoria, they had to *adapt* to the wet weather.
a·dapt (ə dapt′) *verb,* **adapted, adapting.**

add 1. To find the sum of two or more numbers. If you *add* 2 and 7, you get 9. 2. To put one thing with another. Mother *added* cream to her coffee. Wes *added* a new stamp to his collection. 3. To put more onto something written or said. He thanked us for the gift and *added* that it was just what he wanted. ▲ Another word that sounds like this is **ad.**
add (ad) *verb,* **added, adding.**

addend Any number that can be added to another number. In the problem *5 + 3 = 8, 5* and *3* are the addends.
ad·dend (ad′end) *noun, plural* **addends.**

adder A kind of snake. The type of adder found in Europe is poisonous, while the kind found in North America is harmless.
ad·der (ad′ər) *noun, plural* **adders.**

Adder

addict A person taken over by a drug or habit. As an addict you have little control over yourself because the drug or habit controls you. Doctors are trying to find a cure for heroin *addicts.*
ad·dict (ad′ikt) *noun, plural* **addicts.**

▲ The word **addict** used to mean "to deliver" or "to turn over." A judge could *addict* someone to prison. A person could be *addicted* to another person as a servant or slave. Our meaning of *addict* comes from the idea of a person's becoming a slave to a habit.

addition 1. The adding of two or more numbers or things. *9 + 2 + 5 = 16* is an example of addition. 2. The act of adding. The *addition* of salt helped give flavour to the soup. 3. Something that is added. Mr. Jones built an *addition* to his house because he needed more room for his family.
ad·di·tion (ə dish′ən) *noun, plural* **additions.**
in addition or **in addition to.** As well as; also. *In addition to* being on the baseball team, he is also on the hockey team.

additional Added; extra. Frank got *additional* information for his social studies report from the library.
ad·di·tion·al (ə dish′ən əl) *adjective.*

address 1. The place at which a person lives or an organization is located. Carol's *address* is 90 Pine Lane. That store's *address* is 595 Main Street. 2. The writing on a letter or package that tells where it is to be sent. I can't read the *address* on this letter. 3. A speech. The prime minister's *address* to the nation will be on television. *Noun.*
—1. To write on a letter or package the place to which it will be delivered. Father asked me to *address* this letter. 2. To speak to a person or a group. The mayor *addressed* the audience in the town hall. *Verb.*
ad·dress (ə dres′ *or* ad′res *for noun;* ə dres′ *for verb*) *noun, plural* **addresses;** *verb,* **addressed, addressing.**

adenoids Small masses of flesh that grow at the top of the throat in back of the nose. Adenoids are glands, and if they become swollen it is hard to breathe and speak.
ad·e·noids (ad′ən oidz′) *noun plural.*

adept Being very good at doing something; skilled. Janet was an *adept* skater because she practised every morning.
a·dept (ə dept′) *adjective.*

adequate As much as is needed; enough. Those plants will not grow without *adequate* rain. His marks were *adequate,* but not high enough for him to make the honour roll.
ad·e·quate (ad′ə kwət) *adjective.*

adhere 1. To stick tight; become attached. The chewing gum *adhered* to his shoe. 2. To follow closely; be faithful. If you *adhere* to the route on the map, you won't get lost.
ad·here (ad hēr′) *verb,* **adhered, adhering.**

adhesive A substance that makes things stick together. Glue and paste are *adhesives*. *Noun.*
—Having a sticky surface that will hold tight to other things. A postage stamp is *adhesive* on one side. The bandage was held on his skin with *adhesive* tape. *Adjective.*
ad·he·sive (ad hē′siv *or* ad ē′siv) *noun, plural* **adhesives;** *adjective.*

adieu The French word that means "good-bye."
a·dieu (a dyoo′ *or* a dyoo) *interjection.*

adjacent Lying next to or near. The garage is *adjacent* to the house.
ad·ja·cent (ə jā′sənt) *adjective.*

adjective A word that tells something about a noun or a pronoun. An adjective describes a person, place, or thing. Some examples of adjectives are: We own a *red* car. Bill is *tall*. She was *sad*. That is *his* bat. Ann has *many* books. We own *two* dogs.
ad·jec·tive (aj′ək tiv) *noun, plural* **adjectives.**

adjoin To be next to. Things that adjoin are very close to each other. Our farm *adjoins* theirs.
ad·join (ə join′) *verb,* **adjoined, adjoining.**

adjourn To stop and put off something until a time in the future. The class president *adjourned* the meeting until next week. The Senate will *adjourn* for the summer.
ad·journ (ə jurn′) *verb,* **adjourned, adjourning.**

adjust 1. To change and make right or better; arrange in the best way. Helen *adjusted* the length of her new skirt. The mechanic had to *adjust* the brakes on the car. 2. To be comfortable or used to something; adapt. Ben found it hard to *adjust* to the new neighbourhood.
ad·just (ə just′) *verb,* **adjusted, adjusting.**

adjustment 1. A change to make something right or better; correction. He spent an hour making the *adjustments* on the brakes. 2. The act of becoming used to or comfortable in a situation. It took Karen several weeks to make the *adjustment* to her new home in the country.
ad·just·ment (ə just′mənt) *noun, plural* **adjustments.**

ad-lib To do or say something that has not been planned or practised before. He forgot part of his speech, so he had to *ad-lib* as he went along.
ad-lib (ad′lib′) *verb,* **ad-libbed, ad-libbing.**

administer 1. To control the operation of; manage; direct. Her uncle *administers* the company's sales department. 2. To give; pro-

vide. The Canadian Red Cross *administers* first aid. The judge *administered* the oath to the witness.
ad·min·is·ter (ad min′is tər) *verb,* **administered, administering.**

administration 1. The control of the operations of a business, a school, a government, or some other group. He has always worked for another person and has no experience in *administration.* 2. A group of people who are in charge of the operation of something. The principal is the head of the school *administration.* 3. The government in power. In Canada, the prime minister together with the members of the cabinet is called the *administration.* 4. The period of time during which a government holds office. The Canadian flag was introduced during the Pearson *administration.*
ad·min·is·tra·tion (ad min′is trā′shən) *noun, plural* **administrations.**

admiral A navy officer of the highest rank. In the Canadian Armed Forces, the four ranks of admiral are **admiral, vice-admiral, rear admiral,** and **commodore.**
ad·mir·al (ad′mər əl) *noun, plural* **admirals.**

admiration A feeling of approval or respect. We feel *admiration* when we think that a person is very good or a thing is very beautiful.
ad·mi·ra·tion (ad′mə rā′shən) *noun.*

admire 1. To feel a great respect for. I *admire* a person who is always honest. 2. To look at or speak of with pleasure and approval. Sally and Joan *admired* their friend's new coat.
ad·mire (ad mīr′) *verb,* **admired, admiring.**

admission 1. The act of allowing to come in or enter. Her parents held a party to celebrate her *admission* to college. 2. The price that a person has to pay to come in. The *admission* to the soccer game was five dollars. 3. The act of saying that something is true; confession. She found it hard to make the *admission* that she had lost her friend's ring.
ad·mis·sion (ad mish′ən) *noun, plural* **admissions.**

admit 1. To allow to come in; let in. John was *admitted* to the club last week. 2. To

at; āpe; cär; end; mē; it; īce; hot; ōld;
wood; fool; oil; out; up; turn; sing;
thin; this; hw in white; zh in treasure.
ə stands for a in about, e in taken,
i in pencil, o in lemon, and u in circus.

9

confess the truth of. He *admitted* that he had broken the lamp.

ad·mit (ad mit′) *verb*, **admitted, admitting.**

admittance The right to come in; permission to enter. This ticket gives you *admittance* to the movie theatre.

ad·mit·tance (ad mit′əns) *noun.*

adobe 1. A brick made of a sandy kind of clay. Bits of straw are sometimes mixed with the clay, and the bricks are dried in the sun. 2. A building made with adobe.

a·do·be (ə dō′bē) *noun, plural* **adobes.**

Adobe Building

adolescent A young person who is not yet an adult. A person between the ages of twelve and eighteen is an adolescent.

ad·o·les·cent (ad′əl es′ənt) *noun, plural* **adolescents.**

adopt 1. To take a child of other parents as a member of one's own family. The couple *adopted* a boy and a girl from an orphanage. 2. To take and use as one's own. Canada formally *adopted* the British system of government in 1867. 3. To accept or approve. The town council voted to *adopt* the plan for a new library.

a·dopt (ə dopt′) *verb*, **adopted, adopting.**

adoption The act of adopting. The *adoption* of the baby took two months.

a·dop·tion (ə dop′shən) *noun, plural* **adoptions.**

adore To love and admire greatly; worship. She *adores* her grandmother.

a·dore (ə dôr′) *verb*, **adored, adoring.**

adorn To add something beautiful to; decorate. She *adorned* the table with flowers.

a·dorn (ə dôrn′) *verb*, **adorned, adorning.**

adrift Moving freely with the current or wind; drifting. When something is adrift, it is not tied or anchored or held in any way. The boys set the canoe *adrift* by accident.

a·drift (ə drift′) *adverb; adjective.*

adult 1. A person who is fully grown. A man or woman who is more than eighteen years old is an adult. 2. A plant or animal that is fully grown. *Noun.*
—Having grown to full size; mature. An *adult* butterfly develops from a caterpillar. *Adjective.*

a·dult (ə dult′ *or* ad′ult) *noun, plural* **adults;** *adjective.*

adulterate To make weaker or less good by adding something. The restaurant *adulterated* the orange juice by adding water.

a·dul·ter·ate (ə dul′tə rāt′) *verb*, **adulterated, adulterating.**

advance 1. To move forward. He *advanced* the hands of the clock to the correct time. The army *advanced* to the gates of the enemy's city. 2. To help the progress of; add to; improve. The scientist hoped that his experiments would *advance* our knowledge of the sea. 3. To offer; propose. The club's president *advanced* a new plan for a camping trip. 4. To move up in position; promote. The hard-working student *advanced* to the head of her class. 5. To give money before it is due. His mother said she would *advance* him his allowance for the next week so he could buy his friend a present. *Verb.*
—1. A move forward. The army made a steady *advance* toward the city. 2. Progress; improvement. The development of the airplane was an *advance* in long-distance travel. 3. A payment given before it is due. He received an *advance* on his next month's salary. 4. **advances.** Attempts to gain the friendship of someone. Because he was shy, he was nervous when people made *advances*. *Noun.*

ad·vance (ad vans′) *verb*, **advanced, advancing;** *noun, plural* **advances.**

advancement 1. Progress; improvement. Her *advancement* in reading ability pleased the teacher. 2. A move up in position; promotion. That job offers great opportunities for *advancement*.

ad·vance·ment (ad vans′mənt) *noun, plural* **advancements.**

advantage Something that can be of extra help or of use in doing certain things. Being tall is an *advantage* for a basketball player. My older sister's knowledge of typing was an *advantage* when she looked for a job.

ad·van·tage (ad van′təj) *noun, plural* **advantages.**

to take advantage of. 1. To make good use of. He *took advantage of* the opportunity to learn French. **2.** To make unfair use of.

She *took advantage of* her friend's generosity by borrowing her records too often.

advantageous Being of extra help; favourable. Capturing her brother's queen put Jean in an *advantageous* position in their chess game.
ad·van·ta·geous (ad′van tā′jəs *or* ad′vən tā′jəs) *adjective.*

adventure 1. Something a person does that involves danger and difficulties. Columbus' voyage to the New World was a great *adventure*. That book is about the *adventures* of the pioneers. 2. An exciting or unusual experience. Their first trip by airplane was an *adventure* for the boys.
ad·ven·ture (ad ven′chər) *noun, plural* **adventures.**

adventurous 1. Eager to have exciting or dangerous experiences; bold. The *adventurous* campers set off on a canoe trip in the wilderness. 2. Full of danger; risky. The first voyages to the New World were *adventurous* journeys.
ad·ven·tur·ous (ad ven′chər əs) *adjective.*

adverb A word that tells something about a verb, an adjective, or another adverb. An adverb may tell how something is done (The boy walked *quickly*.). It may also tell where or when something is done (She went to bed *early*.). An adverb can also tell how much something is felt (I am *very* tired.).
ad·verb (ad′vurb′) *noun, plural* **adverbs.**

adversary A person or group that is on the other side in a contest or fight; opponent or enemy. Her *adversary* in the tennis match was two games ahead.
ad·ver·sar·y (ad′vər ser′ē) *noun, plural* **adversaries.**

adverse 1. Opposite to what is wanted; not favorable. The football game was played under *adverse* conditions because of the heavy rain. 2. Not friendly or agreeable. Her mother was *adverse* to the idea of a picnic that weekend.
ad·verse (ad vurs′) *adjective.*

adversity Misfortune, suffering, or difficulty. The shipwrecked sailor showed courage in the face of *adversity*.
ad·ver·si·ty (ad vur′sə tē) *noun, plural* **adversities.**

advertise To make known to the public. A business can advertise something by describing what is special or good about it, so that people will learn about it and want to buy it. That company *advertises* its toothpaste on television and in magazines. The school *advertised* the play by putting up posters. Her

mother *advertised* for a babysitter in the town newspaper.
ad·ver·tise (ad′vər tīz′) *verb,* **advertised, advertising.**

advertisement A public announcement describing what is special or good about something. Some advertisements are made to get people to buy a product or use a service, or to support a person or cause. Other advertisements are made in order to find a thing that is wanted or a person to do something.
ad·ver·tise·ment (ad′vər tīz′mənt *or* ad·vur′tiz mənt) *noun, plural* **advertisements.**

advice An idea that is offered to a person telling him or her how to act in a certain situation. The father gave his daughter *advice* about how to take care of her new puppy.
ad·vice (əd vīs′) *noun.*

advisable Being a good or smart thing to do; wise; sensible. It is *advisable* to drive at a slower speed on wet roads.
ad·vis·a·ble (əd vī′zə bəl) *adjective.*

advise 1. To give advice. To advise someone is to suggest a good way to act or the right thing to do in a certain situation. His doctor *advised* him not to eat so much candy. 2. To give information to; notify. The letter *advised* Carol that she had won first prize in the contest.
ad·vise (əd vīz′) *verb,* **advised, advising.**

advisor A person who gives advice. High schools have *advisors* who help students make decisions about what to study. This word is also spelled **adviser.**
ad·vis·or (əd vī′zər) *noun, plural* **advisors.**

advocate To speak in favour of; urge. The politician *advocated* penalties against people who polluted the air. *Verb.*
—A person who speaks in favour of someone or something. Lawyers are *advocates* for people who go to court. *Noun.*
ad·vo·cate (ad′və kāt′ *for verb;* ad′və kət *for noun*) *verb,* **advocated, advocating;** *noun, plural* **advocates.**

adze A tool that looks like an axe. It has a curved blade and is used to shape logs and other large pieces of wood. This word is also spelled **adz.**
adze (adz) *noun, plural* **adzes.**

---

at; āpe; cär; end; mē; it; īce; hot; ōld;
wood; fōōl; oil; out; up; turn; sing;
thin; this; hw in white; zh in treasure.
ə stands for a in about, e in taken,
i in pencil, o in lemon, and u in circus.

aerial In the air. Trapeze artists do *aerial* acrobatics. The helicopter pilot took an *aerial* photograph of the city. *Adjective.*
—A radio or television antenna. *Noun.*
aer·i·al (er′ē əl) *adjective; noun, plural* **aerials.**

aeronautics The science that has to do with flight. Aeronautics is concerned with designing, building, and flying aircraft.
aer·o·nau·tics (er′ə no′tiks) *noun plural.*

aeroplane A machine that flies in the air. This word is usually spelled **airplane.** Look up **airplane** for more information.

Television Aerial

aer·o·plane (er′ə plān′) *noun, plural* **aeroplanes.**

aerosol A mass of very fine particles of a solid or a liquid that are suspended in a gas. Smoke and fog are aerosols that occur in nature. There are also aerosols of paint and other materials that are sealed in cans and released in the form of a fine spray.
aer·o·sol (er′ə sol′) *noun, plural* **aerosols.**

aerospace The earth's atmosphere and outer space. The entire region in which aircraft and spacecraft can be operated is called aerospace.
aer·o·space (er′ō spās′) *noun.*

aesthetic Having to do with art and beauty and things that are beautiful. We can judge a painting from an *aesthetic* point of view.
aes·thet·ic (ez thet′ik *or* es thet′ik) *adjective.*

affable Easy to meet and talk to; friendly. The old country doctor was an *affable* man.
af·fa·ble (af′ə bəl) *adjective.*

affair 1. A thing that is done or has to be done. Moving to a new home can be a confusing *affair.* 2. Something that happens; event. The dance was a formal *affair.*
af·fair (ə fer′) *noun, plural* **affairs.**

affect[1] 1. To make something happen to; have an effect on. The lack of rain may *affect* the crops in a bad way this year. 2. To make you feel something in your heart. The photographs of the hungry children *affected* him very much and made him sad.
af·fect (ə fekt′) *verb,* **affected, affecting.**

▲ The words **affect** and **effect** sound the same and have the same basic meaning, but they cannot be used in the same way. **Affect** is a verb: A poor diet can *affect* your health. **Effect** is a noun: Daily exercise will have a good *effect* on your health.

affect[2] To pretend to have or feel. He *affected* bravery, but he was really afraid.
af·fect (ə fekt′) *verb,* **affected, affecting.**

affection A feeling of love. When you feel affection for people, you like them very much and care about what happens to them.
af·fec·tion (ə fek′shən) *noun, plural* **affections.**

affectionate Full of or showing love. She gave her grandmother an *affectionate* hug.
af·fec·tion·ate (ə fek′shən ət) *adjective.*

affiliate To join or have something to do with. Channel five is *affiliated* with the CBC.
af·fil·i·ate (ə fil′ē āt′) *verb,* **affiliated, affiliating.**

affirmative Saying that something is true; saying "yes." He gave an *affirmative* answer to my question by nodding his head.
af·firm·a·tive (ə fur′mə tiv) *adjective.*

affix To attach to something. He *affixed* the picture to the wall with a thumbtack.
af·fix (ə fiks′) *verb,* **affixed, affixing.**

afflict To cause a person great pain or trouble; make miserable. Helen was *afflicted* by poison ivy for a week.
af·flict (ə flikt′) *verb,* **afflicted, afflicting.**

affliction 1. A cause of pain or trouble. Blindness is a severe *affliction.* 2. The condition of suffering pain or deep unhappiness. The neighbours were very kind to the sick woman during her *affliction.*
af·flic·tion (ə flik′shən) *noun, plural* **afflictions.**

affluent Rich; wealthy. The expensive jewellery store had many *affluent* customers.
af·flu·ent (af′loo ənt) *adjective.*

afford 1. To have enough money to pay for. He cannot *afford* a new car. 2. To be able to do or spare without causing harm. I can only *afford* to watch television for an hour tonight because I have homework to do. 3. To give or provide. A vacation *affords* us time to rest.
af·ford (ə fōrd′) *verb,* **afforded, affording.**

affront A deliberate insult. Her rude comment about my home was an *affront* to me.
af·front (ə frunt′) *noun, plural* **affronts.**

afire On fire; burning. The old house was *afire*. It was hard to set the damp log *afire*.
a·fire (ə fīr′) *adjective; adverb.*

afloat Floating on water. There are fallen leaves *afloat* on the pond. The lifeboat was made so that it would stay *afloat*.
a·float (ə flōt′) *adjective; adverb.*

afoot 1. On foot; by walking. They left their bicycles and continued *afoot*. 2. In action; going on. Secret plans for the attack were *afoot*.
a·foot (ə foot′) *adverb; adjective.*

afraid 1. Feeling fear; frightened. Are you *afraid* of snakes? He is *afraid* to fly in an airplane. 2. Feeling unhappy or sorry about. I'm *afraid* that I will not be able to spend the night at your house.
a·fraid (ə frād′) *adjective.*

Africa A continent south of Europe, between the Atlantic Ocean and the Indian Ocean.
Af·ri·ca (af′ri kə) *noun.*

African Of or having to do with Africa or its people. We saw an exhibit of *African* art. *Adjective.*
—1. A black person who was born in Africa. 2. Any person who is a citizen of an African country. *Noun.*
Af·ri·can (af′ri kən) *adjective; noun, plural* **Africans.**

aft At or toward the rear of a boat or aircraft. The sailor walked *aft*.
aft (aft) *adverb.*

after The dog walked *after* his owner. The police went *after* the thieves. It is ten minutes *after* three o'clock. I came on Sunday and she came one day *after*. It happened *after* you left.
af·ter (af′tər) *preposition; adverb; conjunction.*

Aft · Fore

aftermath Something that comes as a result of something else. Often floods are the *aftermath* of a hurricane.
af·ter·math (af′tər math′) *noun, plural* **aftermaths.**

afternoon The part of the day between noon and evening.
af·ter·noon (af′tər noon′) *noun, plural* **afternoons.**

afterwards At a later time. We chopped wood for an hour, and *afterwards* we rested for an hour. ▲ This word is also spelled **afterward.**
af·ter·wards (af′tər wərdz) *adverb.*

again Once more; another time. She did not hear him the first time, so he called to her *again*.
a·gain (ə gen′ *or* ə gān′) *adverb.*

▲ The word **again** used to mean "back" or "in the opposite direction." A ball that was thrown against a wall was said to bounce *again* to the person who had thrown it. The idea of doing something a second time came from this earlier English meaning.

against He threw the ball *against* the wall. The MP voted *against* the bill. The fish swam *against* the current of the river. She leaned her bicycle *against* the tree.
a·gainst (ə genst′ *or* ə gānst′) *preposition.*

agate 1. A stone that is striped with different colours. It is a kind of quartz. 2. A marble that is made of agate or looks like it, and is used for playing games.
ag·ate (ag′it) *noun, plural* **agates.**

Cross Section of an Agate

age 1. The amount of time that a person, animal, or thing has lived or existed. Her *age* is ten years. He retired from his job at the *age* of sixty-five. 2. A particular period of time. Her grandfather was enjoying his old *age*. Ed wrote a paper about the atomic *age*. 3. A long time. We haven't been to visit them for *ages*. *Noun.*
—1. To make old. Having a hard life can *age* a person. 2. To become old or mature. Some cheese tastes better when it *ages*. *Verb.*
age (āj) *noun, plural* **ages;** *verb,* **aged, aging** *or* **ageing.**

aged 1. Having grown old. The young girl helped take care of her *aged* grandfather. 2. Having the age of. She has a brother *aged* three.
a·ged (ā′jid *for definition 1;* ājd *for definition 2*) *adjective.*

at; āpe; cär; end; mē; it; īce; hot; ōld; wood; fool; oil; out; up; turn; sing; thin; this; hw in white; zh in treasure.
ə stands for a in about, e in taken, i in pencil, o in lemon, and u in circus.

agency A company or a person that does certain work for other companies or people. An employment *agency* helps people to find jobs. An advertising *agency* prepares advertisements for companies that are its clients. The RCMP is the law-enforcement *agency* of the federal government.
a·gen·cy (ā′jən sē) *noun, plural* **agencies.**

agent 1. A person who acts for some other person or company. The real estate *agent* sold the young couple a new house. The secret *agent* acted as a spy in a foreign country. 2. Something that does a certain thing. Soap is a cleaning *agent*.
a·gent (ā′jənt) *noun, plural* **agents.**

aggravate 1. To make worse. Being out in the rain *aggravated* his cold. 2. To make angry; annoy. His constant complaining *aggravates* her.
ag·gra·vate (ag′rə vāt′) *verb*, **aggravated, aggravating.**

aggression An attack or warlike action. Acts of aggression are often made against a person or country that has not done anything to cause such an attack. A country that sends an army to take over the land of another country is guilty of aggression.
ag·gres·sion (ə gresh′ən) *noun, plural* **aggressions.**

aggressive 1. Being warlike and ready to attack without a good reason. The *aggressive* nation sent its troops to attack a neighbouring country. 2. Very forceful and bold. An *aggressive* salesman does not easily accept "no" for an answer.
ag·gres·sive (ə gres′iv) *adjective.*

aghast Feeling great surprise or shock. She was *aghast* at his cheating on the test.
a·ghast (ə gast′) *adjective.*

agile Able to move and react quickly and easily. A cat is an *agile* animal.
ag·ile (aj′əl *or* aj′īl′) *adjective.*

agility Quickness and ease in moving and reacting. An acrobat must have *agility*.
a·gil·i·ty (ə jil′ə tē) *noun.*

agitate 1. To move back and forth; stir up. The wind *agitated* the water and made waves. A washing machine *agitates* clothes. 2. To disturb the feelings of; excite. The report that there might be an earthquake in the area *agitated* the people who lived there.
ag·i·tate (aj′ə tāt′) *verb*, **agitated, agitating.**

agitator A person or thing that stirs up or disturbs. The reporter blamed the riot on *agitators* who aroused the people of the area.
ag·i·ta·tor (aj′ə tā′tər) *noun, plural* **agitators.**

aglow Bright with light or warmth; glowing. The Christmas tree was *aglow* with candles. The room was set *aglow* by the blazing logs in the fireplace.
a·glow (ə glō′) *adjective; adverb.*

agnostic A person who believes that it is not possible to know for sure whether or not God really exists.
ag·nos·tic (ag nos′tik) *noun, plural* **agnostics.**

ago Before the time it is now; past. He left ten minutes *ago*. Dinosaurs lived long *ago*.
a·go (ə gō′) *adjective; adverb.*

agony Great pain or suffering of the mind or body. He was in *agony* from the toothache. She suffered *agony* at the death of her pet.
ag·o·ny (ag′ə nē) *noun, plural* **agonies.**

agree 1. To have the same idea. When you agree, you think or feel the same way about a thing as someone else does. His friends thought it was a good day to go to the beach, but Jim did not *agree*. 2. To say "yes" to something. He *agreed* to lend me his bicycle.
a·gree (ə grē′) *verb*, **agreed, agreeing.**
agree with. To be good for. When he has a stomach ache, cold drinks do not *agree with* him.

agreeable 1. Nice; pleasant. She is a very *agreeable* person. 2. Willing to say "yes." I will come to the party if my mother is *agreeable*.
a·gree·a·ble (ə grē′ə bəl) *adjective.*

agreement 1. An understanding between people or groups. The brothers made an *agreement* about dividing their chores. The two nations signed a peace *agreement* during the meeting. 2. The state of agreeing; having the same ideas. My father is in *agreement* with my mother about what colour to paint the house.
a·gree·ment (ə grē′mənt) *noun, plural* **agreements.**

agricultural Having to do with farming or farms; of agriculture. Because of his interest in farming, the boy went to an *agricultural* college.
ag·ri·cul·tur·al (ag′rə kul′chər əl) *adjective.*

agriculture The raising of crops and farm animals; farming.
ag·ri·cul·ture (ag′rə kul′chər) *noun.*

ahead Jim was way *ahead* of the other runners in the race. Go *ahead* with your plans for the party. Our team is six points *ahead*. A person must work hard to get *ahead* in that company.
a·head (ə hed′) *adverb.*

ahoy An expression used by sailors as a greeting or to attract attention. When the sailors saw the other ship, they yelled "Ship *ahoy!*"
a·hoy (ə hoi′) *interjection.*

aid To give help or support. Jim *aided* the farmer in his search for the lost cattle. Two Boy Scouts *aided* us in putting up the tent. *Verb.*
—**1.** Help or support; assistance. The older boys came to my *aid* when I climbed too high in the tree. **2.** Something that is helpful. A dictionary is an *aid* in learning new words. *Noun.* ▲ Another word that sounds like this is **aide.**
aid (ād) *verb,* **aided, aiding;** *noun, plural* **aids.**

aide A helper or assistant. During the summer, she worked as a nurse's *aide.* ▲ Another word that sounds like this is **aid.**
aide (ād) *noun, plural* **aides.**

ail **1.** To cause illness or trouble for. What *ails* your brother? **2.** To be ill; feel sick. My aunt has been *ailing* for about a month now. ▲ Another word that sounds like this is **ale.**
ail (āl) *verb,* **ailed, ailing.**

ailanthus A tree that has leaves shaped like feathers and clusters of small green flowers. It grows well in city areas where other trees fail to grow.
ai·lan·thus (ā lan′thəs) *noun, plural* **ailanthuses.**

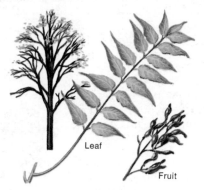

Leaf

Fruit

Ailanthus Tree

aileron A movable part on the back of an airplane wing. By moving up and down, the aileron controls the speed of the airplane in flight.
ai·le·ron (ā′lə ron′) *noun, plural* **ailerons.**

ailment An illness; sickness. His *ailment* was cured by a long rest.
ail·ment (āl′mənt) *noun, plural* **ailments.**

aim **1.** To direct or point a weapon or a blow. The boxer *aimed* a punch at the other fighter's jaw. The hunter *aimed* at the deer but missed him. **2.** To intend for; direct toward. The mayor *aimed* her speech at the young people who would vote in the next election. *Verb.*
—**1.** The act of pointing or directing a weapon or blow. His *aim* was not good enough to hit the bull's-eye. **2.** Goal; purpose. Her *aim* was to become the best player on the team. *Noun.*
aim (ām) *verb,* **aimed, aiming;** *noun, plural* **aims.**

aimless Without purpose or aim. They went on an *aimless* walk through the fields.
aim·less (ām′ləs) *adjective.*

ain't **1.** Am not. **2.** Is not; are not. **3.** Has not; have not.

▲ **Ain't** is not considered to be good English. Because of this, careful speakers and writers avoid using *ain't.*

air **1.** What we breathe. Air is all around us, but we cannot see it, smell it, or taste it. Air is a mixture of many gases, but just two gases, nitrogen and oxygen, make up ninety-nine per cent of the air. **2.** The open space above us; the sky. He threw the ball into the *air.* **3.** Fresh air. Please open the window and let in some *air.* **4.** A song or tune. He whistled a cheerful *air* as he worked. **5.** A way, look, or manner. He has an *air* of mystery about him. **6. airs.** Showy manners used to impress others. She always puts on *airs* when her younger sister's friends are around. *Noun.*
—**1.** To let air through. Please open the windows and *air* out the room before you leave. **2.** To make known. The workers *aired* their complaints about having to work such long hours. *Verb.* ▲ Other words that sound like this are **ere** and **heir.**
air (er) *noun, plural* **airs;** *verb,* **aired, airing.**
on the air. Broadcasting or being broadcast. That programme will be *on the air* at 6:30 tonight.

air conditioner A machine used to cool off and clean the air in a place. Air conditioners are used during the summer in homes,

at; āpe; cär; end; mē; it; īce; hot; ōld;
wood; fo͞ol; oil; out; up; turn; sing;
thin; this; hw in white; zh in treasure.
ə stands for a in about, e in taken,
i in pencil, o in lemon, and u in circus.

cars, stores, and other places to provide air that makes us more comfortable.

aircraft Any machine made to fly in the air. Airplanes, helicopters, gliders, and balloons are all aircraft.
air·craft (er′kraft′) *noun, plural* **aircraft.**

air element *Canadian.* The branch of the Canadian Armed Forces which uses aircraft, formerly known as the Royal Canadian Air Force. It is also called the **air force.**

airfield The landing field of an airport.
air·field (er′fēld′) *noun, plural* **airfields.**

air force The branch of a country's armed forces that uses aircraft. In Canada, this branch is also called the **air element.**

airline A system of carrying people and things from one place to another by airplane.
air·line (er′līn′) *noun, plural* **airlines.**

airliner A large airplane that carries passengers from one place to another.
air·lin·er (er′lī′nər) *noun, plural* **airliners.**

air-mail To send a letter by airplane. My mother is going to *air-mail* this letter to our Member of Parliament. *Verb.*
—Having to do with air mail. I sent an *air-mail* letter to my friend who lives in Japan. *Adjective.*
—By air mail. Please send this package *air-mail* so it will arrive more quickly. *Adverb.*
air-mail (er′māl′) *verb,* **air-mailed, air-mailing;** *adjective; adverb.*

air mail Mail carried between cities by airplane.

airman 1. The pilot or other male crew member of an aircraft. 2. *Canadian.* A person in the air element who is not an officer.

airplane A machine that flies in the air. An airplane has two wings. Because it is heavier than air, it has propellers or jet engines to make it fly. This word is also spelled **aero-plane.**
air·plane (er′plān′) *noun, plural* **airplanes.**

Airplane

airport A place with fields divided into lanes for airplanes to land and take off. An airport has buildings for sheltering and fixing airplanes, and other buildings for people who are waiting to take an airplane flight.
air·port (er′pōrt′) *noun, plural* **airports.**

air pressure The force that air puts on everything it touches. Air pressure is caused by the weight of the air high above the earth pressing down on the air below.

airship An aircraft that is lighter than air. An airship is driven by a motor, and it can be steered.
air·ship (er′ship′) *noun, plural* **airships.**

airstrip A paved or cleared area where aircraft can land and take off.
air·strip (er′strip′) *noun, plural* **airstrips.**

airtight 1. So tight that no air or gases can get in or out. The jelly was packed in an *airtight* jar so that it would stay fresh. 2. Having no weak points that could be easily attacked. The police had an *airtight* case against the man who was accused of robbing the bank.
air·tight (er′tīt′) *adjective.*

airy 1. Light as air; delicate. She wore an *airy* gown that fluttered in the breeze. 2. Open to the air; breezy. We bought the house on Bathurst Street because it was so *airy* and cheerful.
air·y (er′ē) *adjective,* **airier, airiest.**

aisle The space between two rows or sections of something. We walked down the *aisle* between the counters in the grocery store. There were several *aisles* in the movie theatre. ▲ Other words that sound like this are **I'll** and **isle.**
aisle (īl) *noun, plural* **aisles.**

ajar Partly open. The front door was *ajar* and the cat ran out. The door to the safe was left *ajar.*
a·jar (ə jär′) *adjective; adverb.*

akimbo Having one's hands on one's hips with the elbows turned outward.
a·kim·bo (ə kim′bō) *adjective.*

akin 1. Of the same kind; similar. Love and friendship are *akin.* 2. Belonging to the same family; related. She and I are *akin* because our grandmothers were sisters.
a·kin (ə kin′) *adjective.*

alabaster A smooth, whitish stone. It is used mostly to make sculptures.
a·la·bas·ter (al′ə bas′tər) *noun.*

The girl is standing with her arms **akimbo.**

alarm **1.** A bell, buzzer, or other thing used to wake people up or to warn them of danger. He set the *alarm* for seven o'clock before going to bed. The bank has an *alarm* that rings to alert the police if a robbery takes place. **2.** A sudden fear of danger. The loud thunder filled the child with *alarm*. **3.** A warning of danger. The dark clouds and strong winds were an *alarm* that a hurricane was approaching. *Noun.*
—To make afraid. The news that war might break out *alarmed* the people. *Verb.*
    a·larm (ə lärm′) *noun, plural* **alarms;** *verb,* **alarmed, alarming.**

▲ The word **alarm** comes from an old Italian phrase that meant "to arms!" This phrase was used as a warning to tell soldiers to pick up their weapons, or *arms,* and be ready to fight.

alas An expression used to show sorrow or disappointment.
    a·las (ə las′) *interjection.*

Alaska Highway One of the most important highways in the North. It extends from Dawson Creek in British Columbia to Fairbanks in Alaska. The highway was built by the United States during World War II. Afterwards the highway was turned over to Canada.

albatross A large sea bird that has a long, hooked beak and webbed feet. The albatross has large wings and is able to fly for very long distances. It is usually found in the southern oceans of the world.
    al·ba·tross (al′bə tros′) *noun, plural* **albatrosses.**

▲ The name **albatross** is believed to come from a word that meant "bucket of water" or "water carrier." Because the albatross is able to fly for such a long time over the ocean, people once thought that it was somehow able to carry a supply of fresh water in its body to drink as it flew.

Alberta A province in western Canada, between British Columbia and Saskatchewan.
    Al·ber·ta (al ber′tə) *noun.*

▲ **Alberta** became a province of Canada in 1905. The province was named after Queen Victoria's daughter, Princess Louise Caroline Alberta, wife of the Marquess of Lorne, who was Governor General of Canada. Alberta is one of the Prairie Provinces.

Albertan A person born in or living in Alberta. *Noun.*
—Of Alberta. *Albertan* oil reserves are abundant. *Adjective.*
    Al·ber·tan (al ber′tən)   *noun,   plural* **Albertans;** *adjective.*

album **1.** A book with blank pages. People use albums to hold photographs, pictures, or other things that they collect. My uncle has many *albums* filled with postage stamps. **2.** A long-playing phonograph record. Ann gave her brother an *album* by his favourite singer for his birthday.
    al·bum (al′bəm) *noun, plural* **albums.**

alchemy A kind of chemistry practised during the Middle Ages. People who studied alchemy attempted to turn common metals into gold. They also tried to discover a magic substance that could cure all diseases and help other people to live longer.
    al·che·my (al′kə mē) *noun.*

alcohol A liquid that has no colour or smell. It catches fire easily and evaporates very quickly. One kind of alcohol is used in making certain drinks that can cause a temporary change in a person's thoughts and behaviour. Alcohol is also used in making medicines and chemicals, and for many other purposes. Some kinds of alcohol are very poisonous. Alcohol comes from certain grains and fruit. It also can be made from artificial substances.
    al·co·hol (al′kə hol′) *noun, plural* **alcohols.**

alcoholic Containing alcohol. At the party Ted's father served *alcoholic* drinks to the adults and juice to the children. *Adjective.*
—A person who has a strong need for alcohol because he suffers from alcoholism. *Noun.*
    al·co·hol·ic (al′kə hol′ik) *adjective; noun, plural* **alcoholics.**

alcoholism A disease in which your need to drink alcoholic beverages is so strong that you cannot control it.
    al·co·hol·ism (al′kə hol iz′əm) *noun.*

alcool *Canadian.* A kind of alcoholic drink made from grain.
    al·cool (al kōol′) *noun.*

alcove A small room or area that is partly closed off from a larger room.

at; āpe; cär; end; mē; it; īce; hot; ōld;
wood; fōol; oil; out; up; turn; sing;
thin; this; hw in white; zh in treasure.
ə stands for a in about, e in taken,
i in pencil, o in lemon, and u in circus.

alder A tree or shrub that grows in cool and moist places. The alder is similar to the birch tree. It has rough bark and roundish leaves.
al·der (äl′dər) *noun, plural* **alders.**

Leaf

Alder Tree

ale An alcoholic drink that is like beer, but stronger and more bitter. ▲ Another word that sounds like this is **ail.**
ale (āl) *noun, plural* **ales.**

alert **1.** Watching very carefully. An *alert* guard saw the robbers enter the building. **2.** Quick to act or learn; lively; active. Her good work shows that she has an *alert* mind. *Adjective.*
—A signal that warns of possible danger; alarm. The troops remained underground during the air raid *alert. Noun.*
—To make aware of; warn. The weather forecast *alerted* the town to the coming tornado. *Verb.*
a·lert (ə lurt′) *adjective; noun, plural* **alerts;** *verb,* **alerted, alerting.**

alfalfa A plant like clover. It has bluish-purple flowers. Alfalfa is grown as a food for cattle and other livestock.
al·fal·fa (al fal′fə) *noun.*

algae A large group of water plants that do not have roots or flowers. Seaweed is a kind of algae.
al·gae (al′jē) *noun plural.*

algebra A kind of mathematics in which letters are used along with numbers. The letters stand for numbers that are un-

Alfalfa

known. An example of an algebra problem is: 10x − 3 = 17.
al·ge·bra (al′jə brə) *noun.*

alias Another name a person calls himself. A person usually uses an alias to hide his real identity. "Billy the Kid" was the *alias* of an outlaw named William H. Bonney. *Noun.*
—Otherwise called; also known as. Sam Jones, *alias* John Williams, was wanted by the police for questioning. *Adverb.*
a·li·as (ā′lē əs) *noun, plural* **aliases;** *adverb.*

alibi **1.** A claim or proof that one was somewhere else when a crime or other act was going on. When the police questioned the man about the robbery, he had a good *alibi,* so he was not arrested. **2.** An excuse. Do you have an *alibi* for being late?
al·i·bi (al′ə bī′) *noun, plural* **alibis.**

▲ The word **alibi** comes from a Latin word that means "somewhere else." When you were accused of a crime, you would try to prove that you were in another place at the time of the crime. The claim or proof that you were somewhere else became known as your *alibi.*

alien A person who is not a citizen of the country in which he lives; foreigner. That man is an *alien* in Canada because he is still a citizen of France. *Noun.*
—Not familiar; different. The customs of those people are *alien* to me. *Adjective.*
al·ien (ā′lē ən) *noun, plural* **aliens;** *adjective.*

alienate To make someone feel unfriendly or angry. The child's bad temper *alienated* some of his friends.
al·ien·ate (ā′lē ə nāt′ *or* āl′yə nāt′) *verb,* **alienated, alienating.**

alight[1] **1.** To get down; land. The girl *alighted* from her pony. **2.** To come down from the air; land. The bee *alighted* on the flower.
a·light (ə līt′) *verb,* **alighted** or **alit, alighting.**

alight[2] **1.** Lighted up; glowing. Her face was *alight* with joy. **2.** On fire; burning. During the fireworks, the sky seemed *alight* with colour.
a·light (ə līt′) *adjective.*

align To bring into line; put in a line. The captain *aligned* his troops for the parade.
a·lign (ə līn′) *verb,* **aligned, aligning.**

alike In the same way; similarly. She and her twin sister often dress *alike. Adverb.*

always All the time; every time. There is *always* snow and ice at the North Pole.
al·ways (äl′wāz) *adverb.*

am I *am* happy that you can come to my birthday party. I *am* going to the beach tomorrow.
am (am) *verb.*

a.m. The time of day between midnight and noon. She wakes up at 7:30 *a.m.* He met his friend for lunch at 11:30 *a.m.*

▲ **a.m.** comes from the first letters of the Latin words *ante meridiem. Ante meridiem* means "before noon."

amateur A person who does something just for the pleasure of doing it, not for money. Only *amateurs* in sports are allowed to take part in the Olympic games. *Noun.*
—Done by or made up of amateurs. She will run the relay race in the *amateur* track meet. *Adjective.*
am·a·teur (am′ə chər *or* am′ə tər) *noun, plural* **amateurs;** *adjective.*

amaze To surprise greatly; astonish. The girl's speed at solving difficult mathematical problems *amazed* us all.
a·maze (ə māz′) *verb,* **amazed, amazing.**

amazement Great surprise or wonder; astonishment. The children were filled with *amazement* as they watched the circus acrobats perform.
a·maze·ment (ə māz′mənt) *noun.*

ambassador A person in the government who is sent to represent his or her country in a foreign country.
am·bas·sa·dor (am bas′ə dər) *noun, plural* **ambassadors.**

amber A hard yellow-orange or yellow-brown material that is used to make jewellery. Amber is a fossil that is formed from the resin of pine trees that grew millions of years ago.
am·ber (am′bər) *noun.*

ambiguous Having more than one meaning; not clear. The sentence "Tom told Bill that his dog bit the mailman" is *ambiguous.* We cannot be sure which boy the dog belongs to, because we do not know whether "his" refers to Tom or to Bill.
am·big·u·ous (am big′yoo əs) *adjective.*

ambition A strong desire to succeed at something. My sister's *ambition* is to become a doctor.
am·bi·tion (am bish′ən) *noun, plural* **ambitions.**

ambitious Having a strong desire to succeed at something; having ambition. The *ambitious* young worker hoped to be president of the company someday.
am·bi·tious (am bish′əs) *adjective.*

▲ The word **ambitious** goes back to a Latin word. In ancient Rome, men who wanted to be elected to a government job wore white robes. Sometimes a man would walk around the city in his white robes so that people would see him and know he was running for office. The Latin word originally meant "going around trying to get votes."

ambulance A special kind of vehicle used to carry hurt or sick people to a hospital. An ambulance has medical equipment to help people until they can get to the hospital.
am·bu·lance (am′byə ləns) *noun, plural* **ambulances.**

ambush A surprise attack by people who are hidden. *Noun.*
—To make a surprise attack from a hidden place. *Verb.*
am·bush (am′boosh) *noun, plural* **ambushes;** *verb,* **ambushed, ambushing.**

ameba A very tiny animal. This word is usually spelled **amoeba.** Look up **amoeba** for more information.

amen May it be so. *Amen* is said after a prayer. People say *amen* to show that they agree with what has been said and hope it comes true.
a·men (ā′men′ *or* ä′men′) *interjection.*

amend To change something to make it better. In Canada, an act of parliament is required to amend a law.
a·mend (ə mend′) *verb,* **amended, amending.**

amendment A change made to improve something. An *amendment* to a law is necessary when the law is no longer fair to most people because customs have changed.
a·mend·ment (ə mend′mənt) *noun, plural* **amendments.**

amends To make amends. To make up for a wrong. He tried *to make amends* for his rude behaviour by apologizing to his mother.
a·mends (ə mendz′) *noun plural.*

America 1. Another name for the **United States.** 2. Another name for **North America.**
A·mer·i·ca (ə mer′i kə) *noun.*

▲ The name **America** comes from *Amerigo* Vespucci, an Italian explorer.

—Like one another; similar. No two people have fingerprints that are exactly *alike. Adjective.*
a·like (ə līk′) *adverb; adjective.*

alimentary canal A long tube beginning at the mouth. Food moves through this as it is digested and then passed out of the body as waste matter.
al·i·men·ta·ry canal (al′ə men′tər ē *or* al′ə ment′rē).

alimony A fixed sum of money that a person pays to support a spouse during a legal separation or a former spouse after divorce.
al·i·mo·ny (al′ə mō′nē) *noun, plural* **alimonies.**

alive 1. Having life; living. These flowers must be given water if you want them to stay *alive.* 2. Having power; active. They kept *alive* the memory of the dead hero by naming a school after him.
a·live (ə līv′) *adjective.*

Alimentary Canal

all 1. The whole of. We ate *all* the ice cream. 2. Every one. Students from *all* the schools in town were in the swimming meet. *Adjective.*
—Everything or everyone. *All* were saved from the fire. *Noun.*
—The whole amount or number. *All* of us are going to the party. *Pronoun.*
—Completely. The work is *all* finished. *Adverb.* ▲ Another word that sounds like this is **awl.**
all (äl) *adjective; noun; pronoun; adverb.*

Allah God, in the Muslim religion.
Al·lah (al′ə) *noun.*

allege To say or declare positively, but without final proof. It has been *alleged* that the man stole the jewels, but he has not yet been convicted of the crime.
al·lege (ə lej′) *verb,* **alleged, alleging.**

allegiance True and faithful feelings and behaviour; loyalty. When you give your allegiance to someone or something, you promise not to harm that person or thing and to do everything you can to help.
al·le·giance (ə lē′jəns) *noun.*

allergic Having an allergy. She is sneezing because she is *allergic* to dust.
al·ler·gic (ə lur′jik) *adjective.*

allergy A reaction of a person's body against certain foods, plants, or other things that don't bother most other people. If you have an allergy to wool you may get a rash if you wear clothes that are made with wool next to your skin.
al·ler·gy (al′ər jē) *noun, plural* **allergies.**

alley 1. A narrow street or passageway between buildings. There is an *alley* behind those apartments where people can park their cars. 2. A long, narrow path down which bowling balls are rolled. The pins to be knocked down by the ball are at the far end of the alley. This is also called a **bowling alley.**
al·ley (al′ē) *noun, plural* **alleys.**

alliance An agreement between two or more countries, groups, or people to work together in doing something. The two nations had an *alliance* by which each promised to help the other fight if a third country attacked one of them.
al·li·ance (ə lī′əns) *noun, plural* **alliances.**

allied Joined together to do or get something that both or all want. During World War II, Canada, the United States, Britain, and the Soviet Union were *allied* nations in the war against Germany.
al·lied (ə līd′ *or* al′īd) *adjective.*

alligator An animal with a long head and tail and a thick, tough skin. It lives in rivers and marshes in warm parts of America and China. Alligators look like crocodiles but have shorter, wider heads.
al·li·ga·tor (al′ə gā′tər) *noun, plural* **alligators**

Alligator

Crocodile

at; āpe; cär; end; mē; it; īce; hot; ōld;
wood; fōōl; oil; out; up; turn; sing;
thin; this; hw in white; zh in treasure.
ə stands for a in about, e in taken,
i in pencil, o in lemon, and u in circus.

19

allot To give out as a share. Mrs. Smith *allotted* one apple and one candy bar to each child who came to the house at Hallowe'en.
al·lot (ə lot′) *verb,* **allotted, allotting.**

allow 1. To give permission to do or have something; permit. His father does not *allow* him to ride his bicycle on the lawn. Smoking is not *allowed* in that theatre. 2. To add or take away an amount for a special reason. We *allowed* an extra hour to make the trip in case the traffic was heavy.
al·low (ə lou′) *verb,* **allowed, allowing.**

allowance 1. A fixed amount of money given at certain regular times. Billy gets an *allowance* of one dollar a week for helping his father cut the grass. 2. An amount added or taken away for a special reason. The salesman gave us an *allowance* of $600 on the price of a new car because we traded in our old one.
al·low·ance (ə lou′əns) *noun, plural* **allowances.**
to make allowance for. To take into consideration; allow for. The teacher *made allowance for* the boy's being new to the school, and did not blame him for not knowing the rules.

alloy A metal made by mixing two or more different metals and melting them together. Brass is an *alloy* of copper and zinc.
al·loy (al′oi) *noun, plural* **alloys.**

all right 1. Acceptable; good enough. It is *all right* with me if you go. The book was not as good as she had hoped it would be, but it was *all right.* 2. Not hurt or ill; safe; well. His friend asked him if he was *all right* after he fell off his bicycle. 3. Yes. *All right,* I'll do it.

allude To mention briefly or refer to indirectly. Don't even *allude* to the mistake he made in the game; he feels very bad about it.
al·lude (ə lood′) *verb,* **alluded, alluding.**

ally To join together in order to do something. Britain and the United States *allied* themselves during World War II. *Verb.*
—A person, nation, or group who joins with another in order to do something. Canada was an *ally* of Britain during World War II. *Noun.*
al·ly (a lī′ *for verb;* al′ī *for noun) verb,* **allied, allying;** *noun, plural* **allies.**

almanac A book that contains facts and figures on many different subjects. Most almanacs are published every year. Some almanacs are arranged like a calendar and give facts about the weather, the tides, and the rising and setting of the sun for each day of the year.

al·ma·nac (al′mə nak′) *noun, plural* **almanacs.**

almond An oval nut that can be eaten and is used in desserts and candy. It grows on a tree which is also called an almond.
al·mond (ä′mənd) *noun, plural* **almonds.**

almost Very close to; nearly. I am *almost* finished with the work. He is *almost* six years old.
al·most (äl′mōst) *adverb.*

aloft 1. Far above the ground; high up. There were many kites *aloft* at the beach last weekend. 2. High up on the masts of a sailing ship. The sailors climbed *aloft* on ladders made of rope.
a·loft (ə loft′) *adverb.*

aloha *Aloha* is the Hawaiian word that means "love," and it is used to say both "hello" and "good-bye."
a·lo·ha (ə lō′ə *or* ä lō′hä) *noun, plural* **alohas;** *interjection.*

alone Not near or with another or others. She enjoyed being *alone* on the beach. There was just one puppy all *alone* in the window of the pet store. Because all his friends were away, he went to the game *alone.*
a·lone (ə lōn′) *adjective; adverb.*
to leave alone or **to let alone.** To leave undisturbed; not bother or interfere with in any way. Please *leave me alone* for an hour so I can finish reading this book.

along Flowers grew *along* the path. We walked *along* the highway. Don't forget to bring *along* your umbrella. The car moved *along* swiftly.
a·long (ə long′) *preposition; adverb.*

alongside A police car pulled up *alongside* and then passed them. The truck was parked *alongside* the curb.
a·long·side (ə long′sīd′) *adverb; preposition.*

aloof Not warm or friendly; reserved. The old queen had an *aloof* manner toward people. *Adjective.*
—At a distance; apart. When the two brothers argued, their older sister always tried to remain *aloof. Adverb.*
a·loof (ə loof′) *adjective; adverb.*

Fruit

Nut *Kernel*

Almond

aloud So as to be heard; out loud. Each student will read his report *aloud* to the class. He shouted *aloud* from the mountaintop and heard the echo.
a·loud (ə loud′) *adverb.*

alpaca An animal that lives in the mountains of South America and has long, silky wool. The alpaca is related to the camel and the llama.
al·pac·a (al pak′ə) *noun, plural* **alpacas.**

alphabet The letters or symbols that are used to write a language, arranged in their proper order.
al·pha·bet (al′fə bet′) *noun, plural* **alphabets.**

Alpaca

▲ The word **alphabet** comes from the Greek words *alpha* and *beta. Alpha* and *beta* are the names of the first two letters in the Greek alphabet.

alphabetical Arranged in the order of the letters of the alphabet. The words in a dictionary are listed in *alphabetical* order.
al·pha·bet·i·cal (al′fə bet′i kəl) *adjective.*

already He has *already* left. Are you finished *already?*
al·read·y (äl red′ē) *adverb.*

also She swims well and is *also* a good tennis player.
al·so (äl′sō) *adverb.*

altar A table or a raised place that is used for religious services. ▲ Another word that sounds like this is **alter.**
al·tar (äl′tər) *noun, plural* **altars.**

alter To make or become different; change. The tailor *altered* her dress by making it smaller around the waist. ▲ Another word that sounds like this is **altar.**
al·ter (äl′tər) *verb,* **altered, altering.**

alternate 1. To take turns. My brother and I *alternate* at washing the car each week. 2. To happen by turns, with one thing following another in a certain order. Red stripes *alternate* with white stripes on a candy cane. *Verb.*
—1. First one, then the other; every other. I have piano lessons on *alternate* Mondays. 2. Taking the place of another; substitute. Please think of an *alternate* plan in case the first plan doesn't work. *Adjective.*

—A person who takes the place of anot substitute. *Noun.*
al·ter·nate (äl′tər nāt′ *for verb;* äl′tər nə *adjective and noun) verb,* **alternated, a nating;** *adjective; noun, plural* **alternate**

alternating current An electric cu that flows regularly first in one directio then in another.

alternative A choice between two or things. Betsy had the *alternative* of go the beach with her friends or going picnic with her family.
al·ter·na·tive (äl tur′nə tiv) *noun, plu* ternatives.

although *Although* I ate a big dinne hungry again very soon.
al·though (äl tho′) *conjunction.*

altimeter An instrument that sho high above the ground or above s something is. An altimeter is use airplane to show the pilot how high a ground he is.
al·tim·e·ter (al tim′ə tər *or* al′t *noun, plural* **altimeters.**

altitude The height that something the ground or above sea level. The the plane at an *altitude* of two metres. On the mountain we saw a said we were at an *altitude* of one metres above sea level.
al·ti·tude (al′tə tood′ *or* al′tə tyo *plural* **altitudes.**

alto 1. The lowest female voice, est male voice. 2. A singer who voice. 3. A musical instrument th range of an alto voice.
al·to (äl′tō) *noun, plural* **altos.**

altogether His arrow missed th *together.* There were twelve of u at the party.
al·to·geth·er (äl′tə ge′thər) *adve*

aluminum A light, soft, silver al. Aluminum is the most co found in the earth. It is used in different things, such as pots a cooking, trucks, airplanes, or m also used as a building material. a chemical element.
a·lu·mi·num (ə loo′mə nəm) *n*

at; āpe; cär; end; mē; it; īce; wood; fool; oil; out; up; turn thin; this; hw in white; zh in ə stands for a in about, e in i in pencil, o in lemon, and

American 1. Of the United States. 2. Of North America. *Adjective.*
—1. A person who was born or is living in the United States. 2. Any person who was born in North America. *Noun.*
A·mer·i·can (ə mer′i kən) *adjective; noun, plural* **Americans.**

amiable Friendly and kind; good-natured. The owner of the bookstore was an *amiable* man who enjoyed having people come in just to look around and talk.
a·mi·a·ble (ā′mē ə bəl) *adjective.*

amid In the middle of. The house stood *amid* a grove of pine trees not far from the highway.
a·mid (ə mid′) *preposition.*

amigo A Spanish word that means "friend."
a·mi·go (ə mē′gō) *noun, plural* **amigos.**

amiss Not right or proper; wrong. I knew something was *amiss* when Bob said he didn't want to go to the baseball game with me.
a·miss (ə mis′) *adjective.*

ammonia A gas that is a mixture of nitrogen and hydrogen. It has no colour but has a very sharp smell. Many people use a mixture of ammonia in water when they are cleaning their homes.
am·mo·nia (ə mōn′yə) *noun, plural* **ammonias.**

ammunition Bullets, shells, grenades, bombs, and other things that can be fired from guns or exploded in some other way.
am·mu·ni·tion (am′yə nish′ən) *noun.*

amnesia A loss of memory. Amnesia is caused by injury to a person's brain or by sickness or shock.
am·ne·sia (am nē′zhə) *noun.*

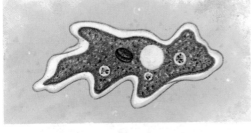

Amoeba

amoeba A very tiny animal. An amoeba is so small that it can only be seen through a microscope. Its body is made up of only one cell. An amoeba is always moving and changing shape. This word is also spelled **ameba.**
a·moe·ba (ə mē′bə) *noun, plural* **amoebas.**

among The campers pitched their tents *among* the trees. Elephants and whales are *among* the largest animals in the world. She divided the cake *among* all her friends at her birthday party.
a·mong (ə mung′) *preposition.*

amount What something adds up to; total quantity. What is the *amount* of money you spent this week? We have a large *amount* of homework to do for tomorrow. *Noun.*
—To equal or add up to. Our family's grocery bill *amounts* to one hundred dollars each week. *Verb.*
a·mount (ə mount′) *noun, plural* **amounts;** *verb,* **amounted, amounting.**

amphibian Any of a group of cold-blooded animals with backbones. Amphibians have moist skin without scales. They usually live in or near water. Frogs and toads are amphibians.
am·phib·i·an (am fib′ē ən) *noun, plural* **amphibians.**

amphibious Able to live on land and in the water. The seal is an *amphibious* animal.
am·phib·i·ous (am fib′ē əs) *adjective.*

Amphitheatre

amphitheatre A circular or oval building. An amphitheatre has seats rising in rows

at; āpe; cär; end; mē; it; īce; hot; ōld;
wood; fo͞ol; oil; out; up; turn; sing;
thin; this; hw in white; zh in treasure.
ə stands for a in about, e in taken,
i in pencil, o in lemon, and u in circus.

around a central open space. Sports contests and plays take place in amphitheatres.

am·phi·the·a·tre (am′fə thē′ə tər) *noun, plural* **amphitheatres.**

ample Enough or more than enough. We bought *ample* food for our camping trip.

am·ple (am′pəl) *adjective,* **ampler, amplest.**

amplify **1.** To add to; make larger. I asked Ruth to *amplify* her short talk by giving more details. **2.** To make sound stronger or louder. The microphone will *amplify* the singers' voices in the arena.

am·pli·fy (am′plə fī′) *verb,* **amplified, amplifying.**

amputate To cut off. The doctor had to *amputate* the soldier's wounded leg.

am·pu·tate (am′pyə tāt′) *verb,* **amputated, amputating.**

amuse To please. When something amuses us, we usually laugh or smile. The silly clowns at the circus *amused* the children.

a·muse (ə myo͞oz′) *verb,* **amused, amusing.**

amusement **1.** The condition of being amused and entertained. The magician did tricks for the *amusement* of the children. **2.** Something that amuses or entertains. Fishing is Joe's favourite *amusement.*

a·muse·ment (ə myo͞oz′mənt) *noun, plural* **amusements.**

an He ate *an* apple. We saw *an* elephant at the zoo. She bought *an* umbrella. We will leave in *an* hour. ▲ **An** means the same thing as **a. An** is used instead of **a** in front of words that have *a, e, i, o,* or *u* as their first letter, or words that sound as if they begin with one of these letters when you say them.

an (an *or* ən) *indefinite article.*

anaconda A very large snake found in South America. The anaconda can coil around and crush an animal to death.

an·a·con·da (an′ə kon′də) *noun, plural* **anacondas.**

Anaconda

anaemia A condition that occurs when the blood does not have enough red cells. Often when you have *anaemia,* you are tired and weak. This word is also spelled **anemia.**

a·nae·mi·a (ə nē′mē ə) *noun.*

anaesthetic A drug or other substance that causes a loss of feeling in the body. The doctor gave her an *anaesthetic* before setting her broken arm. This word is also spelled **anesthetic.**

a·naes·thet·ic (an′əs thet′ik) *noun, plural* **anaesthetics.**

analyse **1.** To find out what something is made of by separating it into parts. If we *analyse* air we find that it is made up mostly of nitrogen and oxygen. **2.** To study something carefully. The detective *analysed* the evidence in the robbery. This word is also spelled **analyze.**

an·a·lyse (an′ə līz′) *verb,* **analysed, analysing.**

analysis A way of finding out what something is made of by separating it into parts. We made an *analysis* of the lake water and found it was very polluted.

a·nal·y·sis (ə nal′ə sis) *noun, plural* **analyses.**

analyze To find out what something is made of. This word is usually spelled **analyse.** Look up **analyse** for more information.

anarchy The condition of a country where there are no laws or government.

an·ar·chy (an′ər kē) *noun.*

anatomy **1.** A branch of science that deals with the structure of animals or plants. **2.** The structure of an animal or plant or one of its parts. We are studying the *anatomy* of a frog in science class.

a·nat·o·my (ə nat′ə mē) *noun, plural* **anatomies.**

ancestor A person from whom one is descended. Your grandparents and great-grandparents are your *ancestors.*

an·ces·tor (an′ses′tər) *noun, plural* **ancestors.**

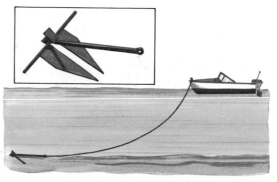

The **anchor** at the top is a close-up of the one in the water.

anchor A very heavy piece of metal that keeps a boat or ship from drifting. *Noun.*

—To hold something in place with an anchor. We will *anchor* the boat while we fish. The sailboat *anchored* in the harbour. *Verb.*

an·chor (ang′kər) *noun, plural* **anchors;** *verb,* **anchored, anchoring.**

ancient Having to do with times very long ago; very old. The workers found the ruins of an *ancient* city when they dug the foundations for the new office building.

an·cient (ān′shənt) *adjective.*

and He is tall *and* strong. Susan *and* Jane came to visit me. Two *and* two make four. Treat her fairly, *and* she'll be fair with you.

and (and *or* ənd) *conjunction.*

andiron Either of two metal supports that are used for holding wood in a fireplace.

and·i·ron (and′ī′ərn) *noun, plural* **andirons.**

anecdote A short story about some event or incident. An anecdote is usually told by a speaker to amuse an audience or to make a point.

an·ec·dote (an′ik-dōt′) *noun, plural* **anecdotes.**

Andirons

anemia A condition that occurs when the blood does not have enough red cells or when a person has lost blood. This word is usually spelled **anaemia.** Look up **anaemia** for more information.

anemometer An instrument used to measure the speed of the wind.

an·e·mom·e·ter (an′ə mom′ə tər) *noun, plural* **anemometers.**

anemone A plant that has white, red, or purple flowers that are shaped like cups.

a·nem·o·ne (ə nem′ə nē) *noun, plural* **anemones.**

anesthetic A drug that causes a loss of feeling. This word is usually spelled **anaesthetic.** Look up **anaesthetic** for more information.

angel 1. A heavenly being who serves God as a helper and messenger. 2. A person who is like an angel in goodness or beauty.

an·gel (ān′jəl) *noun, plural* **angels.**

anger A strong feeling that a person has toward another person or a thing that opposes, insults, or hurts him. In a fit of *anger*, Joan threw a book at her brother. *Noun.*

—To make angry. Jack's rude answer *angered* his father. *Verb.*

an·ger (ang′gər) *noun; verb,* **angered, angering.**

angle 1. The space between two lines or surfaces that meet. When two walls meet in a corner they form an angle. 2. A point of view. Jeff was having trouble solving the problem, so he tried to look at it from another *angle. Noun.*
—To move or bend at an angle. The road *angles* to the right as it goes up the mountain. *Verb.*

an·gle (ang′gəl) *noun, plural* **angles;** *verb,* **angled, angling.**

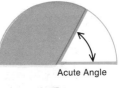
Acute Angle

Right Angle

Obtuse Angle
Angles

Anglophone *Canadian.* A person who speaks English in a country where the English language is one of two or more main languages.

An·glo·phone (ang′glə fōn′) *noun, plural* **Anglophones.**

angry 1. Feeling or showing anger. Tom was *angry* with his sister for breaking his model airplane. 2. Inflamed and painful. He had an *angry* sore on his knee.

an·gry (ang′grē) *adjective,* **angrier, angriest.**

anguish Very great suffering of the body or mind; agony. The child was in *anguish* over the death of his dog.

an·guish (ang′gwish) *noun.*

animal Any living thing that is not a plant. A person, a cow, a bird, a fish, a snake, a fly, and a worm are animals. Most animals can move about freely, use plants and other animals as food, and have sense organs.

an·i·mal (an′ə məl) *noun, plural* **animals.**

animosity Deep hatred. The *animosity* between the two countries led to war.

an·i·mos·i·ty (an′ə mos′ə tē) *noun, plural* **animosities.**

at; āpe; cär; end; mē; it; īce; hot; ōld; wood; fōōl; oil; out; up; turn; sing; thin; this; hw in white; zh in treasure. ə stands for a in about, e in taken, i in pencil, o in lemon, and u in circus.

ankle   The joint that connects the foot and the leg.

an·kle (ang′kəl) *noun, plural* **ankles.**

anklet   A short sock reaching just above the ankle.

an·klet (ang′klit) *noun, plural* **anklets.**

annex   To add or attach to something larger. The owners of the large department store are making plans to *annex* a smaller store nearby. *Verb.*
—A building used as an addition to another building. The school was too small, so the school board built an *annex* for extra classrooms. *Noun.*

Anklets

an·nex (ə neks′ *for verb;* an′eks *for noun*) *verb,* **annexed, annexing;** *noun, plural* **annexes.**

annihilate   To destroy completely; wipe out. The earthquake *annihilated* the town.

an·ni·hi·late (ə nī′ə lāt′) *verb,* **annihilated, annihilating.**

anniversary   The return each year of a special day. The *anniversary* of the day of your birth is your birthday. On February 15th the couple will celebrate the tenth *anniversary* of their wedding.

an·ni·ver·sa·ry (an′ə vur′sər ē) *noun, plural* **anniversaries.**

announce   To make something known. Mr. Jones *announced* that he would run for mayor in the next election.

an·nounce (ə nouns′) *verb,* **announced, announcing.**

announcement   A public notice that announces something. An *announcement* of the winners of the contest will be made soon.

an·nounce·ment (ə nouns′mənt) *noun, plural* **announcements.**

announcer   A person who announces something. The radio *announcer* gave the news every hour.

an·nounc·er (ə noun′sər) *noun, plural* **announcers.**

annoy   To bother or disturb. Her brother's teasing *annoys* her.

an·noy (ə noi′) *verb,* **annoyed, annoying.**

annoyance   **1.** A person or thing that bothers; nuisance. His constant complaining was an *annoyance* to her. **2.** The act of annoying or the state of being annoyed. Signs at the zoo warn against the *annoyance* of animals by visitors. Her angry remark showed her *annoyance* at his silly behaviour.

an·noy·ance (ə noi′əns) *noun, plural* **annoyances.**

annual   **1.** Happening once a year; yearly. My father takes an *annual* vacation. The earth makes an *annual* orbit around the sun. **2.** Measured by the year. The doctor recorded the child's *annual* growth.

an·nu·al (an′yo͞o əl) *adjective.*

anoint   To put oil on during a religious ceremony. The bishop *anointed* the king.

a·noint (ə noint′) *verb,* **anointed, anointing.**

anonymous   **1.** Written or done by someone whose name is not known. The police got an *anonymous* phone call telling them where the criminal was hiding. **2.** Keeping one's name a secret. The man who donated the money wanted to remain *anonymous.*

a·non·y·mous (ə non′ə məs) *adjective.*

anorak   *Canadian.* **1.** A warm waterproof coat, made by Inuit from animal skins. **2.** A parka.

an·or·ak (an′ə rak′) *noun, plural* **anoraks.**

another   I want *another* piece of cake. Joan saw *another* dress that she liked better than the first one. Tom finished his hamburger and then ordered *another.* That plan didn't work, so we'll use *another.*

an·oth·er (ə nuth′ər) *adjective; pronoun.*

Anorak

answer   **1.** Something written, said, or done in reply. Did you get an *answer* to your letter? He would not give an *answer* to my question. **2.** The solution to a problem. To find the right *answer,* multiply by 12. *Noun.*
—**1.** To write or speak in reply to something. She *answered* her friend's long letter. **2.** To act in response to something. The two boys ran to *answer* the doorbell. **3.** To agree with; fit. That man *answers* to the description of the robber. *Verb.*

an·swer (an′sər) *noun, plural* **answers;** *verb;* **answered, answering.**

ant A small insect related to bees and wasps. Ants live together in large groups that are called colonies. ▲ Another word that sounds like this is **aunt**.
  ant (ant) *noun, plural* **ants.**

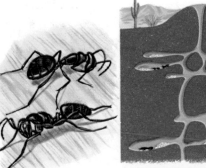
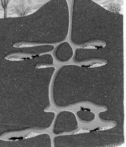

Ants   Underground Ant Colony

antagonism A strong feeling against a person or thing. After their quarrel, the two boys felt great *antagonism* toward each other.
  an·tag·o·nism (an tag′ə niz′əm) *noun, plural* **antagonisms.**

antagonize To make someone feel dislike; irritate. The clerk's rude manner *antagonized* many customers.
  an·tag·o·nize (an tag′ə nīz′) *verb,* **antagonized, antagonizing.**

Antarctica The continent at the South Pole. Antarctica is almost completely covered with ice all year long.
  Ant·arc·ti·ca (ant ärk′ti kə *or* ant är′ti kə) *noun.*

Antarctic Ocean The water around Antarctica which is made up of the most southern parts of the Atlantic, Pacific, and Indian Oceans.
  Ant·arc·tic (ant ärk′tik *or* ant är′tik).

anteater A toothless animal with a long, narrow head, long sticky tongue, and strong front claws. The anteater claws into ant hills and uses its tongue to capture ants and other insects for food.
  ant·eat·er (ant′ē′tər) *noun, plural* **anteaters.**

Anteater

antelope 1. A slender, swift animal that has long horns. Antelopes look like deer, but they are related to goats. 2. An animal of the North American prairies known also as the **pronghorn.**
  an·te·lope (ant′əl ōp′) *noun, plural* **antelopes.**

Antelope

antenna 1. A metal rod or wire used to send out or receive radio and television signals; aerial. 2. One of a pair of long, thin feelers on the head of an insect or a lobster.
  an·ten·na (an ten′ə) *noun, plural* **antennas** (*definition 1*) or **antennae** (*definition 2*).

anthem A song of gladness, praise, or patriotism. The Canadian national *anthem* is "O Canada."
  an·them (an′thəm) *noun, plural* **anthems.**

anther The part of the stamen of a flower that contains the pollen.
  an·ther (an′thər) *noun, plural* **anthers.**

anthology A book or other collection of poems, stories, or articles.
  an·thol·o·gy (an thol′ə jē) *noun, plural* **anthologies.**

anthracite A very hard, shiny black coal that burns with a low, smokeless flame.
  an·thra·cite (an′thrə sīt′) *noun.*

anti- A *prefix* that means "opposed to or against." *Antiwar* means "opposed to war."

at; āpe; cär; end; mē; it; īce; hot; ōld;
wood; fōol; oil; out; up; turn; sing;
thin; this; hw in white; zh in treasure.
ə stands for a in about, e in taken,
i in pencil, o in lemon, and u in circus.

antibiotic A substance that is produced by moulds or bacteria. Antibiotics are used in medicine to kill or slow the growth of germs that cause disease.
an·ti·bi·ot·ic (an′tē bī ot′ik) *noun, plural* **antibiotics.**

anti-body A substance produced by the blood that destroys or weakens germs. Antibodies help protect the body against certain diseases.
an·ti-bod·y (an′tē bod′ē) *noun, plural* **antibodies.**

anticipate To look forward to; expect. I do not *anticipate* any trouble.
an·tic·i·pate (an tis′ə pāt′) *verb,* **anticipated, anticipating.**

anticipation The act of anticipating; expectation. In *anticipation* of a hot summer ahead, we bought an air conditioner.
an·tic·i·pa·tion (an tis′ə pā′shən) *noun, plural* **anticipations.**

antidote A medicine that works against the effects of a poison. After the baby swallowed the poison, the doctor gave him an *antidote* to make him well.
an·ti·dote (an′tē dōt′) *noun, plural* **antidotes.**

antique Of times long ago. We went to an exhibit of *antique* automobiles. *Adjective.*
—Something made very long ago. The museum has *antiques* from the time of Confederation. *Noun.*
an·tique (an tēk′) *adjective; noun, plural* **antiques.**

antiseptic A substance that kills germs or stops their growth. Alcohol and iodine are antiseptics.
an·ti·sep·tic (an′ti sep′tik) *noun, plural* **antiseptics.**

anti-toxin An anti-body produced by the body that protects a person from a particular disease.
an·ti-tox·in (an′tē tok′sən) *noun, plural* **antitoxins.**

antler One of the two branched horns of a deer, elk, or moose. Antlers are shed each year and grow back again the next year.
ant·ler (ant′lər) *noun, plural* **antlers.**

antonym A word that has the opposite meaning of another word. *Sweet* and *sour*, *up* and *down*, and *hot* and *cold* are antonyms.
an·to·nym (an′tə nim′) *noun, plural* **antonyms.**

Antlers

anvil An iron or steel block on which metals are hammered into shape. Metals are usually softened by heating before they are placed on an anvil.
an·vil (an′vəl) *noun, plural* **anvils.**

Anvil

anxiety 1. A feeling of fearful worry or nervousness about what may happen. The mother was filled with *anxiety* because her child was lost. 2. A strong desire; eagerness. His *anxiety* to please his teacher made him work very hard at school.
anx·i·e·ty (ang zī′ə tē) *noun, plural* **anxieties.**

anxious 1. Nervous, worried, or fearful about what may happen. The mother was *anxious* about her children's safety when they were out after dark. 2. Wanting something eagerly. The boy was *anxious* to make friends at his new school.
anx·ious (angk′shəs) *adjective.*

any Take *any* seat. Pick *any* book you want. Did you buy *any* apples? *Any* child can do this problem. He runs faster than *any* of the other boys. Stop before you go *any* farther.
an·y (en′ē) *adjective; pronoun; adverb.*

anybody Has *anybody* seen Jack?
an·y·bod·y (en′ē bud′ē) *pronoun.*

anyhow I didn't want to go to the movies *anyhow.* Our best player was hurt, but we won the game *anyhow.*
an·y·how (en′ē hou′) *adverb.*

anyone *Anyone* who lives in this town can go swimming in the town pool.
an·y·one (en′ē wun′) *pronoun.*

anyplace I couldn't find the book *anyplace.*
an·y·place (en′ē plās′) *adverb.*

anything I'll do *anything* you ask me to. Frank isn't *anything* like his brother.
an·y·thing (en′ē thing′) *pronoun; adverb.*

anytime You may leave for the beach *anytime* you want to.
an·y·time (en′ē tīm′) *adverb.*

anyway It's raining, but we are going for a walk *anyway.*
an·y·way (en′ē wā′) *adverb.*

anywhere Just put the books down *anywhere.*
an·y·where (en′ē wer′ *or* en′ē hwer′) *adverb.*

aorta The main artery of the body. The aorta carries blood from the upper-left side of the heart to all parts of the body except the lungs.
a·or·ta (ā′ôr′tə) *noun, plural* **aortas.**

apart 1. Away from one another. The girls lived two miles *apart*. The trains left three hours *apart*. 2. To pieces. The mechanic took the engine *apart* to find out what was wrong with it.
a·part (ə pärt′) *adverb.*
apart from. Besides. *Apart from* the bad weather, we had a good holiday.

apartment A room or set of rooms to live in. Apartments are usually in a large building.
a·part·ment (ə pärt′mənt) *noun, plural* **apartments.**

apathy A lack of interest or concern; indifference. We listened to the boring speaker with *apathy*.
ap·a·thy (ap′ə thē) *noun.*

ape A large animal that has no tail. An ape is a kind of monkey. It is able to stand and walk almost as straight as a person can. Chimpanzees, gorillas, and orangutans are all types of apes. *Noun.*
—To imitate someone. My brother Chuck is always *aping* people to make his friends laugh. *Verb.*
ape (āp) *noun, plural* **apes;** *verb,* **aped, aping.**

aphid A small insect that lives by sucking juices from plants.
a·phid (ā′fid *or* af′id) *noun, plural* **aphids.**

Aphid

apiece For each one; each. These candy bars are thirty cents *apiece*. Mother gave the boys who raked up the leaves five dollars *apiece* for their work.
a·piece (ə pēs′) *adverb.*

apologize To say one is sorry; make an apology. I *apologized* to my sister when I broke her toy.
a·pol·o·gize (ə pol′ə jīz′) *verb,* **apologized, apologizing.**

apology A statement that one is sorry for having done something that is wrong or that hurts another person. Please accept my *apology* for being late.
a·pol·o·gy (ə pol′ə jē) *noun, plural* **apologies.**

Apostle An early follower of Christ. There were twelve Apostles chosen by Christ to preach the gospel.
A·pos·tle (ə pos′əl) *noun, plural* **Apostles.**

apostrophe A punctuation mark (′) used in the following ways: 1. To show that a letter or letters have been left out in a word or words. For example, "you're" means "you are." The apostrophe has taken the place of the *a* in *are*. 2. To show that something belongs to a person or thing. "Paul's dog" means "the dog that belongs to Paul." 3. To show the plural of letters or numbers. She got four *A's* on her report card.
a·pos·tro·phe (ə pos′trə fē) *noun, plural* **apostrophes.**

apothecary A person who makes and sells medicine; druggist.
a·poth·e·car·y (ə poth′ə ker′ē) *noun, plural* **apothecaries.**

appal To fill with horror or terror; shock. We were *appalled* by the news of the airplane crash. This word is also spelled **appall.**
ap·pal (ə pál′) *verb,* **appalled, appalling.**

apparatus Anything that is used for a particular reason. Gymnasium equipment, chemistry sets, tools, and machinery are all different kinds of apparatus.
ap·pa·rat·us (ap′ə rat′əs *or* ap′ə rā′təs) *noun, plural* **apparatus** or **apparatuses.**

apparel Clothing; clothes. That store sells women's and children's *apparel*.
ap·par·el (ə par′əl) *noun.*

apparent 1. Easily seen or understood. His black eye was *apparent* even though he wore dark glasses. It was *apparent* to us that she was telling the truth about what happened. 2. Seeming real or true even though it may not be. The *apparent* size of a star in the sky is much smaller than its real size.
ap·par·ent (ə par′ənt) *adjective.*

apparently As far as one can tell; seemingly. *Apparently*, it is going to rain.
ap·par·ent·ly (ə par′ənt lē) *adverb.*

appeal 1. A call for help or sympathy. Each year that church makes an *appeal* for money to aid the poor. 2. The power to interest. Sports have a great *appeal* for many boys and girls. 3. A request to have a case heard again by a higher court of law or judge. *Noun.*
—1. To call for help; request strongly. The people of the town *appealed* to the Red Cross

at; āpe; cär; end; mē; it; īce; hot; ōld;
wood; fōōl; oil; out; up; turn; sing;
thin; <u>th</u>is; hw in white; zh in treasure.
ə stands for a in about, e in taken,
i in pencil, o in lemon, and u in circus.

for help after the flood. **2.** To be attractive or interesting. Camping out in the woods does not *appeal* to her. **3.** To ask to have a case heard again before a higher court of law or judge. *Verb.*

ap·peal (ə pēl′) *noun, plural* **appeals;** *verb,* **appealed, appealing.**

appear **1.** To come into sight; be seen. The snowy mountain peaks *appeared* in the distance. **2.** To seem. He *appeared* interested in the game, but he was really bored. **3.** To come before the public. That actor has often *appeared* on television.

ap·pear (ə pēr′) *verb,* **appeared, appearing.**

appearance **1.** The act of appearing or coming into sight. The sun made a sudden *appearance* through the clouds. **2.** Outward look. In spite of his troubles, he gave the *appearance* of being happy. **3.** The act of coming before the public. That was her first *appearance* in the movies.

ap·pear·ance (ə pēr′əns) *noun, plural* **appearances.**

appease To satisfy or calm. The owner of the business *appeased* the striking workers by giving in to their demands for more pay.

ap·pease (ə pēz′) *verb,* **appeased, appeasing.**

appendicitis An inflammation of the appendix, that causes swelling and a bad pain.

ap·pen·di·ci·tis (ə pen′də sī′tis) *noun.*

appendix **1.** A thin growth shaped like a bag or pouch. It is attached to the large intestine. **2.** A part added to the end of a book. An appendix gives more facts about the subject of the book.

ap·pen·dix (ə pen′- diks) *noun, plural* **appendixes** or **appendices.**

appetite **1.** A desire for food. When Bill was sick he had no *appetite* at all. **2.** Any strong desire. Jim has an *appetite* for adventure and excitement.

ap·pe·tite (ap′ə tīt′) *noun, plural* **appetites.**

Appendix

applaud To show approval or enjoyment by clapping the hands. The children *applauded* the clown's funny tricks.

ap·plaud (ə pläd′) *verb,* **applauded, applauding.**

applause Approval or enjoyment shown by clapping the hands. Everyone joined in the *applause* at the end of the magician's act.

ap·plause (ə pläz′) *noun.*

apple A roundish fruit with red, yellow, or green skin. Apples have firm white flesh surrounding a core with small seeds.

ap·ple (ap′əl) *noun, plural* **apples.**

Blossom

Fruit

Apple Tree

appliance A small machine that has a particular use. Most appliances are found in the home. Refrigerators, washing machines, toasters, and irons are appliances.

ap·pli·ance (ə plī′əns) *noun, plural* **appliances.**

application **1.** The act of putting something to use. The *application* of scientific knowledge made it possible for men to walk on the moon. **2.** The act of putting something on. The *application* of paint made the old house look like new. **3.** A request. He made an *application* for the job of delivery boy.

ap·pli·ca·tion (ap′lə kā′shən) *noun, plural* **applications.**

apply **1.** To use. He had to *apply* force to open the locked door. **2.** To put on. They *applied* two coats of paint to the wall. **3.** To ask or request something. He *applied* for a summer job at the grocery store. **4.** To devote oneself with effort. She tried to *apply* herself to her homework. **5.** To be suitable or have to do with. The law against speeding *applies* to all drivers.

ap·ply (ə plī′) *verb,* **applied, applying.**

appoint To decide on something; select. The judge *appointed* the date of the trial. The prime minister *appointed* the members of the cabinet shortly after the election.

ap·point (ə point′) *verb,* **appointed, appointing.**

appointment **1.** The act of naming someone to an office or job. When the principal retired, his position was filled by the *appointment* of Mrs. Brown. **2.** An agreement to meet or see someone at a certain time and place. I have an *appointment* with the doctor at ten o'clock.

ap·point·ment (ə point′mənt) *noun, plural* **appointments.**

appraise To estimate or set the value of something. I asked the jeweller to *appraise* Grandmother's diamond ring because I wanted to sell it.

ap·praise (ə prāz′) *verb,* **appraised, appraising.**

appreciate 1. To recognize the value of something. Everyone *appreciates* loyal friends. 2. To be grateful for something. I *appreciate* your running these errands for me.

ap·pre·ci·ate (ə prē′shē āt′) *verb,* **appreciated, appreciating.**

appreciation 1. The act of recognizing the value of something. The boy had an *appreciation* of good music. 2. A being grateful or thankful. He wrote her a note of thanks in *appreciation* for her present.

ap·pre·ci·a·tion (ə prē′shē ā′shən) *noun.*

apprehend To capture and take to jail. The police *apprehended* the robber as he was running from the bank.

ap·pre·hend (ap′rə hend′) *verb,* **apprehended, apprehending.**

apprehension 1. A fear of what may happen. The thought of going to the dentist filled me with *apprehension.* 2. Arrest or capture. The chase ended with the *apprehension* of the criminal.

ap·pre·hen·sion (ap′rə hen′shən) *noun, plural* **apprehensions.**

apprentice A person who works for a skilled worker in order to learn a trade or skill. In earlier times, an apprentice worked for someone for a certain period of time in return for his training.

ap·pren·tice (ə pren′tis) *noun, plural* **apprentices.**

approach 1. To come near or close to. The car *approached* at a high speed. 2. To go to with a plan or request. He *approached* his father with the hope of getting a larger allowance. *Verb.*
—1. The act of coming closer. I always look forward to the *approach* of summer holidays. 2. A way of doing something. His *approach* to training his dog was to be very patient. 3. A way of reaching a place or person. The only *approach* to the town was blocked by snow. *Noun.*

ap·proach (ə prōch′) *verb,* **approached, approaching;** *noun, plural* **approaches.**

appropriate In keeping with a situation; correct or suitable. Warm clothes are *appropriate* for a cold day. *Adjective.*
—To set apart for a particular use. The principal *appropriated* money for new band uniforms. *Verb.*

ap·pro·pri·ate (ə prō′prē ət *for adjective;* ə prō′prē āt′ *for verb*) *adjective; verb,* **appropriated, appropriating.**

approval 1. A good opinion; approving. The mayor's decision was looked on with *approval* by most people. 2. Permission or consent. We need Father's *approval* before we can use his power tools.

ap·prov·al (ə proo′vəl) *noun, plural* **approvals.**

approve 1. To have or give a good opinion of something. My mother doesn't *approve* of my staying up late on school nights. 2. To consent to something. The town *approved* the school budget for the new year.

ap·prove (ə proov′) *verb,* **approved, approving.**

approximate Nearly correct or exact. The *approximate* cost of the radio is twenty-five dollars. *Adjective.*
—To come near or close to; estimate. Dad asked the man to *approximate* the cost of the paint job. *Verb.*

ap·prox·i·mate (ə prok′sə mət *for adjective;* ə prok′sə māt′ *for verb*) *adjective; verb,* **approximated, approximating.**

approximately Nearly; about. We had *approximately* four centimetres of snow.

ap·prox·i·mate·ly (ə prok′sə mət lē) *adverb.*

apricot A roundish, orange-colored fruit that looks like a small peach. Apricots grow on trees in warm climates.

a·pri·cot (ā′prə kot′ *or* ap′rə kot′) *noun, plural* **apricots.**

Apricots

April The fourth month of the year. April has thirty days.

A·pril (ā′prəl) *noun.*

▲ **April** was named after the Greek goddess of love. This month is in the spring, and many people think of spring as a time of love.

apron A garment worn over the front of the body to protect one's clothing. Cooks and butchers wear aprons.

a·pron (ā′prən) *noun, plural* **aprons.**

Apron

apt 1. Likely; inclined. You're *apt* to hurt yourself if you're not more careful when you're riding your bicycle. 2. Quick to learn. She is an *apt* student in mathematics.

apt (apt) *adjective.*

aptitude 1. A natural ability or talent. It is often said that a person is born with an aptitude for a certain thing. Bill has an *aptitude* for music. 2. Quickness in learning. Joan was a student of great *aptitude.*

ap·ti·tude (ap′tə tōōd′ *or* ap′tə tyōōd′) *noun, plural* **aptitudes.**

aqualung A device used by a person to breathe underwater.

aq·ua·lung (ak′wə lung′) *noun, plural* **aqualungs.**

Aquarium

aquarium 1. A tank, bowl, or other container in which fish, water animals, and water plants are kept. An aquarium is usually made of glass or some other material that one can see through. 2. A building that holds collections of fish, water animals, and water plants.

People visit an aquarium for pleasure or to study the animals and plants kept there.

a·quar·i·um (ə kwer′ē əm) *noun, plural* **aquariums.**

aqueduct A pipe or other channel that carries water over a long distance.

aq·ue·duct (ak′wə dukt′) *noun, plural* **aqueducts.**

Arab 1. A member of a people who live in southwestern Asia and northern Africa. 2. A person who was born or is living in Arabia. *Noun.*
—Of the Arabs or Arabia. *Adjective.*

Ar·ab (ar′əb) *noun, plural* **Arabs;** *adjective.*

Arabia A large peninsula in southwestern Asia.

A·ra·bi·a (ə rā′bē ə) *noun.*

Arabian Having to do with Arabia or the people of Arabia. *Adjective.*
—A person who was born or is living in Arabia. *Noun.*

A·ra·bi·an (ə rā′bē ən) *adjective; noun, plural* **Arabians.**

Arabic Having to do with the Arabs or their language. *Adjective.*
—The language of the Arabs. *Noun.*

Ar·a·bic (ar′ə bik) *adjective; noun.*

Arabic numerals The number symbols 1, 2, 3, 4, 5, 6, 7, 8, 9, and 0. This numbering system is believed to have been developed in India about 2000 years ago. The numerals are called "Arabic" because they were introduced to Western Europe by the Arabs.

arbitrary Based on a person's own opinion or wishes rather than on a rule or law. A judge cannot make *arbitrary* decisions; they must be made according to the law.

ar·bi·trar·y (är′bə trer′ē) *adjective.*

arbitrate To settle a dispute or disagreement for someone else. The umpires *arbitrated* the argument between the two teams.

ar·bi·trate (är′bə trāt′) *verb,* **arbitrated, arbitrating.**

arbitration A way of settling a dispute or disagreement by agreeing to accept the decision of a person or group that is not involved.

ar·bi·tra·tion (är′bə trā′shən) *noun.*

arbour A place that is covered and shaded by trees or shrubs, or by vines growing on a frame. An arbour is usually found in a garden. This word is also spelled **arbor.**

ar·bour (är′bər) *noun, plural* **arbours.**

arc 1. An unbroken curved line between any two points on a circle. 2. Any line curving in this way. The rainbow formed a colourful *arc.*
▲ Another word that sounds like this is **ark.**

arc (ärk) *noun, plural* **arcs.**

arch **1.** A curved structure that is built to support the weight of the material above it. **2.** Anything like an arch in shape or use. The curved part of the foot between the toes and the heel is called the arch. *Noun.*
—To form in an arch. The cat *arched* its back in anger. *Verb.*
arch (ärch) *noun, plural* **arches;** *verb,* **arched, arching.**

Arch

archaeology The study of the way people lived a very long time ago. People who study archaeology are called **archaeologists.** They dig up the remains of ancient cities and towns and then study the tools, weapons, pottery, and other things they find. This word is also spelled **archeology.**
ar·chae·ol·o·gy (är′kē ol′ə jē) *noun.*

archbishop A bishop of the highest rank.
arch·bish·op (ärch′bish′əp) *noun, plural* **archbishops.**

archer A person who shoots with a bow and arrow.
arch·er (är′chər) *noun, plural* **archers.**

archery The skill or sport of shooting with a bow and arrow.
arch·er·y (är′chər ē) *noun.*

Archery

archipelago **1.** A large group of islands. **2.** A large body of water having many islands in it.
ar·chi·pel·a·go (är′kə pel′ə gō′) *noun, plural* **archipelagos** or **archipelagoes.**

architect A person whose work is to design and draw plans for buildings. An architect sees that the buildings are built according to the plans. The *architect* made plans for building a large shopping centre.
ar·chi·tect (är′kə tekt′) *noun, plural* **architects.**

architecture **1.** The science, art, or profession of designing and planning buildings. **2.** A particular style or method of building. Jane studied Greek *architecture* in her art class at college.
ar·chi·tec·ture (är′kə tek′chər) *noun.*

arctic At or near the North Pole; very far north. *Adjective.*
—**the Arctic.** An ice-covered region surrounding the North Pole. *Noun.*
arc·tic (ärk′tik *or* är′tik) *adjective; noun.*

Arctic char *Canadian.* A kind of fish that is like both a salmon and a trout. It is found in the waters of the far North. Arctic char has a delicious taste and is popular in restaurants in Canadian cities.

Arctic char

Arctic Ocean The ocean surrounding the North Pole.

are You *are* late. We *are* glad you could come. How *are* you today?
are (är) *verb.*

area **1.** The amount of surface within a boundary. The *area* of our tree house is ten square metres. **2.** A particular space, region, or section. We eat in the dining *area* of the house. My aunt lives in a farming *area*. **3.** A field of interest or study. My sister is going to

at; āpe; cär; end; mē; it; īce; hot; ōld;
wood; fo͞ol; oil; out; up; turn; sing;
thin; this; hw in white; zh in treasure.
ə stands for a in about, e in taken,
i in pencil, o in lemon, and u in circus.

study in the *area* of science at university.

ar·e·a (er′ē ə) *noun, plural* **areas.**

area code A set of three numbers that stands for one of the areas into which Canada is divided for telephone service. You dial these three numbers before the local number when you call from one area to another.

arena A space that is used for sports contests or entertainment. In the arenas of ancient Rome, men fought with lions. Today, circuses and sports events take place in arenas.

a·re·na (ə rē′nə) *noun, plural* **arenas.**

▲ The word **arena** comes from a Latin word that means "sand." The ancient Romans covered the ground in their arenas with sand.

aren't Why *aren't* you going with us? These shoes *aren't* new.

aren't (ärnt *or* är′ənt) contraction for "are not."

argue 1. To have a disagreement; quarrel. My sister and brother often *argue* over who should walk the dog. 2. To give reasons for or against something. He *argued* against going to the beach because it looked like rain.

ar·gue (är′gyo͞o) *verb,* **argued, arguing.**

argument 1. A discussion of something by people who do not agree. They had an *argument* over whose turn it was to wash the dishes. 2. A reason or reasons given for or against something. His *argument* for getting a bicycle was that he needed it for his job of delivering newspapers.

ar·gu·ment (är′gyə mənt) *noun, plural* **arguments.**

arid Getting very little rain; dry. A desert is an *arid* region.

ar·id (ar′id) *adjective.*

arise 1. To get up; stand up. The audience *arose* and applauded at the end of the play. 2. To move upward; rise. A mist is beginning to *arise* from the lake. 3. To come into being; appear. Questions often *arise* in our minds as we read about new things.

a·rise (ə rīz′) *verb,* **arose, arisen, arising.**

aristocracy 1. A class of persons who are born into a high social position; nobility. Kings, queens, princes, and dukes are members of the aristocracy. 2. Any group of persons who are thought to be outstanding because of wealth, intelligence, or ability.

ar·is·toc·ra·cy (ar′is tok′rə sē) *noun, plural* **aristocracies.**

aristocrat 1. A person who belongs to the aristocracy. 2. A person who has the tastes

and attitudes of the aristocracy. He was an *aristocrat* in his taste for expensive things.

a·ris·to·crat (ə ris′tə krat′) *noun, plural* **aristocrats.**

arithmetic 1. The science of figuring with numbers. When you study arithmetic you learn how to add, subtract, multiply, and divide. 2. The act of adding, subtracting, multiplying, or dividing. You must have made a mistake in your *arithmetic.*

a·rith·me·tic (ə rith′mə tik′) *noun.*

ark The large ship that Noah built to save himself, his family, and two members of every kind of animal from the flood God sent to punish mankind. ▲ Another word that sounds like this is **arc.**

ark (ärk) *noun.*

arm[1] 1. The part of the body between the shoulder and the wrist. 2. Anything shaped or used like an arm. The *arms* of the green chair are loose.

arm (ärm) *noun, plural* **arms.**

arm[2] Any weapon. A gun is an arm. *Noun.* —1. To supply with weapons. The troops *armed* themselves for the battle. 2. To supply with anything that protects or strengthens. A porcupine is *armed* with quills. *Verb.*

arm (ärm) *noun, plural* **arms;** *verb,* **armed, arming.**

armada A large group of warships. The Spanish Armada was defeated by the English.

ar·ma·da (är ma′də) *noun, plural* **armadas.**

Armadillo

armadillo A small, insect-eating animal that digs into the ground looking for food. It has a hard bony shell, a long snout, strong, sharp claws, and a long tail. The armadillo is found in South America and parts of the southern United States.

ar·ma·dil·lo (är′mə dil′ō) *noun, plural* **armadillos.**

▲ The word **armadillo** comes from a Spanish word that means "little armoured animal." Spanish explorers who found this animal in America thought that the armadillo's hard shell looked like armour.

armament The armed forces, equipment, and supplies of a country.

ar·ma·ment (är′mə mənt) *noun, plural* armaments.

armchair A chair with parts on both sides that support a person's arms or elbows.

arm·chair (ärm′cher′) *noun, plural* armchairs.

armed forces The military power of a country. The **Canadian Armed Forces** are made up of land, sea, and air elements that are also called the **army, navy,** and **air force.**

armistice A temporary stop in fighting agreed on by those who are fighting; truce.

ar·mi·stice (är′mi stis) *noun, plural* armistices.

Armour

armour **1.** A covering for the body, usually made from metal. Knights wore it for protection during battle. **2.** Any protective covering. The metal plates on a tank or warship are armour. The hard shell of an armadillo is armour. This word is also spelled **armor.**

ar·mour (är′mər) *noun.*

armoured Protected or equipped with armour. The president rode in an *armoured* car so that he couldn't be hurt. This word is also spelled **armored.**

ar·moured (är′mərd) *adjective.*

armoury **1.** A place where weapons are kept. **2.** A building in which the army reserves are trained. This word is also spelled **armory.**

ar·mour·y (är′mər ē) *noun, plural* armouries.

armpit The hollow part under the arm at the shoulder.

arm·pit (ärm′pit′) *noun, plural* armpits.

arms Weapons. After the battle the defeated troops laid down their *arms* and ran away.

arms (ärmz) *noun plural.*

army **1.** A large, organized group of soldiers who are armed and trained for fighting on land. In the Canadian Armed Forces, the army is also known as the **land element. 2.** Any large group of people or things. An *army* of teenagers came to the concert.

ar·my (är′mē) *noun, plural* armies.

aroma A pleasant or agreeable smell; fragrance. The cookies we were baking gave off a delicious *aroma.*

a·ro·ma (ə rō′mə) *noun, plural* aromas.

arose I *arose* at seven o'clock this morning. Look up **arise** for more information.

a·rose (ə rōz′) *verb.*

around She wore a belt *around* her waist. We walked *around* the block. The horses wandered *around* in the field. I'll meet you *around* ten o'clock. The wheel spun *around* and *around* and Jennifer began to feel dizzy. We spread the news *around* so all our friends would know.

a·round (ə round′) *preposition; adverb.*

arouse To excite or stir up. Her rudeness *aroused* everyone's anger.

a·rouse (ə rouz′) *verb,* aroused, arousing.

arrange **1.** To put in some kind of order. The teacher *arranged* the names of the children in alphabetical order. **2.** To prepare for; plan. Who *arranged* this meeting? Can you *arrange* to meet us at the dance tonight? **3.** To adapt or fit a piece of music for instruments or voices for which it was not originally written.

ar·range (ə rānj′) *verb,* arranged, arranging.

arrangement **1.** The act of putting in order. The *arrangement* of the books took two hours. **2.** Something arranged. They made a flower *arrangement* for the party. **3. arrangements.** Plans or preparations. We made *arrangements* for Joan's surprise birthday party.

ar·range·ment (ə rānj′mənt) *noun, plural* arrangements.

array An orderly grouping, arrangement, or display. This store carries a wide *array* of

at; āpe; cär; end; mē; it; īce; hot; ōld; wood; fool; oil; out; up; turn; sing; thin; this; hw in white; zh in treasure. ə stands for a in about, e in taken, i in pencil, o in lemon, and u in circus.

toys and games. The movie featured an *array* of famous stars. *Noun.*
—To put in order. The officer *arrayed* the troops for battle. *Verb.*

ar·ray (ə rā′) *noun, plural* **arrays;** *verb,* **arrayed, arraying.**

arrest **1.** To seize and hold by authority of the law. The policemen *arrested* the robber. **2.** To stop or hold. We hope to *arrest* pollution in this country. *Verb.*
—The act of seizing by authority of the law. There were ten *arrests* in the city yesterday. *Noun.*

ar·rest (ə rest′) *verb,* **arrested, arresting;** *noun, plural* **arrests.**

arrival **1.** The act of arriving. The reporters were waiting for the *arrival* of the premier. **2.** A person or thing that arrives or has arrived. New *arrivals* waited in line for their baggage at the airport.

ar·riv·al (ə rīv′əl) *noun, plural* **arrivals.**

arrive To come to a place. We will *arrive* in Toronto at midnight. I *arrived* at school on time. Has the jury in that case *arrived* at a decision yet?

ar·rive (ə rīv′) *verb,* **arrived, arriving.**

arrogant Having or showing too much pride or confidence. An arrogant person does not have any respect for other people or their opinions. The boy was quite *arrogant* because his family was very wealthy.

ar·ro·gant (ar′ə gənt) *adjective.*

arrow **1.** A slender stick that has a sharp point at one end and feathers at the other. An arrow is made to be shot from a bow. **2.** Something that is like an arrow. The road sign had an *arrow* to show which way traffic was supposed to go.

ar·row (ar′ō) *noun, plural* **arrows.**

Arrows of North American Indians

arrowhead The pointed tip or head of an arrow.

ar·row·head (ar′ō hed′) *noun, plural* **arrowheads.**

arsenal A place for making or storing weapons and ammunition.

ar·se·nal (är′sə nəl) *noun, plural* **arsenals.**

arsenic A white, tasteless, very poisonous substance. It is used in rat, insect, and weed poisons.

ar·se·nic (är′sə nik) *noun.*

arson The crime of purposely setting fire to a building or other property.

ar·son (är′sən) *noun.*

art **1.** Painting, drawing, and sculpture. We study *art* at school. **2.** The works made by artists; paintings, drawings, and sculptures. We went to an exhibit of North American Indian *art* at the museum. **3.** The making or doing of anything that has beauty or meaning. Poetry, music, and ballet dancing are *arts.* **4.** A special skill, ability, or craft. She has an *art* for making people feel at ease. The *art* of cooking came easily to him.

art (ärt) *noun, plural* **arts.**

artery **1.** One of the tubes that carry blood away from the heart to all parts of the body. **2.** A main road or channel. This highway is the major *artery* between the two cities.

ar·ter·y (är′tər ē) *noun, plural* **arteries.**

arthritis A painful inflammation of a joint or joints of the body.

ar·thri·tis (är thrī′təs) *noun.*

Artichoke

artichoke A plant like a thistle, with large leaves, greenish-yellow flower heads, and purple flowers. The flower head is cooked and eaten as a vegetable.

ar·ti·choke (är′tə chōk′) *noun, plural* **artichokes.**

article **1.** A composition written for a newspaper, magazine, or book. The scientist wrote an *article* on space travel for the encyclopedia. **2.** A particular thing or object; item. Several *articles* were stolen from the house. She bought some new *articles* of

clothing for the camping trip. **3.** A separate section of a formal document. There are articles in treaties, constitutions, and contracts. The first *article* in the club's constitution required a meeting every Tuesday. **4.** The words *a, an,* and *the. A* and *an* are indefinite articles. *The* is a definite article.
 ar·ti·cle (är′ti kəl) *noun, plural* **articles.**

articulate Able to express oneself clearly. The professor was very *articulate* about the subject of her new book. *Adjective.*
—To express oneself clearly. He was so upset that he could not *articulate* his feelings about the argument. *Verb.*
 ar·tic·u·late (är tik′yə lət *for adjective;* är-tik′yə lāt′ *for verb*) *adjective; verb,* **articulated, articulating.**

artificial **1.** Made by people, not by nature; not natural. An electric lamp gives *artificial* light. The *artificial* flowers were made of plastic. **2.** Not sincere or true. His show of interest in the game was *artificial* because all sports really bored him.
 ar·ti·fi·cial (är′tə fish′əl) *adjective.*

artificial respiration The forcing of air into and out of the lungs of a person who has stopped breathing. This helps the person to start breathing normally again. Artificial respiration is used to save people who have almost drowned.

artillery **1.** Large, heavy firearms. Cannons are artillery. **2.** The part of an army that uses such firearms.
 ar·til·ler·y (är til′ər ē) *noun.*

artisan A person who is skilled in a particular craft; craftsman. Carpenters, plumbers, and electricians are artisans.
 ar·ti·san (är′tə zən) *noun, plural* **artisans.**

artist A person who is skilled in painting, music, literature, or any other form of art.
 art·ist (är′tist) *noun, plural* **artists.**

artistic Having to do with art or artists. My brother has *artistic* interests.
 ar·tis·tic (är tis′tik) *adjective.*

as The second movie was not *as* good *as* the first. I have dresses in many colours, such *as* red and blue. Bob arrived *as* we were leaving. I'm speaking to you *as* a friend. He goes to the same school *as* I do.
 as (az) *adverb; conjunction; preposition; pronoun.*

asbestos A greyish substance. Its fibres may be woven or pressed into material that does not burn or conduct electricity. The firemen's clothes were made from a material containing *asbestos.*
 as·bes·tos (az bes′təs) *noun.*

ascend To move or go upward; climb. The elevator *ascended* quickly to the twentieth floor. The hikers *ascended* the hill and rested when they reached the top.
 as·cend (ə send′) *verb,* **ascended, ascending.**

ascent **1.** Movement upward. We watched the *ascent* of the kite high into the sky. **2.** The act of climbing or going up. A heavy snowstorm made an *ascent* of the mountain impossible.
 as·cent (ə sent′) *noun, plural* **ascents.**

ascertain To find out for sure; determine. The police were not able to *ascertain* the identity of the person who wrote the mysterious letter.
 as·cer·tain (as′ər tān′) *verb,* **ascertained, ascertaining.**

ash¹ A greyish-white powder left after something has been burned. An *ash* from Father's cigar fell on the floor.
 ash (ash) *noun, plural* **ashes.**

ash² A tree that has a strong wood. It is used in building. Some baseball bats are made from the wood of the ash.
 ash (ash) *noun, plural* **ashes.**

Leaf

Ash Tree

ashamed **1.** Feeling shame. A person who is ashamed is upset or uncomfortable because of doing something bad or silly. The boy was *ashamed* of the mistake he had made. **2.** Not wanting to do something be-

at; āpe; cär; end; mē; it; īce; hot; ōld;
wood; fōōl; oil; out; up; turn; sing;
thin; <u>th</u>is; hw in white; zh in treasure.
ə stands for **a** in about, **e** in taken,
i in pencil, **o** in lemon, and **u** in circus.

cause of fear or shame. He was *ashamed* to tell his family that he had failed the test.

a·shamed (ə shāmd′) *adjective.*

ashes The greyish-white powder left after something has been burned. The campers poured water on the *ashes* of their fire.

ash·es (ash′əz) *noun plural.*

ashore On or to the shore or land. The children paddled the canoe *ashore.* Most of the sailors are *ashore* on leave.

a·shore (ə shōr′) *adverb; adjective.*

Asia The largest continent. Asia lies between the Pacific Ocean to the east and Europe and Africa to the west.

A·sia (ā′zhə) *noun.*

Asian Of Asia. He is studying *Asian* history. *Adjective.*

—A person who was born or is living in Asia. *Noun.*

A·sian (ā′zhən) *adjective; noun, plural* **Asians.**

aside On or to one side. Father turned *aside* to let the car behind us pass. Put your worries *aside* and have a good time!

a·side (ə sīd′) *adverb.*

ask **1.** To put a question about something; inquire. We *asked* how to get to town. **2.** To put a question to. He *asked* a policeman where the nearest post office was. **3.** To call for an answer to. He *asked* a question about the arithmetic problem. **4.** To make a request. She *asked* for a second piece of cake. May I *ask* for your help? **5.** To invite. Pam *asked* her friends to come to her party.

ask (ask) *verb,* **asked, asking.**

askew At or to one side; turned the wrong way. The picture was hung *askew* until she straightened it. Your hat is *askew.*

a·skew (ə skyo͞o′) *adverb; adjective.*

asleep **1.** Sleeping. Be very quiet because the baby is *asleep.* **2.** Without feeling; numb. His foot was *asleep* because he sat still for so long. *Adjective.*

—Into a condition of sleep. Grandfather fell *asleep* while he was watching television. *Adverb.*

The boy is wearing his cap **askew.**

a·sleep (ə slēp′) *adjective; adverb.*

asparagus The young shoots of a plant. They are cooked and eaten as a vegetable.

The shoots are shaped like spears. They grow from underground stems and have large, scaly leaves at the tip.

as·par·a·gus (əs par′ə gəs) *noun.*

Spears of Asparagus

aspect **1.** A particular way in which something can be looked at and thought about. The mayor's committee considered every *aspect* of the effect of pollution on the city. **2.** Look; appearance. The deserted old house had such a gloomy *aspect* that the children were afraid to go near it.

as·pect (as′pekt) *noun, plural* **aspects.**

aspen A tree whose leaves shake in the slightest breeze. An aspen is a kind of poplar.

as·pen (as′pən) *noun, plural* **aspens.**

Leaves in Autumn

Aspen Tree

asphalt A brown or black substance found in natural deposits or made from petroleum. Asphalt mixed with sand or gravel is used to pave roads.

as·phalt (ash′fält *or* as′fält) *noun.*

aspirin A white drug used to ease pain. Some people take *aspirin* when they have a cold or a headache.

as·pi·rin (as′pər in) *noun, plural* **aspirins.**

ass **1.** An animal that looks like a horse but is smaller and has longer ears; donkey. **2.** A stupid or silly person.

ass (as) *noun, plural* **asses.**

assassin A person who murders another person suddenly and by surprise. An assassin

is someone who kills an important person.
as·sas·sin (ə sas′in) *noun, plural* **assassins.**

assassinate To murder suddenly and by surprise. The police have captured the man who tried to *assassinate* the ambassador.
as·sas·si·nate (ə sas′ə nāt′) *verb,* **assassinated, assassinating.**

assault A sudden, violent attack. The troops gave way under the *assault* of the enemy. *Noun.*
—To make an assault on; attack. The soldiers *assaulted* the fort. *Verb.*
as·sault (ə sôlt′) *noun, plural* **assaults;** *verb,* **assaulted, assaulting.**

assemble 1. To gather or bring together. A crowd began to *assemble* outside the movie theatre. 2. To put or fit together. We had to *assemble* the parts of the bicycle.
as·sem·ble (ə sem′bəl) *verb,* **assembled, assembling.**

assembly 1. A group of people gathered together for some purpose. The school *assembly* was held in the auditorium. 2. A group of people who make laws. In Canada, a provincial parliament is called a **legislative assembly.** The woman being interviewed is a Member of the Legislative *Assembly* of Manitoba. 3. The act of putting or fitting together. Many workers take part in the *assembly* of one automobile.
as·sem·bly (ə sem′blē) *noun, plural* **assemblies.**

assert 1. To state strongly and clearly. The lawyers *assert* that their client is not guilty. 2. To insist on; claim. My little brother *asserted* his independence by demanding that he be allowed to walk to school by himself.
as·sert (ə surt′) *verb,* **asserted, asserting.**

assess 1. To set the value of property for taxation. Mr. Smith's farm is *assessed* at $50 000. 2. To charge or tax. Our library *assesses* a person five cents a day for each day that a book is overdue.
as·sess (ə ses′) *verb,* **assessed, assessing.**

asset 1. Something valuable or useful; advantage. Being tall is a great *asset* for a basketball player. 2. **assets.** Things that have value in money. His *assets* include a house, a car, and a boat.
as·set (as′et) *noun, plural* **assets.**

assign 1. To give out. Our teacher will *assign* a different science project to each student. 2. To appoint. The mayor *assigned* her to the committee on education. 3. To fix definitely; name. The coach *assigned* the date for the game.
as·sign (ə sīn′) *verb,* **assigned, assigning.**

assignment 1. Something that is assigned. My arithmetic *assignment* is to do ten multiplication problems. 2. The act of assigning. The company's *assignment* of my father to a new job meant that we had to move.
as·sign·ment (ə sīn′mənt) *noun, plural* **assignments.**

assist To help; aid. All the people in the town got together to *assist* the family whose house had burned down. 2. *Canadian.* In hockey or lacrosse, to help another player score a goal. Tim *assisted* Jeff in getting the winning goal when Tim passed Jeff the puck. *Verb.*
—*Canadian.* The credit given in hockey to a player who helps score a goal. Henri scored on an *assist* from Pat. *Noun.*
as·sist (ə sist′) *noun, plural* **assists;** *verb,* **assisted, assisting.**

assistance Help; aid. Father will need some *assistance* in carrying the packages.
as·sist·ance (ə sis′təns) *noun.*

assistant A person who helps. The man's *assistant* helps him to run the store. *Noun.*
—Helping. The head football coach has four *assistant* coaches on his staff. *Adjective.*
as·sist·ant (ə sis′tənt) *noun, plural* **assistants;** *adjective.*

associate 1. To connect in one's mind. I always *associate* ice cream and cake with birthday parties. 2. To join as a friend or partner. My brother *associates* mostly with boys who like sports. *Verb.*
—A friend or partner. My aunt has two associates in her new business. *Noun.*
as·so·ci·ate (ə sō′shē āt′ *or* ə sō′sē āt′ *for verb;* ə sō′shət *or* ə sō′shē ət *for noun*) *verb,* **associated, associating;** *noun, plural* **associates.**

association 1. A group of people joined together for a common purpose. I belong to an *association* that helps preserve the forests of our province. 2. Friendship; companionship. Bob was proud of his *association* with the captain of the high school football team. 3. The connection made in the mind between thoughts and feelings. What *associations* do you have with the word "summer"?
as·so·ci·a·tion (ə sō′shē ā′shən *or* ə sō′sē ā′shən) *noun, plural* **associations.**

at; āpe; cär; end; mē; it; īce; hot; ōld;
wood; fōōl; oil; out; up; turn; sing;
thin; this; hw in white; zh in treasure.
ə stands for a in about, e in taken,
i in pencil, o in lemon, and u in circus.

assortment A collection of different kinds. That store carries a large *assortment* of sports equipment.
as·sort·ment (ə sôrt′mənt) *noun, plural* **assortments.**

assume **1.** To take for granted; suppose. I *assume* we will arrive at the station on time if we leave now. **2.** To take upon oneself; undertake. You will have to *assume* the responsibility of feeding the dog. **3.** To take for oneself; seize. The dictator *assumed* control of the country.
as·sume (ə so͞om′) *verb,* **assumed, assuming.**

assumption **1.** The act of assuming. A member of a jury must make the *assumption* that a defendant is innocent until proven guilty. **2.** Something that is assumed. Your *assumption* turned out to be wrong.
as·sump·tion (ə sump′shən) *noun, plural* **assumptions.**

assurance **1.** A statement that is supposed to make a person certain or sure. My father gave the shopkeeper his *assurance* that he would pay for the window I had broken. **2.** Confidence. We had every *assurance* that our team would win the championship.
as·sur·ance (ə sho͝or′əns) *noun, plural* **assurances.**

assure **1.** To tell positively. I *assure* you that I won't be late. **2.** To make certain or sure. He checked the car carefully to *assure* that it was in good condition.
as·sure (ə sho͝or′) *verb,* **assured, assuring.**

aster A flower that has white, pink, purple, or yellow petals around a yellow centre. Asters bloom in the fall.
as·ter (as′tər) *noun, plural* **asters.**

asterisk A star-shaped mark (*) used in printing or writing to tell the reader to look somewhere else on the page for more information.
as·ter·isk (as′tə-risk′) *noun, plural* **asterisks.**

astern **1.** At or toward the rear of a ship. The ship's crew all gathered *astern* to watch the royal yacht pass by. **2.** Behind a ship. A sailboat followed *astern.* **3.** Backward; with the back of the ship forward. The ship pulled *astern* into the dock.
a·stern (ə sturn′) *adverb.*

Asters

asteroid Any of the thousands of small, rocky bodies that revolve around the sun. Most of them are between the orbits of the planets Mars and Jupiter.
as·ter·oid (as′tə roid′) *noun, plural* **asteroids.**

asthma A disease that causes wheezing and coughing and makes breathing difficult.
asth·ma (az′mə) *noun.*

astir In motion; active. Very few people were *astir* as dawn broke over the city.
a·stir (ə stur′) *adjective.*

astonish To surprise very much; amaze. The news that she has won the contest will *astonish* her. It is *astonishing* that such a small boy can throw a ball so far.
as·ton·ish (əs ton′ish) *verb,* **astonished, astonishing.**

astonishment Very great surprise; amazement. The child was filled with *astonishment* when she saw the magician pull a rabbit from a hat.
as·ton·ish·ment (əs ton′ish mənt) *noun.*

astound To surprise very much; amaze; astonish. The first flight in outer space *astounded* the whole world.
as·tound (əs tound′) *verb,* **astounded, astounding.**

astray Off the right way or path. The family was sad because their dog had gone *astray* and gotten lost.
a·stray (ə strā′) *adverb.*

astride With one leg on each side of. The cowboy sat *astride* his horse.
a·stride (ə strīd′) *preposition.*

The boy is sitting **astride** the fence.

astrology The study of the influence that the stars and planets are supposed to have on people and events. Some people use astrology to try to predict what will happen in the future.

as·trol·o·gy (əs trol′ə jē) *noun.*

astronaut A person who flies in a spacecraft. The word *astronaut* is made up of two ancient Greek words that mean "star" and "sailor."

as·tro·naut (as′trə nät′) *noun, plural* **astronauts.**

astronomer A person who knows a great deal about astronomy. An astronomer studies stars and planets by looking at them through a telescope.

as·tron·o·mer (əs tron′ə mər) *noun, plural* **astronomers.**

astronomical 1. Relating to astronomy. Astronauts have collected many important *astronomical* facts during their space flights. 2. Very great or large. For someone with a small allowance, the cost of a bicycle is *astronomical.*

as·tro·nom·i·cal (as′trə nom′i kəl) *adjective.*

astronomy The science that deals with the study of the sun, moon, stars, planets, and other heavenly bodies.

as·tron·o·my (əs tron′ə mē) *noun.*

asylum 1. A place that takes care of people who are not able to care for themselves. People who are mentally ill may live in an asylum. 2. A place of safety or protection. In earlier times, a church was an asylum where anyone was safe from arrest.

a·sy·lum (ə sī′ləm) *noun, plural* **asylums.**

at The race starts *at* the top of the hill. He looked *at* the picture. We eat lunch *at* noon. The Canadians and the Americans were *at* war in the year 1812. She bought the car *at* a low price.

at (at) *preposition.*

ate We *ate* all the pie. Look up **eat** for more information. ▲ Another word that sounds like this is **eight.**

ate (āt) *verb.*

atheist A person who does not believe in God.

a·the·ist (ā′thē ist) *noun, plural* **atheists.**

athlete A person who is good at and trained in sports or exercises that take strength, skill, and speed. Baseball players, hockey players, swimmers, and skiers are athletes.

ath·lete (ath′lēt) *noun, plural* **athletes.**

athletic 1. Relating to an athlete or athletes. Our school has just bought new basketballs, baseball bats, and other *athletic* equipment. 2. Good at sports. Linda is *athletic* and enjoys many outdoor sports.

ath·let·ic (ath let′ik) *adjective.*

atigi *Canadian.* 1. A coat made of skins and worn by Inuit with the fur next to the body. The skin side is decorated with beaded panels. 2. A hooded jacket of fur or cloth; a parka.

a·ti·gi (ə tig′ē) *noun.*

▲ The **atigi** is worn all year by Inuit. In winter they add an outer parka with the fur on the outside.

Atlantic The ocean that separates Europe and Africa from North America and South America. *Noun.*
—Of the Atlantic Ocean. *Adjective.*

At·lan·tic (at lan′tik) *noun; adjective.*

Atlantic Provinces *Canadian.* The provinces of Nova Scotia, New Brunswick, Prince Edward Island, and Newfoundland.

atlas A book of maps.

at·las (at′ləs) *noun, plural* **atlases.**

atmosphere 1. The air that surrounds the earth. Before the first space flights, no person had ever travelled beyond the earth's *atmosphere.* 2. The mass of gases that surrounds any heavenly body. Scientists do not think people could live in the *atmosphere* on Mars. 3. The air in a particular place. This attic has a hot, stuffy *atmosphere.* 4. The mood or influence that surrounds a place. Our house has a happy *atmosphere* at holiday time.

at·mos·phere (at′məs fēr′) *noun, plural* **atmospheres.**

atmospheric Having to do with the atmosphere. A barometer forecasts the weather by measuring the *atmospheric* pressure.

at·mos·pher·ic (at′məs fer′ik) *adjective.*

atoll A ring-shaped coral island that surrounds a shallow body of water.

at·oll (at′ôl *or* ə tôl′) *noun, plural* **atolls.**

atom The smallest particle of a chemical element that has all the qualities of that element. An atom has a central nucleus of protons and neutrons that is surrounded by electrons. All matter in the universe is made up of atoms.

at·om (at′əm) *noun, plural* **atoms.**

atomic 1. Having to do with an atom or atoms. Those scientists are taking part in

at; āpe; cär; end; mē; it; īce; hot; ōld;
wood; fōōl; oil; out; up; turn; sing;
thin; this; hw in white; zh in treasure.
ə stands for a in about, e in taken,
i in pencil, o in lemon, and u in circus.

atomic research. 2. Using atomic energy. An *atomic* submarine can stay underwater for long periods of time.
a·tom·ic (ə tom′ik) *adjective*.

atomic bomb A very powerful bomb. Its great force comes from the energy released by the splitting of atoms. This bomb is also called an **atom bomb.**

atomic energy Energy that can be released from the nucleus of an atom. This kind of energy is usually called **nuclear energy.** Look up **nuclear energy** for more information.

atone To make up for a wrong; make amends. She *atoned* for her rude behaviour by apologizing to me.
a·tone (ə tōn′) *verb*, **atoned, atoning.**

atop On top of. There were ten candles *atop* my birthday cake.
a·top (ə top′) *preposition*.

attach 1. To fasten. You can *attach* the sign to the wall with nails. Bob *attached* the leash to the dog's collar. 2. To add or include. The mayor *attached* his signature to the petition against the new highway. 3. To bind by a strong feeling. Tom is very *attached* to his family.
at·tach (ə tach′) *verb*, **attached, attaching.**

attachment 1. The act of attaching. The *attachment* of the tow truck to the wrecked car was difficult. 2. A strong feeling of affection or devotion. The child showed his *attachment* to his sister by hugging her. 3. A part or device that is connected to a larger thing. The camera had a flash *attachment* for taking pictures indoors.
at·tach·ment (ə tach′mənt) *noun, plural* **attachments.**

attack 1. To begin to fight against. The dog *attacked* the robber. 2. To write or speak against. The newspapers *attacked* the mayor's speech. 3. To begin to work on with energy. The boys *attacked* the job of setting up the tent. 4. To act harmfully on. A plant disease *attacked* all the elm trees in our yard. *Verb.*
—1. The act of attacking. The enemy's *attack* on the fort came without warning. 2. A sudden fit of sickness. She drank the glass of orange juice so fast that she had an *attack* of hiccups. *Noun.*
at·tack (ə tak′) *verb*, **attacked, attacking;** *noun, plural* **attacks.**

attain 1. To arrive at; reach. My great-grandfather *attained* the age of ninety. 2. To get by hard work; achieve. Jim has finally

attained his ambition to be on the football team.
at·tain (ə tān′) *verb*, **attained, attaining.**

attempt To make an effort to do something; try. The prisoner *attempted* to escape from jail. *Verb.*
—1. A try; effort. Bob made an *attempt* to learn how to ski, but he kept falling down. 2. An attack. The assassin made an *attempt* on the prime minister's life. *Noun.*
at·tempt (ə tempt′) *verb*, **attempted, attempting;** *noun, plural* **attempts.**

attend 1. To be present at. She has to *attend* a club meeting this afternoon. 2. To go with. Three bridesmaids *attended* the bride. 3. To take care of; wait on. Doctors and nurses *attended* to the injured man.
at·tend (ə tend′) *verb*, **attended, attending.**

attendance 1. The act of being present. Betty's *attendance* at school was poor last year. 2. The number of people present. The *attendance* at the baseball game was over five hundred.
at·ten·dance (ə ten′dəns) *noun.*

attention 1. Careful watching or listening. The magician had the children's *attention*. He called my *attention* to the airplane flying high above us. 2. Notice or consideration. Pollution of our rivers and lakes calls for immediate *attention*. 3. **attentions.** Kind or polite acts. The host's many *attentions* made every guest at the party feel welcome. 4. A position in which a person stands very straight with his arms at his sides, his feet together, and his eyes looking ahead. The band stood at *attention* waiting for the parade to start.
at·ten·tion (ə ten′shən) *noun, plural* **attentions.**

attest To give proof of. The shelves full of books in his room *attest* to his enjoyment of reading.
at·test (ə test′) *verb*, **attested, attesting.**

attic The space just below the roof of a house. Our *attic* is filled with old clothes, toys, and many other things no one in the family really wants any more.
at·tic (at′ik) *noun, plural* **attics.**

attire Dress; clothing. The queen was clothed in rich *attire*.
at·tire (ə tīr′) *noun.*

attitude A way of thinking, acting, or feeling. Tom's *attitude* toward school is more enthusiastic than mine.
at·ti·tude (at′ə tōōd′ *or* at′ə tyōōd′) *noun, plural* **attitudes.**

attorney A person who has the legal power

to act for another person; lawyer. The prisoner's *attorney* presented his case to the judge and jury.

at·tor·ney (ə tur′nē) *noun, plural* **attorneys.**

attract To draw or pull. A magnet will *attract* an iron bar. The beautiful scenery in these mountains *attracts* many tourists.

at·tract (ə trakt′) *verb,* **attracted, attracting.**

attraction 1. The act or power of attracting. The *attraction* of the magnet drew the nails across the table. 2. A person or thing that attracts. The clowns were the main *attraction* at the circus.

at·trac·tion (ə trak′shən) *noun, plural* **attractions.**

attractive Having a pleasing quality that attracts people; charming. Mary is a very *attractive* girl.

at·trac·tive (ə trak′tiv) *adjective.*

attribute To think of as belonging to or coming from. The coach *attributed* the team's victory to training and practice. Air pollution in cities has been *attributed* partly to car exhaust. *Verb.*
—A quality that is thought of as belonging to a person or thing; characteristic. One of Frank's *attributes* is his friendliness. *Noun.*

at·trib·ute (ə trib′yo͞ot *for verb;* at′rə byo͞ot′ *for noun*) *verb,* **attributed, attributing;** *noun, plural* **attributes.**

auction A public sale at which things are sold to the person who offers the most money. My mother bid five dollars for a rocking chair at the church *auction. Noun.*
—To sell at an auction. When we bought our new house, my parents *auctioned* off some of our old furniture. *Verb.*

auc·tion (äk′shən) *noun, plural* **auctions;** *verb,* **auctioned, auctioning.**

▲ The word **auction** goes back to a Latin word that means "to become bigger or higher." At an auction, the price of something gets higher and higher until someone offers the highest price and the article is sold to him.

audible Loud enough to be heard. The music was barely *audible* after Jim turned down the volume of the record player.

au·di·ble (ä′də bəl) *adjective.*

audience 1. A group of people gathered to hear or see something. The *audience* at the theatre applauded the actors in the play. 2. All the people who give attention to something. That television programme has a large *audience.* 3. A formal meeting with a person

of very high rank. The young man was granted an *audience* with the king.

au·di·ence (ä′dē əns) *noun, plural* **audiences.**

audio Relating to sound. He bought new *audio* equipment for his record player.

au·di·o (ä′dē ō′) *adjective.*

auditor A person who checks business accounts or records to see if they are correct.

au·di·tor (ä′di tər) *noun, plural* **auditors.**

auditorium A large room in a school, church, theatre, or other building where a group of people can gather. We have student meetings in the school *auditorium* once a week.

au·di·to·ri·um (ä′də tôr′ē əm) *noun, plural* **auditoriums.**

auger A tool for boring holes in wood.

au·ger (ä′gər) *noun, plural* **augers.**

augment To make greater; increase. John tries to *augment* his income by working at night as well as during the day.

aug·ment (äg ment′) *verb,* **augmented, augmenting.**

August The eighth month of the year. August has thirty-one days.

Au·gust (ä′gəst) *noun.*

▲ *Augustus,* who was the first emperor of Rome, named the month of **August** after himself.

auk A diving sea bird that lives along northern seacoasts. Auks have webbed feet, short wings that are used as paddles in swimming, and white feathers.

auk (äk) *noun, plural* **auks.**

aunt 1. The sister of one's mother or father. 2. The wife of one's uncle.
▲ Another word that sounds like this is **ant.**

aunt (ant) *noun, plural* **aunts.**

auricle Either of

Auk

at; āpe; cär; end; mē; it; īce; hot; ōld; wood; fo͞ol; oil; out; up; turn; sing; thin; this; hw in white; zh in treasure. ə stands for a in about, e in taken, i in pencil, o in lemon, and u in circus.

the two chambers of the heart. The auricles receive blood from the veins and send it to the ventricles.

au·ri·cle (ōr′i kəl) *noun, plural* **auricles.**

aurora borealis Shimmering lights which appear in the northern sky at night; the northern lights. The aurora borealis is most vivid in the far north where it may appear as shining coloured ribbons of light.

au·ro·ra bo·re·a·lis (ə rō′rə bō′rē al′əs).

Australia 1. A continent southeast of Asia, between the Indian Ocean and the Pacific Ocean. It is the smallest of the continents. 2. A country made up of this continent and the island of Tasmania. Its capital is Canberra.

Aus·tra·lia (äs trāl′yə) *noun.*

authentic Real; genuine; correct. The witness gave an *authentic* account of the accident. She collects *authentic* signatures of famous people.

au·then·tic (ä then′tik) *adjective.*

author A person who writes books, stories, plays, poems, or articles. Who is the *author* of this book?

au·thor (ä′thər) *noun, plural* **authors.**

authority 1. The power or right to act, order, or make decisions. The captain has *authority* over the men on his ship. 2. A person or group having this power or right. We reported the crime to the *authorities,* and they caught the burglar. 3. A good source of information or facts. The dictionary is an *authority* on how to spell words. That professor is an *authority* on the life of Sir John A. Macdonald.

au·thor·i·ty (ə thōr′ə tē) *noun, plural* **authorities.**

authorize 1. To give authority to. My father *authorized* the real-estate agent to sell our house. 2. To approve officially. The provincial cabinet *authorized* the building of the new highway.

au·thor·ize (ä′thə rīz′) *verb,* **authorized, authorizing.**

auto Automobile. Look up **automobile** for more information.

au·to (ä′tō) *noun, plural* **autos.**

autobiography The story of a person's own life written by that person. The politician is writing his *autobiography.*

au·to·bi·og·ra·phy (ä′tō bī og′rə fē) *noun, plural* **autobiographies.**

autograph A person's name written in the person's own handwriting. I got the singer's *autograph* after his performance. *Noun.*
—To write your name in your own hand-

writing. The writer *autographed* a copy of her book for me. *Verb.*

au·to·graph (ä′tə graf′) *noun, plural* **autographs;** *verb,* **autographed, autographing.**

automatic 1. Acting, moving, or operating by itself. We have an *automatic* dishwasher. 2. Done without a person's control. Breathing is an *automatic* action of the body during sleep. *Adjective.*
—A gun that keeps firing and reloading until the trigger is released. *Noun.*

au·to·mat·ic (ä′tə mat′ək) *adjective; noun, plural* **automatics.**

automation The development and use of machines to do jobs that used to be done by people. Machines that can pick corn are an example of the use of automation as an aid in farming.

au·to·ma·tion (ä′tə mā′shən) *noun.*

automobile A vehicle that usually has four wheels and is powered by an engine that uses gasoline; car. An automobile is used mainly to carry passengers.

au·to·mo·bile (ä′tə mə bēl′) *noun, plural* **automobiles.**

An **automobile** that was made years ago.

autopsy A medical examination of a dead body to find the cause of death.

au·top·sy (ä′top′sē) *noun, plural* **autopsies.**

autumn The season of the year coming between summer and winter; fall.

au·tumn (ä′təm) *noun, plural* **autumns.**

auxiliary 1. Giving aid or extra support. This sailboat has an *auxiliary* engine in case there is no wind. 2. Additional; extra. The mayor put *auxiliary* policemen on duty during the president's visit. *Adjective.*
—Something added to give help or support. My mother belongs to the woman's *auxiliary* of my father's club. *Noun.*

aux·il·ia·ry (äk sil′yər ē *or* äg zil′yər ē) *adjective; noun, plural* **auxiliaries.**

available That which can be gotten, had, or used. This shirt is *available* in several different colours. There are still a few seats *available* for Saturday's Grey Cup game at the Olympic Stadium.

a·vail·a·ble (ə vāl′ə bəl) *adjective.*

avalanche The swift, sudden fall of a mass of snow, ice, earth, or rocks down a mountain slope.

av·a·lanche (av′ə lanch′) *noun, plural* **avalanches.**

avenue A wide or main street. Trees line the *avenues* of our city.

av·e·nue (av′ə nyoo′ *or* av′ə noo′) *noun, plural* **avenues.**

average **1.** A number found by dividing the sum of two or more quantities by the number of quantities. The *average* of 2, 4, 6, and 8 is 5. **2.** The usual amount or kind. This year's rainfall came close to the *average. Noun.*
—Usual; typical; ordinary. He is of *average* height and weight. The *average* house in this country has at least one radio. *Adjective.*
—**1.** To find the average of. Jim *averaged* his three bowling scores and wound up with 126. **2.** To have as an average. That basketball player *averages* twenty points a game. *Verb.*

av·er·age (av′ər ij *or* av′rij) *noun, plural* **averages;** *adjective; verb,* **averaged, averaging.**

avert **1.** To turn away or aside. Jim *averted* his eyes from the glare of the sun. **2.** To prevent; avoid. Dad *averted* a crash by slamming on the car's brakes.

a·vert (ə vurt′) *verb,* **averted, averting.**

aviation The science or art of flying aircraft.

a·vi·a·tion (ā′vē ā′shən) *noun.*

aviator A person who flies an airplane or other aircraft; pilot.

a·vi·a·tor (ā′vē ā′tər) *noun, plural* **aviators.**

avocado A pear-shaped tropical fruit that grows on trees. It has a dark-green skin and a pulp with a nutty taste. Avocados are eaten raw in salads.

av·o·ca·do (av′ə kä′dō) *noun, plural* **avocados.**

avoid To keep away from. We took a back road to *avoid* the heavy traffic on the highway.

a·void (ə void′) *verb,* **avoided, avoiding.**

await **1.** To wait for. The parents had long *awaited* the day of

Avocado

their son's graduation from university. **2.** To be ready for. Many changes *await* her in her new school.

a·wait (ə wāt′) *verb,* **awaited, awaiting.**

awake To wake up. It is hard for Bill to *awake* in the morning. *Verb.*
—Not asleep. He was *awake* most of the night because of the noise outside. *Adjective.*

a·wake (ə wāk′) *verb,* **awoke** or **awaked, awaking;** *adjective.*

awaken To wake up. He *awakened* when the dog barked.

a·wak·en (ə wā′kən) *verb,* **awakened, awakening.**

award **1.** To give after careful thought. The judges *awarded* my dog first prize at the dog show. **2.** To give because of a legal decision. The jury *awarded* money to the woman who had been injured in the accident. *Verb.*
—Something that is given after careful thought. He received the *award* for being the best speller. *Noun.*

a·ward (ə wôrd′) *verb,* **awarded, awarding;** *noun, plural* **awards.**

aware Knowing or realizing. The girl was not *aware* that her family was planning a surprise party for her.

a·ware (ə wer′) *adjective.*

away The frightened rabbit hopped *away.* Put the tools *away.* The little boy turned *away* to hide his tears. The sounds of footsteps faded *away.* The town is three miles *away* from our house. My brother has been *away* for three weeks.

a·way (ə wā′) *adverb; adjective.*

awe Great wonder together with fear or deep respect. They read with *awe* the stories of the lives of the early settlers. *Noun.*
—To fill with awe. We were *awed* by the force of the thunderstorm. *Verb.*

awe (ä) *noun; verb,* **awed, awing.**

awful **1.** Causing fear, dread, or awe; terrible. The earthquake caused an *awful* disaster. **2.** Very bad. I thought that movie was *awful.* **3.** Very large; great. A million dollars is an *awful* lot of money.

aw·ful (ä′fəl) *adjective.*

awfully **1.** Terribly; dreadfully. Her knee hurt *awfully* where she had scraped it.

at; āpe; cär; end; mē; it; īce; hot; ōld;
wood; fool; oil; out; up; turn; sing;
thin; this; hw in white; zh in treasure.
ə stands for a in about, e in taken,
i in pencil, o in lemon, and u in circus.

2. Very. I am *awfully* glad that you won first prize.
aw·ful·ly (ä′fə lē *or* äf′lē) *adverb.*

awhile For a short time. They rested *awhile* before playing another game of tennis.
a·while (ə wīl′ *or* ə hwīl′) *adverb.*

awkward **1.** Not graceful; clumsy. The young colt was *awkward* and had trouble standing up. **2.** Difficult or embarrassing. It was an *awkward* moment for Bill when the teacher found out that he hadn't done his homework. **3.** Difficult to use or handle. The large piano was an *awkward* piece of furniture to move.
awk·ward (äk′wərd) *adjective.*

awl A pointed tool used for making small holes in leather or wood. She used an *awl* to put her initials on the belt. ▲ Another word that sounds like this is **all**.
awl (äl) *noun, plural* **awls.**

Azalea

awning A rooflike cover of canvas, metal, or other material over a door or window. An awning is used as a shelter from the sun or rain.
aw·ning (ä′ning) *noun, plural* **awnings.**

awoke I *awoke* at seven-thirty this morning. Look up **awake** for more information.
a·woke (ə wōk′) *verb.*

axe A tool that has a metal blade attached to a handle. An axe is used for cutting down trees and chopping wood. This word is also spelled **ax**.
axe (aks) *noun, plural* **axes.**

axis A straight line around which an object or body turns or seems to turn. The earth turns on an imaginary *axis* that runs from the North Pole through the South Pole.
ax·is (ak′sis) *noun, plural* **axes.**

Axis

axle A bar or shaft on which a wheel or pair of wheels turn. The mechanic is fixing the front *axle* of Cathy's car.
ax·le (ak′səl) *noun, plural* **axles.**

aye Yes. All who are in favour of the plan say "*aye.*" *Adverb.* —A vote of "yes" or a person who votes "yes." The *ayes* won when we counted the votes. *Noun.* ▲ Other words that sound like this are **eye** and **I**.
aye (ī) *adverb; noun, plural* **ayes.**

azalea A small bush with dark-green leaves and clusters of red, pink, or white flowers.
a·za·lea (ə zāl′yə) *noun, plural* **azaleas.**

▲ The name **azalea** goes back to a Latin word that means "dry." At one time it was thought that azaleas grow best in dry soil.

azure A clear blue colour. *Noun.* —Having a clear blue colour. *Adjective.*
az·ure (azh′ər) *noun, plural* **azures;** *adjective.*

at; āpe; cär; end; mē; it; īce; hot; ōld;
wood; fool; oil; out; up; turn; sing;
thin; this; hw in white; zh in treasure.
ə stands for a in about, e in taken,
i in pencil, o in lemon, and u in circus.

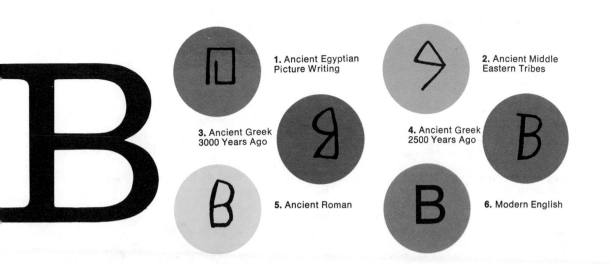

1. Ancient Egyptian Picture Writing

2. Ancient Middle Eastern Tribes

3. Ancient Greek 3000 Years Ago

4. Ancient Greek 2500 Years Ago

5. Ancient Roman

6. Modern English

B is the second letter of the alphabet. The oldest form of the letter **B** was a drawing that the ancient Egyptians **(1)** used in their picture writing nearly 5000 years ago. This drawing was borrowed by several ancient tribes **(2)** in the Middle East. They changed its shape and made it the second letter of their alphabet. The ancient Greeks **(3)** borrowed a form of this letter about 3000 years ago. At first they wrote it like a backwards capital letter **B**. Several hundred years later the Greeks turned their letter **B** around **(4)**. This made it look more like a modern capital letter **B**. The Romans **(5)** borrowed this letter from the Greeks about 2400 years ago. They wrote it in almost the same way that we write the capital letter **B** today **(6)**.

b, B The second letter of the alphabet.
  b, B (bē) *noun, plural* **b's, B's.**

baa The sound that a sheep makes; bleat. *Noun.*
—To make such a sound. *Verb.*
  baa (bä) *noun, plural* **baas;** *verb,* **baaed, baaing.**

babble **1.** To make sounds that have no meaning. The baby *babbles* because he hasn't learned to talk yet. **2.** To talk in a foolish way; chatter. The silly boy *babbled* on about his new bicycle. **3.** To make a low, murmuring sound. The brook *babbled* as it flowed over the pebbles. *Verb.*
—**1.** Sounds that have no meaning. There was a *babble* of voices in the classroom because everyone was talking at once. **2.** A low, murmuring sound. We could hear the *babble* of the brook. *Noun.*
  bab·ble (bab'əl) *verb,* **babbled, babbling;** *noun, plural* **babbles.**

babe A baby.
  babe (bāb) *noun, plural* **babes.**

baboon A large monkey that has a face like a dog. Baboons live in open country in different parts of Africa. They live together in large groups, and they travel great distances in search of food.
  ba·boon (ba bōōn') *noun, plural* **baboons.**

baby **1.** A very young child; infant. The *baby* is learning how to walk. **2.** The youngest person in a family or group. She is the *baby* of the family because her brothers and sisters are all older. **3.** A person who acts in a spoiled way. He is such a *baby* when he can't do what he wants. *Noun.*
—**1.** Of or for a baby. Mother put my little sister in the *baby* carriage. **2.** Very young. Dad bought Susy a *baby* turtle. *Adjective.*
—To treat like a baby. The mother *babied* her son by bringing him supper in bed even though he wasn't sick. *Verb.*
  ba·by (bā'bē) *noun, plural* **babies;** *adjective;* *verb,* **babied, babying.**

babysit To take care of a child or children while the parents are away for a time. My

Baboon

older sister *babysits* for the neighbours.

ba·by·sit (bā′bē sit′) *verb,* **babysat, baby-sitting.**

bachelor A man who has not married.

bach·e·lor (bach′ə lər) *noun, plural* **bachelors.**

back **1.** The part of the body behind the chest. Johnny scratched his *back.* **2.** The upper part of the body of an animal. Alice petted the puppy on its *back.* **3.** The part of anything that is opposite the front part. Jim sat at the *back* of the class. *Noun.*
—1. To help or support. He *backed* his friend in the quarrel with two other boys. **2.** To move backward. The frightened child *backed* away from the growling dog. *Verb.*
—1. Behind the front part. He went around the house to the *back* door. **2.** Past; old. Dad saves *back* copies of magazines. *Adjective.*
—1. Toward the back; backward. Carol moved *back* to let the bicycle rider go past. **2.** In the place where something used to be. She put the keys *back* in her purse. *Adverb.*
back (bak) *noun, plural* **backs;** *verb,* **backed, backing;** *adjective; adverb.*

back bacon *Canadian.* A kind of bacon. It is oval in shape and has very little fat.

backboard The board to which the basket is attached in basketball.
back·board (bak′bōrd′) *noun, plural* **backboards.**

backbone The column of bones in the back; spine. People, dogs, birds, fish, frogs, and snakes all have backbones.
back·bone (bak′bōn′) *noun, plural* **backbones.**

backcheck *Canadian.* A play in hockey or lacrosse. In a backcheck a player who has lost the puck or ball to another player tries to get it back by interfering with the player moving towards the goal.
back·check (bak′chek′) *noun, plural* **backchecks.**

backfire **1.** An explosion in a gasoline engine that causes a loud noise. We heard the *backfire* of the old car. **2.** *Canadian.* A fire set in the path of a prairie fire or a forest fire. A backfire burns the grass or trees on the edge of the fire and helps stop the fire from spreading.
back·fire (bak′fīr′) *noun, plural* **backfires.**

backgammon A game for two people that is played on a special board. The players throw dice to see how to move their pieces.
back·gam·mon (bak′gam′ən) *noun.*

background **1.** The part of a picture or scene that seems to be in the distance. Look up the word **foreground** for a picture of this. **2.** A person's past experience. Because of his many years of playing baseball, he has a good *background* for the job as coach of the team.
back·ground (bak′ground′) *noun, plural* **backgrounds.**

backhand A stroke in tennis and other games. It is made with the back of the hand turned forward.
back·hand (bak′hand′) *noun, plural* **backhands.**

A Backhand Stroke

backward **1.** Toward the back. Mary looked *backward* when she heard the noise behind her. **2.** With the back first. Tom was walking *backward* and fell. This word is also spelled **backwards.** *Adverb.*
—Toward the back. She gave a *backward* glance. *Adjective.*
back·ward (bak′wərd) *adverb; adjective.*

bacon Meat from the back and sides of a pig. Bacon is flavoured with salt and treated with smoke to preserve it.
ba·con (bā′kən) *noun.*

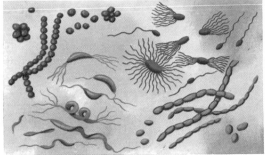

These are different types of **bacteria** as seen under a microscope.

bacteria Very tiny plants. Bacteria are so

small that they can only be seen through a powerful microscope. Some kinds of bacteria cause diseases. Other kinds do useful things, like making soil richer.
bac·te·ri·a (bak tēr′ē ə) *noun plural.*

bacterium One of the bacteria. Look up **bacteria** for more information.
bac·te·ri·um (bak tēr′ē əm) *noun, plural* **bacteria.**

bad Not good. That was a *bad* television program. Stealing the money was a *bad* thing to do. It is *bad* for your teeth to eat too much candy. She felt *bad* because she had hurt her friend's feelings. The *bad* news about his accident upset his friends.
bad (bad) *adjective,* **worse, worst.**

badge Something worn to show that a person belongs to a certain group. The Boy Scout had a merit *badge* on his uniform that he had earned for a science project.
badge (baj) *noun, plural* **badges.**

badger A furry animal with short legs and long claws. Badgers live in holes in the ground which they dig with their claws. They hunt for food at night. *Noun.*
—To bother or annoy. My brother always *badgers* me by trying to borrow money. *Verb.*
badg·er (baj′ər) *noun, plural* **badgers;** *verb,* **badgered, badgering.**

Badger

badlands *Canadian.* A dry, rocky area where almost nothing grows. The badlands are in southern Alberta and southwestern Saskatchewan.
bad·lands (bad′lands′) *noun.*

badly 1. In a bad way. The team played *badly* and lost the game. 2. Very much. He needs new shoes *badly.*
bad·ly (bad′lē) *adverb.*

badminton A game for two or four players. In badminton, the players use rackets to hit a small object called a shuttlecock back and forth over a high net.
bad·min·ton (bad′min′tən) *noun.*

baffle To be too confusing for someone to understand. The magician's trick of pulling a rabbit out of a hat *baffled* the children.
baf·fle (baf′əl) *verb,* **baffled, baffling.**

bag Something used to hold things. Bags are made of paper, cloth, plastic, or other material. She put the groceries in a *bag.* Dad bought a *bag* of grass seed. Edna put her keys in her *bag.* I ate a whole *bag* of popcorn.
bag (bag) *noun, plural* **bags.**

baggage The suitcases, trunks, and bags that a person takes on a trip.
bag·gage (bag′ij) *noun.*

baggy Hanging loosely; sagging. The old man wore *baggy* trousers.
bag·gy (bag′ē) *adjective,* **baggier, baggiest.**

bagpipe A musical instrument made of a leather bag and pipes. A person makes music by blowing air into the bag and then pressing the bag so that the air is forced out through the pipes. The bagpipe is often played in Scotland.
bag·pipe (bag′-pīp′) *noun, plural* **bagpipes.**

Bagpipe

bail¹ Money given to a court of law to get a prisoner out of jail until the time of his trial. The money guarantees that the prisoner will appear for his trial. *Noun.*
—To get a prisoner out of jail until the time of his trial by giving bail. *Verb.* ▲ Another word that sounds like this is **bale.**
bail (bāl) *noun, plural* **bails;** *verb,* **bailed, bailing.**

bail² To take water out of a boat with a pail or other container. The boys will have to *bail* water out of their rowboat or it will sink.
▲ Another word that sounds like this is **bale.**
bail (bāl) *verb,* **bailed, bailing.**

at; āpe; cär; end; mē; it; īce; hot; ōld;
wood; fōol; oil; out; up; turn; sing;
thin; this; hw in white; zh in treasure.
ə stands for a in about, e in taken,
i in pencil, o in lemon, and u in circus.

to bail out. To jump out of an airplane with a parachute. The pilot *bailed out* when his plane caught fire.

bait Something that tempts or attracts. The fisherman used worms as *bait* for fish. *Noun.* —1. To put bait on. We *baited* the trap with cheese to catch the mouse. 2. To tease in a mean way. The other boys tried to *bait* him by calling him a coward. *Verb.*
 bait (bāt) *noun, plural* **baits;** *verb,* **baited, baiting.**

bake 1. To cook by dry heat in an oven. Mother *baked* bread. The potatoes *baked* slowly. 2. To harden or dry by heating. People *bake* bowls and dishes in ovens called kilns. The sun *baked* the grass until it turned brown.
 bake (bāk) *verb,* **baked, baking.**

baker A person who bakes and sells bread, cakes, cookies, and pastries.
 bak·er (bā′kər) *noun, plural* **bakers.**

bakery A place where bread, cakes, cookies, and pastries are baked or sold.
 bak·er·y (bā′kər ē) *noun, plural* **bakeries.**

baking powder A powder used in baking to make dough or batter rise.

balance 1. The condition of having all the parts of something exactly the same in weight, amount, or force. The two children kept the seesaw in *balance.* 2. A steady position. He lost his *balance* and fell down the stairs. 3. An instrument for weighing things. The chemist weighed some powder on the *balance.* 4. The part that is left over. He still has the *balance* of his homework to do after supper. *Noun.* —To put or keep in a steady position. The girl *balanced* a book on her head. *Verb.*
 bal·ance (bal′əns) *noun, plural* **balances;** *verb,* **balanced, balancing.**

The children are **balancing** on the seesaw.

balcony 1. A platform that juts out from the wall of a building. A balcony has a low wall or railing on three sides. 2. An upper floor that juts out into a large room or auditorium. Most theatres have balconies with seats.
 bal·co·ny (bal′kə nē) *noun, plural* **balconies.**

bald 1. Having little or no hair on the head. My father is getting *bald.* 2. Without a natural covering. The *bald* hilltop had no trees or shrubs.
 bald (bäld) *adjective,* **balder, baldest.**

▲ The first meaning of **bald** was "round like a ball." People probably started calling someone without hair *bald* because a smooth, hairless head looks something like a round ball.

bald eagle A large eagle of North America. The bald eagle is brown with a white head, neck, and tail. The bald eagle is the national symbol of the United States.

bale A large bundle of things tied together tightly for shipping or storing. The farmer stored the *bales* of hay in the barn for the winter. ▲ Another word that sounds like this is **bail.**
 bale (bāl) *noun, plural* **bales.**

balk 1. To stop short and refuse to go on. The mule *balked* and would not move. 2. To keep from going on; hinder. The guards *balked* the prisoners' plans to escape from jail.
 balk (bäk) *verb,* **balked, balking.**

ball¹ 1. A round object. Bill wound the kite string into a *ball.* 2. A roundish object used in various games. John brought his *ball* and bat for the baseball game. 3. A game played with a ball. I play *ball* after school every day. 4. A pitch in baseball that does not pass over home plate in the area between the batter's knees and shoulders and that he does not swing at. ▲ Another word that sounds like this is **bawl.**
 ball (bäl) *noun, plural* **balls.**

ball² A large, formal party for dancing. The beautiful princess met the handsome prince at the *ball.* ▲ Another word that sounds like this is **bawl.**
 ball (bäl) *noun, plural* **balls.**

ballad A simple poem or song that tells a story. The cowboy sang a *ballad* about the Red River settlers.
 bal·lad (bal′əd) *noun, plural* **ballads.**

ballast Something heavy used to give balance. Sand or rocks are used as ballast. Ballast is put in a ship to keep it steady in the water.
 bal·last (bal′əst) *noun, plural* **ballasts.**

ball bearing A bearing made up of a number of metal balls, on which the moving part of a machine turns easily. The wheels of my roller skates turn on *ball bearings.*

ballerina A woman or girl who dances ballet.
   bal·le·ri·na (bal′ə rē′nə) *noun, plural* **ballerinas.**

ballet A form of dance. Dancers use certain formal steps and movements when dancing ballet. A ballet usually tells a story.
   bal·let (ba lā′ *or* bal′ā) *noun, plural* **ballets.**

balloon A bag filled with air or other gas. Small balloons are used as children's toys or for decoration. Large balloons are made to rise and float in the air. These balloons have cabins or baskets for carrying passengers or scientific instruments. *Noun.*
—To swell out or grow larger like a balloon. The parachute *ballooned* when it opened. *Verb.*
   bal·loon (bə lōōn′) *noun, plural* **balloons;** *verb,* **ballooned, ballooning.**

Ballerina

ballot A printed form or other thing used in voting. A voter checks or writes down his choice on a paper ballot, and then puts the ballot into a box, or else votes by means of a ballot in a special machine. Later the ballots are counted to see who has won the election. *Noun.*
—To use a ballot for voting. The students *balloted* to choose a class president. *Verb.*
   bal·lot (bal′ət) *noun, plural* **ballots;** *verb,* **balloted, balloting.**

In ancient Greece, people voted by putting a little ball into the voting box. A person used a white ball to vote for someone and a black ball to vote against someone. The word **ballot** comes from the word for these balls.

ball-point pen A pen whose point is a small metal ball that rolls the ink from a container inside the pen onto the paper.
   ball-point pen (bäl′point′).

ballroom A large room where dances and other parties are given.
   ball·room (bäl′rōōm′) *noun, plural* **ballrooms.**

balsa A strong and very light wood from a tropical American tree. Balsa is easy to cut and carve. It is used to make airplane and boat models.
   bal·sa (bäl′sə) *noun.*

balsam An evergreen tree that grows in North America. Wood from the balsam is used to make boxes and crates.
   bal·sam (bäl′səm) *noun, plural* **balsams.**

bamboo A tall, treelike plant that is related to grass. The bamboo has woody stems that are used to make fishing poles, canes, and furniture.
   bam·boo (bam-bōō′) *noun, plural* **bamboos.**

ban To forbid; prohibit. The government *bans* the hunting of animals in that provincial park. *Verb.*
—An official order that forbids something. There is a *ban* on smoking in that theatre. *Noun.*
   ban (ban) *verb,* **banned, banning;** *noun, plural* **bans.**

Bamboo

banana A slightly curved fruit that has a yellow or red skin. Bananas grow in bunches on a treelike plant that has very large leaves. They grow in tropical regions of the world.
   ba·nan·a (bə nan′ə) *noun, plural* **bananas.**

Fruit
Banana Tree

band¹ **1.** A group of persons or animals. A *band* of Gypsies camped outside of town. **2.** A group of musicians playing together. The

at; āpe; cär; end; mē; it; īce; hot; ōld;
wood; fōōl; oil; out; up; turn; sing;
thin; this; hw in white; zh in treasure.
ə stands for a in about, e in taken,
i in pencil, o in lemon, and u in circus.

band played at the football game. **3.** *Canadian.* A number of Indians of one tribe living in the same area and considered by the Department of Indian Affairs as a unit. *Noun.*
—To gather together in a group. The neighbours *banded* together to plant trees. *Verb.*
band (band) *noun, plural* **bands;** *verb,* **banded, banding.**

band² **1.** A strip of cloth or other material. Gail tied a red *band* in her hair. There were metal *bands* around the barrel. **2.** A stripe of colour. A candy cane has *bands* of red and white around it. *Noun.*
—To put a band on. Jack *banded* the leg of the pigeon so he could identify it. *Verb.*
band (band) *noun, plural* **bands;** *verb,* **banded, banding.**

bandage A strip of cloth or other material used to cover or bind a wound or injury. Father put a *bandage* on Jerry's cut finger. *Noun.*
—To cover or bind with a bandage. The nurse *bandaged* Ann's scraped knee. *Verb.*
band·age (ban′dij) *noun, plural* **bandages;** *verb,* **bandaged, bandaging.**

bandanna A large handkerchief with a bright pattern on it. The cowboy wore a red *bandanna* around his neck.
ban·dan·na (ban dan′ə) *noun, plural* **bandannas.**

Bandage

bandit A robber or outlaw. *Bandits* held up the stagecoach.
ban·dit (ban′dit) *noun, plural* **bandits.**

bang A loud, sudden noise or blow. *Noun.*
—**1.** To make a loud, sudden noise. The door *banged* shut. **2.** To strike or hit noisily. She *banged* the table with her fist. *Verb.*
bang (bang) *noun, plural* **bangs;** *verb,* **banged, banging.**

bangs Hair cut short and worn over the forehead.
bangs (bangz) *noun plural.*

banish **1.** To punish someone by making him leave his country. The king *banished* the man who had been a spy for the enemy. **2.** To send or drive away. The boys *banished* the player from the game for being a bad sport.
ban·ish (ban′ish) *verb,* **banished, banishing.**

banister A railing along a staircase, and the posts that support this railing.

ban·is·ter (ban′is tər) *noun, plural* **banisters.**

banjo A musical instrument that has a round body, a long neck, and five strings. A banjo is played by plucking the strings with the fingers or with a pick.
ban·jo (ban′jō) *noun, plural* **banjos** or **banjoes.**

Banjo

bank¹ **1.** A long mound or heap. The bulldozer dug up a *bank* of earth. **2.** The rising ground along a river or lake. We go fishing along the river's *bank*. **3.** A shallow part of the ocean which is good for fishing. The Grand Banks off Newfoundland are famous for cod. *Noun.*
—To form into a bank; pile; heap. The plow *banked* the snow along the side of the road. *Verb.*
bank (bangk) *noun, plural* **banks;** *verb,* **banked, banking.**

bank² A place where people borrow or save money. Dad went to the *bank* to deposit one hundred dollars in his savings account. Johnny was given a toy *bank* to save his pennies in. *Noun.*
—To do business with a bank. She *banks* at the branch of the Royal Bank on Queen Street. *Verb.*
bank (bangk) *noun, plural* **banks;** *verb,* **banked, banking.**

banker **1.** A person who helps run a bank. **2.** *Canadian.* A person who fishes off the Grand Banks. **3.** *Canadian.* A fishing boat which is used for fishing off the Grand Banks near Newfoundland.
bank·er (bang′kər) *noun, plural* **bankers.**

bankrupt Not able to pay what one owes. The businessman was *bankrupt* when his company failed. *Adjective.*
—To make bankrupt. The fire last Thursday in his store *bankrupted* Mr. Comtois. *Verb.*
bank·rupt (bangk′rupt′) *adjective; verb,* **bankrupted, bankrupting.**

▲ The word **bankrupt** comes from two Italian words that mean "broken bench." In the Middle Ages in Italy, each banker had a bench where he kept his money. Supposedly, when a banker could not pay people what he owed them, his bench was broken.

---

banner A flag or other piece of cloth that has a design and sometimes writing on it. The fans at the baseball game hung *banners* from the grandstand. *Noun.*
—Important; outstanding. It was a *banner* year for the high school football team because they won the regional championship. *Adjective.*
ban·ner (ban′ər) *noun, plural* **banners;** *adjective.*

banquet A large formal dinner prepared for many people. A banquet is given for a special occasion. The school gave a *banquet* for the students who won scholarship awards.
ban·quet (bang′kwit) *noun, plural* **banquets.**

baptism A religious ceremony of dipping a person in water or sprinkling him with water. Baptism is a sign of being admitted into a Christian church.
bap·tism (bap′tiz′əm) *noun, plural* **baptisms.**

baptize To make a person a member of a Christian church by dipping him in water or sprinkling him with water. The minister *baptized* the baby.
bap·tize (bap tīz′ *or* bap′tīz) *verb,* **baptized, baptizing.**

bar 1. A piece of metal, wood, soap, or other material that is longer than it is wide. There are *bars* on the windows of the jail. Ken ate a *bar* of candy. 2. Something that blocks the way. The boy's small size was a *bar* to his being on the football team. 3. A stripe or band of colour. Andy's shirt has *bars* of blue and yellow on it. 4. In music, an upright line placed on a staff to mark the division between two measures. 5. A unit of music between two bars; measure. 6. The profession of a lawyer. The young man passed the examination and was admitted to the *bar.* 7. A place where alcoholic drinks are served or sold. *Noun.*
—1. To use a bar to fasten something. Dad *barred* the door with a heavy piece of wood. 2. To keep out. Visitors are *barred* from the hospital in the morning. *Verb.*
bar (bär) *noun, plural* **bars;** *verb,* **barred, barring.**

barb A sharp point that curves backward. The *barb* of the fishhook caught in the fish's mouth.
barb (bärb) *noun, plural* **barbs.**

barbarian A person who belongs to a tribe or a people that is savage or uncivilized. *Barbarians* conquered Rome about 1500 years ago.
bar·bar·i·an (bär ber′ē ən) *noun, plural* **barbarians.**

barbecue A meal cooked outdoors over an open fire. *Noun.*
—To cook a meal outdoors over an open fire. Dad *barbecued* the chicken. *Verb.*
bar·be·cue (bär′bə kyoo′) *noun, plural* **barbecues;** *verb,* **barbecued, barbecuing.**

barbed wire Wire with barbs attached. It is used in fences.

barber A person whose work is cutting hair and trimming or shaving beards.
bar·ber (bär′bər) *noun, plural* **barbers.**

Barbed Wire Fence

bare 1. Without covering or clothing; naked. Joey walked on the beach with *bare* feet. In winter the trees are *bare.* 2. Empty. After we took all the books out, the shelves were *bare.* 3. Just enough; mere. She receives only the *bare* minimum in salary for her work. *Adjective.*
—To uncover. He *bared* his chest by opening his shirt. The cat *bared* its claws. *Verb.*
▲ Another word that sounds like this is **bear.**
bare (ber) *adjective,* **barer, barest;** *verb,* **bared, baring.**

bareback On the back of a horse without a saddle. She is a *bareback* rider in the circus. *Adjective.*
—Without a saddle. The cowboy rode the horse *bareback. Adverb.*
bare·back (ber′bak′) *adjective; adverb.*

barefoot With the feet bare. The *barefoot* boy got a splinter in his toe. She walked *barefoot* on the grass.
bare·foot (ber′foot′) *adjective; adverb.*

---

at; āpe; cär; end; mē; it; īce; hot; ōld;
wood; fool; oil; out; up; turn; sing;
thin; this; hw in white; zh in treasure.
ə stands for a in about, e in taken,
i in pencil, o in lemon, and u in circus.

barely Only just; scarcely. There was *barely* enough food to go around.
bare·ly (ber′lē) *adverb*.

bargain 1. Something offered for sale or bought at a low price. At only ten cents, this ball-point pen is a *bargain*. 2. An agreement. My brother and I made a *bargain* that I would wash the dishes if he would dry them. *Noun.*
—To try to reach a bargain. Betty *bargained* with the salesman in order to get a good price on the used bicycle. *Verb.*
bar·gain (bär′gən) *noun, plural* **bargains;** *verb,* **bargained, bargaining.**

barge A flat-bottomed boat. Barges are used to carry freight on canals and rivers.
barge (bärj) *noun, plural* **barges.**

baritone 1. A man's singing voice that is lower than tenor and higher than bass. 2. A singer who has such a voice.
bar·i·tone (ber′ə tōn′) *noun, plural* **baritones.**

bark¹ The outer covering of the trunk, branches, and roots of a tree. Bark is usually thick and rough. *Noun.*
—To scrape or rub the skin off. He *barked* his shins when he fell on the stairway. *Verb.*
bark (bärk) *noun, plural* **barks;** *verb,* **barked, barking.**

bark² The short, sharp sound that a dog makes. *Noun.*
—1. To make the short, sharp sound that a dog makes. The watchdog *barked* at the stranger. 2. To speak loudly and sharply. The police officer *barked* "Hands up!" at the outlaw. *Verb.*
bark (bärk) *noun, plural* **barks;** *verb,* **barked, barking.**

barley The grain of a plant that is like grass. Barley is often used as animal feed and to make malt.
bar·ley (bär′lē) *noun.*

barn A building on a farm. Barns are used to store hay and grain, and to house cows and horses.
barn (bärn) *noun, plural* **barns.**

Barn

barnyard A yard around a barn. The chickens pecked for food in the *barnyard.*
barn·yard (bärn′yärd′) *noun, plural* **barnyards.**

barometer An instrument for measuring the pressure of the atmosphere. A barometer shows changes in the weather.
ba·rom·e·ter (bə rom′ə tər) *noun, plural* **barometers.**

baron A nobleman of the lowest rank.
▲ Another word that sounds like this is **barren.**
bar·on (bar′ən) *noun, plural* **barons.**

barracks A building or group of buildings where soldiers live. Barracks are found on military bases.
bar·racks (bar′əks) *noun plural.*

barracuda A fierce fish that lives in warm seas. The barracuda has a long, narrow body and a large mouth with sharp teeth. Barracudas have been known to attack swimmers.
bar·ra·cu·da (bar′ə kōō′də) *noun, plural* **barracudas** or **barracuda.**

Barracuda

barrage A heavy amount of cannon, rocket, or gun fire to keep enemy soldiers from moving forward or attacking.
bar·rage (bə räzh′) *noun, plural* **barrages.**

barrel 1. A large, round wooden container with curved sides. The farmer packed the apples in *barrels.* 2. A metal tube that forms part of a gun. Bullets are fired through the barrel.
bar·rel (bar′əl) *noun, plural* **barrels.**

Barrel

barren Not able to produce anything. No plants could grow in the sandy, *barren* soil. The apple tree is *barren* and cannot bear fruit. *Adjective.*
—*Canadian.* **the Barrens.** A bleak stretch of land above the tree line northwest of

Hudson Bay. *Noun.* ▲ Another word that sounds like this is **baron**.

bar·ren (bar′ən) *adjective; noun plural,* **barrens.**

barricade Something that blocks the way. The police set up *barricades* to keep the crowds away from the accident. *Noun.*
—To block the way with a barricade. They piled up logs to *barricade* the fort. *Verb.*

bar·ri·cade (bar′ə kād′) *noun, plural* **barricades;** *verb,* **barricaded, barricading.**

barrier Something that blocks the way. The fallen tree was a *barrier* to traffic on the road.

bar·ri·er (bar′ē ər) *noun, plural* **barriers.**

barter To trade goods for other goods without using money. The early pioneers *bartered* seed for animal skins with the Indians. *Verb.*
—The trading of goods for other goods without the use of money. Early settlers carried on much trade by *barter. Noun.*

bar·ter (bär′tər) *verb,* **bartered, bartering;** *noun.*

base[1] **1.** The part that something rests or stands on; the lowest part. That lamp has a wooden *base*. The boys camped at the *base* of the mountain. **2.** The main part of something. Mother made soup with a chicken *base*. **3.** A starting place. The airplanes got back to the *base* safely. **4.** One of the four corners of a baseball diamond. The batter reached first *base*. **5.** A chemical that joins with an acid to make a salt. A base causes red litmus paper to turn blue. *Noun.*
—To put on a base. The builders *based* the house on concrete. The famous writer *bases* his stories on his own experiences. *Verb.*
▲ Another word that sounds like this is **bass.**

base (bās) *noun, plural* **bases;** *verb,* **based, basing.**

base[2] **1.** Not brave or honourable; cowardly, shameful, or bad. Telling lies about his friend was a *base* thing to do. **2.** Low in value when compared with something else. Iron is a *base* metal; gold is a precious metal. ▲ Another word that sounds like this is **bass.**

base (bās) *adjective,* **baser, basest.**

baseball **1.** A game played with a ball and bat by two teams of nine players each. Baseball is played on a field with four bases that form a diamond. To score a run, you must reach home base by way of first, second, and third bases before you or your team are put out. Each team is allowed three outs in an inning, and a game is made up of nine innings. **2.** The ball used in this game.

base·ball (bās′bäl′) *noun, plural* **baseballs.**

basement The lowest floor of a building. The basement is below or partly below the ground.

base·ment (bās′mənt) *noun, plural* **basements.**

bashful Embarrassed and shy around people. The *bashful* little boy hid behind his mother's skirt.

bash·ful (bash′fəl) *adjective.*

basic Forming the most important part; fundamental. Food is a *basic* human need. The *basic* parts of a bicycle are the wheels, handlebars, and frame. A *basic* difference between the two friends is that Mike likes to play baseball and Bill likes to read.

ba·sic (bā′sik) *adjective.*

basin **1.** A round or oval bowl for holding liquids. Johnny filled the *basin* of the sink with water. **2.** An area containing water. The harbour has a boat *basin*. **3.** All the land that is drained by a river and by all the streams flowing into the river.

ba·sin (bā′sən) *noun, plural* **basins.**

basis The part that something rests or depends on; foundation. The *basis* for my opinion on the matter is something I read about it in a book.

ba·sis (bā′sis) *noun, plural* **bases.**

bask To lie in and enjoy a pleasant warmth. The children *basked* in the sun on the beach. The boys *basked* in front of the campfire.

bask (bask) *verb,* **basked, basking.**

Baseball

at; āpe; cär; end; mē; it; īce; hot; ōld;
wood; fo͞ol; oil; out; up; turn; sing;
thin; this; hw in white; zh in treasure.
ə stands for a in about, e in taken,
i in pencil, o in lemon, and u in circus.

basket **1.** Something to hold things. Baskets are made of twigs, straw, strips of wood, or other material woven together. Phil picked apples and put them in a *basket*. Dad bought a *basket* of pears from the farmer. **2.** A metal hoop with a net hanging from it used in basketball. The ball is thrown through the basket to score a goal.
bas·ket (bas′kət) *noun, plural* **baskets.**

basketball **1.** A game played with a large, round ball on a rectangular court by two teams of five players each. To score a goal, a player must throw the ball through a raised basket at the opponent's end of the court. **2.** The ball used in this game.
bas·ket·ball (bas′kət bäl′) *noun, plural* **basketballs.**

Basketball

bass¹ **1.** The lowest man's singing voice. **2.** A singer who has such a voice. **3.** A musical instrument that has a similar range. ▲ Another word that sounds like this is **base.**
bass (bās) *noun, plural* **basses.**

bass² Any of a number of North American fish. Bass are used for food. They can be found in streams and lakes, and in the sea.
bass (bas) *noun, plural* **bass** or **basses.**

bass drum A very large drum that gives a deep, booming sound when it is struck.
bass drum (bās).

bassoon A musical instrument that makes a low sound when it is played. The bassoon is made up of a long, double wooden tube. It is played by blowing into a curved metal mouthpiece at one end.
bas·soon (ba sōōn′ *or* bə soon′) *noun, plural* **bassoons.**

bass viol The largest stringed musical instrument. It gives a very low sound when it is played. The bass viol is shaped like a violin, but it is played standing upright on the floor because it is very large. The musician plays it with a bow or by plucking with his fingers.
bass vi·ol (bās vī′əl).

Bassoon

baste¹ To pour melted butter, fat, gravy, or other liquid over food to keep it moist while it is roasting. Mother used a large spoon to *baste* the chicken.
baste (bāst) *verb,* **basted, basting.**

baste² To sew with long, loose stitches. She *basted* the seam of the dress in place before sewing it on the sewing machine.
baste (bāst) *verb,* **basted, basting.**

bat¹ **1.** A strong wooden stick or club. A bat is used to hit the ball in baseball and softball. **2.** A turn to hit the ball in baseball and softball. Our team is at *bat. Noun.*
—To hit the ball with a bat. Jack *batted* the ball out of the park. It is her turn to *bat. Verb.*
bat (bat) *noun, plural* **bats;** *verb,* **batted, batting.**

bat² A small, furry animal. A bat has a body like a mouse, and wings of thin skin.
bat (bat) *noun, plural* **bats.**

Bat

batch A group of things or persons. Susan baked a *batch* of cookies. We threw away a *batch* of old newspapers.
batch (bach) *noun, plural* **batches.**

bateau *Canadian.* A boat with a flat bottom, originally made to carry people and goods between Upper and Lower Canada.
ba·teau (ba tō′) *noun, plural* **bateaux.**

bath 1. A washing of something in water. She took a warm *bath.* John gave his dog a *bath.* 2. The water used for bathing. The *bath* was too hot. 3. A place or room for bathing; bathroom. The house has two bedrooms and one *bath.*
bath (bath) *noun, plural* **baths.**

bathe 1. To wash something in water. Mary is going to *bathe* her puppy. He *bathes* each morning before breakfast. 2. To go swimming. The children love to *bathe* in the ocean during the summer. 3. To surround or cover with something. Sweat *bathed* his forehead. She turned on the lamps, and the room was *bathed* in light.
bathe (bāth) *verb,* **bathed, bathing.**

bathing suit A piece of clothing worn while swimming.

bathroom A room that has a sink, toilet, and a bathtub or shower.
bath·room (bath′room′ *or* bath′room′) *noun, plural* **bathrooms.**

bathtub A large tub to bathe in.
bath·tub (bath′tub′) *noun, plural* **bathtubs.**

baton A stick or rod. The conductor used a *baton* to direct the orchestra. The drum majorette twirled her *baton.*
ba·ton (ba ton′ *or* bə ton′) *noun, plural* **batons.**

battalion A large part of an army. A battalion forms part of a regiment.
bat·tal·ion (bə-tal′yən) *noun, plural* **battalions.**

batter¹ To hit over and over again with heavy blows. The sailor was afraid the high waves would *batter* the small boat to pieces.
bat·ter (bat′ər) *verb,* **battered, battering.**

Baton

batter² A mixture of flour, milk or water, and other things. Batter is fried or baked to make pancakes, doughnuts, or cakes.
bat·ter (bat′ər) *noun, plural* **batters.**

batter³ A person whose turn it is to bat in a game of baseball or softball.
bat·ter (bat′ər) *noun, plural* **batters.**

battering ram A heavy beam once used in war to batter down walls or gates.

Battering Ram

battery 1. A device that produces an electric current by chemical changes in the materials inside it. Flashlights must have *batteries* to work. 2. A group of things that are alike or that work together. A *battery* of microphones stood in front of the astronaut as he gave his speech.
bat·ter·y (bat′ər ē) *noun, plural* **batteries.**

battle A fight or struggle. The two armies fought a *battle.* Life in the Arctic is a constant *battle* against the cold. *Noun.*
—To fight or struggle. The ship *battled* the high waves. *Verb.*
bat·tle (bat′əl) *noun, plural* **battles;** *verb,* **battled, battling.**

battle-axe A heavy axe with a wide blade. It was once used as a weapon in war.
bat·tle-axe (bat′əl aks′) *noun, plural* **battle-axes.**

battlefield A place where a battle was fought or is being fought. The Plains of Abraham is a famous Canadian battlefield.
bat·tle·field (bat′əl fēld′) *noun, plural* **battle-fields.**

battlement A low wall built along the top of a fort or tower. A battlement has a series of openings for soldiers to shoot through at someone attacking from outside.
bat·tle·ment (bat′əl mənt) *noun, plural* **battlements.**

at; āpe; cär; end; mē; it; īce; hot; ōld; wood; fo͞ol; oil; out; up; turn; sing; thin; this; hw in white; zh in treasure.
ə stands for a in about, e in taken, i in pencil, o in lemon, and u in circus.

battleship A large warship with very powerful guns and thick, heavy armour.
bat·tle·ship (bat′əl ship′) *noun, plural* battleships.

bawl To cry or shout loudly. The lost child *bawled* for his mother. *Verb.*
—A loud cry or shout. *Noun.* ▲ Another word that sounds like this is **ball.**
bawl (bäl) *verb,* bawled, bawling; *noun.*
to bawl out. To scold loudly. Dad *bawled out* my brother for breaking the window.

bay¹ A part of a sea or lake that stretches into the land.
bay (bā) *noun, plural* bays.

bay² The deep, long barking or howling of a dog. The hunter heard the *bay* of the hounds chasing a rabbit. *Noun.*
—To bark or howl with deep, long sounds. The dog *bayed* at the moon. *Verb.*
bay (bā) *noun, plural* bays; *verb,* bayed, baying.

bayonet A large knife that fits on the end of a rifle. A bayonet is used in fighting.
bay·o·net (bā′ə net′) *noun, plural* bayonets.

Bayonet

bayou A stream that flows slowly through marshy land. Bayous are found in the southern United States.
bay·ou (bī′o͞o *or* bī′ō) *noun, plural* bayous.

bazaar A sale of different things for some special purpose. Mother baked a cake for the church *bazaar.*
ba·zaar (bə zär′) *noun, plural* bazaars.

B.C. An abbreviation meaning "before Christ." It is used in giving dates before the birth of Christ. 100 *B.C.* means 100 years before the birth of Christ.

be That house must *be* the largest one in town. Bill is going to *be* sixteen years old tomorrow. This game should *be* fun. She will *be* home soon. *Be* kind to him. The train may

be late. ▲ Another word that sounds like this is **bee.**
be (bē) *verb,* been, being.

beach The land along the edge of an ocean. A beach is covered with sand or pebbles. We hunted for different kinds of shells along the *beach. Noun.*
—To run a boat onto a beach. We *beached* our sailboat in order to paint it. *Verb.*
▲ Another word that sounds like this is **beech.**
beach (bēch) *noun, plural* beaches; *verb,* beached, beaching.

beacon A light or other signal that warns or guides. The *beacon* from the lighthouse guided the ship through the fog.
bea·con (bē′kən) *noun, plural* beacons.

bead 1. A small round piece of glass, wood, plastic, or other material. A bead has a hole through it so that it can be strung on a wire or string with other pieces like it. Alice wore a necklace of red *beads.* 2. Any small round thing. *Beads* of sweat rolled down the runner's face. *Noun.*
—To decorate with beads. The woman's long dress was *beaded* with silver. *Verb.*
bead (bēd) *noun, plural* beads; *verb,* beaded, beading.

beagle A small dog with short legs, a smooth coat, and drooping ears. Beagles are kept as pets and also are used to hunt squirrels, rabbits, and other small animals.
bea·gle (bē′gəl) *noun, plural* beagles.

Beagle

beak The hard mouth part of a bird. Hawks and eagles have sharp, hooked beaks.
beak (bēk) *noun, plural* beaks.

beaker A glass cup or container with a lip for pouring. Beakers are used in laboratories.
beak·er (bē′kər) *noun, plural* beakers.

beam 1. A long, strong piece of wood or metal. Beams are used in building to support floors or ceilings. 2. A narrow ray of light. *Beams* of sunlight came through the window. The campers could see the path by the *beams* of their flashlights. *Noun.*
—1. To shine brightly. The sun *beamed* down on the cornfield. 2. To smile happily. The girl *beamed* with happiness when her parents gave her a bicycle. *Verb.*
beam (bēm) *noun, plural* beams; *verb,* beamed, beaming.

bean 1. A smooth, flat seed that is eaten as a vegetable. There are many different kinds of beans. Sometimes the long pods that these seeds grow in are also eaten. Some beans that people eat are the lima bean, string bean, and the kidney bean. 2. Any seed that looks like a bean. Mother ground the coffee *beans*.
bean (bēn) *noun, plural* **beans**.

bear¹ 1. To hold up; support or carry. Beams *bear* the weight of the roof of our house. Don't climb that tree because its branches won't *bear* your weight. 2. To bring forth; give birth to. The peach tree *bears* fruit. Our dog will *bear* puppies soon. 3. To put up with patiently; stand. My brother Tom cannot *bear* being teased. The little girl was able to *bear* the pain of her broken arm bravely. ▲ Another word that sounds like this is **bare**.
bear (ber) *verb,* **bore, borne** or **born, bearing**.

bear² A large, heavy animal with thick shaggy fur. A bear has sharp claws and a very short tail. There are many kinds of bears, including the black bear, brown bear, grizzly bear, and the polar bear. ▲ Another word that sounds like this is **bare**.
bear (ber) *noun, plural* **bears**.

Bear

beard 1. The hair that grows on a man's face. 2. Something that looks like a beard. That goat has a *beard* on its chin.
beard (bērd) *noun, plural* **beards**.

bearing 1. The way that a person walks, stands, or acts. The young man has the *bearing* of an athlete. 2. Connection in thought. Jack's silly remark had no *bearing* on what we were talking about. 3. **bearings**. Knowledge of one's position or direction. The campers lost their *bearings* and wandered for hours before they

Beard

found the right path again. 4. A part of a machine that holds a moving part and allows it to move with less friction. Joe replaced a worn *bearing* in the automobile engine.
bear·ing (ber′ing) *noun, plural* **bearings**.

beast 1. Any animal that has four feet. We went to the zoo to see the tigers, elephants, and other *beasts* of the jungle. 2. A person who is coarse or cruel.
beast (bēst) *noun, plural* **beasts**.

beat 1. To hit again and again; pound. He *beat* the drum during the parade. The wicked man *beat* his horse. The ocean waves *beat* against the side of the boat. 2. To do better than; get the better of; defeat. Our soccer team *beat* their team. She *beat* her brother at checkers. 3. To thump or throb. He could feel the kitten's heart *beat*. 4. To move up and down; flap. The eagle *beat* its wings. 5. To stir or mix with force. She *beat* the eggs for the cake. *Verb.*
—1. A blow made over and over again. We could hear the *beat* of the drum. 2. A throb. He pressed his hand to his chest and felt the *beat* of his heart. 3. A regular route or round. Jack saw a policeman patrolling his *beat*. 4. The basic unit of time in music. Jill tapped her foot to the *beat* of the music. *Noun.* ▲ Another word that sounds like this is **beet**.
beat (bēt) *verb,* **beat, beaten** or **beat, beating;** *noun, plural* **beats**.

beaten Their basketball team has *beaten* ours every year. Look up **beat** for more information. *Verb.*
—1. Worn by use. The hunters followed a *beaten* path through the woods. 2. Defeated. The *beaten* football team hoped to do better in the next game. *Adjective.*
beat·en (bēt′ən) *verb; adjective.*

beautiful Pleasing to look at or hear. She has a *beautiful* face. The band played some *beautiful* music. We had *beautiful* weather for our picnic.
beau·ti·ful (byo͞o′ti fəl) *adjective.*

beauty 1. A quality that makes a person or thing pleasing to look at or hear. The garden is a place of *beauty* when all the flowers are in bloom. 2. A person or thing that is beautiful. Steve's new bicycle is a *beauty*.
beau·ty (byo͞o′tē) *noun, plural* **beauties**.

at; āpe; cär; end; mē; it; īce; hot; ōld;
wood; fo͞ol; oil; out; up; turn; sing;
thin; this; hw in white; zh in treasure.
ə stands for a in about, e in taken,
i in pencil, o in lemon, and u in circus.

beaver A furry, brown animal that has a broad, flat tail and webbed hind feet to help it swim. The beaver lives in or near the water in a house built of branches, stones, and mud. The *beaver* has been a national emblem of Canada for years.
bea·ver (bē′vər) *noun, plural* **beavers.**

Beaver

became My older sister *became* a lawyer. Look up **become** for more information.
be·came (bē kām′) *verb.*

because For the reason that. Phil is cold *because* he did not wear his sweater. She drank two glasses of water *because* she was thirsty.
be·cause (bē kuz′) *conjunction.*
because of. On account of. They were late to the party *because of* a flat tire.

beckon To make a sign or signal to someone. He *beckoned* to his friend to join him by waving his hand.
beck·on (bek′ən) *verb,* **beckoned, beckoning.**

become **1.** To grow to be; come to be. Tadpoles *become* frogs. I have *become* tired. **2.** To look well on; flatter; suit. A blue shirt *becomes* him.
be·come (bē kum′) *verb,* **became, become, becoming.**
become of. To happen to. What has *become of* my pencil?

becoming Looking well on; flattering. Jerry's new jacket is *becoming* to him.
be·com·ing (bē kum′ing) *adjective.*

bed **1.** Something used to sleep or rest on. Dad bought Philip a new *bed* with a thick mattress. The deer slept on a *bed* of leaves. **2.** A piece of ground used to grow plants in. Mother planted roses in the flower *bed*. **3.** The ground at the bottom of a river, stream, or lake. The stream had a *bed* of sand and pebbles. **4.** A foundation or support. The road was built on a *bed* of gravel. *Noun.*
—To give a place to sleep to. Johnny decided to *bed* his dog in the garage. *Verb.*

bed (bed) *noun, plural* **beds;** *verb,* **bedded, bedding.**

bedding Sheets, blankets, and other coverings used on a bed.
bed·ding (bed′ing) *noun, plural* **beddings.**

bedraggled Wet, limp, and dirty. We found a *bedraggled* kitten in the street.
be·drag·gled (bē drag′əld) *adjective.*

bedroom A room for sleeping. Our house has three *bedrooms*.
bed·room (bed′room′ *or* bed′room′) *noun, plural* **bedrooms.**

bedside The space beside a bed. The mother waited at the sick little boy's *bedside* until he was asleep.
bed·side (bed′sīd′) *noun, plural* **bedsides.**

bedspread A top cover for a bed.
bed·spread (bed′spred′) *noun, plural* **bedspreads.**

bedtime The time for a person to go to bed. Her *bedtime* is nine o'clock.
bed·time (bed′tīm′) *noun, plural* **bedtimes.**

bee An insect that has a thick, hairy body, four wings, and a stinger. A bee feeds on nectar and pollen. Some bees live in colonies or hives, and make honey and beeswax. ▲ Another word that sounds like this is **be.**
bee (bē) *noun, plural* **bees.**

beech A tree that has smooth, light-grey bark and small, sweet nuts. ▲ Another word that sounds like this is **beach.**
beech (bēch) *noun, plural* **beeches.**

Leaf in Autumn

Beech Tree

beef The meat of a steer, cow, or bull used for food.
beef (bēf) *noun.*

beefsteak A slice of beef to be broiled or fried.
beef·steak (bēf′stāk′) *noun, plural* **beefsteaks.**

beehive   A hive or house for bees.
bee·hive (bē′hīv′) *noun, plural* **beehives.**

Beehive

Inside the Beehive

been   I have *been* sick with a cold.
been (bin *or* bēn) *verb.*

beer   An alcoholic drink made from specially treated grains, called malt, and the fruit of a certain plant, called hops.
beer (bēr) *noun, plural* **beers.**

beer parlour   *Canadian.* A room in a hotel or tavern in which beer is sold by the glass.

beeswax   The yellow wax given out by honeybees, used to make honeycomb.
bees·wax bēz′waks′) *noun.*

beet   A plant with long, thick roots. The leaves and roots of some beets are cooked and eaten as vegetables. ▲ Another word that sounds like this is **beat.**
beet (bēt) *noun, plural* **beets.**

beetle   An insect with hard front wings that protect the thin hind wings when folded. Beetles have biting mouth parts. Some beetles cause much damage to plants.
bee·tle (bēt′əl) *noun, plural* **beetles.**

Beetles

befall   To happen or happen to. The sailors were afraid that some harm might *befall* their ship in the storm.
be·fall (bē fäl′) *verb,* **befell, befallen, befalling.**

before   In front of; ahead of. Ed stood *before* me in line. The letter A comes *before* B. We arrived at the party *before* everyone else. *Preposition.*
—In front; ahead; already. I've seen that movie *before. Adverb.*
—Earlier than the time when. It grew dark *before* the boys finished the game. *Conjunction.*
be·fore bē fōr′) *preposition; adverb; conjunction.*

beforehand   Ahead of time. Paul found out *beforehand* what his birthday present was.
be·fore·hand (bē fōr′hand′) *adverb.*

beg   To ask for; ask. A tramp in our neighborhood sometimes *begs* for a meal. I *beg* your pardon; I didn't mean to hurt your feelings.
beg (beg) *verb,* **begged, begging.**

began   The boy *began* to run. Look up **begin** for more information.
be·gan (bē gan′) *verb.*

beggar   A very poor person. Some beggars ask for money, food, or clothes in order to live.
beg·gar (beg′ər) *noun, plural* **beggars.**

begin   **1.** To do the first part of something; make a start. The builders will *begin* to build the house next month. *Begin* your homework now. **2.** To come into being; start. The movie *begins* at two o'clock.
be·gin (bē gin′) *verb,* **began, begun, beginning.**

beginner   A person who is starting to do something for the first time. My little brother is in a swimming class for *beginners.*
be·gin·ner (bē gin′ər) *noun, plural* **beginners.**

beginning   **1.** The first part. The *beginning* of the story was exciting. **2.** The time when something begins; start. Yesterday was the *beginning* of my vacation.
be·gin·ning (bē gin′ing) *noun, plural* **beginnings.**

at; āpe; cär; end; mē; it; īce; hot; ōld;
wood; fōōl; oil; out; up; turn; sing;
thin; this; hw in white; zh in treasure.
ə stands for a in about, e in taken,
i in pencil, o in lemon, and u in circus.

begonia A tropical plant with large, bright flowers.
be·gon·ia (bə gō′-nē ə) *noun, plural* **begonias.**

Begonia

begun The game has *begun.* Look up **begin** for more information.
be·gun (bē gun′) *verb.*

behalf **On behalf of** or **in behalf of.** For the good of; for. The church held a fair *on behalf of* the town hospital.
be·half (bē haf′) *noun.*

behave **1.** To act; do. The little boy *behaved* bravely when he did not cry after he hurt his knee. **2.** To act in a good way. My little brother promised to *behave* himself at the party.
be·have (bē hāv′) *verb,* **behaved, behaving.**

behaviour A way of behaving or acting. The children's *behaviour* was good. The science class studied the *behaviour* of the grasshopper.
be·hav·iour (bē hāv′yər) *noun.*

behead To cut off someone's head.
be·head (bē hed′) *verb,* **beheaded, beheading.**

behind **1.** At the back of. I sit *behind* my best friend in school. Jim hid *behind* a tree. **2.** Later than; after. The second bus came ten minutes *behind* the first bus. **3.** Not as good as. Our team was *behind* the other team by three points. *Preposition.*
—**1.** At the back. He sneaked up on his friend from *behind.* **2.** In a place just left. In the race, Joe left the other runners far *behind.* **3.** Not on time; late; slow. He is *behind* in his homework. *Adverb.*
be·hind (bē hīnd′) *preposition; adverb.*

behold To look at; see. The campers stayed up late to *behold* the beauty of the stars.
be·hold (bē hōld′) *verb,* **beheld, beholding.**

beige A pale-brown colour. *Noun.*
—Having the colour beige. *Adjective.*
beige (bāzh) *noun, plural* **beiges;** *adjective.*

being The baby is *being* washed. *Verb.*
—**1.** Life. Many of our customs came into *being* years ago. **2.** A person or animal. *Noun.*
be·ing (bē′ing) *verb; noun, plural* **beings.**

belated Late. My aunt sent me a *belated* birthday present a week after my birthday.
be·lat·ed (bē lā′təd) *adjective.*

belfry A tower or a room in a tower where bells are hung. Some churches have a belfry.
bel·fry (bel′frē) *noun, plural* **belfries.**

belief **1.** Trust; faith. She has a *belief* in her brother's honesty. **2.** Something that is believed to be true. Our country was founded on a *belief* in law, order, and good government. It is my *belief* that she is honest.
be·lief (bē lēf′) *noun, plural* **beliefs.**

Belfry

believe **1.** To have trust or faith in the truth of. The police didn't *believe* the thief. Jack *believes* in ghosts. **2.** To think; suppose. I *believe* that Chris went to the ball game.
be·lieve (bē lēv′) *verb,* **believed, believing.**

belittle To make seem less important. The boy *belittled* his younger brother's stamp collection because he was jealous.
be·lit·tle (bē lit′əl) *verb,* **belittled, belittling.**

bell **1.** A hollow metal object that is shaped like a cup. A bell makes a ringing sound when struck. **2.** Something that makes a ringing sound like a bell. He went up to the door and rang the *bell.*
bell (bel) *noun, plural* **bells.**

Bell

belligerent **1.** Wanting to fight. That *belligerent* boy is a bully and always picks on other boys. **2.** Busy fighting; at war. The two *belligerent* countries fought a long battle.
bel·lig·er·ent (bə lij′ər ənt) *adjective.*

bellow To make a loud, deep sound; roar. The bull *bellowed* in the pasture. The angry man *bellowed* at the boys who had broken his window. *Verb.*
—A loud, deep sound; roar. *Noun.*
bel·low (bel′ō) *verb,* **bellowed, bellowing;** *noun, plural* **bellows.**

bellows A device that makes a strong current of air when it is pumped open and closed. Some bellows are used to make fires burn faster. Some musical instruments, such as the accordion, are made to produce sound by means of a bellows.

bel·lows (bel′ōz) *noun plural.*

Bellows

belly 1. The front part of the body below the chest and above the legs; abdomen. 2. The stomach. 3. A curved or bulging part of something. The airplane made an emergency landing on its *belly. Noun.*
—To swell or billow. The sails of the ship *bellied* out. *Verb.*

bel·ly (bel′ē) *noun, plural* **bellies;** *verb,* **bellied, bellying.**

belong 1. To have a special right or place. The lamp *belongs* on that table. The coat *belongs* in the closet, not on the floor. 2. To be owned by. The baseball cap *belongs* to Fred. 3. To be part of. Fran *belongs* to a stamp club.

be·long (bē long′) *verb,* **belonged, belonging.**

belongings Things owned by a person; possessions. Mike packed his *belongings* in a large box.

be·long·ings (bē long′ingz) *noun, plural.*

beloved Loved very much. The little boy had lost his *beloved* puppy.

be·lov·ed (bē luv′əd *or* bē luvd′) *adjective.*

below From my window I could see the street *below.* Jerry's bunk bed is *below* his brother's.

be·low (bē lō′) *adverb; preposition.*

belt 1. A strip or band of cloth, leather, or other material. People wear belts around the waist to hold up clothing. 2. A region or area. We drove through the farm *belt* and saw many cows. 3. An endless band wound around two wheels or pulleys. A belt transfers power or motion from one wheel or pulley to another.

belt (belt) *noun, plural* **belts.**

bench 1. A long seat. We sat on the park *bench.* 2. A long table for working on. The carpenter repaired the broken chair at his *bench.* 3. A judge in a court of law. The thief was brought before the *bench. Noun.*
—To keep a player from playing. The coach *benched* the football player because he had played so badly in the last game. *Verb.*

bench (bench) *noun, plural* **benches;** *verb,* **benched, benching.**

bend 1. To change the shape of something by making it curved or crooked. Terry will *bend* the wire to make a hook. The stream *bends* to the left just beyond those trees. 2. To move the top part of the body forward and down; stoop; bow. Sam *bent* over to tie his shoe. *Verb.*
—Something bent. The boys' tent is just beyond the *bend* in the trail. *Noun.*

bend (bend) *verb,* **bent, bending;** *noun, plural* **bends.**

A Bend in a River

beneath Betty stood *beneath* the tree. He swept the dust *beneath* the rug. The house has an attic above and a basement *beneath.*

be·neath (bē nēth′) *preposition; adverb.*

benefit Something that helps a person or thing. Knowing how to speak Spanish is a great *benefit* if you visit Mexico. *Noun.*
—To be helpful to; be helped by. Rain will *benefit* the farmer's crops. *Verb.*

ben·e·fit (ben′ə fit) *noun, plural* **benefits;** *verb,* **benefited, benefiting.**

bent He *bent* the coat hanger. Look up **bend** for more information. *Verb.*
—1. Curved or crooked. He found a *bent* nail in his tool chest. 2. Determined; set. He was *bent* on going fishing. *Adjective.*

bent (bent) *verb; adjective.*

---

at; āpe; cär; end; mē; it; īce; hot; ōld;
wood; fōōl; oil; out; up; turn; sing;
thin; this; hw in white; zh in treasure.
ə stands for a in about, e in taken,
i in pencil, o in lemon, and u in circus.

beret A soft, round, flat cap.
be·ret (bə rā′) *noun, plural* **berets.**

berry A small, juicy, and fleshy fruit that can be eaten. A berry has many seeds. Blackberries, blueberries, and strawberries are berries. ▲ Another word that sounds like this is **bury.**
ber·ry (ber′ē) *noun, plural* **berries.**

Beret

berth 1. A bed or bunk on a train or ship. I had the upper *berth* on our train trip. 2. A place for a ship to dock. The freighter was in its *berth* in the harbour. ▲ Another word that sounds like this is **birth.**
berth (burth) *noun, plural* **berths.**

beseech To ask someone in a pleading way; beg. I *beseech* you to help me.
be·seech (bē sēch′) *verb,* **besought** or **beseeched, beseeching.**

beset To surround and attack. The hunter and his dogs *beset* the bear.
be·set (bē set′) *verb,* **beset, besetting.**

beside He sat *beside* his friend. The oak tree is *beside* the house.
be·side (bē sīd′) *preposition.*

besides He didn't want to go to the party; *besides*, he had work to do. There were many people at the park *besides* us.
be·sides (bē sīdz′) *adverb; preposition.*

besiege 1. To surround in order to capture. The soldiers *besieged* the fort. 2. To crowd around. The fans *besieged* the hockey player to get his autograph.
be·siege (bē sēj′) *verb,* **besieged, besieging.**

best He is the *best* hitter on the baseball team. I like chocolate ice cream *best*. She is the *best* on the tennis team.
best (best) *adjective; adverb; noun.*

bestow To give. The school *bestowed* a medal on the student.
be·stow (bē stō′) *verb,* **bestowed, bestowing.**

bet An agreement to pay money to another person if he is right about something and you are wrong. I made a *bet* with my friend that our team would win. The other team won, so I lost my *bet. Noun.*
—1. To agree to pay money to another person if he is right about something and you are wrong; make a bet. Paul *bet* George that he could beat him in tennis. 2. To say with confidence; be certain. I *bet* that it won't rain tomorrow. *Verb.*

bet (bet) *noun, plural* **bets;** *verb,* **bet** or **betted, betting.**

betray 1. To give help to the enemy of. The wicked man *betrayed* his country. 2. To be unfaithful to. She will not *betray* her friend by telling others his secret.
be·tray (bē trā′) *verb,* **betrayed, betraying.**

better Our team is *better* than theirs. He is a *better* student than his friend. She swims *better* than I do. Which is the *better* of these two books?
bet·ter (bet′ər) *adjective; adverb; noun, plural* **betters.**

between The table is *between* the chairs. Terry does not eat *between* meals. During an eclipse, the moon is *between* the earth and the sun. There was a quarrel *between* the two brothers. There are two farms with a lake *between.*
be·tween (bē twēn′) *preposition; adverb.*

beverage A liquid for drinking. Orange juice, milk, and coffee are beverages.
bev·er·age (bev′ər ij) *noun, plural* **beverages.**

beware To be on one's guard; be careful. *Beware* of the traffic when you cross the street. *Beware* of that dog or it just might bite you.
be·ware (bē wer′) *verb.*

bewilder To confuse or puzzle; mix up. The hard arithmetic problem *bewildered* the boy.
be·wil·der (bē wil′dər) *verb,* **bewildered, bewildering.**

bewitch 1. To cast a spell over someone by witchcraft or magic. The wicked fairy *bewitched* the prince and turned him into a frog. 2. To charm. The girl's beautiful smile *bewitched* everyone.
be·witch (bē wich′) *verb,* **bewitched, bewitching.**

beyond Our camp is *beyond* those trees. He stayed awake well *beyond* his bedtime. The toys cost far *beyond* what they should. What Dad told us about computers was *beyond* me. Look *beyond,* and you'll see the mountains in the distance.
be·yond (bē ond′) *preposition; adverb.*

bias A strong leaning for or against a person or thing when there is no reason for it. A good judge never shows *bias* when he tries a case in court. *Noun.*
—To cause to have or show bias. That boy's bragging about how smart he is has *biassed* me against him even though I don't know him well. *Verb.*
bi·as (bī′əs) *noun, plural* **biases;** *verb,* **biassed biassing** or **biased, biasing.**

Bible 1. The sacred writings of the Christian religion as contained in the Old Testament and the New Testament. 2. The sacred writings of the Jewish religion as contained in the Old Testament.
Bi·ble (bī′bəl) *noun.*

biblical Found in the Bible; relating to the Bible.
bib·li·cal (bib′li kəl) *adjective.*

bibliography A list of books about a subject.
bib·li·og·ra·phy (bib′lē og′rə fē) *noun, plural* **bibliographies.**

biceps The large muscle in the top part of the upper arm.
bi·ceps (bī′seps) *noun, plural* **biceps** or **bicepses.**

bicker To quarrel in a noisy way about something that is not very important. My brothers always *bicker* about washing dishes.
bick·er (bik′ər) *verb,* **bickered, bickering.**

bicuspid A tooth with two points. A grown person has eight bicuspids.
bi·cus·pid (bī kus′pid) *noun, plural* **bicuspids.**

bicycle A light vehicle to ride on. A bicycle has two wheels, one behind the other. It has a seat, handlebars, and two foot pedals to turn the wheels and make it go forward.
bi·cy·cle (bī′si kəl) *noun, plural* **bicycles.**

bid 1. To give an order to; command. The judge *bid* the prisoner to step forward. 2. To say when meeting or leaving someone. The children *bid* their aunt good-by. 3. To offer to pay. Ted *bid* fifty dollars for the old desk at the auction. *Verb.*
—An offer to pay money. Mary made a *bid* for a lamp at the auction. *Noun.*
bid (bid) *verb* **bid, bidding;** *noun, plural* **bids.**

bidding 1. An order; command. The boy mowed the lawn at his father's *bidding.* 2. The making of bids. The *bidding* at the auction was noisy.
bid·ding (bid′ing) *noun, plural* **biddings.**

bide To bide one's time. To wait for the right moment or chance. She will *bide her time* until spring to buy a winter coat on sale.
bide (bīd) *verb,* **bided, biding.**

big Great in size or amount; large. Montreal is a *big* city. A Douglas fir is a *big* tree. That was a *big* mistake. He is a *big* man in our town. Jack is a *big* talker.
big (big) *adjective,* **bigger, biggest.**

bighorn A kind of wild sheep with very large horns found in the Rocky Mountains. It is also called **Rocky Mountain sheep.**
big·horn (big′horn′) *noun, plural* **bighorns.**

bike A bicycle.
bike (bīk) *noun, plural* **bikes.**

bile A bitter yellow or greenish liquid made in the liver. Bile helps to digest food.
bile (bīl) *noun.*

bill¹ 1. A notice of money owed for something bought or for work done. Mom paid the telephone *bill.* 2. A piece of paper money. Nancy paid for the book with a one-dollar *bill.* 3. A poster or sign with an advertisement. He placed some *bills* on the wall advertising a sale. 4. A suggested law. The new tax *bill* was passed by parliament. *Noun.*
—To send a written notice of money owed to someone. The store will *bill* Susan for the dresses she bought. *Verb.*
bill (bil) *noun, plural* **bills;** *verb,* **billed, billing.**

bill² The hard mouth part of a bird; beak. The woodpecker has a heavy, pointed bill. The duck has a broad, flat bill.
bill (bil) *noun, plural* **bills.**

Bill

billboard A large board placed out of doors for displaying signs or advertisements. You see billboards along highways.
bill·board (bil′bōrd′) *noun, plural* **billboards.**

billfold A folding case for paper money. Many billfolds also have places for a driver's license, cards, and other things.
bill·fold (bil′fōld′) *noun, plural* **billfolds.**

billiards A game played with hard balls that are hit with a long stick called a cue. Billiards is played on a large table with a raised edge.
bil·liards (bil′yərdz) *noun.*

billion A thousand millions; 1 000 000 000.
bil·lion (bil′yən) *noun, plural* **billions;** *adjective.*

billow A great swelling wave of something. *Billows* of smoke poured out of the chimney. *Noun.*

at; āpe; cär; end; mē; it; īce; hot; ōld; wood; fōol; oil; out; up; turn; sing; thin; this; hw in white; zh in treasure. ə stands for a in about, e in taken, i in pencil, o in lemon, and u in circus.

—To rise or swell in billows. Smoke *billowed* from the burning house. The sail of the boat *billowed* in the wind. *Verb.*
bil·low (bil′ō) *noun, plural* **billows;** *verb,* **billowed, billowing.**

bin A closed place or box for holding or storing something. We keep the coal for the furnace in a *bin.*
bin (bin) *noun, plural* **bins.**

binary Having to do with a system of numbers in which any number may be expressed by 0 or 1, or by a combination of these. The ordinary number 2 is the same as the *binary* number 10. Many electronic computers use the *binary* system of numbering.
bi·na·ry (bī′nər ē) *adjective.*

bind 1. To tie together; fasten. He will *bind* the package with string for mailing. Ann always *binds* her hair with ribbon. 2. To tie a bandage around. The nurse will *bind* up Ed's sprained ankle. 3. To fasten together between covers. We watched the machine *bind* the pages into a book.
bind (bīnd) *verb,* **bound, binding.**

bingo A game in which each player covers numbers on a card as they are called out. The winner is the first player to cover a row of numbers.
bin·go (bing′gō) *noun.*

binoculars A device that makes distant objects look larger and closer. Binoculars are made up of two telescopes joined together, so that a person can look at distant objects with both eyes.
bi·noc·u·lars (bə nok′-yə lərz) *noun plural.*

biography A true, written story about a person's life. We enjoyed reading the *biography* of Susanna Moodie.
bi·og·ra·phy (bī og′rə-fē) *noun, plural* **bi·ographies.**

Binoculars

biologist A person who studies biology or who knows a great deal about biology.
bi·ol·o·gist (bī ol′ə jist) *noun, plural* **biologists.**

biology The study of plants and animals. Biology deals with how plants and animals live and grow, how they are made, and where they are found throughout the world. Ellen is studying *biology* in her science class.
bi·ol·o·gy (bī ol′ə jē) *noun.*

bionic Having to do with a mechanical device that replaces or strengthens a part of the human body. The arm that the girl lost in the accident was replaced by a *bionic* arm.
bi·on·ic (bī on′ik) *adjective.*

bionics The study of the parts of the bodies of human beings and other animals in order to make new mechanical or electronic devices or to improve old ones. The design of computers and artificial legs and arms is based on bionics.
bi·on·ics (bī on′iks) *noun plural.*

birch A tree that has hard wood and white bark that peels off in strips. North American Indians used birch bark to make canoes.
birch (burch) *noun, plural* **birches.**

Birch Tree in Autumn

Leaves

bird An animal that has wings and a body covered with feathers. Birds have a backbone, are warm-blooded, and lay eggs. Most birds can fly. Eagles, robins, chickens, and penguins are birds.
bird (burd) *noun, plural* **birds.**

birth 1. The beginning of the life of a person or animal. The cat gave *birth* to five kittens. 2. The beginning of anything. Canada's *birth* took place in 1867. ▲ Another word that sounds like this is **berth.**
birth (burth) *noun, plural* **births.**

birthday 1. The day on which a person is born. Christopher's *birthday* is December 12, 1972. 2. The return each year of this day.
birth·day (burth′dā′) *noun, plural* **birthdays.**

birthplace The place where a person was born. Phil's *birthplace* is Red Deer.
birth·place (burth′plās′) *noun, plural* **birthplaces.**

biscuit A small cake of baked dough.
bis·cuit (bis′kit) *noun, plural* **biscuits.**

bishop 1. A member of the clergy who has a high rank. 2. A piece in the game of chess.
bish·op (bish′əp) *noun, plural* **bishops.**

bison A large animal that has a big shaggy head with short horns and a humped back; buffalo. A bison is a wild ox. Bison are found in North America.
bi·son (bī′sən) *noun, plural* **bison.**

Bison

bit¹ 1. The metal piece of a bridle that goes into the horse's mouth. 2. The part of a tool that makes holes or bores into wood or other material. A bit fits into the part of a tool called the brace.
bit (bit) *noun, plural* **bits.**

bit² 1. A small piece or part. Carl threw a *bit* of meat to the dog. I dropped the glass and it broke into *bits*. 2. A short while. Wait a *bit*.
bit (bit) *noun, plural* **bits.**
a bit. A little; slightly. I am *a bit* tired.

bit³ The girl *bit* into the sandwich.
bit (bit) *verb.*

Bit

bite 1. To seize, cut into, or pierce with the teeth. Did he *bite* off a piece of your candy bar? 2. To wound with teeth, fangs, or a stinger. I killed the mosquito before it could *bite* me. 3. To make something sting. The icy wind will *bite* our cheeks. 4. To take or swallow bait. The fish will not *bite* today. *Verb.*
—1. A seizing or cutting into something with the teeth. The dog's *bite* caused a bad sore. 2. A wound made by biting. The cat scratched at the flea *bite*. 3. A piece bitten off. Do you want a *bite* of my apple? 4. A sting. When I went out I felt the *bite* of the cold air. *Noun.*
bite (bīt) *verb,* **bit, bitten** or **bit, biting;** *noun, plural* **bites.**

bitten He has already *bitten* into the sandwich.
bit·ten (bit′ən) *verb.*

bitter 1. Having a biting, harsh, bad taste. The strong coffee tasted *bitter*. The boy did not like the *bitter* cough medicine. 2. Causing or showing sorrow or pain. The children shivered in the *bitter* cold. 3. Showing anger or hatred. The two men were *bitter* enemies.
bit·ter (bit′ər) *adjective.*

bituminous coal A soft, black coal that burns with a smoky flame. This coal is also called **soft coal.**
bi·tu·mi·nous coal (bī tōō′mə nəs *or* bī-tyōō′mə nəs).

black 1. The darkest of all colours; the opposite of white. 2. A member of one of the major divisions of the human race. *Noun.*
—1. Having the darkest of all colours; having the colour of coal; opposite of white. 2. Having no light; dark. When the lights went out the room was *black*. 3. Of or having to do with black people. *Adjective.*
black (blak) *noun, plural* **blacks;** *adjective,* **blacker, blackest.**

black bear A large bear with thick, black fur. The black bear is the most common bear in North America.

blackberry A sweet, juicy, black berry.
black·ber·ry (blak′ber′ē) *noun, plural* **blackberries.**

blackbird Any of various birds that are mostly black. Some male blackbirds have bright markings, such as red patches on the wings. Female blackbirds have all black or brown feathers.
black·bird (blak′-burd′) *noun, plural* **blackbirds.**

Blackberries

blackboard A hard, smooth board made of slate or other material. Blackboards are used for writing or drawing on with chalk. Some are black, while others are green.
black·board (blak′bōrd′) *noun, plural* **blackboards.**

at; āpe; cär; end; mē; it; īce; hot; ōld;
wood; fōōl; oil; out; up; turn; sing;
thin; this; hw in white; zh in treasure.
ə stands for a in about, e in taken,
i in pencil, o in lemon, and u in circus.

blacken 1. To make or become black. Smoke from the fireplace *blackened* the walls of the room. The white curtains may *blacken* from the smoke. 2. To do harm to. That nasty rumour will *blacken* his reputation.
black·en (blak′ən) *verb*, **blackened, blackening.**

black-fly A small, black fly that gives a sharp, stinging bite. It is common in the North in the late spring and summer.
black-fly (blak′flī′) *noun, plural* **blackflies.**

blackmail The attempt to get money from someone by threatening to tell bad things about him. *Noun.*
—To try to get money from someone by threatening to tell bad things. The men tried to *blackmail* the mayor by saying that they would make it known that he had once been in prison. *Verb.*
black·mail (blak′māl′) *noun; verb*, **blackmailed, blackmailing.**

blacksmith A person who makes things from iron. A blacksmith heats the iron in a forge and then hammers it into shape on an anvil. A blacksmith can make horseshoes.
black·smith (blak′smith′) *noun, plural* **blacksmiths.**

black widow A black spider. The female black widow is poisonous and has a red mark on her body. The female black widow is larger than the male, and often eats the male after mating.

bladder A small baglike part in the body. The bladder holds urine from the kidneys.
blad·der (blad′ər) *noun, plural* **bladders.**

blade 1. The sharp part of anything that cuts. He sharpened the *blade* of his knife. Dad put a new *blade* in his razor. 2. A leaf of grass. 3. The wide, flat part of something. He dipped the *blade* of the oar into the water. String caught in the *blades* of the fan in the kitchen.
blade (blād) *noun, plural* **blades.**

blame 1. To find fault with. Bill didn't *blame* his friend for getting angry. 2. To hold responsible for something wrong or bad. Pete *blamed* me for breaking the window. *Verb.*
—Responsibility for something wrong or bad. He took the *blame* for the accident. *Noun.*
blame (blām) *verb*, **blamed, blaming;** *noun.*

blank 1. Without writing or printing; unmarked. I turned to a *blank* page in my notebook. 2. With empty spaces to be filled in. Bill filled in the *blank* order form. 3. Without thought; vacant. The boy was daydreaming and gave me a *blank* stare. *Adjective.*

—1. An empty space to be filled in. Fill in the *blank* with your name and address. 2. A paper with spaces to be filled in. My friend gave me an application *blank* for joining the stamp club. 3. A cartridge with gunpowder but no bullet. *Noun.*
blank (blangk) *adjective*, **blanker, blankest;** *noun, plural* **blanks.**

blanket 1. A covering made of wool, nylon, or other material. Blankets are used on beds to keep people warm. 2. Anything that covers like a blanket. A *blanket* of fog lay over the town. *Noun.*
—To cover with a blanket. The snowstorm *blanketed* the city with snow. *Verb.*
blan·ket (blang′kət) *noun, plural* **blankets;** *verb*, **blanketed, blanketing.**

blare To make a loud, harsh sound. The car horns *blared* in the busy street. *Verb.*
—A loud, harsh sound. The *blare* of the siren hurt my ears. *Noun.*
blare (bler) *verb*, **blared, blaring,** *noun, plural* **blares.**

blast 1. A strong rush of wind or air. A *blast* of cold air blew into the room. 2. A loud noise made by a horn. We heard the *blast* of trumpets in the marching band. 3. An explosion. When the old building was blown up, the *blast* made the windows of our house rattle. *Noun.*
—1. To blow up with explosives. The workmen *blasted* a hole in the rock with dynamite. 2. To ruin. The rain *blasted* our hopes for a picnic. *Verb.*
blast (blast) *noun, plural* **blasts;** *verb*, **blasted, blasting.**
to blast off. To take off into flight propelled by rockets. The spacecraft will *blast off* in an hour.

blaze¹ 1. A bright flame; a glowing fire. We could see the *blaze* of the burning building. 2. A bright light. We shielded our eyes from the *blaze* of the sun. 3. A bright display. The circus parade was a *blaze* of colour. *Noun.*
—1. To burn brightly. The campfire *blazed* all night. 2. To shine brightly. The tree will *blaze* with lights on Christmas. 3. To show strong feeling. Her eyes *blazed* with anger. *Verb.*
blaze (blāz) *noun, plural* **blazes;** *verb*, **blazed, blazing.**

blaze² A mark made on a tree to show a trail or boundary. You make a *blaze* by chipping off a piece of bark. *Noun.*
—To show a trail or boundary by putting marks on trees. The hikers will *blaze* a trail through the woods. *Verb.*
blaze (blāz) *noun, plural* **blazes;** *verb*, **blazed, blazing.**

bleach To make something white. The sun *bleached* the sheets. Mother will *bleach* the shirts when she washes them. *Verb.*
—A substance used for bleaching. She uses a chemical *bleach* in her wash. *Noun.*
    bleach (blēch) *verb,* **bleached, bleaching;** *noun, plural* **bleaches.**

bleak 1. Open and unprotected from the wind; bare. There were no trees growing on the *bleak* mountaintop. 2. Cold and gloomy. It was a *bleak* December day. Everyone thought that the *bleak* old house was haunted.
    bleak (blēk) *adjective,* **bleaker, bleakest.**

bled Her cut finger *bled.*
    bled (bled) *verb.*

bleed 1. To lose blood. If you cut yourself, you will *bleed.* 2. To lose sap or other liquid. A tree will *bleed* if you cut into its trunk.
    bleed (blēd) *verb,* **bled, bleeding.**

blemish Something that spoils beauty or perfection; flaw. The scar is a *blemish* on his face. One day's absence was the only *blemish* on his school attendance record. *Noun.*
—To spoil the beauty or perfection of something; mar. Worm holes *blemish* an apple. *Verb.*
    blem·ish (blem′ish) *noun, plural* **blemishes;** *verb,* **blemished, blemishing.**

blend 1. To mix together completely. She will *blend* flour, milk, and eggs to make pancakes. The voices in the choir *blend* well. 2. To shade into each other. The sea and sky seemed to *blend* on the horizon. *Verb.*
—A mixture. Dad smokes a strong *blend* of tobacco. *Noun.*
    blend (blend) *verb,* **blended, blending;** *noun, plural* **blends.**

bless 1. To make holy. The minister will *bless* the new chapel. 2. To ask God's help for. The little boy prayed that God would *bless* his mother and father. 3. To make happy or fortunate. Members of our family have been *blessed* with good teeth.
    bless (bles) *verb,* **blessed** or **blest, blessing.**

blessing 1. A prayer to God for His favour or to give thanks. The minister gave a *blessing* at the end of the church service. 2. A person or thing that brings happiness. The helpful child was a *blessing* to her sick grandmother. 3. A wish for happiness or success; good wishes. She sent her *blessings* for a happy new year.
    bless·ing (bles′ing) *noun, plural* **blessings.**

blew Jack *blew* on his hot soup to cool it. Look up **blow** for more information. ▲ Another word that sounds like this is **blue.**
    blew (blōō) *verb.*

blight 1. A disease of plants. Blight makes a plant wither and die. 2. Something that harms or ruins. Those dirty old buildings are a *blight* on our city.
    blight (blīt) *noun, plural* **blights.**

blind 1. Without sight; unable to see. The boy helped the *blind* man across the street. 2. Not easily seen; hidden. The sign warned of a *blind* driveway on the road ahead. 3. Done with instruments only and not with the eyes. The pilot of the airplane had to make a *blind* landing because of the storm. 4. Closed at one end. The thief ran into a *blind* alley and could not escape the police. 5. Without thought or good sense. Tom didn't know the answer to the problem so he made a *blind* guess. *Adjective.*
—1. To make unable to see. The sun will *blind* you if you look at it too long. 2. To take away thought or good sense. Fear *blinded* him. *Verb.*
—Something that blocks a person's sight or keeps the light out. Janet lowered the *blinds* of the window. *Noun.*
    blind (blīnd) *adjective,* **blinder, blindest;** *verb,* **blinded, blinding;** *noun, plural* **blinds.**

Blindfold

blindfold To cover someone's eyes. He *blindfolded* his little sister for the game. *Verb.*
—A cover for the eyes. The *blindfold* was a strip of cloth. *Noun.*
    blind·fold (blīnd′fōld′) *verb,* **blindfolded, blindfolding;** *noun, plural* **blindfolds.**

at; āpe; cär; end; mē; it; īce; hot; ōld;
wood; fōōl; oil; out; up; turn; sing;
thin; this; hw in white; zh in treasure.
ə stands for a in about, e in taken,
i in pencil, o in lemon, and u in circus.

blink 1. To close and open the eyes quickly. The child *blinked* when the photographer took the picture. 2. To flash on and off; twinkle. Stars *blinked* in the sky.
blink (blingk) *verb,* **blinked, blinking.**

bliss Great happiness. The little boy was filled with *bliss* at the thought of going to the circus.
bliss (blis) *noun.*

blister 1. A sore place on the skin that looks like a small bubble. A blister is filled with a watery substance. It is usually caused by rubbing or by a burn. Susan has a *blister* on her heel where her sneaker rubbed it. 2. Any small bubble or swelling. *Blisters* formed on the new coat of paint. *Noun.*
—To form a blister on; have blisters. Touching the hot iron made his finger *blister.* The hot sun *blistered* his nose. *Verb.*
blis·ter (blis′tər) *noun, plural* **blisters;** *verb,* **blistered, blistering.**

blizzard A heavy snowstorm with very strong winds.
bliz·zard (bliz′ərd) *noun, plural* **blizzards.**

bloat To make bigger; cause to swell. Drinking too much water *bloated* his stomach.
bloat (blōt) *verb,* **bloated, bloating.**

blob A drop or small lump of something soft. Sally got a *blob* of paint on her dress.
blob (blob) *noun, plural* **blobs.**

block 1. A piece of something hard and solid. The workmen built the church with *blocks* of stone. The children built a fort with wooden *blocks.* 2. An area in a town or city with four streets around it. Karen walks her dog around the *block* every morning. 3. The length of one side of a block in a town or city. Frank lives three *blocks* from the school. 4. A number of things that are alike. Bill bought a *block*

Blocks

of foreign stamps for his stamp collection. 5. Anything that stops something else. The fallen tree was a *block* to traffic. 6. A pulley in a frame. *Noun.*
—To get in the way of or stop. Patrick's bicycle *blocked* the sidewalk. The house next door *blocks* the view from my window. The football player *blocked* the pass. *Verb.*

block (blok) *noun, plural* **blocks;** *verb,* **blocked, blocking.**

blockade A shutting off of an area to keep people and supplies from going in or out. During a war an enemy may use ships to set up a blockade around the harbour or port of a city. *Noun.*
—To shut off with a blockade. Ships will *blockade* the enemy's harbour. *Verb.*
block·ade (blo kād′) *noun, plural* **blockades;** *verb,* **blockaded, blockading.**

blockhouse 1. A strong building made of wooden timbers or logs. It has holes in the walls to shoot weapons from. Blockhouses were formerly used as forts. 2. A strong building near the launching pad of a rocket. A blockhouse is used to protect people who are watching rocket launchings.
block·house (blok′hoŭs′) *noun, plural* **blockhouses.**

Blockhouse

blond 1. Light-yellow. He has *blond* hair like his mother. 2. Having light-yellow hair and light-coloured eyes and skin. Most of the members of Noreen's family are *blond. Adjective.*
—A person with light-yellow hair and light-coloured eyes and skin. *Noun.* This word is also spelled **blonde.**
blond (blond) *adjective,* **blonder, blondest;** *noun, plural* **blonds.**

blood 1. The bright red liquid that runs from a cut. Blood is pumped by the heart through the veins and arteries to all parts of the body. It carries oxygen and food to the body and takes away waste materials. 2. Family relationship. Susan and I are of the same *blood* because our mothers are sisters.
blood (blud) *noun.*

in cold blood. Without being at all sorry. The prisoner killed the guard *in cold blood* in order to escape.

bloodhound A large dog with long, drooping ears and a wrinkled face. Bloodhounds have such a good sense of smell that they are often used to track down escaped criminals or find people who are lost.

blood·hound (blud′hound′) *noun, plural* **bloodhounds.**

Bloodhound

bloodshed The loss of blood or life. The king's soldiers won the battle without much *bloodshed.*

blood·shed (blud′shed′) *noun.*

bloodstream The blood as it flows through the body.

blood·stream (blud′strēm′) *noun.*

bloodthirsty Eager to cause bloodshed; cruel.

blood·thirst·y (blud′thurs′tē) *adjective.*

blood vessel Any of the tubes in the body through which the blood flows. Arteries and veins are blood vessels.

bloody 1. Covered or stained with blood. The bandage on his cut knee was all *bloody.* 2. Causing much bloodshed. Many men were killed in the *bloody* battle.

blood·y (blud′ē) *adjective,* **bloodier, bloodiest.**

bloom The time of flowering. The roses are in *bloom. Noun.*
—To have flowers; blossom. Cherry trees *bloom* in the spring. *Verb.*

bloom (blo͞om) *noun, plural* **blooms;** *verb,* **bloomed, blooming.**

blossom 1. The flower of a plant or tree that produces fruit. We gathered *blossoms* from the apple trees in the orchard. 2. The time of flowering. The lilacs are in *blossom. Noun.*
—1. To have flowers or blossoms; bloom. The peach trees *blossom* in the spring. 2. To grow; develop. That young writer has *blos-*

somed into one of the country's best novelists. *Verb.*

blos·som (blos′əm) *noun, plural* **blossoms;** *verb,* **blossomed, blossoming.**

blot 1. A spot or stain. Betty got a *blot* of paint on her picture when her brush dripped. 2. Something that spoils or harms. Those billboards along the highway are a *blot* on the beautiful countryside. *Noun.*
—1. To spot or stain. The ink from my pen *blotted* my letter, and I had to copy it over. 2. To soak up or dry with a blotter. He *blotted* his signature carefully so the ink wouldn't smear. *Verb.*

blot (blot) *noun, plural* **blots;** *verb,* **blotted, blotting.**

blotch A large spot or stain. The jelly he spilled left a *blotch* on the tablecloth. The rash covered his arms with red *blotches. Noun.*
—To mark or cover with spots or stains. The hot sun *blotched* her back. *Verb.*

blotch (bloch) *noun, plural* **blotches;** *verb,* **blotched, blotching.**

blotter A piece of soft, thick paper used to soak up or dry wet ink. He used a *blotter* on his signature on the cheque.

blot·ter (blot′ər) *noun, plural* **blotters.**

blouse A piece of clothing for the upper part of the body. Girls and women wear blouses with skirts or slacks.

blouse (blous *or* blouz) *noun, plural* **blouses.**

blow¹ 1. A hard hit or stroke. A blow may be made with the fist, a weapon, or some object. A sudden *blow* on the jaw knocked the champion out. 2. A sudden happening that causes great shock or unhappiness. The death of their dog was a *blow* to the whole family.

blow (blō) *noun, plural* **blows.**

blow² 1. To move with speed or force. The wind

Blouse

at; āpe; cär; end; mē; it; īce; hot; ōld;
wood; fo͞ol; oil; out; up; turn; sing;
thin; this; hw in white; zh in treasure.
ə stands for a in about, e in taken,
i in pencil, o in lemon, and u in circus.

began to *blow* against the sails of the boat. An autumn breeze *blew* the leaves across the yard. **2.** To send out a strong current of air. *Blow* on your hands to warm them. **3.** To move by a current of air. His hat *blew* off as he ran to catch the bus. **4.** To form or shape by a current of air. My little sister loves to *blow* soap bubbles. We are going to *blow* up balloons for my brother's birthday party. **5.** To sound by a blast of air. When the whistle *blows* the race will start. **6.** To break or destroy by an explosion. The soldiers *blew* up the enemy's bridge. **7.** To stop working properly. Our tire *blew* out, and we had to stop to change it.

> **blow** (blō) *verb*, **blew, blown, blowing.**

blower A machine for making a current of air or for forcing air into a place. A *blower* cooled the mine shaft with fresh air.

> **blow·er** (blō′ər) *noun, plural* **blowers.**

blown The wind has *blown* the snow into high drifts. Look up **blow** for more information.

> **blown** (blōn) *verb.*

blowtorch A small torch that shoots out a very hot flame. Blowtorches are used to melt metal and to burn off old paint.

> **blow·torch** (blō′tôrch′) *noun, plural* **blow-torches.**

Blowtorch

blubber A layer of fat under the skin of whales, seals, and some other sea animals. The oil made from whale blubber used to be burned in lamps. Now the oil is used in soaps and other products.

> **blub·ber** (blub′ər) *noun, plural* **blubbers.**

blue The colour of the clear sky in the daytime. The lines on a hockey rink are marked in *blue* and red. *Noun.*
—**1.** Having the colour blue. **2.** Unhappy; sad; discouraged. Mike felt *blue* and lonely during his first week away at summer camp. *Adjective.* ▲ Another word that sounds like this is **blew.**

> **blue** (blōō) *noun, plural* **blues;** *adjective,* **bluer, bluest.**

blueberry A small, dark-blue, sweet berry with tiny seeds. Blueberries grow on a shrub.

> **blue·ber·ry** (blōō′ber′ē) *noun, plural* **blueberries.**

bluebird A small songbird of North America that has blue feathers on its back.

> **blue·bird** (blōō′burd′) *noun, plural* **bluebirds.**

bluegrass A grass that has bluish-green stems.

Blueberries

Bluegrass is raised as food for cattle and horses and is used for lawns.

> **blue·grass** (blōō′gras′) *noun, plural* **blue-grasses.**

Bluebird

blue jay A bird of North America that has a crest on its head and blue feathers with black-and-white markings.

blue jeans Pants or overalls made of blue denim.

blueline The blue line that is halfway between the centre of a hockey rink and each goal. There are two bluelines on each rink.

> **blue·line** (blōō′līn′) *noun, plural* **bluelines.**

blueprint A paper printed with white lines on a blue background. It is used to show the plan for building something. The workmen looked at the *blueprints* so that they would know how the house should be built.

> **blue·print** (blōō′print′) *noun, plural* **blue-prints.**

blues 1. Sadness; low spirits. Jerry has had the *blues* ever since his best friend moved away. **2.** Music that sounds sad and has a rhythm like jazz.

> **blues** (blōōz) *noun plural.*

bluff¹ 1. A high, steep bank or cliff. As the ship pulled closer to shore they saw the *bluffs* jutting up from the sea. **2.** *Canadian.* A grove

of trees on the prairies. *Noun.*
—Rough in a good-natured way; hearty. John's uncle greeted him with a *bluff* slap on the back. *Adjective.*
 bluff (bluf) *noun, plural* **bluffs;** *adjective.*

bluff² To try to fool people about something. A person who bluffs tries to make people think he is braver than he really is or that he knows something that he doesn't. *Verb.*
—Something that is pretended in order to fool other people. All his talk about being able to swim is just a big *bluff. Noun.*
 bluff (bluf) *verb,* **bluffed, bluffing;** *noun, plural* **bluffs.**

blunder A careless or stupid mistake. Forgetting his mother's birthday was an awful *blunder. Noun.*
—**1.** To make a careless or stupid mistake. You really *blundered* when you said that Jacques Cartier was the first prime minister of Canada. **2.** To move in a clumsy way. The lost campers *blundered* through the woods looking for the path. *Verb.*
 blun·der (blun'dər) *noun, plural* **blunders;** *verb,* **blundered, blundering.**

blunderbuss A short gun with a wide muzzle flared at the end. Blunderbusses were used for shooting things at close range without careful aim. They are no longer used.
 blun·der·buss (blun'dər bus') *noun, plural* **blunderbusses.**

Blunderbuss

blunt **1.** Having a dull edge or point; not sharp. This pencil is *blunt* and needs to be sharpened. **2.** Very outspoken and frank about what one thinks. Tom's *blunt* criticism of his sister hurt her feelings. *Adjective.*
—To make less sharp; make dull. Ann *blunted* my scissors by cutting wire. *Verb.*
 blunt (blunt) *adjective,* **blunter, bluntest;** *verb,* **blunted, blunting.**

blur To make hard to see; make less clear. Fog *blurred* the outline of the city. *Verb.*
—Something hard to see. The faces of the crowd were only a *blur* to the runner. *Noun.*

 blur (blur) *verb,* **blurred, blurring;** *noun, plural* **blurs.**

blurt To say suddenly or without thinking. Ted was sorry after he *blurted* out the secret.
 blurt (blurt) *verb,* **blurted, blurting.**

blush To become red in the face. A person blushes because he is ashamed, embarrassed, or confused. Bill *blushed* when the teacher called on him because he was so shy. *Verb.*
—A reddening of the face because of shame, embarrassment, or confusion. Her *blush* showed how shy she was with strangers. *Noun.*
 blush (blush) *verb,* **blushed, blushing;** *noun, plural* **blushes.**

bluster **1.** To blow in a noisy or violent way. The wind *blustered* through the trees. **2.** To talk in a loud or threatening way. When my brother gets angry, you can hear him *bluster* all over the house. *Verb.*
—**1.** A noisy, violent blowing. The *bluster* of the storm kept us awake all night. **2.** Loud, threatening talk. That boy is a bully who is full of *bluster* but scared to fight. *Noun.*
 blus·ter (blus'tər) *verb,* **blustered, blustering;** *noun.*

BNA Act The British North America Act. Look up **British North America Act** for more information.

boa constrictor A large snake that is found in Mexico and in Central and South America. It kills other animals by wrapping itself around them and squeezing them to death.
 bo·a con·stric·tor (bō'ə kən strik'tər).

boar A wild pig or hog that has a hairy coat and a long snout. ▲ Another word that sounds like this is **bore.**
 boar (bōr) *noun, plural* **boars** or **boar.**

Boar

at; āpe; cär; end; mē; it; īce; hot; ōld;
wood; fōōl; oil; out; up; turn; sing;
thin; this; hw in white; zh in treasure.
ə stands for a in about, e in taken,
i in pencil, o in lemon, and u in circus.

board **1.** A long, flat piece of sawed wood. Boards are used in building houses and other things. **2.** A flat piece of wood or other material used for some special purpose. Get the *board* and we'll play a game of checkers. **3.** A group of people who are chosen to manage or direct something. The school *board* helps to run the school. **4.** Meals served daily for pay. Frank found a good room with *board* near the university campus. *Noun.*
—**1.** To cover with boards. We always *board* up the windows of our summer cabin when we go home at the end of the summer. **2.** To get a room to sleep in and meals for pay. He *boarded* with a French family in Paris last summer. **3.** To get on a ship, plane, or train. We will *board* the plane in Montreal. *Verb.*
  board (bōrd) *noun, plural* **boards;** *verb,* **boarded, boarding.**
  on board. On or in a ship, plane, or train; aboard.

boarding The practice in hockey of pushing another player against the boards at the sides of the rink.
  board·ing (bōr′ding) *noun.*

boarding house A house where a person can get a room to sleep in and meals for pay.

boast **1.** To talk too much or with too much pride about oneself; brag. If Bob is going to *boast* all the time about being on the hockey team, his friends will begin to be angry with him. **2.** To be proud of having. Our town *boasts* a big new sports stadium. *Verb.*
—Talk that is too much about oneself. His *boast* that he is the best player on the team is not true. *Noun.*
  boast (bōst) *verb,* **boasted, boasting;** *noun, plural* **boasts.**

boat **1.** A small vessel that is used for traveling on water. A boat is moved by using oars, paddles, sails, or a motor. A boat is usually open. **2.** Any kind of ship. *Noun.*
—To go in a boat; carry in a boat. We want to spend the vacation *boating* and fishing. *Verb.*
  boat (bōt) *noun, plural* **boats;** *verb,* **boated, boating.**

boathouse A small building for sheltering or storing boats.
  boat·house (bōt′hous′) *noun, plural* **boat-houses.**

bob¹ To move up and down or back and forth with a jerky motion. The beach ball *bobbed* on the waves. The hen *bobbed* its head as it pecked its food. *Verb.*
—A jerky motion. Jim answered his mother's question with a *bob* of his head. *Noun.*
  bob (bob) *verb,* **bobbed, bobbing;** *noun, plural* **bobs.**

bob² **1.** A short haircut for a woman or child. **2.** A float or cork at the end of a fishing line. The *bob* moved up and down when the fish bit at the bait. *Noun.*
—To cut hair short. The barber *bobbed* my sister's long hair. *Verb.*
  bob (bob) *noun, plural* **bobs;** *verb,* **bobbed, bobbing.**

bobbin A spool around which yarn or thread is wound. A bobbin is used in weaving, spinning, or sewing on a sewing machine.
  bob·bin (bob′in) *noun, plural* **bobbins.**

bobcat A small wild cat of North America. A bobcat has reddish-brown fur with dark spots and a short tail. It is related to the Canada lynx.
  bob·cat (bob′kat′) *noun, plural* **bobcats.**

Bobcat

bobolink A songbird of North and South America that lives in fields. It is related to the blackbird.
  bob·o·link (bob′ə lingk′) *noun, plural* **bobolinks.**

bobsled A long sled for racing. A bobsled has runners, a steering wheel, and brakes.
  bob·sled (bob′sled′) *noun, plural* **bobsleds.**

Bobsled

bobwhite A North American bird that has a reddish-brown body with white, black, and tan markings. Its call sounds a little like its name. It is a kind of quail.
bob·white (bob′-wīt′ *or* bob′hwīt′) *noun, plural* **bobwhites.**

Bobwhite

bode To be a sign of. The dark clouds *bode* a storm.
bode (bōd) *verb,* **boded, boding.**

bodily Of the body. The people who were in the automobile accident suffered almost no *bodily* harm, but they were very frightened.
bod·i·ly (bod′ə lē) *adjective.*

body 1. All of a person, animal, or plant. An athlete must have a strong *body.* 2. The main part of something. The *body* of the new jet airplane is very large. 3. A group of persons or things. The student *body* at the high school is headed by a president that the students elect. 4. A separate part or mass. The Atlantic Ocean is a huge *body* of water. The sun, the moon, and the stars are heavenly *bodies.*
bod·y (bod′ē) *noun, plural* **bodies.**

bodycheck A move in hockey or lacrosse in which a player bumps an opponent with his body.
bo·dy·check (bod′ē chek′) *noun, plural* **bodychecks.**

bodyguard A person or persons who protect someone from danger or attack. The king's *bodyguard* goes everywhere with him.
bod·y·guard (bod′ē gärd′) *noun, plural* **bodyguards.**

bog Wet, spongy ground; marsh; swamp. A bog is made up mainly of decayed plants. Cranberries grow in *bogs. Noun.*
—To become stuck. The car will *bog* down on those muddy roads. I got *bogged* down on the last arithmetic problem. *Verb.*
bog (bog) *noun, plural* **bogs;** *verb,* **bogged, bogging.**

boil¹ 1. To form bubbles and give off steam. Water will *boil* if you heat it enough. 2. To cause to boil. Mary *boiled* water for tea. 3. To cook by boiling. *Verb.*
—The condition of boiling. Bring the water to a *boil* and then turn off the heat. *Noun.*
boil (boil) *verb,* **boiled, boiling;** *noun.*

boil² A red swelling beneath the skin that hurts. A boil is caused by infection and it is full of pus.
boil (boil) *noun, plural* **boils.**

boiler 1. A large tank in which water is made into steam. The steam made in a boiler is used to heat buildings and to run engines. 2. A pan or pot in which something is heated or boiled. We cooked the ears of corn in a large *boiler.*
boil·er (boi′lər) *noun, plural* **boilers.**

boiling point The temperature at which a liquid begins to boil. The boiling point of water at sea level is 100 degrees Celsius.

bold 1. Not afraid; brave. A person who is bold is willing to do dangerous things. The *bold* explorer pushed on into the deepest part of the jungle. The fireman's rescue of the child from the burning roof was a *bold* thing to do. 2. Not polite; rude; fresh. The *bold* child always talked back to his parents.
bold (bōld) *adjective,* **bolder, boldest.**

boll The seed pod of a cotton or flax plant. ▲ Another word that sounds like this is **bowl.**
boll (bōl) *noun, plural* **bolls.**

bolster A long pillow or cushion. *Noun.*
—To support. The beams *bolstered* the roof of the cabin. The good news *bolstered* Jack's low spirits. *Verb.*
bol·ster (bōl′stər) *noun, plural* **bolsters;** *verb,* **bolstered, bolstering.**

bolt 1. A rod used to hold things together. A bolt usually has a head at one end and screw threads for a nut at the other. 2. A sliding bar for fastening a door. She closed the door and slid the *bolt* shut. 3. The part of a lock that is moved by a key. 4. A sudden spring or start. The frightened deer made a *bolt* for the woods. 5. A flash of lightning; thunderbolt. 6. A roll of cloth or paper. *Noun.*
—1. To fasten with a bolt. *Bolt* the door for the night after you have let the dog in. 2. To start and run off. The horse *bolted* and its rider fell off. 3. To swallow quickly or without chewing. Mother is always telling us not to *bolt* our breakfast. *Verb.*
bolt (bōlt) *noun, plural* **bolts;** *verb,* **bolted, bolting.**

bomb A hollow case filled with something that can explode. It is used as a weapon. A

at; āpe; cär; end; mē; it; īce; hot; ōld;
wood; fōol; oil; out; up; turn; sing;
thin; this; hw in white; zh in treasure.
ə stands for a in about, e in taken,
i in pencil, o in lemon, and u in circus.

bomb is exploded by dropping or throwing it, or by lighting a fuse. *Noun.*
—To throw or drop a bomb on. *Verb.*
  bomb (bom) *noun, plural* **bombs;** *verb,* **bombed, bombing.**

bombard 1. To attack with bombs or artillery. 2. To attack again and again. Reporters *bombarded* the minister with questions.
  bom·bard (bom bärd´) *verb,* **bombarded, bombarding.**

bombardier[1] 1. The person who drops the bombs from a bomber. 2. *Canadian.* A corporal in the artillery.
  bom·bar·dier (bom´bə dēr´) *noun, plural* **bombardiers.**

bombardier[2] *Canadian.* A vehicle used for travelling over snow and ice. It looks like a tank with skis on the front. It was invented by a Canadian named Armand Bombardier.
  bom·bar·dier (bom´bə dēr´) *noun, plural* **bombardiers.**

bomber An airplane used to drop bombs.
  bomb·er (bom´ər) *noun, plural* **bombers.**

bond 1. Something that fastens or holds together. The prisoner's *bonds* were made of rope. There is a *bond* of friendship between the two boys. 2. A written receipt given by a government or a business for a loan of money. A bond is a promise to repay money borrowed at a certain date with interest.
  bond (bond) *noun, plural* **bonds.**

bondage Slavery; lack of freedom.
  bond·age (bon´dəj) *noun.*

bone One of the parts of the skeleton of an animal with a backbone. Bones are hard and stiff. Jack broke one of the *bones* in his ankle playing soccer. *Noun.*
—To take out the bones of. *Verb.*
  bone (bōn) *noun, plural* **bones;** *verb,* **boned, boning.**

bonfire A large fire built outdoors. We sat around the *bonfire* at camp and sang songs.
  bon·fire (bon´fīr´) *noun, plural* **bonfires.**

bongo drums A pair of small drums played with the hands while being held between the knees.
  bon·go drums (bong´gō).

bonnet 1. A covering for the head. A bonnet is usually tied under the chin by ribbons or strings. Bonnets were once worn by children and women. 2. A covering

Bongo Drums

for the head made of feathers. It is worn by North American Indians.
  bon·net (bon´ət) *noun, plural* **bonnets.**

bonspiel A curling tournament.
  bon·spiel (bon´spēl´) *noun, plural* **bonspiels.**

bonus Something extra. A bonus is given or paid in addition to what is due or expected. At Christmas time, the grocer gave each of his delivery boys a twenty dollar *bonus* in addition to their salaries.
  bo·nus (bō´nəs) *noun, plural* **bonuses.**

Bonnet

bony 1. Made of bone. The skeleton is a *bony* structure. 2. Full of bones. The fish we caught was so *bony* that it was hard to eat. 3. Very thin. A *bony* old dog came to our back door begging for food.
  bon·y (bō´nē) *adjective,* **bonier, boniest.**

boo A sound made to frighten or to show dislike. Tom's mother jumped when he leaped out of the closet and yelled *"Boo!" Interjection.*
—To show that one does not like something by shouting "boo." The crowd *booed* the baseball player when he struck out. *Verb.*
  boo (bo͞o) *interjection; verb,* **booed, booing.**

book Sheets of paper fastened together between two covers. The pages of a book have writing or printing on them. Mother read to us from a *book* of fairy tales. We have *books* for arithmetic, science, and geography at school. *Noun.*
—To arrange for ahead of time. Father *booked* rooms at the motel before we left on our trip so we would be sure to have a place to stay for the night. *Verb.*
  book (book) *noun, plural* **books;** *verb,* **booked, booking.**

bookcase A set of shelves for holding books.
  book·case (book´kās´) *noun, plural* **bookcases.**

bookkeeper A person who keeps the records of a business. The *bookkeeper* at the grocery store keeps a record of all the money the owner of the store makes.
  book·keep·er (book´kē´pər) *noun, plural* **bookkeepers.**

booklet A small, thin book. Booklets usually have paper covers. A *booklet* came with the electric knife, telling how to use it.
  book·let (book´lət) *noun, plural* **booklets.**

bookmobile   A bus or large van made into a travelling library.
  book·mo·bile (book′mə bēl′) *noun, plural* **bookmobiles.**

boom¹   **1.** A deep, hollow sound. A boom sounds like the noise an explosion makes. We heard the *boom* of thunder and knew that a storm was coming. **2.** A time of fast growth. The sale of boots at the store has had a *boom* since the heavy snowstorm. *Noun.*
  —**1.** To make a deep, hollow sound. Our voices *boomed* in the empty house. **2.** To grow suddenly and rapidly. Business in the stores *booms* when Christmas comes. *Verb.*
  boom (boom) *noun, plural* **booms;** *verb,* **boomed, booming.**

boom²   **1.** A long pole or beam used to stretch the bottom of a sail. **2.** The long pole on a derrick that holds up the load that is being lifted.
  boom (boom) *noun, plural* **booms.**

boomerang   A flat curved piece of wood. A boomerang can be thrown so that it returns to the thrower. A boomerang is used as a weapon by the native tribes of Australia.
  boom·er·ang (boo′- mə rang′) *noun, plural* **boomerangs.**

Boomerang

boon   A help; benefit. The rain was a big *boon* to my vegetable garden after so much dry weather.
  boon (boon) *noun, plural* **boons.**

boost   A push or shove up. Give me a *boost* to help me climb up the tree. *Noun.*
  —To push or shove up. I *boosted* my little brother over the fence. *Verb.*
  boost (boost) *noun, plural* **boosts;** *verb,* **boosted, boosting.**

boot   A covering for the foot and lower part of the leg. Boots are usually made of leather or rubber. Put on your *boots* if you are going out to play in the snow. *Noun.*
  —To kick. Dave *booted* the football. *Verb.*
  boot (boot) *noun, plural* **boots;** *verb,* **booted, booting.**

booth   **1.** A place where things are sold or shown. Everyone crowded around the refreshment *booth* at the fair. **2.** A small closed place. I made a telephone call from a tele-

phone *booth.* There was a long line of people at the ticket *booth* at the movie theatre.
  booth (booth) *noun, plural* **booths.**

Booth

border   **1.** A boundary line. They crossed the *border* between Ontario and Quebec. **2.** A strip along the edge of anything. Sue's skirt has a pretty red *border. Noun.*
  —**1.** To lie on the edge of. Manitoba *borders* on Saskatchewan. **2.** To put an edging on. She *bordered* the handkerchief with lace. *Verb.*
  bor·der (bôr′dər) *noun, plural* **borders;** *verb,* **bordered, bordering.**

bore¹   **1.** To make by digging. Workmen *bored* a tunnel through the mountain. **2.** To make a hole in. The carpenter *bored* the wood with his drill. ▲ Another word that sounds like this is **boar.**
  bore (bôr) *verb,* **bored, boring.**

bore²   To make very tired by being uninteresting and dull. Bill always *bores* his friends by telling them the same jokes over and over again. *Verb.*
  —A person or thing that is uninteresting and dull. That programme is a *bore. Noun.* ▲ Another word that sounds like this is **boar.**
  bore (bôr) *verb,* **bored, boring;** *noun, plural* **bores.**

bore³   Tom *bore* his defeat in the spelling contest very well and congratulated the winner. Look up **bear** for more information.
  bore (bôr) *verb.*

at; āpe; cär; end; mē; it; īce; hot; ōld; wood; fool; oil; out; up; turn; sing; thin; this; hw in white; zh in treasure. ə stands for a in about, e in taken, i in pencil, o in lemon, and u in circus.

born 1. Brought into life or being. The cat has newly *born* kittens. 2. By birth; natural. Tom is a *born* athlete who plays almost every sport very well. *Adjective.*
—Our cat has *born* six kittens. Look up **bear** for more information. *Verb.* ▲ Another word that sounds like this is **borne**.
born (bōrn) *adjective; verb.*

borne Mary has *borne* the pain of her sprained ankle without crying at all. Look up **bear** for more information. ▲ Another word that sounds like this is **born**.
borne (bōrn) *verb.*

borough In Canada, a town or township that governs itself. East York is a *borough* of Metropolitan Toronto. ▲ Other words that sound like this are **burro** and **burrow**.
bor·ough (bur′ō) *noun, plural* **boroughs.**

borrow 1. To take something from another person with the understanding that it must be given back. I'm allowed to *borrow* my brother's bicycle sometimes. We *borrow* books from the library. 2. To take something and use it as one's own. The name of the animal "chipmunk" was *borrowed* from the North American Indians.
bor·row (bōr′ō *or* bor′ō) *verb,* **borrowed, borrowing.**

bosom The upper, front part of the chest. The mother hugged the frightened child to her *bosom. Noun.*
—Close and dear. Tom and Jack are *bosom* buddies. *Adjective.*
bos·om (bo͞oz′əm *or* booz′əm) *noun, plural* **bosoms;** *adjective.*

boss A person who watches over and plans the work of others. The *boss* hired three new people to help get the job done on time. *Noun.*
—To be the boss of. Jack gets mad at his older sister when she tries to *boss* him around. *Verb.*
boss (bos) *noun, plural* **bosses;** *verb,* **bossed, bossing.**

botany The study of plants. When you study botany you learn about many different kinds of plants and the way they are formed. You also find out how plants grow and where they grow.
bot·a·ny (bot′ən ē) *noun.*

both *Both* boys made the basketball team. Why not invite *both* to the party? They were *both* tired and hungry after their long hike through the bush.
both (bōth) *adjective; pronoun; conjunction.*

bother 1. To trouble or annoy. Meeting new people *bothers* the shy boy. 2. To take the trouble. Don't *bother* to make lunch because I'm not hungry. *Verb.*
—A person or thing that troubles or annoys. I think making my bed every day is a *bother. Noun.*
both·er (both′ər) *verb,* **bothered, bothering;** *noun, plural* **bothers.**

bottle A container to hold liquids. A bottle has a narrow neck that can be closed with a cap or stopper. Bottles are usually made of glass or plastic. *Noun.*
—To put in bottles. That company *bottles* soft drinks. *Verb.*
bot·tle (bot′əl) *noun, plural* **bottles;** *verb,* **bottled, bottling.**

bottom 1. The lowest part. The ball rolled to the *bottom* of the hill. 2. The under or lower part. The *bottom* of the rowboat needs painting. 3. The ground under water. The *bottom* of the pond is sandy. 4. The most important part. The detective tried to get to the *bottom* of the mystery by asking questions. *Noun.*
—Lowest or last. I hid my money in the *bottom* drawer of my dresser. *Adjective.*
bot·tom (bot′əm) *noun, plural* **bottoms;** *adjective.*

bough A large branch of a tree. Father fastened the swing to a *bough* of the old tree in our backyard. ▲ Another word that sounds like this is **bow**.
bough (bou) *noun, plural* **boughs.**

bought We *bought* groceries at the store. Look up **buy** for more information.
bought (bot) *verb.*

boulder A large rock that is rounded and smooth. The *boulder* fell off the cliff and blocked the road below.
boul·der (bōl′dər) *noun, plural* **boulders.**

boulevard A wide city street. A boulevard often has trees growing along its sides.
boul·e·vard (bool′ə värd′) *noun, plural* **boulevards.**

bounce 1. To spring back after hitting something. The ball *bounced* into the street. 2. To cause to spring back. He *bounced* the ball against the wall. *Verb.*
—A spring; bound. With one *bounce* the ball disappeared over the fence. *Noun.*
bounce (bouns) *verb,* **bounced, bouncing;** *noun, plural* **bounces.**

bound[1] 1. Fastened; tied. The bank robbers left the guard *bound* and gagged. 2. Certain; sure. The team is *bound* to lose the game if the players don't practise. 3. Having an obligation; obliged. I am *bound* by my promise to keep the secret. *Adjective.*

—We *bound* the box of books with rope. Look up **bind** for more information. *Verb.*
   bound (bound) *adjective; verb.*

bound² **1.** To leap; spring; jump. The rabbit *bounded* away into the woods. **2.** To spring back after hitting something. The ball *bounded* off the wall. *Verb.*
   —A long or high leap. With one *bound* the deer was across the stream. *Noun.*
   bound (bound) *verb,* **bounded, bounding;** *noun, plural* **bounds.**

bound³ A line that marks the farthest edge; boundary. In the volleyball game, the ball went out of *bounds. Noun.*
   —To form the boundary of. A road *bounds* the farmer's land on the north. *Verb.*
   bound (bound) *noun, plural* **bounds;** *verb,* **bounded, bounding.**

bound⁴ Going toward. The train is *bound* for Vancouver.
   bound (bound) *adjective.*

boundary A line that marks the edge of an area of land; border. Dad built a fence along the *boundary* of our property.
   bound·a·ry (boun′dər ē *or* bound′rē) *noun, plural* **boundaries.**

bountiful More than enough; abundant. The farmer had a *bountiful* harvest.
   boun·ti·ful (boun′ti fəl) *adjective.*

bounty **1.** A reward for killing certain animals. The county government pays a *bounty* of five dollars for every coyote killed. **2.** Generosity; goodness. Many poor people were helped by the rich man's *bounty.*
   boun·ty (boun′tē) *noun, plural* **bounties.**

bouquet A bunch of flowers. The young man brought a *bouquet* of roses to his girlfriend.
   bou·quet (bō kā′ *or* bōō kā′) *noun, plural* **bouquets.**

bout **1.** A trial of skill; contest. The two men will wrestle in the second *bout.* **2.** An attack or outburst; fit; spell. The boy had a *bout* of coughing.
   bout (bout) *noun, plural* **bouts.**

bow¹ **1.** To bend forward. People bow to show respect or to greet someone. **2.** To give in; submit. The small boy *bowed* to his older sister's wishes. *Verb.*

Bouquet

—A bending forward of the head or body. The knight made a *bow* before the queen. *Noun.* ▲ Another word that sounds like this is **bough.**
   bow (bou) *verb,* **bowed, bowing;** *noun, plural* **bows.**

bow² **1.** A weapon for shooting arrows. A bow is made of a strip of wood that is bent by a string fastened to each end. **2.** A knot with two or more loops. Carol tied a pretty green *bow* on the package. **3.** A long piece of wood with horsehairs stretched from one end to the other. This bow is used to play the violin.
   bow (bō) *noun, plural* **bows.**

Bows

bow³ The front end of a boat. ▲ Another word that sounds like this is **bough.**
   bow (bou) *noun, plural* **bows.**

bowels **1.** A long tube in the body; intestines. Food passes from the stomach into the bowels. **2.** The deepest part of something. The coal mine was in the *bowels* of the earth.
   bow·els (bou′əlz) *noun plural.*

bowl¹ **1.** A rounded dish that holds things. Mother put lettuce in the salad *bowl.* Jerry poured milk into a *bowl* for the cat. **2.** Something shaped like a bowl. The round end of a spoon is called a bowl. A football stadium is sometimes called a bowl. ▲ Another word that sounds like this is **boll.**
   bowl (bōl) *noun, plural* **bowls.**

bowl² A wooden ball used in a game. *Noun.*
   —**1.** To play the game of bowling. Tom likes to *bowl* on Saturday night. **2.** To roll a ball in bowling. It is your turn to *bowl. Verb.* ▲ Another word that sounds like this is **boll.**
   bowl (bōl) *noun, plural* **bowls;** *verb,* **bowled, bowling.**

bowlegged Having legs that curve outward. The cowboy was *bowlegged* from riding a horse for many years.
   bow·leg·ged (bō′leg′əd) *adjective.*

at; āpe; cär; end; mē; it; īce; hot; ōld;
wood; fōōl; oil; out; up; turn; sing;
thin; this; hw in white; zh in treasure.
ə stands for a in about, e in taken,
i in pencil, o in lemon, and u in circus.

bowling A game that you play by rolling a heavy ball down an alley to knock down wooden pins at the other end.
bowl·ing (bō′ling) *noun.*

bowman A person who shoots with a bow and arrow; archer.
bow·man (bō′mən) *noun, plural* **bowmen.**

bowstring A strong string fastened to the two ends of a bow for shooting arrows.
bow·string (bō′string′) *noun, plural* **bow-strings.**

box¹ **1.** A container used to hold things. A box is made of cardboard, wood, or another heavy material. It has four sides, a bottom, and sometimes a top. Phil put the books in a large *box.* Mother keeps her rings in a jewellery *box.* **2.** A closed-in area or place. He sat in a *box* at the theatre. *Noun.*
—To put in a box. Andy helped his father *box* apples for the market. *Verb.*
box (boks) *noun, plural* **boxes;** *verb,* **boxed, boxing.**

box² A blow made with the open hand or the fist. The grouchy old man gave the boy a *box* on the ear. *Noun.*
—**1.** To hit with the open hand or the fist. Tom will *box* Bill's ears if he doesn't stop teasing him. **2.** To fight someone with the fists as a sport. The two men will *box* each other for the championship. *Verb.*
box (boks) *noun, plural* **boxes;** *verb,* **boxed, boxing.**

boxcar A car of a railroad train used to carry freight. A boxcar is enclosed on all sides. It is loaded through a sliding door on the side.
box·car (boks′kär′) *noun, plural* **boxcars.**

Boxcars

boxer **1.** A person who boxes. The *boxer* knocked out his opponent in the third round of the fight. **2.** A dog with short hair. The boxer has a tan or reddish-brown coat with white markings. Boxers are related to bull-dogs, but are larger.
box·er (bok′sər) *noun, plural* **boxers.**

boxing The sport of fighting with the fists.
box·ing (bok′sing) *noun.*

Boxing

boy A male child from birth to the time he is a young man.
boy (boi) *noun, plural* **boys.**

boycott To join with others against a person, nation, or business. People sometimes boycott a store whose prices are too high by refusing to buy things from it. *Verb.*
—A planned joining together of people against a person, nation, or business. The people in our neighbourhood led a *boycott* against the bus company because it raised its fares. *Noun.*
boy·cott (boi′kot′) *verb,* **boycotted, boycotting;** *noun, plural* **boycotts.**

▲ About one hundred years ago a man named Captain Charles *Boycott* rented land to farmers in Ireland. The person who owned the land was English, and the Irish farmers thought they should own the land themselves, instead of someone from another country. So they refused to pay their rent to Captain Boycott. None of the people would talk to him or have anything to do with him. Captain Boycott finally had to give up his job and go back to England. Since that time, the word **boycott** has been used in talking about actions of this kind.

boyhood The time of being a boy. He spent his *boyhood* on a farm.
boy·hood (boi′hood′) *noun, plural* **boyhoods.**

boyish Of a boy; like a boy. Jeff and his friends played some *boyish* tricks on Hallowe'en.
boy·ish (boi′ish) *adjective.*

Boy Scout A member of the Boy Scouts.
Boy Scouts An organization for boys. The

Boy Scouts teaches boys outdoor skills, physical fitness, and good citizenship.

brace **1.** Something that holds parts together or holds a thing steady. The roof of the old shack needs a *brace* to hold it up. **2. braces.** Metal wires used to make teeth straight. **3.** A tool that is like a handle. It is used to hold a drill or bit. **4.** A pair. The pirate held a *brace* of pistols. We saw a *brace* of geese. *Noun.*
—**1.** To hold steady; support. The boy *braced* the tent with wires so that the wind wouldn't blow it over. **2.** To prepare for a shock. *Brace* yourself for some bad news. **3.** To give energy to. The cold winter air *braced* us. *Verb.*
brace (brās) *noun, plural* **braces;** *verb,* **braced, bracing.**

bracelet A band or chain worn around the wrist as an ornament. Some bracelets are made of gold and silver.
brace·let (brās′lət) *noun, plural* **bracelets.**

bracket **1.** A piece of wood, metal, plastic, or stone fastened to a wall to support something. The shelf was held up by *brackets.* **2.** One of two marks, [ ], used to enclose words or numbers. **3.** Group. His mother is in a high income *bracket. Noun.*
—**1.** To put words or numbers in brackets. **2.** To group together. The teacher will *bracket* the students according to their reading speeds. *Verb.*
brack·et (brak′ət) *noun, plural* **brackets;** *verb,* **bracketed, bracketing.**

brad A thin nail with a small head.
brad (brad) *noun, plural* **brads.**

brag To speak too well of what one does or owns; boast. She *brags* about how smart she is. The boy *bragged* to his friends about his new bicycle.
brag (brag) *verb,* **bragged, bragging.**

braid A strip made by weaving together three or more long pieces of hair, straw, or cloth. Carol wears her hair in *braids.* Henry's band uniform is decorated with gold *braid. Noun.*
—To weave together long pieces of hair, straw, or cloth. Ralph tried to *braid* a belt from strips of leather. *Verb.*
braid (brād) *noun, plural* **braids;** *verb,* **braided, braiding.**

Braid

braille A system of printing for blind people. The letters of the alphabet in braille are formed by raised dots. Blind people read braille by touching the dots with their fingers.
braille (brāl) *noun.*

▲ The word **braille** comes from the name of a blind Frenchman, Louis *Braille.* He was a teacher of other blind people, and he thought of this way to write for them.

brain **1.** The large mass of nerves and tissue that is inside the head of persons and animals. The brain is the main part of the nervous system. The brain controls the actions of the body. It also lets us think, learn, and remember. **2. brains.** Intelligence. My older sister has real *brains. Noun.*
—To hit on the head. The hunter *brained* the animal with a large club. *Verb.*

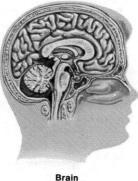

Brain

brain (brān) *noun, plural* **brains;** *verb,* **brained, braining.**

brake¹ Something used to stop or slow the movement of a wheel, or of a car, truck, bicycle, or other vehicle. Many brakes work by pressing against the wheel. *Noun.*
—To cause something to stop or slow down by using a brake. Tony *braked* his bicycle by pressing the pedals backward. *Verb.* ▲ Another word that sounds like this is **break.**
brake (brāk) *noun, plural* **brakes;** *verb,* **braked, braking.**

brake² An area of ground covered with shrubs and bushes. ▲ Another word that sounds like this is **break.**
brake (brāk) *noun, plural* **brakes.**

brakeman A person who helps the conductor of a railroad train. In the past, his job was to operate the train's brakes.
brake·man (brāk′mən) *noun, plural* **brakemen.**

bramble A bush with thorny stems. The blackberry plant is a kind of bramble.
bram·ble (bram′bəl) *noun, plural* **brambles.**

at; āpe; cär; end; mē; it; īce; hot; ōld; wood; fo͞ol; oil; out; up; turn; sing; thin; this; hw in white; zh in treasure. ə stands for a in about, e in taken, i in pencil, o in lemon, and u in circus.

bran The ground-up outer covering of wheat or other grains. The bran is separated from the flour by sifting. Bran is used to feed cows and other livestock. It is also used in breakfast cereals and baking.
bran (bran) *noun.*

branch 1. A part of a tree or bush that grows out from the trunk. 2. Anything that goes out from a main part. A *branch* of the river flows near town. Dad works at a *branch* of the main post office. *Noun.*
—To divide into branches. The tree *branched.* Turn left at the place where the path *branches. Verb.*
branch (branch) *noun, plural* **branches;** *verb,* **branched, branching.**

brand 1. A kind or make of something. She likes that *brand* of ice cream. He bought a new *brand* of soap. 2. A mark made on the skin of cattle or other animals. A brand is made with a hot iron. It shows who owns an animal. 3. A mark of disgrace. In former times a brand was burned on the skin of criminals. *Noun.*
—To mark with a brand. The cowboys will *brand* the cattle. His stealing *brands* him as a criminal. *Verb.*
brand (brand) *noun, plural* **brands;** *verb,* **branded, branding.**

brand-new Completely new. My uncle bought a *brand-new* house that no one has ever lived in.
brand-new (brand′nōō′ *or* brand′nyōō′) *adjective.*

brandy An alcoholic drink. Brandy is made from fermented fruit juice or wine.
bran·dy (bran′dē) *noun, plural* **brandies.**

brass A yellow metal that is a mixture of copper and zinc melted together. Brass is used to make musical instruments, candlesticks, and dishes.
brass (bras) *noun.*

brave Having courage. A person who is brave can face danger or pain without being afraid. The *brave* girl jumped into the water to save the drowning child. *Adjective.*
—To face danger or pain without being afraid. The fireman *braved* the burning house to rescue the trapped child. *Verb.*
brave (brāv) *adjective,* **braver, bravest;** *verb,* **braved, braving.**

bravery The ability to face danger or pain without being afraid; courage.
brav·er·y (brā′vər ē) *noun.*

breach A break made in something. Water poured through the *breach* in the dam. *Noun.*
—To make a break in; break through. The

soldiers *breached* the enemy's lines. *Verb.*
breach (brēch) *noun, plural* **breaches;** *verb,* **breached, breaching.**

bread 1. A food made by mixing flour or meal with water or milk, and then baking it in an oven. 2. The food and other things needed for a person to live. He earns his daily *bread* by writing. ▲ Another word that sounds like this is **bred.**
bread (bred) *noun, plural* **breads.**

breadth The wideness of something measured from one side to the other side; width.
breadth (bredth) *noun.*

break 1. To make come to pieces by force. The clumsy boy may *break* the glass. The cup will *break* if you drop it. Joe did not *break* his ankle, but he has a bad sprain. 2. To harm or damage. The baby will *break* the typewriter if she bangs on it. 3. To fail to obey; fail to keep. Tom will *break* the law if he drives too fast on this road. She never *breaks* a promise. 4. To come or change suddenly. She hopes to *break* the school record at the swimming meet. We are trying to *break* my little brother's habit of sucking his thumb. A rash *broke* out on Mary's back. 5. To force one's way. The prisoner *broke* out of jail. A burglar *broke* into the house by the back door. 6. To fill with sorrow. The little boy's heart will *break* if we do not find his lost kitten. *Verb.*
—1. A broken place; something broken. His arm has a bad *break.* The sun is shining through a *break* in the clouds. The men took a ten-minute *break* from their work. 2. The act of breaking. The puppy made a *break* for the door. *Noun.* ▲ Another word that sounds like this is **brake.**
break (brāk) *verb,* **broke, broken, breaking;** *noun, plural* **breaks.**

breakdown A failing to work. Because of the *breakdown* of the car, we had to walk.
break·down (brāk′doun′) *noun, plural* **breakdowns.**

breaker A large wave that foams as it breaks on rocks or the shore.
break·er (brā′kər) *noun, plural* **breakers.**

Breaker

breakfast The first meal of the day. The children had *breakfast* before going out.
break·fast (brek′fəst) *noun, plural* **breakfasts.**

break-up *Canadian.* The time in spring when the ice melts in the North.
break-up (brāk′up′) *noun, plural* **break-ups.**

breast 1. The front part of the body. The breast is found between the stomach and the neck. 2. A gland that gives milk.
breast (brest) *noun, plural* **breasts.**

breastbone The flat, narrow bone in the centre of the breast to which the ribs are joined.
breast·bone (brest′bōn′) *noun, plural* **breastbones.**

breath 1. Air drawn into and forced out of the lungs when you breathe. 2. The act of breathing. The swimmer held her *breath* under water. 3. The ability to breathe easily. 4. A slight flow of air. There was not a *breath* of fresh air in the room.
breath (breth) *noun, plural* **breaths.**

breathe 1. To draw air into the lungs and then force it out. 2. To whisper. She promised not to *breathe* a word of the secret.
breathe (brēth) *verb,* **breathed, breathing.**

breathless 1. Out of breath. The boy was *breathless* after running all the way home. 2. Excited or fearful. The children were *breathless* as they watched the acrobats.
breath·less (breth′ləs) *adjective.*

bred George *bred* puppies to sell. Look up **breed** for more information. ▲ Another word that sounds like this is **bread.**
bred (bred) *verb.*

breeches Pants that reach to the knees. Men wore breeches in former times.
breech·es (brēch′əz *or* brich′əz) *noun plural.*

breed 1. To raise. She *breeds* roses in her garden. Al *breeds* chickens to sell at the market. 2. To bring forth young. Certain animals *breed* only in the winter.
breed (brēd) *verb,* **bred, breeding.**

breeding The way someone is brought up; training. Her nice manners show good *breeding.*
breed·ing (brēd′ing) *noun.*

breeze A mild, gentle wind. The *breeze* caused the trees to sway. *Noun.*

Breeches

—To move in an easy or quick way. Arthur *breezed* into the room. Mary *breezed* through her homework. *Verb.*
breeze (brēz) *noun, plural* **breezes;** *verb,* **breezed, breezing.**

brew 1. To make beer or ale. Beer and ale are brewed by soaking, boiling, and fermenting malt and hops. 2. To make tea or coffee by soaking in hot or boiling water. 3. To bring about; cause. Those two boys always seem to be *brewing* mischief. 4. To form; gather. A storm is *brewing. Verb.*
—A drink made by brewing. *Noun.*
brew (brōo) *verb,* **brewed, brewing;** *noun, plural* **brews.**

briar A bushy plant with thorns. The blackberry plant is sometimes called a briar. The thorns on the plant are also called briars. This word is also spelled **brier.**
bri·ar (brī′ər) *noun, plural* **briars.**

bribe Money or gifts given to someone to get him to do something wrong or something he does not want to do. *Noun.*
—To give a bribe to. The driver tried to *bribe* the policeman to let him go without a ticket for speeding. *Verb.*
bribe (brīb) *noun, plural* **bribes;** *verb,* **bribed, bribing.**

brick A block of clay baked in an oven or in the sun. Bricks are used in building. The walls of my house are made of *bricks.*
brick (brik) *noun, plural* **bricks.**

bride A woman who has just married or is about to be married.
bride (brīd) *noun, plural* **brides.**

bridegroom A man who has just married or is about to be married.
bride·groom (brīd′grōom′) *noun, plural* **bridegrooms.**

bridge 1. Anything built across a river, road, or railroad track so that people can get from one side to the other. 2. The top bony part of a person's nose. 3. A raised area on the deck of a ship. The captain or another officer steers the ship from the bridge. *Noun.*
—To build a bridge across. The workmen *bridged* the highway. *Verb.*
bridge (brij) *noun, plural* **bridges;** *verb,* **bridged, bridging.**

at; āpe; cär; end; mē; it; īce; hot; ōld;
wood; fōol; oil; out; up; turn; sing;
thin; this; hw in white; zh in treasure.
ə stands for a in about, e in taken,
i in pencil, o in lemon, and u in circus.

bridle The part of a horse's harness that fits over the animal's head. The bridle is used to guide or control the horse. *Noun.*
—**1.** To put a bridle on. Carol will *bridle* her horse. **2.** To hold back; control. John is trying hard to *bridle* his bad temper. *Verb.*

bri·dle (brīd′əl) *noun, plural* **bridles;** *verb,* **bridled, bridling.**

Bridle

brief **1.** Short in time. Aunt Martha came for a *brief* visit. **2.** Using few words. Her letter was very *brief. Adjective.*
—To give last-minute directions or facts to. The officer *briefed* the pilots just before their mission. *Verb.*

brief (brēf) *adjective,* **briefer, briefest;** *verb,* **briefed, briefing.**

brier A thorny shrub. This word is usually spelled **briar.** Look up **briar** for more information.

brig **1.** A sailing ship with two masts. **2.** A prison on a ship. The pirate captain ordered his prisoners to be thrown in the *brig.*

brig (brig) *noun, plural* **brigs.**

Brig

brigade **1.** A part of the army. A brigade is made up of two or more regiments. **2.** A group of people organized for a special purpose. Dad belongs to the volunteer fire *brigade.*

bri·gade (bri gād′) *noun, plural* **brigades.**

bright **1.** Giving much light; filled with light. The *bright* light of the sun hurt her eyes. The waxed floor has a *bright* shine. **2.** Clear; strong. Richard painted the chair a *bright* red.

3. Smart; clever. Sarah is a *bright* student. Kicking that hornet's nest wasn't a very *bright* thing to do.

bright (brīt) *adjective,* **brighter, brightest.**

brilliant **1.** Very bright; sparkling. A *brilliant* light was shining. **2.** Very fine; splendid. We won because of the team's *brilliant* playing. **3.** Very intelligent. She is a *brilliant* scientist.

bril·liant (bril′yənt) *adjective.*

brim An edge or rim. My glass is filled to the *brim.* Mary's beach hat has a wide *brim. Noun.*
—To be full to the brim. The bathtub was *brimming* with water. *Verb.*

brim (brim) *noun, plural* **brims;** *verb,* **brimmed, brimming.**

brine Water that is full of salt. Brine is used for pickling foods.

brine (brīn) *noun.*

bring **1.** To cause something or someone to come with you. Remember to *bring* your books home. Carl will *bring* his records to the party. **2.** To cause something to come or happen. The heavy rains will *bring* floods.

bring (bring) *verb,* **brought, bringing.**

to bring up. 1. To raise someone. My mother was *brought up* on a farm. **2.** To mention; suggest. Don't *bring up* the subject of cleaning my room again.

brink **1.** The edge at the top of a steep place. Joey stood on the *brink* of the cliff to look down at the valley below. **2.** The point just before something happens; verge. He is on the *brink* of tears.

brink (bringk) *noun, plural* **brinks.**

brisk **1.** Quick and lively. The girls walked at a *brisk* pace. **2.** Refreshing; keen; sharp. We went out into the *brisk* winter air.

brisk (brisk) *adjective,* **brisker, briskest.**

bristle A short, stiff hair. Hogs have bristles. My hairbrush and toothbrush are both made of *bristles. Noun.*
—**1.** To have the hairs on the neck or body rise. My dog will *bristle* if he sees your cat. **2.** To stand up stiffly. The porcupine's quills *bristled. Verb.*

bris·tle (bris′əl) *noun, plural* **bristles;** *verb,* **bristled, bristling.**

Britain The countries of England, Scotland, and Wales; Great Britain.

Brit·ain (brit′ən) *noun.*

British Of Great Britain. *Adjective.*
—**the British.** The people of Great Britain. *Noun.*

Brit·ish (brit′ish) *adjective; noun.*

British Columbia The province on the west coast of Canada.
British Co·lum·bi·a (kə lum′bē ə).

▲ The name of the province recalls its early connection with Britain. British Columbia joined Confederation in 1871.

British Columbian A person born in or living in British Columbia. *Noun.*
—Of British Columbia. *Adjective.*
British Col·um·bi·an (kə lum′bē ən).

British North America Act The act of the British Parliament that created the Dominion of Canada in 1867. It united Ontario, Quebec, Nova Scotia, and New Brunswick. In 1982 the British North America Act was renamed the Constitution Act, 1867. Look up **Constitution Act** for more information.

brittle Very easily broken. The *brittle* icicles snapped when I touched them.
brit·tle (brit′əl) *adjective.*

broad 1. Large from one side to the other side; wide. There is a *broad* driveway in front of the school. 2. Wide in range; not limited. John has a *broad* knowledge of foreign stamps and coins. 3. Clear and open. The thief tried to rob the bank in *broad* daylight.
broad (brod) *adjective,* **broader, broadest.**

broadcast 1. To send out music, news, or other kinds of programs by radio or television. That radio station *broadcasts* rock music. 2. To make widely known. Don't *broadcast* that secret to the whole school. *Verb.*
—Something that is broadcast by radio or television. *Noun.*
broad·cast (brod′kast′) *verb,* **broadcast** or **broadcasted, broadcasting;** *noun, plural* **broadcasts.**

brocade A heavy cloth with patterns woven into it. The queen wore a *brocade* robe.
bro·cade (brō kād′) *noun, plural* **brocades.**

broccoli A plant whose thick green stems and flower buds are eaten as a vegetable.
broc·co·li (brok′ə lē) *noun, plural* **broccoli.**

broil 1. To cook over an open fire or under the flame in the broiler of a stove. We will *broil* the steak on our barbecue. 2. To be very hot. We *broiled* in the desert sun.
broil (broil) *verb,* **broiled, broiling.**

broiler A pan, grill, or part of a stove that is used to broil food.
broil·er (broil′ər) *noun, plural* **broilers.**

broke Jack *broke* the dish when he dropped it. Look up **break** for more information.
broke (brōk) *verb.*

broken Mary has *broken* her watch. Look up **break** for more information. *Verb.*
—1. In pieces. You can throw away that *broken* dish. 2. Not kept. You ought to say you're sorry for your *broken* promise. 3. Not working; damaged. Our television set is *broken. Adjective.*
bro·ken (brō′kən) *verb; adjective.*

bronchial tubes The branches of the windpipe. Air flows to and from the lungs through the bronchial tubes.
bron·chi·al tubes (brong′kē əl).

bronchitis A sickness from a cold in the bronchial tubes. When you have bronchitis, you have a bad cough.
bron·chi·tis (brong kī′tis) *noun.*

bronco A small, partly wild horse of the western United States.
bron·co (brong′kō) *noun, plural* **broncos.**

bronze 1. A reddish-brown metal made by melting together copper and tin. Bronze is made into dishes, jewellery, and statues. 2. A reddish-brown colour. *Noun.*
—Reddish-brown. *Adjective.*
—To make reddish-brown. The sun had *bronzed* the lifeguard's back. *Verb.*
bronze (bronz) *noun, plural* **bronzes;** *adjective; verb,* **bronzed, bronzing.**

brooch A pin worn as an ornament. A brooch is fastened with a clasp. Mother wore a silver *brooch* on the collar of her dress.
brooch (brōch) *noun, plural* **brooches.**

Brooch

brood The young birds that are hatched from eggs at the same time. The hen took care of her *brood* of chicks. *Noun.*
—1. To sit on eggs in order to hatch them. Hens, robins, and other birds brood until the baby birds hatch from their eggs. 2. To think or worry about for a long time. Mary *brooded* over the loss of her kitten. *Verb.*
brood (brood) *noun, plural* **broods;** *verb,* **brooded, brooding.**

---

at; āpe; cär; end; mē; it; īce; hot; ōld;
wood; fool; oil; out; up; turn; sing;
thin; this; hw in white; zh in treasure.
ə stands for a in about, e in taken,
i in pencil, o in lemon, and u in circus.

brook A small stream.
  brook (brook) *noun, plural* **brooks.**

broom **1.** A brush with a long handle used for sweeping or in curling. **2.** A bush that has long, thin branches, small leaves, and yellow flowers.
  broom (broom) *noun, plural* **brooms.**

broth A thin soup. Broth is made by boiling meat, fish, or vegetables in water.
  broth (broth) *noun, plural* **broths.**

brother A boy or man having the same parents as another person.
  broth·er (bruth′ər) *noun, plural* **brothers.**

brotherhood **1.** The close feeling between brothers and other men. **2.** A group of men united by common interests or aims.
  broth·er·hood (bruth′ər hood′) *noun, plural* **brotherhoods.**

brother-in-law **1.** The brother of one's husband or wife. **2.** The husband of one's sister.
  broth·er-in-law (bruth′ər in lä′) *noun, plural* **brothers-in-law.**

brought Ted *brought* me a birthday present. Look up **bring** for more information.
  brought (brot) *verb.*

brow **1.** The part of the face above the eyes; forehead. Jack wrinkled his *brow* as he tried to remember the answer. **2.** The curved line of hair above the eye; eyebrow. **3.** The edge of a steep place. From the *brow* of the hill we could see for miles around.
  brow (brou) *noun, plural* **brows.**

brown A dark colour like that of chocolate or coffee. *Noun.*
—Having the colour brown. *Adjective.*
—To make or become brown. *Verb.*
  brown (broun) *noun, plural* **browns;** *adjective,* **browner, brownest;** *verb,* **browned, browning.**

brownie **1.** A kind of fairy. Brownies are supposed to do good things for people. **2.** A small, flat chocolate cake with nuts in it. **3.** Brownie. A girl who belongs to the junior division of the Girl Guides.
  brown·ie (brou′nē) *noun, plural* **brownies.**

browse To look here and there in a book, library, or store. Mary *browsed* through the library books before choosing one.
  browse (brouz) *verb,* **browsed, browsing.**

bruise **1.** An injury that does not break the skin, but makes a bluish or blackish mark on it. A bruise is caused by a fall, blow, or bump. **2.** A mark on the outside of a fruit, vegetable, or plant caused by a blow or bump. *Noun.*
—To cause a bruise on the skin of. Sara *bruised* her arm when she fell. *Verb.*
  bruise (brooz) *noun, plural* **bruises;** *verb,* **bruised, bruising.**

brunette **1.** Dark-brown. Eve has *brunette* hair. **2.** Having dark-brown hair and dark-coloured eyes and skin. Many Spanish people are *brunette. Adjective.*
—A person with dark-brown hair and dark-coloured eyes and skin. Mary and her sisters are *brunettes. Noun.* This word is also spelled **brunet.**
  bru·nette (broo net′) *adjective; noun, plural* **brunettes.**

brush¹ **1.** A tool that is used for scrubbing, smoothing, sweeping, or painting. A brush is made of bristles attached to a stiff back or to a handle. I used a clothes *brush* to get the cat hairs off my skirt. **2.** The act of using a brush. Give your hair a good *brush.* **3.** A light touch in passing. I felt a *brush* on my legs as the cat went by. *Noun.*
—**1.** To scrub, smooth, sweep, or paint with a brush. *Brush* your teeth every day. Henry *brushed* the crumbs from his lap. **2.** To touch lightly in passing. Leaves and branches *brushed* my face as I walked through the heavy woods. *Verb.*
  brush (brush) *noun, plural* **brushes;** *verb,* **brushed, brushing.**

brush² **1.** Shrubs, small trees, and bushes growing together. The frightened rabbit disappeared into the *brush.* **2.** Twigs or branches cut or broken off from trees.
  brush (brush) *noun.*

Brussels sprouts Buds that grow along the thick stem of a leafy plant. Brussels sprouts are cooked and eaten as a vegetable.
  Brus·sels sprouts (brus′əlz).

brutal Like a savage animal; cruel. The *brutal* man beat the dog.
  bru·tal (broot′əl) *adjective.*

brute **1.** An animal. A *brute* cannot reason or feel the way a human does. **2.** A cruel person. I saw that *brute* kicking an old dog.
  brute (broot) *noun, plural* **brutes.**

Brussels Sprouts

bubble A round thing formed from a liquid and filled with air or gas. There are *bubbles* in my ginger ale. The children blew soap *bubbles* with a pipe. *Noun.*
—To form bubbles. Water *bubbles* when it is boiling. *Verb.*
 bub·ble (bub′əl) *noun, plural* **bubbles;** *verb,* **bubbled, bubbling.**

buck A male deer, antelope, rabbit, or goat. *Noun.*
—**1.** To jump into the air with the back arched and the head down. A horse can *buck* to throw off a rider. **2.** To work or push against. We had to *buck* heavy traffic on the highway. *Verb.*
 buck (buk) *noun, plural* **bucks;** *verb,* **bucked, bucking.**

bucket A container used for carrying water, sand, or other things; pail.
 buck·et (buk′ət) *noun, plural* **buckets.**

buckle **1.** A fastening used to hold together the two ends of a belt or strap. My belt has a silver *buckle*. **2.** A bend or bulge. The heat caused a *buckle* in the road. *Noun.*
—**1.** To fasten with a buckle. The pilot told us to *buckle* our seat belts because the plane was about to land. **2.** To bend or bulge. The shelf began to *buckle* because I put too many books on it. *Verb.*
 buck·le (buk′əl) *noun, plural* **buckles;** *verb,* **buckled, buckling.**

buckskin A yellowish-tan leather made from the skins of deer or sheep. Buckskin is strong and soft.
 buck·skin (buk′skin′) *noun, plural* **buckskins.**

buckwheat A plant whose seeds are used as feed for animals or are ground into flour.
 buck·wheat (buk′-wēt′ or buk′-hwēt′) *noun, plural* **buckwheats.**

bud A small swelling on a plant. A bud will later grow into a flower, a leaf, or a branch. The *buds* on the rosebush show that it will bloom soon. *Noun.*
—To form buds. The trees are beginning to *bud. Verb.*
 bud (bud) *noun, plural* **buds;** *verb,* **budded, budding.**

Buckwheat
Seed

buddy A close friend. Jack is my *buddy*.
 bud·dy (bud′ē) *noun, plural* **buddies.**

budge To move even a little. I couldn't *budge* the piano.
 budge (buj) *verb,* **budged, budging.**

budget A plan for using money. A budget shows how much money a person will have and the ways it will be spent. *Noun.*
—To make a plan for the spending of money. Mom *budgets* her salary very carefully. *Verb.*
 budg·et (buj′ət) *noun, plural* **budgets;** *verb,* **budgeted, budgeting.**

budgie *Canadian.* A small, brightly coloured parakeet. Of all the parakeets the budgie is most often kept as a pet.
 budg·ie (buj′ē) *noun, plural* **budgies.**

bud run The third and poorest flow of sap from a maple tree in the spring. It comes after the **robin run** and the **frog run.**

buff **1.** A soft, strong, yellowish-brown leather. Buff was formerly made from the skin of buffalo and is now made from the skin of oxen. **2.** A yellowish-brown colour. *Noun.*
—Having the colour buff; yellowish-brown. *Adjective.*
—To polish; shine. Mary *buffed* her shoes to make them shiny. *Verb.*
 buff (buf) *noun, plural* **buffs;** *adjective; verb,* **buffed, buffing.**

Budgie

buffalo **1.** A North American wild ox; bison. A buffalo has a big shaggy head with short horns and a humped back. **2.** Any of various oxen of Europe, Asia, and Africa.
 buf·fa·lo (buf′ə lō′) *noun, plural* **buffaloes** or **buffalos** or **buffalo.**

buffet **1.** A piece of furniture. A buffet has a flat top to serve food from and drawers or shelves for storing dishes, silver, and table linen. **2.** A meal laid out on a buffet or a table so that guests may serve themselves.
 buf·fet (bu fā′) *noun, plural* **buffets.**

at; āpe; cär; end; mē; it; īce; hot; ōld;
wood; fool; oil; out; up; turn; sing;
thin; this; hw in white; zh in treasure.
ə stands for a in about, e in taken,
i in pencil, o in lemon, and u in circus.

bug **1.** Any of a group of insects with or without wings. Bugs have beaklike mouth parts for sucking. A bedbug is a bug. **2.** Any insect. Ants, spiders, and cockroaches are bugs. **3.** A germ that causes a disease. A lot of pupils missed school because of the flu *bug*. **4.** A fault in the working of a machine. Some *bug* in the car is making it stall. *Noun.*
—To hide a small microphone in. People sometimes *bug* rooms so that they can over-hear other people's conversations. *Verb.*
  bug (bug) *noun, plural* **bugs;** *verb,* **bugged, bugging.**

buggy A light carriage with four wheels. A buggy is pulled by one horse.
  bug·gy (bug′ē) *noun, plural* **buggies.**

bugle A brass musical instrument shaped like a trumpet. Bugles are used in the army and navy to sound signals.
  bu·gle (byo͞o′gəl) *noun, plural* **bu·gles.**

Bugle

bugler A person who plays a bugle.
  bu·gler (byo͞o′-glər) *noun, plural* **buglers.**

build **1.** To make by putting parts or material together. John is going to *build* a bookcase with boards. The province will soon *build* a new highway near our farm. **2.** To form little by little; develop. She is trying to *build* a successful business. *Verb.*
—The way in which something is put to-gether. Jacques has a strong *build. Noun.*
  build (bild) *verb,* **built, building;** *noun, plural* **builds.**

building **1.** Something built. Houses, hotels, schools, stores, and garages are build-ings. **2.** The act of making houses, stores, bridges, and similar things.
  build·ing (bild′ing) *noun, plural* **buildings.**

built The boys *built* a tree hut. Look up **build** for more information.
  built (bilt) *verb.*

bulb **1.** A round, underground part of a plant. Onions, lilies, and tulips grow from bulbs. **2.** Any object with a rounded part. Put a new electric light *bulb* in the lamp.
  bulb (bulb) *noun, plural* **bulbs.**

bulge A rounded part that swells out. The ball made a *bulge* in Tom's pocket. *Noun.*
—To swell out. The bag *bulged* with grocer-ies. *Verb.*

bulge (bulj) *noun, plural* **bulges;** *verb,* **bulged, bulging.**

bulk **1.** Large size. The *bulk* of the fat man in the circus made it hard for him to move around. **2.** The largest or main part. The farmer grew corn on the *bulk* of his land.
  bulk (bulk) *noun.*

bull **1.** The full-grown male of cattle. **2.** The full-grown male of the elephant, moose, or seal.
  bull (bool) *noun, plural* **bulls.**

bulldog A heavily built dog. A bulldog has a large head, square jaws, short legs, and a smooth coat. The bulldog is known for the strong, stubborn grip of its jaws.
  bull·dog (bool′dog′) *noun, plural* **bulldogs.**

bulldozer A tractor with a powerful motor. A bulldozer has a heavy metal blade in front. It is used for clearing land by moving earth and rocks.
  bull·doz·er (bool′dōz′ər) *noun, plural* **bull-dozers.**

Bulldozer

bullet A small piece of rounded or pointed metal. A bullet is made to be shot from a gun.
  bul·let (bool′ət) *noun, plural* **bullets.**

bulletin **1.** A short announcement of the latest news. We heard a *bulletin* on the radio about the coming snow storm. **2.** A small news-paper or magazine published regularly. Our club *bulletin* lists the dates of meetings.
  bul·le·tin (bool′ət in) *noun, plural* **bulletins.**

bullfight A sport in which a man fights a bull in an arena. Bullfights are popular in Spain, Mexico, and South America.
  bull·fight (bool′fīt′) *noun, plural* **bullfights.**

bullfrog A large frog that has a loud, bel-lowing croak. The bullfrog is the largest frog in Canada.
  bull·frog (bool′frog′) *noun, plural* **bull-frogs.**

bull's-eye **1.** The centre circle of a target. John's arrow hit the *bull's-eye.* **2.** A shot that hits this circle.
  bull's-eye (boolz′ī′) *noun, plural* **bull's-eyes.**

bully A person who is tough and likes to fight. A bully is always frightening or hurting people who are smaller or weaker than he or she is. *Noun.*
—To frighten into doing something. Mary *bullies* her little brother into running errands for her. *Verb.*
  bul·ly (bool′ē) *noun, plural* **bullies;** *verb,* **bullied, bullying.**

bumblebee A large bee with a thick, hairy body. Most bumblebees have yellow and black stripes across their backs.
  bum·ble·bee (bum′bəl bē′) *noun, plural* **bumblebees.**

bump **1.** To strike or knock suddenly. The two cars *bumped* into each other. Tom *bumped* his knee on the chair. **2.** To move with jerks and jolts. The wagon *bumped* along the dirt road. *Verb.*
—**1.** A heavy knock or blow. The *bump* on his head made him dizzy. **2.** A swelling or lump. There is a *bump* on my knee where the baseball hit it. *Noun.*
  bump (bump) *verb,* **bumped, bumping;** *noun, plural* **bumps.**

Bumblebee

bumper A heavy metal bar across the front or back of a car or truck. A bumper protects the car or truck from damage if it bumps into something. *Noun.*
—Very large. The farmer had a *bumper* crop of wheat this year. *Adjective.*
  bump·er (bum′-pər) *noun, plural* **bumpers;** *adjective.*

Bumper

bun A sweetened roll. A bun often has raisins, cheese, or fruit in it.
  bun (bun) *noun, plural* **buns.**

bunch **1.** A number of things grouped, fastened, or growing together. We bought a *bunch* of grapes at the fruit store. Put that *bunch* of letters in the desk drawer. **2.** A group of people. A *bunch* of us are going to the movies. *Noun.*
—To gather together. The kittens *bunched* together to keep warm. *Verb.*
  bunch (bunch) *noun, plural* **bunches;** *verb,* **bunched, bunching.**

bundle A number of things tied or wrapped together. Put that *bundle* of newspapers in the garbage can. Mother's arms were full of *bundles* from the store. *Noun.*
—To tie or wrap together. Mary *bundled* some dirty clothes for the laundry. *Verb.*
  bun·dle (bund′əl) *noun, plural* **bundles;** *verb,* **bundled, bundling.**

bungalow A small house. A bungalow usually has only one storey.
  bun·ga·low (bung′gə lō′) *noun, plural* **bungalows.**

bunk A narrow bed that is built against a wall like a shelf.
  bunk (bungk) *noun, plural* **bunks.**

Bunsen burner An instrument that uses a mixture of air and gas to make a very hot, blue flame. Bunsen burners are often used in science laboratories.
  Bun·sen burner (bun′sən).

bunt To tap a baseball so that it goes only a short distance. The batter *bunted* the ball. *Verb.*
—A baseball that has been bunted. *Noun.*
  bunt (bunt) *verb,* **bunted, bunting;** *noun, plural* **bunts.**

buoy **1.** A floating object that is anchored. Buoys are used to warn ships of dangerous rocks or to show the safe way through a channel. **2.** Something used by a person to keep floating in water; life buoy.
  bu·oy (boi *or* bōō′ē) *noun, plural* **buoys.**

bur A prickly covering of a seed. This word is usually spelled **burr.** Look up **burr** for more information.

burden **1.** Something that is carried; load. The mule carried its *burden* of logs easily. **2.** Something very hard to bear. He found it a *burden* to earn enough money to support his large family. *Noun.*

Buoy

at; āpe; cär; end; mē; it; īce; hot; ōld;
wood; fōōl; oil; out; up; turn; sing;
thin; this; hw in white; zh in treasure.
ə stands for a in about, e in taken,
i in pencil, o in lemon, and u in circus.

—To put too heavy a load on. The heavy snow *burdened* the branches of the small tree. *Verb.*

bur·den (burd′ən) *noun, plural* **burdens;** *verb,* **burdened, burdening.**

bureau 1. A chest of drawers. I keep my sweaters, shirts, and socks in my *bureau.* 2. A department of a government. I listen to the reports from the weather *bureau* on the radio. 3. An office or agency. Father bought our airplane tickets at the travel *bureau.*

bu·reau (byoor′ō) *noun, plural* **bureaus.**

burglar A person who breaks into a house, store, or other place to steal something. *Burglars* broke into the hotel room and stole some valuable jewels.

bur·glar (bur′glər) *noun, plural* **burglars.**

burial The act of putting a dead body in the earth, a tomb, or the sea. Many people were present at the *burial* of the famous general.

bur·i·al (ber′ē əl) *noun, plural* **burials.**

buried The dog has *buried* his favourite bone. Look up **bury** for more information.

bur·ied (ber′ēd) *verb.*

burlap A coarse cloth. Burlap is used for making bags, curtains, and wall coverings.

bur·lap (bur′lap) *noun, plural* **burlaps.**

burn 1. To set on fire; be on fire. Joe will *burn* the pile of leaves he has raked in the yard. The damp wood *burned* slowly. 2. To injure by fire or heat. The child *burned* her hand on the hot stove. 3. To make by fire or heat. A spark from the campfire *burned* a hole in Jim's sweater. 4. To feel or cause to feel hot. The child *burned* with fever. The pepper *burned* his tongue. 5. To use for light or heat. Our furnace *burns* oil. *Verb.*

—An injury caused by fire or heat. She got a *burn* on her hand from the hot iron. *Noun.*

burn (burn) *verb,* **burned** or **burnt, burning;** *noun, plural* **burns.**

burner The part of a stove or furnace from which the flame comes. Put the pot on the back *burner* of the stove.

burn·er (bur′nər) *noun, plural* **burners.**

burnt The spark *burnt* a hole in the rug. Look up **burn** for more information.

burnt (burnt) *verb.*

burr 1. A prickly covering of the seed of some plants. Burrs stick to cloth and fur. 2. Any plant that has burrs. This word is also spelled **bur.**

burr (bur) *noun, plural* **burrs.**

burro A small donkey. Burros are used for riding and for carrying loads. ▲ Other words that sound like this are **borough** and **burrow.**

bur·ro (bur′ō) *noun, plural* **burros.**

burrow A hole dug in the ground by an animal. An animal uses its burrow to live in or hide in. *Noun.*

—1. To dig a hole in the ground. Moles and gophers *burrow.* 2. To search. She *burrowed* in her purse for her keys. *Verb.* ▲ Other words that sound like this are **borough** and **burro.**

bur·row (bur′ō) *noun, plural* **burrows;** *verb,* **burrowed, burrowing.**

burst 1. To break open suddenly. The balloon *burst* when I stuck it with a pin. The buds on the roses were ready to *burst* into bloom. 2. To be very full. My closet is *bursting* with clothes. 3. To come or go suddenly. Tom *burst* into my room. The child *burst* into tears when she broke her doll. *Verb.*

—1. The act of bursting; outbreak. There was a *burst* of laughter when he told the joke. 2. A sudden effort. With a *burst* of speed the runner won the race. *Noun.*

burst (burst) *verb,* **burst, bursting;** *noun, plural* **bursts.**

bury 1. To put a dead body in the earth, a tomb, or the sea. The boys *buried* their dead dog in the yard. 2. To cover up; hide. Our dog likes to *bury* its bones. ▲ Another word that sounds like this is **berry.**

bur·y (ber′ē) *verb,* **buried, burying.**

bus A large vehicle with a motor and rows of seats for carrying many passengers. Buses usually go along a regular route. She goes to school by *bus. Noun.*

—To carry or go in a bus. Our town *buses* pupils to school. *Verb.*

bus (bus) *noun, plural* **buses** or **busses;** *verb,* **bussed, bussing** or **bused, busing.**

Bus

bush 1. A woody plant smaller than a tree; a shrub. Berries and roses grow on bushes. 2. *Canadian.* A part of a farm that has not been cleared of trees. 3. *Canadian.* **the bush.** A wilderness area covered with trees.

bush (boosh) *noun, plural* **bushes.**

bushel A measure of volume in the Imperial System of Measure. A *bushel* is equal to four pecks or 32 quarts. We bought a *bushel* of corn to roast for our picnic.

bush·el (boosh′əl) *noun, plural* **bushels.**

bush line *Canadian.* An airline flying into and out of the bush.

bush pilot *Canadian.* A person who flies small planes into and out of the bush.

bushy Thick and spreading like a bush. A squirrel has a *bushy* tail.
bush·y (boosh′ē) *adjective,* **bushier, bushiest.**

business 1. The work that a person does to earn a living. Mr. Brown's *business* is farming. 2. A store, factory, or other similar thing. 3. The buying and selling of things; trade. The garage is doing a big *business* in snow tires this winter. 4. Matter or affair. What *business* is it of yours how he wears his hair?
busi·ness (biz′nəs) *noun, plural* **businesses.**

businessman An owner of or worker in a business. A store manager is a *businessman.*
busi·ness·man (biz′nəs man′) *noun, plural* **businessmen.**

businesswoman A woman who owns or works in a business.
busi·ness·wom·an (biz′nəs woom′ən) *noun, plural* **businesswomen.**

bust A statue of a person's head and shoulders. There is a *bust* of Sir John A. Macdonald near the entrance to our post office.
bust (bust) *noun, plural* **busts.**

bustle To move or hurry in an excited or noisy way. Mother and Father *bustled* around getting everything ready for the birthday party. *Verb.*
—Noisy, excited activity. There was much *bustle* as the family packed to go away on holiday. *Noun.*
bus·tle (bus′əl) *verb,* **bustled, bustling;** *noun.*

Bust

busy 1. Doing something; active. Mary is *busy* making plans to go to the circus. 2. Full of activity. Today was a *busy* day. 3. In use. When I telephoned, her line was *busy. Adjective.*
—To make busy; keep busy. Betty *busied* herself with cleaning the room. *Verb.*
bus·y (biz′ē) *adjective,* **busier, busiest;** *verb,* **busied, busying.**

but Tom is tall, *but* his sister is short. Beth's bruised knee hurt, *but* she did not cry. Jo delivers newspapers every day *but* Sunday. You were there *but* ten minutes ago.
▲ Another word that sounds like this is **butt.**
but (but) *conjunction; preposition; adverb.*

butcher A person who cuts up and sells meat. I went to the *butcher* to buy lamb.
butch·er (booch′ər) *noun, plural* **butchers.**

butler The head servant in a household.
but·ler (but′lər) *noun, plural* **butlers.**

butt¹ 1. The thicker or larger end of something. The boy held the *butt* of the rifle against his shoulder as he aimed at the target. 2. An end that is left over. Please be sure to put your cigarette *butts* in the garbage.
▲ Another word that sounds like this is **but.**
butt (but) *noun, plural* **butts.**

butt² A person or thing that people make fun of. ▲ Another word that sounds like this is **but.**
butt (but) *noun, plural* **butts.**

butt³ To strike hard with the head or the horns. The goat *butted* the gate. *Verb.*
—A push or blow with the head or the horns. The calf gave its mother a playful *butt. Noun.*
▲ Another word that sounds like this is **but.**
butt (but) *verb,* **butted, butting;** *noun, plural* **butts.**

butter 1. A solid, yellowish fat. Butter is separated from cream or milk by churning. 2. A spread that is like butter. Butter can be made from apples or from peanuts. *Noun.*
—To spread with butter. Be sure to *butter* the bread for the sandwiches. *Verb.*
but·ter (but′ər) *noun, plural* **butters;** *verb,* **buttered, buttering.**

buttercup A common plant that has yellow flowers shaped like cups.
but·ter·cup (but′ər kup′) *noun, plural* **buttercups.**

butterfly An insect with a thin body and four large brightly-coloured wings. Butterflies fly in the daytime.
but·ter·fly (but′ər flī′) *noun, plural* **butterflies.**

Butterfly

buttermilk The sour liquid that is left after milk or cream has been churned to make butter.
but·ter·milk (but′ər milk′) *noun, plural* **buttermilks.**

---

at; āpe; cär; end; mē; it; īce; hot; ōld;
wood; fōōl; oil; out; up; turn; sing;
thin; <u>th</u>is; hw in white; zh in treasure.
ə stands for a in about, e in taken,
i in pencil, o in lemon, and u in circus.

butternut   The oily nut of a tree that is related to the walnut.
> **but·ter·nut** (but′ər nut′) *noun, plural* **butternuts.**

butterscotch   A candy made from brown sugar and butter.
> **but·ter·scotch** (but′ər skoch′) *noun.*

button   **1.** A small, round flat thing. A button is used to fasten clothing or to ornament it. Will you please sew the *button* back on my coat? The waiter wore a red uniform with brass *buttons*. **2.** A knob that is turned or pushed to make something work. Press the elevator *button* if you want the elevator to stop at this floor. *Noun.*
—To fasten with buttons. Jack *buttoned* his overcoat because it was cold out. *Verb.*
> **but·ton** (but′ən) *noun, plural* **buttons;** *verb,* **buttoned, buttoning.**

buttress   A strong, heavy thing built against a wall to hold it up or make it stronger. *Noun.*
—To make something stronger with a buttress. The walls of the cathedral were *buttressed. Verb.*
> **but·tress** (but′rəs) *noun, plural* **buttresses;** *verb,* **buttressed, buttressing.**

buy   To get something by paying money for it; purchase. John can *buy* an ice-cream cone for twenty-five cents. Our family *bought* a new car last year. *Verb.*
—A bargain. That used car is a good *buy. Noun.* ▲ Another word that sounds like this is **by.**
> **buy** (bī) *verb,* **bought, buying;** *noun, plural* **buys.**

buyer   A person who buys. Tom put his car up for sale, but there have been no *buyers*.
> **buy·er** (bī′ər) *noun, plural* **buyers.**

buzz   A humming sound. A bee makes a buzz. The *buzz* of talking stopped when the teacher came into the room. *Noun.*
—**1.** To make a humming sound. The mosquito *buzzed* in my ear all night. **2.** To fly an airplane low over something. The pilot *buzzed* the bridge. *Verb.*
> **buzz** (buz) *noun, plural* **buzzes;** *verb,* **buzzed, buzzing.**

buzzard   A very large bird that has a sharp, hooked beak and long, sharp claws. A buzzard is a kind of hawk. Buzzards are birds of prey.
> **buz·zard** (buz′ərd) *noun, plural* **buzzards.**

buzzer   A thing that makes a buzzing sound as a signal. It is worked by electricity. He pressed the *buzzer*, and Joan opened the front door.
> **buzz·er** (buz′ər) *noun, plural* **buzzers.**

by   There is a table *by* the bed. The bus went *by* us. He came *by* train. That book was written *by* Charles Dickens. We buy milk *by* the litre. Please be here *by* eight o'clock. My friend's house is close *by*. A car passed *by*. ▲ Another word that sounds like this is **buy.**
> **by** (bī) *preposition; adverb.*

bygone   Gone by; past; former. The old man thought of his *bygone* school years. *Adjective.*
—**bygones.** Something gone by or past. Let's make up our quarrel and let *bygones* be *bygones. Noun.*
> **by·gone** (bī′gon′) *adjective; noun plural.*

by-pass   A road that turns off the main road. We took the *by-pass* to avoid all the traffic in the centre of town. *Noun.*
—To go around by a by-pass. The highway was built to *by-pass* the town. *Verb.*
> **by-pass** (bī′pas′) *noun, plural* **by-passes;** *verb,* **by-passed, by-passing.**

by-product   Something useful that comes from the making of something else. Buttermilk is a *by-product* of butter.
> **by-prod·uct** (bī′prod′əkt) *noun, plural* **by-products.**

bystander   A person who is at a place while something is happening but does not take part in it. Several *bystanders* watched the fight between the two boys.
> **by·stand·er** (bī′stand′ər) *noun, plural* **bystanders.**

Buzzard

at; āpe; cär; end; mē; it; īce; hot; ōld; wood; fool; oil; out; up; turn; sing; thin; this; hw in white; zh in treasure. ə stands for a in about, e in taken, i in pencil, o in lemon, and u in circus.

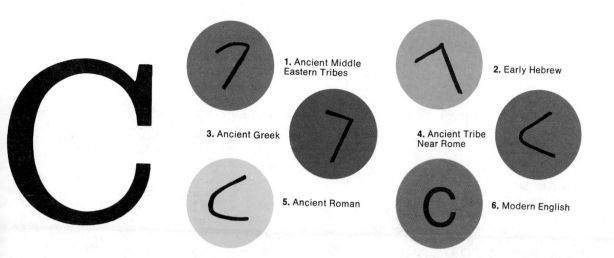

C

1. Ancient Middle Eastern Tribes
2. Early Hebrew
3. Ancient Greek
4. Ancient Tribe Near Rome
5. Ancient Roman
6. Modern English

C is the third letter of the alphabet. Although the letter **C**, as we pronounce it today, was not used before Roman times, the history of the letter goes back to the earliest alphabets. The oldest form of **C** was the third letter in the alphabet used by several ancient tribes (1) in the Middle East. In the early Hebrew alphabet (2) this letter was called *gimel* and was used to stand for the hard *g* sound, such as the *g* in *game*. The ancient Greeks (3) borrowed this letter about 3000 years ago. This letter was then borrowed by an ancient tribe (4) that settled north of Rome about 2800 years ago. These people made no distinction between the hard *g* sound and the *k* sound, such as the *k* in *king*. Because of this, they began to use this early form of **C** to stand for both sounds. When the Romans (5) borrowed the letter, they also used it to stand for both the hard *g* and *k* sounds. The *k* sound was used more often than the hard *g* sound in the language of the Romans. So the Roman letter **C** was used more and more to stand for the *k* sound and was used less and less to stand for the hard *g* sound. About 2200 years ago, the Romans began using **C** to stand for only the *k* sound and made up a new letter, **G**, to stand for the hard *g* sound. Since that time, the capital letter **C** has been written almost exactly as we write it today (6).

c, C The third letter of the alphabet.
c, C (sē) *noun, plural* **c's, C's.**

cab 1. An automobile that can be hired; taxi-cab. We took a *cab* to the airport. 2. A carriage that can be hired. It has a driver and is pulled by one horse. 3. The covered part of a truck, steam shovel, or other machine. The driver or the operator of the machine sits in the cab.
cab (kab) *noun, plural* **cabs.**

cabbage A plant that has thick green or reddish-purple leaves that form a round head. The leaves of the cabbage are eaten as a vegetable.
cab·bage (kab′əj) *noun, plural* **cabbages.**

cabin 1. A small, simple house. Cabins are often built of rough boards or logs. Our family rented a *cabin* on the lake for the summer. 2. A private room on a ship. They were seasick and spent most of the trip across the ocean in their *cabin*. 3. A place in an aircraft for passengers, crew members, or cargo.
cab·in (kab′in) *noun, plural* **cabins.**

cabinet 1. A piece of furniture that has shelves or drawers. Most cabinets have doors. The dishes and glasses are kept in the kitchen *cabinet*. 2. A group of people who are chosen by the prime minister or premier to advise.
cab·i·net (kab′ən ət *or* kab′nət) *noun, plural* **cabinets.**

cabinet minister *Canadian.* A person who heads a department of the federal or a provincial government.

cable 1. A strong, thick rope. Most cables are made up of wires that are twisted to-

Cabin

gether. The ship was held to the dock by huge *cables*. **2.** A bundle of wires with a covering around it for protection. It is used to carry an electric current. Telegraph messages are sent across the ocean by underwater cable. **3.** A message sent under the ocean by cable. *Noun.*

—To send a message by cable. *Verb.*

ca·ble (kā′bəl) *noun, plural* **cables;** *verb,* **cabled, cabling.**

cable car A car drawn by an overhead cable. It is used to carry people or things up and down a hill.

cable TV A system for sending special television programs to the television sets of persons who pay for this service.

caboose **1.** A railroad car that is at the end of a freight train. The trainmen or workmen live, rest, or work in the caboose. **2.** *Canadian.* A kind of cabin on wheels used by work crews of lumberjacks or grain harvesters.

Cable Car

ca·boose (kə-bo͞os′) *noun, plural* **cabooses.**

cacao An evergreen tree found in warm tropical climates. The seeds of this tree are used in making cocoa and chocolate.

ca·ca·o (kə kā′ō *or* kə kā′ō) *noun, plural* **cacaos.**

cache *Canadian.* **1.** A place for keeping food, furs, or other things safe. It is usually in the ground. **2.** The things kept in a cache. *Noun.*

—To hide or store things in a cache. *Verb.*

cache (kash) *noun, plural* **caches;** *verb,* **cached, caching.**

cactus A plant that has a thick stem covered with spines instead of leaves. Cactuses are found in desert areas of North and South America.

cac·tus (kak′təs) *noun, plural* **cactuses** or **cacti.**

Cactuses

cadet A young person who is a student in a military academy. Cadets train to be officers in the armed forces.

ca·det (kə det′) *noun, plural* **cadets.**

▲ The first meaning of **cadet** was "younger son or brother." In the past, the oldest son in a family always inherited his father's land. So a younger son often joined the army as his career. After a while, the word for younger son came to mean "a young man who joins the army to become an officer."

café A small restaurant. They sat at the outdoor *café* to have something to drink.

ca·fé (ka fā′) *noun, plural* **cafés.**

cafeteria A restaurant where a customer buys food at a counter and carries it to his table himself.

caf·e·te·ri·a (kaf′ə tēr′ē ə) *noun, plural* **cafeterias.**

caffeine A bitter white drug found in coffee, tea, and some soft drinks. Caffeine stimulates the body and helps to keep a person from feeling tired and sleepy. This word is also spelled **caffein.**

caf·feine (ka fēn′) *noun.*

cage **1.** An open structure that is closed in with wooden or metal bars or with wire mesh. The lion at the circus was put into a *cage* after the show. **2.** Something that has the same shape or use as a cage. The cashier at the amusement park sat in a *cage. Noun.*

—To put or keep in a cage. The scientist will *cage* the mice during the experiment. *Verb.*

cage (kāj) *noun, plural* **cages;** *verb,* **caged, caging.**

cake **1.** A baked mixture of flour, eggs, sugar, and flavouring. Many cakes are covered with icing. **2.** A flat, thin mass of food that is baked or fried. A pancake is a kind of cake. **3.** A flattened or shaped mass of anything. Please give me a *cake* of soap. *Noun.*

—To make into or become a hard, solid mass. The mud on his boots *caked* as it dried. *Verb.*

cake (kāk) *noun, plural* **cakes;** *verb,* **caked, caking.**

calculate **1.** To find out by using addition, subtraction, multiplication, or division. Karen will *calculate* how much each person owes for the flowers we bought. **2.** To figure out beforehand; estimate. The campers *calculated* that they had packed enough food for five days. **3.** To plan; intend. The politician's speech was *calculated* to make people vote for her.

cal·cu·late (kal′kyə lāt′) *verb,* **calculated, calculating.**

calculation The act of calculating. By the *calculation* of scientists, the sun is about 150 000 000 kilometres away from the earth.
cal·cu·la·tion (kal′kyə lā′shən) *noun, plural* **calculations.**

calculator A machine that can solve mathematical problems.
cal·cu·la·tor (kal′kyə lā′tər) *noun, plural* **calculators.**

calèche *Canadian.* A carriage with one seat, two wheels, and a folding top.
ca·lèche (kə lesh′) *noun, plural* **calèches.**

calendar 1. A chart showing the days, weeks, and months of a year. The *calendar* shows that my birthday falls on a Wednesday this year. 2. A schedule of events that will take place. In a court of law, cases to be tried are listed on a *calendar.*
cal·en·dar (kal′ən dər) *noun, plural* **calendars.**

calf[1] 1. A young cow or bull. 2. A young seal, elephant, or whale. 3. Leather that is made from the skin or hide of a calf.
calf (kaf) *noun, plural* **calves.**

calf[2] The fleshy part of the back of the leg, between the knee and the ankle.
calf (kaf) *noun, plural* **calves.**

Calgary Stampede *Canadian.* A famous rodeo held every July in Calgary, Alberta.
Cal·ga·ry Stampede (kal′gə rē).

calico A cotton material that has small, brightly coloured designs printed on it. I have a bedspread made of *calico. Noun.*
—1. Made of calico. Jane wore a *calico* dress. 2. Having spots; spotted. Sara has a *calico* cat. *Adjective.*
cal·i·co (kal′ə kō′) *noun, plural* **calicoes** or **calicos**; *adjective.*

Calico Cat

call 1. To speak or say in a loud voice. Please raise your hand when I *call* your name. 2. To ask or order to come. The cat will come if you *call.* We will have to *call* a cab if the rain doesn't stop soon. 3. To give a name to; name. She wants to *call* her new puppy "Daisy." 4. To telephone. They will *call* us from the airport when they arrive. 5. To make a short visit or stop. We will *call* at your

house about one o'clock tomorrow afternoon. *Verb.*
—1. A loud shout; cry. We heard Mother's *call* for someone to help her with the packages. 2. A particular sound or cry made by a bird or animal. Jack can recognize many different bird *calls.* 3. The act of getting in touch with someone by telephone. I will expect your *call* at about four o'clock. 4. A short visit or stop. The family doctor made a *call* to look at my little sister, who was ill. *Noun.*
call (käl) *verb,* **called, calling**; *noun, plural* **calls.**

callus A hardened and thickened place on the skin. People get calluses on their hands and feet.
cal·lus (kal′əs) *noun, plural* **calluses.**

calm 1. Not moving; still. The sea was *calm* after the storm. 2. Not excited or nervous; quiet. The people in the building stayed *calm* during the fire and got out safely. *Adjective.*
—A time during which there is quiet or stillness. There was a *calm* before the storm struck the town. *Noun.*
—To make or become calm. Mother sang to the baby to *calm* him after he was frightened. The noisy boys *calmed* down when the movie started. *Verb.*
calm (käm) *adjective,* **calmer, calmest**; *noun, plural* **calms**; *verb,* **calmed, calming.**

calorie 1. A unit that is used to measure the amount of heat in something. 2. A unit that is used to measure the amount of energy produced by food. One slice of white bread has about sixty-five calories.
cal·o·rie (kal′ər ē) *noun, plural* **calories.**

calves More than one calf. Look up **calf** for more information.
calves (kavz) *noun plural.*

came My friend *came* to dinner last night. Look up **come** for more information.
came (kām) *verb.*

camel A large animal that has a humped back, long legs, and a long neck. Camels are found in the deserts of northern Africa and central Asia. They are very strong and can go for days without water. They are used for

at; āpe; cär; end; mē; it; īce; hot; ōld;
wood; fōol; oil; out; up; turn; sing;
thin; this; hw in white; zh in treasure.
ə stands for a in about, e in taken,
i in pencil, o in lemon, and u in circus.

riding and carrying loads. The camel of northern Africa has one hump, and the camel of central Asia has two humps.

cam·el (kam′əl) *noun, plural* **camels.**

Camel

camera A device for taking photographs or motion pictures. Most cameras consist of a box that has an opening at one end to let the light in.

cam·er·a (kam′ər ə *or* kam′rə) *noun, plural* **cameras.**

camouflage A disguise or false appearance that is used to hide something. The camouflage of soldiers and military equipment with paint or leaves hides them from the enemy. The tan coat of a lion is a natural camouflage because it matches the colour of the dry grasses where the lion lives. *Noun.*
—To change the appearance of something in order to hide or trick. The soldiers *camouflaged* the tank by covering it with bushes and branches. *Verb.*

cam·ou·flage (kam′ə fläzh′) *noun, plural* **camouflages;** *verb,* **camouflaged, camouflaging.**

camp An outdoor place with tents or cabins where people live or sleep for a time. The soldiers set up *camp* near the river. Sue will go to a girls' *camp* in the mountains this summer. *Noun.*
—To set up and live in a camp. We *camped* out on our trip through the eastern part of Canada. *Verb.*

camp (kamp) *noun, plural* **camps;** *verb,* **camped, camping.**

campaign A series of actions that are carried on to bring about a special result. He worked on Mr. Lee's *campaign* for election as mayor. *Noun.*
—To carry on or take part in a campaign. Are you going to *campaign* for Jan for class president? *Verb.*

cam·paign (kam pān′) *noun, plural* **campaigns;** *verb,* **campaigned, campaigning.**

camper 1. A person who stays at or lives in a camp. 2. A car, truck, or trailer that is built or used for camping. We slept in the *camper* on our trip.

camp·er (kam′pər) *noun, plural* **campers.**

campfire An outdoor fire that is used for cooking or keeping warm in a camp.

camp·fire (kamp′fīr′) *noun, plural* **campfires.**

camphor A white substance that has a strong odour. Camphor is used in mothballs, in some medicines, and in making plastics.

cam·phor (kam′fər) *noun.*

campus The grounds and buildings of a school, college, or university.

cam·pus (kam′pəs) *noun, plural* **campuses.**

can¹ She *can* walk faster than you. The car *can* hold five people. He *can* speak French.

can (kan) *verb.*

can² A container made of metal. Most cans have lids or covers. Put the old rags in the garbage *can. Noun.*
—To put into or preserve in a can. *Verb.*

can (kan) *noun, plural* **cans;** *verb,* **canned, canning.**

Canada The country in the northern part of North America. Its capital is Ottawa.

Can·a·da (kan′ə də) *noun.*

▲ The word **Canada** comes from an Indian word *canata* which means a village or a community.

Canada balsam A sticky resin from the balsam fir tree.

Canada Day A holiday celebrated on July 1 in honour of Confederation.

Canada Goose

Canada goose A large, wild North American goose with a black head and neck, and a grey-brown body. It is also called a **gronker.**

Canada jay A black and grey North American jay. It is also known as a **whisky-jack.** Look up **whisky-jack** for an illustration.

Canada lynx A kind of lynx found in northern and western Canada.

Canadian A person who was born in or is a citizen of Canada. *Noun.*
—Of Canada. Hockey is a *Canadian* sport. *Adjective.*
Ca·na·di·an (kə nā′ dē ən) *noun, plural* **Canadians;** *adjective.*

Canadian Armed Forces The land, sea, and air forces that defend Canada.

Canadian Broadcasting Corporation The public television and radio network.

Canadian English The English spoken in Canada.

Canadian French The French spoken in Canada.

Canadianism 1. A word or expression which comes from or is most commonly used in Canada. 2. A Canadian custom. 3. The pride of Canadians in Canada or an instance of this pride.
Can·a·di·an·ism (kə nā′dē ən iz′əm) *noun, plural* **Canadianisms.**

Canadian National Railways The public railway system.

Canadian Pacific Railway The private railway system owned by Canadian Pacific Limited.

Canadian Shield The very large formation of ancient rock covering almost half of Canada in the north.

Canadien A French Canadian man or boy.
Can·a·di·en (ka na dyen′) *noun, plural* **Canadiens.**

Canadienne A French Canadian woman or girl.
Can·a·di·enne (ka na dyen′) *noun, plural* **Canadiennes.**

canal A waterway dug across land. A canal is used for boats and ships to travel through, and for carrying water from lakes or rivers to places that need it.
ca·nal (kə nal′) *noun, plural* **canals.**

canary 1. A small yellow songbird. Canaries are often kept as pets. 2. A light, bright yellow colour. *Noun.*
—Having the colour canary; light, bright yellow. *Adjective.*
ca·nar·y (kə ner′ē) *noun, plural* **canaries;** *adjective.*

cancel 1. To do away with or stop. Did you *cancel* your dentist appointment? The foot-ball game was *cancelled* because of snow. 2. To cross out or mark with a line or lines to show that it cannot be used again. The post office will *cancel* the stamp on the letter.
can·cel (kan′səl) *verb,* **cancelled, cancelling** or **canceled, canceling.**

cancer A disease in which a cell or group of cells begin to divide and grow more rapidly than is normal. Cancer destroys healthy tissues and organs and can cause death.
can·cer (kan′sər) *noun.*

candidate A person who seeks or is put forward by others for an office or honour. Mrs. Lachine has agreed to be the Liberal *candidate* for Hochelaga in the next election.
can·di·date (kan′də dāt′) *noun, plural* **candidates.**

candle A stick of wax or tallow formed around a wick, or string that will burn. A candle is burned to give light.
can·dle (kand′əl) *noun, plural* **candles.**

candlestick A holder for a candle.
can·dle·stick (kand′əl stik′) *noun, plural* **candlesticks.**

candy A sweet food made of sugar or syrup with flavourings, nuts, or fruit. I love chocolate *candy.* Ray ate a lemon *candy. Noun.*
—To cover or cook with sugar. Mother is going to *candy* the fruit. *Verb.*
can·dy (kan′dē) *noun, plural* **candies;** *verb,* **candied, candying.**

cane 1. A stick used to help someone walk. Most canes are made of wood. Jenny used a *cane* after she sprained her ankle. 2. The long, woody, jointed stem of the bamboo, reed, and other tall grass plants. Cane is used in making furniture. 3. A plant that has a long, woody, jointed stem. Bamboo is a cane.
cane (kān) *noun, plural* **canes.**

cannibal A person who eats the flesh of humans.
can·ni·bal (kan′ə bəl) *noun, plural* **cannibals.**

cannon A large, heavy gun that is mounted on wheels or some other base.
can·non (kan′ən) *noun, plural* **cannons** or **cannon.**

cannot Can not. I *cannot* come tomorrow.
can·not (kan′ot *or* ka not′) *verb.*

canoe A light, narrow boat that is moved by

at; āpe; cär; end; mē; it; īce; hot; ōld; wood; fōōl; oil; out; up; turn; sing; thin; this; hw in white; zh in treasure. ə stands for a in about, e in taken, i in pencil, o in lemon, and u in circus.

hand with a paddle. Most canoes are pointed at both ends. *Noun.*
—To paddle or go in a canoe. We will *canoe* around the lake after lunch. *Verb.*
> **ca·noe** (kə nōō′) *noun, plural* **canoes;** *verb,* **canoed, canoeing.**

canopy A covering that is made of cloth or other material. A canopy is hung over a bed, throne, or entrance to a building.
> **can·o·py** (kan′ə pē) *noun, plural* **canopies.**

can't I *can't* go with you; I have to study.
> **can't** (kant) contraction for **cannot.**

cantaloupe A kind of melon that has a rough, pale green or yellow skin and sweet, yellowish-orange flesh.
> **can·ta·loupe** (kan′tə lōp′) *noun, plural* **cantaloupes.**

canteen 1. A small metal container for carrying water or other liquids to drink. 2. A store in a school or factory that sells food, drinks, and other things.
> **can·teen** (kan·tēn′) *noun, plural* **canteens.**

Canuck *Canadian.* A Canadian.
> **can·uck** (kə nuk′) *noun, plural* **Canucks.**

canvas A strong, heavy cloth made

Canteen

of cotton, flax, or hemp. It is used to make things that must be strong and last for a long time. Tents, sails, certain pieces of clothing, and boat and truck covers are made of canvas. Oil paintings are usually painted on pieces of canvas.
> **can·vas** (kan′vəs) *noun, plural* **canvases.**

canyon A deep valley with very high, steep sides. A canyon often has a stream running through it.
> **can·yon** (kan′yən) *noun, plural* **canyons.**

cap 1. A close-fitting covering for the head. Most caps have a short brim or no brim. Nurses and policemen wear caps. 2. Something that is used or shaped like a cap. John took the *cap* off the bottle of soda. I lost the *cap* to my fountain pen. 3. A paper wrapping or covering that contains a small amount of explosive. Caps are used in toy guns. *Noun.*
—To put a cap on; cover with a cap. Please *cap* the bottle when you're finished. *Verb.*
> **cap** (kap) *noun, plural* **caps;** *verb,* **capped, capping.**

capable Having or showing ability; able. Joan is a very *capable* driver. Our team is *capable* of winning the city championship.
> **ca·pa·ble** (kā′pə bəl) *adjective.*

capacity The amount that can be held in a space. The car's gas tank has a *capacity* of twenty litres.
> **ca·pac·i·ty** (kə pas′ə tē) *noun, plural* **capacities.**

cape¹ A piece of clothing without sleeves. A cape is worn loosely over the shoulders. The nurse wore a *cape* over her uniform.
> **cape** (kāp) *noun, plural* **capes.**

cape² A pointed piece of land that sticks out from the coastline into the sea or a lake.
> **cape** (kāp) *noun, plural* **capes.**

capital¹ 1. A city or town where the government of a country or province is located. Winnipeg is the *capital* of Manitoba. Ottawa is the *capital* of Canada. 2. A large form of a letter of the alphabet. A, B, C, and D are *capitals.* 3. The total amount of money or property that is owned by a company or person. My father has enough *capital* to start his own business. *Noun.*
—1. Being the most important; main; chief. Madrid is Spain's *capital* city. 2. Having to do with the death penalty. Many countries have done away with *capital* punishment. *Adjective.* ▲ Another word that sounds like this is **Capitol.**
> **cap·i·tal** (kap′it əl) *noun, plural* **capitals;** *adjective.*

Canyon

capital² The top part of a column or pillar. The columns of the building had carved *capitals.* ▲ Another word that sounds like this is **Capitol.**

cap·i·tal (kap′it əl) *noun, plural* **capitals.**

capitalism An economic system in which land, factories, and other means of producing goods are owned and controlled by individual people instead of by the government. The economic system of Canada is based on capitalism.

cap·i·tal·ism (kap′it əl·iz′əm) *noun.*

capitalize To write or print with a capital letter or letters, or begin with a capital letter. You should always *capitalize* proper names.

cap·i·tal·ize (kap′it əl īz′) *verb,* **capitalized, capitalizing.**

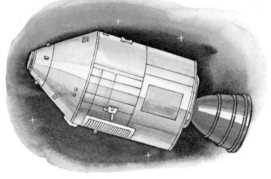

Capital

Capitol 1. The building in which the U.S. Congress meets in Washington, D.C. 2. The building in which a state legislature meets. ▲ Another word that sounds like this is **capital.**

Cap·i·tol (kap′it əl) *noun.*

capsize To turn upside down. The strong wind *capsized* the small sailboat. The sailors held on to the sides of the boat after it *capsized.*

cap·size (kap′sīz *or* kap sīz′) *verb,* **capsized, capsizing.**

Space Capsule

capsule 1. A small case that holds a dose of medicine and can be swallowed whole. When you swallow a capsule, the case dissolves in your stomach and the medicine is used by your body. 2. The part of a spacecraft that carries the astronauts. The capsule is the part that separates from the rocket after the spacecraft is launched.

cap·sule (kap′səl) *noun, plural* **capsules.**

captain 1. A person who is the leader of a group of people. Susan was *captain* of the girl's volleyball team. 2. A person who is in charge of a ship. My uncle is the *captain* of a fishing boat. 3. An officer in the Canadian Armed Forces. In the land and air elements, a captain is next below a major. In the sea element, a captain is below an admiral. *Noun.*
—To be the captain of; lead. John will *captain* the basketball team next year. *Verb.*

cap·tain (kap′tən) *noun, plural* **captains;** *verb,* **captained, captaining.**

caption The word or words under a picture that tell who or what it is. I wasn't sure who the man in the newspaper photograph was until I read the *caption* under it.

cap·tion (kap′shən) *noun, plural* **captions.**

captive A prisoner. The soldiers kept the *captives* in a jail inside the fort. *Noun.*
—Held prisoner. The *captive* lion was kept in a cage. *Adjective.*

cap·tive (kap′tiv) *noun, plural* **captives;** *adjective.*

capture To catch and hold a person, animal, or thing. The hunters *captured* a lion in the jungle. The exciting book *captured* Linda's interest, and she didn't hear her mother call her. *Verb.*
—The act of capturing a person, animal, or thing. The *capture* of the bank robber took place the day after the robbery. *Noun.*

cap·ture (kap′chər) *verb,* **captured, capturing;** *noun, plural* **captures.**

car 1. An automobile. A car is a vehicle with four wheels and an engine. 2. Any kind of vehicle that moves on wheels and is used to carry people or things from one place to another. A railroad train is made up of different cars that are joined together.

car (kär) *noun, plural* **cars.**

caramel 1. Sugar that is browned and melted by being heated slowly. Caramel is used in cooking to colour and flavour gravy, cookies, and other foods. 2. A light-brown,

at; āpe; cär; end; mē; it; īce; hot; ōld;
wood; fōōl; oil; out; up; turn; sing;
thin; this; hw in white; zh in treasure.
ə stands for a in about, e in taken,
i in pencil, o in lemon, and u in circus.

soft candy flavoured with caramel.

car·a·mel (kar′ə məl) *noun, plural* **caramels.**

carat A unit of weight for diamonds and other precious stones. A carat has a mass of 0.2 gm. ▲ Another word that sounds like this is **carrot.**

car·at (kar′ət) *noun, plural* **carats.**

caravan A group of people who travel together. A *caravan* of army trucks and soldiers moved slowly along the highway. The Arab merchants and their camels travelled in a *caravan* across the desert.

car·a·van (kar′ə van′) *noun, plural* **caravans.**

carbohydrate A compound made up of carbon, hydrogen, and oxygen. Carbohydrates are made by green plants. Starches and sugars are carbohydrates.

car·bo·hy·drate (kär′bō hī′drāt) *noun, plural* **carbohydrates.**

carbon A chemical element that is found in coal and charcoal. Diamonds and graphite are carbon in the form of crystals.

car·bon (kär′bən) *noun.*

carbon dioxide A gas that is made up of carbon and oxygen. Carbon dioxide has no colour or odour. It is part of the air we breathe. When we breathe out, we put carbon dioxide in the air. Plants take in carbon dioxide from the air to make food. Carbon dioxide is used in soft drinks, fire extinguishers, and refrigerators.

carbon di·ox·ide (dī ok′sīd).

carbon monoxide A poisonous gas that has no colour or odour. Carbon monoxide is formed when carbon burns but does not burn up completely. Carbon monoxide is found in the gases that come out of the exhaust pipes of automobiles.

carbon mon·ox·ide (mə nok′sīd).

carburetor The part of an engine in which gasoline is mixed with air to make a mixture that is explosive.

car·bu·re·tor (kär′bə rā′tər) *noun, plural* **carburetors.**

carcass The body of a dead animal.

car·cass (kär′kəs) *noun, plural* **carcasses.**

card A flat piece of stiff paper that has words or numbers or some kind of design on it. People have membership cards for libraries and for clubs they belong to. Schools give report cards and stores sell post cards. We play many games with decks of playing cards.

card (kärd) *noun, plural* **cards.**

cardboard A heavy, stiff paper. Cardboard is used to make boxes and posters.

card·board (kärd′bōrd′) *noun.*

cardinal 1. One of the group of important officials who rank just below the Pope in the Roman Catholic Church. They help the Pope govern the church and when he dies, they meet and elect the new Pope. Cardinals wear bright red robes and hats. 2. A songbird that has a crest of feathers on its head. The male cardinal has bright red feathers with a black patch around its bill. 3. A bright, deep red colour. *Noun.*
—1. Of the greatest importance; chief. One of the *cardinal* issues in the town election was the vote on the new park and playground. 2. Having the colour cardinal; bright, deep red. *Adjective.*

Cardinal

car·di·nal (kärd′ən əl) *noun, plural* **cardinals;** *adjective.*

cardinal number A number that tells how many. One, two, three, four, and so on are cardinal numbers.

care 1. A feeling of worry or unhappiness. The girls didn't have a *care* in the world as they ran down the beach splashing in the waves. 2. Close and serious attention. Don dried his mother's good dishes with great *care.* Take *care* when you cross the street. 3. Keeping or custody; protection. When he was on vacation, Brad left his cats in the *care* of his best friend. The sick child was under a doctor's *care. Noun.*
—1. To have an interest, liking, or concern about a person or thing. He doesn't *care* what people think of the way he dresses. 2. To have a feeling against; mind. Do you *care* if I borrow your bicycle? 3. To want or wish. Would you *care* to go to the movies with me? *Verb.*

care (ker) *noun, plural* **cares;** *verb,* **cared, caring.**

career The work that a person chooses to do through life. Eva chose a *career* as a nurse. Newspaper reporters meet many interesting people in their *career.*

ca·reer (kə rēr′) *noun, plural* **careers.**

carefree Happy and gay with nothing to worry about. Margaret and her friends felt absolutely *carefree* as they started off on their picnic.

care·free (ker′frē′) *adjective.*

careful Paying close attention; watchful. When you are careful, you are alert and think about what you are doing or saying. Before you cross a busy intersection, be *careful* and look both ways.

care·ful (ker′fəl) *adjective.*

careless Not paying close enough attention to what one is doing or saying. Jean was *careless* when she ran down the stairs, and she tripped and fell. He did not get a good mark on his book report because he made many *careless* spelling mistakes.

care·less (ker′ləs) *adjective.*

caress To touch or stroke gently and with love; pet. *Verb.*
—A gentle, loving touch or stroke. The *caress* of the boy's hand made the kitten purr. *Noun.*

ca·ress (kə res′) *verb,* caressed, caressing; *noun, plural* caresses.

cargo The goods carried by a ship, airplane, truck, or other vehicle. The ship unloaded a *cargo* of rice.

car·go (kär′gō) *noun, plural* cargoes or cargos.

caribou *Canadian.* The kind of reindeer found in Canada.

car·i·bou (kar′ə boō′) *noun, plural* caribou or caribous.

cariole *Canadian.* 1. A kind of light sleigh pulled by a horse. 2. a kind of sled for one person, drawn by dogs. *Noun.*
—To ride in a cariole. *Verb.*

car·i·ole (kar′ē ōl′) *noun, plural* carioles; *verb,* carioled, carioling or cariolled, cari-olling.

carnation A red, pink, or white flower that has a spicy, fragrant smell. The carnation grows on a plant that has thin, pointed leaves.

car·na·tion (kär nā′-shən) *noun, plural* car-nations.

carnival A fair or festival that has games, rides, and other amusements.

car·ni·val (kär′nə vəl) *noun, plural* carnivals.

carnivorous Eating the flesh of animals. Wolves, lions, dogs, and cats are carnivorous animals.

car·niv·o·rous (kär niv′ər əs) *adjective.*

carol A joyful song. We all sang Christmas *carols* around the tree. *Noun.*

Carnations

—To sing joyously. The children went from house to house *carolling. Verb.*

car·ol (kar′əl) *noun, plural* carols; *verb,* car-olled, carolling or caroled, caroling.

carp A fish that lives in fresh water and is used as food.

carp (kärp) *noun, plural* carps or carp.

carpenter A person who builds and repairs houses and other things made of wood.

car·pen·ter (kär′pən tər) *noun, plural* car-penters.

carpet 1. A covering for a floor, usually made of heavy woven fabric. 2. Anything like a carpet. The lawn was covered with a *carpet* of snow. *Noun.*
—To cover with a carpet. We are going to *carpet* the stairs in our house. *Verb.*

car·pet (kär′pət) *noun, plural* carpets; *verb,* carpeted, carpeting.

Baby Carriage

carriage 1. A vehicle that moves on wheels. Some carriages are used by people to travel from place to place and are pulled by horses. Baby carriages are small and light and are pushed by people. 2. A movable part of a machine that carries or holds up some other part. A carriage on a typewriter holds the paper and moves back and forth.

car·riage (kar′ij) *noun, plural* carriages.

carrier A person or thing that carries something. Railroads are carriers.

car·ri·er (kar′ē ər) *noun, plural* carriers.

at; āpe; cär; end; mē; it; īce; hot; ōld; wood; foōl; oil; out; up; turn; sing; thin; <u>th</u>is; hw in white; zh in treasure. ə stands for a in about, e in taken, i in pencil, o in lemon, and u in circus.

carrot The long, orange-coloured root of a plant. Carrots are eaten as a vegetable. ▲ Another word that sounds like this is **carat**.
car·rot (kar′ət) *noun, plural* **carrots.**

Carrot

carry 1. To hold something while moving it. Evelyn said she would *carry* my suitcase when it got too heavy for me. The pipes in our house *carry* water. 2. To have something. If you *carry* a pen, you have it in your pocket or pocketbook. If a store *carries* rubber boots, it has them there for you to buy. 3. To keep doing something; continue. Sometimes her brother *carries* his teasing too far and makes her angry. 4. To move a number from one column or place and add it where it belongs. When Mary added 23 and 39, she got 52 instead of 62 because she forgot to *carry* the 1 from the first column.
car·ry (kar′ē) *verb,* **carried, carrying.**

cart 1. A strong wagon with two wheels that is used to carry a load. Carts are pulled by horses, mules, or oxen. 2. A light vehicle with four wheels that is pushed by a person. We use carts in supermarkets to hold the groceries we take from the shelves. *Noun.*
—To move something in a cart. In many countries, farmers *cart* the vegetables they grow to the nearest town to sell them. *Verb.*
cart (kärt) *noun, plural* **carts;** *verb,* **carted, carting.**

Cart

cartilage A strong, flexible material that forms parts of the body of man and other animals that have a backbone. Cartilage is not as stiff or as hard as bone. Cartilage is the material that forms much of a person's nose.
car·ti·lage (kärt′əl əj) *noun.*

carton A box or container that is usually made of cardboard and comes in many shapes. Egg cartons are made to hold each egg separately. Milk sometimes comes in cartons. Our new television set was delivered in a strong *carton*. Chris drank a *carton* of orange juice.
car·ton (kärt′ən) *noun, plural* **cartons.**

cartoon A drawing that shows people or things in a way that makes you laugh. Some cartoons are put on movie film and seem to move. Comic strips are cartoons that appear in magazines and newspapers.
car·toon (kär tōon′) *noun, plural* **cartoons.**

cartridge 1. A small case that holds gunpowder and a bullet. Cartridges are made to be shot from a gun. 2. Any small case that holds something. Some pens are loaded with cartridges full of ink. Some cameras have special cartridges that hold the film. The needle of a record player is held in a cartridge.
car·tridge (kär′trij) *noun, plural* **cartridges.**

Cartwheel

cartwheel 1. The wheel of a cart. 2. A kind of jump from one's feet to one's hands and back again. If a person keeps his arms and legs straight when doing a cartwheel, they look like the spokes of a wheel as it turns. Acrobats often do cartwheels.
cart·wheel (kärt′wēl′ *or* kärt′hwēl′) *noun, plural* **cartwheels.**

carve 1. To cut meat into slices or pieces. Father will *carve* the turkey. 2. To make something beautiful by cutting. Artists *carve* statues out of wood and stone. Some furniture is *carved* with designs of flowers and animals.

carve (kärv) *verb*, **carved, carving.**

cascade A small waterfall. *Noun.*
—To flow down in waves like a small waterfall. The water from the flooded stream will *cascade* over the hill. *Verb.*

cas·cade (kas kād′) *noun, plural* **cascades;** *verb*, **cascaded, cascading.**

Cascade

case¹ **1.** An example of something. The forest fire was an obvious *case* of carelessness. **2.** The real facts; state of affairs. He says he has forgotten his keys, and if that is the *case*, we are all locked out. **3.** A person who is sick or hurt; patient. The doctor said that Kate was the third *case* of flu he had treated that day. **4.** A matter to be investigated or decided by law. The police had no suspects in the *case* of the museum robbery. The judge will make her decision on the kidnap *case* tomorrow.

case (kās) *noun, plural* **cases.**

in any case. No matter what happens. *In any case,* you are never to run out into the street without looking first to see if any cars are coming.

in case. In the event that; if. *In case* anything happens, call me right away. Bring your bathing suit *in case* we go swimming.

in case of. If there is. *In case of* rain, we will go to the movies rather than play a game of tennis.

case² A box or other container made to hold or cover something. Her new camera came in a leather *case*. We ordered a *case* of soft drinks for the picnic.

case (kās) *noun, plural* **cases.**

cash Money in the form of coins and paper bills. Instead of charging the dress, she paid *cash* for it. *Noun.*
—To get or give cash for. My father has to stop at the bank and *cash* a cheque before we can buy groceries. *Verb.*

cash (kash) *noun; verb*, **cashed, cashing.**

to cash in on. To take advantage of. The famous skater *cashed in on* her fame by making television commercials.

cashew A sweet nut that is shaped like a lima bean. It grows on an evergreen tree that is found in tropical countries.

cash·ew (kash′oo) *noun, plural* **cashews.**

cashier A person whose job it is to take care of money. In a store or restaurant the cashier takes money from people who are paying for something.

cash·ier (ka shēr′) *noun, plural* **cashiers.**

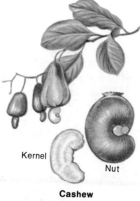
Kernel

Nut

Cashew

cashmere A very soft woollen fabric. Cashmere is woven from the silky hair of goats that live in Asia.

cash·mere (kazh′mēr *or* kash′mēr) *noun, plural* **cashmeres.**

cask A large wooden barrel that is used to hold wine or other liquids.

cask (kask) *noun, plural* **casks.**

casket A box made of wood or metal, in which the body of a dead person is put to be buried; coffin.

cas·ket (kas′kət) *noun, plural* **caskets.**

casserole A deep dish in which food can be cooked and served.

cas·se·role (kas′ə rōl′) *noun, plural* **casseroles.**

cassette **1.** A small case holding recording tape for a tape recorder or player. **2.** A case holding film to put into a camera.

cas·sette (kə set′) *noun, plural* **cassettes.**

cast **1.** To throw through the air. We *cast* our fishing line into the stream. **2.** To cause to fall; throw off. The tree *cast* a long shadow on the ground. **3.** To send or put. She *cast* her vote for her best friend in the election for class president. **4.** To pick the actor or actors who will take different roles in a play. **5.** To shape by pouring a soft material into a mould to harden. The artist *cast* a statue of a horse by pouring melted bronze into a plaster mould. *Verb.*

at; āpe; cär; end; mē; it; īce; hot; ōld;
wood; fool; oil; out; up; turn; sing;
thin; this; hw in white; zh in treasure.
ə stands for a in about, e in taken,
i in pencil, o in lemon, and u in circus.

—**1.** The act of throwing something. Betty made a long *cast* with her fishing line. **2.** Something that is given shape in a mold. He made a plaster *cast* of a deer. **3.** The actors in a play or other show. The whole *cast* came on stage to take a bow together. **4.** A stiff form that is shaped around a part of the body to help a broken bone heal. The doctor put a plaster *cast* on Bill's broken arm. *Noun.*

cast (kast) *verb,* **cast, casting;** *noun, plural* **casts.**

cast iron A hard, brittle kind of iron that is made by melting iron and pouring it into a mould.

castle **1.** A large building or group of buildings having high, thick walls with towers. Many castles had moats around them for defense against attack. Princes and nobles lived in castles in the Middle Ages. **2.** One of the pieces in a chess game; rook.

cas·tle (kas′əl) *noun, plural* **castles.**

casual Done or happening without serious thought or planning. Our neighbours sometimes make a *casual* visit to our house without calling up beforehand.

cas·u·al (kazh′ōō əl) *adjective.*

casualty A person who is injured or killed in an accident or a war. Soldiers who are captured by the enemy are also called casualties. The firemen reported twenty-five *casualties* in the fire.

cas·u·al·ty (kazh′ōō əl tē) *noun, plural* **casualties.**

cat **1.** A small furry animal that has short ears and a long tail. Cats are kept as pets and for catching mice and rats. **2.** Any animal of a group that includes lions, tigers, leopards, and also the kind of cats that are kept as pets in the home.

cat (kat) *noun, plural* **cats.**

catalogue A list. Libraries have *catalogues* of the titles, authors, and subject matter of all their books. Stores publish *catalogues* with pictures and prices of the things they have for sale. *Noun.*

—To make a list of; put in a list. Beverley *catalogued* all the stamps in her collection. *Verb.*

This word is also spelled **catalog.**

cat·a·logue (kat′əl og′) *noun, plural* **catalogues;** *verb,* **catalogued, cataloguing.**

catamaran **1.** *Canadian.* A kind of heavy sled used to haul logs or lumber. **2.** A sailboat with two hulls joined by a frame.

cat·a·mar·an (kat′ə mə ran′) *noun, plural* **catamarans.**

cataract **1.** A large, steep waterfall. **2.** A strong flood or downpour of water. When the dam broke, *cataracts* of water rushed through the streets of the town.

cat·a·ract (kat′ə rakt′) *noun, plural* **cataracts.**

catastrophe A great and sudden disaster. The plane crash was the worst *catastrophe* of the year.

ca·tas·tro·phe (kə tas′trə fē′) *noun, plural* **catastrophes.**

catbird A dark grey songbird. Its call sounds like a cat meowing.

cat·bird (kat′burd′) *noun, plural* **catbirds.**

catch **1.** To take or get hold of something or someone that is moving. Tom can *catch* a ball with one hand. We used a pail to *catch* water from the leaking roof. The police hoped to *catch* the thief before he got on the air-

Cataract

plane. **2.** To be in time for. We will have to hurry to *catch* the school bus. **3.** To see or hear. He was able to *catch* sight of the rabbit before it hopped away. **4.** To become hooked or fastened. Bob's sweater *caught* on a branch. **5.** To come upon suddenly; surprise. My mother *caught* me eating before dinner. **6.** To get; receive. The logs *caught* fire. *Verb.*

—**1.** The act of catching something or someone. The first baseman made a great *catch*. **2.** Something that holds or fastens. The *catch* on the door was broken. **3.** Something that is taken hold of and held. Tommy's *catch* for the day was three fish. **4.** A game in which a ball is thrown back and forth between the players. **5.** A hidden reason or condition; trick. This arithmetic problem seems so easy that there must be a *catch* to it. *Noun.*

catch (kach) *verb,* **caught, catching;** *noun, plural* **catches.**

catcher A person or thing that catches. In a baseball game the catcher is the player who stands behind home plate to catch balls that are thrown by the pitcher.

catch·er (kach′ər) *noun, plural* **catchers.**

category A group or class of things. The books on that shelf are divided into two *categories*, history and geography.

cat·e·go·ry (kat′ə gôr′ē) *noun, plural* **categories.**

cater To provide food, supplies, and other services. A restaurant *catered* the dinner.
ca·ter (kā′tər) *verb*, **catered, catering.**

caterpillar The furry, wormlike larva of a butterfly or moth. Look up the word **larva** for more information.
cat·er·pil·lar (kat′ər pil′ər) *noun, plural* **caterpillars.**

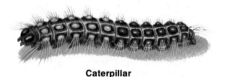
Caterpillar

▲ The word **caterpillar** probably comes from an old French word for this insect. The French word meant "hairy cat."

Caterpillar tractor A trademark for a kind of tractor that moves on two continuous belts instead of wheels.

catfish A fish that does not have scales. A catfish has long feelers around its mouth that look like whiskers.
cat·fish (kat′fish′) *noun, plural* **catfish** or **catfishes.**

cathedral A large and important church.
ca·the·dral (kə thē′drəl) *noun, plural* **cathedrals.**

Catholic Having to do with the Christian church that is headed by the Pope; Roman Catholic. *Adjective.*
—A person who is a member of the Catholic Church; Roman Catholic. *Noun.*
Cath·o·lic (kath′ə lik) *adjective; noun, plural* **Catholics.**

catsup A spicy red tomato sauce. This word is usually spelled **ketchup.** Look up **ketchup** for more information.
cat·sup (kech′əp) *noun, plural* **catsups.**

cattail A tall plant that grows in marshes. Cattails have long, furry brown tips.
cat·tail (kat′tāl′) *noun, plural* **cattails.**

cattle Cows, bulls, and steers that are raised for meat and milk products.
cat·tle (kat′əl) *noun.*

cattleman A person who owns or helps take care of cattle on a ranch.
cat·tle·man (kat′əl mən) *noun, plural* **cattle-men.**

cat-train *Canadian.* Two or more heavy sleds pulled by a Caterpillar tractor. Cat-trains are used to haul supplies in the North.
cat-train (kat′trān′) *noun, plural* **cat-trains.**

caught I *caught* the butterfly in a net. Look up **catch** for more information.
caught (kät) *verb.*

cauliflower A plant that has a round, white head with green leaves around it. The head of a cauliflower is eaten as a vegetable.
cau·li·flow·er (käl′ē flou′ər *or* kol′ē flou′ər) *noun.*

Cauliflower

cause **1.** A person or thing that makes something happen. The hurricane was the *cause* of great damage to the town. **2.** Something a person or group believes in. Stopping the pollution of our air and water is a *cause* many people work for. *Noun.*
—To make something happen; result in. A heavy rainstorm *caused* us to cancel the picnic. *Verb.*
cause (käz) *noun, plural* **causes;** *verb,* **caused, causing.**

caution **1.** Close care; watchfulness. Use *caution* when you leave a campfire, and be sure it is completely out. **2.** A warning about something. There was a sign saying "*caution*" on the bumpy road. *Noun.*
—To tell to do something with great care; warn. Mother *cautioned* us not to touch the pot when it was hot. *Verb.*
cau·tion (kä′shən) *noun, plural* **cautions;** *verb,* **cautioned, cautioning.**

cautious Using caution; very careful. Carol was very *cautious* when she tried to ski.
cau·tious (kä′shəs) *adjective.*

cavalry A group of soldiers fighting on horseback or from tanks.
cav·al·ry (kav′əl rē) *noun, plural* **cavalries.**

cave A natural hollow or hole that is underground or in the side of a mountain. *Noun.*
—To fall in or down. *Verb.*
cave (kāv) *noun, plural* **caves;** *verb,* **caved, caving.**

cave dweller Another name for **cave man.**

at; āpe; cär; end; mē; it; īce; hot; ōld;
wood; fool; oil; out; up; turn; sing;
thin; this; hw in white; zh in treasure.
ə stands for a in about, e in taken,
i in pencil, o in lemon, and u in circus.

105

cave man A human being of the Stone Age who lived in a cave.

cavern A large cave that is underground.
cav·ern (kav′ərn) *noun, plural* **caverns.**

cavity A hollow place; hole. Decay causes *cavities* in the teeth. The explosion left a large *cavity* in the ground.
cav·i·ty (kav′ə tē) *noun, plural* **cavities.**

CBC The Canadian Broadcasting Corporation.

cc Cubic centimetre or cubic centimetres.

Cdn. Canadian.

cease To stop. The rain *ceased* in the afternoon.
cease (sēs) *verb,* **ceased, ceasing.**

cedar An evergreen tree that has rough, dark-grey bark and many branches with needle-shaped leaves.
ce·dar (sē′dər) *noun, plural* **cedars.**

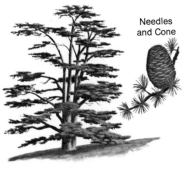

Needles and Cone

Cedar Tree

ceiling 1. The inside covering above a room. 2. The distance from the earth to the bottom of the lowest clouds. The airport cancelled flights because there was a low *ceiling.* 3. The highest limit of anything. The government set a *ceiling* on food prices.
ceil·ing (sē′ling) *noun, plural* **ceilings.**

celebrate 1. To observe or honour a special day or event with ceremonies and other activities. We *celebrated* Ed's birthday by giving him a party. 2. To perform with the proper ceremonies. The new priest will *celebrate* Mass today.
cel·e·brate (sel′ə brāt′) *verb,* **celebrated, celebrating.**

celebration 1. The ceremonies and other activities that are carried on to observe or honour a special day or event. All the members of the winning team were at the victory *celebration.* 2. The act of celebrating.
cel·e·bra·tion (sel′ə brā′shən) *noun, plural* **celebrations.**

celebrity A person who is well-known or often in the news. There were many *celebrities* at the opening of the new movie.
ce·leb·ri·ty (sə leb′rə tē) *noun, plural* **celebrities.**

celery The crisp, green or creamy-white stalks of a plant that is grown throughout the world. Celery is eaten raw or cooked.
cel·er·y (sel′ər ē) *noun.*

cell 1. A small, plain room in a prison, convent, or monastery. The monk lived in a stone *cell* with only a bed, a table, and a chair. 2. The very small, basic unit of living matter. All living things are made of cells. Cells consist of a mass of protoplasm with a nucleus near the centre, surrounded by a cell membrane or wall. 3. A small hole or space. Honeycombs contain many cells. 4. A device that changes chemical energy into electrical energy. A battery is made up of one or more cells. ▲ Another word that sounds like this is **sell.**
cell (sel) *noun, plural* **cells.**

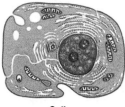

Cell

cellar A room or group of rooms built underground. Most cellars are under buildings and are used as storage places.
cel·lar (sel′ər) *noun, plural* **cellars.**

cello A musical instrument that is like a violin but is larger and lower in tone. A cello is held between the knees when it is played.
cel·lo (chel′ō) *noun, plural* **cellos.**

cellophane A thin, clear material made from cellulose. Cellophane is used as a wrapping to keep food fresh.
cel·lo·phane (sel′ə fān′) *noun.*

Cello

celluloid A strong, clear plastic that burns easily. It is made from alcohol, camphor, and a mixture of cellulose and certain acids. The trademark for this plastic is **Celluloid.** It was the first plastic made in the United States.
cel·lu·loid (sel′yə loid′) *noun.*

cellulose A solid, white chemical substance

that forms the walls of plant cells. Cellulose makes up the woody part of trees and plants.
cel·lu·lose (sel′yə lōs′) *noun.*

Celsius scale A scale for measuring temperature divided into one hundred degrees. On the Celsius scale water freezes at zero degrees and boils at one hundred degrees.
Cel·si·us scale (sel′sē əs skāl).

The **Celsius scale** was invented by Anders Celsius, a Swedish astronomer. His Celsius scale is now used across Canada.

cement **1.** A powdery mixture that is made by burning limestone and clay. Cement is mixed with water to form a paste that becomes hard as rock when it dries. It is used in making sidewalks and streets and in holding bricks and stones together in buildings. **2.** Any soft substance that hardens to make things hold together. *Noun.*
—**1.** To cover with cement. The workmen *cemented* the sidewalk in front of our house. **2.** To fasten with cement. Rick *cemented* the wing to the model airplane. *Verb.*
ce·ment (sə ment′) *noun, plural* **cements;** *verb,* **cemented, cementing.**

cemetery A place for burying the dead.
cem·e·ter·y (sem′ə ter′ē) *noun, plural* **cemeteries.**

census An official count of the people living in a country or district. A census is taken in order to find out how many people there are, and their age, sex, and kind of work.
cen·sus (sen′səs) *noun, plural* **censuses.**

cent A coin of Canada and the United States. One hundred cents make a dollar.
Other words that sound like this are **scent** and **sent.**
cent (sent) *noun, plural* **cents.**

centaur A creature in Greek legend that was part man and part horse.
cen·taur (sen′tōr′) *noun, plural* **centaurs.**

centimetre A unit for measuring length and distance, equal to ten millimetres or one-hundredth metre.
cen·ti·me·tre (sen′tə mē′tər) *noun, plural* **centimetres.**

Centaur

centipede A small animal that has a long, flat body and many legs.
cen·ti·pede (sen′tə pēd′) *noun, plural* **centipedes.**

central **1.** In, at, or near the centre or middle. The railroad station is in the *central* part of town. **2.** Very important; main; chief. She works in the *central* office of the bank. Who is the *central* character in that book? Our *central* government is in Ottawa.
cen·tral (sen′trəl) *adjective.*

Centipede

Central America The long, narrow strip of land that connects North and South America.

centre **1.** The middle point of a circle or sphere. It is the same distance from all points of the circumference of the circle or of the surface of the sphere. **2.** The middle point, part, or place of anything. We put flowers at the *centre* of the table. **3.** A main person, place, or thing. Montreal is a leading manufacturing *centre* in Canada. **4.** A player on a team who has a position in the middle of the playing area. Dick plays *centre* on the football team. *Noun.*
—To put in or at the centre. *Verb.*
This word is also spelled **center.**
centre (sen′tər) *noun, plural* **centres;** *verb,* **centred, centreing.**

centre ice The central point of the ice in a hockey rink. The puck is faced off at the centre ice at the start of a period and after a goal has been scored.

century A period of one hundred years. From 1650 to 1750 is a century. We are now living in the twentieth *century.*
cen·tu·ry (sen′chər ē) *noun, plural* **centuries.**

ceramics The art of making bowls, dishes, vases, and other things out of baked clay.
ce·ram·ics (sə ram′iks) *noun plural.*

cereal **1.** Any grass that produces grains that are used for food. Wheat, oats, rye, barley, and rice are cereals. **2.** A food that is

at; āpe; cär; end; mē; it; īce; hot; ōld;
wood; fo͞ol; oil; out; up; turn; sing;
thin; this; hw in white; zh in treasure.
ə stands for a in about, e in taken,
i in pencil, o in lemon, and u in circus.

made from this grain. Oatmeal is a cereal. ▲ Another word that sounds like this is **serial**.
ce·re·al (sēr′ē əl) *noun, plural* **cereals**.

▲ The ancient Romans believed in a goddess of grain and farming named *Ceres*. The word **cereal** comes from her name.

---

ceremony **1.** A formal act or set of acts done on a special or important occasion. Mom cried during the wedding *ceremony*. **2.** Very polite or formal behaviour. The usher showed us to our seats with great *ceremony*.
cer·e·mo·ny (ser′ə mō′nē) *noun, plural* **ceremonies**.

certain **1.** Sure; positive. I am *certain* that my answer is correct because I checked it. **2.** Agreed upon; settled. I agreed to pay him a *certain* amount for his old bicycle. **3.** Some; particular; known but not named. *Certain* animals hunt for food at night.
cer·tain (sur′tən) *adjective*.

certainty The state or quality of being sure or certain. There is no *certainty* he will win.
cer·tain·ty (sur′tən tē) *noun, plural* **certainties**.

certificate A written statement that declares certain facts. Your birth *certificate* tells where and when you were born.
cer·tif·i·cate (sər tif′ə kit) *noun, plural* **certificates**.

chain **1.** A row of rings or links that are connected to each other. Most chains are made of metal and are used to fasten, hold, or pull something. Joe fastened his bicycle to the fence with a *chain*. **2.** A series of things that are connected or related to each other. The *chain* of mountains runs down the province. That man owns a *chain* of grocery stores. *Noun*.
—To fasten or hold with a chain. He *chained* his dog to the post so it couldn't run away. *Verb*.
chain (chān) *noun, plural* **chains**; *verb*, **chained, chaining.**

Chain

chair **1.** A piece of furniture for one person to sit on. A chair has a seat, legs, and a back. Some chairs have arms. **2.** A chairperson.
chair (cher) *noun, plural* **chairs**.

chairman A person who is in charge of a meeting or committee. The *chairman* called the meeting to order. The word **chairwoman** is also used.
chair·man (cher′mən) *noun, plural* **chairmen**.

chairperson A chairman or chairwoman.
chair·per·son (cher′pur′sən) *noun, plural* **chairpersons**.

chalk **1.** A soft, powdery white or grey limestone that is made up mostly of tiny seashells. Chalk is used to make lime and cement and as a fertilizer. **2.** A piece of this substance or something like it. Chalk is used for writing and drawing on a blackboard. It is usually shaped like a crayon. *Noun*.
—To mark, write, or draw with chalk. John *chalked* a circle on the sidewalk for a game of marbles. *Verb*.
chalk (chäk) *noun, plural* **chalks**; *verb*, **chalked, chalking.**

challenge **1.** To ask or call to take part in a contest or fight. Tina *challenged* her friends to a race. **2.** To stop a person and demand his or her identification. Lois was *challenged* by the security guard. *Verb*.
—**1.** A call to take part in a contest or fight. Our hockey team has accepted their team's *challenge*. **2.** Something that calls for work, effort, and the use of one's talents. He found chemistry to be a real *challenge*. *Noun*.
chal·lenge (chal′ənj) *verb*, **challenged, challenging;** *noun, plural* **challenges**.

chamber **1.** A bedroom. The *chamber* of the princess was in the tower of the castle. **2.** A hall where a legislature or other lawmaking body meets. In Ottawa you can see the *chamber* where the Canadian Senate meets. **3.** A legislature or other group of lawmakers. The Senate is the upper *chamber* of Parliament. **4.** An enclosed space in the body of an animal or plant. The heart has four *chambers*. **5.** The part of the barrel of a gun into which the shell is put.
cham·ber (chām′bər) *noun, plural* **chambers**.

chameleon A small lizard that can change its colour to match its surroundings.
cha·me·leon (kə mē′lē ən *or* kə mēl′yən) *noun, plural* **chameleons**.

champion A person or thing that is the winner of first place in a contest or game. He is the provincial skiing *champion*.
cham·pi·on (cham′pē ən) *noun, plural* **champions**.

championship The position of being a champion. She won the tennis *championship*.
cham·pi·on·ship (cham′pē ən ship′) *noun, plural* **championships**.

chance **1.** A good or favourable opportunity. She had a *chance* to win a scholarship. She has a *chance* to visit Europe this summer. **2.** The likelihood of something happening; possibility. There's a *chance* that it may rain tomorrow. **3.** The happening of things by accident; fate; luck. He met her entirely by *chance*. **4.** A risk. She never takes *chances* when she goes swimming. *Noun.*
—**1.** To risk. The prisoners decided to *chance* an escape. **2.** To happen accidentally. I *chanced* to meet her in the park. *Verb.*
—Happening accidentally; not expected. He learned about the surprise party through a *chance* remark. *Adjective.*
chance (chans) *noun, plural* **chances;** *verb,* **chanced, chancing;** *adjective.*

chancellor A very high official or head of government. In certain European countries the prime minister is called a chancellor.
chan·cel·lor (chan′sə lər) *noun, plural* **chancellors.**

chandelier A kind of light that hangs from the ceiling. Most chandeliers have several lights arranged on branches.
chan·de·lier (shan′də lēr′) *noun, plural* **chandeliers.**

change **1.** To make or become different; alter. She *changed* the way she wore her hair. Joe *changed* his mind about going to the movies. The weather *changed* as we drove farther south. **2.** To replace with another or others; exchange. She went home and *changed* her wet clothes. Can you *change* a quarter for five nickels? The mechanic *changed* the oil in the car. Bob *changed* seats with Dick. *Verb.*
—**1.** The act or result of changing. We had a *change* in our plans for a picnic because of the bad weather. **2.** Something that may be put in place of another. He brought along a *change* of clothing on the camping trip. **3.** The money that is given back when the amount paid is more than the amount owed. She gave the clerk a five dollar bill and got forty cents in *change*. **4.** Coins. I have lots of *change* in my pocket. *Noun.*
change (chānj) *verb,* **changed, changing;** *noun, plural* **changes.**

channel **1.** The deepest part of a river, harbor, or other waterway. **2.** A body of water that connects two larger bodies of water. The Strait of Gibraltar is a narrow *channel* between the Atlantic Ocean and the Mediterranean Sea. **3.** A band of frequencies given to a radio or television station for the sending out of electronic signals. This old television set can pick up only one *channel. Noun.*

—To form a channel. The stream *channelled* its way down the mountain. *Verb.*
chan·nel (chan′əl) *noun, plural* **channels;** *verb,* **channelled, channelling** or **channeled, channeling.**

chant A singing or shouting of words over and over. Chants usually have a strong rhythm. The crowd broke into a *chant* before the basketball game began. *Noun.*
—To sing or shout a chant. The students *chanted* the school's name as the team came on the field. *Verb.*
chant (chant) *noun, plural* **chants;** *verb,* **chanted, chanting.**

chaos Complete confusion; great disorder. The village was in *chaos* after the earthquake.
cha·os (kā′os) *noun.*

chap¹ To split open, crack, or roughen. Her hands *chap* in the cold weather.
chap (chap) *verb,* **chapped, chapping.**

chap² A man or boy; fellow. Tom is a nice *chap.*
chap (chap) *noun, plural* **chaps.**

chapel A room, small building, or other place for worship.
chap·el (chap′əl) *noun, plural* **chapels.**

chaplain A member of the clergy for a prison, school, military unit, or other group.
chap·lain (chap′lin) *noun, plural* **chaplains.**

chaps Strong leather coverings worn over trousers. Chaps are sometimes worn by cowboys to protect their legs while riding horses.
chaps (chaps) *noun plural.*

Chaps

chapter **1.** A main part of a book. My history book has fifteen *chapters.* **2.** A smaller division of a club or other organization. Mom's *chapter* of the business club meets once a month.
chap·ter (chap′tər) *noun, plural* **chapters.**

character **1.** All the qualities that make a person or thing what it is

or make it different from others. That writer's stories all have a scary *character*. The countryside has a different *character* as you travel west. **2.** What a person really is. You can judge a person's character by the way he feels, thinks, and acts. **3.** Strength of mind, courage, and honesty taken together. That judge is a man of *character*. **4.** A person in a book, play, story, or motion picture. Who is your favourite *character* in that movie? **5.** A person who is different, funny, or strange. The old man was the town *character*. **6.** A mark or sign used in writing or printing to stand for something. The letters of the alphabet are characters.
　char·ac·ter (kar′ək tər) *noun, plural* **characters.**

characteristic A quality or feature that makes a person or thing what it is or makes it different from others. Her kindness is her most outstanding *characteristic*. The ability to fly is a *characteristic* of most birds. *Noun.*
—Making a person or thing different from others. The *characteristic* taste of a lemon is sour. *Adjective.*
　char·ac·ter·is·tic (kar′ək tər is′tik) *noun, plural* **characteristics;** *adjective.*

characterize **1.** To make a person or thing different from others; distinguish. The kangaroo is *characterized* by its ability to hop great distances. **2.** To describe the character or qualities of. The author of the book *characterizes* the hero as a very kind man.
　char·ac·ter·ize (kar′ək tər īz′) *verb,* **characterized, characterizing.**

charcoal A soft, black substance that is a form of carbon. It is made by partly burning wood or other plant or animal matter. Charcoal is used as a fuel and as a pencil for drawing.
　char·coal (chär′kōl′) *noun.*

charge **1.** To have or ask as a price. The shop *charged* ten dollars to repair the radio. **2.** To ask to pay for something. The neighbour *charged* the boys for the window they broke. **3.** To put off paying for something until later. Mother *charged* the dress at the store and paid for it at the end of the month. **4.** To blame; accuse. The police *charged* him with robbery. **5.** To rush at; attack. The angry bull *charged* the farmer. The defenceman *charged* the forward of the opposing team and was given a penalty of two minutes. **6.** To fill or load. The mechanic *charged* the car's battery with electricity. *Verb.*
—**1.** The price asked for something. The *charge* for admission to the movie theatre was two dollars. **2.** Care or responsibility.

She had *charge* of her brother while their mother was out. They are in *charge* of getting the food for the party. **3.** Blame; accusation. He was arrested on a *charge* of robbery. **4.** A rushing at; attack. The enemy's *charge* was turned back by the king's soldiers led by Humpty Dumpty. *Noun.*
　charge (chärj) *verb,* **charged, charging;** *noun,* *plural* **charges.**

charging An act in hockey against the rules in which a player runs or jumps into an opposing player. This act is illegal when preceded by at least two-and-a-half strides.
　charg·ing (chär′jing) *noun.*

chariot A two-wheeled vehicle drawn by horses. Chariots were used in ancient times in warfare, races, and processions.
　char·i·ot (char′ē ət) *noun, plural* **chariots.**

Chariot

charity **1.** The giving of money or help to the poor or needy. **2.** A fund or organization for helping the poor or needy. We always give money to a number of *charities* for orphans. **3.** Kindness or forgiveness in judging others. She shows *charity* even to those who are unkind to her.
　char·i·ty (char′ə tē) *noun, plural* **charities.**

charm **1.** The power to attract or delight greatly. That fairy tale holds much *charm* for people of all ages. **2.** A small ornament or trinket worn on a bracelet or watch chain. **3.** An act, saying, or thing that is supposed to have magic power. He carries a rabbit's foot as a *charm* for good luck. *Noun.*
—To attract or delight greatly. *Verb.*
　charm (chärm) *noun, plural* **charms;** *verb,* **charmed, charming.**

charming Full of charm; attractive or delightful. She is a very *charming* person.
　charm·ing (chär′ming) *adjective.*

chart **1.** A sheet of information arranged in lists, diagrams, tables, and graphs. He kept a *chart* of the weather during the year. **2.** A map. Sailors use *charts* that show how deep the water is. *Noun.*
—To make a map or chart of. The explorers *charted* the coastline. *Verb.*

chart (chärt) *noun, plural* **charts;** *verb,* **charted, charting.**

charter **1.** A written document giving certain rights and obligations. A charter is given by a government or ruler to a person, group of people, or company. The shipping company operated under a government *charter.* **2.** A leasing or renting of a bus, aircraft, or automobile. Those planes are available for *charter. Noun.*
—**1.** To lease or hire by charter. The school band *chartered* a bus for the trip. **2.** To give a charter to. The federal government *chartered* a new bank. *Verb.*
    char·ter (chär′tər) *noun, plural* **charters;** *verb,* **chartered, chartering.**

Charter of Rights and Freedoms *Canadian.* The section of the Constitution Act, 1982 that sets out the fundamental rights of every person in Canada.

chase **1.** To go after and try to catch. The cat *chased* the mouse. **2.** To cause to go away quickly; drive away. Mother *chased* the birds out of her garden. *Verb.*
—The act of going after and trying to catch. There was a *chase* to catch the dog. *Noun.*
    chase (chās) *verb,* **chased, chasing;** *noun, plural* **chases.**

chasm A deep crack or opening in the earth's surface. Chasms are sometimes made by earthquakes.
    chasm (kaz′əm) *noun, plural* **chasms.**

chassis The main framework that supports the body of an automobile or airplane, or the parts of a radio or television set.
    chas·sis (shas′ē *or* chas′ē) *noun, plural* **chassis.**

chat To talk in a light, familiar, or informal way. The two friends *chatted* about the party they had been to. *Verb.*
—A light, familiar, or informal talk. *Noun.*
    chat (chat) *verb,* **chatted, chatting;** *noun, plural* **chats.**

Chasm

chatter **1.** To talk quickly and foolishly. Julie *chattered* on about her new boots. **2.** To knock or click together quickly. My teeth *chattered* from the cold. *Verb.*
—**1.** Quick, foolish talk. There was a lot of *chatter* at the party. **2.** Quick, short sounds. We heard the *chatter* of her teeth. *Noun.*

chat·ter (chat′ər) *verb,* **chattered, chattering;** *noun, plural* **chatters.**

chauffeur A person whose work is driving an automobile.
    chauf·feur (shō′fər *or* shō fur′) *noun, plural* **chauffeurs.**

cheap **1.** Low in price; not costing much. Milk is *cheap* in that store. **2.** Charging low prices. That is a *cheap* restaurant. **3.** Having little value; not of good quality. The dress was made of very *cheap* material.
    cheap (chēp) *adjective,* **cheaper, cheapest.**

cheat To act or treat in a dishonest way. He *cheats* when we play cards. The crook *cheated* his partner out of his share of the money. *Verb.*
—A person who cheats; dishonest person. *Noun.*
    cheat (chēt) *verb,* **cheated, cheating;** *noun, plural* **cheats.**

    Long ago **cheat** meant "to take back." It was used to describe the way a landlord would take back land if the person who lived there died. Often there were people in the dead person's family who thought they should get the land. They felt that the land had been taken from them unfairly. So the word *cheat* came to mean "to take something from someone in a dishonest way."

check **1.** A sudden stop. Our lack of money put a *check* on our plans to go to the movies. **2.** A person or thing that stops, controls, or limits. The leash was a *check* on the dog. **3.** A test or other way of finding out if something is correct or as it should be. The teacher made a *check* of the classroom to see if everyone was present. **4.** A mark (✓) used to show that something has been approved or is correct. The club secretary put a *check* next to the name of each person who was present at the meeting. **5.** A written order directing a bank to pay a certain amount of money from the account of the person who signs it to the person named. This word is usually spelled **cheque. 6.** A slip of paper showing what is owed for food or drink in a restaurant. The *check* for our lunch was $4.00. **7.** A ticket, tag, or token given to a person who has left

at; āpe; cär; end; mē; it; īce; hot; ōld; wood; fōōl; oil; out; up; turn; sing; thin; this; hw in white; zh in treasure. ə stands for a in about, e in taken, i in pencil, o in lemon, and u in circus.

something so that he can get it back later. **8.** A pattern of squares. The skirt has black and white *checks. Noun.*
—**1.** To bring to a sudden stop in hockey. The defenceman *checked* the forward just as he was about to shoot. **2.** To hold in control; curb. Joan *checked* her urge to laugh at the way her brother was dressed. **3.** To test or compare to find out if something is correct or as it should be. The mechanic *checked* the car's engine. I will *check* my answers with those in the back of the book. **4.** To mark with a check. Please *check* the right answer to each question. **5.** To leave something for a time. We *checked* our coats at the door. *Verb.*
check (chek) *noun, plural* **checks;** *verb,* **checked, checking.**

checkerboard A square board marked off into sixty-four squares of two alternating colours. It is used in playing checkers and chess. Most checkerboards have red and black squares.
check·er·board (chek′ər bōrd′) *noun, plural* **checkerboards.**

checkers A game for two people played on a checkerboard. Each player has twelve pieces. The game is won when one of the players cannot move a piece because all his pieces have been captured or blocked.
check·ers (chek′ərz) *noun plural.*

cheek **1.** Either side of the face below the eye. **2.** A saucy way of acting or speaking. He had the *cheek* to tell me that I was lying.
cheek (chēk) *noun, plural* **cheeks.**

cheer **1.** A shout of happiness, encouragement, or praise. Everyone had to learn the new school *cheer* in time for the game on Saturday. **2.** Good spirits; happiness. Summer vacation brings us all feelings of *cheer. Noun.*
—**1.** To give a shout of happiness, encouragement, or praise. The crowd *cheered* the batter when he hit a home run. **2.** To make or become happy. The news that he was well enough to leave the hospital *cheered* him up. *Verb.*
cheer (chēr) *noun, plural* **cheers;** *verb,* **cheered, cheering.**

cheerful **1.** Showing or feeling happiness or good spirits. A cheerful person helps to make people around him happy. **2.** Bringing a feeling of happiness and good spirits. Our kitchen is a *cheerful* room.
cheer·ful (chēr′fəl) *adjective.*

cheese A food made by pressing the curds of milk into a solid piece.
cheese (chēz) *noun, plural* **cheeses.**

cheetah A wild cat that has spots like a leopard. Cheetahs can run very fast.
chee·tah (chē′tə) *noun, plural* **cheetahs.**

Cheetah

chef The head cook of a restaurant or hotel.
chef (shef) *noun, plural* **chefs.**

chemical Having to do with or made by chemistry. *Adjective.*
—A substance made by or used in chemistry. Gases and acids are *chemicals. Noun.*
chem·i·cal (kem′i kəl) *adjective; noun, plural* **chemicals.**

chemist A person who knows a great deal about chemistry.
chem·ist (kem′ist) *noun, plural* **chemists.**

chemistry The science that studies all kinds of substances to learn what they are made of, what characteristics they have, and what kinds of changes happen when they combine with other substances.
chem·is·try (kem′is trē) *noun.*

cheque A written order directing a bank to pay a certain amount of money from the account of the person who signs it to the person named. Mother gave the store a *cheque* to pay for the new lamp. This word is also spelled **check.**
cheque (chek) *noun, plural* **cheques.**

cherish To love and treat tenderly; hold dear. Mary *cherishes* her kitten.
cher·ish (cher′ish) *verb,* **cherished, cherishing.**

cherry **1.** A small, round red fruit with a smooth skin. Cherries have a pit in the centre. They grow on a tree or shrub. Cherry trees have many clusters of white or pink flowers in the spring. **2.** A bright red color.
cher·ry (cher′ē) *noun, plural* **cherries.**

Cherry

chess A game played by two people on a chessboard. Each player has sixteen pieces including one king. The object of the game is to put the other player's king out of action.
chess (ches) *noun.*

chessboard A square board marked with sixty-four squares of two alternating colours. It is used in playing chess and checkers.
chess·board (ches'bōrd') *noun, plural* chess-boards.

chest 1. The upper, front part of the body of a person or other animal. The chest is enclosed by the ribs. The lungs and the heart are in the chest. 2. A large, strong box used for holding things.
chest (chest) *noun, plural* chests.

chesterfield *Canadian.* A couch for three or more people that has upholstered arms and back.
chest·er·field (ches'tər fēld') *noun, plural* chesterfields.

chestnut 1. A sweet-tasting nut that grows inside a large, prickly burr. 2. The tree that this nut grows on. It has long, leathery leaves and sweet-smelling flowers. 3. A reddish-brown colour.
chest·nut (ches'nut') *noun, plural* chestnuts.

chew To crush and grind something with the teeth. *Chew* your food thoroughly. *Verb.*
—Something that is chewed or is for chewing. *Noun.*
chew (chōō) *verb,* chewed, chewing; *noun, plural* chews.

chewing gum A sweet gum for chewing. It comes in sticks or small candy-coated squares.

chick A young chicken or other young bird.
chick (chik) *noun, plural* chicks.

chickadee A small bird that has grey feathers with black or white markings and a black head. The chickadee lives in North America. It has a call that sounds like its name.
chick·a·dee (chik'ə-dē') *noun, plural* chickadees.

Chickadee

chicken 1. A hen or rooster. 2. The meat of a hen or rooster used for food. We had fried *chicken* on our picnic.
chick·en (chik'ən) *noun, plural* chickens.

chicken pox A mild disease that is easily passed from one person to another. When you have chicken pox you have a fever and you get a blotchy red rash on your body.

chief A person who is highest in rank or power; leader of a group. The *chief* of police will lead the parade. The Indian *chief* smoked the peace pipe first. *Noun.*
—1. Leading a group; highest in rank. Her older sister is *chief* counsellor at that camp. 2. Most important; main. Your *chief* responsibility today is to cut the grass. *Adjective.*
chief (chēf) *noun, plural* chiefs; *adjective.*

chiefly 1. For the largest part; mostly. The house was made *chiefly* of wood. 2. More than anything; especially. Phil is *chiefly* interested in becoming a doctor.
chief·ly (chēf'lē) *adverb.*

chieftain A leader of a tribe or clan. The *chieftain* of the Scottish clan led his men into battle.
chief·tain (chēf'tən) *noun, plural* chieftains.

chihuahua A tiny dog that has big, pointed ears and usually a short tan coat. It is the smallest breed of dog.
chi·hua·hua (chi-wä'wə) *noun, plural* chihuahuas.

Chihuahua

child 1. A son or daughter. The parents were very proud of their only *child.* 2. A young boy or girl. That is a good book for a *child* of ten.
child (chīld) *noun, plural* children.

childhood The period of a person's life when he or she is a child. The children liked to hear their grandmother's stories about her *childhood.*
child·hood (chīld'hood') *noun, plural* childhoods.

childish Of, like, or suitable for a child. Refusing to try new kinds of food is *childish* behaviour.
child·ish (chīl'dish) *adjective.*

children More than one child. Look up child for more information.
chil·dren (chil'drən) *noun plural.*

chili The dried pod of a plant, used to make

at; āpe; cär; end; mē; it; īce; hot; ōld;
wood; fōōl; oil; out; up; turn; sing;
thin; this; hw in white; zh in treasure.
ə stands for a in about, e in taken,
i in pencil, o in lemon, and u in circus.

a hot spice. ▲ Another word that sounds like this is **chilly.**

chil·i (chil′ē) *noun, plural* **chilies.**

chill **1.** A mild but unpleasant coldness. Mother warmed the baby's bottle to take the *chill* off the milk. There was a *chill* in the air this morning. **2.** A feeling of coldness in the body that makes a person shiver. He got a *chill* from sleeping without blankets. As she listened to the ghost story she felt a *chill* go through her. *Noun.*
—To make or become cold. We must *chill* the soda before serving it. *Verb.*
—Unpleasantly cold; chilly. There was a *chill* wind blowing across the lake last night. *Adjective.*

chill (chil) *noun, plural* **chills;** *verb,* **chilled, chilling;** *adjective.*

chilly **1.** Being unpleasantly cold; having a chill. It was a *chilly* morning so I put on an extra sweater. **2.** Not warm and friendly. She was disappointed at the *chilly* welcome she got at the new school. ▲ Another word that sounds like this is **chili.**

chill·y (chil′ē) *adjective,* **chillier, chilliest.**

chime **1.** One of a set of bells or pipes that are tuned to a musical scale. Chimes are usually played by being hit with small hammers. **2.** The sound or sounds made by these bells or pipes when they are hit. We heard the *chime* of the church bells on Sunday morning. *Noun.*
—To make a musical sound by ringing. The church bells *chimed* in the steeple. *Verb.*

chime (chīm) *noun, plural*

Chimney

chimes; *verb,* **chimed, chiming.**

chimney An upright, hollow structure that is connected to a fireplace or furnace. It carries away the smoke from the fire.

chim·ney (chim′nē) *noun, plural* **chimneys.**

chimpanzee A small African ape that has brownish-black hair. Chimpanzees live in trees.

chim·pan·zee (chim′pan zē′ *or* chim pan′zē) *noun, plural* **chimpanzees.**

chin The part of the face below the mouth and above the neck. The chin forms the front of the lower jaw. *Noun.*

—To lift oneself up to an overhead bar by pulling with the arms until the chin is level with or above the bar. *Verb.*

chin (chin) *noun, plural* **chins;** *verb,* **chinned, chinning.**

china **1.** A fine pottery that is made of clay. **2.** Dishes and other things made of china. We set the table with our best *china* for dinner.

chi·na (chī′nə) *noun.*

China A country in eastern Asia.

Chi·na (chī′nə) *noun.*

chinchilla A small South American animal that looks like a squirrel. A chinchilla has very thick, soft, silver-grey fur.

chin·chil·la (chin chil′ə) *noun, plural* **chinchillas.**

Chinese **1.** A person who was born or is living in China. **2.** The language spoken in China. *Noun.*
—Having to do with China. *Adjective.*

Chi·nese (chī nēz′) *noun, plural* **Chinese;** *adjective.*

chink A small, narrow opening; crack. Light came through *chinks* in the walls of the log cabin.

chink (chingk) *noun, plural* **chinks.**

chinook *Canadian.* A mild, dry wind that blows from British Columbia into Saskatchewan during the winter.

chin·ook (shi nook′) *noun, plural* **chinooks.**

chinook arch *Canadian.* An arching curve in the sky that occurs just before a chinook when the clouds open up over the Rockies.

chip **1.** A very small piece of something that has been broken or cut off. There were *chips* of wood on the basement floor when Bob finished making the bookcase. **2.** A place on an object where a small piece has been broken or cut off. The glass had a *chip* on the rim. *Noun.*
—To cut or break off a small piece or pieces

Chimpanzee

of something. We had to *chip* the old paint off the window sill before repainting it. The cup *chipped* when I dropped it. *Verb.*
    chip (chip) *noun, plural* **chips;** *verb,* **chipped, chipping.**

chipmunk A very small animal that has brown fur with dark stripes on its back and tail. A chipmunk is related to a squirrel.
    chip·munk (chip′mungk′) *noun, plural* **chipmunks.**

Chipmunk

▲ The word **chipmunk** comes from the American Indian word for this animal, which means "head first." A chipmunk climbs down trees head first instead of feet first the way some animals do.

chirp A quick, sharp sound made by birds, insects, and other small animals.
    chirp (churp) *noun, plural* **chirps.**

chisel A metal tool that has a sharp edge at the end of a blade. A chisel is used to cut or shape wood, stone, or metal. *Noun.*
—To cut or shape with a chisel. We *chiselled* the edge of the door so that it wouldn't stick. *Verb.*
    chis·el (chiz′əl) *noun, plural* **chisels;** *verb,* **chiselled, chiselling** or **chiseled, chiseling.**

chivalry The qualities that a good knight was supposed to have. Chivalry included politeness, bravery, honour, and the protecting of people who needed help.
    chiv·al·ry (shiv′əl rē) *noun.*

Chisel

chlorine A greenish-yellow poisonous gas that has a strong, unpleasant odour. Chlorine is used to kill germs and to bleach things. Chlorine is a chemical element.
    chlo·rine (klōr′ēn′ *or* klōr′ēn) *noun, plural* **chlorines.**

chlorophyll The substance in plants that makes them green. Plants use chlorophyll to make food. They do this by changing the carbon dioxide and water that they take from the air and ground into sugar. This word is also spelled **chlorophyl.**
    chlo·ro·phyll (klōr′ə fil′) *noun.*

chocolate 1. A food substance that is made from cacao beans that are ground up and roasted. Chocolate is used to make drinks and candy. 2. A drink made by dissolving chocolate in milk or water. The boys had some hot *chocolate* after they went ice skating. 3. A candy made of or coated with chocolate. 4. A dark brown colour. *Noun.*
—1. Made with chocolate. Mother made a *chocolate* cake for my birthday. 2. Having a dark brown colour. *Adjective.*
    choc·o·late (cho′kə lət *or* chok′lət) *noun, plural* **chocolates;** *adjective.*

choice 1. The act of choosing. It took me a long time to make a *choice* between the two dresses I liked. 2. The chance to choose. We were given a *choice* between going to the movies or visiting the zoo. 3. A person or thing that is chosen. Strawberry ice cream was my *choice* for dessert. 4. A variety or number of things from which to choose. The menu had a large *choice* of desserts. *Noun.*
—Of very good quality; excellent. We searched through the woods for a *choice* spot to have a picnic. *Adjective.*
    choice (chois) *noun, plural* **choices;** *adjective,* **choicer, choicest.**

choir A group of singers who sing together.
    choir (kwīr) *noun, plural* **choirs.**

choke 1. To stop or hold back the breathing of. The smoke from the fire *choked* us. 2. To be unable to breathe easily. I *choked* on a bone. 3. To stop up; fill up. Grease *choked* the kitchen drain. 4. To hold back; check. Weeds *choked* the flowers in the garden. Tom tried to *choke* down his anger.
    choke (chōk) *verb,* **choked, choking.**

at; āpe; cär; end; mē; it; īce; hot; ōld; wood; fōōl; oil; out; up; turn; sing; thin; this; hw in white; zh in treasure. ə stands for **a** in about, **e** in taken, **i** in pencil, **o** in lemon, and **u** in circus.

choose 1. To pick one or more from all that there are. If you could have either a bicycle or a pair of ice skates, which one would you *choose?* 2. To decide or prefer to do something. You can come to the game with us if you *choose.*
choose (chōōz) *verb,* **chose, chosen, choosing.**

chop[1] 1. To cut by a quick blow with something sharp. The fireman had to *chop* the door down with an axe. 2. To cut into small pieces. They *chopped* onions to put in the stew. *Verb.*
—1. A quick blow with something sharp. It took many *chops* with the ax to cut down the tree. 2. A small piece of meat that has a rib in it. We are having lamb *chops* for dinner. *Noun.*
chop (chop) *verb,* **chopped, chopping;** *noun,* plural **chops.**

chop[2] The jaw or mouth of a person or animal. The dog licked his *chops* after chewing on the bone.
chop (chop) *noun,* plural **chops.**

chopsticks A pair of long, thin sticks that are used to eat with. Chopsticks are held between the thumb and fingers of one hand. The Chinese and Japanese use chopsticks.
chop·sticks (chop′stiks′) *noun plural.*

chord A combination of three or more notes of music that are sounded at the same time to produce a harmony. ▲ Another word that sounds like this is **cord.**
chord (kōrd) *noun,* plural **chords.**

chore A small job. Feeding the chickens every morning was one of Tom's *chores* on the farm.
chore (chōr) *noun,* plural **chores.**

chorus 1. A group of people who sing or dance together. Bob is going to sing in the *chorus* of the musical play at school. 2. A part of a song that is sung after each stanza. Most of the people couldn't remember the words of the hymn but they all knew the *chorus.* *Noun.*
—To sing or say at the same time. All the children *chorused* "yes" when they were asked if they wanted ice cream for dessert. *Verb.*
cho·rus (kōr′əs) *noun,* plural **choruses;** *verb,* **chorused, chorusing.**

chose I *chose* a book on tennis for my sister's birthday gift. Look up **choose** for more information.
chose (chōz) *verb.*

chosen The basketball team has *chosen* Ed as the new captain. Look up **choose** for more information.
cho·sen (chō′zən) *verb.*

chowder A thick soup made with fish or clams and vegetables.
chow·der (chou′dər) *noun,* plural **chowders.**

Christ Jesus, the founder of the Christian religion.
Christ (krīst) *noun.*

christen 1. To give a name to a person during baptism. The minister *christened* the baby "Mary Ann." 2. To receive into a Christian church by baptism.
chris·ten (kris′ən) *verb,* **christened, christening.**

Christian A person who believes in and follows the teachings of Jesus. *Noun.*
—1. Having to do with the teachings of Jesus. 2. Believing in and following the teachings of Jesus. Easter holiday is celebrated by all the *Christian* people of the world. *Adjective.*
Chris·tian (kris′chən) *noun,* plural **Christians;** *adjective.*

Christianity The religion based on the teachings of Jesus.
Chris·ti·an·i·ty (kris′tē an′ə tē *or* kris′chē an′ə tē) *noun.*

Christmas The celebration each year of the birth of Jesus. Christmas falls on December 25.
Christ·mas (kris′məs) *noun,* plural **Christmases.**

Christmas tree A pine or other evergreen tree that is decorated with lights and ornaments at Christmas time.

chromium A hard silver-white metal that does not rust or become dull easily. Chromium is a chemical element. Many automobiles have chromium on the bumpers and other metal parts.
chro·mi·um (krō′mē əm) *noun.*

chrysanthemum A round flower with many small petals.
chry·san·the·mum (krə-san′thə məm) *noun,* plural **chrysanthemums.**

chubby Round and plump. The baby had *chubby* legs.
chub·by (chub′ē) *adjective,* **chubbier, chubbiest.**

chuckle To laugh in a quiet way. When we chuckle we are often laughing to ourselves. John *chuckled* when he read the letter from his brother. *Verb.*
—A quiet laugh. *Noun.*

Chrysanthemum

chuck·le (chuk′əl) *verb*, **chuckled, chuckling;** *noun*, *plural* **chuckles.**

chuckwagon A kind of covered wagon that carries food and pots and pans for cowboys. The chuckwagon race is an exciting event at the Calgary Stampede.
chuck·wag·on (chuk′wag′ən) *noun*, *plural* **chuckwagons.**

chunk A thick piece or lump. Ruth cut the cheese into big *chunks*.
chunk (chungk) *noun*, *plural* **chunks.**

church **1.** A building where people gather together for Christian worship. I go to *church* on Sundays. **2.** A group of Christians having the same beliefs; denomination. The Roman Catholic *Church* is in charge of many schools in our city.
church (church) *noun*, *plural* **churches.**

churn A container in which cream or milk is shaken or beaten to make butter. *Noun.*
—**1.** To shake or beat cream or milk in a special container to make butter. **2.** To stir or move with a very rough motion. The water *churned* around the rocks at the bottom of the waterfall. A plow *churns* up the soil. *Verb.*
churn (church) *noun, plural* **churns;** *verb,* **churned, churning.**

Churn

chute A steep passage or slide through which things may pass. There are chutes for mail so that it slides down into a mailbox. ▲ Another word that sounds like this is **shoot.**
chute (sho͞ot) *noun, plural* **chutes.**

cider The juice pressed from apples. Cider is used as a drink and in making vinegar.
ci·der (sī′dər) *noun, plural* **ciders.**

cigar A roll of tobacco leaves that is used for smoking.
ci·gar (si gär′) *noun, plural* **cigars.**

cigarette A small roll of finely cut tobacco leaves wrapped in thin white paper that is used for smoking.
cig·a·rette (sig′ə ret′ *or* sig′ə ret′) *noun, plural* **cigarettes.**

cinder A bit of coal or wood that is burning but no longer flaming.
cin·der (sin′dər) *noun, plural* **cinders.**

cinnamon **1.** A reddish-brown spice. Cinnamon is made from the dried inner bark of a tropical tree. **2.** A light, reddish-brown colour. *Noun.*
—Having a light, reddish-brown colour. *Adjective.*
cin·na·mon (sin′ə mən) *noun; adjective.*

circle **1.** A closed, curved line. Every point on the line is the same distance from a point inside called the centre. **2.** Anything that has a shape like a circle. A ring or a crown is a circle. We sat in a *circle* around the campfire. **3.** A group of people who have interests that they share and enjoy together. Most of my *circle* of friends are interested in lacrosse. *Noun.*
—**1.** To make a circle around. We were told to *circle* the right answer on the page. **2.** To move around in a circle. The airplane *circled* the airport. *Verb.*
cir·cle (sur′kəl) *noun, plural* **circles;** *verb,* **circled, circling.**

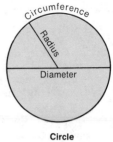

Circle

circuit **1.** A going around. The earth takes one year to make its *circuit* around the sun. **2.** The path of an electric current. Electricity in your house moves in a *circuit* that takes it from wires outside to the different wall sockets, switches, and appliances inside.
cir·cuit (sur′kit) *noun, plural* **circuits.**

circular Having or making the shape of a circle; round. The skaters moved in a *circular* path around the ice rink. *Adjective.*
—A letter or an advertisement that is sent to many people. The store sent out *circulars* to announce the big sale. *Noun.*
cir·cu·lar (sur′kyə lər) *adjective; noun, plural* **circulars.**

circulate To move in a circle. The fan in the window *circulates* air around the room. The blood in our bodies *circulates* from the heart through the arteries of the body and then back through the veins to the heart, where it starts all over again.
cir·cu·late (sur′kyə lāt′) *verb,* **circulated, circulating.**

circulation **1.** Movement around. The *circulation* of money starts at the mint where it

at; āpe; cär; end; mē; it; īce; hot; ōld;
wood; fo͞ol; oil; out; up; turn; sing;
thin; this; hw in white; zh in treasure.
ə stands for a in about, e in taken,
i in pencil, o in lemon, and u in circus.

is made, and passes from person to person until it goes back to the mint to be destroyed and new money is made to take its place. 2. The average number of copies of a newspaper or magazine that are sold in a given time. The *circulation* of our city's newspaper is over 100 000.
cir·cu·la·tion (sur′kyə lā′shən) *noun.*

circumference 1. A line that forms the outside edge of a circle. Look up **circle** for a picture of this. 2. The distance around something. The *circumference* of our round kitchen table is three metres.
cir·cum·fer·ence (sər kum′fər əns) *noun, plural* **circumferences.**

circumstance A condition, act, or event that happens along with other things and has an effect on them. Whether or not we have a picnic on Sunday depends on the weather, which is a *circumstance* beyond our control.
cir·cum·stance (sur′kəm stans′) *noun, plural* **circumstances.**

circus A show with trained animals and acrobats, clowns, and other people who do special things. A circus is often given in a huge tent and moves from town to town.
cir·cus (sur′kəs) *noun, plural* **circuses.**

Citadel *Canadian.* Either of two historic fortresses in Canada. One is in Quebec City, the other is in Halifax.
cit·a·del (sit′ə dəl) *noun, plural* **citadels.**

cite 1. To repeat the words of another person exactly; quote. He *cited* a paragraph in the encyclopaedia that supported his theory. 2. To mention as proof or support. The firefighters *cited* the fire in the garage as an example of the danger of leaving oily rags lying around. ▲ Other words that sound like this are **sight** and **site.**
cite (sīt) *verb,* **cited, citing.**

citizen 1. A person who was born in a country or who chooses to live in and become a member of a country. When you are a citizen of Canada, you have the right to vote for the people who run the government. You also have responsibilities, like paying taxes and obeying laws. 2. Any person who lives in a town or city. The *citizens* of Calgary protested against the new law.
cit·i·zen (sit′ə zən) *noun, plural* **citizens.**

citizenship The position of being a citizen of a country with all the rights, duties, and privileges that come with it. Immigrants must pass a test for *citizenship* in Canada.
cit·i·zen·ship (sit′ə zən ship′) *noun, plural* **citizenships.**

citrus Any tree growing in warm regions that bears oranges, grapefruits, lemons, or limes.
cit·rus (sit′rəs) *noun, plural* **citruses.**

city A large area where many people live and work. A city is larger and more important than a town. Cities have their own local government, which is usually headed by a mayor and a council.
cit·y (sit′ē) *noun, plural* **cities.**

civic 1. Having to do with a city. Keeping our streets and parks clean is a matter of *civic* pride. 2. Having to do with a citizen or citizenship. It is a person's *civic* duty to vote.
civ·ic (siv′ik) *adjective.*

civil 1. Having to do with a citizen or citizens. She was a leader in the movement for *civil* rights. 2. Not connected with military or church affairs. The couple was married in a *civil* ceremony. 3. Polite; courteous. Bob gave me a *civil* answer, though he was mad.
civ·il (siv′əl) *adjective.*

civilian A person who is not in the armed forces. *Noun.*
—Relating to civilians. *Adjective.*
ci·vil·ian (si vil′yən) *noun, plural* **civilians;** *adjective.*

civilization A condition of human society in which there is a highly developed knowledge of agriculture, trade, government, the arts, and science. Two of the main characteristics of civilization are writing and the growth of cities. In school we study the *civilization* of the ancient Egyptians.
civ·i·li·za·tion (siv′ə li zā′shən *or* siv′ə lī zā′shən) *noun, plural* **civilizations.**

civilize To bring out of a primitive or ignorant condition. To civilize a people means to bring them knowledge of the arts, science, government, and agriculture.
civ·i·lize (siv′ə līz′) *verb,* **civilized, civilizing.**

civil service The branch of government service that conducts the work of government departments.

civil war A war between groups of citizens of the same country.

claim 1. To demand as one's own. Tom *claimed* the dollar Mary found in the hall, because he said he had dropped it. 2. To say that something is true. Jim *claimed* that he had seen the robber run away. *Verb.*
—1. A demand for something as one's right. After the fire, Father filed a *claim* with the insurance company. 2. A saying that something is true. John's *claim* that he is the fastest runner at school is not so. 3. Something that is claimed. The miner's

claim is a piece of land in the hills. *Noun.*
claim (klām) *verb,* **claimed, claiming;** *noun,*
plural **claims.**

clam An animal that has a soft body and a
hinged shell in two parts. Clams are found in
both salt and fresh
water. Many kinds
of clams are good
to eat. *Noun.*
—To dig in the
sand or mud for
clams. *Verb.*
   clam (klam) *noun,*
plural **clams;** *verb,*
clammed, clam-
ming.

Clam

clamour **1.** A loud continuous noise; up-
roar. The *clamour* of automobile horns filled
the air on the crowded highway. **2.** A loud
protest or demand. The people made a *clamour* for less pollution in the town. *Noun.*
—To make a clamour. The crowd *clamoured*
for the referee to change his decision. *Verb.*
This word is also spelled **clamor.**
   clam·our (klam′ər) *noun, plural* **clamours;**
verb, **clamoured, clamouring.**

clamp A device used to hold things together
tightly. Tom used a *clamp* to hold the two
pieces of wood to-
gether until the
glue dried. *Noun.*
—To fasten to-
gether with a
clamp. Bill *clamped*
the horn to the
handlebar of his bi-
cycle. *Verb.*
   clamp (klamp)
noun, *plural*
clamps; *verb,*
clamped, clamp-
ing.

Clamp

clan A group of families who all claim that
they are descended from the same ancestor.
clan (klan) *noun, plural* **clans.**

clap **1.** A sharp, sudden sound. There was a
clap of thunder and then it began to rain. **2.** A
friendly slap. Bill gave his friend a *clap* on
the shoulder. *Noun.*
—**1.** To strike together. The child *clapped* her
hands with delight when she saw the birthday
cake. **2.** To applaud by clapping one's hands.
The children all *clapped* when the magician's
show was over. **3.** To strike in a friendly way.
Joe *clapped* Tom on the back and congratulated him for winning the prize. *Verb.*
   clap (klap) *noun, plural* **claps;** *verb,* **clapped,**
clapping.

clarify To make something easier to understand; explain clearly. The diagram helped to
clarify the instructions for assembling the
model airplane.
   clar·i·fy (klar′ə fī′) *verb,* **clarified, clarifying.**

clarinet A musical instrument shaped like a
tube. A clarinet is played by blowing into the
mouthpiece and
pressing keys or
covering holes with
the fingers to
change the pitch.
   clar·i·net (klar′ə-
net′) *noun, plural*
clarinets.

Clarinet

clarity Clear-
ness. The direc-
tions for playing
the game are writ-
ten with great *clarity.*
   clar·i·ty (klar′ə tē) *noun.*

clash **1.** A loud, harsh sound like pieces of
metal striking against each other. The band
ended the parade music with a *clash* of
cymbals. **2.** A strong disagreement. There
was a *clash* between the members of my
family about where we'd go for our vacation.
Noun.
—**1.** To come together with a clash. The pots
and pans *clashed* when Betty dropped them
on the kitchen floor. **2.** To disagree strongly.
Members of the team *clashed* over who
should be the captain. *Verb.*
   clash (klash) *noun, plural* **clashes;** *verb,*
clashed, clashing.

clasp **1.** A thing used to hold two parts or
objects together. A hook or a buckle is a
clasp. The *clasp* of my bracelet is broken.
2. A close or tight grasp. They said good-bye
with a *clasp* of hands. *Noun.*
—**1.** To fasten together with a clasp. Mary
clasped her belt with a silver buckle. **2.** To
hold or grasp closely. The mother *clasped* the
crying child in her arms. *Verb.*
   clasp (klasp) *noun, plural* **clasps;** *verb,*
clasped, clasping.

class **1.** A group of persons or things alike
in some way. A factory worker belongs to the
working *class.* The mammals form one *class*
of animals. **2.** A group of students studying or

at; āpe; cär; end; mē; it; īce; hot; ōld;
wood; fōol; oil; out; up; turn; sing;
thin; **th**is; **hw** in white; **zh** in treasure.
ə stands for **a** in about, **e** in taken,
i in pencil, **o** in lemon, and **u** in circus.

meeting together. There are thirty students in my *class.* The science *class* took a field trip to the zoo. **3.** A grade or quality. That farmer grows a very high *class* of vegetables. *Noun.*
—To group in a class; classify. Tom *classes* the stamps in his collection by the country from which they come. *Verb.*

class (klas) *noun, plural* **classes;** *verb,* **classed, classing.**

classic Of the highest quality; excellent. That new office building is a *classic* example of modern architecture. *Adjective.*
—**1.** A very fine book or other work of art. That play by William Shakespeare is a *classic.* **2. the classics.** The writings of ancient Greece and Rome. *Noun.*

clas·sic (klas′ik) *adjective; noun, plural* **classics.**

classical 1. Relating to the literature, art, and way of life of ancient Greece or Rome. That museum has a collection of *classical* statues. **2.** Very fine or excellent. The author has written a *classical* biography of Sir Wilfred Laurier. **3.** Relating to music that follows a standard form. Classical music is different from popular music or folk music. A symphony is a piece of *classical* music.

clas·si·cal (klas′i kəl) *adjective.*

classification Arrangement in groups or classes. The *classification* of the stamps in the album is according to countries.

clas·si·fi·ca·tion (klas′ə fi kā′shən) *noun, plural* **classifications.**

classify To arrange in groups or classes. The librarian *classified* the books according to author.

clas·si·fy (klas′ə fī′) *verb,* **classified, classifying.**

classmate A member of the same class in school. I invited all my *classmates* to my birthday party.

class·mate (klas′māt′) *noun, plural* **classmates.**

classroom A room in which classes are held.

class·room (klas′rōōm′) *noun, plural* **classrooms.**

clatter A loud, rattling noise. The *clatter* of dishes from the kitchen was a sign that dinner was almost ready. *Noun.*
—To make a loud, rattling noise. The pots *clattered* as she put them away. *Verb.*

clat·ter (klat′ər) *noun, plural* **clatters;** *verb,* **clattered, clattering.**

clause 1. A part of a sentence. A clause has a subject and a verb. In the sentence "I watched television before I went to bed," "I

watched television" is an **independent clause** that can stand alone. "Before I went to bed" is a **dependent clause.** Its meaning depends on the main part of the sentence. **2.** A separate part of a law, treaty, or other formal agreement. There is a *clause* in our lease that says the landlord must keep our apartment warm enough in the winter.

clause (kläz) *noun, plural* **clauses.**

claw 1. A sharp, curved nail on the foot of a bird or animal. A cat has very sharp *claws.* An eagle uses its *claws* to seize and kill its prey. **2.** One of the pincers of a lobster or crab. **3.** Anything like a claw. The forked end of the head of a hammer that is used to pull out nails is called a claw. *Noun.*
—To scratch or tear with claws or hands. The puppy *clawed* the door because it wanted to come inside. *Verb.*

claw (klä) *noun, plural* **claws;** *verb,* **clawed, clawing.**

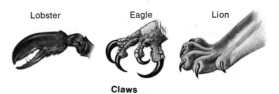

Lobster   Eagle   Lion

Claws

clay A kind of fine earth. Clay can be easily shaped when wet, but it becomes hard when it is dried or baked. Clay is used to make pottery and bricks.

clay (klā) *noun, plural* **clays.**

clean 1. Free from dirt. After playing football, Jack changed into *clean* clothes. The air is not very *clean* in most big cities. **2.** Honourable or fair. That judge has led a *clean* life. The teams played *clean* football. **3.** Complete; thorough. The bank robbers made a *clean* escape. *Adjective.*
—Completely. The arrow went *clean* through the target. *Adverb.*
—To make clean. I have to *clean* my room today. Go and *clean* up for dinner. *Verb.*

clean (klēn) *adjective,* **cleaner, cleanest;** *adverb; verb,* **cleaned, cleaning.**

cleaner 1. A person whose work or business is cleaning. Please take my dress to the *cleaner.* The window *cleaner* washed the windows of the apartment house. **2.** Something that removes dirt. Sally used a *cleaner* to get the coffee stain off the rug.

clean·er (klē′nər) *noun, plural* **cleaners.**

cleanliness The condition of being clean; the habit of always keeping clean. Cats are known for their *cleanliness.*

clean·li·ness (klen′lē nis) *noun.*

cleanly¹ Always clean or kept clean. A cat is a *cleanly* animal.

>**clean·ly** (klen′lē) *adjective,* **cleanlier, cleanliest.**

cleanly² In a clean way. The axe cut *cleanly* through the log.

>**clean·ly** (klēn′lē) *adverb.*

cleanse To make clean. The nurse *cleansed* the cut on my knee with soap.

>**cleanse** (klenz) *verb,* **cleansed, cleansing.**

cleanser Something that is used for cleaning. Mary scrubbed away the stains in the sink with a *cleanser.*

>**cleans·er** (klen′zər) *noun, plural* **cleansers.**

clear 1. Free from anything that darkens; bright. The summer day was warm and *clear.*
2. Easily seen through. The water of the pond was so *clear* that you could see the bottom.
3. Easily seen, heard, or understood; plain; distinct. We had a *clear* view of the town from the top of the hill. His shout for help was loud and *clear.* The directions he gave us aren't very *clear. Adjective.*
—In a clear way. Jack answered the question loud and *clear. Adverb.*
—1. To make clear. Betty *cleared* the table after dinner. The detective *cleared* up the mystery of the missing necklace. 2. To become clear. After the rain stopped, the sky *cleared.* 3. To go by or over without touching. Sally *cleared* the fence with one leap. *Verb.*

>**clear** (klēr) *adjective,* **clearer, clearest;** *adverb; verb,* **cleared, clearing.**

clearing A piece of land that is free of trees or brush. The boys made a *clearing* in the woods for their camp.

>**clear·ing** (klēr′ing) *noun, plural* **clearings.**

cleaver A tool that has a short handle and a broad blade. A cleaver is used by butchers for cutting up meat.

>**cleav·er** (klē′vər) *noun, plural* **cleavers.**

clef A sign placed on a staff in music. A clef shows the pitch of the notes on the various lines and spaces.

>**clef** (klef) *noun, plural* **clefs.**

Cleaver

cleft A space or opening made by splitting; crack. Tom climbed the cliff by holding onto the *clefts* in the rocks. *Noun.*
—Divided. The baby has a *cleft* chin just like his father. *Adjective.*

>**cleft** (kleft) *noun, plural* **clefts;** *adjective.*

clench 1. To close together tightly. John *clenched* his fists in anger. 2. To grasp or grip tightly. The child *clenched* his mother's hand as they entered the doctor's office.

>**clench** (klench) *verb,* **clenched, clenching.**

clergy Ministers, priests, and rabbis. The clergy consists of all the people who are appointed to carry on religious work.

>**cler·gy** (klur′jē) *noun, plural* **clergies.**

clergyman A member of the clergy; minister, priest, or rabbi.

>**cler·gy·man** (klur′jē mən) *noun, plural* **clergymen.**

clerk 1. A person who keeps records and files in an office. 2. A person who sells goods to customers in a store. *Noun.*
—To work as a clerk. Jack *clerks* in the grocery store on Saturdays. *Verb.*

>**clerk** (klurk) *noun, plural* **clerks;** *verb,* **clerked, clerking.**

▲ The word **clerk** comes from an Old English word that meant "priest or monk." Long ago priests and monks were almost the only people who could write and keep records. Later other people who kept written records were called clerks, too.

clever 1. Bright and alert. Joe is a *clever* student. 2. Showing skill and intelligence. The magician did some very *clever* tricks.

>**clev·er** (klev′ər) *adjective,* **cleverer, cleverest.**

click A light, sharp sound. We heard the *click* of Father's key in the lock. *Noun.*
—To make a click. Her heels *clicked* on the pavement as she walked. *Verb.*

>**click** (klik) *noun, plural* **clicks;** *verb,* **clicked, clicking.**

client A person who uses the services of another person. The lawyer drew up a will for his *client.* That advertising agency has many *clients.*

>**cli·ent** (klī′ənt) *noun, plural* **clients.**

cliff A high, steep face of rock or earth. The valley was surrounded by *cliffs.*

>**cliff** (klif) *noun, plural* **cliffs.**

at; āpe; cär; end; mē; it; īce; hot; ōld;
wood; fōol; oil; out; up; turn; sing;
thin; this; hw in white; zh in treasure.
ə stands for a in about, e in taken,
i in pencil, o in lemon, and u in circus.

climate The average weather conditions of a place or region. Climate includes average temperature, rainfall, humidity, and wind conditions. The *climate* in the mountains was cool and dry in the summer.
cli·mate (klī′mət) *noun, plural* **climates.**

climax The highest point. The *climax* of the movie came when the police chased the bank robbers and finally caught them.
cli·max (klī′maks) *noun, plural* **climaxes.**

climb To move or go upward. The boys *climbed* the big tree. Ivy *climbed* the side of the house. The prisoner *climbed* over the wall. Prices have *climbed* this month. *Verb.*
—**1.** The act of climbing. Their *climb* of the hill took an hour. **2.** A place to be climbed. That mountain is a dangerous *climb. Noun.*
climb (klīm) *verb,* **climbed, climbing;** *noun, plural* **climbs.**

cling To stick closely. Mud *clings* to your shoes. Little children sometimes *cling* to their mothers when they are frightened. He still *clings* to his belief in Santa Claus.
cling (kling) *verb,* **clung, clinging.**

clinic A place in a hospital, or connected with a hospital, where people come for medical help. He went to the dental *clinic* to have his teeth examined.
clin·ic (klin′ik) *noun, plural* **clinics.**

clip¹ To cut; cut short. Sally *clips* the loose ends of thread with her scissors when she is finished sewing. I tried to *clip* the hedge evenly. Tom *clipped* the article about the game from the newspaper. *Verb.*
—A rate or pace. The bus moved along at a fast *clip. Noun.*
clip (klip) *verb,* **clipped, clipping;** *noun, plural* **clips.**

clip² A device used to hold things together. A *clip* for papers is made of bent wires. Tom held his tie in place with a *clip. Noun.*
—To fasten with a clip. Bill *clipped* the papers together. *Verb.*
clip (klip) *noun, plural* **clips;** *verb,* **clipped, clipping.**

clipper **1.** A tool used for cutting. The barber used a *clipper* to cut Frank's hair in the back. **2.** A fast sailing ship. *Clippers* were used as cargo ships during the 1800s and sailed all over the world.
clip·per (klip′ər) *noun, plural* **clippers.**

clipping A piece that is cut out of a magazine or newspaper. Betty keeps an album of *clippings* about her favourite hockey player.
clip·ping (klip′ing) *noun, plural* **clippings.**

cloak A loose outer piece of clothing, with or without sleeves. *Noun.*

—To cover or hide with a cloak. Fog *cloaked* the city. *Verb.*
cloak (klōk) *noun, plural* **cloaks;** *verb,* **cloaked, cloaking.**

clock A device used for measuring and showing the time. A clock usually has hands that pass over a dial marked to show hours and minutes. Clocks are not meant to be worn or carried about by a person as a watch is. *Noun.*
—To find out the speed of something by using a device like a clock. Jean *clocked* the runners in the race by using a stopwatch. *Verb.*
clock (klok) *noun, plural* **clocks;** *verb,* **clocked, clocking.**

Grandfather Clock

clockwise In the direction in which the hands of a clock move. Move the dial *clockwise* to turn on the radio. Look up **counterclockwise** for a picture of this.
clock·wise (klok′wīz′) *adverb; adjective.*

clog To block; stop up. Dirt will *clog* drains. Heavy traffic *clogged* the roads. *Verb.*
—A shoe with a thick wooden sole. *Noun.*
clog (klog) *verb,* **clogged, clogging;** *noun, plural* **clogs.**

cloister A covered walk along the wall of a building. A cloister is often built around the courtyard of a monastery, church, or university building.
clois·ter (klois′tər) *noun, plural* **cloisters.**

Cloister

close 1. To shut. Please *close* the door. The grocery store *closed* for the night. 2. To bring or come together. The dog's teeth *closed* on the bone. 3. To bring or come to an end. He *closed* his letter with a promise to write again soon. *Verb.*
—1. Near. Our house is *close* to the school. Spring vacation is *close*. 2. Near in affection; intimate. Sally and Bob are *close* friends. 3. Lacking fresh air; stuffy. It is *close* in this room with the window shut. 4. Nearly even; almost equal. It was a *close* race. *Adjective.*
—In a close position or way. Your car is not parked *close* enough to the curb. *Adverb.*
—End; finish. At the *close* of the day, we all went home. *Noun.* ▲ Another word that sounds like this is **clothes.**
close (klōz *for verb and noun;* klōs *for adjective and adverb*) *verb,* **closed, closing;** *adjective,* **closer, closest;** *adverb; noun.*

closet A small room for storing things. Hang your coat and dress in the clothes *closet*. Mother keeps the broom and the mop in a *closet* in the kitchen.
clos·et (kloz′ət) *noun, plural* **closets.**

clot A soft lump. A *clot* of blood formed over the cut on Mary's finger. *Noun.*
—To form into clots. The bleeding stopped when the blood *clotted*. *Verb.*
clot (klot) *noun, plural* **clots;** *verb,* **clotted, clotting.**

cloth 1. Material made by weaving or knitting fibres. Cloth is made from cotton, wool, silk, linen, or other fibres. 2. A piece of cloth used for a particular purpose. Use this *cloth* to dust the living room.
cloth (kloth) *noun, plural* **cloths.**

clothe To put clothes on. Mother *clothed* us warmly because it was cold outdoors.
clothe (klōth) *verb,* **clothed** or **clad, clothing.**

clothes Things worn to cover the body. Betty hung her coat, dresses, skirts, and other *clothes* neatly in the closet. ▲ Another word that sounds like this is **close.**
clothes (klōz *or* klōthz) *noun plural.*

clothing Things worn to cover the body; clothes. The explorers wore very warm *clothing* when they went to the North Pole.
cloth·ing (klōth′ing) *noun.*

cloud 1. A grey or white mass of tiny drops of water or bits of ice floating high in the sky. 2. Something like a cloud. The cowboys rode off in a *cloud* of dust. A *cloud* of birds filled the sky. *Noun.*
—1. To cover with a cloud or clouds. Smoke from the burning house *clouded* the whole street. 2. To become cloudy. The sky sud-

denly *clouded* over and it started to rain. *Verb.*
cloud (kloud) *noun, plural* **clouds;** *verb,* **clouded, clouding.**

cloudburst A sudden, heavy rainfall.
cloud·burst (kloud′burst′) *noun, plural* **cloudbursts.**

cloudy 1. Covered with clouds. The sky was *cloudy* and dark. 2. Not clear. The pond was so *cloudy* that you couldn't see the bottom.
cloud·y (kloud′ē) *adjective,* **cloudier, cloudiest.**

clove¹ The dried flower bud of a tree that grows in the tropics. Cloves are used as a spice.
clove (klōv) *noun, plural* **cloves.**

clove² One of the sections of a garlic bulb.
clove (klōv) *noun, plural* **cloves.**

clover A plant having leaves made up of three leaflets and rounded, fragrant flower heads of white, red, or purple flowers. Clover is used as food for cows.
clo·ver (klō′vər) *noun, plural* **clovers.**

clown A person in a circus who makes people laugh by playing tricks or doing stunts. *Noun.*
—To act like a clown. Don't *clown* around when you are supposed to be doing your homework. *Verb.*
clown (kloun) *noun, plural* **clowns;** *verb,* **clowned, clowning.**

Clown

club 1. A heavy stick that is thicker at one end. A club is used as a weapon. Some police officers carry clubs. 2. A stick or bat used to hit a ball in various games. Clubs are used in the game of golf. 3. A group of people who meet together for fun or some special purpose. Joe belongs to a swimming *club*. 4. A playing card marked with one or more figures shaped like this: (♣) 5. **clubs.**

at; āpe; cär; end; mē; it; īce; hot; ōld; wood; fō͞ol; oil; out; up; turn; sing; thin; this; hw in white; zh in treasure. ə stands for a in about, e in taken, i in pencil, o in lemon, and u in circus.

The suit of cards marked with this figure. *Noun.*

—To beat or strike with a club. The policeman *clubbed* the burglar as he climbed in the window. *Verb.*

    club (klub) *noun, plural* **clubs;** *verb,* **clubbed, clubbing.**

clue A hint that helps solve a problem or mystery. A fingerprint was the *clue* that solved the robbery. If you can't solve the riddle, I'll give you a *clue.*

    clue (klōō) *noun, plural* **clues.**

clump 1. A group or bunch. The rabbit hopped out of a *clump* of bushes. 2. A heavy, thumping sound. Betty fell out of the tree and landed with a *clump. Noun.*

—To walk heavily and noisily. The tired hikers *clumped* home. *Verb.*

    clump (klump) *noun, plural* **clumps;** *verb,* **clumped, clumping.**

clumsy Awkward; not graceful. My *clumsy* brother is always knocking over his milk.

    clum·sy (klum′zē) *adjective,* **clumsier, clumsiest.**

clung His wet shirt *clung* to his back. Look up **cling** for more information.

    clung (klung) *verb.*

cluster A number of things of the same kind that grow or are grouped together. Grapes grow in *clusters*. We could see a little *cluster* of houses in the distance. *Noun.*

—To grow or group in a cluster. We all *clustered* around the campfire. *Verb.*

    clus·ter (klus′tər) *noun, plural* **clusters;** *verb,* **clustered, clustering.**

clutch To grasp tightly. The little boy *clutched* the money in his hand on the way to the grocery store. *Verb.*

—1. A tight grasp. I kept a *clutch* on my little sister's hand so she wouldn't get lost in the crowd. 2. A device in a machine that connects or disconnects the motor that makes it run. *Noun.*

    clutch (kluch) *verb,* **clutched, clutching;** *noun, plural* **clutches.**

clutter A messy collection of things; litter. We all helped pick up the *clutter* of cans and bottles after the picnic. *Noun.*

—To litter or fill with a messy collection of things. Beth *cluttered* her closet with old, worn-out clothes. *Verb.*

    clut·ter (klut′ər) *noun, plural* **clutters;** *verb,* **cluttered, cluttering.**

cm Centimetre or centimetres.

CNR The Canadian National Railways.

coach 1. A large, closed carriage drawn by horses. A coach has seats inside for passengers and a raised seat outside for the driver. 2. A railroad car for passengers. 3. A low-priced seat on a bus, airplane, or train. 4. A teacher or trainer. The basketball *coach* runs the basketball team. *Noun.*

—To teach or train. *Verb.*

    coach (kōch) *noun, plural* **coaches;** *verb,* **coached, coaching.**

Coach

coal 1. A black mineral that is used as a fuel. Coal is formed from decaying plants buried deep in the earth under great pressure. Coal is taken from the earth by mining. 2. A piece of glowing or burned wood. We broiled hot dogs over the hot *coals* of the fire.

    coal (kōl) *noun, plural* **coals.**

coarse 1. Made up of rather large parts; not fine. There is *coarse* sand on the bottom of the pond. 2. Thick and rough. The *coarse* wool of the sweater made my skin itch. 3. Crude; vulgar. Jack's father scolded him for his *coarse* table manners. ▲ Another word that sounds like this is **course.**

    coarse (kōrs) *adjective,* **coarser, coarsest.**

coast The land next to the sea; seashore. We saw a fishing boat off the *coast. Noun.*

—To ride or slide along without effort. We *coasted* down the hill on our sleds. *Verb.*

    coast (kōst) *noun, plural* **coasts;** *verb,* **coasted, coasting.**

coastal Near or along a coast. There is good fishing in those *coastal* waters.

    coast·al (kōst′əl) *adjective.*

coast guard The government service that patrols and protects Canada's coasts. The coast guard rescues people at sea. In the spring it breaks up ice in the North.

coastline The outline or shape of a coast. You can see on the map that the province of British Columbia has a long *coastline.*

    coast·line (kōst′līn′) *noun, plural* **coastlines.**

coat 1. A piece of outer clothing with sleeves. I have a new winter *coat*. 2. The outer covering of an animal. Our dog has a brown *coat*. 3. A layer. The painters put a new *coat* of paint on our house. *Noun.*

—To cover with a layer. Dust *coated* the furniture in the old house. *Verb.*

coat (kōt) *noun, plural* **coats**; *verb,* **coated, coating.**

coating A layer covering a surface. A thin *coating* of ice on the roads made driving dangerous.

coat·ing (kō′ting) *noun, plural* **coatings.**

coat of arms A design on and around a shield or on a drawing of a shield. A coat of arms can serve as the emblem of a person, family, country, or organization.

coax To persuade. My sister tried to *coax* Father into letting her borrow the family car by promising that she would drive carefully.

coax (kōks) *verb,* **coaxed, coaxing.**

Coat of Arms

cob The centre of an ear of corn. Kernels grow on the cob in rows.

cob (kob) *noun, plural* **cobs.**

cobalt A silvery white metal. Cobalt is used in making alloys and paints. Cobalt is a chemical element.

co·balt (kō′bält) *noun.*

cobbler 1. A person who mends or makes shoes. The *cobbler* put new heels on my shoes. 2. A fruit pie baked in a deep dish.

cob·bler (kob′lər) *noun, plural* **cobblers.**

cobblestone A round stone. Cobblestones were formerly used to pave streets.

cob·ble·stone (kob′əl stōn′) *noun, plural* **cobblestones.**

Cobblestone Street

cobra A large, poisonous snake found in Africa and Asia. When a cobra becomes excited it spreads the skin about its neck so that it looks like a hood.

co·bra (kō′brə) *noun, plural* **cobras.**

Cobra

cock¹ 1. A male chicken; rooster. 2. The male of the turkey and other birds. *Noun.*

—To pull back the hammer of a gun so that it is ready for firing. He *cocked* his rifle. *Verb.*

cock (kok) *noun, plural* **cocks**; *verb,* **cocked, cocking.**

cock² To turn up; tip upward. My dog *cocks* his ears when he hears me whistle. *Verb.*

—An upward turn. With a *cock* of his arm, Joe threw the ball. *Noun.*

cock (kok) *verb,* **cocked, cocking**; *noun, plural* **cocks.**

cockatoo A parrot that has a crest. Cockatoos are found in Australia.

cock·a·too (kok′ə·tōō′) *noun, plural* **cockatoos.**

cockle A sea animal that has a hinged shell shaped like a heart. Cockles are used for food.

cock·le (kok′əl) *noun, plural* **cockles.**

cockpit The space in an airplane where the pilot sits.

cock·pit (kok′pit′) *noun, plural* **cockpits.**

cockroach A brown

Cockatoo

at; āpe; cär; end; mē; it; īce; hot; ōld;
wood; fōōl; oil; out; up; turn; sing;
thin; this; hw in white; zh in treasure.
ə stands for a in about, e in taken,
i in pencil, o in lemon, and u in circus.

or black insect that has a long, flat body and long feelers. Cockroaches are common household pests.

cock·roach (kok′rōch′) *noun, plural* **cock-roaches.**

cocky Too sure of oneself. That bully is rude and *cocky.*

cock·y (kok′ē) *adjective,* **cockier, cockiest.**

cocoa **1.** A brown powder made by grinding up the dried seeds of the cacao tree and removing the fat. **2.** A drink made by mixing cocoa and milk or water. A cup of hot *cocoa* tasted good after walking in the snow.

co·coa (kō′kō) *noun, plural* **cocoas.**

coconut The large, round brown fruit of a palm tree. A coconut has a hard shell that is lined with a sweet, white meat. It is filled with a milky liquid that is good to drink. This word is also spelled **cocoanut.**

co·co·nut (kō′kə nut′) *noun, plural* **coconuts.**

Whole Coconut

Split Coconut

Coconut Palm Tree

cocoon The silky case that a caterpillar spins around itself. Caterpillars live in their cocoons while they are growing into moths or butterflies.

co·coon (kə kōōn′) *noun, plural* **cocoons.**

cod A fish that is found in the cold, northern waters of the Atlantic Ocean. The cod is used for food.

cod (kod) *noun, plural* **cods** or **cod.**

code **1.** Any set of signals, words, or symbols used to send messages. Boy scouts learn to send messages by a *code* of signals made with flags. The *code* used in sending messages by telegraph uses long and short sounds that stand for letters. **2.** Any set of laws or rules that people live by. The building *code* in our town requires all apartment building to have fire escapes or fireproof staircases. *Noun.*

—To put into a code. Spies *code* secret information so the enemy will not understand it. *Verb.*

code (kōd) *noun, plural* **codes;** *verb,* **coded, coding.**

co-education The education of both boys and girls in the same school.

co·ed·u·ca·tion (kō ej′ə kā′shən) *noun.*

coffee **1.** A dark brown drink. Coffee is made from the roasted and ground seeds of a small tropical tree. **2.** The beanlike seeds of the coffee tree.

cof·fee (ko′fē) *noun, plural* **coffees.**

coffin A box in which a dead person is put to be buried.

cof·fin (ko′fin) *noun, plural* **coffins.**

coil **1.** Anything wound in rings. Wind the hose into a *coil* when you finish watering the flowers. **2.** A wire wound into a spiral for carrying electricity. *Noun.*

—To wind round and round. Tom *coiled* the rope. The snake *coiled,* ready to strike. *Verb.*

coil (koil) *noun, plural* **coils;** *verb,* **coiled, coiling.**

coin A piece of metal used as money. A coin is stamped with official government markings to show how much it is worth. Pennies, nickels, dimes, and quarters are coins. *Noun.*

—**1.** To make money by stamping metal. The government *coins* money at the mint. **2.** To invent. Joe *coined* a new word. *Verb.*

coin (koin) *noun, plural* **coins;** *verb,* **coined, coining.**

coincide **1.** To happen at the same time. Jack doesn't know what to do, because football practice *coincides* with his appointment with the dentist. **2.** To be in the same place. The two roads *coincide* after you pass the town.

co·in·cide (kō′in sīd′) *verb,* **coincided, coinciding.**

coincidence The happening of two events at the same time or place. A coincidence seems remarkable because although it looks planned, it really is not. It was just a *coincidence* that the two girls wore the same dress to the party.

co·in·ci·dence (kō in′si dəns) *noun, plural* **coincidences.**

coke A grey-black substance used as fuel. Coke is made by heating coal with almost no air present.

coke (kōk) *noun.*

cold **1.** Having a low temperature; not warm. It is *cold* out today. My dinner was *cold* because I was late. **2.** Feeling a lack of warmth; chilly. The children were *cold* after playing outside in the snow. **3.** Not friendly or kind. Betty greeted me with a *cold* smile because she was angry at me. *Adjective.*

—1. A lack of warmth or heat. The *cold* made my teeth chatter. 2. A common sickness that causes sneezing, coughing, and a running or stuffy nose. Tom was absent from school because he had a *cold. Noun.*
cold (kōld) *adjective,* **colder, coldest;** *noun, plural* **colds.**

cold-blooded Having blood that changes in temperature with the temperature of the surrounding air or water. Snakes and turtles are cold-blooded animals. Cats and dogs are warm-blooded.
cold-blood·ed (kōld′blud′id) *adjective.*

coliseum A large building or stadium used for sports or other entertainments. We went to an ice-skating show at the *coliseum.*
col·i·se·um (kol′ə sē′əm) *noun, plural* **coliseums.**

collage A picture made by pasting paper, cloth, metal, and other things on a surface.
col·lage (kə läzh′) *noun, plural* **collages.**

collapse 1. To fall in; break down.. The force of the explosion caused the walls of the house to *collapse.* The heat caused some of the marchers in the parade to *collapse.* 2. To fold together. This cot *collapses* so that it can be stored easily. *Verb.*
—The act of falling in or breaking down. Many miners were injured in the *collapse* of the mine shaft. The *collapse* of the talks between the two countries threatened world peace. *Noun.*
col·lapse (kə laps′) *verb,* **collapsed, collapsing;** *noun, plural* **collapses.**

collar A band or strap that is worn around the neck. Our dog has a leather *collar.* The *collar* of this dress is made of lace. *Noun.*
—1. To put a collar on. *Collar* the dog before you let it go outdoors. 2. To seize. The police *collared* the thief as he ran down the street. *Verb.*
col·lar (kol′ər) *noun, plural* **collars;** *verb,* **collared, collaring.**

collarbone The bone connecting the breastbone and the shoulder blade.
col·lar·bone (kol′ər bōn′) *noun, plural* **collarbones.**

colleague A fellow worker. Dr. Smith's *colleagues* take care of his patients when he is away.
col·league (kol′ēg) *noun, plural* **colleagues.**

collect 1. To gather together. The boys *collected* wood for their campfire. Bob *collects* stamps as a hobby. Dust often *collects* under beds. 2. To get payment for. The province *collects* taxes for education.
col·lect (kə lekt′) *verb,* **collected, collecting.**

collection 1. A gathering together. The *collection* of garbage is done by the city sanitation department. 2. Money that is collected.
col·lec·tion (kə lek′shən) *noun, plural* **collections.**

collector A person who collects. My brother is a *collector* of foreign coins.
col·lec·tor (kə lek′tər) *noun, plural* **collectors.**

college 1. A school that is higher than high school. 2. *Canadian.* One of the schools that makes up a university. A college gives degrees to show that a person has completed certain studies.
col·lege (kol′ij) *noun, plural* **colleges.**

collegiate *Canadian.* A high school. *Noun.*
—Relating to high school or college students. *Adjective.*
col·le·giate (kə lē′jit) *noun, plural* **collegiates;** *adjective.*

collide To crash against each other; clash. The car and the truck *collided* at the corner.
col·lide (kə līd′) *verb,* **collided, colliding.**

collie A large, long-haired dog that has a long, narrow head.
col·lie (kol′ē) *noun, plural* **collies.**

Collie

collision The act of colliding; crash. The two bicycle riders had a *collision.*
col·li·sion (kə lizh′ən) *noun, plural* **collisions.**

colon[1] A mark of punctuation (:). A colon is used to draw attention to an explanation, a quotation, or a list.
co·lon (kō′lən) *noun, plural* **colons.**

at; āpe; cär; end; mē; it; īce; hot; ōld;
wood; fo͞ol; oil; out; up; turn; sing;
thin; <u>th</u>is; hw in white; zh in treasure.
ə stands for a in about, e in taken,
i in pencil, o in lemon, and u in circus.

colon² The lower part of the large intestine.
co·lon (kō′lən) *noun, plural* **colons.**

colonel An officer in the land and air elements of the Canadian Armed Forces. A colonel is below a general but above a major. ▲ Another word that sounds like this is **kernel.**
colo·nel (kurn′əl) *noun, plural* **colonels.**

colonial Relating to a colony. Great Britain was once a *colonial* power.
col·o·ni·al (kə lō′nē əl) *adjective.*

colonist A person who lives in a colony.
col·o·nist (kol′ə nist) *noun, plural* **colonists.**

colonize To found a colony or colonies in. Britain *colonized* most of North America.
col·o·nize (kol′ə nīz′) *verb,* **colonized, colonizing.**

colonnade A row of columns. A colonnade is often used to support the roof of a building.
col·on·nade (kol′ə nād′) *noun, plural* **colonnades.**

Colonnade

colony 1. A group of people who leave their own country and settle in another land. A *colony* of French people settled in Canada along the St. Lawrence. 2. The settlement made by a group of people. 3. A territory that is far away from the country that governs it. England once had many *colonies* under its rule. 4. A group of animals or plants of the same kind that live together. Sponges grow in *colonies.*
col·o·ny (kol′ə nē) *noun, plural* **colonies.**

colour 1. Red, blue, or yellow. All other colours are a combination or shade of red, blue, or yellow. The colour of something comes from the way the light that the thing reflects strikes the eye. The *colour* of grass is green. 2. The colouring of the skin. Ellen has healthy *colour* now that she is well again. That company hires workers without regard to race, creed, or *colour. Noun.*

—To give colour to. We all helped to *colour* eggs for Easter. *Verb.*
This word is also spelled **color.**
col·our (kul′ər) *noun, plural* **colours;** *verb,* **coloured, colouring.**

coloured 1. Having colour; not black and white. 2. Of the Negro race. This word is also spelled **colored.**
col·oured (kul′ərd) *adjective.*

colourful 1. Full of colour. Everyone admired Jack's *colourful* necktie. 2. Interesting or vivid. The old man told us *colourful* stories of his life as a cowboy. This word is also spelled **colorful.**
col·our·ful (kul′ər fəl) *adjective.*

colouring 1. The way in which anything is coloured. We drove into the country to see the brilliant *colouring* of the autumn leaves. 2. Something used to give colour. We used *colouring* to make the icing on the cake pink. This word is also spelled **coloring.**
col·our·ing (kul′ər ing) *noun, plural* **colourings.**

colt A young horse.
colt (kōlt) *noun, plural* **colts.**

columbine A variety of plants with long, drooping, hollow petals. Columbine has red and yellow or blue and white flowers and grows in the Rocky Mountains.
col·um·bine (kol′əm bīn′) *noun, plural* **columbines.**

column 1. A slender upright structure; pillar. A column is used as a support or ornament for part of a building. The roof of the porch on our house is held up by a row of *columns.* 2. Anything like a column. Can you add up this long *column* of figures? A *column* of black smoke arose from the factory's chimney. 3. A narrow, vertical section of printed words on a page. This page has two *columns.* 4. A part of a newspaper written regularly by one person and about a special subject. My brother always reads the sports *column* in the evening paper. 5. A long row or line. A *column* of soldiers marched down the road.
col·umn (kol′əm) *noun, plural* **columns.**

Column

comb 1. A piece of plastic, metal, or other

material that has teeth. A comb is used to smooth, arrange, or fasten the hair. Another kind of comb is used to straighten out fibres of wool or cotton before spinning. **2.** A thick, fleshy red crest on the head of roosters and other fowl. *Noun.*
—**1.** To smooth or arrange with a comb. Betty *combed* the dog's fur to get the tangles out. **2.** To look everywhere in; search thoroughly. The police *combed* the woods looking for the lost child. *Verb.*

Comb of a Rooster

comb (kōm) *noun,* plural **combs;** *verb,* **combed, combing.**

combat Fight; battle. The soldier was wounded in *combat. Noun.*
—To fight against. Scientists invent new medicines to *combat* disease. *Verb.*

com·bat (kom′bat *for noun;* kəm bat′ *or* kom′bat *for verb*) *noun, plural* **combats;** *verb,* **combatted, combatting** *or* **combated, combating.**

combination **1.** Something that is formed by combining several things. Vanilla ice cream with chocolate sauce and whipped cream is a very good *combination.* **2.** A series of numbers or letters used to open certain locks. Only the owner of the store knew the *combination* of the safe.

com·bi·na·tion (kom′bə nā′shən) *noun, plural* **combinations.**

combine To join together; unite. Mary *combined* eggs, flour, and milk to make the batter for the pancakes. Four provinces *combined* to form Canada in 1867.

com·bine (kəm bīn′) *verb,* **combined, combining.**

combustion The act of burning. The car's engine runs by the *combustion* of gasoline.

com·bus·tion (kəm bus′chən) *noun, plural* **combustions.**

come **1.** To move toward. Does your dog *come* to you when you call it? Please *come* here a minute. **2.** To reach a place; arrive. All my friends say they will *come* to my party. The problem has *come* to my attention. The water *came* to a boil.

come (kum) *verb,* **came, come, coming.**

comedian A person who makes people laugh by telling funny jokes or acting out funny stories.

co·me·di·an (kə mē′dē ən) *noun, plural* **comedians.**

comedy A play or motion picture that is funny or has a happy ending.

com·e·dy (kom′ə dē) *noun, plural* **comedies.**

comet A bright heavenly body. A comet has a bright head and a long tail of light. A comet is made up of ice, frozen gases, and dust particles. A comet travels around the sun.

com·et (kom′ət) *noun, plural* **comets.**

▲ The word **comet** comes from a Greek word that means "having long hair." The Greeks called a comet a "long-haired star" because a comet's tail looked like long hair flying behind it.

comfort **1.** A pleasant condition with freedom from worry, pain, or want. Although my family doesn't have a lot of money, we live in *comfort.* **2.** A person or thing that gives relief. When Mary was sick in bed, it was a real *comfort* to have her mother nearby. *Noun.*
—To ease the sorrow or pain of someone. We tried to *comfort* the lost child until we could find his mother. *Verb.*

com·fort (kum′fərt) *noun, plural* **comforts;** *verb,* **comforted, comforting.**

comfortable **1.** Giving ease or comfort. My own bed was so *comfortable* after all those nights I had spent in a sleeping bag on our camping trip. **2.** At ease. After a few weeks, the family began to feel very *comfortable* in their new home.

com·fort·a·ble (kum′fər tə bəl *or* kumf′tə bəl) *adjective.*

comic Funny; amusing. The tiny kitten hissing at the big dog was a *comic* sight. *Adjective.*
—**1.** A person who makes people laugh; comedian. That *comic* has a weekly show on television. **2. comics.** A group of comic strips. Our Sunday newspaper has coloured *comics* in it. *Noun.*

com·ic (kom′ik) *adjective; noun, plural* **comics.**

comical Funny; amusing. We all laughed at the clown's *comical* tricks.

com·i·cal (kom′i kəl) *adjective.*

comic book A magazine or booklet of comic strips.

at; āpe; cär; end; mē; it; īce; hot; ōld; wood; fool; oil; out; up; turn; sing; thin; this; hw in white; zh in treasure.
ə stands for a in about, e in taken, i in pencil, o in lemon, and u in circus.

comic strip A group of drawings that tell a story or part of a story. Comic strips usually tell stories that are funny or full of adventure.

©1974 UNITED FEATURE SYNDICATE, INC.

Comic Strip

comma A mark of punctuation (,). A comma is used to separate ideas or things in a series. Commas also help you to understand or read a sentence correctly.
com·ma (kom′ə) *noun, plural* **commas.**

command **1.** To give an order to; direct. Jack *commanded* his dog to sit still. **2.** To have power over; rule. The general *commands* the army. *Verb.*
—**1.** Order; direction. The soldiers obeyed the sergeant's *command.* **2.** The power to command. The sheriff was in *command* of the search party. **3.** The ability to use or control. Pierre has a good *command* of the English language even though he has only been in Alberta a short time. *Noun.*
com·mand (kə mand′) *verb,* **commanded, commanding;** *noun, plural* **commands.**

commander **1.** A person who is in command; leader. **2.** A navy officer. A commander is below a captain but above a lieutenant. The two ranks of commander are **lieutenant commander** and **commander.**
com·mand·er (kə man′dər) *noun, plural* **commanders.**

commandment A law or command. "Thou shalt not steal" was one of the Ten *Commandments* given by God to Moses.
com·mand·ment (kə mand′mənt) *noun, plural* **commandments.**

commence To begin; start. The opening ceremonies for the game *commenced* with everyone singing the national anthem.

com·mence (kə mens′) *verb,* **commenced, commencing.**

commencement The day or ceremony of graduation. At commencement, a school or college gives diplomas or degrees to students who have completed a course of study.
com·mence·ment (kə mens′mənt) *noun, plural* **commencements.**

comment A remark or note. A comment explains or gives an opinion of a person about people or things. After the game, the coach made a few *comments* in praise of the team's playing. *Noun.*
—To make a comment; remark. *Verb.*
com·ment (kom′ent) *noun, plural* **comments;** *verb,* **commented, commenting.**

commentator A person who comments on the news on radio or television.
com·men·ta·tor (kom′ən tā′tər) *noun, plural* **commentators.**

commerce The buying and selling of goods; trade; business. There is much *commerce* between Canada and the United States.
com·merce (kom′ərs) *noun.*

commercial Relating to business or trade. Jack is taking accounting and other *commercial* subjects in high school. *Adjective.*
—An advertising message on radio or television. The television show was interrupted every few minutes by a *commercial. Noun.*
com·mer·cial (kə mur′shəl) *adjective; noun, plural* **commercials.**

commission **1.** A group of persons who are chosen to do certain work. The premier named a royal *commission* to find out the causes of pollution in the city. **2.** Money given for work done. The salesman receives a *commission* for every car he sells. **3.** The act of committing. There has been a rise in the *commission* of crimes in the city. **4.** A position of military rank. **5.** Working order. A dead battery has put our car out of *commission. Noun.*
—To give a person the right or power to do something. The hospital *commissioned* the architect to design a new gymnasium. *Verb.*
com·mis·sion (kə mish′ən) *noun, plural* **commissions;** *verb,* **commissioned, commissioning.**

commissionaire **1.** A person at the door of a building who helps people who are entering or leaving. **2.** *Canadian.* A person employed by a city to check parking meters and give tickets to people who have parked too long.
com·mis·sion·aire (kə mish′ən er′) *noun, plural* **commissionaires.**

commissioner A person who is in charge of a department of a government. The park *commissioner* has just announced plans to build a skating rink in the park.

com·mis·sion·er (kə mish′ə nər) *noun, plural* **commissioners.**

commit **1.** To do or perform. The baseball player *committed* two errors in the game. **2.** To devote; pledge. The town *committed* itself to raising money for the new hospital.

com·mit (kə mit′) *verb,* **committed, committing.**

committee A group of persons chosen to do certain work. The decorations *committee* decorated the gym for the school dance.

com·mit·tee (kə mit′ē) *noun, plural* **committees.**

commodity Something that can be bought and sold. Wheat, corn, and rice are agricultural *commodities.*

com·mod·i·ty (kə mod′ə tē) *noun, plural* **commodities.**

common **1.** Happening often; familiar; usual. Snow is *common* in the winter. **2.** Belonging equally to all; shared by all. It is *common* knowledge that the earth is round. **3.** Ordinary; average. The dandelion is a *common* weed.

com·mon (kom′ən) *adjective,* **commoner, commonest.**

in common. Shared equally. The two friends had many interests *in common.*

commonplace Ordinary; not interesting, new, or remarkable. Snow is *commonplace* in Montreal but not in Vancouver.

com·mon·place (kom′ən plās′) *adjective.*

Commons *Canadian.* The House of Commons.

Com·mons (kom′ənz) *noun.*

common sense Ordinary good judgement. A person learns common sense from experience, not from school or study. It is only *common sense* to make sure a campfire is completely out before leaving it.

Commonwealth An association of countries, like Canada, most of which are now independent, but which were once ruled by Britain.

Com·mon·wealth (kom′ən welth′) *noun, plural* **Commonwealths.**

commotion A noisy confusion; disorder. There was a *commotion* at the ball park as the crowd booed the umpire's decision.

com·mo·tion (kə mō′shən) *noun, plural* **commotions.**

communicate To exchange or pass along feelings, thoughts, or information. People communicate with each other by speaking or writing. When I was away at camp, I *communicated* with my family by writing letters and telephoning.

com·mu·ni·cate (kə myōō′ni kāt′) *verb,* **communicated, communicating.**

communication **1.** An exchanging or sharing of feelings, thoughts, or information. The telephone makes *communication* over great distances possible. The Indians used smoke signals as a means of *communication.* **2. communications.** A system for sending messages by telephone, telegraph, radio, or television. *Communications* in the flooded town are still not working.

com·mu·ni·ca·tion (kə myōō′ni kā′shən) *noun, plural* **communications.**

communion **1.** A sharing of feelings or thoughts. There was a close *communion* between the father and his son. **2. Communion.** A religious service commemorating the last meal of Jesus and His apostles on the night before the Crucifixion.

com·mun·ion (kə myōōn′yən) *noun, plural* **communions.**

communism A system of social organization in which all property and goods are owned by the government and are shared equally by all the people. The government of the Soviet Union is based on this system.

com·mu·nism (kom′yə niz′əm) *noun.*

communist A person who believes in communism as a way of life or who belongs to a Communist Party.

com·mu·nist (kom′yə nist) *noun, plural* **communists.**

Communist Party A political party that is in favour of communism.

community A group of people who live together in the same place. Our *community* voted to build a new library.

com·mu·ni·ty (kə myōō′nə tē) *noun, plural* **communities.**

commute To travel regularly to and from work over quite a long distance. Father *commutes* to the city every day by train.

com·mute (kə myōōt′) *verb,* **commuted, commuting.**

compact¹ **1.** Tightly packed together; dense. *Compact* snow is good for making snowballs. **2.** Taking up a small amount of space. We have very *compact* cooking equipment for camping. *Adjective.*

at; āpe; cär; end; mē; it; īce; hot; ōld;
wood; fōōl; oil; out; up; turn; sing;
thin; this; hw in white; zh in treasure.
ə stands for a in about, e in taken,
i in pencil, o in lemon, and u in circus.

—**1.** A small case for face powder. **2.** An automobile that is smaller than a standard model. *Noun.*

com·pact (kom′pakt) *adjective; noun, plural* **compacts.**

compact² An agreement made by a group of people. The Metis made a *compact* among themselves as to how they would govern their settlement.

com·pact (kom′pakt) *noun, plural* **compacts.**

companion A person who often goes along with another; friend; comrade. Tom and Jack were constant *companions* at camp last summer.

com·pan·ion (kəm pan′yən) *noun, plural* **companions.**

companionship The relation between good companions; friendship. Sue missed the *companionship* of her friends when she moved to a new town.

com·pan·ion·ship (kəm pan′yən ship′) *noun.*

company **1.** A guest or guests. We are having *company* for dinner. **2.** A business firm or organization. My father works for a lumber *company.* **3.** Companionship. When all my family is away, I am grateful for my dog's *company.* **4.** A group of performers. A *company* of musicians is giving a concert tonight. **5. the Company.** *Canadian.* The Hudson's Bay Company.

com·pa·ny (kum′pə nē) *noun, plural* **companies.**

comparative **1.** That compares one thing with another. We made a *comparative* study of a frog and a worm in science class. **2.** Measured or judged by comparing. Jack is a *comparative* stranger to me, because I've only met him once. *Adjective.*

—The form of an adjective or adverb that gives the idea of "more." For example, the comparative of "short" is "shorter": Mary is shorter (more short) than Sue. *Noun.*

com·par·a·tive (kəm par′ə tiv) *adjective; noun, plural* **comparatives.**

compare **1.** To study to find out how persons or things are alike or different. Tom and Jack *compared* their watches and saw that Jack's watch was five minutes ahead of Tom's. **2.** To say or think that something is like something else; liken. The writer *compared* the sound of the thunder to the boom of big guns.

com·pare (kəm per′) *verb,* **compared, comparing.**

comparison **1.** The finding out of the likenesses and the differences between persons or things. A *comparison* of the two teams seems to show that Saturday's game will be close. **2.** A likeness; similarity. There is no *comparison* between those two cars when it comes to speed.

com·par·i·son (kəm par′ə sən) *noun, plural* **comparisons.**

compartment A separate division or section. My desk drawer has *compartments* for pencils, rubber bands, and paper clips.

com·part·ment (kəm pärt′mənt) *noun, plural* **compartments.**

compass **1.** An instrument for showing directions. A compass has a needle that points to the north. Airplane pilots, ship captains, and hikers all use a compass so they will always know in what direction they are going. **2.** An instrument for drawing circles or measuring distances. A compass is made up of two arms joined together at the top. One of the arms ends in a point and the other one holds a pencil.

Compass

com·pass (kum′pəs) *noun, plural* **compasses.**

compassion Sympathy for someone else's suffering or misfortune, together with the desire to help. Ruth had such *compassion* for the lonely old woman that she visited her every week in the hospital and brought her presents.

com·pas·sion (kəm pash′ən) *noun.*

compel To force. The policemen *compelled* the crowds to stay away from the burning building.

com·pel (kəm pel′) *verb,* **compelled, compelling.**

compensate **1.** To pay. The company *compensated* Mary for the extra hours she worked. The government *compensated* the farmer for the land they took from him to build the highway. **2.** To make up for something. The soccer player's speed *compensated* for his small size.

com·pen·sate (kom′pən sāt′) *verb,* **compensated, compensating.**

compensation Something that makes up for something else. The company gave the employee money as a *compensation* for the extra work she had done.

com·pen·sa·tion (kom′pən sā′shən) *noun, plural* **compensations.**

132

compete To try to win or gain something from another or others. The two girls *competed* against each other for first prize in the spelling contest.
 com·pete (kəm pēt′) *verb,* **competed, competing.**

competent Able and capable. Only *competent* swimmers should use the deep end of the pool.
 com·pe·tent (kom′pə tənt) *adjective.*

competition 1. The act of trying to win or gain something from another or others; rivalry. Our team was in *competition* with three others for the championship. 2. A contest. George is going to enter the swimming *competition.*
 com·pe·ti·tion (kom′pə tish′ən) *noun, plural* **competitions.**

competitive Involving or using competition. Most sports are *competitive.*
 com·pet·i·tive (kəm pet′ə tiv) *adjective.*

competitor A person or thing that tries to win or gain something from another or others. Sarah's main *competitor* in running for school president was her best friend. My father's gas station has two *competitors* within two blocks.
 com·pet·i·tor (kəm pet′ə tər) *noun, plural* **competitors.**

compile To collect or put together in a list or report. Libraries *compile* facts about all the books they have on their shelves.
 com·pile (kəm pīl′) *verb,* **compiled, compiling.**

complacent Pleased with oneself; satisfied. The boxing champion was so *complacent* that he did not even bother to train for his match with the challenger.
 com·pla·cent (kəm plā′sənt) *adjective.*

complain 1. To say that something is wrong; find fault. My father *complains* that his train is never on time. My brother *complained* all day about a stomachache. 2. To make an accusation or charge. We *complained* to the police about our noisy neighbours.
 com·plain (kəm plān′) *verb,* **complained, complaining.**

complaint 1. A finding fault. We took our *complaint* about the rude clerk to the store manager. 2. A cause for complaining. I have no *complaints* about the food in this restaurant. 3. An accusation or charge. The storekeeper made a *complaint* against the man that had robbed his store.
 com·plaint (kəm plānt′) *noun, plural* **complaints.**

complement Something that makes complete. The football team now has its full *complement* of players. *Noun.*
—To make complete. The background music nicely *complements* the acting in the movie. *Verb.* ▲ Another word that sounds like this is **compliment.**
 com·ple·ment (kom′plə mənt *for noun;* kom′plə ment′ *for verb) noun, plural* **complements;** *verb,* **complemented, complementing.**

complete 1. Having all its parts; whole; entire. Our school library has the *complete* writings of William Shakespeare. 2. Ended; finished. Rick promised his parents he would not go out and play until his homework was *complete.* 3. Thorough; perfect. The new play promised to be a *complete* success. *Adjective.*
—1. To make whole or perfect. Joe is trying to *complete* his collection of baseball cards. 2. To bring to an end; finish. Lucy wanted to *complete* the first chapter of her book before going to bed. *Verb.*
 com·plete (kəm plēt′) *adjective; verb,* **completed, completing.**

completely 1. Wholly; entirely. Jill was being *completely* honest when she told the teacher that she had not tripped Pam on purpose. 2. Thoroughly; perfectly. Anne was *completely* exhausted after skiing all day.
 com·plete·ly (kəm plēt′lē) *adverb.*

completion 1. The act of completing. The early *completion* of our house meant that we would be able to move in sooner. 2. The condition of being completed. Steve hoped to bring his science project to *completion* before the holidays.
 com·ple·tion (kəm plē′shən) *noun.*

complex 1. Hard or difficult to understand or do. I don't know how to solve this *complex* arithmetic problem. 2. Made up of many parts. My brother studied for months before he learned to fix such a *complex* machine as a computer.
 com·plex (kom′pleks′ *or* kom′pleks′) *adjective.*

complexion 1. The colour and look of a person's skin. Alice has a lovely rosy *complexion.* 2. The general look or character of anything. The substitution of two new players on

at; āpe; cär; end; mē; it; īce; hot; ōld;
wood; fōōl; oil; out; up; turn; sing;
thin; this; hw in white; zh in treasure.
ə stands for a in about, e in taken,
i in pencil, o in lemon, and u in circus.

our team changed the whole *complexion* of the game, and we won.

com·plex·ion (kəm plek′shən) *noun, plural* **complexions.**

complexity The quality of being complex. The *complexity* of the arithmetic problem puzzled all the students in the class.

com·plex·i·ty (kəm plek′sə tē) *noun, plural* **complexities.**

complicate To make harder to understand or do. His little brother's attempts to help only *complicated* John's job of washing the car.

com·pli·cate (kom′plə kāt′) *verb,* **complicated, complicating.**

complicated Hard to understand or do. The directions for putting together the bicycle were too *complicated* for me to follow.

com·pli·cat·ed (kom′plə kāt′id) *adjective.*

complication A confused or difficult condition. The snowstorm that closed the airport caused a *complication* in our travel plans.

com·pli·ca·tion (kom′plə kā′shən) *noun, plural* **complications.**

compliment Something good that is said in praise or admiration. Joan receives many *compliments* on her cooking. *Noun.*
—To praise or admire. The teacher *complimented* Ellen on her well-written composition. *Verb.* ▲ Another word that sounds like this is **complement.**

com·pli·ment (kom′plə mənt *for noun;* kom′plə ment′ *for verb*) *noun, plural* **compliments;** *verb,* **complimented, complimenting.**

complimentary 1. Containing or expressing praise or admiration. The teacher made a *complimentary* remark to Mr. Smith about his daughter's work. 2. Without charge; free. The coach gave us two *complimentary* tickets to the football game.

com·pli·men·ta·ry (kom′plə men′tə rē *or* kom′plə men′trē) *adjective.*

comply To act in agreement with a request or rule. I *complied* with the doctor's orders and stayed home until my cold was better.

com·ply (kəm plī′) *verb,* **complied, complying.**

compose 1. To make up. The material in this dress is *composed* of cotton and rayon. Twelve people *compose* a jury. 2. To put together; create. Jack and Betty *composed* a new school cheer. The musician *composed* an opera. 3. To make quiet or calm. She tried to *compose* herself after hearing the sad news.

com·pose (kəm pōz′) *verb,* **composed, composing.**

composer A person who composes a musical work or anything else. Johann Sebastian Bach is a very famous *composer.*

com·pos·er (kəm pō′zər) *noun, plural* **composers.**

composite Made up of various parts. The photographer made a *composite* picture by putting together parts of a few old snapshots.

com·pos·ite (kom′pə zit *or* kəm poz′it) *adjective.*

composite school *Canadian.* A high school that offers training in business and technical courses, as well as the usual high school courses.

composition 1. The making of anything. The *composition* of the musician's new opera took two years. 2. The parts that make up something. The scientist studied the moon rock to find out its *composition.* 3. Something that is put together or created. Steve wrote a *composition* for his English class.

com·po·si·tion (kom′pə zish′ən) *noun, plural* **compositions.**

composure Self-control; calmness. The mother's *composure* when the fire broke out helped her to save all her children.

com·po·sure (kəm pō′zhər) *noun.*

compound Made up of two or more parts. "Football" is a *compound* word. A grasshopper has *compound* eyes that allow it to see in almost all directions at once. *Adjective.*
—To mix or combine. A druggist's job is to *compound* medicines. *Verb.*
—1. A mixture or combination. Steel is a *compound* of iron and carbon. 2. A substance that is formed by the chemical combination of two or more elements. Water is a *compound* of hydrogen and oxygen. *Noun.*

com·pound (kom′pound′ *for adjective and noun;* kəm pound′ *for verb*) *adjective; verb,* **compounded, compounding;** *noun, plural* **compounds.**

comprehend To understand. The teacher felt that her students still did not *comprehend* how to add and subtract fractions.

com·pre·hend (kom′prə hend′) *verb,* **comprehended, comprehending.**

▲ The word **comprehend** used to mean "to catch" or "to take hold of." For example, one horseman could ride fast enough to *comprehend* another. This led to our use of *comprehend* to mean "to take hold of with the mind" or "to understand."

comprehension The power of understanding. Joe said that a knowledge of how com-

puters work was beyond his *comprehension.*
com·pre·hen·sion (kom′prə hen′shən) *noun,*
plural **comprehensions.**

compress To press or squeeze together.
The city has big machines to *compress* garbage so it will take up less room. *Verb.*
—A pad or cloth used to put pressure, heat,
or cold on some part of the body. The mother
put a cold *compress* on her child's head when
he had a fever. *Noun.*
    com·press (kəm pres′ *for verb;* kom′pres′ *for*
noun) *verb,* **compressed, compressing;** *noun,*
plural **compresses.**

comprise To consist of. Canada *comprises*
ten provinces and two huge territories.
    com·prise (kəm prīz′) *verb,* **comprised, com-
prising.**

compromise The settlement of an argument or disagreement. A compromise is
reached by having each side give up part of
its demands. When Rick refused to eat his
spinach, his mother offered him a *compromise* and made him eat only half of it. *Noun.*
—To reach a settlement by agreeing that each
side will give up some part of its demands.
When the two boys wanted to watch different television programs, they *compromised*
and watched parts of both. *Verb.*
    com·pro·mise (kom′prə mīz′) *noun, plural*
compromises; *verb,* **compromised, com-
promising.**

compulsory Required by law or rules. Gym
class is *compulsory* in this school.
    com·pul·so·ry (kəm pul′sər ē) *adjective.*

compute To find out or calculate by using
mathematics. The builder *computed* the cost
of a new garage. Scientists have *computed*
how far away the moon is from the earth.
    com·pute (kəm pyo͞ot′) *verb,* **computed,
computing.**

computer An electronic machine for storing, organizing, and retrieving information.
Computers can solve mathematical problems
very quickly, and show words and pictures
on a TV screen.
    com·put·er (kəm pyo͞ot′ər) *noun, plural*
computers.

comrade A close friend who shares the
same work or interests with another.
    com·rade (kom′rad) *noun, plural* **comrades.**

▲ The word **comrade** comes from the Latin
word for "room." *Comrade* first meant
"someone who shares a room with another
person."

concave Curving inward. The inside of a
bowl is *concave.* The arch of a person's foot
is *concave.*
    con·cave (kon kāv′ *or*
kon′kāv) *adjective.*

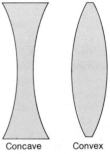

Concave   Convex

conceal To put or keep
out of sight; hide. Father
concealed the car keys
under the seat. Helen
concealed her anger by
smiling.
    con·ceal (kən sēl′) *verb,*
concealed, concealing.

concede To admit as
true. The candidate for
mayor would not *concede* that he had lost the
election until all the votes were counted.
    con·cede (kən sēd′) *verb,* **conceded, conced-
ing.**

conceited Having too high an opinion of
oneself or of one's ability to do things. The
conceited boy was always talking about how
good-looking he was.
    con·ceit·ed (kən sēt′id) *adjective.*

conceive To think or imagine; think up.
Scientists *conceived* the plan for the first
spacecraft.
    con·ceive (kən sēv′) *verb,* **conceived, conceiv-
ing.**

concentrate 1. To bring together in one
place. The population in our country is *concentrated* in the cities. The team *concentrated*
their efforts on winning the game. 2. To make
stronger or thicker. That company *concen-
trates* orange juice and sells it in small cans.
3. To pay attention. Bill could not *concentrate* on his homework because of the noise.
    con·cen·trate (kon′sən trāt′) *verb,* **concen-
trated, concentrating.**

concentration 1. The act of concentrating
or the state of being concentrated. Because
of the shampoo's *concentration,* you don't
have to use very much of it to get a lot of
suds. 2. Close attention. Jim's *concentration*
on the television program was so deep that he
didn't hear the doorbell.
    con·cen·tra·tion (kon′sən trā′shən) *noun,*
plural **concentrations.**

concept A general idea; thought. My cousin
is always late for everything because he has

at; āpe; cär; end; mē; it; īce; hot; ōld;
wood; fo͞ol; oil; out; up; turn; sing;
thin; <u>th</u>is; hw in white; zh in treasure.
ə stands for a in about, e in taken,
i in pencil, o in lemon, and u in circus.

no *concept* of what time it is.

con·cept (kon′sept) *noun, plural* **concepts.**

conception An idea; concept. Learning about travel in space gives you some *conception* of how enormous the universe must be.

con·cep·tion (kən sep′shən) *noun, plural* **conceptions.**

concern 1. To be important to; have to do with. What Mother said about saving money *concerns* our whole family. 2. To worry. Her bad cough *concerned* her son. *Verb.*
—1. Something that is important to a person. Taking care of the puppy is my *concern.* 2. Worried interest. He was full of *concern* for his sick brother. 3. A business. Mr. Smith owns a clothing *concern. Noun.*

con·cern (kən surn′) *verb,* **concerned, con-cerning;** *noun, plural* **concerns.**

concerning About; regarding. Mike wrote me a long letter *concerning* his new school.

con·cern·ing (kən surn′ing) *preposition.*

concert A performance of music by a number of musicians. We went to a band *concert.*

con·cert (kon′sərt) *noun, plural* **concerts.**

concerto A piece of music for one or more musical instruments accompanied by an orchestra.

con·cer·to (kən cher′tō) *noun, plural* **concer-tos.**

concession[1] 1. The act of conceding or granting. As a *concession,* Dad let Sally go camping with her older sisters. 2. Something conceded. Father made a *concession* and let me stay up late to watch wrestling. 3. The right to something granted by a government or other authority. The town gave Mom the *concession* to sell hot dogs in the park.

con·ces·sion (kən sesh′ən) *noun, plural* **con-cessions.**

concession[2] 1. *Canadian.* A subdivision of rural land in a township of Ontario or Quebec. 2. *Canadian.* A road in a concession.

con·ces·sion (kən sesh′ən) *noun, plural* **con-cessions.**

conch The large, coiled shell of a sea animal.

conch (kongk *or* konch) *noun, plural* **conchs** or **conches.**

concise Saying much in few words. The coach's instructions to the team were clear and *concise.*

con·cise (kən sīs′) *ad-jective.*

Conch

conclude 1. To bring to

an end; finish. When the band *concluded* the playing of the national anthem, the baseball game began. 2. To decide after thinking. After hearing all the facts, he *concluded* that he had been wrong.

con·clude (kən klood′) *verb,* **concluded, con-cluding.**

conclusion 1. The end of something. The *conclusion* of the movie was very happy. 2. Arrangement; settlement. The *conclusion* of the treaty between the two countries took many months. 3. Something decided after thinking. Tom eventually came to the *conclu-sion* that he wanted to be a doctor when he grew older.

con·clu·sion (kən kloo′zhən) *noun, plural* **conclusions.**

concrete Able to be seen and touched; real. A chair is a *concrete* object. *Adjective.*
—A mixture of cement, pebbles, sand, and water. Concrete becomes very hard when it dries. Concrete is used in building office buildings and bridges and in paving roads and sidewalks. *Noun.*

con·crete (kon′krēt′) *adjective; noun.*

concussion 1. A sudden, violent shaking. The house shook from the *concussion* of the explosion. 2. An injury to the brain or spine caused by a fall or blow. Falling out of the tree on his head caused him to have a *concus-sion.*

con·cus·sion (kən kush′ən) *noun, plural* **con-cussions.**

condemn 1. To be against; disapprove of. Many people *condemn* smoking. 2. To find someone guilty. The judge *condemned* the thief to ten years in jail. 3. To declare to be no longer safe or fit for use. The city government *condemned* the old building because it was falling down.

con·demn (kən dem′) *verb,* **condemned, con-demning.**

condensation 1. The act of condensing something. The *condensation* of steam causes it to change into water. 2. Something condensed. Alice read a *condensation* of the long novel.

con·den·sa·tion (kon′den sā′shən) *noun, plu-ral* **condensations.**

condense 1. To make less; thicken; shorten. You can *condense* milk by boiling away much of the water in it. The writer *condensed* the long story to a short story. 2. To change from a gas to a liquid or solid form. Steam *con-denses* to water when cooled.

con·dense (kən dens′) *verb,* **condensed, con-densing.**

condition 1. The way that a person or thing is. That athlete keeps in good *condition* by doing exercises. 2. Something needed for something else; a thing that something else depends on. Being a good skater is one of the *conditions* for getting on the hockey team. 3. conditions. State of affairs; circumstances. Poor working *conditions* caused the employees to go on strike. *Noun.*
—1. To put in a healthy or good condition. Carl exercises to *condition* his body. 2. To make used to something; accustom. Living at the North Pole soon *conditioned* the explorers to cold weather. *Verb.*
con·di·tion (kən dish′ən) *noun, plural* conditions; *verb,* conditioned, conditioning.

condor A large bird with a hooked bill and a bare head and neck. A condor is a kind of vulture. It is found in the mountains of South America and California.
con·dor (kon′dər) *noun, plural* condors.

Condor

conduct The way someone behaves. My mother was thankful for my little brother's good *conduct* in front of the guests. *Noun.*
—1. To behave. The spoiled child *conducted* himself badly. 2. To direct or lead. Our music teacher will *conduct* the school orchestra. 3. To take charge of; control; manage. Mrs. Smith *conducts* a successful hardware business. 4. To carry or transmit. Cast iron *conducts* heat evenly. *Verb.*
con·duct (kon′dukt *for noun;* kən dukt′ *for verb*) *noun, plural* conducts; *verb,* conducted, conducting.

conductor 1. A person who conducts. Our music teacher is also the *conductor* of the school orchestra. 2. A person on a train or bus who collects fares. The conductor also calls out the names of stops. 3. Something that transmits heat, electricity, or sound. Plastic is a poor *conductor* of heat.
con·duc·tor (kən duk′tər) *noun, plural* conductors.

cone 1. A solid, pointed object that has a flat, round base. 2. Something shaped like a cone. I like to eat ice cream in a *cone.* 3. A fruit with scales, that grows on a pine tree or other evergreen tree. The cone bears the seeds.
cone (kōn) *noun, plural* cones.

The teepee has the shape of a **cone.**

confederacy A group of countries, states, or people joined together for a common purpose. The five Indian tribes joined to form a *confederacy.*
con·fed·er·a·cy (kən fed′ər ə sē) *noun, plural* confederacies.

confederate 1. A person or group that joins with another for a common purpose. The bank robber and his *confederates* were arrested by the police. 2. *Canadian.* A person who supports Canadian Confederation. *Noun.*
—Joined together for a common purpose. *Adjective.*
con·fed·er·ate (kən fed′ər it) *noun, plural* confederates; *adjective.*

confederation 1. The act of joining together to form a confederacy. The two small countries began plans for *confederation.* 2. A group of countries, states, or provinces that are joined together for a common purpose. After gaining independence from Britain, the American states formed a *confederation.*
con·fed·er·a·tion (kən fed′ə rā′shən) *noun, plural* confederations.

Confederation *Canadian.* The joining together of New Brunswick, Nova Scotia, Ontario, and Quebec in 1867 to become Canada.

confer 1. To meet and talk together. The coach of the football team will *confer* with his assistants about the new player. 2. To give. The general will *confer* a medal on the brave soldier.
con·fer (kən fur′) *verb,* conferred, conferring.

at; āpe; cär; end; mē; it; īce; hot; ōld;
wood; fōol; oil; out; up; turn; sing;
thin; this; hw in white; zh in treasure.
ə stands for a in about, e in taken,
i in pencil, o in lemon, and u in circus.

conference A meeting. A *conference* of doctors from all over the country was held to discuss new ways to treat disease.
con·fer·ence (kon′fər əns) *noun, plural* conferences.

confess 1. To admit. The crook *confessed* his guilt. She *confessed* that she really liked him. 2. To tell a priest your sins.
con·fess (kən fes′) *verb,* confessed, confessing.

confession The confessing of something. The man made a full *confession* to the crime.
con·fes·sion (kən fesh′ən) *noun, plural* confessions.

confide To tell a secret to someone; trust. Janet always *confides* in her best friends. He *confided* his worries to his mother.
con·fide (kən fīd′) *verb,* confided, confiding.

confidence 1. Trust or faith. I have *confidence* in his honesty. 2. Faith in oneself. Mary gave the answer with *confidence*. 3. Trust that a person will not tell a secret. Sue told me her plans for the surprise party in *confidence*.
con·fi·dence (kon′fə dəns) *noun.*

confident Having trust or faith; sure. I am *confident* that our team will win the game.
con·fi·dent (kon′fə dənt) *adjective.*

confidential Secret. The ambassador sent a *confidential* letter to the prime minister.
con·fi·den·tial (kon′fə den′shəl) *adjective.*

confine To hold or keep in; limit. The police *confined* the outlaw in a jail cell. Jean's bad cold *confined* her to her bed. *Verb.*
—A limit; boundary. The dog was not allowed to go outside the *confines* of the yard. *Noun.*
con·fine (kən fīn′ *for verb;* kon′fīn *for noun*) *verb,* confined, confining; *noun, plural* confines.

confirm 1. To show to be true or correct. The newspaper *confirmed* reports of a flood. 2. To consent to; approve. Parliament *confirmed* the trade agreement. 3. To admit a person to full membership in a church or synagogue.
con·firm (kən furm′) *verb,* confirmed, confirming.

confirmation 1. The act of confirming something. He called the hotel for *confirmation* of his reservation. 2. The ceremony of admitting a person to full membership in a church or synagogue.
con·fir·ma·tion (kon′fər mā′shən) *noun, plural* confirmations.

confiscate To take something by authority. The government *confiscated* the man's property when he couldn't pay his taxes.
con·fis·cate (kon′fis kāt′) *verb,* confiscated, confiscating.

conflict 1. A long fight; war. The *conflict* between the two countries lasted a long time. 2. A strong disagreement. The two newspaper stories about the fire are in *conflict*. *Noun.*
—To disagree strongly. The two accounts of the accident *conflict*. *Verb.*
con·flict (kon′flikt *for noun;* kən flikt′ *for verb*) *noun, plural* conflicts; *verb,* conflicted, conflicting.

conform 1. To act or think in a way that agrees with a rule or a standard. New students were told that they must *conform* to the rules of the school. 2. To be the same; be like. The house *conformed* to the architect's plans.
con·form (kən fōrm′) *verb,* conformed, conforming.

confront To meet or face. The soldiers *confronted* the enemy soldiers. A hard problem *confronted* her.
con·front (kən frunt′) *verb,* confronted, confronting.

confuse 1. To mix up; bewilder. The hard rules for the game *confuse* me. The street signs *confused* the driver and he took a wrong turn. 2. To mistake one for another. People are always *confusing* the twins.
con·fuse (kən fyo͞oz′) *verb,* confused, confusing.

confusion 1. Disorder or bewilderment. Everything in my desk drawer was in *confusion*. In his *confusion*, he gave the wrong answer. 2. A mistaking of one person or thing for another. Mrs. Young's *confusion* of David with his brother embarrassed her.
con·fu·sion (kən fyo͞o′zhən) *noun, plural* confusions.

congratulate To give a person one's good wishes or praise for success or for something nice that has happened. We *congratulated* Ruth on doing such a good job on her science project.
con·grat·u·late (kən grach′ə lāt′) *verb,* congratulated, congratulating.

congratulations Good wishes or praise given for a person's success or for something nice that has happened. We offered *congratulations* to Phil when he won the race.
con·grat·u·la·tions (kən grach′ə lā′shənz) *noun plural.*

congregate To come together in a crowd. People *congregated* around the famous movie star to get her autograph.

con·quer (kong′kər) *verb,* **conquered, conquering.**

conqueror A person who conquers. In ancient times, Alexander the Great was a powerful *conqueror.*
con·quer·or (kong′kər ər) *noun, plural* **conquerors.**

conquest **1.** The act of conquering something. The *conquest* of the country took the invading army many months. **2.** Something conquered. Mexico was once a *conquest* of Spain.
con·quest (kon′kwest *or* kong′kwest) *noun, plural* **conquests.**

conscience A feeling about what is right and what is wrong. Your conscience tells you to do right and warns when you are doing something wrong. The lie that he told troubled his *conscience.*
con·science (kon′shəns) *noun, plural* **consciences.**

conscientious Showing honesty, thought, and care. Agnes does *conscientious* work at school.
con·sci·en·tious (kon′shē en′shəs) *adjective.*

conscious **1.** Knowing or realizing; aware. He was *conscious* of someone tapping his shoulder. **2.** Able to see and feel things; awake. He remained *conscious* even though he was hit hard on the head. **3.** Done on purpose. She made a *conscious* effort to stop laughing.
con·scious (kon′shəs) *adjective.*

consecutive Following one after another without a break. 1, 2, 3, and 4 are *consecutive* numbers.
con·sec·u·tive (kən sek′yə tiv) *adjective.*

consent To give permission; agree to. Mother would not *consent* to my going camping by myself. *Verb.*
—Permission. My parents had to give their *consent* before I could go on the field trip with my class. *Noun.*
con·sent (kən sent′) *verb,* **consented, consenting;** *noun, plural* **consents.**

consequence **1.** Outcome; result. He climbed over the barbed-wire fence and as a *consequence* he ripped his pants. She suffered the *consequences* of her bad behaviour.

---

at; āpe; cär; end; mē; it; īce; hot; ōld;
wood; fōōl; oil; out; up; turn; sing;
thin; this; hw in white; zh in treasure.
ə stands for a in about, e in taken,
i in pencil, o in lemon, and u in circus.

---

electrician looked for the bad *connection* in the wiring.
con·nec·tion (kə nek′shən) *noun, plural* **connections.**

conquer To overcome; defeat. He tried to *conquer* the habit of biting his nails.

2. Importance. What he thinks is of little *consequence* to me.

con·se·quence (kon′sə kwens′) *noun, plural* **consequences.**

consequently As a result; therefore. He did not wear his boots when it rained, and *consequently* he got his shoes wet.

con·se·quent·ly (kon′sə kwent′lē) *adverb.*

conservation The protection and wise use of the forests, rivers, minerals, and other natural resources of a country.

con·ser·va·tion (kon′sər vā′shən) *noun.*

conservative Wanting things to be as they used to be or to stay as they are; being against changes or new ideas. *Adjective.*
—A person who is conservative. *Noun.*

con·serv·a·tive (kən sur′və tiv) *adjective; noun, plural* **conservatives.**

Conservative *Canadian.* A member of the Progressive Conservative Party.

conserve To keep and protect. Terry *conserved* his energy for the hike.

con·serve (kən surv′) *verb,* **conserved, conserving.**

consider **1.** To think carefully about before deciding. Tom's older sister will *consider* going to university. **2.** To think of as; believe to be. The boys *consider* Ed the best player on the team.

con·sid·er (kən sid′ər) *verb,* **considered, considering.**

considerate Thoughtful of other people and their feelings. The *considerate* boy offered his seat to the old man.

con·sid·er·ate (kən sid′ər ət) *adjective.*

consideration **1.** Thoughtfulness for other people and their feelings. Jean shows *consideration* for the neighbours by not playing her record player too loudly. **2.** Careful thought before deciding about something. After much *consideration*, my sister decided to study law.

con·sid·er·a·tion (kən sid′ə rā′shən) *noun, plural* **considerations.**

consist To be made up. Bricks *consist* mostly of clay. A year *consists* of twelve months.

con·sist (kən sist′) *verb,* **consisted, consisting.**

consistency **1.** Thickness or stiffness. This paint has the *consistency* of glue. **2.** A keeping to one way of thinking or acting. Since he changes his mind so often, there is no *consistency* to what he says or believes.

con·sist·en·cy (kən sis′tən sē) *noun, plural* **consistencies.**

consistent **1.** Keeping to one way of thinking or acting. The boy remained *consistent* in his love of animals, and when he grew up he became a veterinarian. **2.** In agreement. What

he said about the accident is not *consistent* with what really happened.

con·sist·ent (kən sis′tənt) *adjective.*

console[1] To comfort or cheer. You try to console a person who is sad or disappointed about something. The mother tried to *console* the weeping child for the loss of his kitten.

con·sole (kən sōl′) *verb,* **consoled, consoling.**

console[2] The cabinet of a radio, television set, or phonograph that rests on the floor.

con·sole (kon′sōl) *noun, plural* **consoles.**

Console

consolidate To join together; combine. The two stores *consolidated* to form one large store.

con·sol·i·date (kən sol′ə dāt′) *verb,* **consolidated, consolidating.**

consonant A letter of the alphabet that is not a vowel. Consonants include the letters *b, d, f, g, m, p,* and *t.*

con·so·nant (kon′sə nənt) *noun, plural* **consonants.**

conspicuous Easily seen; attracting attention; striking. The blue ink left a *conspicuous* stain on the tablecloth.

con·spic·u·ous (kən spik′yo͞o əs) *adjective.*

conspiracy Secret planning together with others to do something wrong. They caught the leader of the *conspiracy* to rob the bank.

con·spir·a·cy (kən spir′ə sē) *noun, plural* **conspiracies.**

constable A member of the police force in England; police officer.

con·sta·ble (kon′stə bəl) *noun, plural* **constables.**

constant Not changing; continuing. The boy's *constant* talking made the teacher angry.

con·stant (kon′stənt) *adjective.*

constellation A group of stars. A constellation forms a pattern in the sky that looks like a picture. The Big Dipper and the Little Dipper are parts of constellations.

con·stel·la·tion (kon′stə lā′shən) *noun, plural* **constellations.**

constituency *Canadian.* **1.** The riding represented by a Member of Parliament or a Member of the Legislative Assembly. **2.** The voters in a riding.
con·stit·u·en·cy (kən stich′o͞o ən sē) *noun, plural* **constituencies.**

constituent Forming a needed part. Hydrogen and oxygen are the *constituent* parts of water. *Adjective.*
—1. A needed part. Pulp is an important *constituent* of paper. **2.** A voter. *Noun.*
con·stit·u·ent (kən stich′o͞o ənt) *adjective; noun, plural* **constituents.**

constitute To make up; form. Twelve months *constitute* a year.
con·sti·tute (kon′stə to͞ot′ *or* kon′stə tyo͞ot′) *verb,* **constituted, constituting.**

constitution **1.** The way in which a person or thing is made. The healthy boy has a strong *constitution*. **2.** The basic principles used to govern an organization or country.
con·sti·tu·tion (kon′stə to͞o′shən *or* kon′stə-tyo͞o′shən) *noun, plural* **constitutions.**

Constitution Act *Canadian.* Any act passed by Parliament to change the constitution of Canada. Since 1982 Canada has had the power to pass Constitution Acts without the approval of the British Parliament. Each Constitution Act is followed by a date that tells the year it was enacted. The Constitution Act, 1982 contains our Charter of Rights and Freedoms.

constitutional Having to do with a constitution. She is an expert in *constitutional* law.
con·sti·tu·tion·al (kon′stə to͞o′shən əl *or* kon′stə tyo͞o′shən əl) *adjective.*

constrict To make smaller or narrower by pressing together. The dog's tight collar *constricted* its neck.
con·strict (kən strikt′) *verb,* **constricted, constricting.**

constrictor A large snake that can kill small animals by squeezing them in its coils. The python is one kind of constrictor.
con·stric·tor (kən strik′tər) *noun, plural* **constrictors.**

Constrictor

construct To make by putting parts together; build. Kim and her father *constructed* a tool shed in the back yard. The province will *construct* a new highway to the town.
con·struct (kən strukt′) *verb,* **constructed, constructing.**

construction The act of constructing something; building. The *construction* of the new gym was started last summer.
con·struc·tion (kən struk′shən) *noun, plural* **constructions.**

constructive Serving to make better; helpful. The coach always gives *constructive* criticism so that the players can improve their game.
con·struc·tive (kən struk′tiv) *adjective.*

consul A person appointed by a government to live in a foreign city. A consul protects his country's citizens and business there.
con·sul (kon′səl) *noun, plural* **consuls.**

consult To go to for advice or information. When you are ill, you *consult* a doctor. We *consulted* a map to find out where the town was located.
con·sult (kən sult′) *verb,* **consulted, consulting.**

consume To use up or destroy. A car *consumes* gasoline. The fire *consumed* the garage and part of the house.
con·sume (kən soom′ *or* kən syo͞om′) *verb,* **consumed, consuming.**

consumer A person who buys and uses up things. A person who shops for food in a grocery store is a consumer. People who buy radios, books, cars, and many other things are consumers.
con·sum·er (kən so͞o′mər *or* kən syo͞om′ər) *noun, plural* **consumers.**

consumption The using up of something. The *consumption* of gasoline is greater in a big car than in a small car.
con·sump·tion (kən sump′shən) *noun, plural* **consumptions.**

contact A touching or meeting. When the baby came in *contact* with the hot stove, he burned his hand. Ann lost *contact* with her friends when she moved away. *Noun.*
—To get in touch with; communicate with;

at; āpe; cär; end; mē; it; īce; hot; ōld;
wood; fo͞ol; oil; out; up; turn; sing;
thin; <u>th</u>is; hw in white; zh in treasure.
ə stands for a in about, e in taken,
i in pencil, o in lemon, and u in circus.

reach. Mary tried to *contact* her friend by telephone. *Verb.*
con·tact (kon′takt) *noun, plural* **contacts;** *verb,* **contacted, contacting.**

contagious Spread from person to person. Everyone in the class caught chicken pox because it is so *contagious.*
con·ta·gious (kən tā′jəs) *adjective.*

contain 1. To hold. The jar *contains* candy. The shelf *contains* books. 2. To be made up of. Candy *contains* sugar. A litre *contains* one thousand millilitres. 3. To keep or hold back. She tried to *contain* her laughter when the boy's chair tipped over backwards.
con·tain (kən tān′) *verb,* **contained, containing.**

container A box, can, or jar that holds something. I bought a *container* of milk at the grocery store.
con·tain·er (kən tā′nər) *noun, plural* **containers.**

contaminate To make dirty; pollute. If the town throws garbage in the river it will *contaminate* the water.
con·tam·i·nate (kən tam′ə nāt′) *verb,* **contaminated, contaminating.**

contemplate To think about something carefully for a long time. The young man sat and *contemplated* his future.
con·tem·plate (kon′təm plāt′) *verb,* **contemplated, contemplating.**

contemporary Belonging to the same time. Sir Robert Borden and Sir Wilfrid Laurier were *contemporary* figures in our history. *Adjective.*
—A person who belongs to the same time as another person. *Noun.*
con·tem·po·rar·y (kən tem′pə rer′ē) *adjective; noun, plural* **contemporaries.**

contempt A feeling that a person or act is bad, mean, or worth nothing; scorn. He has *contempt* for people who are cruel to animals.
con·tempt (kən tempt′) *noun.*

contend 1. To compete. Sally and Mike *contended* for the swimming championship. 2. To argue. Tom *contended* that he could run the fastest. 3. To struggle. The explorers had to *contend* with very cold weather at the North Pole.
con·tend (kən tend′) *verb,* **contended, contending.**

content Happy and satisfied. Bill and Jane are not *content* to stay home and play games on rainy days. *Adjective.*
—To make happy; satisfy. A pat on the head and a kind word *contents* my dog. *Verb.*

—A feeling of being happy or satisfied. After eating, the baby went to sleep in complete *content. Noun.*
con·tent (kən tent′) *adjective; verb,* **contented, contenting;** *noun.*

contented Happy and satisfied. A contented person is happy with what he is and what he has. The *contented* kitten purred and rubbed against my leg.
con·tent·ed (kən ten′tid) *adjective.*

contents 1. What something holds. When the bag broke, its *contents* fell all over the floor. 2. What is written or spoken about. This book has a table of *contents* in the front.
con·tents (kon′tents) *noun plural.*

contest 1. A game or race that people try to win. Our team won the hurdles *contest.* Jim won the pie-eating *contest* at the church fair. 2. A struggle; fight. The *contest* between the two countries lasted for more than twenty years.
con·test (kon′test) *noun, plural* **contests.**

contestant A person who takes part in a contest. Barbara was a *contestant* in the swimming meet. The *contestant* on the television quiz show won a car and a trip to Hawaii.
con·test·ant (kən tes′tənt) *noun, plural* **contestants.**

continent One of the seven large land areas on the earth. The continents are Asia, Africa, North America, South America, Antarctica, Europe, and Australia.
con·ti·nent (kont′ən ənt) *noun, plural* **continents.**

continual Going on without stopping. The electric clock made a *continual* humming noise.
con·tin·u·al (kən tin′yo͞o əl) *adjective.*

continue To keep on happening or doing; go on without stopping. The snowfall *continued* for two days. Tom *continued* his work in spite of a bad headache.
con·tin·ue (kən tin′yo͞o) *verb,* **continued, continuing.**

continuous Going on without a break; unbroken. The river has a *continuous* flow of water.
con·tin·u·ous (kən tin′yo͞o əs) *adjective.*

contour The outline or shape of something. The astronauts could see the curved *contour* of the earth.
con·tour (kon′toor) *noun, plural* **contours.**

contract 1. To make or become shorter or smaller. A turtle can *contract* his neck so that his head can be drawn into its shell. We *contract* words like "are not" to form

"aren't" and "she had" to form "she'd."
2. To make an agreement. The painter *contracted* to paint the house for $600. *Verb.*
—An agreement. The singer signed a *contract* to make records for the record company. *Noun.*
  con·tract (kən trakt′ *for verb, definition 1;*
kən trakt′ *or* kon′trakt *for verb, definition 2;*
kon′trakt *for noun*) *verb,* **contracted, contracting;** *noun, plural* **contracts.**

contraction **1.** The act of contracting or the state of being contracted. The *contraction* of the heart forces blood into the arteries. **2.** A shortened form. "Wouldn't" is the contraction of "would not."
  con·trac·tion (kən trak′shən) *noun, plural* **contractions.**

contradict To say the opposite of; disagree with. The boy *contradicted* what he had said earlier about the accident.
  con·tra·dict (kon′trə dikt′) *verb,* **contradicted, contradicting.**

contralto **1.** The lowest female singing voice. **2.** A singer who has such a voice.
  con·tral·to (kən tral′tō) *noun, plural* **contraltos.**

contrary **1.** Entirely different; opposite. My brother's ideas about sports and music are *contrary* to my own. **2.** Liking to argue and oppose. That *contrary* boy never agrees with what other people say.
  con·trar·y (kon′trer ē *for definition 1;*
kon′trer ē *or* kən trer′ē *for definition 2*) *adjective.*

contrast To show differences by comparing. The teacher *contrasted* life in a big city and life on a farm. *Verb.*
—A difference. There is a great *contrast* between the weather at the North Pole and the weather in the tropics. *Noun.*
  con·trast (kən trast′ *for verb;* kon′trast *for noun*) *verb,* **contrasted, contrasting;** *noun, plural* **contrasts.**

contribute To give. The townspeople *contributed* food and clothing to the family whose house had burned down. The children *contributed* ideas for the school picnic.
  con·trib·ute (kən trib′yo͞ot) *verb,* **contributed, contributing.**

contribution **1.** The act of contributing; giving something. The wealthy man's *contribution* of money will help build a new hospital. **2.** Something contributed. We gave *contributions* to help hungry children in other countries.
  con·tri·bu·tion (kon′trə byo͞o′shən) *noun, plural* **contributions.**

control **1.** Power or authority. The dictator had complete *control* over the country. **2.** A holding back; check. She has no *control* over her temper. **3.** **controls.** Instruments for guiding a machine. An airplane or spacecraft has controls. *Noun.*
—**1.** To have power or authority over. In some countries, the government tries to *control* the way people act and think. **2.** To hold back. He tried to *control* his temper. *Verb.*
  con·trol (kən trōl′) *noun, plural* **controls;** *verb,* **controlled, controlling.**

control tower A tower on an airfield. The movement of airplanes landing or taking off is directed from the control tower.

controversial Causing an argument. Politics is often a *controversial* subject.
  con·tro·ver·sial (kon′trəvur′shəl) *adjective.*

controversy A disagreement; dispute. The new tax caused much *controversy.*
  con·tro·ver·sy (kon′trəvur′sē) *noun, plural* **controversies.**

convene To come or bring together for a meeting; assemble. Parliament will *convene* again after the Christmas holidays.
  con·vene (kən vēn′) *verb,* **convened, convening.**

Control Tower

convenience Ease and comfort. The boys liked the *convenience* of canned foods when they went camping.
  con·ven·ience (kən vēn′yəns) *noun, plural* **conveniences.**

convenient Giving ease and comfort; useful; handy. A dishwasher is very *convenient* if you have lots of dishes to be washed.
  con·ven·ient (kən vēn′yənt) *adjective.*

convent A building where a group of nuns live.
  con·vent (kon′vent *or* kon′vənt) *noun, plural* **convents.**

at; āpe; cär; end; mē; it; īce; hot; ōld;
wood; fo͞ol; oil; out; up; turn; sing;
thin; this; hw in white; zh in treasure.
ə stands for a in about, e in taken,
i in pencil, o in lemon, and u in circus.

convention 1. A formal meeting for some special purpose. At a recent *convention* dentists in the province decided to open more free clinics. 2. An accepted way of acting or doing something; custom. Shaking hands when you are introduced to someone is a *convention*.
con·ven·tion (kən ven′shən) *noun, plural* **conventions.**

conventional Following practices or customs. Saying "hello" is a *conventional* thing to do when you meet someone.
con·ven·tion·al (kən ven′shən əl) *adjective.*

conversation A friendly and informal talk. Joan and Sarah had a long *conversation* about their summer vacations.
con·ver·sa·tion (kon′vər sā′shən) *noun, plural* **conversations.**

converse To talk together in a friendly and informal way. Mother and Aunt Ruth *conversed* by telephone about the day's events.
con·verse (kən vurs′) *verb,* **conversed, conversing.**

conversion The changing of something. The *conversion* of water into ice happens when the temperature of the water goes below zero degrees Celsius.
con·ver·sion (kən vur′zhən) *noun, plural* **conversions.**

convert 1. To change something into something different. The new owner *converted* the large house into a hotel. 2. To cause a person to change a belief. The missionary tried to *convert* the tribe to the Christian faith.
con·vert (kən vurt′) *verb,* **converted, converting.**

convertible Able to be changed. The *convertible* sofa can be made into a bed. *Adjective.*
—An automobile with a roof that can be folded back. *Noun.*
con·vert·i·ble (kən vur′tə bəl) *adjective; noun, plural* **convertibles.**

convex Curving outward. The outside of a bowl is *convex.* Look up **concave** for a picture of this.
con·vex (kon veks′ *or* kon′veks) *adjective.*

convey 1. To take from one place to another; carry. These pipes *convey* water from the well to the house. 2. To make known; express. My older brother *conveys* his feelings about his life at university in the letters he writes home to the family.
con·vey (kən vā′) *verb,* **conveyed, conveying.**

convict To declare or prove that a person is guilty of a crime. The jury *convicted* the thief of robbery. *Verb.*
—A person who is serving a prison sentence. The police were looking for two *convicts* who had escaped from a nearby prison. *Noun.*
con·vict (kən vikt′ *for verb;* kon′vikt *for noun*) *verb,* **convicted, convicting;** *noun, plural* **convicts.**

conviction 1. The act of declaring or proving that a person is guilty of a crime. The jury's verdict resulted in the *conviction* of the thief. 2. The state of being found guilty of a crime. After his *conviction* for robbery, the man was sentenced to five years in jail. 3. A strong belief. Bill has the *conviction* that most people are good at heart.
con·vic·tion (kən vik′shən) *noun, plural* **convictions.**

convince To cause a person to believe something; persuade. She argued with her brother until she *convinced* him that she was right.
con·vince (kən vins′) *verb,* **convinced, convincing.**

▲ The word **convince** used to mean "to overcome or conquer." For example, one army could *convince* another army in battle. This meaning later led to the meaning "to overcome by persuading."

convulse To shake or disturb violently. The boy was *convulsed* with laughter by his friend's jokes.
con·vulse (kən vuls′) *verb,* **convulsed, convulsing.**

cook 1. To make food ready for eating by using heat. You can cook food by broiling, roasting, baking, boiling, or frying it. 2. To be cooked. The peas will *cook* quickly. *Verb.*
—A person who cooks. *Noun.*
cook (kook) *verb,* **cooked, cooking;** *noun, plural* **cooks.**

cookie A small, flat sweet cake. Mother baked raisin *cookies.* This word is also spelled **cooky.**
cook·ie (kook′ē) *noun, plural* **cookies.**

cool 1. Somewhat cold. The *cool* breeze felt good on the hot summer day. She brought us a *cool* drink of lemonade. 2. Not excited; calm. Everyone kept *cool* and got out of the burning building safely. 3. Not warm or friendly. She was very *cool* to him after he insulted her. *Adjective.*
—Something cool. We took a walk in the *cool* of the early morning. *Noun.*
—To make or become cool. Phil tried to *cool* his soup by blowing on it. *Verb.*
cool (kōōl) *adjective,* **cooler, coolest;** *noun; verb,* **cooled, cooling.**

coop   A cage or pen for chickens or other small animals. Bob keeps his rabbits in a *coop* in the back yard. *Noun.*
—To put or keep in a coop or other small space. We *cooped* the dog up in the kitchen until the guests left. *Verb.*
   coop (ko͞op) *noun, plural* **coops;** *verb,* **cooped, cooping.**

co-operate   To work together. The three classes *co-operated* in planning a picnic at the end of the school year.
   co·op·er·ate (kō op′ə rāt′) *verb,* **co-operated, co-operating.**

co-operation   The act of working together. Keeping the streets of our town clean requires the *co-operation* of all the people who live here.
   co·op·er·a·tion (kō op′ə rā′shən) *noun.*

co-ordinate   To work or cause to work well together; bring or put into proper working order. A good athlete's muscles *co-ordinate* well. In dancing, it is important to *co-ordinate* the movements of the feet to the beat of the music.
   co·or·di·nate (kō ôr′də nāt′) *verb,* **co-ordinated, co-ordinating.**

cope   To struggle or handle with success. She had trouble *coping* with the extra homework.
   cope (kōp) *verb,* **coped, coping.**

copper   **1.** A reddish-brown metal. Copper is easy to form in different shapes, and it is an excellent conductor of heat and electricity. Copper is a chemical element. **2.** A reddish-brown colour. *Noun.*
—Having the colour copper; reddish-brown. *Adjective.*
   cop·per (kop′ər) *noun; adjective.*

copperhead   A poisonous snake found in the eastern part of the United States. It has a copper-coloured head and a light brown body with dark brown markings.
   cop·per·head (kop′ər hed′) *noun, plural* **copperheads.**

Copperhead

copy   **1.** Something that is made to look exactly like something else; imitation; duplicate. He used carbon paper to make a *copy* of the letter he typed. **2.** One of a number of books, magazines, or newspapers printed at the same time. He bought two *copies* of the new book on football. *Noun.*
—**1.** To make a copy of. *Copy* the book report neatly. **2.** To make or do something that is exactly like something else. Mary *copied* her older sister's way of dressing. *Verb.*
   cop·y (kop′ē) *noun, plural* **copies;** *verb,* **copied, copying.**

copyright   The sole right to print, sell, or copy a literary, musical, or artistic work. Copyrights are granted by law for a certain number of years. The writer has a *copyright* on the song he wrote.
   cop·y·right (kop′ē rīt′) *noun, plural* **copyrights.**

coral   **1.** A hard stony substance. Coral is made up of the skeletons of tiny sea animals. **2.** The tiny sea animal that makes coral. **3.** A pinkish-red colour. *Noun.*
—Having the colour coral; pinkish-red. *Adjective.*
   cor·al (kôr′əl) *noun, plural* **corals;** *adjective.*

Coral Snake

coral snake   A poisonous American snake that has a narrow head and red, black, and yellow bands on its body.

cord   **1.** A string or thin rope. Cord is made of several strands twisted or woven together. She tied the books together with *cord.* **2.** A covered wire that is used to connect a toaster, lamp, or other appliance to an electrical outlet. **3.** A structure in the body that is like a cord. The spinal *cord* extends from the brain. **4.** An amount of cut wood equalling

at; āpe; cär; end; mē; it; īce; hot; ōld;
wood; fo͞ol; oil; out; up; turn; sing;
thin; this; hw in white; zh in treasure.
ə stands for **a** in about, **e** in taken,
i in pencil, **o** in lemon, and **u** in circus.

128 cubic feet. A cord is a pile of wood that is 4 feet wide, 4 feet high, and 8 feet long in the Imperial System of Measure. It is about three cubic metres. *Noun.*

—To fasten together with cord. *Verb.* ▲ Another word that sounds like this is **chord.**

cord (kōrd) *noun, plural* **cords;** *verb,* **corded, cording.**

cordial Warm and friendly; hearty. He gave us a *cordial* greeting when we arrived.

cor·dial (kōr′jəl *or* kōr′dyəl) *adjective.*

corduroy A cloth with rows of ribs. It is usually made of cotton and is used for clothing.

cor·du·roy (kōr′də roi′) *noun.*

core 1. The hard, middle part of apples, pears, and certain other fruits. The seeds are in the core. 2. The central, most important, or deepest part of anything. The *core* of the coach's talk was that the team needed more practice. *Noun.*

—To remove the core of. She *cored* the apples before baking them. *Verb.* ▲ Another word that sounds like this is **corps.**

core (kōr) *noun, plural* **cores;** *verb,* **cored, coring.**

cork 1. The light, thick, outer bark of a kind of oak tree. Cork is used for such things as insulation, bottle stoppers, and floats for rafts. 2. A stopper made of cork for a bottle or other thing. Please put the *cork* back in the bottle. *Noun.*

—To stop with a cork. *Verb.*

cork (kōrk) *noun, plural* **corks;** *verb,* **corked, corking.**

The **corkscrew** on the right is a close-up of the one being used to open the bottle.

corkscrew A device for taking corks out of bottles.

cork·screw (kōrk′skroo′) *noun, plural* **corkscrews.**

corn 1. A grain that grows in rows on the large ears of a tall plant. Corn is used for food. 2. The plant that corn grows on.

corn (kōrn) *noun.*

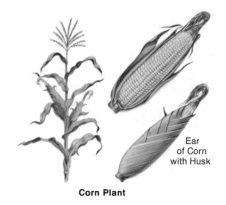

Ear of Corn with Husk

Corn Plant

corncob The woody core of an ear of corn. The corn kernels grow in rows on the corncob.

corn·cob (kōrn′kob′) *noun, plural* **corncobs.**

cornea The clear or transparent outer covering of the front of the eyeball. The cornea covers the iris and the pupil.

cor·ne·a (kōr′nē ə) *noun, plural* **corneas.**

corner 1. The place or point where two lines or surfaces come together. She hit her leg on the sharp *corner* of the box. The table is in the *corner* of the room. 2. The place where two streets come together. There is a mailbox on the *corner. Noun.*

—At or near a corner. Tom works at the *corner* drugstore after school. *Adjective.*

—To force or drive into a dangerous or difficult place or position. The dog *cornered* the cat under the bed. *Verb.*

cor·ner (kōr′nər) *noun, plural* **corners;** *adjective; verb,* **cornered, cornering.**

cornet A brass musical instrument that is like a trumpet.

cor·net (kōr net′) *noun, plural* **cornets.**

Cornet

coronation The ceremony of crowning a king or queen. My parents remember the *coronation* of Queen Elizabeth II.
co·ro·na·tion (kōr′ə nā′shən) *noun, plural* **coronations.**

corporal An officer in the land and air elements of the Canadian Armed Forces. A corporal is below a sergeant but above a private.
cor·po·ral (kōr′pər əl *or* kōr′prəl) *noun, plural* **corporals.**

corporation An organization made up of a number of people who are allowed by law to act as a single person. A corporation is created by a government charter and has the right to buy and sell property, borrow and lend money, and to enter into contracts.
cor·po·ra·tion (kōr′pə rā′shən) *noun, plural* **corporations.**

corps 1. A group of soldiers trained for special service. He belongs to the medical *corps*. 2. A group of persons who act or work together. That restaurant has a large *corps* of waiters and waitresses. ▲ Another word that sounds like this is **core.**
corps (kōr) *noun, plural* **corps.**

corpse A dead human body.
corpse (kōrps) *noun, plural* **corpses.**

corpuscle A small cell that is part of the blood. Red and white blood cells are corpuscles.
cor·pus·cle (kōr′pus′əl) *noun, plural* **corpuscles.**

corral A space with a fence around it. A corral is used for cattle, horses, and other animals. *Noun.*
—1. To drive or put into a corral. The cowboys *corralled* the herd of horses. 2. To capture by surrounding. The police *corralled* the gang of bank robbers. *Verb.*
cor·ral (kə ral′) *noun, plural* **corrals;** *verb,* **corralled, corralling.**

Corral

correct 1. Not having any mistakes; accurate. This is the *correct* answer to the arithmetic problem. 2. Proper. It is *correct* to thank people for gifts that they give you. *Adjective.*
—1. To mark the mistakes in; change to make right. The teacher *corrected* our spelling tests. 2. To make agree with some standard. The doctor *corrected* my poor eyesight with glasses. *Verb.*
cor·rect (kə rekt′) *adjective; verb,* **corrected, correcting.**

correction 1. The act of correcting. *Correction* of the trouble in the car's engine took the mechanic several hours. 2. A change that is made to correct an error. I kept a list of the *corrections* I made in the report.
cor·rec·tion (kə rek′shən) *noun, plural* **corrections.**

correspond 1. To agree; match. His answer to the question does not *correspond* with mine. 2. To be similar. The gills of a fish *correspond* to the lungs of man. 3. To write letters to one another. Jack and Bill *corresponded* when Bill was away at summer camp.
cor·re·spond (kōr′ə spond′) *verb,* **corresponded, corresponding.**

correspondence 1. Agreement or similarity. The police found a close *correspondence* between the stories of the two witnesses. 2. The writing of letters to one another. We kept up a *correspondence* for many years after he moved.
cor·re·spon·dence (kōr′ə spon′dəns) *noun.*

corridor A long hallway or passageway in a building. A corridor often has rooms opening onto it.
cor·ri·dor (kōr′ə dor) *noun, plural* **corridors.**

corrode To eat or wear away, little by little. Rust *corroded* our patio furniture.
cor·rode (kə rōd′) *verb,* **corroded, corroding.**

corrupt Able to be bribed; crooked; dishonest. The *corrupt* mayor was eventually found out and sent to jail. *Adjective.*
—To cause to be dishonest. That judge cannot be *corrupted. Verb.*
cor·rupt (kə rupt′) *adjective; verb,* **corrupted, corrupting.**

at; āpe; cär; end; mē; it; īce; hot; ōld;
wood; fōōl; oil; out; up; turn; sing;
thin; this; hw in white; zh in treasure.
ə stands for a in about, e in taken,
i in pencil, o in lemon, and u in circus.

corsage A flower or small bunch of flowers worn by a woman at the shoulder or waist, or on the wrist. He bought her a *corsage* to wear to the dance. cor·sage (kōr′säzh′) *noun, plural* cor·sages.

corset A close-fitting undergarment worn by women to shape and support the waist and hips. cor·set (kōr′sət) *noun, plural* corsets.

Corsage

cosmetic A preparation used to beautify the face, hair, or some other part of the body. cos·met·ic (koz met′ik) *noun, plural* cosmetics.

cosmic Of or relating to the whole universe. *Cosmic* dust is very small particles of matter from outer space that fall to earth. cos·mic (koz′mik) *adjective.*

cost 1. An amount of money paid or charged for something; price. The *cost* of that book is five dollars. 2. Something lost. The war was won at the *cost* of many lives. *Noun.*
—1. To be gotten or bought at the price of. The bicycle *cost* too much, so my father didn't buy it. 2. To cause the loss of. The motorcycle accident almost *cost* him his life. *Verb.*
cost (kost) *noun, plural* costs; *verb,* cost, costing.

costly Costing much. Collecting rare stamps can be a *costly* hobby. cost·ly (kost′lē) *adjective,* costlier, costliest.

costume 1. Clothes worn in order to look like someone or something else. She wore a ghost *costume* to the Hallowe'en party. 2. Clothes worn at a particular time or place or by particular people. She collects dolls dressed in Victorian *costumes.* cos·tume (kos′tōom *or* kos′tyōom) *noun, plural* costumes.

cosy Warm and comfortable; snug. The kitten slept in a *cosy* spot by the fire. This word is also spelled cozy. co·sy (kō′zē) *adjective,* cosier, cosiest.

cot A narrow bed. Cots are usually made of canvas stretched on a frame. cot (kot) *noun, plural* cots.

cottage A small house. cot·tage (kot′ij) *noun, plural* cottages.

cottage cheese A soft, white cheese. It is made from the curds of sour skim milk.

cotton A fluffy mass of soft white or grey fibres that grow in the large seed pod of a tall plant. Cotton is used to make thread or cloth. cot·ton (kot′ən) *noun.*

cottontail An American rabbit that has brown or greyish fur and a short, fluffy, white tail. cot·ton·tail (kot′ən tāl′) *noun, plural* cottontails.

cottonwood A tree that grows near rivers and streams in North America. It has tiny brown seeds covered with tufts of silky white hairs like cotton. cot·ton·wood (kot′ən wood′) *noun, plural* cottonwoods.

Cotton Plant

couch A piece of furniture that two or more people can sit on at the same time. Couches usually have soft cushions. couch (kouch) *noun, plural* couches.

cougar A golden-brown American animal that has a small head, long legs, and a slender, strong body. A cougar is a member of the cat family. A cougar is also called a **puma** and a **mountain lion.** cou·gar (kōo′gər) *noun, plural* cougars.

Cougar

cough To force air from the lungs with a sudden, sharp sound. Beth stayed home today because she has a cold and *coughs* all the time. *Verb.*
—1. The sharp sound that is made when air is suddenly forced from the lungs. 2. A sickness that causes a person to cough. *Noun.*
cough (kof) *verb,* coughed, coughing; *noun, plural* coughs.

could I *could* tell that he was angry. could (kood) *verb.*

couldn't I *couldn't* reach the high shelf.
could·n't (kood′ənt) contraction for "could not."

council **1.** A group of people called together. A council can give advice, discuss a problem, or make a decision. **2.** A group of people elected to govern a city or town. Our town *council* discussed widening the main street at their meeting last night. ▲ Another word that sounds like this is **counsel.**
coun·cil (koun′səl) *noun, plural* **councils.**

counsel **1.** Ideas or suggestions about what to do; advice. A good friend can often give you wise *counsel.* **2.** A lawyer or group of lawyers who give legal advice. The *counsel* for the defense summed up the case. *Noun.*
—To give ideas or suggestions to; advise. Her brother *counselled* her to start working harder. *Verb.* ▲ Another word that sounds like this is **council.**
coun·sel (koun′səl) *noun, plural* **counsels;** *verb,* **counselled, counselling** or **counseled, counseling.**

counsellor A person who helps or gives advice. Our *counsellor* at summer camp taught us how to paddle a canoe. This word is also spelled **counselor.**
coun·sel·lor (koun′sə lər) *noun, plural* **counsellors.**

count¹ **1.** To find out how many of something there are; add up. *Count* the number of cookies in the box. **2.** To say or write down numbers in order. He can *count* up to 100 really fast. **3.** To include or be included when things are added up. There were forty people in the bus, *counting* the driver. **4.** To depend; rely. Can I *count* on you if I need help? *Verb.*
—The number of things there are when you add them up; total. *Noun.*
count (kount) *verb,* **counted, counting;** *noun, plural* **counts.**

count² A European nobleman.
count (kount) *noun, plural* **counts.**

countdown The counting of time backward from a certain time to zero. This is done to tell people how much time is left before the start of something. The *countdown* for the launching of the spacecraft will begin soon.
count·down (kount′doun′) *noun, plural* **countdowns.**

counter¹ **1.** A long table. Stores have counters on which things are sold. Some restaurants have counters on which meals are served. **2.** Something used for counting. Some games have round, coloured disks called counters to help keep score.
count·er (koun′tər) *noun, plural* **counters.**

counter² Opposite. He acted *counter* to instructions and wrote in pencil instead of ink. Your idea is *counter* to my idea. *Adverb, Adjective.*
—To go against; oppose. My friend *countered* my idea for a picnic and said he wanted to go to the movies instead. *Verb.*
coun·ter (koun′tər) *adverb; adjective; verb,* **countered, countering.**

counterclockwise In the direction opposite to the direction the hands of a clock move. You turn a screw *counterclockwise* if you want to take it out.
coun·ter·clock·wise (koun′tər klok′wīz′) *adverb; adjective.*

counterfeit To make a copy or imitation of something in order to cheat or fool other people. It is a crime to *counterfeit* money. *Verb.*
—A copy or imitation made in order to cheat or fool someone. The shopkeeper had a twenty dollar bill that was a *counterfeit. Noun.*
—Not genuine. The man was put in jail for making *counterfeit* money. *Adjective.*
coun·ter·feit (koun′tər fit′) *verb,* **counterfeited, counterfeiting;** *noun, plural* **counterfeits;** *adjective.*

counterpart A person or thing that is very much like or equal to another. The United States Congress is the *counterpart* of the Canadian Parliament.
coun·ter·part (koun′tər pärt′) *noun, plural* **counterparts.**

country **1.** Any area of land; region. We have a summer cabin in mountain *country.* **2.** An area of land that has boundaries and has a government that is shared by all the people; nation. Canada and the United States are *countries.* **3.** The land outside of cities and towns. We decided to go for a drive in the *country. Noun.*
—Having to do with land outside of cities and towns; rural. We drove along narrow *country* roads. *Adjective.*
coun·try (kun′trē) *noun, plural* **countries;** *adjective.*

at; āpe; cär; end; mē; it; īce; hot; ōld;
wood; fool; oil; out; up; turn; sing;
thin; this; hw in white; zh in treasure;
ə stands for a in about, e in taken,
i in pencil, o in lemon, and u in circus.

countryman A person who lives in one's own country. The word **countrywoman** is also used.
　coun·try·man (kun′trē mən) *noun, plural* **countrymen.**

countryside The land outside of cities and towns.
　coun·try·side (kun′trē sīd′) *noun, plural* **countrysides.**

county One of the sections into which a province, state, or country is divided.
　coun·ty (koun′tē) *noun, plural* **counties.**

couple 1. Two things that are the same or go together in some way; pair. 2. A man and woman who are married, engaged, or partners in a dance or game. My father and mother are a happy *couple. Noun.*
—To join together. We *coupled* the trailer and the car. *Verb.*
　cou·ple (kup′əl) *noun, plural* **couples;** *verb,* **coupled, coupling.**

coupon A ticket or part of a ticket. A coupon can be exchanged for a gift or for a discount on the price of something. The *coupon* in the box of cereal was good for ten cents toward the price of the next box.
　cou·pon (kōō′pon *or* kyōō′pon) *noun, plural* **coupons.**

courage The strength to face danger without fear; bravery. She showed great *courage* in swimming in the rough water to save the child.
　cour·age (kur′əj) *noun.*

courageous Brave. A courageous person can face something that is dangerous, very hard, or painful without fear. The *courageous* firefighter went into the burning building to save the old man.
　cou·ra·geous (kə rā′jəs) *adjective.*

coureur de bois *Canadian.* A French or Métis woodsman who lived in early Canada.
　cour·eur de bois (kōō′ər də bwä′) *noun, plural* **coureurs de bois.**

course 1. A moving onward from one point to the next; progress. He grew ten centimetres in the *course* of a year. 2. A way; route; track. The airplane flew off its *course.* The river had a winding *course.* 3. A way of acting. The most sensible *course* would be to go home now before it starts to rain. 4. An area used for certain sports or games. We are going to the golf *course* this afternoon. 5. A series of classes or lessons. I am taking a *course* in cooking. 6. A part of a meal that is served at one time. Our first *course* was fruit cup and the second *course* was soup. ▲ Another word that sounds like this is **coarse.**
　course (kōrs) *noun, plural* **courses.**

of course. Certainly; naturally. *Of course* I'll help you with your work.

court 1. An open space that is surrounded by walls or buildings; courtyard. Our apartment building is built around a *court.* 2. A space or area marked off for certain games. The gym has a basketball *court.* 3. The place where a king or queen and their attendants live. 4. A room or building where trials are held or legal matters are decided. *Noun.*
—To try to win the favour or love of a person. He *courted* the voters in his riding. *Verb.*
　court (kōrt) *noun, plural* **courts;** *verb,* **courted, courting.**

courteous Having good manners; polite. A courteous person is always thoughtful of the feelings of others.
　cour·te·ous (kur′tē əs) *adjective.*

courtesy A way of behaving that shows good manners and thoughtfulness toward other people; politeness. Everyone likes that grocery clerk because of his *courtesy* to all his customers.
　cour·te·sy (kur′tə sē) *noun.*

courthouse 1. A building in which courts of law are held. 2. A building in which the offices of a county government are located.
　court·house (kōrt′hous′) *noun, plural* **courthouses.**

courtyard An open area that is surrounded by walls or buildings. The rooms of the palace looked out onto the *courtyard.*
　court·yard (kōrt′yärd′) *noun, plural* **courtyards.**

cousin The son or daughter of an aunt or uncle. **First cousins** have the same grandparents; **second cousins** have the same great-grandparents.
　cou·sin (kuz′in) *noun, plural* **cousins.**

cove A small sheltered bay or inlet. The sailors anchored their boat in a *cove* where they were protected from the wind.
　cove (kōv) *noun, plural* **coves.**

Cove

cover **1.** To put something over or on. The girl *covered* her hair with a bright red scarf. Snow *covered* the ground during the night. **2.** To hide. She tried to *cover* up her mistake with a lie. Darkness *covered* the hills. **3.** To travel over. Sally *covered* the distance from her house to mine in five minutes on her bicycle. **4.** To deal with; include. The book I'm reading *covers* the history of airplanes. That magazine *covers* sports. *Verb.*
—**1.** Something that is put on or over something else. Put a *cover* on the pot. What is the picture on the *cover* of that book? **2.** Something that hides or protects. The prisoner escaped from jail under the *cover* of darkness. The hikers took *cover* in a barn when the storm broke. *Noun.*
cov·er (kuv′ər) *verb,* **covered, covering;** *noun, plural* **covers.**

covered wagon A large wagon with a canvas top that is spread over hoops. American pioneers travelled in covered wagons when they moved westward.

Covered Wagon

covering Anything that covers. A rug is a *covering* for a floor. Our new car has plastic seat *coverings.*
cov·er·ing (kuv′ər ing) *noun, plural* **coverings.**

covet To want something very much that belongs to another person. Jack *coveted* his brother's new baseball glove.
cov·et (kuv′ət) *verb,* **coveted, coveting.**

cow **1.** The full-grown female of cattle. Cows are raised for their milk. **2.** The female of some other large animals. A female moose, elephant, or whale is called a cow.
cow (kou) *noun, plural* **cows.**

coward A person who lacks courage. A coward is often shamefully afraid of anything that is dangerous or hard to do.
cow·ard (kou′ərd) *noun, plural* **cowards.**

cowardly Not courageous; showing fear in a shameful way.
cow·ard·ly (kou′ərd lē) *adjective.*

cowboy A man who herds and takes care of cattle on a ranch. Cowboys work on horseback.
cow·boy (kou′boi′) *noun, plural* **cowboys.**

cowgirl A girl or woman who herds and takes care of cattle on a ranch.
cow·girl (kou′gurl′) *noun, plural* **cowgirls.**

Cowichan sweater *Canadian.* A heavy wool sweater knitted by the Indians on Vancouver Island.
cow·i·chan sweater (kou′i chən).

Coyote

coyote An animal that looks like a wolf and lives in the prairies of North America.
coy·o·te (kī ō′tē *or* kī′ōt) *noun, plural* **coyotes** or **coyote.**

cozy Warm and comfortable. Look up **cosy** for more information.

CPR The Canadian Pacific Railway.

Crab

crab An animal that lives in the water and is covered by a hard shell. Crabs have a wide, flat body, four pairs of legs, and a pair of claws. Many kinds of crabs are good to eat.
crab (krab) *noun, plural* **crabs.**

at; āpe; cär; end; mē; it; īce; hot; ōld; wood; fool; oil; out; up; turn; sing; thin; this; hw in white; zh in treasure. ə stands for a in about, e in taken, i in pencil, o in lemon, and u in circus.

crab apple A small, hard, sour-tasting apple that is used to make jelly. Crab apples grow on trees that have many beautiful clusters of flowers in the spring.

crack **1.** A break or narrow opening between the parts of something. A crack does not make a thing fall into parts. The window has a *crack* in it where the ball hit it. There are *cracks* between the floor boards in my room. **2.** A sudden, sharp noise like that made by something breaking. When a bat hits a baseball you hear a crack. **3.** A sharp, hard blow. The swinging door gave him a painful *crack* on the head. *Noun.*
—**1.** To break without coming completely apart; split. The cup *cracked* when I hit it against the sink. The squirrel *cracked* the acorn with his teeth. **2.** To make a sudden, sharp noise. The cowboy showed us how he *cracked* the whip. **3.** To hit with a sharp, hard blow. He *cracked* his head on the door. *Verb.*
crack (krak) *noun, plural* **cracks;** *verb,* **cracked, cracking.**

cracker A thin, crisp biscuit.
crack·er (krak′ər) *noun, plural* **crackers.**

crackle To make slight, sharp snapping sounds. Dry leaves *crackle* when you walk on them. Some cold cereals *crackle* when you pour on milk. *Verb.*
—A slight, sharp snapping sound. The *crackle* of the burning logs was a pleasant sound. *Noun.*
crack·le (krak′əl) *verb,* **crackled, crackling;** *noun, plural* **crackles.**

cradle **1.** A small bed for a baby. Most cradles are set on rockers so the baby can be rocked to sleep. **2.** Anything like a cradle in shape or use. A box on rockers used to wash gold from earth is a cradle. **3.** The part of a phone that holds the receiver. *Noun.*
—To hold in a cradle. Mother *cradled* the baby in her arms until he fell asleep. *Verb.*
cra·dle (krād′əl) *noun, plural* **cradles;** *verb,* **cradled, cradling.**

Cradle

craft **1.** A special skill that a person has. The chair was carved with great *craft.* **2.** A trade or work that needs special skill. Carpentry is a *craft* that takes years to master. **3.** Skill in deceiving people; cunning. The thief showed great *craft* because he left no clues. **4.** A boat or airplane. The harbour was filled with small sailing *craft.*
craft (kraft) *noun, plural* **crafts.**

craftsman A person who has a special skill in making or doing something; artisan. The person who made this beautiful antique furniture was a fine *craftsman.*
crafts·man (krafts′mən) *noun, plural* **craftsmen.**

crag a steep, rugged rock or cliff. Eagles live on high mountain *crags.*
crag (krag) *noun, plural* **crags.**

cramp¹ The sudden, painful contraction of a muscle. She got a *cramp* in her leg when she was swimming, and had to be helped out of the water. *Noun.*
—To cause a sharp pain in a muscle. Holding the pencil tightly for so long *cramped* his hand. *Verb.*
cramp (kramp) *noun, plural* **cramps;** *verb,* **cramped, cramping.**

Cranberries

cramp² To limit. We left too late and were very *cramped* for time.
cramp (kramp) *verb,* **cramped, cramping.**

cranberry A sour, red berry that grows on low shrubs and bushes in bogs and swamps. Cranberries are used to make sauce, juice, and jelly.
cran·ber·ry (kran′ber′ē) *noun, plural* **cranberries.**

crane **1.** A large bird that has very long thin legs and a long neck and bill. Cranes live near water, and wade along the shore looking for food in the water. **2.** A large machine with a long arm that can be moved up and down and in a circle. Cranes are used to lift and move heavy objects that are attached to cables at the end of the arm. *Noun.*
—To stretch out the neck in order to see better. The people standing in back of the crowd had to *crane* their necks to see the parade. *Verb.*

crane (krān) *noun, plural* **cranes;** *verb,* **craned, craning.**

Crane

crank **1.** A part of a machine that has a handle attached to a rod. When the handle is turned, the rod turns with it and makes the machine work. The storekeeper turned the *crank* of the store's awning to lower it. **2.** A person who has queer ideas. The police said that the strange telephone calls were the work of a *crank*. **3.** A person who is always grouchy or cross. She said that her brother was being a *crank* today and we should leave him alone. *Noun.*
—To turn a crank so that something will work. Years ago people had to *crank* the engine of a car to start it. *Verb.*
crank (krangk) *noun, plural* **cranks;** *verb,* **cranked, cranking.**

crash **1.** A sudden, loud noise like something breaking or smashing. There was a *crash* when the ball broke the window. **2.** A violent collision. We read about the terrible plane *crash. Noun.*
—**1.** To make a sudden, loud noise. The lamp *crashed* to the floor. **2.** To collide violently. The car *crashed* into a wall. *Verb.*
crash (krash) *noun, plural* **crashes;** *verb,* **crashed, crashing.**

crate A box made of slats of wood. Crates are used to hold and protect things that are being stored or moved. My uncle sent us a *crate* of apples from British Columbia. *Noun.*
—To pack in a crate or crates. The farmer *crated* the lettuce before he shipped it to the market. *Verb.*
crate (krāt) *noun, plural* **crates;** *verb,* **crated, crating.**

crater A hollow area that looks like the inside of a bowl. There are many *craters* on the surface of the moon.
cra·ter (krā′tər) *noun, plural* **craters.**

crawl **1.** To move very slowly. Babies *crawl* by moving on their hands and knees. Worms *crawl* by pulling their bodies along the ground. Traffic *crawled* along the highway for twelve kilometres. **2.** To be covered with crawling things. The picnic table *crawled* with ants. *Verb.*
—**1.** A very slow movement. **2.** A fast swimming stroke. When a person does the crawl his face is down, he lifts his arms over his head one after the other, and he keeps kicking his feet. *Noun.*
crawl (kräl) *verb,* **crawled, crawling;** *noun, plural* **crawls.**

Crayfish

crayfish A small animal that looks like a lobster and lives in fresh water. Crayfish are a kind of shellfish and are used as food.
cray·fish (krā′fish′) *noun, plural* **crayfish** or **crayfishes.**

crayon A coloured stick made of a waxy material used for drawing or writing. Crayons come in all different colours.
cray·on (krā′on *or* krā′ən) *noun, plural* **crayons.**

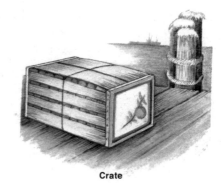

Crate

at; āpe; cär; end; mē; it; īce; hot; ōld;
wood; fōōl; oil; out; up; turn; sing;
thin; this; hw in white; zh in treasure.
ə stands for a in about, e in taken,
i in pencil, o in lemon, and u in circus.

crazy 1. Having a mind that is sick; insane; mentally ill. The prisoner almost became *crazy* after spending twenty years in an enemy prison. 2. Foolish. Putting three dogs and two cats in the same room was a *crazy* thing to do. 3. Very enthusiastic. My brother is *crazy* about fishing.
cra·zy (krā′zē) *adjective,* **crazier, craziest.**

creak To make a sharp, squeaking sound. The old stairs *creak* when you step on them. *Verb.*
—A sharp, squeaking sound. The rusty gate opened with a loud *creak. Noun.* ▲ Another word that sounds like this is **creek.**
creak (krēk) *verb,* **creaked, creaking;** *noun, plural* **creaks.**

cream 1. The yellowish-white part of milk. Cream has fat in it and is thicker than milk. Butter is made from cream. 2. A soft, thick lotion or foam that is put on the skin. My father uses shaving *cream* that smells like mint.
cream (krēm) *noun, plural* **creams.**

crease 1. A line or mark made by folding or wrinkling something. 2. *Canadian.* In hockey and lacrosse, the area in front of the goal. *Noun.*
—To make or get a line or mark in by folding or wrinkling. I *creased* my shirt badly when I packed it. *Verb.*
crease (krēs) *noun, plural* **creases;** *verb,* **creased, creasing.**

create To cause something new to exist or happen. The lack of rain that summer *created* a shortage of wheat the next winter. An author *creates* characters in his books.
cre·ate (krē āt′) *verb,* **created, creating.**

creation 1. The act of causing something new to exist or happen. The *creation* of the motion picture took many months to complete. 2. Anything that has been made. A sculpture, a painting, or a book is a creation.
cre·a·tion (krē ā′shən) *noun, plural* **creations.**

creative Having or showing ability to make something new. A poet must be *creative.*
cre·a·tive (krē ā′tiv) *adjective.*

creator 1. A person who makes something new. That author is the *creator* of many novels. 2. **the Creator.** God.
cre·a·tor (krē ā′tər) *noun, plural* **creators.**

creature A living person or animal. Deer, bears, and wolves are *creatures* of the forest.
crea·ture (krē′chər) *noun, plural* **creatures.**

credit 1. Belief in the truth of something; faith. His friends gave full *credit* to his story. 2. Reputation. His *credit* was not good at the store because he didn't pay his bills. 3. Praise or honour. She deserves the *credit* for the dinner because she did most of the cooking. 4. Something that is owed to a person. I have a five dollar *credit* at the bookstore. *Noun.*
—1. To believe; trust. I *credit* his story of the accident because he is always honest. 2. To put an amount of money that is owed to someone into an account for him. The store *credited* his account with ten dollars when he returned the shirt. *Verb.*
cred·it (kred′it) *noun, plural* **credits;** *verb,* **credited, crediting.**

creed A statement of what a person or group of people believe in.
creed (krēd) *noun, plural* **creeds.**

creek A small stream. A creek is bigger than a brook but smaller than a river. ▲ Another word that sounds like this is **creak.**
creek (krēk *or* krik) *noun, plural* **creeks.**

creep 1. To move slowly and quietly; crawl. The baby *creeps* on his hands and knees. The last days before vacation seemed to *creep* by. 2. To grow along the ground or over a surface. The ivy *creeps* over the fence in our yard. 3. To feel as if things were crawling over one's skin. The howling of the dog made my flesh *creep.*
creep (krēp) *verb,* **crept, creeping.**

crepe A cloth that has a crinkled surface.
crepe (krāp) *noun, plural* **crepes.** This word is also spelled **crêpe.**

crepe paper A thin paper with a crinkled surface. Crepe paper can be stretched to take on different shapes and is used for decorating. The spelling **crêpe paper** is also used.

crept The crabs *crept* along the sand. Look up **creep** for more information.
crept (krept) *verb.*

crescent The shape the moon has when you can only see a thin, curved part of it.
cres·cent (kres′ənt) *noun, plural* **crescents.**

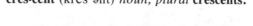
The moon has a **crescent** shape.

crest 1. A bunch of feathers on the head of a bird. Bluejays have a *crest* on their head. 2. A plume or other decoration on the top of a helmet. 3. The highest part of something. We have a long way to climb before we reach the *crest* of the hill. We watched Susan on her surfboard riding the *crest* of the big wave.
crest (krest) *noun, plural* **crests.**

Crest

crew A group of people who work together to make something run. The people who work on a ship, airplane, or train are called the crew. A team of men who row a racing boat are its crew.
crew (krōō) *noun, plural* **crews.**

crib 1. A small bed for a baby. Cribs have high sides that can be moved up and down. 2. A box or rack that holds food for cattle and horses to eat from. 3. A small building that grain or corn is stored in on a farm.
crib (krib) *noun, plural* **cribs.**

Crib

cricket[1] A black or brown insect that looks like a short grasshopper. Crickets have strong back legs that are used for hopping. The male makes a chirping noise by rubbing his front wings together.
crick·et (krik′ət) *noun, plural* **crickets.**

cricket[2] A game like baseball played with a ball and bats on a grass field. Each team has eleven players and instead of home base, there is a goal, called a wicket, at each end of the field. Cricket is popular in England and in certain countries that were once ruled by England.
crick·et (krik′ət) *noun.*

cried My baby sister *cried* when she fell and hurt her knee. Look up **cry** for more information.
cried (krīd) *verb.*

crime Something that is very wrong and against the law to do. Robbery is a crime, and a person who robs someone else can be sent to jail.
crime (krīm) *noun, plural* **crimes.**

criminal A person who does something that is a crime. The robber was a *criminal* and was sent to prison. *Noun.*
—Having to do with crime or the laws about crime. Linda is studying to be a *criminal* lawyer. *Adjective.*
crim·i·nal (krim′ən əl) *noun, plural* **criminals;** *adjective.*

crimson A deep red colour. *Noun.*
—Having the colour crimson. The setting sun was *crimson. Adjective.*
crim·son (krim′zən) *noun, plural* **crimsons;** *adjective.*

cripple A person or animal that cannot move some part of the body in the proper way because of an injury or a disease. The fox was a *cripple* after his leg was crushed in the trap. *Noun.*
—1. To badly injure a person or animal. Polio *crippled* many children years ago. 2. To cause damage to something so that it cannot work properly. The heavy snowstorm *crippled* the airlines for several days. *Verb.*
crip·ple (krip′əl) *noun, plural* **cripples;** *verb,* **crippled, crippling.**

crisis 1. A very important turning point that helps decide what will happen in the future. Having to decide whether or not to go to university was the first real *crisis* in his life. 2. A difficult or dangerous situation. The murder of the prime minister caused a *crisis* in that country.
cri·sis (krī′sis) *noun, plural* **crises.**

crisp 1. Hard but breaking easily into bits. Fresh lettuce, celery, and radishes should be *crisp. Crisp* bacon has most of the fat cooked out of it. 2. Clear and cool; brisk. John likes to go fishing on *crisp* autumn days. 3. Short and to the point. The coach gave *crisp* instructions to the team.
crisp (krisp) *adjective,* **crisper, crispest.**

at; āpe; cär; end; mē; it; īce; hot; ōld;
wood; fōōl; oil; out; up; turn; sing;
thin; this; hw in white; zh in treasure.
ə stands for a in about, e in taken,
i in pencil, o in lemon, and u in circus.

crisscross Marked with lines that cross one another. The game of tic-tac-toe is played on a *crisscross* diagram. *Adjective.*
—A design made by crossing lines. A plaid is a *crisscross* of lines and *colours. Noun.*
—To mark with or make lines that cross one another. We could see where their footprints *crisscrossed* in the snow. *Verb.*
  criss·cross (kris′kros′) *adjective; noun, plural* **crisscrosses;** *verb,* **crisscrossed, crisscrossing.**

critic A person whose job is to say or write what he thinks is good or bad about books, motion pictures, music, art, or plays. We looked in the newspaper to see what the movie *critic* said about the new movie.
  cri·tic (krit′ik) *noun, plural* **critics.**

critical **1.** Always finding something wrong with things. He was *critical* of every plan that we suggested. She is always *critical* of the way other people dress. **2.** Having to do with a person whose job is to be a critic. There is a good *critical* review of his new book in the newspaper. **3.** Dangerous or serious. There is a *critical* shortage of water in the town.
  crit·i·cal (krit′i kəl) *adjective.*

criticism **1.** The act of saying what is good or bad about something. Don read with interest the newspaper's *criticism* of the artist's work. **2.** Disapproval. Her brother's *criticism* of the way she dressed made her angry.
  crit·i·cism (krit′ə siz′əm) *noun, plural* **criticisms.**

criticize **1.** To say what is good or bad about something. His job on television is to *criticize* new movies. **2.** To find fault with something. Peggy *criticized* her brother's table manners.
  crit·i·cize (krit′ə sīz′) *verb,* **criticized, criticizing.**

croak A deep, hoarse sound like one made by a frog or crow. *Noun.*
—To make a deep, hoarse sound. The frogs *croaked* in the pond. *Verb.*
  croak (krōk) *noun, plural* **croaks;** *verb,* **croaked, croaking.**

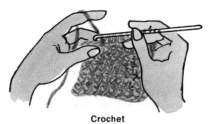
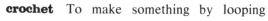
Crochet

crochet To make something by looping thread or yarn into connected stitches with a needle that has a hook at one end. Aunt Agnes *crocheted* a beautiful blanket for the baby.
  cro·chet (krō shā′) *verb,* **crocheted, crocheting.**

crocodile A long animal with short legs, thick, scaly skin, and a long, strong tail. A crocodile has strong jaws with long rows of teeth. Crocodiles live in and near water in Asia, Africa, and America. They look like and are related to alligators. Look up **alligator** for a picture of this animal.
  croc·o·dile (krok′ə dīl′) *noun, plural* **crocodiles.**

crocus A small flower that grows from an underground bulb. Crocuses grow in many colours and have thin leaves like blades of grass. They are one of the first flowers to bloom in the spring.
  cro·cus (krō′kəs) *noun, plural* **crocuses.**

Crocus

crook **1.** A bent part; curve. Barbara carried the umbrella in the *crook* of her arm. **2.** A person who is not honest. The *crook* broke into their house and stole the television set. *Noun.*
—To bend; curve; hook. Jean *crooked* her finger at us to tell us to come over. *Verb.*
  crook (krook) *noun, plural* **crooks;** *verb,* **crooked, crooking.**

crooked **1.** Not straight; bent or curving. The path that we followed through the woods was very *crooked.* **2.** Not honest. The *crooked* man cheated at cards.
  crook·ed (krook′id) *adjective.*

crop **1.** Plants that are grown to be used as food or to make something else. We harvested a huge *crop* of tomatoes this year. Wheat is an important *crop* in the West. **2.** A group of persons or things that come at the same time. We had a large *crop* of new students come to our school this fall. **3.** A pouch near the bottom of the throat of a bird. Food is held in the crop and is prepared for digestion. **4.** A short whip that has a loop at the end

instead of a lash. Some horseback riders use crops. *Noun.*
—To cut or bite off the top part of something. Dad *cropped* the bushes in our yard. *Verb.*
crop (krop) *noun, plural* **crops;** *verb,* **cropped, cropping.**

croquet An outdoor game played with sticks called mallets that are used to hit wooden balls along the ground and through wire hoops called wickets.
cro·quet (krō kā′) *noun.*

Croquet

cross 1. A post or stake that has another bar across it. The cross is the symbol of Christianity because Christ died on a cross. 2. Anything shaped like a cross. On some tests you make a *cross* next to the right answer. 3. A mixing of two or more animals or plants of different kinds. A mule is a *cross* between a horse and a donkey. *Noun.*
—1. To move or go from one side of something to the other. The ship *crossed* the ocean in seven days. 2. To draw a line across. You *cross* a "t" in writing. 3. To put or lay one thing across another. She *crossed* her legs when she sat down. *Verb.*
—1. In a bad temper. My sister gets *cross* when people criticize her. 2. Lying or going from one side of something to another. *Adjective.*
cross (kros) *noun, plural* **crosses;** *verb,* **crossed, crossing;** *adjective,* **crosser, crossest.**

crossbow A bow mounted across a wooden stock along which arrows were shot. This weapon was used in the Middle Ages.
cross·bow (kros′bō′) *noun, plural* **crossbows.**

cross-checking An illegal act in hockey in which a player, having both hands on his stick, lifts it not less than six inches (about eighteen centimetres) above the ice and hits an opposing player.
cross-check·ing (kros′chek′ing) *noun.*

crossing 1. A place where two lines or other things cross each other. We stopped at the railroad *crossing* to let the train go through. 2. A place where a street or river may be crossed. There is a shallow *crossing* just down the stream.
cross·ing (kros′ing) *noun, plural* **crossings.**

crossroad 1. A road that crosses another road or a road that leads from one main road to another. 2. **crossroads.** The place where two or more roads cross each other. There was a traffic light at the *crossroads.*
cross·road (kros′rōd′) *noun, plural* **crossroads.**

cross section 1. A slice or piece made by cutting straight across something. When you slice a banana you make cross sections. 2. A sample of people or things that is thought to show what the whole group of people or things is like. A poll of a *cross section* of voters in the state showed that the senator would probably be elected to another term in office.

crotch The place where the body divides into two legs, or where a branch of a tree divides from the trunk or from another branch.
crotch (kroch) *noun, plural* **crotches.**

crouch To stoop or bend low with the knees bent. The cat *crouched* in the bushes, ready to spring if a bird came close.
crouch (krouch) *verb,* **crouched, crouching.**

Crow

crow¹ 1. To make the loud, sharp cry of a rooster. The farmer's rooster *crows* every morning when the sun rises. 2. To make a happy yell or cry. Steve *crowed* with delight when he won the contest.
crow (krō) *verb,* **crowed, crowing.**

crow² A large bird with shiny, black feathers and a harsh cry.
crow (krō) *noun, plural* **crows.**

at; āpe; cär; end; mē; it; īce; hot; ōld; wood; fōōl; oil; out; up; turn; sing; thin; this; hw in white; zh in treasure. ə stands for a in about, e in taken, i in pencil, o in lemon, and u in circus.

crowbar A heavy steel or iron bar that has one flattened end. A crowbar is used to lift things up or pry things apart.
crow·bar (krō′bär′) *noun, plural* **crowbars.**

Crowbar

crowd A large number of people gathered together. *Noun.*
—**1.** To put or force too many people or things into too small a space. Roberta *crowded* her shelf with books. **2.** To move by pushing or shoving. She asked the man behind her in line not to *crowd* her. *Verb.*
crowd (kroud) *noun, plural* **crowds;** *verb,* **crowded, crowding.**

crown **1.** A covering for the head worn by kings and queens. A crown is often made of gold and silver set with jewels. **2.** The highest or top part of anything. The hikers climbed to the *crown* of the hill. **3.** The part of a tooth that can be seen above the gums. **4. the Crown.** *Canadian.* The authority of the king or queen or the power of government officials who represent the king or queen. The Crown in Canada is represented by the Governor General. *Noun.*
—To make a person a king or queen at a special ceremony during which a crown is put on his or her head. *Verb.*
crown (kroun) *noun, plural* **crowns;** *verb,* **crowned, crowning.**

Crown corporation *Canadian.* A company owned by a provincial or the federal government. Air Canada and the CBC are Crown corporations.

Crown land *Canadian.* Land which is not settled and is owned by the government.

crow's-nest A small platform near the top of a ship's mast. Sailors use it as a lookout.
crow's-nest (krōz′nest′) *noun, plural* **crow's-nests.**

CRTC The Canadian Radio-Telecommunications Commission.

crucial Very important; decisive. When a thing is crucial it means that it will decide whether something else succeeds or fails.

The last minutes of the hockey game were *crucial* to our team.
cru·cial (krōō′shəl) *adjective.*

crucifixion **1.** The act of crucifying a person. **2. Crucifixion.** The putting to death of Christ on a cross.
cru·ci·fix·ion (krōō′sə fik′shən) *noun, plural* **crucifixions.**

crucify To put a person to death by nailing or tying the hands and feet to a cross.
cru·ci·fy (krōō′sə fī′) *verb,* **crucified, crucifying.**

crude **1.** In a natural or raw state. *Crude* rubber is rubber as it is drained from the bark of rubber trees. **2.** Done or made without skill; rough. The boys built a *crude* shack out of bits of wood. **3.** Not polite or in good taste; not refined; rude. It was *crude* of them to laugh at the girl when she fell off the chair.
crude (krōōd) *adjective,* **cruder, crudest.**

cruel **1.** Willing to cause pain or suffering to others. The *cruel* man beat his dog. **2.** Causing pain or suffering. A *cruel,* biting cold wind swept across the plains.
cru·el (krōō′əl) *adjective,* **crueler, cruelest.**

cruelty **1.** Being willing to cause pain to others. That girl is hated because of her *cruelty* to animals. **2.** A cruel act. They suffered many *cruelties* in the enemy prison camp.
cru·el·ty (krōō′əl tē) *noun, plural* **cruelties.**

cruet A small glass bottle that vinegar, oil, or other dressings are served in.
cru·et (krōō′it) *noun, plural* **cruets.**

cruise **1.** To sail from place to place. We *cruised* along the coast until we found a place to anchor for a while. **2.** To move or ride from place to place. A police car *cruises* through our neighbourhood each night. *Verb.*
—A trip in a boat taken for pleasure.

Cruets

We would love to take a *cruise* to Victoria. *Noun.*
cruise (krōōz) *verb,* **cruised, cruising;** *noun, plural* **cruises.**

cruiser **1.** A warship that is faster than a battleship and carries fewer guns. **2.** A motorboat with a cabin, that is used for pleasure.
cruis·er (krōō′zər) *noun, plural* **cruisers.**

crumb A tiny piece of bread, cake, cracker, or cookie. We put out *crumbs* for the birds.
crumb (krum) *noun, plural* **crumbs.**

crumble 1. To break into small pieces. The muffin *crumbled* when I tried to butter it. 2. To fall apart or be destroyed. The old house is slowly *crumbling.* The team's hopes for winning the game *crumbled* when the best player got sick.
crum·ble (krum′bəl) *verb,* **crumbled, crumbling.**

crumple 1. To press or crush into wrinkles or folds. We *crumpled* sheets of newspaper to start the fire. 2. To fall down or collapse. Susan *crumpled* to the ground when she hit her head on the low branch.
crum·ple (krum′pəl) *verb,* **crumpled, crumpling.**

crunch To chew or crush with a noisy, crushing sound. The rabbit *crunched* on a carrot. *Verb.*
—A crushing, crackling sound. We heard the *crunch* of the hiker's boots in the snow. *Noun.*
crunch (krunch) *verb,* **crunched, crunching;** *noun, plural* **crunches.**

crusade 1. Any of the military expeditions undertaken by the Christian people of Europe between the years 1095 and 1291 to take the Holy Land away from the Muslims. 2. A strong fight against something evil or for something good. We started a *crusade* to clean up the town parks. *Noun.*
—To fight in a crusade. He is *crusading* against the pollution of the province's lakes and rivers. *Verb.*
cru·sade (krōō sād′) *noun, plural* **crusades;** *verb,* **crusaded, crusading.**

crusader A person who fights in a crusade. She is a *crusader* for civil rights.
cru·sad·er (krōō sād′ər) *noun, plural* **crusaders.**

crush 1. To squeeze very hard. When you crush something, it is broken, put out of shape, or hurt in some way. We have a machine that *crushes* ice into small bits. The garbage can was *crushed* when the truck ran over it. 2. To put down; subdue. Her hopes of going to the circus were *crushed* when she got sick and had to stay in bed. *Verb.*
—1. A very strong pressure or squeezing. The *crush* of the crowd pushed him against the door of the bus. 2. A sudden, strong liking for a person. My sister has a *crush* on a handsome movie actor. *Noun.*
crush (krush) *verb,* **crushed, crushing;** *noun, plural* **crushes.**

crust 1. The hard, crunchy outside part of bread, rolls, or other food. A pie has a *crust* of dough. We fed the birds *crusts* of bread. 2. Any hard outside part or coating. The pond was covered with a *crust* of ice. The *crust* of the earth is a layer of rock thirty kilometres deep. *Noun.*
—To cover with a crust. Ice *crusted* the pond. *Verb.*
crust (krust) *noun, plural* **crusts;** *verb,* **crusted, crusting.**

crustacean An animal that has a hard shell and lives mostly in water. Lobsters, crabs, shrimp, and barnacles are crustaceans.
crus·ta·cean (krus tā′shən) *noun, plural* **crustaceans.**

crutch A support that helps a lame person in walking. A crutch is a pole that usually has a padded part at the top that fits under the arm so a person can lean on it.
crutch (kruch) *noun, plural* **crutches.**

Crutches

cry 1. To shed tears; weep. The baby will *cry* when he is hungry. She *cried* when she lost her ring on the beach. 2. To call loudly; shout. The man in the burning building *cried* for help. *Verb.*
—1. A loud call or shout. Sarah gave a *cry* of joy when she saw the bicycle under the Christmas tree. The boys heard a *cry* for help from the lake. 2. The special sound that an animal or bird makes. Late at night we listened to the *cries* of the owls. *Noun.*
cry (krī) *verb,* **cried, crying;** *noun, plural* **cries.**

crystal 1. A clear kind of rock that has no colour. Crystal is a kind of quartz. 2. A body that is formed by certain substances when they solidify. Crystals have flat surfaces. Salt forms in crystals. Snowflakes are crystals. 3. A very fine, clear glass used to make drinking glasses, bowls, plates, and vases. Crystal sparkles in the light.
crys·tal (kris′təl) *noun, plural* **crystals.**

at; āpe; cär; end; mē; it; īce; hot; ōld;
wood; fōōl; oil; out; up; turn; sing;
thin; this; hw in white; zh in treasure.
ə stands for a in about, e in taken,
i in pencil, o in lemon, and u in circus.

cub   A very young bear, fox, wolf, lion, or tiger.
cub (kub) *noun, plural* **cubs.**

cube   **1.** A solid figure with six equal, square sides. **2.** Something shaped like a cube. Put more ice *cubes* in my iced tea, please. **3.** The product of a number that is multiplied by itself two times. The cube of 2 is 8 because $2 \times 2 \times 2 = 8$. *Noun.*
—To cut or make into cubes. Alan *cubed* potatoes to make potato salad. *Verb.*
cube (ky$\overline{oo}$b) *noun, plural* **cubes;** *verb,* **cubed, cubing.**

The building block is a **cube.**

cubic   **1.** Shaped like a cube. These building blocks are *cubic.* **2.** Having length, width, and height. The volume of a cube can be measured in *cubic* centimetres or metres.
cu·bic (ky$\overline{oo}$′bik) *adjective.*

cub scout   A boy who is a junior member of the Boy Scouts.

cuckoo   A bird that has a long tail and a call that sounds like its name. Most cuckoos have brown feathers and lay their eggs in the nests of other birds.
cuck·oo (k$\overline{oo}$′k$\overline{oo}$ *or* kook′$\overline{oo}$) *noun, plural* **cuckoos.**

Cuckoo

cucumber   A long, green vegetable with white flesh and many seeds inside. The cucumber grows on a vine. Cucumbers are eaten raw in salads or made into pickles.
cu·cum·ber (ky$\overline{oo}$′kum′bər) *noun, plural* **cucumbers.**

cud   Food that comes back into the mouth from the first stomach of cows and some other animals so that they can chew it again.
cud (kud) *noun, plural* **cuds.**

cue¹   A signal that tells someone to begin to do something. The ring of the telephone was the actor's *cue* to walk on stage. *Noun.*
—To give a signal to someone to tell them to begin to do something. Betty's job was to stand backstage and *cue* the actors. *Verb.*
cue (ky$\overline{oo}$) *noun, plural* **cues;** *verb,* **cued, cuing.**

cue²   A long, thin stick that is used to strike the ball in playing pool or billiards.
cue (ky$\overline{oo}$) *noun, plural* **cues.**

cuff¹   **1.** A band of material at the bottom of a sleeve. **2.** A turned-up fold of material at the bottom of a trouser leg.
cuff (kuf) *noun, plural* **cuffs.**

cuff²   To hit with the hand. The grocer *cuffed* the boy on the head for stealing an apple. *Verb.*
—A hit with the hand; slap. She gave the dog a *cuff* when he snapped at her. *Noun.*
cuff (kuf) *verb,* **cuffed, cuffing;** *noun, plural* **cuffs.**

culprit   A person who is guilty of doing something that is wrong. The woman identified the two men as the *culprits* who stole her purse.
cul·prit (kul′prit) *noun, plural* **culprits.**

cultivate   **1.** To prepare and use land for growing vegetables, flowers, or other crops. To cultivate land, you plow and fertilize it and get rid of weeds in it before you plant seeds. **2.** To work hard to improve or develop. Tom tried to *cultivate* good study habits.
cul·ti·vate (kul′tə vāt′) *verb,* **cultivated, cultivating.**

cultivator   A tool or machine used to loosen the soil and pull up weeds around growing plants.
cul·ti·va·tor (kul′tə vā′tər) *noun, plural* **cultivators.**

cultural   Having to do with culture. We read a book about the *cultural* history of ancient Greece.
cul·tur·al (kul′chər əl) *adjective.*

Cultivator

culture   **1.** The arts, beliefs, and customs that make up a way of life for a group of people at a certain time. We are studying the *cultures* of North American Indians. **2.** The good taste and manners, and the knowledge and appreciation of the arts that come as a result of good education. The family sent their son to Europe to gain *culture.* **3.** The improvement and development of something. Gymnastics are a part of physical *culture.*

cul·ture (kul′chər) *noun, plural* **cultures.**

cunning **1.** Very clever at fooling or deceiving others. The *cunning* thief disguised herself as a maid and robbed people at the party. **2.** Very cute; charming. Everyone said that Katherine was such a *cunning* baby. *Adjective.*
—Cleverness at fooling or deceiving others. Foxes are said to show much *cunning* in escaping from hunters. *Noun.*

cun·ning (kun′ing) *adjective; noun.*

cup **1.** A small bowl with a handle that is used to drink from. **2.** Anything that has the shape of a cup. A silver *cup* was the prize for the winner of the sailing race. *Noun.*
—To shape like a cup. Dan *cupped* his hands under the hose to fill them with water to drink. *Verb.*

cup (kup) *noun, plural* **cups;** *verb,* **cupped, cupping.**

cupboard A closet with shelves to store dishes or food.

cup·board (kub′ərd) *noun, plural* **cupboards.**

cupcake A small cake. Cupcakes are baked in metal pans with several cup-shaped hollows.

cup·cake (kup′kāk′) *noun, plural* **cupcakes.**

Cupid The god of love. Cupid is usually pictured as a young boy who has wings and carries a bow and arrow. Valentines often have a picture of Cupid on them.

Cu·pid (kyōō′pid) *noun.*

Cupid

curb **1.** A border of concrete or stone along the side of a road or sidewalk. We were lucky to find a place to park along the *curb* in front of the restaurant. **2.** Anything that holds back or controls an action. We decided to put a *curb* on our spending by following a strict budget. **3.** A chain or strap that is fastened to a horse's bit. It is used to control the horse when the reins are pulled. *Noun.*
—To hold back or control. She *curbed* her anger at what he said by counting silently to ten before she answered him. *Verb.*

curb (kurb) *noun, plural* **curbs;** *verb,* **curbed, curbing.**

cure **1.** To make a person or animal healthy again. The veterinarian *cured* our dog. **2.** To get rid of. My mother says to *cure* a cold you have to stay in bed and rest. **3.** To preserve or prepare meat and fish for use by drying, smoking, or salting. Farmers *cure* the meat of pigs to make bacon. *Verb.*
—Something that makes a person or animal healthy again. Aspirin is the best *cure* for my headache. *Noun.*

cure (kyoor) *verb,* **cured, curing;** *noun, plural* **cures.**

curfew A fixed time at night when a person has to be indoors or at home. At camp we had a 10:00 *curfew* to be in bed.

cur·few (kur′fyōō) *noun, plural* **curfews.**

▲ The word **curfew** comes from two early French words that meant "cover" and "fire." In the Middle Ages, a bell rang at night to tell people that it was time for them to put out or cover their fires. This signal became known as the "cover-fire" or *curfew.*

curiosity **1.** A strong wish to learn about things that are new, strange, or interesting. The children had a great *curiosity* about what was in the locked closet. **2.** Something that is interesting because it is unusual. A horse-drawn carriage is a *curiosity* today.

cu·ri·os·i·ty (kyoor′ē os′ə tē) *noun, plural* **curiosities.**

curious **1.** Eager to learn about things that are new, strange, or interesting. I was really *curious* to know more about the new girl in class. **2.** Strange or unusual. Tom has a collection of *curious* old coins.

cu·ri·ous (kyoor′ē əs) *adjective.*

curl **1.** To twist in curved rings or coils. She *curled* her hair for the party. **2.** To play the game of curling. *Verb.*
—**1.** A curved lock of hair; ringlet. My little sister has *curls* all over her head. **2.** Something shaped like a ring or coil. A *curl* of smoke rose upward out of the chimney. *Noun.*

curl (kurl) *verb,* **curled, curling;** *noun, plural* **curls.**

at; āpe; cär; end; mē; it; īce; hot; ōld; wood; fōōl; oil; out; up; turn; sing; thin; this; hw in white; zh in treasure. ə stands for a in about, e in taken, i in pencil, o in lemon, and u in circus.

curler 1. Anything around which hair is wound to make it curl. 2. A person who plays the game of curling.
curl·er (kurl′ər) *noun, plural* **curlers.**

curling A game in which large, smooth stones with handles are slid over ice at a target. There are two teams of four players each.
curl·ing (kur′ling) *noun.*

curling stone One of the large, smooth stones used in curling.

curly Forming or having curls. She has *curly* hair.
curl·y (kur′lē) *adjective,* **curlier, curliest.**

currant 1. A small, sour berry that grows in bunches on a bush. Currants are used to make jelly. 2. A small seedless raisin used in cakes, pies, and buns. ▲ Another word that sounds like this is **current.**
cur·rant (kur′ənt) *noun, plural* **currants.**

currency 1. The money that is used in a country. Dollar bills, quarters, and dimes are part of the currency of Canada. 2. General use or acceptance. As more and more people use a new slang word, they begin to give it *currency.*
cur·ren·cy (kur′ən sē) *noun, plural* **currencies.**

current Being part of the present time. If something is happening, used, or believed in now it is current. The *current* belief is that there is probably no life on the planet Venus. *Adjective.*
—1. A part of the air or of a body of water that is moving along in a path. A cold *current* of air flowed through the room when she opened the door. 2. A flow of electricity in a wire or through anything. When a fuse burns out it stops the electric *current* in the circuit. 3. The way events or thoughts seem to move along a path. The *current* of public opinion today seems to be that the mayor should not run for re-election. *Noun.* ▲ Another word that sounds like this is **currant.**
cur·rent (kur′ənt) *adjective; noun, plural* **currents.**

curse 1. A wish that something evil or harmful will happen to a person or thing. A curse is often made by calling on God or gods. 2. A word or words used in swearing. A curse is usually said when you are very angry. *Noun.*
—1. To wish that something evil or harmful will happen to a person or thing. The soldier *cursed* the enemy. 2. To say a word or words that show hate or anger; swear. He *cursed* when he hit his thumb with the hammer. 3. To

cause evil, harm, or suffering to. He had been *cursed* with a weak back for years. *Verb.*
curse (kurs) *noun, plural* **curses;** *verb,* **cursed, cursing.**

curtain 1. A piece of cloth hung across an open space. Curtains are hung at windows, in doorways, and across the front part of a stage. 2. Anything like a curtain. A *curtain* of fog hid the tops of the tall buildings. *Noun.*
—To put a curtain over; screen. We *curtained* off a part of the basement as a workshop. *Verb.*
cur·tain (kur′tən) *noun, plural* **curtains;** *verb,* **curtained, curtaining.**

Curtsy

curtsy A bow showing respect made by bending the knees and lowering the body slightly, Women and girls curtsy and men and boys bow. This word is also spelled *curtsey.*
curt·sy (kurt′sē) *noun, plural* **curtsies.**

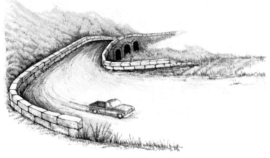
A **curve** in a road

curve 1. A line that keeps bending in one direction. A curve has no straight parts or angles. 2. Something that has the shape of a curve. The river has a *curve* in it further on. The baby rested his head in the *curve* of his mother's arm. *Noun.*
—To bend or move in a curved line. The road *curves* as you come off the bridge. The base-

ball *curved* to the left as it came near the batter. *Verb.*

curve (kurv) *noun, plural* **curves;** *verb,* **curved, curving.**

cushion **1.** A pillow or soft pad used to sit, lie, or rest on. Our couch has three *cushions* on the seat. **2.** Anything that softens a blow or protects against harm. A savings account in a bank can be a *cushion* if you lose your job. *Noun.*
—**1.** To make a pillow or soft pad for. We are going to *cushion* the rocking chair so that it is more comfortable. **2.** To soften a blow or shock. The pile of leaves *cushioned* my fall from the tree. *Verb.*

cush·ion (koosh′ən) *noun, plural* **cushions;** *verb,* **cushioned, cushioning.**

custard A sweet dessert made of eggs, milk, and sugar that are cooked together into a pudding.

cus·tard (kus′tərd) *noun, plural* **custards.**

custodian A person who is responsible for the care of a person or thing. The school *custodian* made sure the buildings were kept clean and in good repair.

cus·to·di·an (kəs tō′dē ən) *noun, plural* **custodians.**

custody The care and keeping of a person or thing. She was in her grandmother's *custody* while her parents lived in China for a year. The suspected bank robber was taken into the *custody* of the police until bail was arranged.

cus·to·dy (kus′tə dē) *noun, plural* **custodies.**

custom **1.** A way of acting that has become accepted by many people. Customs are learned and passed down from one generation to another. Decorating trees and giving presents at Christmas is a *custom* shared by many people in this country. **2.** The usual way that something is done; habit. It is my *custom* to walk to school every morning. **3. customs.** Taxes that a government collects on products that are brought in from a foreign country. We had to pay *customs* on the sweaters we had bought in Scotland.

cus·tom (kus′təm) *noun, plural* **customs.**

customary Usual. It is *customary* in our family to have Thanksgiving dinner at our grandmother's house.

cus·tom·ar·y (kus′tə mer′ē) *adjective.*

customer A person who buys something. That store thinks of us as regular *customers* because we shop there at least once a week.

cus·tom·er (kus′tə mər) *noun, plural* **customers.**

cut **1.** To divide, pierce, open, or take away a part with something sharp. We could not untie the knot, so we had to *cut* the string. Laura *cut* the pie into six slices. I *cut* my foot on the sharp rock. We have to *cut* the grass today. The cold wind *cut* through her light jacket. **2.** To make by using a sharp tool. We *cut* a hole in the door so the cat could come in and go out. **3.** To make shorter or smaller. He *cut* his speech because it was too long. The store will *cut* all its prices for the big sale. **4.** To cross or pass. The river *cuts* through the valley. Let's *cut* through the park instead of walking around it. *Verb.*
—**1.** An opening or slit made with something sharp. He got a *cut* on his hand from the broken glass. **2.** A decrease. Father asked if I would mind taking a *cut* in my allowance. *Noun.*

cut (kut) *verb,* **cut, cutting;** *noun, plural* **cuts.**

cute Adorable; charming; appealing. All the puppies were so *cute* that it was hard to choose which one to buy.

cute (kyo͞ot) *adjective,* **cuter, cutest.**

cuticle A tough layer of skin. We have cuticles around the edges of our fingernails.

cu·ti·cle (kyo͞o′ti kəl) *noun, plural* **cuticles.**

cutlass A sword with a wide, flat, curved blade.

cut·lass (kut′ləs) *noun, plural* **cutlasses.**

Cutlass

cutter **1.** A person whose job it is to cut out things. A diamond *cutter* cuts away bits of

at; āpe; cär; end; mē; it; īce; hot; ōld;
wood; fo͞ol; oil; out; up; turn; sing;
thin; this; hw in white; zh in treasure.
ə stands for a in about, e in taken,
i in pencil, o in lemon, and u in circus.

the stone to give a diamond a special shape. A dress *cutter* cuts out dresses from fabric. **2.** A tool or machine that is used to cut out things. It is fun to use cookie *cutters* to make different shapes. **3.** A small, fast ship. The cutters are used to rescue people who are having trouble at sea. **4.** *Canadian.* A small sleigh. She attached the *cutter* to the snowmobile to take the children to school. *Adjective.*

cut·ter (kut′ər) *noun, plural* **cutters.**

cutting **1.** Able to make a slit or other opening in; sharp. The *cutting* edge of a knife is thinner than the other edge. **2.** Hurting a person's feelings. He made a *cutting* remark about his friend's new jacket. *Adjective.*
—**1.** A small part cut from a plant and used to grow a new one. If you take a *cutting* from ivy and put it in water, it will grow roots and can be planted. **2.** An article or picture cut out of a newspaper or magazine; clipping. *Noun.*

cut·ting (kut′ing) *adjective; noun, plural* **cuttings.**

cycle A series of events that happen one after another in the same order, over and over again. Spring, summer, autumn, and winter are the *cycle* of the four seasons of the year. *Noun.*
—To ride a bicycle, tricycle, or motorcycle. We plan to *cycle* in the park. *Verb.*

cy·cle (sī′kəl) *noun, plural* **cycles;** *verb,* **cycled, cycling.**

cyclone A very powerful windstorm. The winds in a cyclone move around and around and can cause much damage.

cy·clone (sī′klōn′) *noun, plural* **cyclones.**

cylinder A solid or hollow object that is shaped like a roller or a soup can.

cyl·in·der (sil′ən dər) *noun, plural* **cylinders.**

cymbal A metal musical instrument that is shaped like a plate. One cymbal is hit against another to make a ringing sound. ▲ Another word that sounds like this is **symbol.**

cym·bal (sim′bəl) *noun, plural* **cymbals.**

Leaves and Cone

Cypress Tree

cypress Any of various evergreen trees that have small scalelike leaves. The wood of the cypress is very hard and is used for building.

cy·press (sī′prəs) *noun, plural* **cypresses.**

czar One of the emperors who once ruled Russia. This word is also spelled **tsar.**

czar (zär) *noun, plural* **czars.**

czarina **1.** The wife of a czar. **2.** A Russian empress.

czarina (zä rē′nə) *noun, plural* **czarinas.**

---

at; āpe; cär; end; mē; it; īce; hot; ōld;
wood; fōol; oil; out; up; turn; sing;
thin; this; hw in white; zh in treasure.
ə stands for a in about, e in taken,
i in pencil, o in lemon, and u in circus.

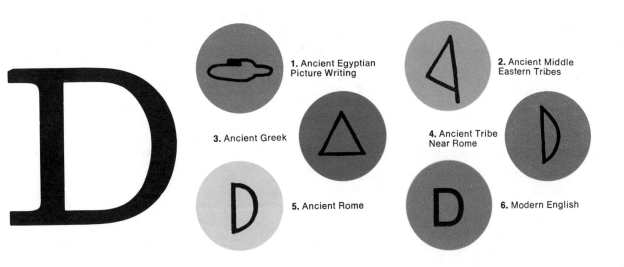

1. Ancient Egyptian Picture Writing
2. Ancient Middle Eastern Tribes
3. Ancient Greek
4. Ancient Tribe Near Rome
5. Ancient Rome
6. Modern English

D is the fourth letter of the alphabet. The oldest form of the letter **D** was a drawing that the ancient Egyptians (**1**) used in their picture writing nearly 5000 years ago. This drawing was borrowed by several ancient tribes (**2**) in the Middle East. They drew this letter like a triangle. The ancient Greeks (**3**) borrowed this letter and called it *delta*. We use the word "delta" for soil that builds up at the mouth of a river. The Greek letter was borrowed by an ancient tribe (**4**) that settled north of Rome about 2800 years ago. They changed the shape of *delta* by rounding two of the sides of the triangle. The Romans (**5**) borrowed this letter and, by about 2400 years ago, were writing it almost exactly the way we write the capital letter **D** today (**6**).

d, D The fourth letter of the alphabet.
d, D (dē) *noun, plural* **d's, D's.**

dab **1.** To touch lightly and gently; tap. Tim's mother *dabbed* his cut knee with cotton. **2.** To put on lightly and gently. Betty *dabbed* lotion on her sunburn. *Verb.*
—**1.** A small, moist mass of something. The girl formed a *dab* of clay into the shape of a bowl. **2.** A little bit. Alice wanted only a *dab* of butter on her mashed potatoes. *Noun.*
dab (dab) *verb,* **dabbed, dabbing;** *noun, plural* **dabs.**

dabble **1.** To work at or do something a little, but not in a serious way. He only *dabbled* at playing the piano because he would never take the time to practise. **2.** To splash in and out of the water. The girls sat on the dock to *dabble* their feet in the water.
dab·ble (dab′əl) *verb,* **dabbled, dabbling.**

dachshund A small dog with a long body, very short legs, and drooping ears.
dachs·hund (däks′hoont′ *or* däks′hoond′) *noun, plural* **dachshunds.**

▲ The word **dachshund** comes from the German name for the dog, which means "badger dog." These dogs were first raised for hunting badgers.

---

dad Father. Children often call their father *Dad.*
dad (dad) *noun, plural* **dads.**

daddy Father. Mary and Jack call their father *Daddy.*
dad·dy (dad′ē) *noun, plural* **daddies.**

daddy-longlegs An animal that looks like a spider. It has a small round body and very long, thin legs.
dad·dy-long·legs (dad′ē long′legz′) *noun, plural* **daddy-longlegs.**

daffodil A plant that has long, thin leaves and yellow or white flowers.
daf·fo·dil (daf′ə dil′) *noun, plural* **daffodils.**

dagger A small weapon that looks like a knife. A dagger is used for stabbing.
dag·ger (dag′ər) *noun, plural* **daggers.**

daily Appearing, done, or happening every day. Mr. Smith reads the *daily* newspaper on his way to work. Peggy does her *daily* job of making her bed before she leaves for school. *Adjective.*
—Day after day; every day. That train runs *daily. Adverb.*
—A newspaper published every day or every weekday. *Noun.*
dai·ly (dā′lē) *adjective; adverb; noun, plural* **dailies.**

Daffodil

dainty Delicate and pretty. Joan's older sis-

165

ter wore a *dainty* gold bracelet to the school dance.

dain·ty (dān′tē) *adjective,* **daintier, daintiest.**

dairy 1. A place where milk and cream are stored or made into butter and cheese. 2. A store or company that sells milk, cream, butter, and cheese. 3. A farm where cows are raised, milk and cream are produced, and butter and cheese are made.

dair·y (der′ē) *noun, plural* **dairies.**

dais A slightly raised platform for a throne, a speaker's desk, or seats for guests of honour.

da·is (dā′is) *noun, plural* **daises.**

daisy A plant that has a flower of pink, white, or yellow petals around a yellow centre.

dai·sy (dā′zē) *noun, plural* **daisies.**

Dalmatian A large dog that has a short-haired white coat covered with small black or brown spots.

Dal·ma·tian (dal-mā′shən) *noun, plural* **Dalmatians.**

Daisy

dam A wall built across a stream or river to hold back the water. *Noun.*
—To hold back by a dam. Beavers *dam* streams with mud and sticks. *Verb.* ▲ Another word that sounds like this is **damn.**

dam (dam) *noun, plural* **dams;** *verb,* **dammed, damming.**

Dam

damage Harm or injury that makes something less valuable or useful. The flood caused great *damage* to the farms in the area. *Noun.*
—To harm or injure. Rain came through the open window and *damaged* the books that were on the window sill. *Verb.*

dam·age (dam′əj) *noun, plural* **damages;** *verb,* **damaged, damaging.**

dame 1. A woman who has a position of rank. 2. An elderly woman.

dame (dām) *noun, plural* **dames.**

damn 1. To say that something is very bad or of little worth. The critics *damned* the new movie. 2. To curse or swear at. ▲ Another word that sounds like this is **dam.**

damn (dam) *verb,* **damned, damning.**

damp A little wet; moist. He wiped up the spilled milk with a *damp* sponge. Karen put on a warm sweater because it was such a *damp* and chilly day. *Adjective.*
—Slight wetness; moisture. *Noun.*

damp (damp) *adjective,* **damper, dampest;** *noun.*

dampen 1. To make a little wet or moist. *Dampen* the rag before you wipe the table. 2. To lessen the force or strength of. Losing the game *dampened* the team's spirits.

damp·en (dam′pən) *verb,* **dampened, dampening.**

dance 1. To move the body or feet in time to music. Alice likes to *dance.* 2. To move or jump about quickly or lightly. Waves *danced* on the lake. *Verb.*
—1. A particular set of steps or movements done in time to music. The waltz is a hard *dance* to learn. 2. A party where people dance. There will be a *dance* Friday night at the high school. *Noun.*

dance (dans) *verb,* **danced, dancing;** *noun, plural* **dances.**

dancer A person who dances. Jill wants to study to be a *dancer.*

danc·er (dan′sər) *noun, plural* **dancers.**

dandelion A plant with a bright yellow flower and long leaves. Dandelion leaves are sometimes eaten in salads or cooked as a vegetable.

dan·de·li·on (dand′əl ī′ən *or* dand′ē lī′ən) *noun, plural* **dandelions.**

▲ The word **dandelion** comes from the French name for this flower, which means "lion's teeth." The French probably called the plant by this name because its leaves have sharp edges like teeth.

dandruff Small white or grey pieces of dead skin that fall from the scalp.

dan·druff (dan′drəf) *noun.*

dandy A man who is too fussy about his clothes and the way he looks.

dan·dy (dan′dē) *noun, plural* **dandies.**

danger 1. The chance that something bad or

harmful will happen. The children knew the *danger* of skating on thin ice. **2.** Something that may cause harm or injury. Icy roads are a *danger* to drivers.

dan·ger (dān′jər) *noun, plural* **dangers.**

dangerous Likely to cause something bad or harmful to happen. Driving too fast is *dangerous.*

dan·ger·ous (dān′jər əs) *adjective.*

dangle To hang or swing loosely. Paul sat down on the edge of the swimming pool to *dangle* his feet in the water.

dan·gle (dang′gəl) *verb,* **dangled, dangling.**

dare **1.** To challenge someone to do something. Bill *dared* Joe to jump off the high diving board. **2.** To be bold enough to try; have the courage for. The boys did not *dare* to skate on the thin ice. *Verb.*

—A challenge. Alice took her brother's *dare* and jumped across the stream. *Noun.*

dare (der) *verb,* **dared, daring;** *noun, plural* **dares.**

daring Courage or boldness; bravery. The first explorers of the North Pole are famous for their *daring. Noun.*

—Courageous and bold; brave; fearless. The girl was given a medal for her *daring* rescue of the drowning child. *Adjective.*

dar·ing (der′ing) *noun; adjective.*

dark **1.** Having little or no light. The night is very *dark* because the clouds are covering the moon. **2.** Not light in colour; almost the colour of black. Nancy has *dark* hair and brown eyes. *Adjective.*

—**1.** A lack of light. We keep a light on in my little brother's room at night because he is afraid of the *dark.* **2.** Night or nightfall; the end of daylight. Bob's mother told him to be home before *dark. Noun.*

dark (därk) *adjective,* **darker, darkest;** *noun.*
in the dark. Without knowledge; not aware. The teacher kept us *in the dark* about the party because she wanted to surprise us.

darken To make or become dark or darker. Janet watched the rain clouds *darken* the sky. The white paint had *darkened* with age.

dark·en (därk′ən) *verb,* **darkened, darkening.**

darling A person who is loved very much. A husband and wife may call each other *darling. Noun.*

—**1.** Very much loved; dear. The mother wrote a letter to her daughter at camp that began with the words "My *darling* Amy." **2.** Cute and attractive; charming. Everyone thought the kittens were *darling. Adjective.*

dar·ling (där′ling) *noun, plural* **darlings;** *adjective.*

darn To mend by making stitches back and forth across a hole or tear. She *darned* the holes in her sweater.

darn (därn) *verb,* **darned, darning.**

dart A thin, pointed object that looks like a small arrow. Darts are thrown at targets in certain games. *Noun.*

—**1.** To jump or move suddenly and quickly. We watched the rabbit *dart* into the bushes. **2.** To throw or send suddenly and quickly. The frog *darted* out its tongue to catch the fly. She *darted* an angry look at her friend for giving away her secret. *Verb.*

dart (därt) *noun, plural* **darts;** *verb,* **darted, darting.**

Dart

dash **1.** To move fast; rush. We tried to teach our dog not to *dash* after cars. **2.** To hit or throw with force; smash. High waves *dashed* against the ship during the storm. **3.** To destroy or ruin. Spraining her ankle *dashed* her hopes of winning the race. *Verb.*

—**1.** A fast movement or sudden rush. The hikers made a *dash* for cover when the rain started. **2.** A small amount that is added or mixed in. Add another *dash* of salt to the beef stew. **3.** A short race. Both schools had runners in the 50-metre *dash. Noun.*

dash (dash) *verb,* **dashed, dashing;** *noun, plural* **dashes.**

dashboard A panel in front of the driver in an automobile. It has dials and instruments to help the driver operate the car. They tell how fast the car is going, how much gas there is in the gas tank, and other things.

dash·board (dash′bôrd′) *noun, plural* **dashboards.**

at; āpe; cär; end; mē; it; īce; hot; ōld;
wood; fool; oil; out; up; turn; sing;
thin; this; hw in white; zh in treasure.
ə stands for a in about, e in taken,
i in pencil, o in lemon, and u in circus.

data Facts, figures, and other information. Students' names, ages, and other *data* were stored in our school's microcomputer.
da·ta (dā′tə *or* dat′ə) *noun plural.*

date¹ **1.** The day, month, year, or time when something happened or happens. The *date* of Jane's birthday is June 3. The *date* of Canada's one-hundredth birthday was 1967. Your library card shows the *date* on which it will expire. **2.** An agreement to meet or be with someone at a certain time and place. The two friends made a *date* to meet for lunch on Thursday. **3.** A person with whom one has such an agreement. My brother doesn't have a *date* for the dance yet. *Noun.*
—**1.** To mark with a time or date. Jim *dated* his test paper. **2.** To find out or fix the time of. The scientists at the museum were able to *date* the dinosaur bones they found. **3.** To belong to or come from a certain time. The old chair in the living room *dates* from the late 1800s. *Verb.*
date (dāt) *noun, plural* **dates;** *verb,* **dated, dating.**
out of date. No longer in fashion or use. The woman's dress was old and *out of date.*
up to date. In fashion or use; modern; current. This telephone book is revised and *up to date.*

date² **1.** A sweet fruit that grows on a kind of palm tree. **2.** The tree that this fruit grows on. This tree is also called a **date palm.**
date (dāt) *noun, plural* **dates.**

Date Palm Tree

Fruit

daughter A female child. A girl or woman is the daughter of her mother and father.
daugh·ter (dät′ər) *noun, plural* **daughters.**

daughter-in-law The wife of a son.
daugh·ter-in-law (dät′ər in lä′) *noun, plural* **daughters-in-law.**

dawn **1.** The first light that appears in the morning; daybreak. **2.** The beginning or first sign. The *dawn* of civilization took place thousands and thousands of years ago. *Noun.*
—**1.** To begin to get light in the morning; become day. We sat on the beach and watched the day *dawn.* **2.** To begin to be clear or understood. It *dawned* on him that he was being tricked. *Verb.*
dawn (dän) *noun, plural* **dawns;** *verb,* **dawned, dawning.**

day **1.** The period of light between the rising and setting of the sun; daylight. **2.** The 24 hours of one day and night. We have a holiday of ten *days* in the spring when we go skiing. **3.** The part of a day spent working. Jean's school *day* ends at three o'clock in the afternoon. **4.** A time or period. In the present *day,* more people live in cities than on farms.
day (dā) *noun, plural* **days.**

daybreak The time each morning when light first appears; dawn.
day·break (dā′brāk′) *noun, plural* **daybreaks.**

day-care centre A place where small children are taken care of during the day; nursery school. Day-care centres are used most often by children whose parents work away from home during the day. This is also called a **day nursery.**

daydream Pleasant thinking or wishing about things one would like to do or have happen. Janet had a *daydream* of being a famous writer someday. *Noun.*
—To think about pleasant things in a dreamy way. Bill's father told him to get to work and not to *daydream* all day. *Verb.*
day·dream (dā′drēm′) *noun, plural* **daydreams;** *verb,* **daydreamed, daydreaming.**

daylight **1.** The light of day; daytime. **2.** The dawn; daybreak. The farmer was up doing his chores before *daylight.*
day·light (dā′līt′) *noun.*

daytime The time when it is day and not night; daylight.
day·time (dā′tīm′) *noun.*

daze To confuse or stun; bewilder. The fall from the tree *dazed* her. *Verb.*
—A confused or stunned condition. The car accident left him in a *daze. Noun.*
daze (dāz) *verb,* **dazed, dazing;** *noun, plural* **dazes.**

dazzle To daze or make almost blind by too much light. Tom always wears sunglasses when he goes to the beach so the sun will not *dazzle* his eyes. *Verb.*
—Something that dazzles. Each time he visi-

ted the city, the *dazzle* of the lights excited the little boy. *Noun.*

daz·zle (daz′əl) *verb,* **dazzled, dazzling;** *noun,* *plural* **dazzles.**

deacon 1. A church officer who helps a minister. 2. A member of the clergy who ranks just below a priest.

dea·con (dē′kən) *noun, plural* **deacons.**

dead 1. No longer living or having life. The plant was *dead* because it had not gotten enough water and sun. 2. Never having had life. Rocks are *dead* matter. 3. Without power, usefulness, or interest. I can't call my mother because the telephone is *dead.* Summer is never a *dead* time for Jean because she visits her uncle's farm during July and August. 4. Complete; total. The patients waited in the doctor's office in *dead* silence. 5. Sure or certain; exact. He hit the target at *dead* centre. *Adjective.*
—1. Completely. The hikers were *dead* tired. 2. Directly; straight. The exit from the highway is *dead* ahead. *Adverb.*
—1. People who are no longer living. The minister led us in a prayer for the *dead.* 2. The time of greatest darkness or coldness. Thunder woke him up in the *dead* of night. On long, cold nights in the *dead* of winter, Alice likes to sit by the fire with a good book. *Noun.*

dead (ded) *adjective,* **deader, deadest;** *adverb; noun.*

deaden To dull or weaken. The dentist gave John an injection to *deaden* the pain in his sore tooth.

dead·en (ded′ən) *verb,* **deadened, deadening.**

dead end A street or passage that is closed at one end.

deadline A set time by which something must be finished; time limit. The *deadline* for handing in our book reports is this Friday.

dead·line (ded′līn′) *noun, plural* **deadlines.**

deadly 1. Causing or likely to cause death. The policeman took *deadly* aim at the fleeing murderer. 2. Meaning to kill or destroy. The two countries became *deadly* enemies when they went to war.

dead·ly (ded′lē) *adjective,* **deadlier, deadliest.**

deaf 1. Not able to hear, or not able to hear well. The *deaf* man knew what people were saying to him because he could read their lips. When you call our old dog you have to shout because she is *deaf.* 2. Not willing to hear or listen. He was *deaf* to her call for help.

deaf (def) *adjective,* **deafer, deafest.**

deafen To make deaf. The noise of the machines in the factory *deafened* us for a moment.

deaf·en (def′ən) *verb,* **deafened, deafening.**

deal 1. To have to do with; be about. Mary wanted to read a book that would *deal* with dogs and cats. 2. To act or behave. The principal tried to *deal* fairly with the boys who had been making too much noise in the halls. 3. To do business; trade. That store *deals* in candy, newspapers, and magazines. 4. To give or deliver. Whose turn is it to *deal* the cards? *Verb.*
—A bargain or agreement. My uncle made a *deal* with a man from Winnipeg to sell his house. *Noun.*

deal (dēl) *verb,* **dealt, dealing;** *noun, plural* **deals.**

a great deal or **a good deal.** A large amount or quantity. Sally spent *a great deal* of time making her own Christmas cards.

dealer 1. A person who buys or sells something for a living. We bought our new car from the car *dealer* in town. 2. A person who gives out cards in a card game.

deal·er (dēl′ər) *noun, plural* **dealers.**

dealt I read a book that *dealt* with the discovery of North America. Look up **deal** for more information.

dealt (delt) *verb.*

dear Much or greatly loved. Polly has been my *dear* friend ever since elementary school. I began my letter to my friend in Saint John with the words "*Dear* Michael." *Adjective.*
—A much loved person. You are such a *dear* to come over and help with the party. *Noun.*
—An exclamation of surprise, disappointment, or trouble. Oh *dear!* I've missed the bus. *Interjection.* ▲ Another word that sounds like this is **deer.**

dear (dēr) *adjective,* **dearer, dearest;** *noun, plural* **dears;** *interjection.*

dearly Very much; a great deal. Ruth *dearly* loves her mother.

dear·ly (dēr′lē) *adverb.*

death 1. The end of life in people, plants, or animals. Highway accidents cause many *deaths.* 2. Anything like death. The *death* of King Louis XIV's hopes for New France came with the British victory in 1763.

death (deth) *noun, plural* **deaths.**

at; āpe; cär; end; mē; it; īce; hot; ōld;
wood; fōōl; oil; out; up; turn; sing;
thin; this; hw in white; zh in treasure.
ə stands for a in about, e in taken,
i in pencil, o in lemon, and u in circus.

debate A talk or argument. There was much *debate* in the province on whether to build a new highway. The television station asked the two candidates for mayor to have a *debate* on the ban on smoking. *Noun.*
—**1.** To argue about or discuss at a public meeting. The two speakers *debated* the advantages of building a new city hall. **2.** To think about; consider. They *debated* whether or not they would go to the movies. **3.** To discuss something in parliament. The members of the House of Commons *debated* the tax bill. *Verb.*
 de·bate (dē bāt′) *noun, plural* **debates;** *verb,* **debated, debating.**

debris The scattered remains of something that has been broken or destroyed; rubbish. The earthquake destroyed so many buildings that the streets were filled with *debris.*
 de·bris (de brē′) *noun.*

debt **1.** Something that is owed to another. After paying all his *debts,* he still has money in the bank. I owe you a *debt* of gratitude for all your help. **2.** The condition of owing. We are in *debt* to the bank for our new car.
 debt (det) *noun, plural* **debts.**

decade A period of ten years. The period of time between 1970 and 1980 is a *decade.*
 dec·ade (dek′ād) *noun, plural* **decades.**

decanter A fancy glass bottle with a top that is used as a stopper. Decanters are usually used to hold wine or liquor.
 de·cant·er (dē kan′tər) *noun, plural* **decanters.**

decay A slow rotting of plant and animal matter. The dentist told Bill to brush his teeth at least twice a day to prevent tooth decay. The wooden beams of the old house showed decay. *Noun.*

Decanter

—To rot slowly. The oranges in the cellar turned mouldy and began to *decay. Verb.*
 de·cay (dē kā′) *noun, plural* **decays;** *verb,* **decayed, decaying.**

deceased Dead. The children of the *deceased* man have already been told of his death. *Adjective.*
—**the deceased.** A dead person or persons. *Noun.*
 de·ceased (dē sēst′) *adjective; noun.*

deceit **1.** The act of lying or cheating. The salesman was guilty of *deceit* when he told the customer that the used bicycle for sale was a new one. **2.** The quality that makes someone lie or cheat. The girl was full of *deceit* as she tried to put the blame for the missing money on someone else.
 de·ceit (dē sēt′) *noun, plural* **deceits.**

deceive To make someone believe something that is not true. He *deceived* his parents by telling them he had no homework to do, because he wanted to watch television instead of studying.
 de·ceive (dē sēv′) *verb,* **deceived, deceiving.**

December The twelfth and last month of the year. December has thirty-one days.
 De·cem·ber (dē sem′bər) *noun.*

▲ In the early Roman calendar, March was the first month of the year, and **December** was the tenth month. The word *December* comes from the Latin word for "ten."

---

decent **1.** Proper and respectable. It is not *decent* to listen in on other people's private conversations. It was very *decent* of Nancy to help her brother with his homework. **2.** Fairly good; satisfactory. She'll never be an A student, but she gets *decent* grades in school.
 de·cent (dē′sənt) *adjective.*

deceptive Misleading; meant to trick. Ellen hid her anger with a *deceptive* smile.
 de·cep·tive (dē sept′əv) *adjective.*

decide **1.** To make up one's mind. Alice has *decided* to study to be a doctor. **2.** To settle or judge a question or argument. The judge *decided* in favour of the prisoner.
 de·cide (dē sīd′) *verb,* **decided, deciding.**

decided Definite; sure. The taller basketball player had a *decided* advantage over the others.
 de·cid·ed (dē sī′dəd) *adjective.*

decimal Based on the number 10. Money in Canada and the United States is based on the *decimal* system. *Adjective.*
—A fraction with a denominator of 10, or a multiple of 10 such as 100 or 1000. This is also called a **decimal fraction.** The decimal fraction .5 is another way of writing $^5/_{10}$. *Noun.*
 dec·i·mal (des′ə məl) *adjective; noun, plural* **decimals.**

decimal point A period put before a decimal fraction. The periods in .5, .30, and .052 are decimal points.

decimetre A measure of length equal to one tenth metre, or ten centimetres. This word is also spelled **decimeter**.

dec·i·metre (des′ə mēt′ər) *noun, plural* **decimetres**.

decipher 1. To make out the meaning of something difficult to understand. The teacher handed the spelling test back to Jim to write again because she could not *decipher* his handwriting. 2. To change secret writing into ordinary writing. The officer *deciphered* the enemy's secret message and found out the plans for the attack.

de·ci·pher (də sī′fər) *verb,* **deciphered, deciphering**.

decision The act or result of making up one's mind. John likes to think carefully about a problem before he makes a *decision*.

de·ci·sion (də sizh′ən) *noun, plural* **decisions**.

decisive 1. Deciding something finally and completely. The army suffered a *decisive* defeat and was forced to surrender to the enemy. 2. Showing firmness and determination. The boy defended his innocence in such a *decisive* manner that no one believed that he had stolen the money.

de·ci·sive (dē sīs′əv) *adjective*.

deck 1. The floor on a ship or boat. A deck may have a roof or covering over it or be completely open. 2. A platform that is like the deck of a ship or boat. Father built a *deck* onto the back of the house so we could sit out in the sun. 3. A set of playing cards. Bob shuffled the *deck* and then dealt the cards. *Noun.*

—To dress or decorate. We all *decked* ourselves out in funny costumes for Hallowe'en. *Verb.*

deck (dek) *noun, plural* **decks**; *verb,* **decked, decking**.

declaration The act of announcing or of making something known. In Canada, a *declaration* of war can be made only with the approval of Parliament.

dec·la·ra·tion (dek′lə rā′shən) *noun, plural* **declarations**.

declare 1. To announce or make something known. The two countries *declared* war. 2. To say strongly and firmly. She *declared* that she was right and nothing would change her mind.

de·clare (dē kler′) *verb,* **declared, declaring**.

decline 1. To refuse politely. Alice wrote Jack a note to *decline* the invitation to his birthday party. 2. To grow less or weaker; decrease. The power of kings and queens has *declined* in modern times. Food prices *declined* again this month. *Verb.*

—A lessening or weakening of power, health, value, or amount. We've noticed a *decline* in the old man's health ever since his accident. *Noun.*

de·cline (dē klīn′) *verb,* **declined, declining**; *noun, plural* **declines**.

decode To change secret writing into ordinary language. The spy *decoded* the secret message.

de·code (dē kōd′) *verb,* **decoded, decoding**.

decompose To rot or decay. Steve cut down the tree for firewood but left the stump behind to *decompose*.

de·com·pose (dē′kəm pōz′) *verb,* **decomposed, decomposing**.

decorate 1. To make more beautiful; ornament. The children *decorated* the Christmas tree with lights and ornaments. Mother *decorated* the living room by painting the walls and choosing a new rug and drapes. 2. To give a badge or medal to. The city *decorated* the policeman for bravery.

dec·o·rate (dek′ə rāt′) *verb,* **decorated, decorating**.

decoration 1. The act of making more beautiful; decorating. The *decoration* of the gym for the dance took all day. 2. Something that is used to decorate; ornament. We took down the balloons, crepe paper, and other *decorations* after the party was over. 3. A badge or medal. All the boys in the Boy Scout troop wore their *decorations* for the Dominion Day parade.

dec·o·ra·tion (dek′ə rā′shən) *noun, plural* **decorations**.

decoy 1. A model of a bird used to attract real birds into a trap or to within shooting distance of a hunter. The hunter floated a wooden *decoy* on the lake and waited in the bushes for it to attract a duck. 2. A person who leads another person into danger or into a trap. Police departments in big cities use policemen in everyday clothes as *decoys* for criminals in dangerous neighbourhoods. *Noun.*

—To attract or lead into danger or into a trap. Jane tried to *decoy* the rabbit that was eating the lettuce in her garden. *Verb.*

de·coy (dē′koi *for noun;* də koi′ *for verb*) *noun, plural* **decoys**; *verb,* **decoyed, decoying**.

---

at; āpe; cär; end; mē; it; īce; hot; ōld;
wood; fo͞ol; oil; out; up; turn; sing;
thin; <u>this</u>; hw in white; zh in treasure.
ə stands for a in about, e in taken
i in pencil, o in lemon, and u in circus.

decrease To make or become less. Father *decreased* the speed of the car as we came to our exit on the highway. We hope that the number of car accidents on our block will *decrease* because of the new stop sign at the end of the street. *Verb.*
—1. The act of becoming less. The *decrease* in Christmas shopping for this year will mean less money for the stores. 2. The amount by which something becomes less. There was a *decrease* of ten degrees in the temperature during the night. *Noun.*
de·crease (də krēs′ *for verb;* dē′krēs′ *for noun*) *verb,* **decreased, decreasing;** *noun, plural* **decreases.**

decree An official order or decision. The mayor issued a *decree* that banned smoking at city hall. *Noun.*
—To order or decide officially. The Governor General *decreed* a holiday to celebrate his visit to the town. *Verb.*
de·cree (dē krē′) *noun, plural* **decrees;** *verb,* **decreed, decreeing.**

dedicate To set apart for or devote to a special purpose or use. Two floors of the new hospital will be *dedicated* to medical research.
ded·i·cate (ded′ə kāt′) *verb,* **dedicated, dedicating.**

dedication A setting apart for or devotion to a special purpose or use. All the teachers, students, and parents were invited to the *dedication* of the new school this Friday afternoon.
ded·i·ca·tion (ded′ə kā′shən) *noun, plural* **dedications.**

deduct To take away or subtract from a total. The teacher told the class that she would *deduct* five points for each wrong answer on the test.
de·duct (dē dukt′) *verb,* **deducted, deducting.**

deduction The taking away from a total; subtraction. The store made a *deduction* of ten dollars from the regular price of fifty dollars for the radio.
de·duc·tion (dē duk′shən) *noun, plural* **deductions.**

deed 1. Something done; act; action. Sue did a good *deed* by helping the blind woman across the street. 2. A written, legal agreement. When Father bought our house, he got a *deed* to show that he owned it.
deed (dēd) *noun, plural* **deeds.**

deep 1. Far down from the top. Jane warned her little brother not to go near the *deep* end of the swimming pool where the water was over his head. 2. Great in degree; intense; extreme. Ruth fell into a *deep* sleep. 3. Difficult to understand. My sister's chemistry book is too *deep* for me. 4. Completely taken up with something; occupied; absorbed. He didn't hear the doorbell ring because he was *deep* in thought. 5. Low in pitch. Don could easily sing the low notes in the song because he had such a *deep* voice. *Adjective.*
—In, at, or to a great depth. The explorers went *deep* into the jungle. *Adverb.*
deep (dēp) *adjective,* **deeper, deepest;** *adverb.*

deer An animal that has hoofs and chews its cud. A male deer has antlers that are shed every year and grow back the next year. Deer can run very fast. ▲ Another word that sounds like this is **dear.**
deer (dēr) *noun, plural* **deer.**

Deer

deface To spoil or mar. The policeman made the boys wash their names off the statue and warned them never to *deface* public property again.
de·face (dē fās′) *verb,* **defaced, defacing.**

defeat To win a victory over; overcome in a contest of any kind. Our basketball coach told us he thought we could easily *defeat* the visiting team. The troops defending the fort *defeated* the attacking enemy. *Verb.*
—The state of being defeated in a contest of any kind. Our team's *defeat* ended our hopes of winning the championship for yet another year. *Noun.*
de·feat (dē fēt′) *verb,* **defeated, defeating;** *noun, plural* **defeats.**

defect A flaw or weakness. These dishes are for sale cheap because they have *defects* in them.
de·fect (dē′fekt) *noun, plural* **defects.**

defective Having a flaw or weakness; not perfect. *Defective* electric wiring is the cause of many fires in people's homes.
de·fec·tive (dē fekt′iv) *adjective.*

defence 1. The act of guarding against attack or danger. The Canadian Armed Forces are responsible for the *defence* of our country against attack. 2. A person or thing that protects. The dam was the city's only *defence* against floods. 3. Support. The premier spoke in *defence* of his plan to give more public aid to public transportation. 4. The defending team or players in a game. Our hockey team has a good *defence*. This word is also spelled **defense**.
de·fence (dē fens′ *or* də fens′) *noun, plural* **defences**.

defenceman *Canadian.* A player in certain games, such as hockey, whose job is to stop an opponent from reaching the goal. This word is also spelled **defenseman**.
de·fence·man (dē fens′mən) *noun, plural* **defencemen**.

defend 1. To guard against attack or danger; protect. The soldiers did their best to *defend* the people in the town from the attacking army. 2. To speak or act in support of. The lawyer agreed to *defend* the woman accused of robbery because he believed she was innocent.
de·fend (dē fend′) *verb*, **defended, defending**.

defensive Guarding or protecting against attack. Knights used to put on *defensive* armour before going into battle. The Canadiens moved on the *defensive* when the Boston forward grabbed the puck.
de·fen·sive (də fens′iv) *adjective*.

defer[1] To put off to a future time; delay. The judge asked the jury to *defer* judgement in the case until they had heard all the facts.
de·fer (dē fur′) *verb*, **deferred, deferring**.

defer[2] To yield in judgement or opinion. Bob thought he should *defer* to his father on what to buy his mother for a Christmas present.
de·fer (dē fur′) *verb*, **deferred, deferring**.

defiance Bold refusal to obey or respect authority. The man showed his *defiance* by deliberately breaking the law.
de·fi·ance (dē fī′əns) *noun, plural* **defiances**.

deficiency 1. A lack of something needed or necessary. Diane takes vitamin pills every morning to help keep her healthy and prevent a vitamin *deficiency*. 2. The amount by which something is lacking. The banker counted the money in the safe after the robbery and found a *deficiency* of $10 000.
de·fi·cien·cy (dē fish′ən sē) *noun, plural* **deficiencies**.

define 1. To give the meaning or meanings of. A dictionary *defines* words. 2. To describe or fix exactly. The Ottawa River *defines* part of the boundary between Ontario and Quebec.
de·fine (dē fīn′) *verb*, **defined, defining**.

definite Certain; clear. It is *definite* that Mary is going to college next fall.
def·i·nite (def′ə nit) *adjective*.

definite article The word *the* is the definite article. *The* is used to point out one or more particular persons or things. *The* train is late. *The* boys are fighting.

definition An explanation of the meaning of a word or group of words. A definition for the word *family* is "a father, mother, and their children."
def·i·ni·tion (def′ə nish′ən) *noun, plural* **definitions**.

deform To spoil the form or shape of. Constant winds had *deformed* and bent the tree.
de·form (dē fōrm′) *verb*, **deformed, deforming**.

defrost To make free of ice or frost; thaw. We have to *defrost* the refrigerator to keep the freezer free of ice.
de·frost (dē frost′) *verb*, **defrosted, defrosting**.

deft Skilful and clever; nimble. The girl's *deft* fingers raced over the piano keys.
deft (deft) *adjective*.

defy To oppose or challenge boldly. To *defy* his mother, Dick went out without a jacket even though she had told him to wear one.
de·fy (dē fī′) *verb*, **defied, defying**.

degrade To lower in character, quality, or rank. Telling lies *degrades* a person.
de·grade (dē grād′) *verb*, **degraded, degrading**.

degree 1. A stage or step in a process or series. A young child learns to walk by *degrees*. 2. Amount or extent. To what *degree* is Bob interested in becoming a doctor? 3. A unit for measuring temperature. A person's normal body temperature is 37 *degrees* Celsius. 4. A unit for measuring angles, or arcs of a circle. Two perpendicular lines form a 90 *degree* angle.
de·gree (dē grē′) *noun, plural* **degrees**.

deity A god or goddess. Mars was the Roman *deity* of war.
de·i·ty (dē′ə tē) *noun, plural* **deities**.

at; āpe; cär; end; mē; it; īce; hot; ōld;
wood; fōōl; oil; out; up; turn; sing;
thin; <u>th</u>is; hw in white; zh in treasure.
ə stands for a in about, e in taken,
i in pencil, o in lemon, and u in circus.

dejected Depressed or sad. The basketball team felt *dejected* after losing the game.
de·ject·ed (dē jek′təd) *adjective.*

deke *Canadian.* To fake a play in hockey in order to fool another player. *Verb.*
—A fake play or a misleading move in hockey. *Noun.*
▲ This word is used only in everyday speech.
deke (dēk) *verb,* **deked, deking;** *noun, plural* **dekes.**

delay 1. To put off to a later time. The officials had to *delay* the start of the game because of the rain. 2. To make late. We would have come sooner, but we were *delayed* by a flat tire. 3. To slow down. Jane will miss the bus if she *delays* any longer. *Verb.*
—The act of delaying or the state of being delayed. There will be a short *delay* of fifteen minutes before the train arrives. *Noun.*
de·lay (dē lā′) *verb,* **delayed, delaying;** *noun, plural* **delays.**

delegate A person who is chosen to act for others. Each country at the United Nations is represented by a *delegate. Noun.*
—To choose or send as a delegate. The club *delegated* Bill to make arrangements for a Christmas party. *Verb.*
del·e·gate (del′ə gāt′ *or* del′ə gət *for noun;* del′ə gāt′ *for verb*) *noun, plural* **delegates;** *verb,* **delegated, delegating.**

delegation A group of delegates or representatives. A *delegation* from the fire department marched in the Santa Claus parade.
del·e·ga·tion (del′ə gā′shən) *noun, plural* **delegations.**

deliberate 1. Done or said on purpose. He told his mother a *deliberate* lie and blamed the broken window on his brother. 2. Careful and slow; not hasty or rash. He walked down the street with *deliberate* steps. *Adjective.*
—To think over or discuss carefully. The young man *deliberated* whether or not he should study to be a lawyer. *Verb.*
de·lib·er·ate (də lib′ər ət *for adjective;* də-lib′ə rāt′ *for verb*) *adjective; verb,* **deliberated, deliberating.**

delicacy 1. Fineness; daintiness. The *delicacy* of the lace made it look like a cobweb. 2. A rare or choice food. Snails are thought to be a *delicacy* by some people.
del·i·ca·cy (del′i kə sē) *noun, plural* **delicacies.**

delicate 1. Fine or dainty. The threads of a spider's web are *delicate.* 2. Pleasing in smell, taste, or colour; mild or soft. There was a *delicate* scent of roses in the air. Mary's dress is a *delicate* shade of pink. 3. Easily damaged; fragile. Mother never puts her *delicate* wine glasses in the dishwasher because they break too easily. 4. Very sensitive. Scientists have *delicate* instruments that can detect an earthquake thousands of kilometres away.
del·i·cate (del′i kət) *adjective.*

delicatessen A store that sells food that is ready to eat. Cold meats, cheeses, and salads are sold in a delicatessen.
del·i·ca·tes·sen (del′i kə tes′ən) *noun, plural* **delicatessens.**

▲ The word **delicatessen** is really a German word which is now used in English. It comes from the French word *délicatesse* meaning "delicacy." At one time, *delicatessen* meant the delicacies and relishes served at the table. Now the word is more often used to mean the store in which foods like these are sold.

---

delicious Pleasing or delightful to the taste or smell. The stew cooking for dinner smelled *delicious* to the hungry boy.
de·li·cious (də lish′əs) *adjective.*

delight Great pleasure; joy. Joan beamed with *delight* as she watched the circus. *Noun.*
—1. To give great pleasure or joy to. The puppet show in the park *delighted* the children. 2. To have or take great pleasure. Tom was *delighted* to go fishing with his father. *Verb.*
de·light (dē līt′) *noun, plural* **delights;** *verb,* **delighted, delighting.**

delightful Very pleasing. We all had a *delightful* time at the party.
de·light·ful (dē līt′fəl) *adjective.*

delirious Wildly excited. Rick's high fever made him *delirious.* Betty was *delirious* with happiness when she won the prize.
de·lir·i·ous (də lēr′ē əs) *adjective.*

deliver 1. To carry or take. The department store promised it would *deliver* our new television set this week. 2. To say; utter. Father is going to *deliver* a speech to a meeting of business people. 3. To strike or throw. The pitcher *delivered* a curve ball that the batter swung at and missed.
de·liv·er (də liv′ər) *verb,* **delivered, delivering.**

delivery 1. The act of carrying or taking something to a place or person. The letter carrier makes a mail *delivery* every day except weekends and holidays. The eggs were missing from the grocery *delivery.* 2. A way of speaking or singing. The singer's *delivery* was excellent.
de·liv·er·y (də liv′rē *or* də liv′ər ē) *noun, plural* **deliveries.**

delta An area of land at the mouth of a river. A delta is formed by deposits of earth, sand, and stone. A delta is usually shaped like a triangle.
del·ta (del′tə) *noun, plural* **deltas.**

▲ The word **delta** comes from the Greek name for the fourth letter in the Greek alphabet. The letter delta was drawn as a triangle, and deltas in rivers are often in the shape of a triangle.

demand 1. To ask for urgently or forcefully; claim as a right. The angry customer asked to see the store manager to *demand* an apology from the rude clerk. The judge *demanded* silence in the courtroom. 2. To call for; need. Bill's new job *demands* hard work. *Verb.*
—1. The act of demanding. The workers' *demand* for higher salaries was turned down. 2. Something that is demanded. The butcher said that the *demand* for turkeys was very high at Thanksgiving and at Christmas time. *Noun.*
de·mand (də mand′) *verb,* **demanded, demanding;** *noun, plural* **demands.**

democracy 1. A government that is run by the people who live under it. In a democracy, the people may run the government indirectly by electing representatives who govern for them. Or they may run it directly by having meetings which everyone can come to. The government of Canada is an indirect democracy because we elect representatives to do the work of a government for us. 2. A country in which the government is a democracy. Britain is a *democracy.*
de·moc·ra·cy (də mok′rə sē) *noun, plural* **democracies.**

democrat 1. A person who believes that a government should be run by the people who live under it. 2. A person who believes that all people should be treated as equals.
dem·o·crat (dem′ə krat′) *noun, plural* **democrats.**

democratic 1. Of or supporting a democracy. Canada is a *democratic* country. 2. Believing that all people should be treated as equals. In Canada, we believe in the *democratic* idea that all people have equal rights as human beings.
de·mo·crat·ic (dem′ə krat′ik) *adjective.*

demolish To tear down or destroy. The workmen's job was to *demolish* the old factory to make way for a new office building.
de·mol·ish (də mol′ish) *verb,* **demolished, demolishing.**

demon 1. An evil spirit; devil. 2. A person who does something with great skill or energy. Henry is such a *demon* for work that he spends nearly every evening and every weekend at the office.
de·mon (dē′mən) *noun, plural* **demons.**

demonstrate 1. To explain, prove, or show clearly. The science teacher dropped a pencil out the window to *demonstrate* the law of gravity. A salesman *demonstrated* the new coffee pot at the department store. 2. To take part in a public meeting or parade to protest something or make demands. An angry group of citizens from all over the province *demonstrated* against pollution of the river by wastes from the factory.
dem·on·strate (dem′ən strāt′) *verb,* **demonstrated, demonstrating.**

demonstration 1. Something that explains, proves, or shows clearly. The fireman's rescue of the child from the burning house was a *demonstration* of his bravery. 2. A public meeting or parade to protest something or make demands. On Saturday the secretaries at the university held a *demonstration* to demand a raise in pay.
dem·on·stra·tion (dem′ən strā′shən) *noun, plural* **demonstrations.**

den 1. A place where wild animals live. Bears use caves as a *den* during their long sleep in winter. 2. A small, cosy room for reading or studying. 3. A group of about eight Wolf Cubs.
den (den) *noun, plural* **dens.**

denial The act of denying. The judge listened to the prisoner's *denial* of the charges against him.
de·ni·al (dē nī′əl) *noun, plural* **denials.**

denim 1. A heavy cotton cloth used for work or sports clothes. 2. denims. Pants or overalls made of this cloth.
den·im (den′im) *noun, plural* **denims.**

denomination 1. A religious group or sect. The Lutherans are a *denomination* of the Protestant church. 2. One kind of unit. A dime and a nickel are coins of different *denominations.*
de·nom·i·na·tion (dē nom′ə nā′shən) *noun, plural* **denominations.**

at; āpe; cär; end; mē; it; īce; hot; ōld;
wood; fōōl; oil; out; up; turn; sing;
thin; this; hw in white; zh in treasure.
ə stands for a in about, e in taken,
i in pencil, o in lemon, and u in circus.

denominator The number below the line in a fraction. The denominator shows the number of equal parts into which the whole is divided. In the fraction $1/2$, 2 is the denominator.
de·nom·i·na·tor (dē nom′ə nā′tər) *noun*, *plural* **denominators**.

denote 1. To be a sign of; show. A dark sky and high winds usually *denote* the coming of a storm. 2. To be a name for; mean. The word "dentist" *denotes* a doctor who takes care of people's teeth.
de·note (dē nōt′) *verb*, **denoted, denoting**.

denounce To speak against in public; accuse. The speaker *denounced* living conditions in the slums.
de·nounce (dē nouns′) *verb*, **denounced, denouncing**.

dense Packed closely together; thick. The boys wandered away from the camp and got lost in the *dense* woods.
dense (dens) *adjective*, **denser, densest**.

density Closeness; thickness. Pea soup has a greater *density* than water. The *density* of population is greater in a big city than it is in the country.
den·si·ty (den′sə tē) *noun*, *plural* **densities**.

dent A small hollow made in the surface of something by a blow or pressure. Roy got a *dent* in the front of his bicycle when he hit the tree. *Noun*.
—To make a dent or hollow in. *Verb*.
dent (dent) *noun*, *plural* **dents**; *verb*, **dented, denting**.

dental 1. Having to do with the teeth. Good *dental* care helps prevent tooth decay. 2. Having to do with a dentist's work. Our dentist has an X-ray machine and other *dental* equipment in his office.
den·tal (dent′əl) *adjective*.

dentine The hard, bony material that forms the main part of the tooth. It is covered by the enamel.
den·tine (den′tin) *noun*.

dentist A doctor who takes care of people's teeth. A dentist cleans teeth, fills cavities, pulls teeth that are diseased, and makes teeth to take the place of real ones that have been pulled.
den·tist (den′tist) *noun*, *plural* **dentists**.

deny 1. To say that something is not true. The prisoner *denied* that he had robbed the bank. 2. To refuse to give or grant. The company *denied* the workers' request for longer holidays.
de·ny (dē nī′) *verb*, **denied, denying**.

depart 1. To go away; leave. The train is due to *depart* from the station at ten o'clock. 2. To change or differ. Jim *departed* from his usual routine of getting up early and was late for school.
de·part (dē pärt′) *verb*, **departed, departing**.

department A separate part; division. The English *department* at school will have three new teachers this fall. In Canada, the *department* of education of each province is in charge of what is taught in the schools.
de·part·ment də pärt′mənt) *noun*, *plural* **departments**.

department store A large store that sells many different kinds of goods in different departments.

departure The act of departing. The plane's *departure* was delayed two hours because of the thick fog that surrounded the airport. Sue's taking a bus to work was a *departure* from her habit of walking the whole way.
de·par·ture (dē pär′chər) *noun*, *plural* **departures**.

depend 1. To rely or trust. You can always *depend* on Jane to be on time. 2. To get help or support. Children *depend* on their parents until they can earn their own living. 3. To be influenced or determined. Whether or not we go on the hike *depends* on the weather.
de·pend (dē pend′) *verb*, **depended, depending**.

dependable Reliable or trustworthy. A person who is dependable can be trusted to do a job without being watched or checked.
de·pend·a·ble (dē pen′də bəl) *adjective*.

dependant A person who relies on someone else for help or support. My sister and I are our parents' *dependants* because we are too young to take care of ourselves.
de·pend·ant (dē pen′dənt) *noun*, *plural* **dependants**.

dependence The state of being dependent. A baby's *dependence* on his mother grows less as he gets older.
de·pend·ence (dē pen′dəns) *noun*.

dependent 1. Relying on someone else for what is needed or wanted. Jim was *dependent* on his parents to pay for his university education. 2. Influenced by something. Our plans for the picnic are *dependent* on the weather.
de·pend·ent (dē pen′dənt) *adjective*.

depict To show by drawing or painting. The artist tried to *depict* the breaking of the ocean's waves on the beach.
de·pict (dē pikt′) *verb*, **depicted, depicting**.

deposit 1. To put money or valuable things in a bank or other safe place. Ted *deposited*

twenty dollars in his savings account at the bank. **2.** To put or set down; place. Ruth *deposited* the groceries on the table. *Verb.*
—**1.** Something put in a bank or other safe place. Pat made a *deposit* of fifty dollars. **2.** Something given as part of a payment or promise to pay more later. Susan put down a *deposit* of twenty dollars on the new bicycle and planned to pay the rest by the end of the month. **3.** Something that has settled and is left as a layer. There was a thick *deposit* of dust in the vacant house. **4.** A large amount of mineral in rock or in the ground. Alberta has large *deposits* of oil underground. *Noun.*
de·pos·it (dē poz′ət) *verb*, **deposited, depositing;** *noun, plural* **deposits.**

depot A railroad or bus terminal.
dep·ot (dē′pō *or* de′pō) *noun, plural* **depots.**

depress To make sad or gloomy. The death of their dog *depressed* the whole family.
de·press (dē pres′) *verb*, **depressed, depressing.**

depression **1.** Sadness; gloom. Failing to make the team caused Jack to have a fit of *depression.* **2.** A low place or hollow. The car bumped over a *depression* in the road. **3.** A time when business is slow and people are out of work. Many people lost their jobs during the *Depression* of the 1930s.
de·pres·sion (dē presh′ən) *noun, plural* **depressions.**

deprive To keep from having or doing. The dictator *deprived* the people of their right to vote. The new highway will *deprive* the children of their playground.
de·prive (dē prīv′) *verb*, **deprived, depriving.**

depth **1.** The distance from top to bottom or from front to back. The *depth* of the pool was four metres at the deep end. The *depth* of our back yard is ten metres. **2.** The quality of being deep. The mother's *depth* of understanding helped her son with his problems.
depth (depth) *noun, plural* **depths.**

deputy **1.** A person appointed to take the place of another. The cabinet minister appointed a *deputy* to do some of her work. **2. Deputy.** *Canadian.* A member of the National Assembly of Quebec. The *Deputies* voted on the French-language bill.
dep·u·ty (dep′yə tē) *noun, plural* **deputies.**

derby A man's stiff round hat with a narrow rolled brim.
der·by (dur′bē) *noun, plural* **derbies.**

derive To get from a source; obtain. The word "democracy" is *derived* from a Greek word. Jack *derives* pleasure from camping.
de·rive (də rīv′) *verb*, **derived, deriving.**

derrick **1.** A machine for lifting and moving heavy objects. It has a long arm attached to the base of an upright post. **2.** The framework over an oil well or other drill hole that supports the drilling machinery.
der·rick (der′ik) *noun, plural* **derricks.**

Oil Derrick

descend **1.** To move or come from a higher place to a lower one. They rode up the hill on horseback but *descended* on foot. **2.** To come down from an earlier source or ancestor. The farm *descended* from the father to his son.
de·scend (dē send′) *verb*, **descended, descending.**

descendant A person who comes from a particular ancestor or group of ancestors. Jack is a *descendant* of the early French settlers in the Maritimes.
de·scend·ant (dē sen′dənt) *noun, plural* **descendants.**

descent **1.** A coming from a higher place to a lower one. The quick *descent* of the elevator made my stomach feel funny. **2.** A downward slope. There was a steep *descent* down the stairs of the old tower. **3.** Ancestry or birth. He is of Polish *descent* because his parents were born in Poland.
de·scent (dē sent′) *noun, plural* **descents.**

describe To give a picture of something in words; tell or write about. The boy *described* his adventures at camp. Can you *describe* the man you saw at the window?
de·scribe (də skrīb′) *verb*, **described, describing.**

▲ The word **describe** used to mean "to write down." When a person writes something down, he puts it in words. So *describe* came to mean "to tell about in words," whether the words are written or spoken.

at; āpe; cär; end; mē; it; īce; hot; ōld; wood; fo͞ol; oil; out; up; turn; sing; thin; this; hw in white; zh in treasure.
ə stands for a in about, e in taken, i in pencil, o in lemon, and u in circus.

description 1. The act of giving a picture using words. Betty's *description* of the movie she had seen was very complete. 2. A statement that describes. My father sent a *description* of our lost dog to the newspaper. 3. Kind; sort; variety. There were cats of every *description* in the show.
de·scrip·tion (də skrip′shən) *noun, plural* descriptions.

descriptive Giving a picture in words. The tourists were given *descriptive* pamphlets about places to visit in the city.
de·scrip·tive (də skrip′tiv) *adjective.*

desegregate To do away with the system or practice of having different schools and other facilities for different races. The state government ordered the town to *desegregate* its public schools.
de·seg·re·gate (dē seg′rə gāt′) *verb,* desegregated, desegregating.

desert[1] A hot, dry sandy area of land with few or no plants growing on it. *Noun.*
—Not lived in or on; desolate. The man was shipwrecked on a *desert* island when his boat sank. *Adjective.*
des·ert (dez′ərt) *noun, plural* deserts; *adjective.*

desert[2] To go away and leave a person or thing that should not be left; abandon. The man *deserted* his wife and children. The soldier *deserted* the army. ▲ Another word that sounds like this is **dessert.**
de·sert (də zurt′) *verb,* deserted, deserting.

deserve To have a right to; be worthy of. The girl *deserves* praise for working so hard.
de·serve (dē zurv′) *verb,* deserved, deserving.

design 1. A plan, drawing, or outline made to serve as a guide or pattern. Everyone liked the architect's *design* for the new school. 2. An arrangement of different parts or colours; pattern. The carpet in the living room has a blue and green *design. Noun.*
—To make a plan, drawing, or outline of; make a pattern for. She *designed* beautiful costumes for the play. *Verb.*
de·sign (dē zīn′) *noun, plural* designs; *verb,* designed, designing.

The pillows have a North American Indian **design.**

designate 1. To mark or point out; show. Jack used a blue pencil to *designate* rivers and lakes on the map he was drawing. 2. To call by a particular name or title. The head of the government of Canada is *designated* "prime minister." 3. To choose; name. He was *designated* chairman of the fund drive.
des·ig·nate (dez′ig nāt′) *verb,* designated, designating.

designated hitter A baseball player who bats in place of the pitcher. A designated hitter is usually a powerful hitter.

desirable Worth having or wishing for; pleasing. That corner lot is a *desirable* place to lay out a baseball field.
de·sir·a·ble (dē zīr′ə bəl) *adjective.*

desire To wish for; long for. Jack *desires* a university education. *Verb.*
—A longing; wish. The cold and hungry man had a *desire* for a bowl of hot soup. *Noun.*
de·sire (dē zīr′) *verb,* desired, desiring; *noun, plural* desires.

desk A piece of furniture used for reading or writing. It has a flat or sloping top and usually drawers.
desk (desk) *noun, plural* desks.

desolate 1. Without people; deserted. In the winter, that beach is really *desolate.* 2. Destroyed; ruined. The fire left the forest *desolate.* 3. Miserable; cheerless. The lost child was *desolate.*
des·o·late (dez′ə lət) *adjective.*

Desk

despair A complete loss of hope. The family was filled with *despair* when their house was destroyed by the fire. *Noun.*
—To give up or lose hope. She *despaired* of ever finding her lost puppy. *Verb.*
de·spair (dē sper′) *noun; verb,* despaired, despairing.

desperate 1. Reckless because of having no hope. A desperate person is ready or willing to take any risk. The *desperate* thief ran from the policeman who was chasing him. 2. Very bad or hopeless. The mountain climbers who were trapped by the snowstorm were in a *desperate* position.
des·per·ate (des′pər ət) *adjective.*

desperation A reckless feeling coming from loss of hope. In *desperation,* the cowgirl tried to stop the stampede.
des·per·a·tion (des′pə rā′shən) *noun.*

despise To look down on as hateful; scorn. She *despised* the cruel way he treated his dog and cat.
de·spise (də spīz′) *verb*, **despised, despising.**

despite In spite of. He went to school *despite* his bad cold.
de·spite (də spīt′) *preposition.*

dessert A sweet food served at the end of a meal. Cake, pie, fruit, pudding, and ice cream are desserts. ▲ Another word that sounds like this is **desert²**.
des·sert (də zurt′) *noun, plural* **desserts.**

destination A place to which a person or thing is going or being sent. The airplane's *destination* is Paris.
des·ti·na·tion (des′tə nā′shən) *noun, plural* **destinations.**

destine 1. To set apart for a particular purpose or use; intend. That land is *destined* for a new hospital. 2. To be decided ahead of time. She is *destined* to become a musician.
des·tine (des′tin) *verb*, **destined, destining.**

destiny What happens to a person or thing; fortune. He felt that it was his *destiny* to become a great surgeon.
des·ti·ny (des′tə nē) *noun, plural* **destinies.**

destroy To ruin completely; wreck. The earthquake *destroyed* the city. Locusts *destroyed* the crops.
de·stroy (dē stroi′) *verb*, **destroyed, destroying.**

destroyer A small, fast warship.
de·stroy·er (dē stroi′ər) *noun, plural* **destroyers.**

destruction 1. The act of destroying. Chemical sprays are sometimes used for the *destruction* of the breeding places of mosquitoes. 2. Great damage or ruin. The earthquake caused the total *destruction* of the city.
de·struc·tion (dē struk′shən) *noun, plural* **destructions.**

destructive Causing destruction. Moths are *destructive* to clothes made of wool.
de·struc·tive (dē struk′tiv) *adjective.*

detach To unfasten and separate; take off. She *detached* the price tag from the gift before wrapping it.
de·tach (dē tach′) *verb*, **detached, detaching.**

detached 1. Not attached; not connected. The *detached* house was surrounded by a large yard. 2. Not taking sides in an argument. The reporter was a *detached* observer at the murder trial.
de·tached (dē tacht′) *adjective.*

detail 1. A small or less important part of a whole; item. The newspaper gave few *details*

about the accident. 2. A dealing with matters one by one. He told us he spent the summer at camp, but he didn't have time to go into *detail*. 3. A small group of persons sent on some special duty. A police *detail* patrols the park at night. *Noun.*
—1. To tell or describe item by item. She *detailed* her experiences as a writer to the students. 2. To assign to or send on special duty. The captain *detailed* soldiers to guard the gate. *Verb.*
de·tail (dē′tāl *for noun;* də tāl′ *or* dē tāl′ *for verb*) *noun, plural* **details;** *verb*, **detailed, detailing.**

detain 1. To keep from going; hold back; delay. A flat tire *detained* him on his way home. 2. To keep in custody. The police *detained* the man suspected of robbery.
de·tain (dē tān′) *verb*, **detained, detaining.**

detect To find out; discover. I called the fire department after I *detected* smoke coming from the garage.
de·tect (dē tekt′) *verb*, **detected, detecting.**

detective A police officer or other person who searches for information in order to solve a crime and catch a criminal. *Noun.*
—Having to do with detectives and their work. Bob likes to read *detective* stories. *Adjective.*
de·tec·tive (dē tek′tiv) *noun, plural* **detectives;** *adjective.*

deter To discourage from doing something because of fear or doubt. The huge waves *deterred* him from going swimming.
de·ter (dē tur′) *verb*, **deterred, deterring.**

detergent A chemical substance used for washing. A detergent acts like soap.
de·ter·gent (dē tur′jənt) *noun, plural* **detergents.**

deteriorate To make or become worse. Nancy's car *deteriorated* as it got older.
de·te·ri·o·rate (dē tēr′ē ə rāt′) *verb*, **deteriorated, deteriorating.**

determination 1. A definite and firm purpose. Her *determination* to become a doctor was encouraged by her parents. 2. The act of deciding or settling ahead of time. The campers' *determination* of what to take on their trip took a long time.

at; āpe; cär; end; mē; it; īce; hot; ōld;
wood; fōōl; oil; out; up; turn; sing;
thin; this; hw in white; zh in treasure.
ə stands for a in about, e in taken,
i in pencil, o in lemon, and u in circus.

de·ter·mi·na·tion (dē tur′mi nā′shən) *noun, plural* **determinations**.

determine 1. To decide or settle definitely or ahead of time. The members of the club *determined* the date for their next meeting. 2. To find out by watching or checking. She *determined* the name of the flower by looking for its picture in a book about plants. 3. To be the cause of. The number of votes each candidate gets will *determine* who will be the class president.
de·ter·mine (dē tur′min) *verb*, **determined, determining**.

determined Having one's mind made up; firm. The basketball team made a *determined* effort to win.
de·ter·mined (dē tur′mind) *adjective*.

detest To dislike very much; hate. Bill *detests* being teased by his older brother.
de·test (dē test′) *verb*, **detested, detesting**.

detour A roundabout or indirect way. We had to take a *detour* because the main highway was being repaired. *Noun.*
—To cause to make a detour. The police *detoured* the traffic because of the accident. *Verb.*
de·tour (dē′tŏŏr) *noun, plural* **detours**; *verb*, **detoured, detouring**.

detract To take away from the value or beauty of something. The ugly advertisements along the road *detracted* from the beauty of the countryside.
de·tract (dē trakt′) *verb*, **detracted, detracting**.

devastate To destroy; ruin. The hurricane *devastated* the small towns along the coast.
dev·as·tate (dev′əs tāt′) *verb*, **devastated, devastating**.

develop 1. To bring or come into being or activity; grow. She *developed* an interest in poetry at an early age. He *developed* his muscles by exercising. The widespread use of the automobile has *developed* the nation's highway system. 2. To treat an exposed photographic film, plate, or print with a chemical so that the picture can be seen.
de·vel·op (dē vel′əp) *verb*, **developed, developing**.

development 1. The act or process of developing. The *development* of a spacecraft that could reach the moon took many years. 2. An event or happening. The radio station reported new *developments* in the search for the missing child. 3. A group of houses or other buildings on a large piece of land. The houses often look alike and are built by one builder.

de·vel·op·ment (dē vel′əp ment) *noun, plural* **developments**.

deviate To move or turn away from an action, thought, or statement. He *deviated* from the truth just to impress me.
de·vi·ate (dē′vē āt′) *verb*, **deviated, deviating**.

device 1. Something made or invented for a particular purpose. A can opener is a device. 2. A plan or scheme; trick. She used the *device* of pretending to have a sore throat to stay home from school.
de·vice (dē vīs′) *noun, plural* **devices**.

devil 1. **the Devil.** The evil spirit that is thought to be the ruler of hell. 2. An evil spirit. 3. A wicked, cruel, or mean person.
dev·il (dev′əl) *noun, plural* **devils**.

devise To think out; invent; plan. We *devised* a code no one else would understand.
de·vise (dē vīz′) *verb*, **devised, devising**.

devote To give effort, attention, or time to some person or purpose. She *devoted* all her energy to studying dancing.
de·vote (dē vōt′) *verb*, **devoted, devoting**.

devoted Loyal; faithful. My *devoted* friend would do anything for me.
de·vot·ed (dē vō′təd) *adjective*.

devotion A strong affection; loyalty; faithfulness. He felt great *devotion* to his parents.
de·vo·tion (dē vō′shən) *noun, plural* **devotions**.

devour 1. To eat with vigour or greed; consume. The hungry boy *devoured* his dinner. 2. To destroy. Fire *devoured* the house.
de·vour (dē vour′) *verb*, **devoured, devouring**.

devout 1. Very religious. 2. Sincere; earnest. You have my *devout* thanks for all your help.
de·vout (dē vout′) *adjective*.

dew Moisture from the air that forms drops on cool surfaces. Dew gathers on grass, plants, and trees during the night. ▲ Another word that sounds like this is **due**.
dew (dŏŏ *or* dyŏŏ) *noun, plural* **dews**.

DEW Line A radar network set up for defence. DEW Line stands for **Distant Early Warning Line.** Look up **Distant Early Warning Line** for more information.

dew-worm *Canadian.* A large earthworm used as bait for fish. The dew-worm can be found in grassy areas when the dew forms in the evening.
dew-worm (dŏŏ′wurm *or* dyŏŏ′wurm) *noun, plural* **dew-worms**.

dexterous Having or showing skill in using the hands, body, or mind. Both magicians and surgeons are dexterous with their hands.
dex·ter·ous (deks′tər əs) *adjective*.

diabetes A disease in which there is not enough of a certain substance called insulin in the blood. As a result of diabetes, there is too much sugar in the blood.
di·a·be·tes (dī′ə bē′təs *or* dī′ə bē′tēz) *noun.*

diacritical mark A mark or sign such as ¨ , ˆ , ¯ , ′, or ′ placed over, under, or across a letter either as part of the spelling or to show pronunciation. The pronunciation of the word "skate" using a diacritical mark is *skāt.*
di·a·crit·i·cal mark (dī′ə krit′i kəl).

diagnosis The act of finding out what is wrong with a person or animal by examination and the study of symptoms. The doctor's *diagnosis* showed that Jane had chicken pox.
di·ag·no·sis (dī′əg nō′sis) *noun, plural* **diagnoses.**

diagonal Having a slanting direction. Her dress had a pattern of *diagonal* stripes. *Adjective.*
—A straight line that connects the opposite corners of a rectangle. *Noun.*
di·ag·o·nal (dī ag′ən-əl) *adjective; noun, plural* **diagonals.**

The necktie has **diagonal** stripes.

diagram A plan or sketch that shows the parts of a thing. A diagram shows how something is put together or how it works. He had a *diagram* of the model airplane that showed how to put it together. *Noun.*
—To show by a diagram; make a diagram of. The engineer *diagrammed* the parts of the automobile engine. *Verb.*
di·a·gram (dī′ə gram′) *noun, plural* **diagrams;** *verb,* **diagrammed, diagramming** or **diagramed, diagraming.**

dial 1. The face of an instrument. A dial is marked with numbers, letters, or other signs. A pointer moves over these markings and shows how much there is of something. A clock, compass, or meter has a dial. 2. The disk on a radio or television set that tunes in a station or channel. 3. The disk on some telephones that you turn. *Noun.*
—1. To tune in by using a radio or television dial. *Dial* the channel the movie is being shown on. 2. To call by means of a telephone dial. My sister *dialled* a wrong number. *Verb.*
di·al (dī′əl *or* dīl) *noun, plural* **dials;** *verb,* **dialled, dialling** or **dialed, dialing.**

dialect A type of language that is spoken in a particular area or by a particular group of people. A dialect differs from other forms of the same language in the way some words are spoken, or in the way words are used in sentences, or in what certain words mean.
di·a·lect (dī′ə lekt′) *noun, plural* **dialects.**

dialogue A conversation. That play was full of funny *dialogue.*
di·a·logue (dī′ə log′) *noun, plural* **dialogues.**

dial tone The steady humming sound in a telephone that tells the caller that he may dial his number.

diameter 1. A straight line passing through the centre of a circle or other round object, from one side to the other. 2. The length of such a line; the width or thickness of something round. Scientists think that the *diameter* of the earth is about thirteen thousand kilometres.
di·am·e·ter (dī am′ə tər) *noun. plural* **diameters.**

The two lines on the sign are **diameters.**

diamond 1. A mineral that is usually colourless. A diamond comes from pure carbon in the form of a crystal. It is the hardest natural material known. Diamonds are used in industry for cutting and grinding. Cut and polished diamonds are used as jewels. 2. A playing card marked with one or more figures shaped like this: ♦. 3. The suit of cards marked with this figure. 4. The space on a baseball field that is inside the lines that connect the bases.
di·a·mond (dī′mənd *or* dī′ə mənd) *noun, plural* **diamonds.**

The sign has a **diamond** shape.

diaper A baby's undergarment made of soft, folded cloth or other material.
di·a·per (dī′pər *or* dī′ə pər) *noun, plural* **diapers.**

---

at; āpe; cär; end; mē; it; īce; hot; ōld; wood; fōōl; oil; out; up; turn; sing; thin; this; hw in white; zh in treasure.
ə stands for a in about, e in taken, i in pencil, o in lemon, and u in circus.

diaphragm **1.** A wall of muscle that divides the chest from the abdomen. It is used in breathing. **2.** A disk used to change sound into electrical signals, or to change electrical signals into sound. It is used in telephones and microphones.

di·a·phragm (dī′ə fram′) *noun, plural* diaphragms.

diary A written record of the things that one does each day. Mary kept a *diary* when she was away at summer camp.

di·a·ry (dī′ər ē) *noun, plural* diaries.

dice Small cubes of wood, plastic, or other material marked on each side with from one to six dots. Dice are used in some games. *Noun.*
—To cut into small cubes. Please help me *dice* the potatoes for the stew. *Verb.*

dice (dīs) *noun plural; verb,* diced, dicing.

A Pair of Dice

dictate **1.** To say or read something aloud to be written down or recorded by another. A businessman often *dictates* letters to his secretary. **2.** To order by authority. The victorious nation *dictated* the terms of the peace treaty. *Verb.*
—A rule or command that must be obeyed. He believes in following the *dictates* of the law. *Noun.*

dic·tate (dik′tāt) *verb,* dictated, dictating; *noun, plural* dictates.

dictator A person who has complete authority. The *dictator* took away the peoples' right to vote.

dic·ta·tor (dik′tā′tər) *noun, plural* dictators.

dictionary A book that has words of a language arranged in alphabetical order, together with information about them. This dictionary tells what words mean, how they are spelled, how they are used, how they are pronounced, and where they come from.

dic·tion·ar·y (dik′shə ner′ē) *noun, plural* dictionaries.

did *Did* you know that man? I *did* not see him. Look up **do** for more information.

did (did) *verb.*

didn't I *didn't* do my homework.

did·n't (did′ənt) contraction for "did not."

die¹ **1.** To stop living; become dead. Many soldiers *died* in the war. The flowers *died* during the cold spell. **2.** To lose force or strength; come to an end. The wind suddenly *died* as the sailboat neared the shore. The music *died* away in the distance. **3.** To want

very much. The hikers were *dying* for a cold drink of water. ▲ Another word that sounds like this is **dye.**

die (dī) *verb,* died, dying.

die² **1.** A small cube used in games. Look up the word **dice** for more information. **2.** A metal block or plate used to stamp designs or letters on coins. ▲ Another word that sounds like this is **dye.**

die (dī) *noun, plural* dice (*for definition 1*) or dies (*for definition 2*).

diesel engine An engine that burns fuel oil. The oil is set on fire by heat produced by the compression of air in the engine.

die·sel engine (dē′zəl).

diet **1.** The food and drink usually eaten by a person or animal. Her *diet* is made up of meat, vegetables, and fruit. A giraffe's *diet* is mostly leaves. **2.** A special selection of food and drink chosen by a person for reasons of health or for losing or gaining weight. Because he is too heavy, his doctor told him to go on a *diet. Noun.*
—To eat according to a special diet in order to be healthy or to lose or gain weight. She *dieted* for many weeks and lost twelve kilograms. *Verb.*

di·et (dī′ət) *noun, plural* diets; *verb,* dieted, dieting.

dietitian A person who is trained to plan balanced meals. A dietitian usually works at a hospital or school.

di·e·ti·tian (dī′ə tish′ən) *noun, plural* dietitians.

differ **1.** To be unlike; not be the same. Michael and Edward *differ* greatly in looks, even though they are brothers. **2.** To have a different opinion; disagree. My sister *differs* with the rest of our family about where to go on our vacation.

dif·fer (dif′ər) *verb,* differed, differing.

difference **1.** The state or quality of being unlike or different. Was there a *difference* between her answer and his? **2.** A way of being unlike or different. One of the *differences* between the sisters is the colour of their hair. **3.** The amount left after one quantity is subtracted from another. The *difference* between 16 and 12 is 4. **4.** A disagreement about something. They were able to settle their *differences* without a fight.

dif·fer·ence (dif′ər əns *or* dif′rəns) *noun, plural* differences.

different **1.** Not alike or similar. A bicycle and a motorcycle are *different.* **2.** Not the same; separate. It rained two *different* times this afternoon.

dif·fer·ent (dif′ər ənt *or* dif′rənt) *adjective.*

difficult 1. Hard to do, solve, or understand; not easy. Carrying the heavy bed upstairs was a *difficult* job. This is a *difficult* arithmetic problem. 2. Hard to get along with or please. He becomes very *difficult* when he can't have his own way.
dif·fi·cult (dif′ə kult′) *adjective.*

difficulty 1. The fact of being difficult. The *difficulty* of learning how to ride a bicycle discouraged him. 2. Something that is hard to do, understand, or deal with. Ruth had *difficulty* fitting everything into her small suitcase.
dif·fi·cul·ty (dif′ə kul′tē) *noun, plural* **difficulties.**

dig 1. To break up or turn over the earth with a shovel, the hands, or claws. Our dog likes to *dig* in the yard for bones. I *dig* in the vegetable garden with a spade. 2. To make or get by digging. The men had to *dig* a well for water. The workmen will *dig* through the mountain to finish the highway. We *dig* clams at the seashore when the tide is low. 3. To find or discover by searching or by study. It took the reporter weeks to *dig* up enough facts to write a story on the jewel robbery. 4. To poke or thrust. The cat loved to *dig* her claws into the tree and scratch.
dig (dig) *verb,* **dug, digging.**

digest To break down food in the mouth, stomach, and intestines. When we digest food, we change it into a form that can be taken in and used by the body. *Verb.*
—A summary of a longer book or document. I am reading a *digest* of that long novel. *Noun.*
di·gest (di jest′ *or* dī jest′ *for verb;* dī′jest *for noun) verb,* **digested, digesting;** *noun, plural* **digests.**

digestion The process of digesting. Digestion starts in the mouth and is completed in the small intestine.
di·ges·tion (di jes′chən *or* dī jes′chən) *noun, plural* **digestions.**

digestive Relating to or helping digestion. Saliva from the mouth is the first of the *digestive* juices that break down pieces of food.
di·ges·tive (di jes′tiv *or* dī jes′tiv) *adjective.*

digit One of the numerals 0, 1, 2, 3, 4, 5, 6, 7, 8, or 9. Sometimes 0 is not called a digit.
dig·it (dij′it) *noun, plural* **digits.**

dignified Having dignity; noble. The wedding party walked down the aisle of the church in a *dignified* manner.
dig·ni·fied (dig′nə fīd′) *adjective.*

dignity The state of being noble, worthy, or honourable. Despite great hardship and poverty, their mother kept her *dignity.*
dig·ni·ty (dig′nə tē) *noun, plural* **dignities.**

dike A dam or high wall of earth built to hold back the waters of a sea or river.
dike (dīk) *noun, plural* **dikes.**

Dike

dilapidated Fallen into ruin or decay; broken down. Father is going to build a new tool shed to replace the *dilapidated* one we have now.
di·lap·i·dat·ed (di lap′ə dāt′əd) *adjective.*

diligent Careful and hard-working. Janet is a *diligent* student.
dil·i·gent (dil′ə jənt) *adjective.*

dilute To make thin or weaker by adding a liquid. The directions on the can of frozen orange juice say to *dilute* the contents with three cans of cold water.
di·lute (di lōōt′ *or* dī lōōt′) *verb,* **diluted, diluting.**

dim 1. Having or giving little light; not bright. There was only a *dim* light in the hallway. 2. Not clear; indistinct. He could see a *dim* outline of the building through the fog. 3. Not seeing, hearing, or understanding clearly. The old man's eyes were growing *dim. Adjective.*
—To make or become dim. Ann always *dimmed* her car headlights at night when she passed cars going in the other direction. *Verb.*
dim (dim) *adjective,* **dimmer, dimmest;** *verb,* **dimmed, dimming.**

at; āpe; cär; end; mē; it; īce; hot; ōld;
wood; fōōl; oil; out; up; turn; sing;
thin; this; hw in white; zh in treasure.
ə stands for a in about, e in taken,
i in pencil, o in lemon, and u in circus.

183

dime A coin in Canada and the United States that is worth ten cents.
  dime (dīm) *noun, plural* **dimes.**

dimension Measurement of length, width, or height. The *dimensions* of the room are five metres long, four metres wide, and three metres high.
  di·men·sion (di men′shən) *noun, plural* **dimensions.**

diminish To make or become smaller. The camper's supply of food *diminished* as the days wore on.
  di·min·ish (di min′ish) *verb,* **diminished, diminishing.**

diminutive Very small; tiny. A baby has *diminutive* hands and feet.
  di·min·u·tive (di min′yə tiv) *adjective.*

dimple A small hollow on or in something. Linda had *dimples* in her cheeks whenever she smiled. *Noun.*
  —To mark with or form dimples. The pebbles we threw *dimpled* the surface of the water. *Verb.*
  dim·ple (dim′pəl) *noun, plural* **dimples;** *verb,* **dimpled, dimpling.**

din A loud noise that goes on for some time. The *din* of car horns kept us awake. *Noun.*
  —To say over and over. Mother *dinned* into our ears that we must stand up straight. *Verb.*
  din (din) *noun, plural* **dins;** *verb,* **dinned, dinning.**

dine To eat dinner. Mom and Dad *dined* at a restaurant on their anniversary.
  dine (dīn) *verb,* **dined, dining.**

diner 1. A person who is eating dinner. The *diners* in the restaurant were not aware that the kitchen was dirty. 2. A small restaurant that is usually beside a road or highway. That *diner* is a favourite stop for truck drivers.
  din·er (dīn′ər) *noun, plural* **diners.**

dinghy A small rowboat or lifeboat.
  din·ghy (ding′ē *or* ding′gē) *noun, plural* **dinghies.**

dingy Having a dirty and dull appearance; not bright and cheery. The white curtains were *dingy* from the dirt and soot that came in through the window.
  din·gy (din′jē) *adjective,* **dingier, dingiest.**

dining room A room where meals are served and eaten.

dinner 1. The main meal of the day. 2. A formal meal in honour of some person or event. The school gave the members of the football team a *dinner* to celebrate their winning season.
  din·ner (din′ər) *noun, plural* **dinners.**

dinosaur One of a large group of extinct reptiles that lived millions of years ago. Some dinosaurs were the largest land animals that have ever lived.
  din·o·saur (dī′nə sōr′) *noun, plural* **dinosaurs.**

Dinosaur

diocese A church district that is under the authority of a bishop.
  di·o·cese (dī′ə sis *or* dī′ə sēs′) *noun, plural* **dioceses.**

dip 1. To put into water or another liquid for a moment. Nancy *dipped* her hand in the clear water of the stream. 2. To go in water and come out quickly. Peter *dipped* in the swimming pool to cool off. 3. To lower and raise again. The soldier *dipped* the flag in salute as the Governor General of Canada rode by. 4. To sink or go down. The sun *dipped* below the horizon as evening came. *Verb.*
  —1. The act of dipping. Ruth took one last *dip* in the ocean before she went home. 2. A liquid into which something is dipped for cleaning or colouring. We put the eggs in a *dip* to colour them for Easter. 3. A sinking or drop. The car ahead of us suddenly disappeared because of a *dip* in the road. *Noun.*
  dip (dip) *verb,* **dipped, dipping;** *noun, plural* **dips.**

diphthong Two vowel sounds in one syllable that are pronounced as one speech sound. The *ou* in *out* and the *oy* in *boy* are diphthongs.
  diph·thong (dif′thong′ *or* dip′thong′) *noun, plural* **diphthongs.**

diploma A printed piece of paper given by a school or university to a graduating student that says he or she has successfully finished a course of study.
  di·plo·ma (di plō′mə) *noun, plural* **diplomas.**

diplomat A person whose job is to handle relations between his country and other countries of the world. A diplomat must be very skilful in dealing with people.
dip·lo·mat (dip′lə mat′) *noun, plural* **diplomats.**

dipper 1. A cup with a long handle that is used to lift water or other liquids. 2. **Dipper.** Either of two groups of stars in the northern sky that are in the shape of a dipper. The larger of these groups is called the **Big Dipper,** and the smaller is called the **Little Dipper.**
dip·per (dip′ər) *noun, plural* **dippers.**

Dipper

direct 1. To manage or control; guide. There is a policeman on each busy corner downtown to *direct* traffic. Our school drama club asked the music teacher to *direct* the Christmas play. 2. To order; command. The general *directed* the troops to attack. 3. To tell or show someone the way. Can you *direct* me to the nearest bus stop? 4. To turn or send in a particular direction or to a particular place. Jim *directed* the hose at the flowers. *Verb.*
—1. Going in a straight line or by the shortest way. We are taking a *direct* flight to London. King Street is a *direct* route between my house and Janet's. 2. Honest; straightforward. The witness gave *direct* answers to all the lawyer's questions. *Adjective.*
—Directly. This plane goes *direct* to Toronto from Vancouver. *Adverb.*
di·rect (di rekt′ *or* dī rekt′) *verb,* **directed, directing;** *adjective; adverb.*

direct current An electric current that flows only in one direction. A flashlight and a radio with batteries run on direct current.

direction 1. Management or control; guidance. The young doctor performed the operation under the *direction* of an older, more experienced doctor. 2. The line or course along which something moves, faces, or lies. We decided to walk in the *direction* of the lake. 3. An order or instruction on how to do something or how to act. Follow the doctor's *directions* and take the pills four times a day. The *directions* on the package are to cook the vegetables in boiling water.
di·rec·tion (di rek′shən *or* dī rek′shən) *noun, plural* **directions.**

directly 1. In a direct line or manner; straight. The third baseman threw the ball *directly* to his teammate covering first base. 2. At once; without delay. Amy came home *directly* after the concert. 3. Exactly; absolutely. Tim's likes and dislikes in music are *directly* opposite to his father's.
di·rect·ly (di rekt′lē *or* dī rekt′lē) *adverb.*

director A person or thing that manages or controls. A person who directs a play, movie, or television show is called a director.
di·rec·tor (di rek′tər *or* dī rek′tər) *noun, plural* **directors.**

directory A list of names and addresses. A telephone directory lists the telephone numbers of people living in a particular area.
di·rec·to·ry (di rek′tə rē *or* dī rek′tə rē) *noun, plural* **directories.**

dirigible A large balloon that is in the shape of a cigar. It is driven by a motor and can be steered.
dir·i·gi·ble (dir′ə jə bəl *or* də rij′ə bəl) *noun, plural* **dirigibles.**

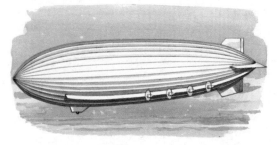
Dirigible

dirt 1. Mud, dust, or other material that makes something unclean. Tommy washed the *dirt* off his hands before coming to dinner. 2. Loose earth or soil. The gardener filled the pots with *dirt* before planting the flowers in them.
dirt (durt) *noun.*

dirty Soiled; not clean. Fred put all his *dirty* clothes in a pile for the laundry. Cleaning out the garage was a hard and *dirty* job.
dirt·y (dur′tē) *adjective,* **dirtier, dirtiest.**

disable To take away ability; cripple. A broken leg can *disable* a person for months.
dis·a·ble (dis ā′bəl) *verb,* **disabled, disabling.**

disadvantage 1. Something that makes it

at; āpe; cär; end; mē; it; īce; hot; ōld;
wood; fool; oil; out; up; turn; sing;
thin; this; hw in white; zh in treasure.
ə stands for a in about, e in taken,
i in pencil, o in lemon, and u in circus.

harder to succeed. Being short is a *disadvantage* to a basketball player. **2.** A loss or injury; harm. It will be to Ann's *disadvantage* if she turns down that offer for free skiing lessons.

dis·ad·van·tage (dis′əd van′təj) *noun, plural* **disadvantages.**

disagree **1.** To differ in opinion; argue. Mike *disagreed* with his brother over which television show to watch at seven o'clock. **2.** To be different or unlike. The stories of the two witnesses *disagreed* so much that the policeman didn't know which one to believe. **3.** To be harmful. Hot, spicy foods *disagree* with me.

dis·a·gree (dis′ə grē′) *verb,* **disagreed, disagreeing.**

disagreement A difference of opinion; argument. Mary had a *disagreement* with her father over whether or not she could use the family car for the weekend.

dis·a·gree·ment (dis′ə grē′mənt) *noun, plural* **disagreements.**

disappear **1.** To go out of sight. We watched the sun *disappear* behind a cloud. **2.** To pass away; end. Dinosaurs *disappeared* from the earth millions of years ago.

dis·ap·pear (dis′ə pēr′) *verb,* **disappeared, disappearing.**

disappearance The act or fact of disappearing. The *disappearance* of the two mountain climbers made everyone fear that they were dead.

dis·ap·pear·ance (dis′ə pēr′əns) *noun, plural* **disappearances.**

disappoint To fail to live up to one's hopes. You will *disappoint* your sister if you do not take her to the movies as you promised.

dis·ap·point (dis′ə point′) *verb,* **disappointed, disappointing.**

disappointment **1.** A feeling of being disappointed. Kate couldn't hide her *disappointment* when it rained and the picnic was called off. **2.** A person or thing that disappoints. The coach thought the new player would be very good, but he turned out to be a *disappointment.*

dis·ap·point·ment (dis′ə point′mənt) *noun, plural* **disappointments.**

disapprove To have a feeling against. Jan's parents *disapprove* of smoking.

dis·ap·prove (dis′ə prōōv′) *verb,* **disapproved, disapproving.**

disaster An event that causes much suffering or loss. Floods, fires, and earthquakes are disasters.

dis·as·ter (di zas′tər) *noun, plural* **disasters.**

The word **disaster** comes from two Greek words. One word means "against," and the other word means "star." Long ago, people believed that the stars had an effect on their lives. When the stars were "against" a person, something very bad would happen to him.

disbelief Lack of belief; refusal to believe. Helen's face showed *disbelief* when she heard that her experiment had been awarded first prize at the science fair.

dis·be·lief (dis′bə lēf′) *noun, plural* **disbeliefs.**

disc A flat, round object. This word is usually spelled **disk.** Look up **disk** for more information.

discard To throw aside or give up as useless, worthless, or unwanted. Jane went through her closet and *discarded* all her worn-out clothes.

dis·card (dis kärd′) *verb,* **discarded, discarding.**

discern To make out or recognize. We could barely *discern* the person in the fog.

dis·cern (di surn′) *verb,* **discerned, discerning.**

discharge **1.** To let go or release; dismiss. When the company went out of business it had to *discharge* all its workers. **2.** To unload or remove. The ship *discharged* its cargo of bananas and other fruits at the dock. **3.** To fire or shoot. **4.** To send off or let out. The factory should not be allowed to *discharge* its wastes into the river. *Verb.*
—The act of discharging. The *discharge* of the airplane's passengers will be at gate ten. *Noun.*

dis·charge (dis chärj′ *for verb;* dis′chärj′ *for noun*) *verb,* **discharged, discharging;** *noun, plural* **discharges.**

disciple **1.** A person who follows and believes in a leader or his teachings. The young doctor was a devoted *disciple* of the famous surgeon. **2.** One of the followers of Jesus.

dis·ci·ple (di sī′pəl) *noun, plural* **disciples.**

discipline Training or punishment that develops orderly behaviour. Those children have had no *discipline* from their parents. *Noun.*
—To train to be obedient. An officer in the army must be able to *discipline* the troops under his command. *Verb.*

dis·ci·pline (dis′ə plin) *noun, plural* **disciplines;** *verb,* **disciplined, disciplining.**

disclose To make known. Mary promised her best friend that she would not *disclose* her secret to anyone.

dis·close (dis klōz′) *verb*, **disclosed, disclosing.**

disconnect To separate; undo. The repairman had to *disconnect* the television set before fixing it.
dis·con·nect (dis′kə nekt′) *verb*, **disconnected, disconnecting.**

discontented Unhappy and restless. Ann started looking for a new job because she was *discontented* with the one she had.
dis·con·tent·ed (dis′kən ten′təd) *adjective*.

discontinue To put an end to; stop. The owners of our town newspaper are going to *discontinue* publishing it because not enough people buy the paper.
dis·con·tin·ue (dis′kən tin′yо̄о̄) *verb*, **discontinued, discontinuing.**

discount The amount taken off the regular price. Nancy bought a dress on sale at a twenty-five per cent *discount*.
dis·count (dis′kount′) *noun*, *plural* **discounts.**

discourage 1. To cause to lose courage, hope, or confidence. Failing to have her first story published did not *discourage* Pam from wanting to become a writer. 2. To try to keep a person from doing something. They *discouraged* us from starting out on our trip because of the heavy snowstorm.
dis·cour·age (dis kur′ij) *verb*, **discouraged, discouraging.**

discover To see or find out for the first time. Marie Curie and her husband *discovered* the chemical element radium. Dick *discovered* his mistake in the arithmetic problem and corrected it.
dis·cov·er (dis kuv′ər) *verb*, **discovered, discovering.**

discovery 1. The act of seeing or finding out something for the first time. Christopher Columbus's *discovery* of America happened in 1492. 2. Something that is seen or found out for the first time. Electricity was an important *discovery*.
dis·cov·er·y (dis kuv′ər ē) *noun*, *plural* **discoveries.**

discriminate To treat a person differently from others because of unfair feelings. It is against the law to *discriminate* against people because of their colour, religion, or sex.
dis·crim·i·nate (dis krim′ə nāt′) *verb*, **discriminated, discriminating.**

discrimination An unfair difference in treatment. That company hires people without *discrimination*.
dis·crim·i·na·tion (dis krim′ə nā′shən) *noun*.

discuss To talk over; speak about. The city

council held a meeting to *discuss* the building plans for the new city hall.
dis·cuss (dis kus′) *verb*, **discussed, discussing.**

discussion The act of talking something over. Jane's question about the new school rules started a *discussion* that continued for half an hour.
dis·cus·sion (dis kush′ən) *noun*, *plural* **discussions.**

disdain A feeling of dislike or scorn for a person or thing. The bully treated the younger girls with *disdain*. *Noun*.
—To look down on. He *disdained* all help from his friends. *Verb*.
dis·dain (dis dān′) *noun*; *verb*, **disdained, disdaining.**

disease Sickness or illness. Chicken pox is a *disease* that many children get. That tree with brownish leaves is suffering from a *disease*.
dis·ease (di zēz′) *noun*, *plural* **diseases.**

disgrace 1. The loss of honour or respect; shame. The president of the company resigned in *disgrace* when the police learned about the money he had stolen. 2. A person or thing that causes a loss of honour or respect. Living conditions in that slum are a *disgrace* to our city. *Noun*.
—To bring shame to. He *disgraced* his family when he was caught stealing a car. *Verb*.
dis·grace (dis grās′) *noun*, *plural* **disgraces**; *verb*, **disgraced, disgracing.**

disguise 1. To change or hide the way one looks in order to look like someone or something else. The children wore animal costumes to *disguise* themselves on Hallowe'en. 2. To hide. Mother tried to *disguise* the bitter taste of the cough medicine by mixing it with orange juice. *Verb*.
—Something that changes or hides the way one looks. A mustache was part of the thief's *disguise*. *Noun*.
dis·guise (dis gīz′) *verb*, **disguised, disguising**; *noun*, *plural* **disguises.**

disgust A sickening feeling of strong dislike. She felt *disgust* when she saw the man beating his dog with a stick. *Noun*.
—To cause strong dislike in; sicken. The awful smell from the polluted river *disgusted* us. *Verb*.

at; āpe; cär; end; mē; it; īce; hot; ōld;
wood; fо̄о̄l; oil; out; up; turn; sing;
thin; this; hw in white; zh in treasure.
ə stands for a in about, e in taken,
i in pencil, o in lemon, and u in circus.

dis·gust (dis gust′) *noun; verb,* **disgusted, disgusting.**

dish **1.** A plate or shallow bowl used for holding food. A dish can be made out of china, glass, or metal. **2.** Food made in a particular way. Spaghetti with tomato sauce is my brother's favourite *dish. Noun.*
—To put or serve in a dish. Mother *dished* up dinner as soon as everyone sat down. *Verb.*
dish (dish) *noun, plural* **dishes;** *verb,* **dished, dishing.**

dishonest Not fair or honest. A student who cheats on a test is being *dishonest.* The salesman used *dishonest* methods to sell cars.
dis·hon·est (dis on′əst) *adjective.*

dishonour Loss of honour or reputation; shame. It is no *dishonour* to admit you are wrong if you have made a mistake. *Noun.*
—To disgrace or shame. The teacher *dishonoured* herself by slapping a student. *Verb.*
dis·hon·our (dis on′ər) *noun, plural* **dishonours;** *verb,* **dishonoured, dishonouring.**

dishwasher A machine that washes dishes, glasses, and pots.
dish·wash·er (dish′wosh′ər) *noun, plural* **dishwashers.**

disinfect To destroy germs that cause disease. The nurse *disinfected* my cut.
dis·in·fect (dis′in fekt′) *verb,* **disinfected, disinfecting.**

disintegrate To break up into many small pieces. A blow with the heavy hammer caused the stone to *disintegrate.*
dis·in·te·grate (dis in′tə grāt′) *verb,* **disintegrated, disintegrating.**

disinterested Free from selfish interest; fair. A judge should take a *disinterested* view of the cases that come before him.
dis·in·ter·est·ed (dis in′tər əs təd *or* dis in′tə res′təd *or* dis in′trəs təd) *adjective.*

disk A flat, thin, round object that is shaped like a coin or phonograph record. The sun shone like a bright, golden *disk* in the sky. This word is also spelled **disc.**
disk (disk) *noun, plural* **disks.**

diskette A small, thin, magnetic disk for storing computer programs or data.
disk·ette (dis ket′) *noun, plural* **diskettes.**

dislike A feeling of not liking or of being against something. My brother has a *dislike* of spinach. *Noun.*
—To have a feeling of not liking or of being against. Susan *dislikes* housework. *Verb.*
dis·like (dis līk′) *noun, plural* **dislikes;** *verb,* **disliked, disliking.**

dislocate To put a bone out of joint. The man *dislocated* his hip when he slipped and fell on the ice.
dis·lo·cate (dis′lō kāt′) *verb,* **dislocated, dislocating.**

dislodge To move or force out of a place or position. The flood threatened to *dislodge* two of the supports that held up the bridge.
dis·lodge (dis loj′) *verb,* **dislodged, dislodging.**

disloyal Not loyal; unfaithful. It was *disloyal* not to help your best friend.
dis·loy·al (dis loi′əl) *adjective.*

dismal Causing gloom or sadness; dreary; miserable. The weather this week has been so rainy and *dismal* that we haven't been outside to play.
dis·mal (diz′məl) *adjective.*

▲ The word **dismal** comes from two old French words that meant "unlucky days" or "evil days." In the Middle Ages, certain days on the calendar were marked "unlucky days" because people thought the position of the stars on those days would bring them bad luck. The two French words were put together to make the English word *dismal,* and the English called these days "dismal days." Later the word was used to talk about anything gloomy or unlucky.

dismay To make afraid or discouraged because of danger or trouble. The rising flood waters *dismayed* the people of the town. *Verb.*
—A feeling of fear or discouragement in the face of danger or trouble. The family was filled with *dismay* when they learned that the fire was near their house. *Noun.*
dis·may (dis mā′) *verb,* **dismayed, dismaying;** *noun.*

dismiss To send away or allow to leave. The teacher decided to *dismiss* the class early because it was the last day before summer holidays.
dis·miss (dis mis′) *verb,* **dismissed, dismissing.**

dismount To get off or down from. The RCMP officer gave the order to *dismount.*
dis·mount (dis mount′) *verb,* **dismounted, dismounting.**

disobedient Refusing or failing to obey. The *disobedient* child crossed the highway without his mother's permission.
dis·o·be·di·ent (dis′ə bē′dē ənt) *adjective.*

disobey To refuse or fail to obey. He *disobeyed* the traffic laws by driving through a red light.

dis·pos·al (dis pō′zəl) *noun, plural* **disposals.**

spose To dispose of. 1. To get rid of. My rother was able *to dispose of* his old car for hundred dollars more than he had paid for . 2. To deal with or settle. Mother quickly *isposed of* her work so that we could all go the zoo for the afternoon.
dis·pose (dis pōz′) *verb,* **disposed, disposing.**

sposition A person's usual way of acting, hinking, or feeling. My sister always has a ery cheerful *disposition,* even when she first yakes up in the morning.
dis·po·si·tion (dis′pə zish′ən) *noun, plural* **dispositions.**

ispute To argue against; disagree with. ack *disputed* Bill's statement that he was a aster swimmer. *Verb.*
—An argument or quarrel. A judge had to ettle the *dispute* between the two farmers ver who owned the land. *Noun.*
dis·pute (dis pyo͞ot′) *verb,* **disputed, disput- ing;** *noun, plural* **disputes.**

squalify To make or declare unfit or un- ble to do something. The judges had to *isqualify* the runner from the race for nocking down another runner.
dis·qual·i·fy (dis kwol′ə fī′) *verb,* **disquali- fied, disqualifying.**

sregard To pay no attention to; ignore. om tried to *disregard* the other children's nean comments about his new shirt. *Verb.*
—Lack of attention; neglect. Playing the adio very loudly late at night shows a *disre- ard* for other people. *Noun.*
dis·re·gard (dis′rə gärd′) *verb,* **disregarded, disregarding;** *noun.*

srupt To break up or apart. The teacher old the two boys to stop talking because they vere beginning to *disrupt* the whole class.
dis·rupt (dis rupt′) *verb,* **disrupted, disrupt- ing.**

ssatisfied Not content; displeased. Ted ook his new television set back to the store ecause he was *dissatisfied* with the picture e got.
dis·sat·is·fied (di sat′əs fīd′) *adjective.*

ssect To cut apart or divide in order to tudy or examine. Each biology student was

at; āpe; cär; end; mē; it; īce; hot; ōld;
wood; fo͞ol; oil; out; up; turn; sing;
thin; this; hw in white; zh in treasure.
ə stands for a in about, e in taken,
i in pencil, o in lemon, and u in circus.

Programs like this go beyond the medical aspect of cancer. They touch

...One of our outstanding accomplishments is our support of Camp Trillium, a year-round program for children who have cancer and their families.

...We are a partner in the Cancer Information Service which is bilingual, toll-free, nationwide -- 1-888-939-3333 -- that anyone can call to get up-to-date information on all types of cancer, cancer-related issues and Canadian Cancer Society programs and services.

difference in defeating cancer, and I can't tell you how glad I am that we're able to promote them. But we don't stop there....

garbage.

given a frog to *dissect* in order to study its digestive system.

dis·sect (di sekt´ *or* dī sekt´) *verb*, **dissected, dissecting.**

dissent To differ strongly in opinion; disagree. The dictator did not allow anyone to *dissent* from the actions of the government. *Verb.*
—A strong difference of opinion; disagreement. John's suggestion to use the club's dues for a party met with *dissent* at the meeting. *Noun.*

dis·sent (di sent´) *verb*, **dissented, dissenting;** *noun.*

dissolve 1. To mix and make or become liquid. Sugar will *dissolve* in a cup of hot tea. *Dissolve* the powder in milk to make the instant pudding. 2. To bring to an end. The club members voted to *dissolve* the dance committee once the dance was over.

dis·solve (di zolv´) *verb*, **dissolved, dissolving.**

distance 1. The amount of space between two things or points. The *distance* from Jane's house to the school is two blocks. 2. A far-off point or place. The driver slowed down because he saw a slow-moving truck in the *distance* ahead of him.

dis·tance (dis´təns) *noun, plural* **distances.**

distant 1. Far away in space or time; not near. Pluto is the most *distant* planet from the sun. Dinosaurs lived in the *distant* past. 2. Away. The farm was ten kilometres *distant* from the nearest town. 3. To or from a distance. Golda was disappointed when she heard a *distant* rumble of thunder. 4. Not friendly. She has been very *distant* since our quarrel last Canada Day.

dis·tant (dis´tənt) *adjective.*

Distant Early Warning Line A network of radar stations built for defence. It extends from Point Barrow, Alaska, to Baffin Island. This network is also called the **DEW Line.**

distil To make a liquid pure by heating it until it becomes a vapour and then cooling it until it becomes a liquid again. Gasoline is *distilled* from petroleum. This word is also spelled **distill.**

dis·til (dis til´) *verb*, **distilled, distilling.**

distinct 1. Not the same; separate; different. The letters were sorted into three *distinct* piles. 2. Easy to see, hear, or understand; clear. The words on the street sign became *distinct* when we walked closer. The sound of the drums was *distinct* even from a distance. The coach noticed a *distinct* improvement in the team's playing.

dis·tinct (dis tingkt´) *adjective.*

distinction 1. The act of making or noticing a difference between things. It is not always easy to make a *distinction* between poison ivy and other plants that look like it. 2. Something that makes a thing different from other things; difference. The ability to fly is one of the *distinctions* between birds and other animals. 3. Excellence; worth. The senator was a man of *distinction.*

dis·tinc·tion (dis tingk´shən) *noun, plural* **distinctions.**

distinctive Making or showing a difference between things. I recognized the *distinctive* smell of roast turkey coming from the kitchen.

dis·tinc·tive (dis tingk´tiv) *adjective.*

distinguish 1. To know or show that there is a difference between certain things. The jeweller quickly *distinguished* the real diamond from the fake one. 2. To make something special or different. The cardinal's bright red feathers *distinguish* it from other birds. 3. To see or hear clearly. He could see three men walking toward him, but he could not *distinguish* their faces in the dark. 4. To make famous or deserving of special honour or attention; make well known. The doctor *distinguished* herself by her work in cancer research.

dis·tin·guish (dis ting´gwish) *verb*, **distinguished, distinguishing.**

distort To twist or bend out of shape. The curved mirror *distorted* the way she looked. The witness tried to *distort* the facts.

dis·tort (dis tôrt´) *verb*, **distorted, distorting.**

distract To draw someone's attention away from what he is doing or thinking. The noise *distracted* Tom from his homework.

dis·tract (dis trakt´) *verb*, **distracted, distracting.**

distraction Something that draws someone's attention away from what he is doing or thinking. I find telephone calls a *distraction* when I am trying to write a letter.

dis·trac·tion (dis trak´shən) *noun, plural* **distractions.**

distress 1. Great pain or sorrow; misery. My friend's illness was a great *distress* to me. 2. Danger, trouble, or great need. The sinking ship sent a message that it was in *distress.* *Noun.*
—To cause pain, sorrow, or misery. The bad news from home *distressed* the traveller. *Verb.*

dis·tress (dis tres´) *noun; verb*, **distressed, distressing.**

distribute 1. To give something out in shares; deal out. The teacher *distributed* new books to the class. 2. To spread something out over a large area; scatter. The farmer *distributed* seed over the ploughed field. 3. To arrange or sort into groups. The post office *distributed* the letters according to which town they were going to.
   dis·trib·ute (dis trib′yo͞ot) *verb,* **distributed, distributing.**

distribution The act of distributing. The Canadian Red Cross supervised the *distribution* of food and clothing to the flood victims, so that each family received its share.
   dis·tri·bu·tion (dis′trə byo͞o′shən) *noun, plural* **distributions.**

district An area that is a special part of a larger area. That store is in the business *district* of the city. Jim had to go to a different school when his family moved to a new school *district.*
   dis·trict (dis′trikt) *noun, plural* **districts.**

disturb 1. To make uneasy or nervous; worry. Having to take a test *disturbs* Richard, even though he is a good student. 2. To break in on; interrupt. The telephone call *disturbed* his sleep. 3. To upset or change the order or arrangement of things. The children *disturbed* the books on the shelf.
   dis·turb (dis turb′) *verb,* **disturbed, disturbing.**

disturbance 1. A disturbing; interruption. The writer hoped that there would be no more *disturbance* of his work. 2. Something that disturbs. The noise was a *disturbance* to the students who were trying to concentrate. The policeman went to investigate the *disturbance.*
   dis·turb·ance (dis tur′bəns) *noun, plural* **disturbances.**

ditch A long, narrow hole dug in the ground. Ditches are used to drain off water.
   ditch (dich) *noun, plural* **ditches.**

dive 1. To plunge headfirst into water. At first, I was afraid to *dive* from the high board into the pool. 2. To plunge downward quickly and at a steep angle. We watched the eagle *dive* down from the sky. 3. To go, move, or drop suddenly and quickly. The sound of thunder made the frightened puppy *dive* under the bed. *Verb.*
   —1. A headfirst plunge into water. Ellen did a *dive* from the rocks into the lake. 2. A quick, steep plunge. The plane went into a *dive* when it was hit by enemy fire. *Noun.*
   dive (dīv) *verb,* **dived** or **dove, dived, diving;** *noun, plural* **dives.**

diver 1. A person who dives. 2. A person who works or explores underwater. Divers usually carry tanks of air on their backs or wear special suits and helmets with an air hose so that they can breathe underwater. 3. A bird that dives into water to get its food.
   div·er (dī′ər) *noun, plural* **divers.**

Diver

diverse Not the same; different. The students in the class come from *diverse* backgrounds.
   di·verse (di vurs′) *adjective.*

diversion 1. A changing of the direction in which something is going. The *diversion* of the train to a different track was necessary because the regular tracks were then being repaired. 2. Something that turns the attention in a different direction. The second robber created a *diversion* while the first picked the man's pocket. 3. Entertainment; amusement; pastime. Ronald's favorite *diversion* is fishing.
   di·ver·sion (di vur′zhən) *noun, plural* **diversions.**

diversity Difference; unlikeness. The *diversity* of our interests makes it hard for my sister and me to agree on which television show to watch.
   di·ver·si·ty (di vur′sə tē) *noun, plural* **diversities.**

divert 1. To change the direction in which something is going. The police *diverted* traffic from the street where the accident happened. 2. To turn the attention in a different direction. The ringing of the telephone *diverted* Tom from the book he was reading. 3. To entertain; amuse. The television show *diverted* me for a few minutes, but then I got bored.
   di·vert (di vurt′) *verb,* **diverted, diverting.**

divide 1. To separate into parts, pieces, or

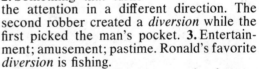

at; āpe; cär; end; mē; it; īce; hot; ōld;
wood; fo͞ol; oil; out; up; turn; sing;
thin; this; hw in white; zh in treasure.
ə stands for a in about, e in taken,
i in pencil, o in lemon, and u in circus.

groups. The baker *divided* the pie into ten slices. The class *divided* into two teams for the spelling contest. **2.** To separate into parts or pieces and give some to each; share. The three girls who found the lost dog *divided* the reward money. **3.** To show how many times one number contains another number. For example, when you *divide* 6 by 2 you get 3, because the number 6 contains the number 2 three times. **4.** To split up into opposing sides because of different feelings or ideas. The team *divided* on the choice of a new captain. *Verb.*

—A ridge of land that separates two areas that are drained by different rivers. The Great Divide in the Rocky Mountains separates the areas drained by the rivers flowing east and west. *Noun.*

di·vide (di vīd′) *verb,* **divided, dividing; noun, plural divides.**

dividend **1.** A number that is to be divided by another number. When you divide 6 by 3, the *dividend* is 6. **2.** Money that is earned by a business and is divided among the owners as their share of the profit.

div·i·dend (div′ə dend′) *noun, plural* **dividends.**

divine **1.** Of or from God or a god. The old man prayed for *divine* mercy. **2.** Religious; sacred. The church bell called the people to *divine* worship.

di·vine (di vīn′) *adjective.*

divisible Capable of being divided. The number 8 is *divisible* by the numbers 8, 4, 2, and 1.

di·vis·i·ble (di viz′ə bəl) *adjective.*

division **1.** The act of dividing or the state of being divided. The *division* of the house into apartments provided homes for five families. **2.** One of the parts into which something is divided. Asian history is one of the *divisions* of our social studies course. **3.** Something that divides or separates. The wooden fence formed a *division* between the farms. **4.** A unit of the army that is made up of different regiments.

di·vi·sion (di vizh′ən) *noun, plural* **divisions.**

divisor A number by which another number is to be divided. When you divide the number 6 by the number 3, the *divisor* is 3.

di·vi·sor (di vī′zər) *noun, plural* **divisors.**

divorce The legal ending of a marriage. *Noun.*

—To legally end a marriage. *Verb.*

di·vorce (di vōrs′) *noun, plural* **divorces; verb,** **divorced, divorcing.**

dizzy Having the feeling of spinning and

falling. The children ran in circles until they were *dizzy.*

diz·zy (diz′ē) *adjective,* **dizzier, dizziest.**

do **1.** The teacher helped Susan *do* the arithmetic problem. It was kind of Harry to *do* me a favour. It will *do* her good to take a holiday. **2.** *Do* is used to ask questions. *Do* you know John's last name? *Do* horses run faster than dogs? **3.** *Do* is used to make something that is said stronger. *Do* be quiet! **4.** *Do* is used with *not* to show that something is not real or true. I *do* not want to go. **5.** *Do* is used in place of a word or phrase that has already been used. Jan ice-skates as well as I *do.*

do (do͞o) *verb,* **did, done, doing.**

Doberman Pinscher

Doberman pinscher A dog that has a long head, thin legs, and a shiny black or brown coat. It was first bred in Germany.

Do·ber·man pin·scher (dō′bər mən pin′shər).

docile Easy to teach, train, or handle. Jack has a *docile* pony that is easy to ride.

do·cile (do′sīl, dos′əl, *or* dō′sīl) *adjective.*

Dock

dock¹ **1.** A platform where boats or ships are tied up. A dock is built along the shore or out into the water. Docks are used for loading and unloading a ship's cargo and passengers. **2.** An area of water between two piers where

boats and ships tie up. The tugboat towed the ocean liner into the *dock. Noun.*
—**1.** To bring a boat or ship to a dock. The tanker *docked* and unloaded its cargo. **2.** To bring two spacecraft together in space. *Verb.*
dock (dok) *noun, plural* **docks;** *verb,* **docked, docking.**

dock² **1.** To take some away; make less. The company *docked* the man's salary because he missed two days of work. **2.** To make shorter by cutting off the end. The veterinarian *docked* the puppy's tail.
dock (dok) *verb,* **docked, docking.**

doctor **1.** A person who has been trained and licensed to treat sickness or injury. A physician or a dentist is a doctor. **2.** A person who has the highest degree from a university.
doc·tor (dok′tər) *noun, plural* **doctors.**

doctrine Something that is believed by a group of people. The beliefs of a religion and the ideals of a political party are doctrines.
doc·trine (dok′trin) *noun, plural* **doctrines.**

document A written or printed statement that gives official proof and information about something. A birth certificate, a deed to a house, and a diploma are documents.
doc·u·ment (dok′yə mənt) *noun, plural* **documents.**

dodge **1.** To keep away from something by moving aside quickly. Jane *dodged* the snowball that Jack threw at her. **2.** To get away from something in a tricky way. The witness *dodged* the lawyer's question by pretending that he didn't remember. *Verb.*
—**1.** A quick move to the side. The boxer avoided being hit by making a *dodge* to the left. **2.** A trick that is used to fool or cheat someone. The man used a clever *dodge* to keep from paying his taxes. *Noun.*
dodge (doj) *verb,* **dodged, dodging;** *noun, plural* **dodges.**

dodo A large bird that no longer exists. The dodo had a heavy hooked bill and a short tail of curly feathers. Its wings were so small that it was not able to fly.
do·do (dō′dō) *noun, plural* **dodos** or **dodoes.**

Dodo

doe **1.** A female deer. **2.** The female of several other animals, such as the antelope or hare.
▲ Another word that sounds like this is **dough.**
doe (dō) *noun, plural* **does.**

does She *does* beautiful paintings.
does (duz) *verb.*

doesn't Alan *doesn't* like cold weather.
does·n't (duz′ənt) contraction for "does not."

dog An animal that has four legs and makes a barking noise. There are more than 200 different kinds of dogs. People keep dogs in their homes as pets or guards. Dogs are closely related to wolves, foxes, and coyotes. *Noun.*
—To follow closely in the way a hunting dog would. Michael *dogged* his little sister's footsteps to make sure she didn't get lost. *Verb.*
dog (dog) *noun, plural* **dogs;** *verb,* **dogged, dogging.**

dogwood A tree that has flowers with a greenish-yellow centre and pink or white leaves that look like petals. The Pacific dogwood is the provincial flower of British Columbia.
dog·wood (dog′wood′) *noun, plural* **dogwoods.**

Blossom
Dogwood Tree

doily A small piece of linen, lace, paper, or some other material. Doilies are usually placed under something, such as a vase or plate, as a decoration or to protect furniture.
doi·ly (doi′lē) *noun, plural* **doilies.**

doll A toy that looks like a baby, a child, or a grown person.
doll (dol) *noun, plural* **dolls.**

dollar A unit of money in Canada and the United States. A dollar is worth one hundred cents.
dol·lar (dol′ər) *noun, plural* **dollars.**

---

at; āpe; cär; end; mē; it; īce; hot; ōld;
wood; fo͞ol; oil; out; up; turn; sing;
thin; this; hw in white; zh in treasure.
ə stands for a in about, e in taken,
i in pencil, o in lemon, and u in circus.

dolphin   An animal that lives in the sea and is related to the whale. Dolphins have a snout that is like a beak, and two flippers. Although a dolphin looks like a fish, it is a mammal. Dolphins are very intelligent animals.
   dol·phin (dol′fin) *noun, plural* **dolphins.**

Dolphin

domain   All the land that is controlled by a ruler or government. The young knight was the bravest man in the king's *domain.*
   do·main (dō mān′) *noun, plural* **domains.**

dome   A round roof that looks something like an upside-down cup. Domes are built on a base that is circular or has many sides. Some churches and some public buildings have domes.
   dome (dōm) *noun, plural* **domes.**

Dome

domestic   **1.** Having to do with the home and family. Mr. and Mrs. Brown take turns doing the cleaning, cooking, and other *domestic* chores in their house. **2.** Not wild; tame. Dogs and cats are *domestic* animals. **3.** Having to do with one's own country; not foreign. The Prime Minister of Canada must make decisions on both foreign and *domestic* affairs.
   do·mes·tic (də mes′tik) *adjective.*

domesticate   To train or change a wild animal so that it can live with or be used by people; tame. Man first *domesticated* wild horses to pull loads and help him in farming.
   do·mes·ti·cate (də mes′tə kāt′) *verb,* **domesticated, domesticating.**

dominant   Most powerful or important. Britain was the *dominant* country in the world for many years. Blue is the *dominant* colour in our kitchen.
   dom·i·nant (dom′ə nənt) *adjective.*

dominate   To rule or control because of power, strength, or importance. The Roman Empire *dominated* a large part of the world 2000 years ago.
   dom·i·nate (dom′ə nāt′) *verb,* **dominated, dominating.**

dominion   A land or territory that is controlled by a ruler or government.
   do·min·ion (də min′yən) *noun, plural* **dominions.**

Dominion Day   A holiday celebrated on July 1 in honour of Confederation. This holiday is now called **Canada Day.**

domino   **1.** One of a set of small black tiles marked with dots used in playing a game. **2. dominoes.** The game played with these tiles.
   dom·i·no (dom′ə nō′) *noun, plural* **dominoes.**

donate   To give to; contribute. The family *donated* their old clothes to the poor.
   do·nate (dō′nāt) *verb,* **donated, donating.**

donation   A gift; contribution. The hospital fund received *donations* of more than $1000 from the businessmen in our town.
   do·na·tion (dō nā′shən) *noun, plural* **donations.**

done   The carpenters have *done* a very good job on our house. Look up **do** for more information. *Verb.*
   —Cooked. When the meat is *done,* we can start our dinner. *Adjective.*
   done (dun) *verb; adjective.*

donkey   An animal that looks very much like a small horse. Donkeys have longer ears and a shorter mane than horses do. They are often used to pull or carry loads.
   don·key (dong′kē) *noun, plural* **donkeys.**

Donkey

don't   Please *don't* tell anyone else the secret I told you.
   don't (dōnt) contraction for "do not."

doom   Something causing pain, ruin, or

death; a terrible fate. The mountain climber met his *doom* when the rope he was holding snapped. *Noun.*
—To fix the result of something before it happens, especially when the result is bad. Until his recent success, the writer felt that he was *doomed* to fail. *Verb.*

doom (dōōm) *noun, plural* **dooms;** *verb,* **doomed, dooming.**

door A movable part that is used to open or close an entrance in something. Doors are usually made of wood, metal, or glass.

door (dōr) *noun, plural* **doors.**

doorbell A bell or buzzer that someone who is outside a door rings to show that he wants to come in.

door·bell (dōr′bel′) *noun, plural* **doorbells.**

doorstep A step or flight of steps leading from the outside door of a building to the ground or sidewalk.

door·step (dōr′step′) *noun, plural* **doorsteps.**

doorway An opening in a wall that leads in and out of a room or building and is closed by a door.

door·way (dōr′wā′) *noun, plural* **doorways.**

dope 1. A very stupid person. 2. Opium, heroin, or some similar drug. ▲ These two meanings are used mostly in everyday conversation. 3. A varnish or similar liquid. Dope is used in building models of airplanes.

dope (dōp) *noun, plural* **dopes.**

dormant Not active for a period of time. The volcano which had been *dormant* for years suddenly erupted.

dor·mant (dōr′mənt) *adjective.*

dormitory A building in which there are many bedrooms. Many universities have dormitories where students live.

dor·mi·to·ry (dōr′mə tōr′ē) *noun, plural* **dormitories.**

dormouse A small animal that is like a squirrel. Dormice have brown or grey fur. They go to sleep, or hibernate, in the winter.

dor·mouse (dōr′mous′) *noun, plural* **dormice.**

dory A rowboat that has a flat bottom and high sides. Fishermen often use dories.

do·ry (dōr′ē) *noun, plural* **dories.**

Dormouse

dose The amount of medicine that a person is given at one time. The doctor prescribed a small *dose* of aspirin for the boy who had a fever.

dose (dōs) *noun, plural* **doses.**

dot A small, round mark; small spot or speck. When the ink spattered, it left *dots* of ink on the desk. The *dot* on the map showed the exact location of the town. *Noun.*
—1. To mark with a dot or dots. In the summer, Michael's face is *dotted* with freckles. 2. To be scattered here and there. Small houses *dotted* the seashore. *Verb.*

dot (dot) *noun, plural* **dots;** *verb,* **dotted, dotting.**

dote To give too much affection. The grandparents *doted* on their only grandchild and spoiled him a little.

dote (dōt) *verb,* **doted, doting.**

double 1. Twice as many or as much; twice as large or as strong. A person who is six years old is *double* the age of a person who is three years old. 2. Having or made up of two parts. People stood in a *double* line in front of the theatre. The man led a *double* life as a businessman and a spy. *Adjective.*
—Two instead of one; in pairs. The ride on the merry-go-round made Helen feel dizzy and see everything *double. Adverb.*
—1. Something that is twice as much. Ten is the *double* of five. 2. A person or thing that is very much or just like another. Christopher is the *double* of his father. 3. A hit in baseball in which the batter goes to second base. *Noun.*
—1. To make or become twice as many or as much. John's parents *doubled* his weekly allowance from twenty-five cents to fifty cents. 2. To bend, fold, or turn over or back. The funny story made Harry *double* over with laughter. 3. To hit a double in baseball. *Verb.*

dou·ble (dub′əl) *adjective; adverb; noun, plural* **doubles;** *verb,* **doubled, doubling.**

double-cross To cheat or betray someone by not doing what one has promised. The robber *double-crossed* his partner by running off with the money that they were supposed to share.

dou·ble-cross (dub′əl krôs′) *verb,* **double-crossed, double-crossing.**

at; āpe; cär; end; mē; it; īce; hot; ōld; wood; fōōl; oil; out; up; turn; sing; thin; this; hw in white; zh in treasure. ə stands for a in about, e in taken, i in pencil, o in lemon, and u in circus.

195

double-header Two baseball games between the same teams that are played one right after the other on the same day.
dou·ble-head·er (dub′əl hed′ər) *noun, plural* **double-headers.**

double play A play in baseball in which two runners are put out.

doubt To not believe or trust; be unsure. The judge *doubted* that the prisoner was telling the truth. I brought my umbrella with me, even though I *doubt* that it will rain. *Verb.*
—**1.** A feeling of not believing or trusting. Jim had *doubts* about the honesty of the man who was trying to sell him the car. **2.** A state of being undecided or unsure. The result of the race was in *doubt* until the horses reached the finish line. *Noun.*
doubt (dout) *verb,* **doubted, doubting;** *noun, plural* **doubts.**

doubtful Feeling, showing, or causing doubt; not sure or certain. The team was *doubtful* about its chances of winning the big game.
doubt·ful (dout′fəl) *adjective.*

doubtless Without doubt; certainly. Maria draws so well that she will *doubtless* become an artist someday.
doubt·less (dout′ləs) *adverb.*

dough A thick mixture of flour, liquid, and other ingredients that is used to make bread, cookies, pie crusts, and other food. ▲ Another word that sounds like this is **doe.**
dough (dō) *noun, plural* **doughs.**

doughnut A small, round cake that usually has a hole in the middle. A doughnut is cooked in fat.
dough·nut (dō′nut′) *noun, plural* **doughnuts.**

Douglas fir *Canadian.* A large fir tree. It is the largest tree native to Canada.
Doug·las fir (dug′ləs).

Doukhobor A member of a Christian church founded in Russia. Thousands of Doukhobors settled in western Canada about a hundred years ago. One branch of the Doukhobors is **Sons of Freedom.** This word is also spelled **Dukhobor.**
Douk·ho·bor (doo′kə bōr) *noun, plural* **Doukhobors.**

dove[1] A bird that has a thick body and short legs. It makes a cooing sound. A dove is a kind of pigeon. A white dove is sometimes used as a symbol of peace.
dove (duv) *noun, plural* **doves.**

dove[2] The girl *dove* from the rocks into the lake. Look up **dive** for more information.
dove (dōv) *verb.*

down[1] From a higher to a lower place. The painter climbed *down* from the ladder. The noisy crowd quieted *down*. The price of milk has gone *down*. *Adverb.*
—Down along, through, or into something. Jeff met a friend of his as he walked *down* the street. *Preposition.*
—To bring or put down. Father tackled the escaping burglar and *downed* him. *Verb.*
—One of three chances that a football team gets to move the ball ten yards (about nine metres). If it does not move the ball that far, the other team gets possession of the ball. *Noun.*
down (doun) *adverb; preposition; verb,* **downed, downing;** *noun, plural* **downs.**

down[2] Fine, soft feathers. Baby birds have *down* until their regular feathers grow in.
down (doun) *noun.*

down East *Canadian.* **1.** The Maritimes. My uncle is a cod fisherman *down East.* **2.** Central Canada, to anyone living in the West.

downpour A very heavy rain.
down·pour (doun′pōr′) *noun, plural* **downpours.**

downright Thorough; complete. The rumour about him is a *downright* lie. *Adjective.*
—Thoroughly; completely. She was *downright* nasty when I asked her to help me. *Adverb.*
down·right (doun′rīt′) *adjective; adverb.*

downstairs **1.** Down the stairs. **2.** On or to a lower floor. While Sandy was in her room, she could hear her parents talking *downstairs.*
down·stairs (doun′sterz′) *adverb.*

downstream In the direction in which a stream flows. Dick didn't have to paddle the canoe as it drifted *downstream.* The *downstream* current is very strong.
down·stream (doun′strēm′) *adverb; adjective.*

downtown To or in the main part or business district of a town. Peter went *downtown* to see a movie. The *downtown* stores are larger than the ones in our neighbourhood.
down·town (doun′toun′) *adverb; adjective.*

downward From a higher to a lower place. The road is level and then goes *downward* into the valley. This word is also spelled **downwards.** *Adverb.*
—Moving from a higher place to a lower place. The hikers followed the *downward* course of the stream from the mountain top. *Adjective.*
down·ward (doun′wərd) *adverb; adjective.*

dowry The money or property that a woman brings to her husband when she gets married.
dow·ry (dour′ē) *noun, plural* **dowries.**

doze To sleep lightly or for a short time; take a nap. The truck driver pulled off the road when he realized that he was starting to *doze.*
doze (dōz) *verb,* **dozed, dozing.**

Dragon

dozen A group of twelve. The grocery store sells eggs by the *dozen.* She bought three *dozen* doughnuts.
doz·en (duz′ən) *noun, plural* **dozens** or **dozen.**

drab Not cheerful or bright; dull. The dark, *drab* room was much nicer after we put up new curtains.
drab (drab) *adjective,* **drabber, drabbest.**

draft 1. A current of air in an enclosed space. Emily felt a cold *draft* from the open window. 2. A device that controls the flow of air in something. Furnaces, fireplaces, and some stoves have drafts. 3. A sketch, plan, or rough copy of something. The author wrote three different *drafts* of his novel. 4. The selecting of a person or persons for some special purpose. *Noun.*
—1. To make a sketch, plan, or rough copy of something. David *drafted* the letter in pencil and then typed it. 2. To select a person or persons for some special purpose. The politician was *drafted* by his party to run for mayor. *Verb.*
—Used for pulling loads. Elephants are used as *draft* animals in some countries. *Adjective.*
draft (draft) *noun, plural* **drafts;** *verb,* **drafted, drafting;** *adjective.*

draftsman A person who draws or designs plans for machinery, buildings, and other things.
drafts·man (drafts′mən) *noun, plural* **draftsmen.**

drag 1. To pull or move along slowly or heavily. He *dragged* the heavy trunk across the room. Time *dragged* on while we waited for the train that was late. 2. To search the bottom of a body of water with a hook or net. The fisherman anxiously *dragged* the bottom of the lake looking for the sunken rowboat. *Verb.*
drag (drag) *verb,* **dragged, dragging.**

dragon An imaginary beast that is supposed to look something like a giant lizard with claws and wings. Dragons are supposed to breathe out fire.
drag·on (drag′ən) *noun, plural* **dragons.**

dragonfly A large insect that has a thin body and two pairs of wings. Dragonflies eat mosquitoes and other insects. They live near fresh water.
drag·on·fly (drag′ən-flī′) *noun, plural* **dragonflies.**

Dragonfly

drain 1. To empty water or other liquid from something. The workers *drained* the water from the swimming pool at the end of the summer. 2. To tire or use up; exhaust. The long hike *drained* our energy. *Verb.*
—1. An opening, pipe, or other device that draws off water or another liquid. The *drain* in the sink is clogged. 2. Something that uses up or exhausts. Buying the bicycle was a *drain* on my savings. *Noun.*
drain (drān) *verb,* **drained, draining;** *noun, plural* **drains.**

drainage A drawing off or emptying of water or other liquid. The *drainage* of the swamp land made it possible for the farmer to plant crops there.
drain·age (drān′ij) *noun.*

drake A male duck.
drake (drāk) *noun, plural* **drakes.**

drama 1. A story that is written for actors to perform on the stage; play. 2. A happening that is as exciting or interesting as a play. The newspaper story reported the *drama* of the

at; āpe; cär; end; mē; it; īce; hot; ōld;
wood; fōōl; oil; out; up; turn; sing;
thin; this; hw in white; zh in treasure.
ə stands for a in about, e in taken,
i in pencil, o in lemon, and u in circus.

firemen's rescue of the family from the burning building.

dra·ma (dra′mə *or* dräm′ə) *noun, plural* **dramas.**

dramatic **1.** Of or having to do with plays or acting. My older brother is taking *dramatic* lessons. **2.** As exciting and interesting as a play. Our team won a *dramatic* victory by tying the score and then going ahead in the last minutes of the game.

dra·mat·ic (drə mat′ik) *adjective.*

dramatist A person who writes plays.

dram·a·tist (dram′ə tist) *noun, plural* **dramatists.**

dramatize **1.** To write or perform something as a play. The members of the Sunday school class *dramatized* several stories from the Bible. **2.** To make something seem very exciting. Pat *dramatized* what happened on her vacation so that it sounded like a real adventure.

dram·a·tize (dram′ə tīz′) *verb,* **dramatized, dramatizing.**

drank Mark *drank* three glasses of water. Look up **drink** for more information.

drank (drangk) *verb.*

drape To cover or decorate with cloth that hangs loosely. The woman *draped* a shawl over her shoulders. *Verb.*
—Cloth that is hung at a window; drapery. Christine opened the *drapes* to let sunlight into the room. *Noun.*

drape (drāp) *verb,* **draped, draping;** *noun, plural* **drapes.**

drapery Cloth that is hung in loose folds. Draperies are usually used as window curtains.

drap·er·y (drā′pər ē) *noun, plural* **draperies.**

drastic Very strong or harsh; extreme. Forbidding automobiles on the main street was the *drastic* measure that the town took to stop air pollution.

dras·tic (dras′tik) *adjective.*

draw **1.** To bring or move in a particular direction or to a particular position. The farmer used horses to *draw* his wagon. The cowboy *drew* his gun and fired. I will have to *draw* money from my savings to pay for my brother's birthday present. The popular singer always *draws* a large crowd to his concerts. **2.** To make a picture of something. People usually *draw* with a pencil, pen, or crayons. **3.** To cause or allow a current of air to pass. The chimney does not *draw* well because it is blocked with dead leaves. *Verb.*
—**1.** The act of drawing. The cowboy was quick on the *draw* and fired first. **2.** A game or

contest in which the players or teams have the same score; tie. The chess game ended in a *draw. Noun.*

draw (drä) *verb,* **drew, drawn, drawing;** *noun, plural* **draws.**

drawback A thing that makes something more difficult or unpleasant; disadvantage. The main *drawback* of our new house is that it is so far away from my school.

draw·back (drä′bak′) *noun, plural* **drawbacks.**

drawbridge A kind of bridge that can be raised or lowered, or moved to one side. Drawbridges are sometimes used over water so that tall boats or ships can pass through when the bridge is raised. In olden times, castles had drawbridges which could be raised to keep enemies from crossing the water around the castle.

draw·bridge (drä′brij′) *noun, plural* **drawbridges.**

Drawbridge

drawer A box that fits into a piece of furniture and can be pulled out and pushed in. Bureaus, desks, and cabinets have drawers.

draw·er (drôr) *noun, plural* **drawers.**

drawing **1.** A picture or design made with a pencil, pen, crayon, or similar thing. **2.** The choosing of a winning chance or ticket in a lottery or raffle. The *drawing* for the winning number will be next Saturday night.

draw·ing (drä′ing) *noun, plural* **drawings.**

drawl To speak in a slow or lazy way. The sleepy boy *drawled* his answer to the question. *Verb.*
—A slow way of speaking. Many people from the southern part of the United States speak with a *drawl. Noun.*

drawl (dräl) *verb,* **drawled, drawling;** *noun,* *plural* **drawls.**

drawmaster The person in charge of organizing a curling tournament.
draw·mas·ter (drä′mas′tər) *noun,* *plural* **drawmasters.**

drawn The artist has *drawn* many sketches of the church. Look up **draw** for more information.
drawn (drän) *verb.*

dread To look forward to with fear; be afraid about something that has not happened yet. I *dread* going to the dentist. *Verb.*
—A feeling of fear about what may happen. Jimmy thought of the airplane trip with *dread* because he was scared of flying. *Noun.*
—Causing fear; dreadful. Polio is one of the *dread* diseases that modern medicine has almost completely wiped out. *Adjective.*
dread (dred) *verb,* **dreaded, dreading;** *noun;* *adjective.*

dreadful 1. Very frightening; terrible. The *dreadful* storm caused floods that destroyed many homes. 2. Very bad; awful. I saw a *dreadful* movie on television last night.
dread·ful (dred′fəl) *adjective.*

dream 1. A series of thoughts or feelings that a person has while asleep. Linda had a *dream* last night that she was able to fly. 2. An idea that is like a dream but is thought by a person who is awake; daydream. Peter's great *dream* is to become an actor. *Noun.*
—1. To see, feel, or think about in a dream. Fred dozed off and *dreamed* about riding a horse. 2. To imagine. I never *dreamed* it would rain, so I didn't take an umbrella. *Verb.*
dream (drēm) *noun,* *plural* **dreams;** *verb,* **dreamed** or **dreamt, dreaming.**

The word **dream** probably comes from an old German word that means "to fool or trick." Often dreams are so real that they fool us and make us think that something that was only a dream really did happen.

dreamt Robin *dreamt* that she and Jack had a fight.
dreamt (dremt) *verb.*

dreary Sad or dull; gloomy. Painting the dark room bright yellow made it less *dreary.*
drear·y (drēr′ē) *adjective,* **drearier, dreariest.**

dredge A large machine that scoops up mud, sand, and other material from the bottom of a body of water. The engineers used a *dredge* to make the canal deeper. *Noun.*
—To clean out or deepen with a dredge. The machine *dredged* mud from the river. *Verb.*

dredge (drej) *noun,* *plural* **dredges;** *verb,* **dredged, dredging.**

dregs Small pieces that settle at the bottom of a liquid. There was nothing left of the coffee but the *dregs* at the bottom of the cup.
dregs (dregz) *noun plural.*

drench To make something completely wet; soak. The big wave *drenched* the boys on the raft.
drench (drench) *verb,* **drenched, drenching.**

dress 1. A garment for a woman or girl. A dress usually looks like a blouse and skirt that have been sewn together. 2. Clothing or a particular style of clothing. The guests at the ball were all wearing formal *dress. Noun.*
—1. To put clothes on. Lisa *dressed* quickly because she was late for school. 2. To arrange, prepare, or treat something. The butcher *dressed* the turkey by cutting off its head and feet. The doctor *dressed* the boy's wound and bandaged it. *Verb.*
dress (dres) *noun,* *plural* **dresses;** *verb,* **dressed, dressing.**

dresser A piece of furniture that has drawers for storing clothes and other things. A dresser often has a large mirror attached to it.
dress·er (dres′ər) *noun,* *plural* **dressers.**

dressing 1. A sauce that is put on salads and some other foods. 2. A mixture of bread crumbs and seasonings used to stuff turkey or chicken. 3. A medicine or bandage that is put on a wound or sore.
dress·ing (dres′ing) *noun,* *plural* **dressings.**

drew Mitchell *drew* a funny picture of his uncle. Look up **draw** for more information.
drew (drōō) *verb.*

dribble 1. To flow or let flow in small drops; trickle. Rain *dribbled* through the cracks in the roof. 2. To move a ball along by bouncing or kicking it. Players *dribble* the ball in basketball and soccer. *Verb.*
—A dripping; trickle. A *dribble* of juice from the plum ran down Kevin's chin. *Noun.*
drib·ble (drib′əl) *verb,* **dribbled, dribbling;** *noun,* *plural* **dribbles.**

dried Mary washed her hair and then *dried* it. Look up **dry** for more information.
dried (drīd) *verb.*

at; āpe; cär; end; mē; it; īce; hot; ōld; wood; fōōl; oil; out; up; turn; sing; thin; this; hw in white; zh in treasure. ə stands for a in about, e in taken, i in pencil, o in lemon, and u in circus.

drier The clothes were *drier* after they had been hanging on the line for an hour. Look up **dry** for more information. *Adjective.*
—A machine that dries something. This word is usually spelled **dryer**. Look up **dryer** for more information. *Noun.*

dri·er (drī′ər) *adjective; noun, plural* **driers.**

dries Short hair *dries* faster than long hair.

dries (drīz) *verb.*

driest The cave was the *driest* place we could find during the storm. Look up **dry** for more information.

dri·est (drī′əst) *adjective.*

drift To move or pile up because of a current of air or water. The fisherman stopped rowing and let his boat *drift* downstream. Smoke from the fire *drifted* up into the sky. *Verb.*
—Something that has been moved along or piled up by air or water currents. The storm caused *drifts* of snow more than two metres deep. *Noun.*

drift (drift) *verb,* **drifted, drifting;** *noun, plural* **drifts.**

driftwood Wood that floats on water or is brought to the shore by water.

drift·wood (drift′wood′) *noun, plural* **driftwoods.**

Drill

drill 1. A tool that is used to cut holes in wood, plastic, and other hard material. A drill usually has a long, pointed end that is turned with a crank or by an electric motor. 2. Training or teaching by making someone do something again and again; practice. For our social studies *drill,* the teacher asked us to name the capital of each province. *Noun.*
—1. To make a hole in something with a drill; use a drill. The carpenter *drilled* a hole in the wood. The company *drilled* for oil in Alberta. 2. To train or teach a person by having him do something again and again. The school band *drilled* by marching back and forth. *Verb.*

drill (dril) *noun, plural* **drills;** *verb,* **drilled, drilling.**

drink 1. To swallow a liquid. I *drink* a glass of milk with every meal. 2. To soak up. The plants *drank* in the rain. 3. To drink an alcoholic beverage. *Verb.*
—1. A liquid for drinking. Lemonade is my favourite *drink* in the summer. 2. A portion of liquid. The tennis players stopped to have a *drink* of orange juice. 3. An alcoholic beverage. *Noun.*

drink (dringk) *verb,* **drank, drunk, drinking;** *noun, plural* **drinks.**

drip To fall or let fall in drops. Raindrops *dripped* from the trees. He *dripped* paint from the brush onto his shirt. *Verb.*
—A falling of liquid in drops. There was a *drip* of water from the broken pipe. *Noun.*

drip (drip) *verb,* **dripped, dripping;** *noun, plural* **drips.**

drive 1. To use and steer a car or other vehicle. My father says he will teach me to *drive* when I am sixteen years old. The farmer *drove* his truck to the market. 2. To go or be carried in a car or other vehicle. We plan to *drive* to the city on Saturday. 3. To cause to move, work, or go. Strong winds *drove* the sailboat onto the rocks. The carpenter used a hammer to *drive* the nail into the board. The baseball player tried to *drive* the ball over the fence for a home run. My brother's constant teasing *drives* me crazy. *Verb.*
—1. A trip in a car or other vehicle. The *drive* to the city was unpleasant because there was so much traffic. 2. A road or driveway. She parked the car in the *drive* and walked to the front door. 3. A strong hit. In the golf tournament, Johnny hit a *drive* more than 250 metres. 4. A special effort to do something. The town started a *drive* to raise money for a new hospital. *Noun.*

drive (drīv) *verb,* **drove, driven, driving;** *noun, plural* **drives.**

drive-in A restaurant, movie theatre, or bank that can take care of customers in their cars.

drive-in (drīv′in′) *noun, plural* **drive-ins.**

driver A person who drives an automobile, truck, or other vehicle.

driv·er (drīv′ər) *noun, plural* **drivers.**

driveway A private road that leads to a house, garage, or other building from a road or street.

drive·way (drīv′wā′) *noun, plural* **driveways.**

dromedary A kind of camel that has one hump. Dromedaries live in Arabia and North Africa.

drom·e·dar·y (drom′ə der′ē) *noun, plural* **dromedaries.**

Dromedary

drone¹ A male bee that does no work.

drone (drōn) *noun, plural* **drones.**

drone² **1.** To make a low, continuous humming sound. The small airplane *droned* as it climbed higher. **2.** To talk in a dull, boring way. People began to leave when the speaker *droned* on and on about his experiences. *Verb.*
—A low, continuous humming sound. The *drone* of the car's engine could be heard down the road. *Noun.*

drone (drōn) *verb,* **droned, droning;** *noun, plural* **drones.**

drool To let saliva drip from the mouth. The baby *drooled* on his bib.

drool (drōol) *verb,* **drooled, drooling.**

droop To hang or sink down; sag. The little girl's eyelids *drooped* and she was soon asleep.

droop (drōop) *verb,* **drooped, drooping.**

drop **1.** To fall or cause to fall to a lower position; move or fall down. The wet dish *dropped* from Kathy's hand. Philip tripped and *dropped* the book he was carrying. The temperature *dropped* to below freezing on Hallowe'en. **2.** To stop doing something. Ricky decided to *drop* out of school and get a job. **3.** To do or give something in a casual way. My aunt *dropped* in to see us last week. Natalie always *drops* a hint about what she wants for her birthday. **4.** To leave out. Although Susan knits carefully, she sometimes accidentally *drops* a stitch. *Verb.*
—**1.** A very small amount of liquid. A drop is usually shaped like a tiny ball. There was a *drop* of blood on Margaret's hand where the cat had scratched her. **2.** The act of dropping

or falling. The weatherman said there would be a *drop* in temperature tonight. **3.** The distance between one thing and another thing that is below it. From the tree branch to the ground was a *drop* of three metres. *Noun.*

drop (drop) *verb,* **dropped** or **dropt, dropping;** *noun, plural* **drops.**

drought A long period of time when there is very little rain or no rain at all.

drought (drout) *noun, plural* **droughts.**

drove¹ We *drove* downtown in the car. Look up **drive** for more information.

drove (drōv) *verb.*

drove² **1.** A group of animals that move or are driven along together. The cowboys brought a *drove* of cattle to the ranch. **2.** A large number of people; crowd. People went to the beach in *droves* on the hot summer day.

drove (drōv) *noun, plural* **droves.**

drown **1.** To die in water because there is no air to breathe. The lifeguard saved the girl as she was about to *drown.* **2.** To kill by keeping under water or another liquid. Two people were *drowned* in the flood. **3.** To cover up the sound of something by a louder sound. We tried to say good-bye, but the roar of the airplane engines *drowned* out our words.

drown (droun) *verb,* **drowned, drowning.**

drowsy Half asleep; sleepy. George felt *drowsy* after dinner and decided to take a nap.

drow·sy (drou′zē) *adjective,* **drowsier, drowsiest.**

drug **1.** A chemical or other substance that makes a change in a person's body. Most drugs are used to treat or cure diseases. **2.** A substance to which a person can become addicted. Heroin is a drug. *Noun.*
—To give a drug to a person. The nurse *drugged* the patient so that he would sleep. *Verb.*

drug (drug) *noun, plural* **drugs;** *verb,* **drugged, drugging.**

druggist **1.** A person who has a licence to make and sell medicine; pharmacist. **2.** A person who owns or runs a drugstore.

drug·gist (drug′ist) *noun, plural* **druggists.**

drugstore A store where medicines and drugs are sold. Drugstores often also sell

at; āpe; cär; end; mē; it; īce; hot; ōld;
wood; fōol; oil; out; up; turn; sing;
thin; this; hw in white; zh in treasure.
ə stands for a in about, e in taken,
i in pencil, o in lemon, and u in circus.

201

cosmetics, candy, cigarettes, magazines, and various other things.

drug·store (drug′stōr′) *noun, plural* **drug-stores.**

drum **1.** A musical instrument that makes a sound when it is beaten. A drum is a hollow object that is covered at the top and at the bottom with material that is stretched very tight. A person who plays a drum hits the material with a stick or with his hand. **2.** Something that is shaped like a drum. The oil was stored in large metal *drums. Noun.*
—**1.** To beat or play on a drum. **2.** To make a sound like a drum. The bored student *drummed* on the desk with his fingers. **3.** To force into a person's head by repeating. He finally *drummed* the idea into her head that he didn't like to be called by his nickname. *Verb.*
  drum (drum) *noun, plural* **drums;** *verb,* **drummed, drumming.**

A Set of Drums

drum major A person who leads a marching band.

drum majorette A girl who twirls a baton while marching with a band in a parade.
  drum ma·jor·ette (mā′jə ret′).

drumstick **1.** A stick used for beating a drum. **2.** The lower part of the leg of a cooked chicken or turkey.
  drum·stick (drum′stik′) *noun, plural* **drum-sticks.**

drunk Have you *drunk* your milk yet? Look up **drink** for more information. *Verb.*
—Having had too much alcoholic liquor to drink. *Adjective.*
—A person who has had or often has too much alcoholic liquor to drink. *Noun.*
  drunk (drungk) *verb; adjective,* **drunker, drunkest;** *noun, plural* **drunks.**

dry **1.** Not wet or damp; with very little or

no water or other liquid. The farmer had to bring water from the stream because the well was *dry.* Cactus plants grow well in a *dry* desert climate. **2.** Not in or under water. After the long voyage, the sailors were happy to be back on *dry* land again. **3.** Thirsty. Frank was so *dry* after playing tennis that he drank three glasses of water. **4.** Not interesting; dull. The book was so *dry* that Janet fell asleep while reading it. *Adjective.*
—To make or become dry. If you wash the dishes, I'll *dry* them. *Verb.*
  dry (drī) *adjective,* **drier, driest;** *verb,* **dried, drying.**

dry cell An electric cell in which the substance that conducts the electrical current is made of a paste so that it will not spill.

dry-clean To clean clothes by using chemicals instead of water.
  dry-clean (drī′klēn′) *verb,* **dry-cleaned, dry-cleaning.**

dryer A machine or device for drying something. Jim put the wet laundry in the clothes *dryer.* This word is also spelled **drier.**
  dry·er (drī′ər) *noun, plural* **dryers.**

dry goods Cloth, thread, lace, ribbons, and the like.

dual Made up of or having two parts. The driving instructor used a car that had *dual* controls so that he could stop the car if a student made a bad mistake in driving. ▲ Another word that sounds like this is **duel.**
  du·al (dōō′əl *or* dyōō′əl) *adjective.*

duchess The wife or widow of a duke.
  duch·ess (duch′əs) *noun, plural* **duchesses.**

duck¹ **1.** A bird that has a broad, flat bill and webbed feet that help it to swim. There are both wild and tame ducks. Tame ducks are often raised for food. **2.** A female duck. The male is often called a drake.
  duck (duk) *noun, plural* **ducks.**

duck² **1.** To push someone under water suddenly. Jake swam behind Don and playfully *ducked* him. **2.** To lower the head or bend down quickly. Jerry *ducked* his head to keep from being hit by the ball.
  duck (duk) *verb,* **ducked, ducking.**

Duck

duckling A young duck.
    duck·ling (duk′ling) *noun, plural* **ducklings.**

duct A tube, pipe, or channel that carries a liquid or air. Tears are formed in glands behind the eyes and are carried to the eyes by tiny ducts. Ducts are used in some buildings to carry hot or cold air to rooms.
    duct (dukt) *noun, plural* **ducts.**

due **1.** Owed or owing. If you don't return your library book when it is *due*, you will have to pay a fine. **2.** Expected or supposed to arrive or be ready. *Adjective.*
—**1.** Something that is owed. You should give him his *due* and congratulate him for beating you in the contest. **2. dues.** A fee that a person pays to a club to be a member. *Noun.*
—Straight; directly. The explorers walked *due* west toward the setting sun. *Adverb.*
    due (dōō *or* dyōō) *adjective; noun, plural* **dues;** *adverb.*

duel A formal fight between two people with swords or pistols. *Noun.*
—To fight a duel. *Verb.* ▲ Another word that sounds like this is **dual.**
    du·el (dōō′əl *or* dyōō′əl) *noun, plural* **duels;** *verb,* **duelled, duelling** *or* **dueled, dueling.**

duet A piece of music written for two singers or two musical instruments.
    du·et (dōō et′ *or* dyōō et′) *noun, plural* **duets.**

dug The men *dug* a hole and planted a tree in it. Look up **dig** for more information.
    dug (dug) *verb.*

dugout **1.** A long shelter in which baseball players sit when they are not playing. Dugouts are built at the side of the field and usually have a roof and three sides. **2.** A rough shelter that is made by digging a hole in the ground or in the side of a hill. **3.** A canoe or boat that is made by hollowing out a large log. **4.** *Canadian.* A long, shallow hole to catch raindrops or melting snow and ice. On the Prairies dugouts are used to supply water for cattle or for crops.
    dug·out (dug′out′) *noun, plural* **dugouts.**

duke A nobleman who has the highest rank below a prince.
    duke (dōōk *or* dyōōk) *noun, plural* **dukes.**

Dukhobor A member of a Christian church founded in Russia. This word is usually spelled **Doukhobor.** Look up **Doukhobor** for more information.

dull **1.** Not sharp or pointed; blunt. The knife was so *dull* that Matthew could not cut the steak. **2.** Not interesting; plain or boring. The movie was so *dull* that Keith left before it was over. **3.** Slow to learn or understand;

not intelligent. A person would have to be very *dull* not to understand that joke. **4.** Not bright, clear, or distinct. The barn was painted a *dull* red. Marcia felt a *dull* ache in her legs for several days after the long hike. *Adjective.*
—To make or become dull. Using the kitchen scissors for cutting wire *dulled* them. *Verb.*
    dull (dul) *adjective,* **duller, dullest;** *verb,* **dulled, dulling.**

dumb **1.** Not able to speak. Although she was born deaf and *dumb*, she learned to communicate through sign language. We were struck *dumb* by the surprising news. **2.** Stupid. You have to be really *dumb* to fall for such a silly trick.
    dumb (dum) *adjective,* **dumber, dumbest.**

dummy **1.** A figure that is made to look like a person. The *dummy* in the department store window was dressed in a wedding dress. **2.** Something that is made to look like something else that is real. The actor's gun was a *dummy.*
    dum·my (dum′ē) *noun, plural* **dummies.**

dump To drop, unload, or empty. The truck *dumped* the gravel on the sidewalk. Michael *dumped* his books on the table. *Verb.*
—A place where garbage and trash are dumped. At the end of the day, the garbage trucks unloaded at the city *dump. Noun.*
    dump (dump) *verb,* **dumped, dumping;** *noun, plural* **dumps.**

dune A mound or ridge of sand that has been piled up by the wind.
    dune (dōōn *or* dyōōn) *noun, plural* **dunes.**

Dune

dungaree **1.** A heavy cotton cloth that is used to make work clothes, sportswear, and sails. **2. dungarees.** Pants or work clothes that are made from this cloth.

at; āpe; cär; end; mē; it; īce; hot; ōld;
wood; fōōl; oil; out; up; turn; sing;
thin; this; hw in white; zh in treasure.
ə stands for a in about, e in taken,
i in pencil, o in lemon, and u in circus.

dun·ga·ree (dung′gə rē′) *noun, plural* **dun-garees.**

dungeon A dark prison or cell that is built underground. The king's guards captured the traitor and put him in the *dungeon* of the castle.

dun·geon (dun′jən) *noun, plural* **dungeons.**

duplicate Just like something else. My parents gave me a *duplicate* key to our front door. *Adjective.*
—Something that is just like something else; exact copy. William liked the snapshot so much that I had a *duplicate* made for him. *Noun.*
—To make an exact copy of something. The secretary *duplicated* the letter so that she would have a copy after she mailed it. *Verb.*

du·pli·cate (doo′pli kət *or* dyoo′pli kət *for adjective and noun;* doo′pli kāt′ *or* dyoo′pli-kāt′ *for verb*) *adjective; noun, plural* **duplicates;** *verb,* **duplicated, duplicating.**

durable Able to last a long time in spite of much use or wear. My mother bought my brother *durable* shoes with heavy soles.

du·ra·ble (door′ə bəl *or* dyoor′ə bəl) *adjective.*

duration The length of time during which something continues. The doctor said that Nancy should stay in bed for the *duration* of her illness.

du·ra·tion (doo rā′shən *or* dyoo rā′shən) *noun, plural* **durations.**

during My grandparents always go away to the country *during* the summer. Joseph was awakened by a telephone call *during* the night.

dur·ing (door′ing *or* dyoor′ing) *preposition.*

dusk The time of day just before the sun goes down; twilight. The farmer worked in the fields from dawn to *dusk.*

dusk (dusk) *noun.*

dust Tiny pieces of earth, dirt, or other matter. The horse kicked up a cloud of *dust* as it galloped along the dirt road. *Noun.*
—**1.** To remove the dust from something by brushing or wiping. I *dusted* the table and then polished it with wax. **2.** To cover or sprinkle. The baker *dusted* the doughnuts with sugar. The farmer *dusted* his crops with a chemical that killed insects. *Verb.*

dust (dust) *noun; verb,* **dusted, dusting.**

Dutch Of or relating to the Netherlands, its people, or their language. *Adjective.*
—**1. the Dutch.** The people of the Netherlands. **2.** The language of the Netherlands. *Noun.*

Dutch (duch) *adjective; noun.*

duty **1.** Something that a person is supposed to do. Mr. Robinson said it was his *duty* as a citizen to vote in every election. Locking up the store at night was one of the manager's *duties.* **2.** A tax that is paid on goods that are brought into or taken out of a country.

du·ty (doo′tē *or* dyoo′tē) *noun, plural* **duties.**

dwarf **1.** A person, animal, or plant that is much smaller than the normal size. **2.** A little man in fairy tales who has magical powers. *Noun.*
—To make seem small. The skyscraper *dwarfed* the buildings around it. *Verb.*

dwarf (dwôrf) *noun, plural* **dwarfs** or **dwarves;** *verb,* **dwarfed, dwarfing.**

dwell To live in. After living in the country for many years, they decided to *dwell* in the city.

dwell (dwel) *verb,* **dwelt** or **dwelled, dwelling.**

dwelling A place where a person lives. We live in a two-family *dwelling.*

dwell·ing (dwel′ing) *noun, plural* **dwellings.**

dwindle To become less or smaller; shrink slowly. The crowd began to *dwindle* after the parade passed by.

dwin·dle (dwind′əl) *verb,* **dwindled, dwindling.**

dye A substance that is used to give a particular colour to cloth, hair, food, or other materials. *Noun.*
—To colour or stain something with a dye. When the blue curtains faded, my mother *dyed* them red. *Verb.* ▲ Another word that sounds like this is **die.**

dye (dī) *noun, plural* **dyes;** *verb,* **dyed, dyeing.**

dying Our sailboat slowed because the wind was *dying* down. Look up **die** for more information.

dy·ing (dī′ing) *verb.*

dynamic Having or showing a lot of energy; active; forceful. That *dynamic* young woman is sure to become a leader.

dy·nam·ic (dī nam′ik) *adjective.*

dynamite A substance that explodes with great force. Dynamite is used to blow up rocks. *Noun.*
—To blow something up with dynamite. The builders *dynamited* the rocks so that they could put a road through. *Verb.*

dy·na·mite (dī′nə mīt′) *noun; verb,* **dynamited, dynamiting.**

dynamo An electric motor or generator. Dynamos usually produce a direct current.

dy·na·mo (dī′nə mō′) *noun, plural* **dynamos.**

dynasty A series of rulers who belong to the same family.

dy·nas·ty (dī′nəs tē) *noun, plural* **dynasties.**

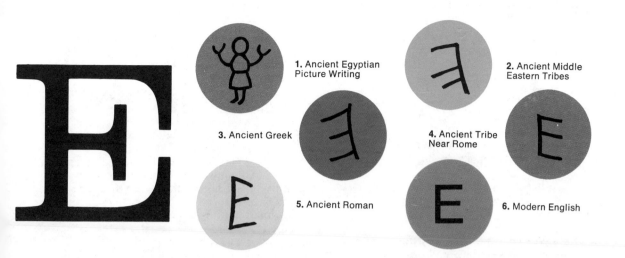

1. Ancient Egyptian Picture Writing
2. Ancient Middle Eastern Tribes
3. Ancient Greek
4. Ancient Tribe Near Rome
5. Ancient Roman
6. Modern English

E is the fifth letter of the alphabet. The oldest form of the letter **E** was a drawing that the ancient Egyptians (**1**) used in their picture writing nearly 5000 years ago. The drawing showed a person with his arms stretched out. Several ancient tribes (**2**) in the Middle East borrowed the drawing for their alphabet. They changed its shape by drawing it as a tall line with three or, sometimes, four short lines on the left side. This letter was used to stand for the *h* sound. When the ancient Greeks (**3**) borrowed this letter, they used it to stand for both the *h* sound and the *e* sound. Because they had another letter that stood for the *h* sound, the Greeks began to use this letter to stand for only the *e* sound. This Greek letter was borrowed by an ancient tribe (**4**) that settled north of Rome about 2800 years ago. They gave this letter its modern shape by turning the Greek letter around. The Romans (**5**) borrowed this new form of **E.** By about 2400 years ago, they were writing it almost the same way that we write the capital letter **E** today (**6**).

e, E   The fifth letter of the alphabet.
　e, E (ē) *noun, plural* **e's, E's.**

each   *Each* player gets a turn to hit the ball. My aunt gave *each* of us a piece of pie. These candies are ten cents *each.*
　each (ēch) *adjective; pronoun; adverb.*
　each other. One another. We see *each other* every day.

eager   Wanting very much to do something. A person who is eager is full of interest and enthusiasm. The boys were *eager* to go to the ball game.
　ea·ger (ē′gər) *adjective.*

eagle   A large, powerful bird. Eagles hunt and feed on small animals. They are known for their sharp eyesight and have strong claws. Eagles have large, strong wings, and they can fly very high in the sky.
　ea·gle (ē′gəl) *noun, plural* **eagles.**

ear¹   **1.** The part of the body with which people and animals hear. **2.** The sense of hearing. Her voice is soft and pleasing to the *ear.*
　ear (ēr) *noun, plural* **ears.**

ear²   The part of certain plants on which the grains or seeds grow. The grains of corn and wheat grow on ears.
　ear (ēr) *noun, plural* **ears.**

eardrum   The thin layer of tissue between the outer and middle parts of the ear. It moves back and forth when sound waves strike it.
　ear·drum (ēr′drum′) *noun, plural* **eardrums.**

earl   A nobleman in Britain.
　earl (url) *noun, plural* **earls.**

Eagle

205

early **1.** In or near the beginning. We started out on the hike in the *early* morning. Linda's birthday is *early* in March. **2.** Before the usual time. We had an *early* dinner so we all could watch the movie on television.
ear·ly (ur′lē) *adjective*, **earlier, earliest;** *adverb*.

earn **1.** To get as pay for work done. Larry *earned* fifty dollars mowing lawns. **2.** To deserve or win because of hard work. Leslie *earned* her high marks by studying hard. ▲ Another word that sounds like this is **urn.**
earn (urn) *verb*, **earned, earning.**

earnest Not joking or fooling about something. An earnest person is sincere and serious about what he says and does. John was being *earnest* when he said he was sorry for what he did.
ear·nest (ur′nəst) *adjective*.

earnings Money that has been earned; pay. Charlie put all his *earnings* in the bank to save up for a car.
earn·ings (ur′ningz) *noun plural*.

earphone A part of a machine that receives sound. Earphones are placed over or held at a person's ear so that he can listen.
ear·phone (ēr′fōn′) *noun, plural* **earphones.**

earring A piece of jewellery worn on the ear.
ear·ring (ēr′ring′) *noun, plural* **earrings.**

earth **1.** The planet that we live on. The earth is the fifth largest planet in the solar system. It is the third in order of distance from the sun. **2.** Dry land; the ground. After many weeks at sea, the sailors were glad to feel the *earth* under their feet again. **3.** Soil; dirt. Tom planted the seeds in the *earth*.
earth (urth) *noun, plural* **earths.**

earthen **1.** Made out of earth. The log cabin had an *earthen* floor. **2.** Made out of clay that has been baked and made hard. In the museum we saw *earthen* bowls made by Indians.
earth·en (ur′thən) *adjective*.

earthly **1.** Having to do with the earth or this world, rather than with heaven. The old man left all his *earthly* goods to his grandchildren. **2.** Possible; imaginable. These shoes are so old that they're of no *earthly* use to anyone.
earth·ly (urth′lē) *adjective*.

earthquake A shaking or trembling of the ground. Earthquakes are caused by rock, lava, or hot gases moving deep inside the earth. Some earthquakes are so large that they cause the ground to split and buildings to fall down.
earth·quake (urth′kwāk′) *noun, plural* **earthquakes.**

earthworm A worm that has a long body and lives in the soil.
earth·worm (urth′wurm′) *noun, plural* **earthworms.**

ease Freedom from trouble, pain, or hard work; comfort. After working for many years, my grandfather sold his business and lived a life of *ease*. Michael rides a bicycle with *ease*. *Noun*.
—**1.** To make free from trouble, pain, or worry. The news that Paul's plane had landed safely *eased* his mother's mind. **2.** To move slowly or carefully. Norma *eased* the car into the small parking space. *Verb*.
ease (ēz) *noun; verb*, **eased, easing.**

easel A tall stand or rack. Easels are used to hold blackboards, signs, and paintings.
ea·sel (ē′zəl) *noun, plural* **easels.**

Easel

easily **1.** Without trying hard. I can touch my toes *easily*. **2.** Without any doubt; for sure. Warren is *easily* the best player on the team. **3.** Very likely; possibly. If the books are too heavy, you could *easily* drop them.
eas·i·ly (ēz′ə lē) *adverb*.

east **1.** The direction a person faces when he watches the sun rise in the morning. East is one of the four main points of the compass. It is directly opposite west. **2. East.** Any area or place that is in the east. **3. the East.** The eastern part of Canada, along the Atlantic coast; central Canada and the Maritimes, to anyone living in the West. **4. the East.** Asia and the islands close to it. *Noun*.
—**1.** Toward or in the east. Our school is on the *east* side of town. **2.** Coming from the east. An *east* wind was blowing. *Adjective*.
—Toward the east. We bicycled *east* to get to the park. *Adverb*.
east (ēst) *noun; adjective; adverb*.

Easter A Christian holy day that celebrates the rising of Christ from the grave. Easter is on a Sunday between March 22 and April 25, but it does not come on the same date each year. It falls on the Sunday after the first full moon on or following March 21.
East·er (ēs′tər) *noun, plural* **Easters.**

eastern 1. In or toward the east. There is a large river in the *eastern* part of that province. 2. Coming from the east. An *eastern* breeze was blowing. 3. **Eastern.** Of or in the part of Canada that is in the east. 4. **Eastern.** Of or in Asia and the islands close to it.
east·ern (ēs′tərn) *adjective.*

easterner 1. A person living in the east. 2. **Easterner.** A person living in the eastern part of Canada.
east·ern·er (ēs′tər nər) *noun, plural* **easterners.**

Eastern Hemisphere The eastern half of the earth. It includes Europe, Asia, Africa, and Australia.

eastward Toward the east. The river flows *eastward* through the province.
east·ward (ēst′wərd) *adverb; adjective.*

easy 1. Needing only a little work; not hard to do. The math problems were *easy.* 2. Without pain, trouble, or worry. The clerk felt *easy* in his mind once the money was locked in the safe. 3. Not strict. She is an *easy* teacher.
eas·y (ēz′ē) *adjective,* **easier, easiest.**

eat 1. To chew on and swallow. I like to *eat* popcorn when I'm at the movies. 2. To have a meal. Our family usually *eats* at six o'clock. 3. To wear away or use up. Rust has *eaten* away the surface of the metal porch furniture.
eat (ēt) *verb,* **ate, eaten, eating.**

eaves The under part of a roof that hangs over the side of a building.
eaves (ēvz) *noun plural.*

eavesdrop To listen to other people talking and not let them know about it. The girl learned about her own surprise party next Thursday by *eavesdropping* as her friends planned it.
eaves·drop (ēvz′drop′) *verb,* **eavesdropped, eavesdropping.**

▲ The word **eavesdrop** once meant the area at the side of a house, where rainwater on the roof would *drop* from the *eaves* to the ground. A person who stood in this place to listen in secret to people talking inside the house was said to be *eavesdropping.*

ebb The flowing out of the ocean from the shore. The beach was covered with seaweed and shells at the tide's *ebb. Noun.*
—1. To flow out. We sat on the beach and watched the tide *ebb.* 2. To become less or weaker. Hope of finding the lost plane began to *ebb. Verb.*
ebb (eb) *noun, plural* **ebbs;** *verb,* **ebbed, ebbing.**

ebony A hard, black wood. It comes from trees that grow in Africa and Asia. Ebony is used to make black piano keys.
eb·on·y (eb′ən ē) *noun, plural* **ebonies.**

eccentric Not like other people; different and odd. Everyone thought the man was *eccentric* because he used to go swimming outdoors in the middle of winter.
ec·cen·tric (ek sen′trik) *adjective.*

echo The repeating of a sound. Echoes are caused when sound waves strike a surface that blocks them and they are thrown back. We shouted "hello" toward the hill and soon heard the *echo* of our own voices. *Noun.*
—1. To send back the sound of something. The walls of the cave *echoed* with voices and footsteps. 2. To be heard again. His warning *echoed* in her ears. *Verb.*
ech·o (ek′ō) *noun, plural* **echoes;** *verb,* **echoed, echoing.**

eclipse A darkening or hiding of the sun or the moon. In an eclipse of the sun, the moon passes between the sun and the earth. In an eclipse of the moon, the earth passes between the sun and the moon.
e·clipse (ē klips′) *noun, plural* **eclipses.**

ecology A science that is part of biology. Ecology studies how plants and animals live in relation to each other and to their environment.
e·col·o·gy (ē kol′ə jē) *noun.*

economic Having to do with economics. The prime minister spoke on television about his new *economic* programme.
ec·o·nom·ic (ek′ə nom′ik *or* ē′kə nom′ik) *adjective.*

economical Using only a small amount of something; not wasting anything. A person who is economical is very careful about spending money. A car that is economical

at; āpe; cär; end; mē; it; īce; hot; ōld;
wood; fool; oil; out; up; turn; sing;
thin; this; hw in white; zh in treasure.
ə stands for a in about, e in taken,
i in pencil, o in lemon, and u in circus.

doesn't use very much gasoline and doesn't cost a lot of money to run.

ec·o·nom·i·cal (ek′ə nom′i kəl *or* ē′kə nom′i-kəl) *adjective.*

economics The science that studies how money and goods are produced, how they are divided up among people, and how they are used.

ec·o·nom·ics (ek′ə nom′iks *or* ē′kə nom′iks) *noun plural.*

economist A person who knows a great deal about economics.

e·con·o·mist (ē kon′ə mist) *noun, plural* **economists.**

economize 1. To cut down on spending money; save. Our family has to *economize* because prices are so high. 2. To be careful to use only a small amount of something; not waste any. Everyone had to *economize* on water because there was a shortage.

e·con·o·mize (ē kon′ə mīz′) *verb,* **economized, economizing.**

economy 1. The way a country produces, divides up, and uses its money and goods. The *economy* of Canada is different from that of China. 2. The careful use of money and other things to cut down on waste and to save. He tries to practise *economy* in buying groceries.

e·con·o·my (ē kon′ə mē) *noun, plural* **economies.**

ecstasy A feeling of being so happy that you are thrilled. The children were in *ecstasy* when their mother brought the puppy home.

ec·sta·sy (ek′stə sē) *noun, plural* **ecstasies.**

-ed A *suffix* that is added to a verb to show that an action is in the past. The word *walked* in "He walked to work yesterday" is the past tense of *walk.* The word *walked* in "She has walked to work every day this week" is the past participle of *walk.*

edge 1. A line or place where something ends; side. Ron wrote his name along the *edge* of his notebook. The pencil rolled off the *edge* of the desk. The lake is over by the *edge* of the woods. 2. The side of a tool that cuts. That knife has a sharp *edge. Noun.*
—1. To move slowly or carefully, little by little. Sally *edged* toward the door, hoping that no one would see her leave. 2. To put an edge on; form an edge on. Jane *edged* the handkerchief with lace. *Verb.*

edge (ej) *noun, plural* **edges;** *verb,* **edged, edging.**

edible Fit or safe to eat. Not all kinds of berries are *edible.*

ed·i·ble (ed′ə bəl) *adjective.*

edit To correct and check something written so that it is ready to be printed. Before that story can be put in a book, it must be *edited.* Henry's father *edits* the town newspaper.

ed·it (ed′it) *verb,* **edited, editing.**

edition 1. The form in which a book is printed. That dictionary is now for sale in a paperback *edition.* 2. One of the copies of a book, newspaper, or magazine printed at one time. Jim bought the morning *edition* of the newspaper.

e·di·tion (ə dish′ən) *noun, plural* **editions.**

editor A person who edits. The newspaper *editor* wrote an article in favour of raising city taxes.

ed·i·tor (ed′ə tər) *noun, plural* **editors.**

editorial 1. An article in a newspaper or magazine written by the editor. An editorial gives an opinion on some subject. The *editorial* praised Parliament for passing the new law. 2. A statement on a television or radio programme that gives the opinion of the management of the station. *Noun.*
—Of or having to do with editors or their work. The article is on the *editorial* page of the newspaper. *Adjective.*

ed·i·to·ri·al (ed′ə tôr′ē əl) *noun, plural* **editorials;** *adjective.*

educate 1. To teach or train. Teachers *educate* children. 2. To send to school. The cost of *educating* children is increasing every year.

ed·u·cate (ej′ə kāt′) *verb,* **educated, educating.**

education 1. The act or process of gaining knowledge. A person's university *education* takes three or four years. 2. The knowledge gained. He has little *education* in science.

ed·u·ca·tion (ej′ə kā′shən) *noun, plural* **educations.**

educational 1. Of or having to do with education. This province's *educational* system requires every student to study English. 2. That is meant to teach something; giving knowledge. Our class saw an *educational* film about how steel is made.

ed·u·ca·tion·al (ej′ə kā′shən əl) *adjective.*

eel A long, thin fish that looks like a snake.

eel (ēl) *noun, plural* **eels** or **eel.**

Eel

208

eerie Strange in a scary way; making people frightened or nervous. It was *eerie* that a black cat wandered into our yard on Hallowe'en.
ee·rie (ēr′ē) *adjective,* **eerier, eeriest.**

effect **1.** Something that happens as a result of something else. One *effect* of prices going up was that people began to buy less. **2.** The power to change something or to make something happen; influence. Punishment has no *effect* on that naughty child. That new traffic law doesn't go into *effect* until next month. *Noun.*
—To make happen; bring about; cause. The medicine *effected* a cure of her sore throat. *Verb.* Look up the word **affect** for more information.
ef·fect (ə fekt′) *noun, plural* **effects;** *verb,* **effected, effecting.**

effective Able to change something or to make something happen. Rhoda used very *effective* arguments and got everyone to agree with her. The medicine was not *effective* in bringing his fever down.
ef·fec·tive (ə fek′tiv) *adjective.*

efficient Able to get the results wanted without wasting time or effort. With our *efficient* new washing machine, the laundry gets done much faster.
ef·fi·cient (ə fish′ənt) *adjective.*

effort **1.** Hard work. Climbing the steep hill took much *effort.* **2.** A hard try. Make an *effort* to get there on time.
ef·fort (ef′ərt) *noun, plural* **efforts.**

egg¹ **1.** A round or roundish body out of which young animals hatch. Eggs are laid by female birds, insects, fish, and snakes. **2.** The inside of a hen's egg that is used for food. I like bacon and *eggs* for breakfast. **3.** A cell that is produced in the bodies of female animals. Human beings, horses, dogs, and many kinds of other animals grow from these cells.
egg (eg) *noun, plural* **eggs.**

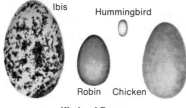

Ibis
Hummingbird
Robin Chicken
Kinds of Eggs

egg² To urge. The two boys began to fight after they were *egged* on by the others in the playground.
egg (eg) *verb,* **egged, egging.**

eggplant A vegetable that has a shiny, purple skin and is shaped like an egg.
egg·plant (eg′plant′) *noun, plural* **eggplants.**

ego **1.** All of one's own thoughts and feelings; one's own unique self. **2.** Great liking or admiration for oneself; conceit. That famous actor is known for his *ego.*
e·go (ē′gō) *noun, plural* **egos.**

Eggplant

Egypt A country in northeastern Africa.
E·gypt (ē′jipt) *noun.*

Egyptian **1.** A person who was born or is living in Egypt. **2.** The language of the people of Egypt in ancient times. *Noun.*
—Of or having to do with Egypt or its people. *Adjective.*
E·gyp·tian (ē jip′shən) *noun, plural* **Egyptians;** *adjective.*

eh A word used to express surprise, doubt, or failure to hear what was said. *Eh,* I can hardly hear you. What do you mean, *eh?*
eh (ā) *interjection.*

eight One more than seven; 8. ▲ Another word that sounds like this is **ate.**
eight (āt) *noun, plural* **eights;** *adjective.*

eighteen Eight more than ten; 18.
eight·een (ā′tēn′) *noun, plural* **eighteens;** *adjective.*

eighteenth **1.** Next after the seventeenth. **2.** One of eighteen equal parts; 1/18.
eight·eenth (ā′tēnth′) *adjective; noun, plural* **eighteenths.**

eighth **1.** Next after the seventh. **2.** One of eight equal parts; 1/8.
eighth (ātth) *adjective; noun, plural* **eighths.**

eightieth **1.** Next after the seventy-ninth. **2.** One of eighty equal parts; 1/80.
eight·i·eth (ā′tē əth) *adjective; noun, plural* **eightieths.**

eighty Eight times ten; 80.
eight·y (ā′tē) *noun, plural* **eighties;** *adjective.*

either She didn't want *either* dress. There were no houses on *either* side of the road.

at; āpe; cär; end; mē; it; īce; hot; ōld;
wood; fōōl; oil; out; up; turn; sing;
thin; this; hw in white; zh in treasure.
ə stands for a in about, e in taken,
i in pencil, o in lemon, and u in circus.

Either is fine with me. *Either* be quiet or leave the library. He didn't see what happened and she didn't *either*.

ei·ther (ē′thər *or* ī′thər) *adjective; pronoun; conjunction; adverb.*

elaborate Worked out or made with great care and in great detail. *Elaborate* plans were made for the wedding. *Adjective.*
—To work out with great care; add details to. The reporter asked the prime minister to *elaborate* on what he had said in answer to an earlier question. *Verb.*

e·lab·o·rate (ə lab′ər ət *for adjective;* ə lab′ə-rāt′ *for verb*) *adjective; verb,* **elaborated, elaborating.**

elapse To go by; pass. Three years *elapsed* before they saw each other again.

e·lapse (ē laps′) *verb,* **elapsed, elapsing.**

elastic Able to go back to its own shape soon after being stretched, squeezed, or pressed together. Rubber bands, balloons, and metal springs are elastic. *Adjective.*
—A tape or fabric that can stretch. Her skirt had *elastic* around the waist. *Noun.*

e·las·tic (ə las′tik) *adjective; noun, plural* **elastics.**

elbow 1. The part of the arm where the bones of the lower arm joins the bone of the upper arm. 2. Something having the same shape as a bent elbow. A pipe that curves at a sharp angle is sometimes called an elbow. *Noun.*
—To push with the elbows; shove. Chuck tried to *elbow* me off the line in the lunchroom. *Verb.*

el·bow (el′bō) *noun, plural* **elbows;** *verb,* **elbowed, elbowing.**

elder Born earlier; older. My *elder* sister wants to be a lawyer. *Adjective.*
—A person who is older. She has great respect for her *elders. Noun.*

eld·er (el′dər) *adjective; noun, plural* **elders.**

elderly Rather old. That *elderly* man uses a cane.

eld·er·ly (el′dər lē) *adjective.*

eldest Born first; oldest. Matthew is the *eldest* of three children.

eld·est (el′dəst) *adjective.*

elect 1. To choose by voting. The people of the town *elected* a new mayor. 2. To make a choice; choose; decide. John *elected* history as his main study in university.

e·lect (ə lekt′) *verb,* **elected, electing.**

election The act of electing. There is an *election* in each class every fall so that the students can choose a class president.

e·lec·tion (ə lek′shən) *noun, plural* **elections.**

electric Having to do with electricity; run or produced by electricity. An *electric* clock keeps good time. I have a set of *electric* trains. Joel got an *electric* shock when he plugged in the lamp.

e·lec·tric (ə lek′trik) *adjective.*

electrical Having to do with electricity; electric. Irons and other *electrical* appliances are now on sale at that store.

e·lec·tri·cal (ə lek′tri kəl) *adjective.*

electric eel A long fish that looks like an eel. It is able to give off electric shocks to protect itself and to catch small fish for food.

Electric eel

electrician A person who works with or repairs things that are electric.

e·lec·tri·cian (ə lek′trish′ən) *noun, plural* **electricians.**

electricity 1. One of the basic forms of energy in our world. Electricity can run motors and produce light and heat. It makes radios, televisions, and telephones work. Electricity is carried by electrons and protons. 2. Electric current. *Electricity* is running through those wires.

e·lec·tric·i·ty (ə lek tris′ə tē) *noun.*

electrocute To kill by means of a very strong electric shock.

e·lec·tro·cute (ə lek′trə kyoot′) *verb,* **electrocuted, electrocuting.**

electrode A place where electric current enters or leaves a battery or other electrical device.

e·lec·trode (ə lek′trōd) *noun, plural* **electrodes.**

electromagnet A piece of iron with wire wound around it. It becomes a magnet when an electric current is passed through the wire.

e·lec·tro·mag·net (ə lek′trō mag′nət) *noun, plural* **electromagnets.**

electron A very tiny particle that is too small to be seen. An electron is one of the basic pieces of all matter. An electron carries a negative electrical charge and forms the part of an atom outside the nucleus. An electric current is really a flow of a large number of electrons.

e·lec·tron (ə lek′tron) *noun, plural* **electrons.**

electronics The science that studies electrons and how they act and move. The study of electrons has led to the development of radio, television, and computers.

e·lec·tron·ics (ə lek tron′iks) *noun plural.*

elegant Rich and fine in quality. The queen was dressed in *elegant* robes.

el·e·gant (el′ə gənt) *adjective.*

element 1. One of the materials out of which all other things are made up. Iron, oxygen, gold, and carbon are elements. Every element is made up of only one kind of atom, so it cannot be broken down into simpler materials by chemicals. There are more than 100 known elements. 2. One of the parts that something is made of. Words are the *elements* used to build sentences. This story is exciting and has all the *elements* of a good mystery. 3. The natural or most comfortable place to be. The ocean is the whale's *element.* 4. *Canadian.* One of the three branches of the Canadian Armed Forces: sea, land, and air. 5. **the elements.** Rain, wind, snow, and other forces of nature. The explorers struggled against *the elements* to make their way across the mountains.

el·e·ment (el′ə mənt) *noun, plural* **elements.**

elementary Dealing with the simple parts or beginnings of something. We learned about addition and subtraction when we studied *elementary* arithmetic.

el·e·men·ta·ry (el′ə men′tər ē *or* el′ə-men′trē) *adjective.*

elementary school A school for children from the ages of about six to twelve or fourteen. Elementary schools usually cover the first six or eight grades. An elementary school is also called a **grade school** or a **public school.**

elephant A huge grey animal. An elephant has a long trunk, large, floppy ears, and two ivory tusks. It makes a sound like a trumpet. Elephants come from Asia and Africa.

el·e·phant (el′ə fənt) *noun, plural* **elephants** or **elephant.**

elevate To raise to a higher level; lift up. The worker in the garage *elevated* the car so that he could repair the wheel.

el·e·vate (el′ə vāt′) *verb,* **elevated, elevating.**

elevation 1. A raising or lifting up. The cranes beside those docks are used for the *elevation* of boats from the water. 2. A raised thing or place. The cabin is on a slight *elevation* that looks over the lake. 3. The height above the earth's surface or above sea level. The plane flew at an *elevation* of nine thousand metres.

el·e·va·tion (el′ə vā′shən) *noun, plural* **elevations.**

elevator 1. A small room or cage that can be raised or lowered. It is used for carrying people and things from one floor to another in a building, mine, or other place. 2. A building for storing grain.

el·e·va·tor (el′ə vā′tər) *noun, plural* **elevators.**

eleven One more than ten; 11.

e·lev·en (ə lev′ən) *noun, plural* **elevens;** *adjective.*

eleventh 1. Next after the tenth. 2. One of eleven equal parts; $1/11$.

e·lev·enth (ə lev′ənth) *adjective; noun, plural* **elevenths.**

elf A kind of fairy who has magical powers. In legends and folk tales, elves are usually small and full of mischief.

elf (elf) *noun, plural* **elves.**

eligible Having the qualities needed for something; fit to be chosen. You must live in this town to be *eligible* for a public library card.

el·i·gi·ble (el′ə jə bəl) *adjective.*

Elephant

at; āpe; cär; end; mē; it; īce; hot; ōld; wood; fōōl; oil; out; up; turn; sing; thin; this; hw in white; zh in treasure. ə stands for a in about, e in taken, i in pencil, o in lemon, and u in circus.

eliminate To get rid of; remove or leave out. The city is trying to *eliminate* pollution. When the family was deciding which house to buy, they *eliminated* all those that didn't have a back yard.
　e·lim·i·nate (ə lim′ə nāt′) *verb*, **eliminated, eliminating.**

Elk

elk A large deer of North America. The male elk has very large antlers.
　elk (elk) *noun, plural* **elk** or **elks.**

ellipse A figure that looks like a narrow or flattened circle.
　el·lipse (ə lips′) *noun, plural* **ellipses.**

elm A tall tree. Elms are often planted to shade streets and lawns. The hard, heavy wood of this tree is used to make boxes and crates.
　elm (elm) *noun, plural* **elms.**

Leaves

Elm Tree

eloquent Having or showing an ability to use words well. The mayor is an *eloquent* speaker. The lawyer made an *eloquent* plea to the jury to find his client innocent of the crime.
　el·o·quent (el′ə kwənt) *adjective.*

else He looks just like someone *else* I know. If anyone *else* comes, we won't have enough chairs. Where *else* did you go on Saturday? Dress warmly when you go out, or *else* you'll catch cold.
　else (els) *adjective; adverb.*

elsewhere The librarian said we'd have to look *elsewhere* for that book because the school library did not have it.
　else·where (els′wer′ *or* els′hwer′) *adverb.*

elude To avoid or escape by being clever or quick. The bandit *eluded* the police by hiding in an abandoned building.
　e·lude (ə lo̅o̅d′) *verb,* **eluded, eluding.**

elves More than one elf. Look up **elf** for more information.
　elves (elvz) *noun plural.*

emancipate To set free from slavery or control. Abraham Lincoln's proclamation *emancipated* all slaves in the United States.
　e·man·ci·pate (ə man′sə pāt′) *verb,* **emancipated, emancipating.**

embankment A mound of earth, stones, or bricks used to hold up a road or to hold back water.
　em·bank·ment (em bangk′mənt) *noun, plural* **embankments.**

Embankment

embargo An order by a government that forbids certain ships from entering or leaving its ports. In time of war, a government may place an *embargo* on the ships of those countries that have helped the enemy.
　em·bar·go (em bär′gō) *noun, plural* **embargoes.**

embark **1.** To go on board a ship for a trip. The passengers *embarked* at Quebec City. **2.** To start out or set out. The explorers *embarked* upon a dangerous journey. Doug *embarked* on a career in business after he finished university.
　em·bark (em bärk′) *verb,* **embarked, embarking.**

embarrass To make someone feel shy, uncomfortable, or ashamed. Her foolish mistake *embarrassed* her.
　em·bar·rass (em bar′əs) *verb,* **embarrassed, embarrassing.**

embarrassment A feeling of shyness or being ashamed. He turned red with *embarrassment* when he realized what a silly thing he had said.
　em·bar·rass·ment (em bar′əs mənt) *noun,* *plural* **embarrassments.**

embassy The official home and office in a foreign country of an ambassador and the people who work for him.
　em·bas·sy (em′bə sē) *noun, plural* **embassies.**

embed To place or set firmly in something. The workmen *embedded* the flagpole in cement.
　em·bed (em bed′) *verb,* **embedded, embedding.**

ember A piece of wood or coal that is glowing in the ashes of a fire. The campers put water on the *embers* of their fire before they left.
　em·ber (em′bər) *noun, plural* **embers.**

embezzle To steal money or goods that one was supposed to take care of. The teller *embezzled* thousands of dollars from the bank.
　em·bez·zle (em bez′əl) *verb,* **embezzled, embezzling.**

emblem A sign or figure that stands for something. The shamrock is the *emblem* of Ireland. A country's flag is an *emblem* of the nation.
　em·blem (em′bləm) *noun, plural* **emblems.**

emboss To decorate or cover a surface with a design that is raised. Susan's stationery was *embossed* with her initials.
　em·boss (em bos′) *verb,* **embossed, embossing.**

embrace To take or hold in the arms as a sign of love or friendship; hug. The returning soldier *embraced* his parents as soon as he got off the plane. *Verb.*
　—A holding in the arms; hug. The puppy wiggled out of the child's *embrace. Noun.*
　em·brace (em brās′) *verb,* **embraced, embracing;** *noun, plural* **embraces.**

embroider **1.** To decorate cloth with designs sewn on with thread. Donna *embroidered* the napkins with flowers. **2.** To make a story more interesting by adding parts that have been made up. Uncle Henry always *embroiders* his stories about his childhood to make us laugh.
　em·broi·der (em broi′dər) *verb,* **embroidered, embroidering.**

Embroider

embroidery Designs that have been sewn on cloth with thread. The *embroidery* on her wedding dress was beautiful.
　em·broi·der·y (em broi′dər ē) *noun, plural* **embroideries.**

embryo An animal or plant that is just starting to live and grow, before its birth. A baby inside its mother, a chicken inside an egg, and a plant inside a seed are embryos.
　em·bry·o (em′brē ō′) *noun, plural* **embryos.**

emerald **1.** A bright-green, clear stone that is very valuable. Emeralds are often used in jewellery. **2.** A bright-green colour. *Noun.*
　—Having a bright-green colour. *Adjective.*
　em·er·ald (em′ər əld) *noun, plural* **emeralds;** *adjective.*

emerge To come into view, come out, or come up. The sun *emerged* from behind a cloud. Ten people *emerged* from the elevator. New facts about the case *emerged* during the trial.
　e·merge (ē murj′) *verb,* **emerged, emerging.**

emergency Something serious that comes without warning and calls for fast action. In case of an *emergency,* the doctor can be reached at his home. *Noun.*
　—Having to do with an emergency; used during an emergency. There is an *emergency* exit at the back of the theatre. *Adjective.*
　e·mer·gen·cy (ə mur′jən sē) *noun, plural* **emergencies;** *adjective.*

---

at; āpe; cär; end; mē; it; īce; hot; ōld; wood; fool; oil; out; up; turn; sing; thin; this; hw in white; zh in treasure. ə stands for a in about, e in taken, i in pencil, o in lemon, and u in circus.

213

emery A hard black or brown mineral in the form of a powder. Emery is used for grinding and polishing metals or stones. It is also put on pieces of cardboard to be used in filing the fingernails.
em·er·y (em′ər ē) *noun.*

emigrant A person who leaves his own country to live in another. Peggy's parents were *emigrants* from Ireland.
em·i·grant (em′ə grənt) *noun, plural* **emigrants.**

emigrate To leave one's own country to live in another. Her family plans to *emigrate* from Canada to Australia.
em·i·grate (em′ə grāt′) *verb,* **emigrated, emigrating.**

eminent Above others in rank, power, or achievement; outstanding. Doctors Banting and Best were *eminent* in Canadian medical research. Mrs. Lewis is an *eminent* lawyer in our town.
em·i·nent (em′ə nənt) *adjective.*

emit To send forth or give out. The sun *emits* heat and light. Boiling water *emits* steam.
e·mit (ē mit′) *verb,* **emitted, emitting.**

emotion A strong feeling. Love, hate, happiness, sorrow, and fear are emotions. The talented actress was able to act out any *emotion.*
e·mo·tion (ə mō′shən) *noun, plural* **emotions.**

emotional 1. Having to do with the emotions or feelings a person has. *Emotional* problems kept him from doing as good a job as he usually did. 2. Easily moved by emotion. My aunt is an *emotional* person who always cries during sad movies. 3. That moves or touches the emotions. The general made an *emotional* speech at the ceremony honouring men who had died in battle.
e·mo·tion·al (ə mō′shən əl) *adjective.*

emperor A man who is the ruler of an empire.
em·per·or (em′pər ər) *noun, plural* **emperors.**

emphasis 1. Special attention or importance given to something. Father always placed much *emphasis* on telling the truth. There is an *emphasis* on reading and arithmetic in elementary school. 2. Special force used when saying a particular word or syllable; stress. The *emphasis* is on the first syllable in the word "empty" and on the second syllable in the word "employ."
em·pha·sis (em′fə sis) *noun, plural* **emphases.**

emphasize To put emphasis on; stress. The mayor's speech *emphasized* the need for a new hospital.
em·pha·size (em′fə sīz′) *verb,* **emphasized, emphasizing.**

empire A group of countries, lands, or peoples under one government or ruler. The *empire* of ancient Rome was powerful.
em·pire (em′pīr) *noun, plural* **empires.**

employ 1. To pay someone to do work; hire. The store *employed* extra workers at Christmas. 2. To make use of; use. The gardener *employed* a shovel and a hoe in his work. *Verb.*
—Service for pay; employment. George is in the *employ* of a large shipping company. *Noun.*
em·ploy (em ploi′) *verb,* **employed, emloying;** *noun.*

employee A person who works for some person or business for pay. The store gives its *employees* a raise twice a year.
em·ploy·ee (em ploi′ē *or* em′ploi ē′) *noun, plural* **employees.**

employer A person or business that pays a person or group of people to work. Mr. Green's *employer* promoted him to a higher position.
em·ploy·er (em ploi′ər) *noun, plural* **employers.**

employment 1. The act of employing or the state of being employed. The automobile company's *employment* of more men made it possible to manufacture cars faster. 2. The work that a person does; job. After the factory closed, it was hard for many of the workers to find new *employment.*
em·ploy·ment (em ploi′mənt) *noun, plural* **employments.**

empress A woman who is the ruler of an empire.
em·press (em′prəs) *noun, plural* **empresses.**

empty Having nothing in it; without what is usually inside. The bottom drawer of the dresser is *empty,* and you can use it for your shirts. The house was *empty* in August because the whole family was away on holiday. *Adjective.*
—1. To take out the contents of; make empty. Steve *emptied* out his pockets. Janet *emptied* the glass of milk. 2. To become empty. The theatre *emptied* when the movie was over. 3. To take out all that is in something. Joan *emptied* the water out of the bathtub. 4. To pour or flow out. That river *empties* into the sea. *Verb.*
emp·ty (emp′tē) *adjective,* **emptier, emptiest;** *verb,* **emptied, emptying.**

emu A bird of Australia that is like an ostrich. An emu cannot fly, but it can run very fast.
e·mu (ē′myo͞o) *noun, plural* **emus.**

Emu

enable To make able. The school raised enough money to *enable* the library to buy many new books.
en·a·ble (en ā′bəl) *verb,* **enabled, enabling.**

enact **1.** To make into law. Parliament *enacted* a new defence bill this year. **2.** To act out on stage; play. Sandra *enacted* the part of the queen in this year's class play.
en·act (en akt′) *verb,* **enacted, enacting.**

enamel **1.** A smooth, hard coating like glass. Enamel is put on metal, glass, or other material to protect or decorate it. **2.** A paint that dries to form a hard, glossy surface. They painted the kitchen with white *enamel.* **3.** The hard, white outer layer of the teeth. Decay can eat through a tooth's *enamel.*
e·nam·el (ə nam′əl) *noun, plural* **enamels.**

-ence A *suffix* that means "the state of being." *Independence* means "the state of being independent."

enchant **1.** To put a magical spell on. The witch had *enchanted* the handsome prince and turned him into a frog. **2.** To delight; charm. The children were *enchanted* by the beautiful costumes the dancers wore in the play.
en·chant (en chant′) *verb,* **enchanted, enchanting.**

encircle **1.** To form a circle around; surround. The soldiers *encircled* the enemy's camp. **2.** To move in a circle around. Many satellites *encircle* the earth.
en·cir·cle (en sur′kəl) *verb,* **encircled, encircling.**

enclose **1.** To shut in or surround on all sides. The back yard was *enclosed* by a picket fence. **2.** To put inside something. Aunt Jean *enclosed* some photographs with her letter.
en·close (en klōz′) *verb,* **enclosed, enclosing.**

encompass To form a circle around; surround. A stone wall *encompasses* the castle.
en·com·pass (en kum′pəs) *verb,* **encompassed, encompassing.**

encore **1.** A demand made by an audience to a performer to go on performing. People usually clap for a long time to call for an encore. The singer received four *encores* at the end of her performance. **2.** Something that is performed in answer to such a demand. As an *encore,* he sang the song that had made him famous.
en·core (än′kōr) *noun, plural* **encores.**

encounter To meet; come upon or against. The soldiers *encountered* the enemy and defeated them. The sailors *encountered* stormy weather on their voyage. *Verb.*
—A coming upon or against; meeting. Susan's *encounter* with the movie star was the talk of the neighbourhood. *Noun.*
en·coun·ter (en koun′tər) *verb,* **encountered, encountering;** *noun, plural* **encounters.**

encourage **1.** To give courage, hope, or confidence to; urge on. The coach *encouraged* Jack to try out for the swimming team. **2.** To give help to; help bring about. The low price of homes *encouraged* many people to settle in that town.
en·cour·age (en kur′əj) *verb,* **encouraged, encouraging.**

encouragement Something that encourages. His father's praise of his marks at school was an *encouragement* to Al.
en·cour·age·ment (en kur′əj mənt) *noun, plural* **encouragements.**

encyclopaedia A book or set of books giving a great deal of information about many things. An encyclopaedia is usually made up of a large number of articles about various subjects. This word is also spelled **encyclopedia.**
en·cy·clo·pae·di·a (en sī′klə pē′dē ə) *noun, plural* **encyclopaedias.**

end **1.** The last part. The *end* of the movie was happy. **2.** The part where something starts or stops. They each held an *end* of the rope. Make a left turn at the *end* of the road.

at; āpe; cär; end; mē; it; īce; hot; ōld;
wood; fo͞ol; oil; out; up; turn; sing;
thin; this; hw in white; zh in treasure.
ə stands for **a** in about, **e** in taken,
i in pencil, **o** in lemon, and **u** in circus.

My vacation is at an *end*. **3.** Purpose; goal; outcome. The *end* of all his hard studying is to get into university. **4.** One of the divisions of a game in curling. *Noun.*
—To bring or come to an end. The rain *ended* their picnic. The game *ended* at ten. *Verb.*
> **end** (end) *noun, plural* **ends;** *verb,* **ended, ending.**

endanger To put in danger. The flood *endangered* the lives of hundreds of people.
> **en·dan·ger** (en dān′jər) *verb,* **endangered, endangering.**

endeavour To make an effort; try. The judge always *endeavoured* to be fair and just. *Verb.*
—A serious effort to do or achieve something. His *endeavours* to do well on the test were rewarded with a high mark. *Noun.*
> **en·deav·our** (en dev′ər) *verb,* **endeavoured, endeavouring;** *noun, plural* **endeavours.**

ending The last or final part. I like stories that have happy *endings*.
> **end·ing** (en′ding) *noun, plural* **endings.**

endless 1. Having no limit or end; going on forever. There were *endless* miles of desert as far as the eye could see. Our teacher has *endless* patience and never loses her temper. **2.** Without ends. A circle is *endless*.
> **end·less** (end′ləs) *adjective.*

end of steel *Canadian.* The farthest point reached by railway service. They lived at the *end of steel* until the railway was extended.

endorse 1. To sign one's name on the back of a cheque or similar paper. You have to *endorse* the cheque or the bank won't cash it. **2.** To give support or approval to. The senator *endorsed* the premier's statement.
> **en·dorse** (en dōrs′) *verb,* **endorsed, endorsing.**

endow 1. To give money or property to. Many wealthy people have *endowed* that museum with valuable paintings. **2.** To give an ability, a talent, or some other good quality to at birth. The ballerina was *endowed* with natural grace.
> **en·dow** (en dou′) *verb,* **endowed, endowing.**

endurance The power to stand anything. The pioneers who crossed this country in covered wagons had much *endurance*.
> **en·dur·ance** (en door′əns *or* en dyoor′əns) *noun.*

endure 1. To bear; stand; put up with. The first explorers of the North Pole had to *endure* many hardships. **2.** To continue; last. A great artist's name will *endure* forever.
> **en·dure** (en door′ *or* en dyoor′) *verb,* **endured, enduring.**

enemy 1. A person who hates or wishes to harm another. The dictator's cruelty caused him to have many *enemies*. **2.** A country that is at war with another country. France and Germany were *enemies* in World War II. **3.** Something that is dangerous or harmful. A lack of rain can be a farmer's *enemy*.
> **en·e·my** (en′ə mē) *noun, plural* **enemies.**

energetic Full of energy. An energetic person is eager and ready to work or do things. After a good rest, the hikers felt *energetic* enough to go on.
> **en·er·get·ic** (en′ər jet′ik) *adjective.*

energy 1. The strength or eagerness to work or do things. Carol has so much *energy* that she gets up early to do exercises. **2.** The capacity for doing work. Some forms of energy are light, heat, and electricity.
> **en·er·gy** (en′ər jē) *noun, plural* **energies.**

enforce To make certain that a law or rule is carried out; put or keep in force. The police in that town *enforce* the traffic laws strictly.
> **en·force** (en fōrs′) *verb,* **enforced, enforcing.**

engage 1. To hire. The automobile factory *engaged* more workers. **2.** To take up the time or attention of. A stranger *engaged* him in a conversation at the bus stop. Practising the piano *engages* much of her time. **3.** To promise; pledge. They are *engaged* to be married.
> **en·gage** (en gāj′) *verb,* **engaged, engaging.**

engagement 1. The act of engaging or the state of being engaged. The *engagement* of workers at the printing plant was the job of the foreman. **2.** A promise to marry. That young couple's *engagement* was announced last week by their parents. **3.** A meeting with someone at a certain time; appointment. I have an *engagement* for dinner this evening.
> **en·gage·ment** (en gāj′mənt) *noun, plural* **engagements.**

Automobile Engine

engine 1. A machine that uses energy to run other machines. Engines can get their energy

from the burning of oil or gasoline or from steam. The part of a car that makes it go is the engine. **2.** A machine that pulls a railway train; locomotive.
en·gine (en′jən) *noun, plural* **engines.**

engineer **1.** A person who is trained in engineering. An engineer may plan and build bridges, roads, or airplanes. **2.** A person who drives a locomotive.
en·gi·neer (en′jə nēr′) *noun, plural* **engineers.**

engineering The work that uses scientific knowledge for building bridges and dams, drilling for oil, or designing machines.
en·gi·neer·ing (en′jə nēr′ing) *noun.*

England The largest part of Britain.
Eng·land (ing′glənd) *noun.*

English **1.** One of the two main languages in Canada. **2.** The language spoken in England and in some other countries, such as the United States, Australia, and New Zealand. **3. the English.** The people of England. *Noun.*
—**1.** Of England or its people. **2.** Of the English language. The book was written in French, but you can buy an *English* translation of it. *Adjective.*
Eng·lish (ing′glish) *noun; adjective.*

English Canada **1.** All the people in Canada who speak English. **2.** The part of Canada where the majority of people speak English.

English Canadian **1.** A Canadian who speaks English. **2.** A Canadian whose ancestors came from England. *Noun.*
—Of English Canada or English Canadians. *Adjective.*

English horn A long, thin musical instrument.

engrave **1.** To cut or carve letters, figures, or designs into a surface. The jeweller *engraved* her name on the back of her watch. **2.** To print something from a metal plate or other material· that has been cut with letters or figures. The printer *engraved* the invitations to the wedding.
en·grave (en grāv′) *verb,* **engraved, engraving.**

English Horn

engulf To flow over and fill or cover completely. The waves *engulfed* the small boat.
en·gulf (en gulf′) *verb,* **engulfed, engulfing.**

enhance To make greater; add to. The rose bushes by the front door *enhance* the beauty of the house.
en·hance (en hans′) *verb,* **enhanced, enhancing.**

enjoy **1.** To get joy or pleasure from; be happy with. The whole family *enjoys* going to the beach. **2.** To have as an advantage. That region *enjoys* mild weather the year round.
en·joy (en joi′) *verb,* **enjoyed, enjoying.**
to enjoy oneself. To have a good time. We all *enjoyed ourselves* at the movies.

enjoyable Giving joy or happiness; pleasant. The class had an *enjoyable* time at the museum.
en·joy·a·ble (en joi′ə bəl) *adjective.*

enjoyment Pleasure; joy. Many people find *enjoyment* in collecting stamps.
en·joy·ment (en joi′mənt) *noun, plural* **enjoyments.**

enlarge To make or become larger. We are *enlarging* our house by adding an extra bedroom.
en·large (en lärj′) *verb,* **enlarged, enlarging.**

enlighten To give knowledge or wisdom to. The news reports *enlightened* us about what was really happening.
en·light·en (en līt′ən) *verb,* **enlightened, enlightening.**

enlist **1.** To join the armed forces. He *enlisted* in the armed forces as soon as the war broke out. **2.** To get the help or support of. The mayor *enlisted* the entire town in the drive to clean up the streets.
en·list (en list′) *verb,* **enlisted, enlisting.**

enormous Much greater than the usual size or amount; very large. Some dinosaurs were *enormous.* The flood caused an *enormous* amount of damage.
e·nor·mous (ə nōr′məs) *adjective.*

enough As much or as many as needed. There is not *enough* room for all of us in the car. There were *enough* players for a game of soccer. *Adjective.*
—An amount that is as much or as many as

at; āpe; cär; end; mē; it; īce; hot; ōld;
wood; fōol; oil; out; up; turn; sing;
thin; **th**is; **hw** in white; **zh** in treasure.
ə stands for **a** in about, **e** in taken,
i in pencil, **o** in lemon, and **u** in circus.

needed. There is *enough* here to feed the whole family. *Noun.*
—**1.** To an amount or degree big enough to fill a need. The meat is not cooked *enough.* **2.** Quite; very. The path up the mountain is certainly steep *enough. Adverb.*
> **e·nough** (ə nuf') *adjective; noun; adverb.*

enrage To make very angry. My father was *enraged* when he realized we'd been cheated.
> **en·rage** (en rāj') *verb,* **enraged, enraging.**

enrich To improve or make better by adding something. They *enrich* bread at this bakery by adding vitamins to it.
> **en·rich** (en rich') *verb,* **enriched, enriching.**

enrol To make or become a member. The teacher *enrolled* seven new students in the class. This word is also spelled **enroll.**
> **en·rol** (en rōl') *verb,* **enrolled, enrolling.**

enrolment **1.** The act of enrolling. *Enrolment* at the school takes place the first week in September. **2.** The number of persons enrolled. The class has an *enrolment* of 25. This word is also spelled **enrollment.**
> **en·rol·ment** (en rōl'mənt) *noun, plural* **enrolments.**

ensign **1.** A flag or banner. The Red Ensign was Canada's flag for many years. **2.** A badge which shows a person's position or rank.
> **en·sign** (en'sīn' *or* en'sən) *noun, plural* **ensigns.**

Ensign

ensure **1.** To make sure or certain; guarantee. Careful planning helped to *ensure* the success of the project. **2.** To make safe; protect. A shot of vaccine will *ensure* you against getting that disease.
> **en·sure** (en shur' *or* en shoor') *verb,* **ensured, ensuring.**

entangle To catch in a tangle or net. The kitten *entangled* its claws in the yarn.
> **en·tan·gle** (en tang'gəl) *verb,* **entangled, entangling.**

enter **1.** To go or come into or in. The train *entered* the tunnel. A sudden thought *entered* his mind. **2.** To pass through something; pierce. The rusty nail *entered* the bottom of his foot. **3.** To become a member or part of; join. Frances will *enter* high school next year.

4. To enrol; register. Vic *entered* his dog in the contest. **5.** To put down in writing; make a record of. The bank *enters* in your bankbook the amount of money you put in or take out.
> **en·ter** (en'tər) *verb,* **entered, entering.**

enterprise Something that a person plans or tries to do. Our school's annual march for charity is a money-making *enterprise.*
> **en·ter·prise** (en'tər prīz') *noun, plural* **enterprises.**

entertain **1.** To keep interested and amused. The clown *entertained* the children. **2.** To have as a guest. On the weekends, they often *entertain* people in their house in the country. **3.** To keep in mind; consider. Harry is *entertaining* an offer for a new job.
> **en·ter·tain** (en'tər tān') *verb,* **entertained, entertaining.**

entertainer Someone who entertains people for a living like singers and dancers.
> **en·ter·tain·er** (en'tər tā'nər) *noun, plural* **entertainers.**

entertainment **1.** The act of entertaining. The *entertainment* of guests is something Mother does very well. **2.** Something that interests and amuses. The *entertainment* at the party was a puppet show.
> **en·ter·tain·ment** (en'tər tān'mənt) *noun, plural* **entertainments.**

enthral To hold the attention and interest of someone completely. The audience was *enthralled* as they watched the lion tamer's act. This word is also spelled **enthrall.**
> **en·thral** (en thräl') *verb,* **enthralled, enthralling.**

enthusiasm A strong feeling of excitement and interest about something. She looked forward to the puppet show with *enthusiasm.*
> **en·thu·si·asm** (en thoo'zē az'əm) *noun.*

enthusiastic Full of enthusiasm. A person who is enthusiastic is very excited, interested, and eager about something. We were all *enthusiastic* about going on a picnic.
> **en·thu·si·as·tic** (en thoo'zē as'tik) *adjective.*

entire Having all the parts; whole. Joe ate the *entire* box of cookies. It took an *entire* morning to clean the attic.
> **en·tire** (en tīr') *adjective.*

entirely Completely; totally. It will be *entirely* your fault if you are late.
> **en·tire·ly** (en tīr'lē) *adverb.*

entitle **1.** To give a right to. Buying a ticket to the amusement park *entitles* you to one free ride. **2.** To give the title of; call. Sinclair Ross *entitled* his short story "One's a Heifer."
> **en·ti·tle** (en tīt'əl) *verb,* **entitled, entitling.**

entrance¹ 1. A place through which one enters. The *entrance* to the building is in the middle of the block. Only one *entrance* to the park was open. 2. The act of entering. Everyone stood up at the judge's *entrance*. 3. The power, right, or permission to enter. Students were given free *entrance* to the game.
en·trance (en′trəns) *noun, plural* **entrances.**

entrance² To fill with delight or wonder. The children were *entranced* by the clown and his trick dog.
en·trance (en trans′) *verb,* **entranced, entrancing.**

entreat To ask earnestly; beg. The prisoner *entreated* the king to let him go.
en·treat (en trēt′) *verb,* **entreated, entreating.**

entry 1. The act of entering. At the queen's *entry* into the hall, the band began to play. 2. A place through which one enters; entrance. The workman's ladder blocked the *entry* to the building. 3. Something written in a book, list, diary, or other record. Sam made an *entry* in his diary. Each word explained in this dictionary is an *entry*. 4. Something that is entered in a contest or race. The judges must have all *entries* for the art show by next Friday.
en·try (en′trē) *noun, plural* **entries.**

enunciate To speak or pronounce words. It is difficult to understand someone who does not *enunciate* his words clearly.
e·nun·ci·ate (ē nun′sē āt′) *verb,* **enunciated, enunciating.**

envelop To wrap or cover completely. Fog *enveloped* the city.
en·vel·op (en vel′əp) *verb,* **enveloped, enveloping.**

envelope A flat covering or container made of paper. Envelopes are used for mailing letters and other papers. Envelopes can usually be folded over and sealed up.
en·ve·lope (en′və lōp′ *or* än′və lōp′) *noun, plural* **envelopes.**

envious Feeling or showing envy; jealous. When people are envious, they often feel dislike for a person who has something they would like to have. All the girls on the block were *envious* of Lynn's new bicycle.
en·vi·ous (en′vē əs) *adjective.*

environment The surrounding in which a person, animal, or plant lives. Environment can affect the growth of a person, animal, or plant. The zoo in our city tries to make each animal's cage like its natural *environment*.
en·vi·ron·ment (en vī′rən mənt) *noun, plural* **environments.**

envy 1. A feeling of jealousy and not being happy about someone else's good luck. He was filled with *envy* when he saw his friend's birthday presents. 2. A person or thing that makes one feel envy. Andy's new bicycle made him the *envy* of his friends. *Noun.*
—To feel envy toward or because of. Everyone in the class *envies* her because of her good marks. He *envies* his friend's new camera. *Verb.*
en·vy (en′vē) *noun, plural* **envies;** *verb,* **envied, envying.**

eon A very long period of time. That deposit of coal was formed *eons* ago.
e·on (ē′ən *or* ē′on) *noun, plural* **eons.**

epic A long poem. It tells of the adventures and deeds of a great hero in legend or history. *Noun.*
—1. Being an epic. The class read an *epic* poem about a great king and his knights. 2. Like something in an epic; great. We admire the *epic* courage of the early Canadian pioneers who settled Upper and Lower Canada. *Adjective.*
ep·ic (ep′ik) *noun, plural* **epics;** *adjective.*

epidemic The very fast spread of a disease. During an epidemic, many people have the same disease at the same time. We had an *epidemic* of chicken pox in our town.
ep·i·dem·ic (ep′ə dem′ik) *noun, plural* **epidemics.**

▲ The word **epidemic** goes back to a Greek word that means "among the people." An epidemic is a very fast spreading of a disease among many people.

episode One part of a series of events in a story or real life. I watched the third *episode* of that television series.
ep·i·sode (ep′ə sōd′) *noun, plural* **episodes.**

epoch A period of time during which something developed or took place. The first airplane flight marked a new *epoch* in travel.
ep·och (ep′ək *or* ē′pok) *noun, plural* **epochs.**

equal 1. That is the same in amount, number, size, or value. One metre is *equal* to one hundred centimetres. Both girls have an *equal* chance to win the tennis match because they are both good players. 2. Having enough

at; āpe; cär; end; mē; it; īce; hot; ōld; wood; fo͞ol; oil; out; up; turn; sing; thin; <u>th</u>is; hw in white; zh in treasure.
ə stands for **a** in about, **e** in taken, **i** in pencil, **o** in lemon, and **u** in circus.

strength or ability to do something. Artie was not *equal* to running in the race after he hurt his foot. *Adjective.*

—A person that is equal. Joan is Kevin's *equal* in softball because she plays as well as he does. *Noun.*

—To be equal to. Two plus two *equals* four. *Verb.*

e·qual (ē′kwəl) *adjective; noun, plural* **equals;** *verb,* **equaled, equaling.**

equality The quality of being equal. Recent changes in laws in Canada provide Canadian men and women with greater *equality* under the law.

e·qual·i·ty (ē kwäl′ə tē) *noun.*

equation A statement in mathematics that two quantities are equal. 5 + 4 = 9 is an equation.

e·qua·tion (ē kwā′zhən) *noun, plural* **equations.**

equator An imaginary line around the earth. It is halfway between the North and South Poles. Canada and the United States are north of the equator. Most of South America is south of the equator.

The dotted line represents the **equator.**

e·qua·tor (ē kwā′-tər) *noun, plural* **equators.**

△ In the Middle Ages, people used a Latin name for the **equator** that meant "something that makes night and day equal." On the days each year when the sun is exactly over the equator, night and day are the same length.

equatorial At or near the equator. All the countries in Central America are equatorial countries.

e·qua·to·ri·al (ē′kwə tōr′ē əl) *adjective.*

equilibrium Balance. The tightrope walker carried a pole to help him keep his *equilibrium.*

e·qui·lib·ri·um (ē′kwə lib′rē əm) *noun.*

equinox One of the two times of the year when day and night are equal in length all over the earth. During these two times the sun is exactly above the equator. The equinoxes take place about March 21 and September 23.

e·qui·nox (ē′kwə noks′) *noun, plural* **equinoxes.**

equip To provide with whatever is needed. The ship was *equipped* with hoses to be used in case of fire.

e·quip (ē kwip′) *verb,* **equipped, equipping.**

equipment 1. Anything that is provided for a particular purpose or use; supplies. Jed bought a tent, a sleeping bag, and other camping *equipment.* 2. The act of equipping. The *equipment* of the entire football team with new uniforms cost the school a lot of money.

e·quip·ment (ē kwip′mənt) *noun.*

equivalent Equal. A quarter is *equivalent* to five nickels. Shaking your head from side to side is *equivalent* to saying "no." *Adjective.*

—Something that is equal. Ten dimes are the *equivalent* of one dollar. *Noun.*

e·quiv·a·lent (ē kwiv′ə lənt) *adjective; noun, plural* **equivalents.**

-er[1] A *suffix* that means "a person or thing that does something." *Teacher* means "a person who teaches." *Opener* means "a thing that opens."

-er[2] A *suffix* that means "more." *Colder* means "more cold." It shows that an adjective or adverb is in its comparative form. The word *colder* is the comparative form of *cold.* The word *faster* is the comparative form of *fast.*

era A period of time or of history. Our class is studying the Depression *era* in Canadian history.

e·ra (er′ə) *noun, plural* **eras.**

erase To rub out; scratch or wipe off. He *erased* the word that was spelled wrong and wrote in the correct spelling. Would you please *erase* the blackboard?

e·rase (ē rās′) *verb,* **erased, erasing.**

eraser Something used to rub out or remove marks. This pencil has a rubber *eraser* on one end.

e·ras·er (ē rās′ər) *noun, plural* **erasers.**

ere Before. ▲ This word is used mainly in poetry and other writing. ▲ Other words that sound like this are **air** and **heir.**

ere (er) *preposition; conjunction.*

erect Upright; raised. The dog's ears became *erect* when its owner whistled. *Adjective.*

—1. To build. A new apartment house will be *erected* on that lot. 2. To put or raise into an upright position. They hurried to *erect* the tent so they could get inside before the rain began. *Verb.*

e·rect (ē rekt′) *adjective; verb,* **erected, erecting.**

ermine An animal that is valued for its fur. It has brown fur that turns white in winter.
er·mine (ur′min) *noun, plural* **ermines** or **ermine.**

Ermine

Ermite *Canadian.* A salty cheese streaked with blue mould. It is made by monks in Quebec.
Er·mite (ur′mīt) *noun.*

erode To wear or wash away slowly; eat away. Ocean waves *eroded* the shore. Rust had *eroded* the tin roof of the shed.
e·rode (ē rōd′) *verb,* **eroded, eroding.**

erosion A slow wearing, washing, or eating away. The trees and grass helped prevent the *erosion* of soil on the hill by protecting it from the wind and rain.
e·ro·sion (ē rō′zhən) *noun.*

errand A short trip to do something. I have to go to the grocery store, stop at the cleaners, and do several other *errands* today.
er·rand (er′ənd) *noun, plural* **errands.**

error 1. Something that is wrong; mistake. 2. A wrong play made by a fielder in baseball. An error lets a base runner get to base safely or lets a batter remain at bat when he would have been put out if the play had been made correctly.
er·ror (er′ər) *noun, plural* **errors.**

erupt To break out suddenly and with force. The volcano *erupted* and covered the land around it with lava.
e·rupt (ē rupt′) *verb,* **erupted, erupting.**

escalator A moving stairway. It is made of a series of steps pulled by a continuous chain. An escalator is used to carry people from one floor to another.
es·ca·la·tor (es′kə lā′tər) *noun, plural* **escalators.**

escape To get away; get free. The bird *escaped* from the cage and flew into the woods. The bicycle rider *escaped* getting hurt when he avoided the truck that was coming toward him. *Verb.*
—**1.** The act of escaping. The rabbit made its *escape* when its owner forgot to lock the cage door. **2.** A way of escaping. A rope ladder served as an *escape* from the burning house. *Noun.*
es·cape (es kāp′) *verb,* **escaped, escaping;** *noun, plural* **escapes.**

escort A person or persons who go along with others. An escort does this to be polite or to honour or to protect someone. The prime minister's car had a police *escort.* My *escort* to the party made sure I got home safely. *Noun.*
—To act as an escort. John *escorted* Ann to the dance. *Verb.*
es·cort (es′kôrt *for noun;* es kôrt′ *for verb*) *noun, plural* **escorts;** *verb,* **escorted, escorting.**

Eskimo 1. A member of a people living in northern Canada, Alaska, and other arctic regions. 2. The language spoken by these people. *Noun.*
—Having to do with the Eskimos or their language. *Adjective.*
Es·ki·mo (es′kə mō′) *noun, plural* **Eskimos** or **Eskimo;** *adjective.*

◢ The word **Eskimo** comes from an Indian word meaning "eater of raw flesh." In Canada, we now call the Eskimos *Inuit,* which means "the people," because this is the name they have always called themselves.

Eskimo dog A wolf-like dog used by Inuit to pull sleds.

esophagus A tube leading from the mouth to the stomach. This word is usually spelled **oesophagus.** Look up **oesophagus** for more information.

especially More than usually; particularly. Kathy came over *especially* to see my new dress. Be *especially* careful not to slip on the icy sidewalk.
es·pe·cial·ly (es pesh′ə lē) *adverb.*

essay A short written composition on a subject. Sally wrote an *essay* about the need for world peace.
es·say (es′ā) *noun, plural* **essays.**

at; āpe; cär; end; mē; it; īce; hot; ōld; wood; fōōl; oil; out; up; turn; sing; thin; this; hw in white; zh in treasure.
ə stands for a in about, e in taken, i in pencil, o in lemon, and u in circus.

221

essence 1. Something that makes a thing what it is; necessary and basic part. Love of others is the *essence* of brotherhood. 2. A concentrated substance or solution. We used *essence* of peppermint to add flavouring to the candy we made.
es·sence (es′əns) *noun, plural* **essences.**

essential Very important or necessary. It is *essential* that we leave now or we'll miss the last train. *Adjective.*
—A necessary or basic part. We brought food, sleeping bags, a tent, and other *essentials* for our camping trip. *Noun.*
es·sen·tial (ə sen′shəl) *adjective; noun, plural* **essentials.**

-est A *suffix* that means "most." *Coldest* means "most cold." It shows that an adjective or adverb is in its superlative form. The word *coldest* is the superlative of *cold.* The word *fastest* is the superlative of *fast.*

establish 1. To set up. The college *established* a new course for students interested in computers. The young doctor *established* himself in his new offices. 2. To show or prove to be true. The lawyer *established* the fact that his client was innocent by showing that he was out of town on the day of the crime.
es·tab·lish (es tab′lish) *verb,* **established, establishing.**

establishment 1. An establishing. The *establishment* of a new health centre for the town took longer than was planned. 2. Something established. A department store, a school, a business, and a household are establishments.
es·tab·lish·ment (es tab′lish mənt) *noun, plural* **establishments.**

estate 1. A piece of land in the country with a large house. That rich man owns a fine *estate* with a swimming pool, tennis courts, and stables. 2. Everything that a person owns. The woman left her entire *estate* to her children.
es·tate (es tāt′) *noun, plural* **estates.**

esteem To think highly of. The captain's men *esteemed* him for his bravery. *Verb.*
—High respect and admiration. Everyone in town had great *esteem* for the mayor's honesty. *Noun.*
es·teem (es tēm′) *verb,* **esteemed, esteeming;** *noun, plural* **esteems.**

estimate An opinion of the value, quality, or cost of something. The repairman gave an *estimate* on what it would cost to patch the roof. *Noun.*
—To form an opinion. We *estimated* that the trip would take an hour, but it took longer because of heavy traffic. *Verb.*
es·ti·mate (es′tə mət *for noun;* es′tə māt′ *for verb) noun, plural* **estimates;** *verb,* **estimated, estimating.**

estimation An opinion or judgement. In her *estimation,* the project will be finished in two weeks.
es·ti·ma·tion (es′tə mā′shən) *noun, plural* **estimations.**

etc. An abbreviation that means "and so forth" or "and the rest." We saw a film about animals that live in Africa, such as elephants, lions, monkeys, *etc.*

etch To engrave a picture or design on metal by letting acid burn into parts of it. The artist *etched* a likeness of an old man.
etch (ech) *verb,* **etched, etching.**

eternal 1. Lasting forever. God is thought to be *eternal.* 2. That seems to last or go on forever. She complained about the *eternal* noise that her neighbours made.
e·ter·nal (ē tur′nəl) *adjective.*

eternity Time without beginning or end; all time.
e·ter·ni·ty (ē tur′nə tē) *noun, plural* **eternities.**

ether A colourless liquid that burns easily and has a strong smell. It is used in medicine to put people to sleep during operations.
e·ther (ē′thər) *noun.*

ethnic Having to do with a group of people who have the same language and culture. There are many different *ethnic* groups in Montreal.
eth·nic (eth′nik) *adjective.*

etiquette Rules of proper behaviour. It is not good *etiquette* to wipe your nose on your sleeve.
et·i·quette (et′i kət *or* et′i ket′) *noun, plural* **etiquettes.**

etymology The history of a word from its beginning to its present form. An etymology tells what other language a word has come from. It also tells about any changes in spelling or meaning that have taken place in the word over the years. An example of an etymology is as follows. The word *pigeon* originally came from the Latin word *pipire,* which meant "to chirp." This word later passed into the French language as *pijon,* which meant "a young chirping bird." By the time it came into English, it was spelled *pejon* and meant "a young dove." The way we now spell it is the same way it is spelled in French today, *pigeon.*
et·y·mol·o·gy (et′ə mol′ə jē) *noun, plural* **etymologies.**

eucalyptus A tall tree that grows in warm climates. Its hard wood is used to make floors, ships, and buildings. Oil made from its leaves is used in medicine.
eu·ca·lyp·tus (yo͞o′kə lip′təs) *noun, plural* **eucalyptuses.**

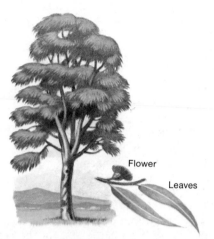

Flower

Leaves

Eucalyptus Tree

Europe The continent that is between Asia and the Atlantic Ocean.
Eu·rope (yoor′əp) *noun.*

European Of Europe. *Adjective.*
—A person who was born or is living in Europe. *Noun.*
Eu·ro·pe·an (yoor′ə pē′ən) *adjective; noun, plural* **Europeans.**

evacuate To leave or cause to leave; empty or remove. Firemen *evacuated* the tenants from the burning building.
e·vac·u·ate (ē vak′yo͞o āt′) *verb,* **evacuated, evacuating.**

evade To get away from by clever planning. The escaped prisoner *evaded* the police by hiding on the roof of an old building. The man tried to *evade* paying his income taxes.
e·vade (ē vād′) *verb,* **evaded, evading.**

evaluate To judge or discover the value of. That test is used to *evaluate* how well students are doing in the reading programme.
e·val·u·ate (ē val′yo͞o āt′) *verb,* **evaluated, evaluating.**

evaporate To change from a liquid or solid into a gas. Water evaporates when it is boiled and becomes steam.
e·vap·o·rate (ē vap′ə rāt′) *verb,* **evaporated, evaporating.**

eve The evening or day before a holiday or other important day. On Christmas *Eve* we all wrapped presents. On the *eve* of the school elections, John seemed likely to be elected class president.
eve (ēv) *noun, plural* **eves.**

even **1.** Completely flat. Our house is built on a piece of *even* ground. **2.** At the same height. The snow drifts were *even* with the tops of the parked cars. **3.** Free from changes; regular. We were able to keep up an *even* speed on the highway. Sally has an *even* temper. **4.** That is the same or equal. At the end of the second period the score in the game was *even*. **5.** Able to be divided by 2 without a remainder. 4, 28, and 72 are *even* numbers. *Adjective.*
—**1.** As a matter of fact; actually. She was willing, *even* eager, to help us. **2.** Though it may seem unlikely. He was always friendly, *even* to strangers. **3.** Still; yet. Her mark on the test was *even* better than his. *Adverb.*
—To make even. The workers *evened* the bumpy road by filling in the holes with gravel. That last goal *evened* the score of the hockey game. *Verb.*
e·ven (ē′vən) *adjective; adverb; verb,* **evened, evening.**

evening The late afternoon and early nighttime. *Noun.*
—Having to do with evening. The family eats its *evening* meal at seven o'clock. *Adjective.*
eve·ning (ēv′ning) *noun, plural* **evenings;** *adjective.*

event **1.** Anything that happens that is important. We studied the *events* leading up to World War I. The first time he went to the circus was a real *event* in his life. **2.** A contest in a programme of sports. The mile run was the main *event* at the track meet.
e·vent (ē vent′) *noun, plural* **events.**
in the event of. If something should happen; in case of. *In the event of* rain, the baseball game will be played tomorrow.

eventual Happening in the end; final. The *eventual* decision on whether to build a public swimming pool depends on how much money the town can raise.
e·ven·tu·al (ē ven′cho͞o əl) *adjective.*

eventually In the end; finally. We waited and waited for Lisa; *eventually* we went to the movies without her.
e·ven·tu·al·ly (ē ven′cho͞o ə lē) *adverb.*

at; āpe; cär; end; mē; it; īce; hot; ōld;
wood; fo͞ol; oil; out; up; turn; sing;
thin; this; hw in white; zh in treasure.
ə stands for a in about, e in taken,
i in pencil, o in lemon, and u in circus.

ever Has she *ever* visited Ottawa before? They lived happily *ever* after. How did you *ever* lift that heavy trunk by yourself?
ev·er (ev′ər) *adverb.*

evergreen Having green leaves or needles all year long. We have three *evergreen* trees in our back yard. *Adjective.*
—An evergreen shrub, tree, or other plant. Pine trees, spruce trees, and holly trees are evergreens. Evergreens are used for Christmas trees because they stay green and don't lose their needles in the winter. *Noun.*
ev·er·green (ev′ər grēn′) *adjective; noun, plural* **evergreens.**

every *Every* student in the class is here today.
eve·ry (ev′rē) *adjective.*
every other. Each second one; skipping one. The garbage collector comes to our house *every other* day.

everybody *Everybody* in the family went next door to meet the new neighbours.
eve·ry·bod·y (ev′rē bod′ē) *pronoun.*

everyday **1.** Having to do with every day; daily. Walking the dog is an *everyday* chore for me. Saving people's lives is an *everyday* happening for a fireman. **2.** Fit for regular days; not special. Most people get dressed up to go to a party instead of wearing their *everyday* clothes.
eve·ry·day (ev′rē dā′) *adjective.*

everyone He bought ice cream for *everyone* who was at the party.
eve·ry·one (ev′rē wun′) *pronoun.*

everything She showed her mother *everything* she had bought.
eve·ry·thing (ev′rē thing′) *pronoun.*

everywhere They want to travel *everywhere* in Canada before they visit any other country.
eve·ry·where (ev′rē wer′ *or* ev′rē hwer′) *adverb.*

evidence Proof of something. The footprints were used by the police as *evidence* that the suspect had been near the scene of the crime.
ev·i·dence (ev′ə dəns) *noun.*

evident Easily seen or understood; clear. It was *evident* that they didn't like the movie since they walked out before the end.
ev·i·dent (ev′ə dənt) *adjective.*

evil Bad, wicked, or harmful. The *evil* witch turned the prince into a frog. *Adjective.*
—Wickedness. The minister's sermon spoke out against *evil.* War is a great *evil* of mankind. *Noun.*
e·vil (ē′vəl) *adjective; noun, plural* **evils.**

evolution **1.** A very slow development, growth, or change. The *evolution* of the automobile was shown at the museum with pictures of early cars and pictures of cars of today. **2.** The idea that all living animals and plants slowly developed over millions of years from much earlier and simpler forms of life.
ev·o·lu·tion (ev′ə lōō′shən) *noun, plural* **evolutions.**

evolve To develop or grow gradually. Elephants *evolved* from huge animals called mammoths.
e·volve (ē volv′) *verb,* **evolved, evolving.**

ewe A female sheep. ▲ Other words that sound like this are **yew** and **you.**
ewe (yōō) *noun, plural* **ewes.**

ex- A *prefix* that means "former." *Ex-partner* means "a former partner."

exact Without anything wrong; very accurate. This clock gives the *exact* time.
ex·act (eg zakt′) *adjective.*

exactly **1.** Without any mistake; accurately. He measured the boards for the bookcase *exactly.* **2.** In the exact way; quite. The accident happened *exactly* as I told him.
ex·act·ly (eg zakt′lē) *adverb.*

exaggerate To make something seem larger or greater than it is. The fisherman *exaggerated* the size of the fish he had caught. She *exaggerated* when she said she had eaten five bowls of ice cream yesterday.
ex·ag·ger·ate (eg zaj′ə rāt′) *verb,* **exaggerated, exaggerating.**

examination **1.** The act of examining. The dentist's *examination* of my teeth showed that I had no cavities. **2.** A test. My sister in university has three *examinations* each term.
ex·am·in·a·tion (eg zam′ə nā′shən) *noun, plural* **examinations.**

examine **1.** To look at closely and carefully; check. Tony *examined* the skis before buying them to be sure they were the right length. The doctor *examined* the child to see if she had the flu. **2.** To test. The teacher said she would *examine* the class in arithmetic the next day.
ex·am·ine (eg zam′in) *verb,* **examined, examining.**

example **1.** One thing that is used to show what other similar things are like. Sherry's picture was hung up as an *example* of the work the class was doing in art. **2.** A problem. The arithmetic *example* on the blackboard was hard to understand.
ex·am·ple (eg zam′pəl) *noun, plural* **examples.**

to set an example. To serve as a model for others. John's hard work in class *set an example* for the other students.

exasperate   To annoy greatly; make angry. She always became *exasperated* when her brother teased her.

ex·as·per·ate (eg zas′pər āt′) *verb,* **exasperated, exasperating.**

excavate   **1.** To remove by digging. The workmen *excavated* dirt and rocks with a steam shovel. **2.** To uncover by digging. The museum sent a group of men to *excavate* the ruins of the ancient city. **3.** To make by digging. The miners *excavated* a tunnel in the side of the mountain.

ex·ca·vate (eks′kə vāt′) *verb,* **excavated, excavating.**

excavator   A big machine used for digging.

ex·ca·va·tor (eks′-kə vā′tər) *noun, plural* **excavators.**

Excavator

exceed   To go ahead of; be greater than. The driver *exceeded* the speed limit because he was in a hurry. Gloria's skill as a speller *exceeds* everyone else's in the class.

ex·ceed (ek sēd′) *verb,* **exceeded, exceeding.**

excel   To be better or greater than others. Pete *excels* at soccer.

ex·cel (ek sel′) *verb,* **excelled, excelling.**

excellence   The state of being better or greater. His *excellence* as a runner was known by the whole school.

ex·cel·lence (ek′sə ləns) *noun.*

Excellency   The title used to speak to the Governor General and some other people of high rank, such as bishops.

Ex·cel·len·cy (ek′sə lən sē) *noun, plural* **Excellencies.**

excellent   Very, very good; outstanding. The teacher told Jim's parents that his work in arithmetic was *excellent.*

ex·cel·lent (ek′sə lənt) *adjective.*

except   The store is open every day *except* Sunday. He would go with us, *except* he has work to do.

ex·cept (ek sept′) *preposition; conjunction.*

exception   **1.** The state of being left out. Everyone went on the picnic with the *exception* of Mary, who was sick. **2.** A person or

thing that is left out or that is different from others. Most birds can fly, but the penguin is an *exception.*

ex·cep·tion (ek sep′shən) *noun, plural* **exceptions.**

exceptional   Not ordinary; unusual; extraordinary. He is an *exceptional* piano player.

ex·cep·tion·al (ek sep′shən əl) *adjective.*

excess   An amount greater than what is needed or usual; extra amount or degree. An *excess* of water in the fish tank caused it to overflow. Linda's savings were in *excess* of $300. *Noun.*

—Greater than what is needed or usual; extra. When you travel on an airplane you have to pay for *excess* luggage. *Adjective.*

ex·cess (ek ses′ *for noun;* ek ses′ *or* ek′səs *for adjective) noun, plural* **excesses;** *adjective.*

excessive   More than is necessary or usual. He spends an *excessive* amount of money on candy.

ex·ces·sive (ek ses′iv) *adjective.*

exchange   To give or give up for something else; change. He *exchanged* the shirt he had been given as a present and got a belt instead. Jerry *exchanged* hockey cards with his friend. *Verb.*

—**1.** The act of giving one thing in return for another. The two friends enjoyed their *exchange* of letters. **2.** A place where things are bought, sold, or traded. Stocks are bought and sold at the Stock *Exchange* in Toronto. **3.** A central office where telephone lines are connected for a town or part of a city. *Noun.*

ex·change (eks chānj′) *verb,* **exchanged, exchanging;** *noun, plural* **exchanges.**

excite   To stir up; arouse. The home team's great play *excited* the fans. The old, deserted house *excited* the children's curiosity.

ex·cite (ek sīt′) *verb,* **excited, exciting.**

excitement   **1.** The state of being excited. Tom could hardly sleep because of his *excitement* over being made captain of the team. **2.** Something that stirs up or excites. Winning the contest was an *excitement* she would never forget.

ex·cite·ment (ek sīt′mənt) *noun.*

exciting   Causing excitement; thrilling. For

at; āpe; cär; end; mē; it; īce; hot; ōld;
wood; fōōl; oil; out; up; turn; sing;
thin; this; hw in white; zh in treasure.
ə stands for a in about, e in taken,
i in pencil, o in lemon, and u in circus.

me, the tightrope walkers are the most *exciting* part of the circus.

ex·cit·ing (ek sīt′ing) *adjective.*

exclaim To speak or cry out suddenly. A person usually exclaims because he is angry, excited, or surprised. "You took my baseball bat without asking!" Phil *exclaimed* angrily.

ex·claim (eks klām′) *verb*, **exclaimed, exclaiming.**

exclamation Something exclaimed. In the sentence "Hurrah, our team won again!" "Hurrah" is an exclamation.

ex·cla·ma·tion (eks′klə mā′shən) *noun*, *plural* **exclamations.**

exclamation mark A punctuation mark (!). It is used after a word, group of words, or sentence to show an exclamation of anger, surprise, or excitement. This mark of punctuation is also called an **exclamation point.**

exclude To keep from entering; shut out. All those who aren't eighteen or over are *excluded* from voting.

ex·clude (eks klōōd′) *verb*, **excluded, excluding.**

exclusive 1. Belonging to a single person or group. She has *exclusive* ownership of the house and property. 2. Open to a certain kind of person or group only. That is an *exclusive* club for lawyers only.

ex·clu·sive (eks klōō′siv) *adjective.*

excuse 1. To forgive; pardon; overlook. Please *excuse* me for stepping on your toe. We *excused* her rude remark because we knew she was very tired. 2. To let off from duty. He was *excused* from volleyball practice because he had hurt his knee. 3. To serve as a reason or explanation for. Her being sick *excused* her absence from school. *Verb.*
—A reason given to explain something. Oversleeping is not a good *excuse* for being late for school. *Noun.*

ex·cuse (eks kyōōz′ *for verb;* eks kyōōs′ *for noun*) *verb*, **excused, excusing;** *noun*, *plural* **excuses.**

execute 1. To carry out; put into effect. The captain *executed* the colonel's orders. 2. To put to death by order of the law. The murderer was *executed* for his crime.

ex·e·cute (ek′sə kyōōt′) *verb*, **executed, executing.**

execution 1. The act of executing. The *execution* of the plan to clean up the neighbourhood will call for everyone's help. 2. The act of putting to death by order of the law.

ex·e·cu·tion (ek′sə kyōō′shən) *noun*, *plural* **executions.**

executive Having to do with directing or managing matters in business or government. Mr. Carter had an *executive* position as vice-president of the company. *Adjective.*
—1. A person who directs or manages. All the *executives* of the company met to discuss ways of selling their new product. 2. The branch of government that manages the affairs of a nation and sees that the laws are carried out. *Noun.*

ex·ec·u·tive (eg zek′yə tiv) *adjective; noun*, *plural* **executives.**

Executive Council The cabinet of a provincial government. The Executive Council is made up of the premier and his ministers.

exempt To excuse. He was *exempted* from taking the final test because of his good marks during the year. *Verb.*
—Freed from doing or giving something; excused. Church land is usually *exempt* from real estate taxes. *Adjective.*

ex·empt (eg zempt′) *verb*, **exempted, exempting;** *adjective.*

exercise 1. Activity that trains or improves the body or the mind. Walking is good *exercise*. That book has arithmetic *exercises* at the end of each chapter. 2. Use or practice. The dictator's *exercise* of power made him many enemies. 3. A ceremony or programme. Graduation *exercises* included speeches by teachers and students. *Noun.*
—1. To put or go through exercises. I *exercise* my dog in the park. He *exercises* by walking three kilometres every day. 2. To make use of. You should *exercise* your rights as a citizen by voting. *Verb.*

ex·er·cise (ek′sər sīz′) *noun*, *plural* **exercises;** *verb*, **exercised, exercising.**

exert To make use of; use. The firemen had to *exert* all their strength to break down the door.

ex·ert (eg zurt′) *verb*, **exerted, exerting.**

exhale To breathe out. His doctor listened to his heart as he inhaled and *exhaled.*

ex·hale (eks hāl′) *verb*, **exhaled, exhaling.**

exhaust 1. To make very weak or tired. The long, hot hike *exhausted* us. 2. To use up completely. The campers *exhausted* their supply of water. *Verb.*
—The used steam or gases that escape from an engine. *Noun.*

ex·haust (eg zäst′) *verb*, **exhausted, exhausting;** *noun*, *plural* **exhausts.**

exhaustion An exhausting or being exhausted. Jack's *exhaustion* was caused by his five-kilometre run.

ex·haus·tion (eg zäs′chən) *noun.*

exhibit To show. The school *exhibited* the best art work of the students for all the parents to see. Donna *exhibited* great talent in playing the piano. *Verb.*
—Something shown. We went to see the *exhibit* of African art at the museum. Jack's science *exhibit* won first prize. *Noun.*
ex·hib·it (eg zib'it) *verb,* **exhibited, exhibiting;** *noun, plural* **exhibits.**

exhibition **1.** The act of exhibiting; showing. Her being rude to the guests was an *exhibition* of bad manners. **2.** A public show. The class went to an *exhibition* of rare books shown at the public library.
ex·hi·bi·tion (ek'sə bish'ən) *noun, plural* **ex-hibition**

exhilar
cited. T
rated th
trail.
ex·hil·a
exhilar

exile T
try or k
exiled hi
—1. The
ment de
ment fo
away fr
ex·ile (
noun, p

exist 1
ghosts e
exist for
Outside
arctic re
ex·ist (e

existenc
existence
because
2. A way
New Fra
ex·ist·en
ences.

exit 1.
the *exit*
exit from
—To go
side doo
ex·it (eg
exited, e

exotic F
otic flow
ex·ot·ic (

expand
out. Hea
its wings and flew away.

ex·pand (eks pand') *verb,* **expanded, expanding.**

expanse A wide, open area. The snowmobile had to cross a large *expanse* of ice and snow to reach the closest town.
ex·panse (eks pans') *noun, plural* **expanses.**

expansion **1.** The act of expanding or the state of being expanded. After its *expansion*, the school had thirty new classrooms. **2.** The amount that something expands.
ex·pan·sion (eks pan'shən) *noun, plural* **expansions.**

expect **1.** To look forward to. He *expects* to get a new bicycle for his birthday. **2.** To want something because it is right or necessary.
an apology from the
; suppose. I *expect* he
hool because he has a

b, **expected, expecting.**
of expecting. The man
rely in *expectation* of

tā'shən) *noun, plural*

made for a particular
made an *expedition* to
animals in the area.
lish'ən) *noun, plural*

e out. They will *expel*
continues to disobey

expelled, expelling.
nding of time, money,
w house requires the
eal of money.
'di chər) *noun, plural*

nt to buy or do some-
cannot afford the *ex-*
A cause or reason for
ng the swimming pool

un, plural **expenses.**
gh price; very costly.
sive new radio.
) *adjective.*

ng that a person has

it; īce; hot; ōld;
p; turn; sing;
; zh in treasure.
t, e in taken,
, and u in circus.

done, seen, or taken part in. Their *experience* with the bear in the Algonquin Park is something they won't soon forget. The old man told us about his *experiences* as a soldier. **2.** The knowledge or skill a person gains from doing something. Jack has three years' *experience* as a salesman. Ken is the only one on the hockey team with *experience* because all the other players are new. *Noun.*
—To have something happen to one; feel; undergo. I didn't *experience* much pain when the dentist drilled my tooth. *Verb.*
ex·pe·ri·ence (eks pēr′ē əns) *noun, plural* experiences; *verb,* experienced, experiencing.

experiment A test that is used to discover or prove something. We did an *experiment* in class to show that a fire needs oxygen to burn. *Noun.*
—To make an experiment or experiments. Scientists tested the new drug by *experimenting* with mice. *Verb.*
ex·per·i·ment (eks per′ə mənt *for noun;* eks per′ə ment′ *for verb*) *noun, plural* experiments; *verb,* experimented, experimenting.

experimental Having to do with experiments. There is *experimental* proof that water becomes steam when it is heated.
ex·per·i·men·tal (eks per′ə ment′əl) *adjective.*

expert A person who knows a great deal about some special thing. That professor is an *expert* on Canadian history. *Noun.*
—Having or showing a great deal of knowledge. The swimming coach gave me *expert* advice about how to learn how to dive. *Adjective.*
ex·pert (eks′purt *for noun;* eks′purt *or* eks purt′ *for adjective*) *noun, plural* experts; *adjective.*

expire To come to an end. Your library card will *expire* at the end of the month if you don't renew it.
ex·pire (eks pīr′) *verb,* expired, expiring.

explain **1.** To make something plain or clear; tell the meaning of. Can you *explain* how you got your answer to this math problem? **2.** To give or have a reason for. Can she *explain* why she was late for school?
ex·plain (eks plān′) *verb,* explained, explaining.

explanation **1.** The act of making something plain or clear. My brother's *explanation* of how to make a kite helped me understand how to do it. **2.** A reason or meaning. Mother wanted an *explanation* for the broken vase.
ex·pla·na·tion (eks′plə nā′shən) *noun, plural* explanations.

explicit Stated or shown clearly. He gave *explicit* instructions on how we should do the work.
ex·plic·it (eks plis′it) *adjective.*

explode **1.** To burst suddenly and with a loud noise; blow up. The pop bottle *exploded* because of the heat. The amusement park *exploded* firecrackers to celebrate Canada Day. **2.** To break forth noisily or with force. He *exploded* with anger when he saw that his bicycle had been stolen.
ex·plode (eks plōd′) *verb,* exploded, exploding.

exploit A brave deed or act. The story is about the exciting *exploits* of a knight who saves the life of his king.
ex·ploit (eks′ploit) *noun, plural* exploits.

exploration The act of exploring. Columbus's *explorations* led to his discovery of America.
ex·plo·ra·tion (eks′plə rā′shən) *noun, plural* explorations.

explore **1.** To travel in unknown lands for the purpose of discovery. Astronauts *explored* the moon to learn what it is like. **2.** To look through closely; examine. Jack and his friends *explored* the deserted house. Doctors *explore* the causes of disease.
ex·plore (eks plōr′) *verb,* explored, exploring.

explorer A person who explores.
ex·plor·er (eks plōr′ər) *noun, plural* explorers.

explosion **1.** The act of bursting or expanding suddenly and noisily. The *explosion* of the bomb broke windows in all the buildings nearby. **2.** A sudden outburst. We didn't know what had caused his *explosion* of anger.
ex·plo·sion (eks plō′zhən) *noun, plural* explosions.

explosive Likely to explode or cause an explosion. A bomb is an *explosive* device. His *explosive* temper frightens me. *Adjective.*
—Something that can explode or cause an explosion. Dynamite is an *explosive. Noun.*
ex·plo·sive (eks plō′siv) *adjective; noun, plural* explosives.

export To send goods to other countries to be sold or traded. Some South American countries *export* large amounts of coffee to Canada. *Verb.*
—Something that is sold or traded to another country. Wheat is an *export* of this country. *Noun.*
ex·port (eks pōrt′ *or* eks′pōrt′ *for verb;* eks′pōrt′ *for noun*) *verb,* exported, exporting; *noun, plural* exports.

expose 1. To leave open or without protection. She was *exposed* to the mumps when her best friend had them. He *exposed* himself to the laughter of his classmates when he made such a foolish mistake. 2. To make something known; reveal. The police *exposed* a gang of thieves who were stealing cars. 3. To allow light to reach a photographic film or plate. I *exposed* the film of my camera when I loaded it under the lamp.
ex·pose (eks pōz′) *verb,* **exposed, exposing.**

exposition A large public display. There was an *exposition* of camping equipment at the trade centre.
ex·po·si·tion (eks′pə zish′ən) *noun, plural* **expositions.**

exposure 1. The act of exposing. The newspaper's *exposure* of the mayor's tax fraud shocked the public. 2. The condition of being exposed. The mountain climbers were suffering from *exposure* after the climb in the terrible cold and wind. 3. A position in relation to the sun or wind. This room has a southern *exposure,* so it gets a lot of sunlight. 4. The act of exposing a photographic film to light.
ex·po·sure (eks pō′zhər) *noun, plural* **exposures.**

express To say or show. He *expressed* his happiness by smiling. The artist's paintings of plants and animals *express* her love of nature. *Verb.*
—1. Special or particular. He came here for the *express* purpose of seeing her. 2. Having to do with fast transportation or delivery. We took an *express* bus into the city. *Adjective.*
—1. A system of fast transportation or delivery. I sent my trunk to camp by *express.* 2. A train, bus, or elevator that is fast and makes few stops. *Noun.*
ex·press (eks pres′) *verb,* **expressed, expressing;** *adjective; noun, plural* **expresses.**

expression 1. The act of putting thoughts or feelings into words or actions. The letter was an *expression* of his thanks to us. 2. An outward show; look. Robin had a disappointed *expression* on her face when the kitten jumped out of her arms. 3. A common word or group of words. "Look before you leap" and "He who hesitates is lost" are well-known *expressions.*
ex·pres·sion (eks presh′ən) *noun, plural* **expressions.**

expressive Full of expression. The poet read his poem to the audience in a very *expressive* voice.
ex·pres·sive (eks pres′iv) *adjective.*

expressway A wide highway built for fast and direct travelling.
ex·press·way (eks pres′wā′) *noun, plural* **expressways.**

Expressway

extend 1. To make or be longer; stretch out. The bird *extended* its wings and flew away. The driveway *extends* from the house to the street. 2. To offer or give. We *extended* our welcome to the new neighbours.
ex·tend (eks tend′) *verb,* **extended, extending.**

extension 1. A stretching out; addition. They built an *extension* to the house so they would have a room for the new baby. 2. An extra telephone added to the same line as the main telephone.
ex·ten·sion (eks ten′shən) *noun, plural* **extensions.**

extensive Large; broad. The flood caused *extensive* damage to the farms in the area.
ex·ten·sive (eks ten′siv) *adjective.*

extent The space, amount, degree, or limit to which something extends. Betty would go to any *extent* to help a friend. The manager explained the *extent* of their duties to the new workers.
ex·tent (eks tent′) *noun, plural* **extents.**

exterior The outer part; outward look or manner. The *exterior* of the building is made of brick. Although he has a calm *exterior,* Jack often feels nervous. *Noun.*
—Having to do with the outside; outer. The *exterior* walls were painted white. *Adjective.*

at; āpe; cär; end; mē; it; īce; hot; ōld; wood; fōōl; oil; out; up; turn; sing; thin; this; hw in white; zh in treasure. ə stands for a in about, e in taken, i in pencil, o in lemon, and u in circus.

ex·te·ri·or (eks tēr′ē ər) *noun, plural* **exteriors;** *adjective.*

exterminate To wipe out; destroy. Dad used a spray to *exterminate* the bugs.
ex·ter·mi·nate (eks tur′mə nāt′) *verb,* **exterminated, exterminating.**

external Having to do with the outside; outer. The skin of a banana is its *external* covering.
ex·ter·nal (eks tur′nəl) *adjective.*

extinct 1. No longer existing. Leopards will become *extinct* if people keep killing them to make fur coats. 2. No longer active or burning. The village is built on an *extinct* volcano.
ex·tinct (eks tingkt′) *adjective.*

extinguish To put out. The firemen *extinguished* the fire in about twenty minutes.
ex·tin·guish (eks ting′gwish) *verb,* **extinguished, extinguishing.**

extra More than what is usual, expected, or needed; additional. I spent *extra* time studying to get a better grade on that test. She did *extra* work to get more pay. *Adjective.*
—1. Something added to what is usual, expected, or needed. That car has many *extras,* such as a clock, a radio, and air conditioning. 2. A special edition of a newspaper that is printed to report something important. The paper printed an *extra* to announce that the war was over. *Noun.*
—Unusually. My mother bought an *extra* large cake for my birthday party. *Adverb.*
ex·tra (eks′trə) *adjective; noun, plural* **extras;** *adverb.*

extract To take or pull out. The dentist *extracted* her tooth. Scientists have found a way to *extract* salt from sea water. *Verb.*
—Something that is extracted. The cake was flavoured with *extract* of vanilla. *Noun.*
ex·tract (eks trakt′ *for verb;* eks′trakt *for noun*) *verb,* **extracted, extracting;** *noun, plural* **extracts.**

extraordinary Very unusual; remarkable. Ann's art teacher said that she had *extraordinary* talent.
ex·traor·di·nar·y (eks trôr′də ner′ē *or* eks′trə ôr′də ner′ē) *adjective.*

extravagance The spending of too much money. When Mother goes shopping, she avoids all *extravagance* and buys only what she needs.
ex·trav·a·gance (eks trav′ə gəns) *noun, plural* **extravagances.**

extravagant Spending too much money; spending in a careless way. The *extravagant* man bought only very expensive clothes.
ex·trav·a·gant (eks trav′ə gənt) *adjective.*

extreme 1. Going beyond what is usual; very great or severe. Vic and Mike were in *extreme* danger when they were caught in the rock slide. 2. Very far; farthest. She lives at the *extreme* end of the block. *Adjective.*
—1. The greatest or highest degree of something. Starvation is the *extreme* of hunger. 2. **extremes.** Complete opposites. Hot and cold are *extremes* of each other. *Noun.*
ex·treme (eks trēm′) *adjective; noun, plural* **extremes.**

extremely Very. He was *extremely* happy when he won the contest.
ex·treme·ly (eks trēm′lē) *adverb.*

eye 1. The part of the body by which people and animals see. 2. The coloured part of the eye; iris. Joe has brown *eyes.* 3. The part of the face around the eye. When he fell, he got a black *eye.* 4. A look. She kept her *eye* on the cake in the oven to be sure it would not burn. 5. Something like an eye in shape, position, or use. The bud of a potato and the hole in a needle are called *eyes. Noun.*
—To watch carefully or closely. The detective *eyed* every move the suspect made. *Verb.*
▲ Other words that sound like this are **aye** and **I.**
eye (ī) *noun, plural* **eyes;** *verb,* **eyed, eying** or **eyeing.**

eyeball The part of the eye that the eyelids close over.
eye·ball (ī′bäl′) *noun, plural* **eyeballs.**

eyebrow The hair that grows on the bony part of the face above the eye.
eye·brow (ī′brou′) *noun, plural* **eyebrows.**

eyeglasses A pair of lenses in a frame that help make a person's eyesight better.
eye·glass·es (ī′glas′əz) *noun plural.*

eyelash One of the small, stiff hairs growing on the edge of the eyelid. The baby has very long *eyelashes.*
eye·lash (ī′lash′) *noun, plural* **eyelashes.**

eyelet A small hole in a material for a cord or lace to go through. Shoe laces are put through eyelets. ▲ Another word that sounds like this is **islet.**
eye·let (ī′lət) *noun, plural* **eyelets.**

eyelid The fold of skin that can open and close over the eye.
eye·lid (ī′lid′) *noun, plural* **eyelids.**

eyesight The ability to see; vision. They tested our *eyesight* in school by asking us to read a chart.
eye·sight (ī′sīt′) *noun.*

eyetooth Either of the two pointed teeth in the upper, front part of the mouth.
eye·tooth (ī′tooth′) *noun, plural* **eyeteeth.**

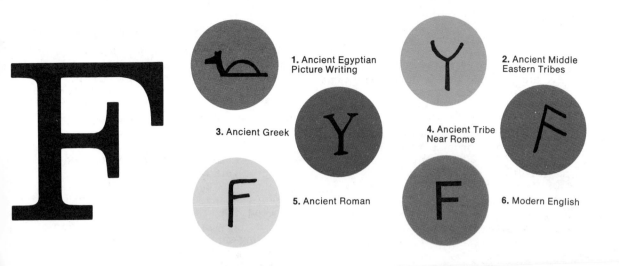

1. Ancient Egyptian Picture Writing

2. Ancient Middle Eastern Tribes

3. Ancient Greek

4. Ancient Tribe Near Rome

5. Ancient Roman

6. Modern English

F is the sixth letter of the alphabet. The oldest form of the letter **F** was a drawing that the ancient Egyptians (**1**) used in their picture writing nearly 5000 years ago. This drawing was borrowed by several ancient tribes (**2**) in the Middle East. They used it to stand for both the consonant sound *w*, as the *w* in *water*, and the vowel sound *u*, as the *u* in *rude*. The ancient Greeks (**3**) borrowed this letter, writing it very much like a modern capital letter *Y*. They used it to stand for the *u* sound only. Another letter, which was called *digamma*, was used to stand for the *w* sound. *Digamma* looked very much like a modern capital letter *F*. These letters were borrowed by an ancient tribe (**4**) that settled north of Rome about 2800 years ago. They used both the letter that looked like a capital *Y* and the letter called *digamma* to stand for the *f* sound. This was probably the first time in the history of the alphabet that the *f* sound was used. The Romans (**5**) borrowed the letter called *digamma* to stand for the *f* sound in their alphabet. By about 2400 years ago the Roman letter **F** was written in almost the same way that we write the capital letter **F** today (**6**).

f, F The sixth letter of the alphabet.
f, F (ef) *noun, plural* **f's, F's.**

fable A story that is meant to teach a lesson. The characters in fables are usually animals that talk and act like people.
fa·ble (fā′bəl) *noun, plural* **fables.**

fabric A material that is woven or knitted; cloth. Fabric is made from natural or man-made fibres. Cotton, silk, and felt are fabrics.
fab·ric (fab′rik) *noun, plural* **fabrics.**

fabulous Too much to believe; seeming impossible; amazing. He read a story about dragons and other *fabulous* creatures. She spent *fabulous* amounts of money on toys.
fab·u·lous (fab′yə ləs) *adjective.*

face **1.** The front of the head. The eyes, nose, and mouth are parts of the face. **2.** A look on the face; expression. The boy's *face* was happy when he saw his friends. The children made funny *faces* in the mirror. **3.** The front, main, or outward part of something. We could see many people skiing down the *face* of the mountain. There are numbers on the *face* of a clock. *Noun.*
—1. To have or turn the face toward. Please *face* the camera. The school *faces* the park. **2.** To meet openly and with courage. He always *faces* his problems. *Verb.*

face (fās) *noun, plural* **faces;** *verb,* **faced, facing.**

face off. To start the play in hockey by dropping the puck between the sticks of two opposing players.

face-off The start of the play in hockey when the referee drops the puck between the sticks of two opposing players facing each other.
face-off (fās′of′) *noun, plural* **face-offs.**

facet One of the small, polished flat surfaces of a cut gem.
fac·et (fas′ət) *noun, plural* **facets.**

facial Of or for the face. A smile is a happy *facial* expression.
fa·cial (fā′shəl) *adjective.*

Facets

facilitate To make easier; help in the doing of. Postal codes *facilitate* mail service throughout Canada.
fa·cil·i·tate (fə sil′ə tāt′) *verb,* **facilitated, facilitating.**

facility **1.** Ease or skill in doing something. He rides his new bicycle with great *facility.* **2. facilities.** Something that makes a job easier to do or serves a particular purpose.

The kitchen *facilities* in our summer cabin consist of a stove, refrigerator, and sink. There are very good playground *facilities* in our town for younger children.

fa·cil·i·ty (fə sil′ə tē) *noun, plural* **facilities.**

fact Something that is known to be true or real; something that has really happened. Is it a *fact* that you won first prize? The police were interested in finding out the *facts* of the accident. It is a scientific *fact* that the earth revolves around the sun.

fact (fakt) *noun, plural* **facts.**

factor **1.** One of the things that causes something else. Sunny weather and good food were important *factors* in the success of the picnic. **2.** Any of the numbers that form a product when multiplied together. The *factors* of 12 are 12 and 1, 6 and 2, and 3 and 4.

fac·tor (fak′tər) *noun, plural* **factors.**

factory A building or group of buildings where things are manufactured. Automobiles are made in factories.

fac·to·ry (fak′tər ē) *noun, plural* **factories.**

factual Containing or having to do with facts. The witness gave a *factual* account of the accident.

fac·tu·al (fak′chōō əl) *adjective.*

faculty **1.** A natural power of the mind or body. Hearing and speaking are two human *faculties*. **2.** A special talent or skill for doing something. She has a great *faculty* for making friends. **3.** All the teachers of a school, college, or university. The *faculty* had a meeting before the school year began.

fac·ul·ty (fak′əl tē) *noun, plural* **faculties.**

fad Something that is very popular for a short period of time. My sister and her friends don't do that dance anymore; it was last year's *fad*.

fad (fad) *noun, plural* **fads.**

fade **1.** To lose colour or brightness. Some coloured materials will *fade* when they are washed. The strong sunlight *faded* the curtains. **2.** To lose strength or energy; disappear gradually. The sound of music *faded* away.

fade (fād) *verb,* **faded, fading.**

Fahrenheit Of or according to the temperature scale on which 32 degrees is the freezing point of water and 212 degrees is the boiling point of water.

Fahr·en·heit (far′ən hīt′) *adjective.*

fail **1.** To not succeed in doing or getting something. He *failed* the test the first time he wrote it. We *failed* to get to the station in time to catch our train. **2.** To be of no use or help to; disappoint. Her friends *failed* her when she needed their help. **3.** To not be enough;

run out. The water supply *failed* during the emergency. **4.** To become weaker in strength or health. My grandfather's eyesight is beginning to *fail*. **5.** To not be able to pay what one owes; go bankrupt. Her father's small store *failed* when the new department store opened nearby.

fail (fāl) *verb,* **failed, failing.**

failure **1.** The act of not succeeding in doing or getting something. She was disappointed at her *failure* to get on the swimming team. **2.** A person or thing that does not succeed. The school play will not be a *failure* if everyone works hard. **3.** The condition of not being enough. The bad weather caused a crop *failure*.

fail·ure (fāl′yər) *noun, plural* **failures.**

faint **1.** Not clear or strong; weak. We heard the *faint* cry of a puppy from the basement. There was a *faint* light at the end of the road. **2.** Weak and dizzy. After playing all morning, the children were *faint* with hunger by noon. *Adjective.*
—A condition in which a person seems to be asleep and does not know what is going on around him. *Noun.*
—To be as if asleep and not know what is going on around one. He *fainted* when he heard the news of his wife's accident. *Verb.* ▲ Another word that sounds like this is **feint.**

faint (fānt) *adjective,* **fainter, faintest;** *noun, plural* **faints;** *verb,* **fainted, fainting.**

fair¹ **1.** Not in favour of any one more than another or others; just. The judges made a *fair* decision in choosing Jim the winner of the race. **2.** According to the rules. The referee said it was a *fair* tackle. **3.** Neither too good nor too bad; average. She has a *fair* chance of winning the tennis match. **4.** Light in colouring; not dark. He has *fair* hair. **5.** Not cloudy; clear; sunny. The weather for the weekend will be *fair*. **6.** Pleasing to the eye; attractive; beautiful. The prince married the *fair* young princess. *Adjective.*
—In a fair manner; according to the rules. Jack always plays *fair. Adverb.* ▲ Another word that sounds like this is **fare.**

fair (fer) *adjective,* **fairer, fairest;** *adverb.*

fair² **1.** A public showing of farm products. Fairs are held to show and judge crops and cows, pigs, and other livestock. Fairs often have shows, contests, and entertainment. **2.** Any large showing of products or objects. Father took us to see the Manitoba exhibit at the *fair*. **3.** The showing and selling of things for a particular cause or reason. Our school *fair* is going to raise money for a new playground. ▲ Another word that sounds like this is **fare**.

fair (fer) *noun, plural* **fairs.**

fairly 1. In a fair manner; honestly; justly. That teacher always treats each pupil *fairly.* 2. Somewhat; rather. John has saved a *fairly* large amount of money.

fair·ly (fer′lē) *adverb.*

fairy A tiny being in stories who has magic powers.

fair·y (fer′ē) *noun, plural fairies.*

fall 1. To come down from a higher place; drop. The lamp will *fall* off the table if the baby keeps playing with it. The mountain climber held the rope tightly so that he would not *fall.* 2. To become lower or less. Their voices *fell* to a whisper when the band started to play. The price of eggs has *fallen* by five cents. 3. To take place; happen. Christmas *falls* on December 25. 4. To pass into a particular state or condition; become. He *fell* in love with her. She couldn't come to the [party be]cause she *fell* ill. 5. To be defeated, [capture]d, or overthrown. The city *fell* after a [long ba]ttle. 6. To hang down. The dress *fell* in [fol]ds. *Verb.*

[The act of] coming down from a higher place. He [hurt him]self in the *fall* from the ladder. The [child to]ok a *fall* on the ice. 2. The amount of [something] that comes down. We had a six-[inch] *fall* of rain on Saturday. 3. A loss [of powe]r; capture or defeat. The whole coun[try was] in confusion after the *fall* of the [governm]ent. 4. A lowering or lessening. [There w]as a *fall* in the price of apples last [week.] 5. The season of the year coming [between] summer and winter; autumn. The [weather] begins to get cooler in the fall. [6. A] fall of water from a higher place; [waterfall.] *Noun.*

[Having] to do with the fall season. We went [shopping] for new *fall* clothes. *Adjective.*

[fall (fôl)] *verb,* **fell, fallen, falling;** *noun, plural* [falls; adj]*ective.*

[**fallen** T]he leaves of the trees have *fallen.* [fall·en (fô]l′ən) *verb.*

[**fallout** T]he radioactive material that falls [to the eart]h after a nuclear bomb explodes. [fall·out (fô]l′out′) *noun.*

[**false** 1. N]ot true or correct; wrong. The [children sw]ore not to make a *false* statement. [2. Fake]; artificial. Her grandmother wears [false teeth.] 3. Used to fool or trick. He gave a [false impr]ession when he acted as if the [car bel]onged to him.

[false (fôls)] *adjective,* **falser, falsest.**

[**falter** To] act or speak as if one is not [sure; he]sitate. The baby *faltered* for a [moment be]fore trying to take a step. The man [faltered eve]ry time he spoke of the accident.

[fal·ter (fôl′]tər) *verb,* **faltered, faltering.**

[A falcon has sharp cl]aws. A falcon can fly very fast. Falcons are good hunters and many have been trained to hunt birds and small animals.

fal·con (fäl′kən *or* fal′kən) *noun, plural* **fal·cons.**

at; āpe; cär; end; mē; it; īce; hot; ōld;
wood; fo͞ol; oil; out; up; turn; sing;
thin; this; hw in white; zh in treasure.
ə stands for a in about, e in taken,
i in pencil, o in lemon, and u in circus.

fame The quality of being famous or well-known. The poet's *fame* spread to Europe.
fame (fām) *noun*.

familiar 1. Often heard or seen. I can't remember the name of the song, but the tune is *familiar*. 2. Knowing something well. I am *familiar* with that story. 3. Friendly or close. She is on *familiar* terms with all her neighbours.
fa·mil·iar (fə mil′yər) *adjective*.

family 1. A father and mother and their children. Twenty *families* live on our street. 2. The children of a father and mother. My parents raised a large *family*. 3. A group of people who are related to each other; relatives. The whole *family* will get together for the holidays. 4. A group of people living in the same household. The *family* works and plays together. 5. A group of related animals or plants. Zebras and donkeys belong to the horse *family*. 6. Any group of things that are the same or similar. English and German belong to the same *family* of languages.
fam·i·ly (fam′ə lē *or* fam′lē) *noun, plural* **families**.

Family Compact *Canadian*. A small group of families that governed Upper Canada before 1837.

famine A very great lack of food in an area or country. Many people died of starvation during the *famine* in that country.
fam·ine (fam′in) *noun, plural* **famines**.

famous Very well-known; having great fame. Thomas Edison is *famous* for having invented the electric light.
fa·mous (fā′məs) *adjective*.

fan¹ 1. A device shaped like part of a circle that is held in the hand and waved back and forth to make air move. 2. A mechanical device having several blades that are turned by an electric motor. Fans are used to make air move for cooling or heating. 3. Anything that looks like a fan. The open tail of the peacock is called a fan. *Noun*.
—To move air toward or on. He *fanned* the flames to make the fire burn more. *Verb*.
fan (fan) *noun, plural* **fans**; *verb*, **fanned, fanning**.

Fan

fan² A person who is very enthusiastic about something. My brother is a real football *fan* and watches the games on television every Sunday.
fan (fan) *noun, plural* **fans**.

fanatic A person who is much too devoted to a cause or too enthusiastic about something. That man is such a *fanatic* about being clean that he will not shake hands with other people for fear of getting their germs. Mike is a sports *fanatic* who can watch one game on television while listening to another on the radio. *Noun*.
—Much too devoted or enthusiastic. She is a *fanatic* follower of that political leader. *Adjective*.
fa·nat·ic (fə nat′ik) *noun, plural* **fanatics**; *adjective*.

fancy 1. The power to picture something in the mind; imagination. A unicorn is a creature of *fancy*. 2. Something that is imagined. Being a princess was the little girl's favourite *fancy*. 3. A liking or fondness. Andrew has a *fancy* for cowboy movies. The two girls took a *fancy* to each other. *Noun*.
—Not plain; very decorated. Nancy wore a *fancy* dress to the party. *Adjective*.
—1. To imagine. Tom likes to *fancy* himself as a famous soccer player. 2. To be fond of; like. Which of the dresses do you *fancy* the most? *Verb*.
fan·cy (fan′sē) *noun, plural* **fancies**; *adjective*, **fancier, fanciest**; *verb*, **fancied, fancying**.

fang A long, pointed tooth. The fangs of certain snakes contain poison.
fang (fang) *noun, plural* **fangs**.

fantastic 1. Very strange; odd. The wood in the fireplace took on *fantastic* shapes as it burned. 2. Very good; excellent. The hikers had a *fantastic* view of the town from the top of the mountain.
fan·tas·tic (fan tas′tik) *adjective*.

fantasy Something that is imagined or not real. The author wrote *fantasies* about life on other planets.
fan·ta·sy (fan′tə sē) *noun, plural* **fantasies**.

far 1. At a great distance; not near. She travelled *far* from home to visit her uncle. 2. To or at a certain place, distance, or time. Read as *far* as chapter two for tomorrow. As *far* as I can tell, she's right. The meeting lasted *far* into the afternoon. 3. Very much. It would be *far* better if you waited to leave until the rain stops. *Adverb*.
—1. At a great distance; distant. He lives in the *far* northern part of the country. 2. More distant; farther away. The spacecraft landed on the *far* side of the moon. *Adjective*.

far (fär) *adverb,* **farther** or **further, farthest** or **furthest;** *adjective,* **farther** or **further, farthest** or **furthest.**

fare 1. The cost of a ride on a bus, train, airplane, ship, or taxi. The bus driver collected the *fares.* 2. A passenger who pays a fare. *Noun.*
—To get along; do. He is *faring* well at his new school. *Verb.* ▲ Another word that sounds like this is **fair.**
fare (fer) *noun, plural* **fares;** *verb,* **fared, faring.**

farewell Good-bye and good luck. The guests said their *farewells* and left.
fare·well (fer'wel') *interjection; noun, plural* **farewells.**

farm A piece of land that is used to raise crops and animals for food. *Noun.*
—To raise crops and animals on a farm. Most of the people in this valley *farm* for a living. *Verb.*
farm (färm) *noun, plural* **farms;** *verb,* **farmed, farming.**

farmer A person who lives on and runs a farm.
farm·er (färm'ər) *noun, plural* **farmers.**

farming The business of raising crops or animals on a farm; agriculture. Most of the people in that area make a living by *farming.*
farm·ing (färm'ing) *noun.*

farsighted Able to see things that are far away more clearly than things that are close. Grandmother is *farsighted* and must wear glasses to read.
far·sight·ed (fär'sīt'id) *adjective.*

farther The little boat drifted *farther* and *farther* from the dock. They live at the *farther* side of town. Look up **far** for more information.
far·ther (fär'thər) *adverb; adjective.*

farthest Jane sat *farthest* from the front of the room. He lives *farthest* away from school. The town lies just over the *farthest* hill. Look up **far** for more information.
far·thest (fär'thəst) *adverb; adjective.*

fascinate To attract and hold the interest of; charm. The magician's tricks *fascinated* the children in the audience.
fas·ci·nate (fas'ə nāt') *verb,* **fascinated, fascinating.**

fascism A form of government in which a dictator rules. Under fascism there is strict government control of labour and business, a great stress on national interests, and the putting down by force of all opposition to the government.
fas·cism (fash'iz'əm) *noun.*

fashion 1. The newest custom or style in dress or behaviour. He always bought the latest *fashion* in men's clothing. 2. Manner or way. She decorated her room in her own *fashion. Noun.*
—To give form to; make; shape. Grandfather *fashioned* a little boat out of a block of wood. *Verb.*
fash·ion (fash'ən) *noun, plural* **fashions;** *verb,* **fashioned, fashioning.**

fast[1] 1. Acting, moving, or done very quickly; rapid. Hockey is a very *fast* game. If she catches a *fast* train, she will be here in an hour. He is a very *fast* thinker who can make decisions quickly. 2. Ahead of the correct time. My watch is ten minutes *fast.* 3. Faithful; loyal. Those two men have been *fast* friends since they were in school. 4. Not easily faded. Are the colours in this material *fast? Adjective.*
—1. In a firm way; tightly; securely. The tent was held *fast* by poles driven into the ground. 2. Soundly; deeply. He has been *fast* asleep since nine o'clock. 3. With speed; quickly. The horse ran *fast. Adverb.*
fast (fast) *adjective,* **faster, fastest;** *adverb.*

fast[2] To eat little or no food, or only certain kinds of food. In many religions, people *fast* on certain holy days. *Verb.*
—A day or period of fasting. Many Roman Catholics observe a *fast* each year on Good Friday. *Noun.*
fast (fast) *verb,* **fasted, fasting;** *noun, plural* **fasts.**

fasten To attach, close, or put firmly. Mother *fastened* the gold pin to her dress. Please *fasten* the door when you leave. She *fastened* her attention on the book she was reading.
fas·ten (fas'ən) *verb,* **fastened, fastening.**

fat A yellow or white oily substance. Fat is found mainly in certain body tissues of animals and in some plants. *Noun.*
—1. Having much fat or flesh on the body. That *fat* man has a mass of 130 kilograms. We had a *fat* 10-kilogram turkey for Thanksgiving. 2. Having much in it; full. All that money made his wallet *fat. Adjective.*
fat (fat) *noun, plural* **fats;** *adjective,* **fatter, fattest.**

at; āpe; cär; end; mē; it; īce; hot; ōld; wood; fōōl; oil; out; up; turn; sing; thin; this; hw in white; zh in treasure. ə stands for a in about, e in taken, i in pencil, o in lemon, and u in circus.

fatal 1. Causing death. There are many *fatal* accidents on highways. 2. Causing harm; very bad. He broke his arm when he made the *fatal* mistake of jumping out of the tree.
fa·tal (fāt′əl) *adjective.*

fate The power that is believed to control what is going to happen or how things will turn out. People have no control over fate. The team blamed its loss on *fate.*
fate (fāt) *noun, plural* **fates.**

father 1. The male parent of a child. 2. A priest.
fa·ther (fä′thər) *noun, plural* **fathers.**

father-in-law The father of one's husband or wife.
fa·ther-in-law (fä′thər in lä′) *noun, plural* **fathers-in-law.**

Fathers of Confederation *Canadian.* The group of men mainly responsible for the creation of Canada in 1867.

fathom A measure equal to six feet in the Imperial System of Measure. It is slightly less than two metres. Fathoms are used mainly in measuring the depth of the ocean.
fath·om (fath′əm) *noun, plural* **fathoms.**

fatigue A being tired. Fatigue can be caused by working too hard. *Noun.*
—To cause to be tired. The long hours of studying *fatigued* him. *Verb.*
fa·tigue (fə tēg′) *noun; verb,* **fatigued, fatiguing.**

fatten To make or become fat. The farmer *fattened* the turkeys for Thanksgiving.
fat·ten (fat′ən) *verb,* **fattened, fattening.**

faucet A device for turning water or another liquid on or off; a tap.
fau·cet (fä′sət) *noun, plural* **faucets.**

fault 1. Something that is wrong with and spoils something else. The roof fell in because of a *fault* in the beams. His bad temper is his main *fault.* 2. The responsibility for a mistake. The driver of the speeding car was at *fault* in the accident. 3. A mistake; error. He corrected the *faults* in his spelling.
fault (fält) *noun, plural* **faults.**

faun A god of the woods and fields in Roman myths. A faun had the body of a man and the ears, horns, legs, and tail of a goat. ▲ Another word that sounds like this is **fawn.**
faun (fän) *noun, plural* **fauns.**

favour 1. An act of kindness. He did her a *favour* by giving her a ride to school. 2. Friendliness or approval; liking. The candidate won the *favour* of the voters and was elected. 3. A small gift. The children at the party were given horns and other *favours. Noun.*

—1. To show kindness or favour to; oblige. Please *favour* us with an answer to our letter. 2. To approve of; like. She *favours* the colour red. 3. To show special treatment or kindness. The mother cat *favoured* the sick kitten over the others. 4. To look like; resemble. The baby *favours* his father. *Verb.*
This word is also spelled **favor.**
fa·vour (fā′vər) *noun, plural* **favours;** *verb,* **favoured, favouring.**
in one's favour. To one's advantage. The score was three to nothing *in our favour.*

favourable 1. Showing approval or liking; approving. I hoped she would give me a *favourable* answer and say she could come to the party. 2. In one's favour, benefiting. If the weather is *favourable,* we'll go on a picnic.
This word is also spelled **favorable.**
fa·vour·a·ble (fā′vər ə bəl) *adjective.*

favourite Liked best. Summer is her *favourite* time of year. *Adjective.*
—A person or thing that is liked best. Mystery stories are my *favourites. Noun.*
This word is also spelled **favorite.**
fa·vour·ite (fā′vər it) *adjective; noun, plural* **favourites.**

fawn A young deer. ▲ Another word that sounds like this is **faun.**
fawn (fän) *noun, plural* **fawns.**

Fawn

fear A strong feeling caused by knowing that danger, pain, or evil is near. He felt great *fear* when he saw the escaped lion. *Noun.*
—1. To be afraid of. He *fears* snakes. 2. To be worried or anxious. She *feared* we would be late for the show if we didn't hurry. *Verb.*
fear (fēr) *noun, plural* **fears;** *verb,* **feared, fearing.**

fearful 1. Feeling or showing fear; afraid. The cat was *fearful* of the barking dog. 2. Causing fear; frightening; scary. The thunder and lightning were *fearful.*
fear·ful (fēr′fəl) *adjective.*

feast A large, rich meal for many people on a special occasion. The king invited his knights to a *feast. Noun.*
—To have a feast; eat richly. We *feasted* on turkey and stuffing on Thanksgiving. *Verb.*
feast (fēst) *noun, plural* **feasts;** *verb,* **feasted, feasting.**

feat An act or deed that shows great courage, strength, or skill. Climbing that mountain was quite a *feat.*
▲ Another word that sounds like this is **feet.**
feat (fēt) *noun, plural* **feats.**

feather One of the light growths that cover a bird's skin. Feathers protect the bird's skin from injury and help keep the bird warm.
feath·er (feth′ər) *noun, plural* **feathers.**
feather in one's cap. An act to be proud of. Winning the spelling contest was a *feather in his cap.*

▲ Long ago when a soldier was very brave in battle, he was awarded a feather to wear in his cap or helmet. Wearing a **feather in one's cap** was a great honour. After a while, people began to use a *feather in one's cap* for anything that a person should be proud of.

feature 1. An important or outstanding part or quality of something. One of the most important *features* of the camel is its ability to go for days without water. Among the *features* of that new house are air conditioning in every room and a swimming pool in the back yard. 2. A part of the face. The eyes, nose, mouth, and chin are *features.* 3. A full-length motion picture. *Noun.*
—To give an important place to. The concert *features* a singer and a guitar player. *Verb.*
fea·ture (fē′chər) *noun, plural* **features;** *verb,* **featured, featuring.**

February The second month of the year. February has twenty-eight days except in leap year, when it has twenty-nine.
Feb·ru·ar·y (feb′roo er′ē *or* feb′yoo er′ē) *noun.*

▲ The word **February** comes from the Latin name of a religious holiday that the ancient Romans held in the middle of this month.

fed The dog has not been *fed* its dinner yet. Look up **feed** for more information.
fed (fed) *verb.*

federal 1. Having to do with the national government of Canada, thought of as separate from the government of each province. The power to conduct foreign affairs and provide for defence are *federal* powers.
2. Formed by an agreement between smaller groups to join together as one nation. Canada has a *federal* government.
fed·er·al (fed′ər əl) *adjective.*

federal government The government of Canada. It is made up of the prime minister and the cabinet.

federation A union formed by agreement between provinces, states, or other groups. The various nations formed a *federation* to work for world peace.
fed·er·a·tion (fed′ə rā′shən) *noun, plural* **federations.**

fee Money asked or paid for some service or right. We paid a *fee* of two dollars for a licence for our dog. The admission *fee* to the circus is four dollars.
fee (fē) *noun, plural* **fees.**

feeble Not strong; weak. The *feeble* old woman walked with a cane. We heard the *feeble* cry of a cat from the basement.
fee·ble (fē′bəl) *adjective,* **feebler, feeblest.**

feed 1. To give food to. Can I *feed* the baby? The mother lion *fed* her baby cubs. 2. To give as food. She *fed* oats to the horse. 3. To supply with something necessary or important. Melting snow from the mountains *feeds* the rivers each spring. My sister is learning how to *feed* information into a computer at school. 4. To eat. The cows are *feeding* in the pasture. Frogs *feed* on flies. *Verb.*
—Food for farm animals. Grass, hay, and grains are *feed* for cattle. *Noun.*
feed (fēd) *verb,* **fed, feeding;** *noun, plural* **feeds.**

feel 1. To find out about by touching or handling; touch. I can *feel* the difference between wool and cotton. 2. To be aware of by touch. She could *feel* the rain on her face. 3. To have or cause the sense of being something. The water *feels* warm. He *feels* happy when he thinks of his new bicycle. 4. To think; believe. Many people *feel* that our team should have won the game. 5. To try to find by touching. She *felt* her way up the stairs in the dark. *Verb.*
—The way something seems to the touch. I like the *feel* of velvet on my skin. *Noun.*
feel (fēl) *verb,* **felt, feeling;** *noun, plural* **feels.**

at; āpe; cär; end; mē; it; īce; hot; ōld; wood; fōōl; oil; out; up; turn; sing; thin; this; hw in white; zh in treasure.
ə stands for a in about, e in taken, i in pencil, o in lemon, and u in circus.

feeler   A part of an animal's body that is used for touch. An insect has feelers.
feel·er (fēl′ər) *noun, plural* **feelers.**

feeling   1. The ability to feel by touching; sense of touch. He rubbed his cold hands to bring back the *feeling*. 2. A being aware of; sense of being. Having missed breakfast, I had a *feeling* of hunger around noon. 3. An emotion. Joy, fear, and anger are feelings. 4. **feelings.** The tender or sensitive part of a person's nature. She hurt his *feelings* when she didn't even say hello to him. 5. A way of thinking; opinion; belief. It is my *feeling* that you are right about what happened.
feel·ing (fēl′ing) *noun, plural* **feelings.**

feet   More than one foot. Look up **foot** for more information. ▲ Another word that sounds like this is **feat.**
feet (fēt) *noun plural.*

feign   To put on a false show of; pretend. She *feigned* sickness so that she wouldn't have to go to the dentist.
feign (fān) *verb,* **feigned, feigning.**

feint   A blow or movement meant to trick or take away attention from the main point of attack. *Noun.*
—To make a feint. The boxer *feinted* with his left hand and then hit with his right. *Verb.*
▲ Another word that sounds like this is **faint.**
feint (fānt) *noun, plural* **feints;** *verb,* **feinted, feinting.**

fell¹   She slipped on the ice and *fell.* Look up **fall** for more information.
fell (fel) *verb.*

fell²   1. To hit and knock down; cause to fall. The fighter *felled* his opponent. 2. To cut down. The lumberjack *felled* the tree.
fell (fel) *verb,* **felled, felling.**

fellow   1. A man or boy. He is certainly a clever *fellow* to come up with such a good idea. 2. A person who is like another; companion; associate. *Noun.*
—Being the same or very much alike. He got along well with his *fellow* classmates. *Adjective.*
fel·low (fel′ō) *noun, plural* **fellows;** *adjective.*

felt¹   I *felt* the cold wind against my face. Look up **feel** for more information.
felt (felt) *verb.*

felt²   A material made of wool, hair, or fur that is pressed together in layers instead of being woven or knitted. Felt is used to make hats.
felt (felt) *noun, plural* **felts.**

female   1. Of or having to do with the sex that gives birth to young or produces eggs. A mare is a *female* horse. 2. Having to do with

women or girls; feminine. *Adjective.*
—A female person or animal. Her dog is a *female*. There was an even number of *females* and males in the class. *Noun.*
fe·male (fē′māl) *adjective; noun, plural* **females.**

feminine   Of or having to do with women or girls.
fem·i·nine (fem′ə nin) *adjective.*

fence   1. A structure that is used to surround, protect, or mark off an area. A fence may be made of wire or wood. There was a white picket *fence* in front of the house. The farmer put up a *fence* around the pasture to keep the cows from straying. 2. A person who buys and sells stolen goods. The thief took the stolen diamonds to a *fence. Noun.*
—1. To put a fence around. Mother *fenced* her vegetable garden to keep the rabbits out. In the spring, part of the park is *fenced* off for a ball field. 2. To fight with a sword or foil; take part in the sport of fencing. The two boys *fenced* as the other members of the class watched. *Verb.*
fence (fens) *noun, plural* **fences;** *verb,* **fenced, fencing.**

fencing   The art or sport of fighting with a sword or foil.
fenc·ing (fen′sing) *noun.*

Fencing

fender   1. A metal piece that sticks out over the wheel of an automobile or bicycle for protection against splashed water or mud. 2. A metal screen in front of a fireplace to protect against sparks.
fend·er (fen′dər) *noun, plural* **fenders.**

ferment   1. To go through or cause a chemical change that results in the forming of bubbles of gas. When milk *ferments*, it turns sour. When the juice of grapes *ferments*, it turns into wine. 2. To cause by stirring up or exciting feelings. The rebel leaders tried to *ferment* a revolution by blaming the government for the lack of food in the country. *Verb.*

—Something that causes a substance to ferment. Certain bacteria and moulds are used as ferments in making some cheeses. *Noun.*

fer·ment (fər ment′ *for verb;* fur′ment *for noun*) *verb,* **fermented, fermenting;** *noun, plural* **ferments.**

fern A plant that has large feathery leaves and no flowers. Ferns reproduce from spores instead of seeds.

fern (furn) *noun, plural* **ferns.**

ferocious Extremely cruel or mean; savage; fierce. A hungry lion can be *ferocious.*

fe·ro·cious (fə-rō′shəs) *adjective.*

Fern

ferret An animal that looks like a weasel. Ferrets have yellowish-white fur and pink eyes. They are sometimes trained to hunt rats, mice, and rabbits. *Noun.*
—**1.** To hunt with ferrets. **2.** To look for; search. He *ferreted* through his drawers looking for the missing sock. *Verb.*

fer·ret (fer′ət) *noun, plural* **ferrets;** *verb,* **ferreted, ferreting.**

Ferret

Ferris wheel A large, revolving wheel with seats hung from its rim. It is used at fairs and amusement parks to give people rides.

Fer·ris wheel (fer′is).

ferry A boat used to carry people, cars, and goods across a river, channel, or other narrow body of water. This is also called a **ferryboat.** *Noun.*
—To go or carry in a ferry. The rescue workers *ferried* the storm victims to land. *Verb.*

fer·ry (fer′ē) *noun, plural* **ferries;** *verb,* **ferried, ferrying.**

fertile **1.** Able to produce crops and plants easily and plentifully. There is very *fertile* soil in this valley. **2.** Able to produce eggs, seeds, pollen, or young. An animal is *fertile* when it is able to give birth to young. **3.** Able to develop into or become a new person or animal. An egg must be *fertile* in order for a chick to hatch from it.

fer·tile (fur′təl *or* fur′tīl) *adjective.*

fertilize **1.** To make fertile. A chick hatched from the *fertilized* egg. **2.** To put fertilizer on. The farmer *fertilized* the field with manure.

fer·ti·lize (furt′əl īz′) *verb,* **fertilized, fertilizing.**

fertilizer A substance that is added to soil to make it better for the growing of crops. Manure and certain chemicals are used as fertilizers.

fer·ti·liz·er (furt′əl ī′zər) *noun, plural* **fertilizers.**

festival A celebration or holiday. Many religious *festivals,* such as Christmas and Easter, take place every year. Ten new movies are being shown at this year's film *festival.*

fes·ti·val (fes′tə vəl) *noun, plural* **festivals.**

fetch To go after and bring back; get. Please *fetch* two more chairs from the other room.

fetch (fech) *verb,* **fetched, fetching.**

fetter A chain or piece of iron put on the feet to prevent movement.

fet·ter (fet′ər) *noun, plural* **fetters.**

feud A bitter, violent quarrel between two persons, families, or groups. A feud lasts for many years. The *feud* between the two tribes resulted in the deaths of many people.

feud (fyo͞od) *noun, plural* **feuds.**

feudalism A political system in the western part of Europe during the Middle Ages. Under feudalism, a lord provided land and protection for people under his rule, who were known as vassals. In return they promised loyalty and service to the lord.

feu·dal·ism (fyo͞od′əl iz′əm) *noun.*

fever A body temperature that is higher than normal. A person has a fever if his temperature is more than 37 degrees. The sick boy had a *fever* of 39 degrees.

fe·ver (fē′vər) *noun, plural* **fevers.**

at; āpe; cär; end; mē; it; īce; hot; ōld;
wood; fo͞ol; oil; out; up; turn; sing;
thin; this; hw in white; zh in treasure.
ə stands for a in about, e in taken,
i in pencil, o in lemon, and u in circus.

few Not many. *Few* dogs are here. *Adjective.*
—Not many persons or things. He sold only a *few* of the newspapers. *Noun.*
　few (fyōō) *adjective,* **fewer, fewest;** *noun.*

fez A round, red felt hat that has a tassel. Fezzes used to be worn by men in Turkey.
　fez (fez) *noun, plural* **fezzes.**

fiancé A man to whom a woman is engaged to be married.
　fi·an·cé (fē′än sā′) *noun, plural* **fiancés.**

Fez

fiancée A woman to whom a man is engaged to be married.
　fi·an·cée (fē′än sā′) *noun, plural* **fiancées.**

fibre A fine, threadlike part. The rope was made of hemp *fibres.* This word is also spelled **fiber.**
　fi·bre (fī′bər) *noun, plural* **fibres.**

fibreglass A strong material that is made of fine threads of glass. Fibreglass will not burn easily. It is used for insulation. This word is also spelled **fiberglass.**
　fi·bre·glass (fī′bər glas′) *noun.*

fiction A written work that tells a story about characters and events that are not real. Novels and short stories are fiction.
　fic·tion (fik′shən) *noun.*

fiddle A violin. *Noun.*
—To play a violin. *Verb.*
　fid·dle (fid′əl) *noun, plural* **fiddles;** *verb,* **fiddled, fiddling.**

fiddlehead The young, curled-up leaves of certain kinds of ferns. They are found in Nova Scotia and New Brunswick. Fiddleheads are eaten as a vegetable.
　fid·dle·head (fid′el hed′) *noun, plural* **fiddleheads.**

Fiddlehead

field 1. A piece of open or cleared land. 2. Land that contains or gives a natural resource. There were about ten oil wells in the oil *field.* 3. An area or piece of land on which certain games are played. The players have just come out on the football *field.* 4. An area of interest or activity. Jack will work in the *field* of physics when he graduates. *Noun.*
—To catch, stop, or pick up a ball that has been hit in baseball. *Verb.*
　field (fēld) *noun, plural* **fields;** *verb,* **fielded, fielding.**

field glasses A pair of small binoculars used outdoors.

field hockey A kind of hockey played on a field by two teams of eleven players each. Curved sticks are used to hit a ball along the ground into the other team's goal. It is also called **grass hockey.**

field trip A trip away from the classroom to see things that have been studied. We took a *field trip* to the zoo to study birds.

fierce 1. Cruel or dangerous; savage. The hungry animal was *fierce.* 2. Very strong or violent; raging. There was a *fierce* storm last night that blew down several trees.
　fierce (fērs) *adjective,* **fiercer, fiercest.**

fife A musical instrument like a flute. The fife makes a shrill tone and is most often used with drums in a marching band.
　fife (fīf) *noun, plural* **fifes.**

fifteen Five more than ten; 15.
　fif·teen (fif′tēn′) *noun, plural* **fifteens;** *adjective.*

fifteenth 1. Next after the fourteenth. 2. One of fifteen equal parts; 1/15.
　fif·teenth (fif′tēnth′) *adjective; noun, plural* **fifteenths.**

Fife

fifth 1. Next after the fourth. 2. One of five equal parts; 1/5.
　fifth (fifth) *adjective; noun, plural* **fifths.**

fiftieth 1. Next after the forty-ninth. 2. One of fifty equal parts; 1/50.
　fif·ti·eth (fif′tē əth) *adjective; noun, plural* **fiftieths.**

fifty Five times ten; 50.
　fif·ty (fif′tē) *noun, plural* **fifties;** *adjective.*

fig The sweet fruit of a shrub or small tree that grows in warm regions. Figs have many tiny seeds.
　fig (fig) *noun, plural* **figs.**

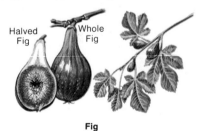

Halved Fig　　Whole Fig

Fig

fight 1. A battle or struggle. The two boys had a fist *fight*. 2. A quarrel. The two sisters had a *fight* over which television programme to watch. *Noun.*
—1. To take part in a battle with. The British *fought* the American colonists in 1776. The policeman *fought* with the thief. 2. To struggle against; try to overcome. The firemen *fought* the blaze for hours. 3. To carry on a battle, contest, or struggle. The sick man *fought* for his life. *Verb.*
  fight (fīt) *noun, plural* **fights;** *verb,* **fought, fighting.**

fighter 1. A person who fights. 2. A person who boxes for a living.
  fight·er (fīt′ər) *noun, plural* **fighters.**

figurative Using words in a way that is different from their actual meanings. *Her head is in the clouds* is a figurative expression because her "head" is not really in the "clouds;" she's only daydreaming.
  fig·ur·a·tive (fig′yər ə tiv *or* fig′ər ə tiv) *adjective.*

figure 1. A symbol that stands for a number. 0, 1, 2, 3, 4, and 5 are figures. 2. An amount given in figures. The population *figures* of the cities and towns are given on the back of the map. 3. A form or outline; shape. He saw the *figure* of a dog in the moonlight. 4. A person; character. The mayor is a public *figure*. 5. A design; pattern. The cloth had bright red *figures* on it. *Noun.*
—1. To find an answer by using numbers. Father and Mother *figured* the cost of the trip. 2. To stand out; have importance; appear. Several well-known people *figured* in the news today. *Verb.*
  fig·ure (fig′yər *or* fig′ər) *noun, plural* **figures;** *verb,* **figured, figuring.**
  to figure out. To come to know or understand. She *figured out* who the murderer was before she got to the end of the book.

figurehead 1. A carved wooden figure placed on the bow of a ship for decoration. 2. A person who has a position of authority but who has no real power or responsibility. In Canada the queen is a *figurehead;* Parliament governs the country.
  fig·ure·head (fig′yər hed′ *or* fig′ər hed′) *noun, plural* **figureheads.**

figure of speech An expression in which words are used in a way that is different from their actual meanings. Figures of speech are used to make writing or speaking fresher and more expressive. "When she saw she was late, she flew out of the house" is a *figure of speech.*

filament A very fine thread, or a part that is like a thread. The filament in an electric light bulb is a fine wire that gives off light when an electric current passes through it.
  fil·a·ment (fil′ə mənt) *noun, plural* **filaments.**

file¹ 1. A folder, drawer, cabinet, or other container in which papers, cards, or records are arranged in order. 2. A set of papers, cards, or records arranged in order. Mother keeps a *file* of recipes. 3. A line of persons, animals, or things placed one behind the other. *Noun.*
—1. To keep papers, cards, or records arranged in order. The secretary *filed* the letters in alphabetical order. 2. To hand in or put on a record. The policeman *filed* a report of the accident. Father must *file* his income tax return. 3. To march or move in a file. The passengers *filed* off the airplane. *Verb.*
  file (fīl) *noun, plural* **files;** *verb,* **filed, filing.**

file² A steel tool having many tiny ridges on one or two sides. A file is used to cut, smooth, or grind down a hard substance. *Noun.*
—To cut, smooth, or grind down with a file. I *filed* my fingernails. *Verb.*
  file (fīl) *noun, plural* **files;** *verb,* **filed, filing.**

filings Small bits that have been removed by a file. A magnet attracts iron *filings.*
  fil·ings (fīl′ingz) *noun plural.*

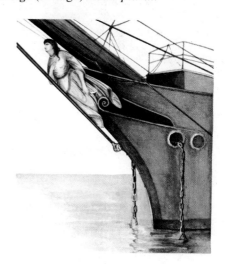

Figurehead

at; āpe; cär; end; mē; it; īce; hot; ōld;
w**oo**d; f**oo**l; oil; out; up; turn; sing;
thin; **th**is; hw in white; zh in treasure.
ə stands for **a** in about, **e** in taken,
i in pencil, **o** in lemon, and **u** in circus.

fill 1. To make or become full. Please *fill* the bucket with water. He will *fill* the box with books. The room *filled* with fresh air when we opened the window. 2. To take up the whole space of. The students *filled* the auditorium. The smell of roses *filled* the room. 3. To give or have whatever is asked for or needed. The grocery store *filled* our order. 4. To stop up or close up by putting something in. The painter *filled* the hole in the wall with plaster before painting. The dentist *filled* a cavity in my tooth. 5. To have or hold a position or office. Mr. Smith will *fill* the office of company treasurer after my father retires. *Verb.*
—Something used to fill. Gravel was used as *fill* for the hole in the road. *Noun.*
   fill (fil) *verb,* **filled, filling;** *noun, plural* **fills.**

fillet A slice of meat or fish without bones or fat. *Noun.* This word is also spelled **filet.**
—To cut meat or fish into fillets. *Verb.*
   fil·let (fi lā′ *or* fil′ā) *noun, plural* **fillets;** *verb,* **filleted, filleting.**

filling A thing used to fill something. Mother used cherries as a pie *filling.* He broke the *filling* in one of his teeth when he bit into the hard candy.
   fill·ing (fil′ing) *noun, plural* **fillings.**

filly A female colt.
   fil·ly (fil′ē) *noun, plural* **fillies.**

film 1. A very thin layer or covering. The windows were covered with a *film* of dirt. 2. A thin roll or strip of material coated with a substance that is sensitive to light. It is used to take photographs. 3. A motion picture. *Noun.*
—1. To cover or become covered with a thin layer of something. The windows of the car were *filmed* with dust from the road. 2. To take pictures of with a motion-picture camera. He *filmed* the ballet class. *Verb.*
   film (film) *noun, plural* **films;** *verb,* **filmed, filming.**

filter 1. A device through which a liquid or air is passed in order to clean out any dirt or other unclean matter. Our swimming pool at school has a *filter.* 2. A material through which a liquid or air passes in a filter. Paper, sand, cloth, and charcoal are often used as filters. *Noun.*
—1. To pass a liquid or air through a filter; strain. The water was *filtered* through charcoal. 2. To take out or separate by a filter. The solid pieces of dirt were *filtered* from the water. 3. To go through slowly. The sunlight *filtered* through the trees. *Verb.*
   fil·ter (fil′tər) *noun, plural* **filters;** *verb,* **filtered, filtering.**

filth Disgusting or sickening dirt. The pond was filled with garbage and other *filth.*
   filth (filth) *noun.*

filthy Extremely dirty; foul. The streets were *filthy.*
   filth·y (fil′thē) *adjective,* **filthier, filthiest.**

fin 1. One of the movable parts that look like wings, sticking out from the body of a fish. A fish uses its fins to swim and balance itself in the water. Certain other water animals, such as whales and porpoises, have fins. 2. Something that has the same shape or use as a fin. Rockets often have fins to give them balance during flight.
   fin (fin) *noun, plural* **fins.**

final 1. Coming at the end; last. I just finished reading the *final* chapter of the book. What was the *final* score of the game? 2. Deciding completely. The decision of the judges is *final. Adjective.*
—1. The last examination of a school, college, or university course of study. My brother Jim is studying for his history *final.* 2. The last or deciding game or match in a series. Our team reached the *finals* of the basketball tournament. *Noun.*
   fi·nal (fīn′əl) *adjective; noun, plural* **finals.**

finale The last part of something; conclusion. The music programme included a piano solo as its *finale.*
   fi·na·le (fi nal′ē *or* fi nä′lē) *noun, plural* **finales.**

finally At the end; at last. We *finally* finished our homework.
   fi·nal·ly (fī′nəl ē) *adverb.*

finance 1. The management of money matters for people, businesses, or governments. The president of that bank is an expert in *finance.* 2. **finances.** The amount of money had by a person, business, or government; funds. The company's *finances* were very low. *Noun.*
—To provide money for. His parents *financed* his university education. *Verb.*
   fi·nance (fi nans′ *or* fī′nans) *noun, plural* **finances;** *verb,* **financed, financing.**

financial Having to do with money matters. Banks, stock exchanges, and insurance companies handle *financial* dealings. Newspapers often have a *financial* section.
   fi·nan·cial (fi nan′shəl *or* fī nan′shəl) *adjective.*

finch A small songbird. The sparrow, canary, and cardinal are kinds of finches.
   finch (finch) *noun, plural* **finches.**

find 1. To come upon by accident; happen on. Where did you *find* that four-leaf clover?

She *found* a wallet on the sidewalk. **2.** To get or learn by adding, subtracting, multiplying, or dividing. Please *find* the sum of this column of numbers. **3.** To learn or discover. I *found* that I could not study well with the radio on. **4.** To look for and get something lost or left. The police *found* the missing money in an old warehouse. **5.** To come to a decision about and declare. The jury *found* the man guilty. *Verb.*
—Something that is found. She came up with some great *finds* when she looked through the attic. *Noun.*

> **find** (fīnd) *verb,* **found, finding;** *noun, plural* **finds.**
> **to find out.** To learn; discover. Try to *find out* what time the meeting is.

fine¹ **1.** Of very high quality; very good; excellent. John is a *fine* musician. **2.** Very small or thin. Betty used a *fine* thread to sew on the button. That book has *fine* print. *Adjective.*
—Very well. He is doing *fine* in school. *Adverb.*

> **fine** (fīn) *adjective,* **finer, finest;** *adverb.*

fine² An amount of money paid as a punishment for breaking a rule or law. There is a *fine* of fifty dollars for littering. *Noun.*
—To punish by making pay a fine. The judge *fined* the driver for going through a red light. *Verb.*

> **fine** (fīn) *noun, plural* **fines;** *verb,* **fined, fining.**

finger **1.** One of the five separate parts at the end of the hand. Usually, a person is said to have four fingers and a thumb. **2.** Anything that has the same shape or use as a finger. *Fingers* of sunlight came through the window. *Noun.*
—To touch, handle, or play with the fingers. The witness *fingered* his handkerchief nervously as the lawyer questioned him. *Verb.*

> **fin·ger** (fing′gər) *noun, plural* **fingers;** *verb,* **fingered, fingering.**

fingernail A hard layer on the end of a finger.

> **fin·ger·nail** (fing′gər nāl′) *noun, plural* **fingernails.**

fingerprint An impression of the markings on the inner surface of the tip of a finger. Fingerprints help to identify people because no two people have the same fingerprints. *Noun.*
—To take the fingerprints of. The police *fingerprinted* the suspected thief. *Verb.*

> **fin·ger·print** (fing′gər print′) *noun, plural* **fingerprints;** *verb,* **fingerprinted, fingerprinting.**

finish **1.** To bring to an end; come to the end of; complete. When will you *finish* your homework? When he *finished* speaking, we all applauded. **2.** To use up completely. We *finished* the jar of peanut butter. **3.** To treat the surface of in some way. He used clear varnish to *finish* the cabinet. *Verb.*
—**1.** The last part of anything; end. We watched the *finish* of the race. **2.** The surface of something. The table has a shiny *finish.* *Noun.*

> **fin·ish** (fin′ish) *verb,* **finished, finishing;** *noun, plural* **finishes.**

fiord A deep, narrow inlet of the sea between high, steep cliffs. The country of Norway has many fiords.

> **fiord** (fyôrd) *noun, plural* **fiords.**

fir An evergreen tree that is related to the pine. Firs have cones and are often used as Christmas trees. ▲ Another word that sounds like this is **fur.**

> **fir** (fur) *noun, plural* **firs.**

Fir Tree

Needles and Cone

fire **1.** The flame, heat, and light given off in burning. **2.** Something burning. He added another log to the *fire.* **3.** Burning that destroys or causes damage. The bad wiring in the old house started a *fire.* **4.** A very strong emotion or feeling; passion. The angry man's eyes were full of *fire.* **5.** The shooting of guns. We heard the sound of rifle *fire* in the distance. *Noun.*
—**1.** To set on fire; cause to burn. We *fired* the heap of dead leaves. **2.** To dismiss from a job. The company *fired* seven employees. **3.** To

at; āpe; cär; end; mē; it; īce; hot; ōld;
wood; fŏŏl; oil; out; up; turn; sing;
thin; this; hw in white; zh in treasure.
ə stands for a in about, e in taken,
i in pencil, o in lemon, and u in circus.

cause to be excited or stirred up. Stories about pirates *fired* the child's imagination. **4.** To shoot a firearm. He *fired* the gun once. *Verb.*
fire (fīr) *noun, plural* **fires;** *verb,* **fired, firing.**

firearm A weapon used for shooting. A firearm is usually a weapon that can be carried and fired by one person. Rifles, pistols, and shotguns are firearms.
fire·arm (fīr′ärm′) *noun, plural* **firearms.**

firebreak A strip of land ploughed or cleared to stop the spread of a fire on the prairie or in the forest.
fire·break (fīr′brāk′) *noun, plural* **firebreaks.**

firecracker A paper tube containing gunpowder and a fuse. Firecrackers are often exploded on holidays and at celebrations.
fire·crack·er (fīr′krak′ər) *noun, plural* **firecrackers.**

fire engine A truck that carries equipment for fighting and putting out fires. Most fire engines have a machine that pumps water or chemicals on a fire to put it out.

fire escape A metal stairway attached to the outside of a building. It is used for escape in case of fire.

fire extinguisher A device containing chemicals that can be sprayed on a fire to put it out.
fire ex·tin·guish·er (eks ting′gwish ər).

firefighter A person whose work is to put out fires; a fireman.
fire·fight·er (fīr′fīt′ər) *noun, plural* **firefighters.**

firefly A small beetle that gives off short flashes of light.
fire·fly (fīr′flī′) *noun, plural* **fireflies.**

Fire Escape

fire hall A building for firefighters, trucks, and equipment.

fireman **1.** A person whose work is to put out and prevent fires. He is usually called a firefighter. **2.** A person who takes care of the fire in a furnace or steam engine.
fire·man (fīr′mən) *noun, plural* **firemen.**

fireplace **1.** An opening in a room with a chimney leading up from it. Fires are built in fireplaces. **2.** An outdoor structure for fires.
fire·place (fīr′plās′) *noun, plural* **fireplaces.**

fireproof That will not burn or will not burn easily. The new hospital is *fireproof.*
fire·proof (fīr′proof′) *adjective.*

fire-reels *Canadian.* A truck that is equipped to put out fires; a fire engine.
fire-reels (fīr′rēlz′) *noun.*

fireside **1.** The area around a fireplace; hearth. **2.** The home or family life.
fire·side (fīr′sīd′) *noun, plural* **firesides.**

fire truck A truck that carries equipment for putting out fires; a fire engine.

fireweed A plant with a bright pink flower. It is the emblem of the Yukon.
fire·weed (fīr′wēd′) *noun, plural* **fireweeds.**

firewood Wood that is used for fires.
fire·wood (fīr′wood′) *noun.*

fireworks Firecrackers and other such devices that are burned or exploded to make loud noises or brilliant shows of light. Fireworks are used in Canada Day celebrations.
fire·works (fīr′wurks′) *noun plural.*

firm[1] **1.** Not giving in to pressure; solid. This is a very *firm* mattress. **2.** Not easily moved; secure. We made sure the fence posts were *firm* in the ground. **3.** Not changing; staying the same. It is my *firm* belief that he is honest. **4.** Steady or strong. During her speech, Mary's voice was *firm. Adjective.*
—So as not to move or change. The post was stuck *firm* in the ground. She stayed *firm* in her belief that he was wrong. *Adverb.*
firm (furm) *adjective,* **firmer, firmest;** *adverb.*

firm[2] A company in which two or more people go into business together. There are five partners in my father's law *firm.*
firm (furm) *noun, plural* **firms.**

first Before all others. Our team finished in *first* place. Sir John A. Macdonald was the *first* prime minister of Canada. *Adjective.*
—**1.** Before all others. She was ranked *first* in her class in mathematics. **2.** For the first time. I *first* heard the news yesterday. *Adverb.*
—**1.** A person or thing that is first. This invention is the *first* of its kind. **2.** The beginning. I liked the new boy from the *first. Noun.*
first (furst) *adjective; adverb; noun, plural* **firsts.**

first aid Emergency treatment that is given to a sick or injured person before a doctor comes.

first-class **1.** Of the highest rank or best quality. The singer gave a *first-class* performance. **2.** Having to do with a class of mail that includes mainly letters, packages, and

other written or sealed matter. **3.** Having to do with the best and most expensive seats or rooms on a ship, train, or airplane. We bought *first-class* tickets for our plane trip. *Adjective.*
—By first-class mail or travel seats or rooms. I sent the package *first-class. Adverb.*
first-class (furst′klas′) *adjective; adverb.*

first-hand Direct from the first or original source. He has *first-hand* knowledge of the accident from talking to the victims.
first-hand (furst′hand′) *adjective; adverb.*

fish **1.** An animal that lives in the water. Fish have backbones, gills for breathing, fins, and, usually, an outer covering of thin bony scales for protection. Fish are cold-blooded animals and are found in almost all fresh and salt waters of the world. **2.** The flesh of fish used as food. *Noun.*
—**1.** To catch or try to catch fish. We *fished* for trout. **2.** To look or search. He *fished* around in his pocket for the key. *Verb.*
fish (fish) *noun, plural* **fish** or **fishes**; *verb,* **fished, fishing.**

fisherman A person who fishes for a living or for sport.
fish·er·man (fish′ər mən) *noun, plural* **fishermen.**

fishery **1.** A fishing business. The cod *fisheries* are important to the economy of Newfoundland. **2.** A place for catching fish.
fish·er·y (fish′ər ē) *noun, plural* **fisheries.**

fish flake *Canadian.* A platform on which fish are dried in the Maritimes.

fish-hawk A kind of hawk that eats fish. This bird is also called an **osprey.** Look up **osprey** for more information.
fish-hawk (fish′häk′) *noun, plural* **fish-hawks.**

fishing rod A pole made of wood, metal, or fibreglass and used for fishing. It has a hook, line, and usually a reel on it.

fishy **1.** Like a fish in odour or taste. His hands smelled *fishy* after cleaning the fish. **2.** Not likely to be true. He gave us a *fishy* excuse for being late.
fish·y (fish′ē) *adjective,* **fishier, fishiest.**

fission The splitting or breaking in two of an atomic nucleus. Large amounts of energy are released during fission.
fis·sion (fish′ən) *noun.*

fist A hand that is tightly closed with the fingers doubled into the palm.
fist (fist) *noun, plural* **fists.**

fit¹ **1.** Suitable, right, or proper. This water is not *fit* to drink. She is *fit* for the job. **2.** In good health; healthy. We should exercise to keep *fit. Adjective.*

—**1.** To be suitable, right, or proper for. The part of the witch in the play does not *fit* her. **2.** To be the right or correct size or shape for. That coat *fits* you well. **3.** To make right, proper, or suitable. He *fit* his speech to the serious nature of the occasion. **4.** To supply with what is necessary or suitable; equip. The campers were *fitted* with all the supplies needed for the trip. **5.** To join, adjust, or put in. We *fitted* the pieces of the jigsaw puzzle together. *Verb.*
—The way in which something fits. The jacket has a tight *fit. Noun.*
fit (fit) *adjective,* **fitter, fittest;** *verb,* **fitted, fitting;** *noun, plural* **fits.**

fit² **1.** A sudden, sharp attack of something. She had a *fit* of coughing. **2.** A sudden burst. He yelled at us in a *fit* of anger.
fit (fit) *noun, plural* **fits.**

five One more than four; 5.
five (fīv) *noun, plural* **fives;** *adjective.*

fivepins *Canadian.* A game of bowling in which the player tries to knock down five pins by rolling a large ball down an alley. The game was first played in Toronto early this century.
five·pins (fīv′pinz′) *noun.*

fix **1.** To make firm or secure; fasten tightly. The campers *fixed* the pegs for the tent in the ground. **2.** To arrange definitely; settle. He *fixed* the price for the used car at $1000. **3.** To direct or hold steadily. He *fixed* his eyes straight ahead. **4.** To place; put. The police *fixed* the responsibility for the accident on the driver of the blue car. **5.** To repair; mend. Can you *fix* the broken chair? **6.** To get ready or arrange; prepare. I will *fix* dinner tonight. She *fixed* up the room before the guests arrived. **7.** To try to get something to come out the way one wants. The dishonest man tried to *fix* the boxing match by bribing one of the boxers to lose on purpose. *Verb.*
—Trouble; difficulty. I got myself into a *fix* by lying to my teacher. *Noun.*
fix (fiks) *verb,* **fixed, fixing;** *noun, plural* **fixes.**

fixture Something that is firmly fastened into place to stay. A bathtub, a toilet, and a washbowl are bathroom fixtures.
fix·ture (fiks′chər) *noun, plural* **fixtures.**

---

at; āpe; cär; end; mē; it; īce; hot; ōld;
wood; fool; oil; out; up; turn; sing;
thin; this; hw in white; zh in treasure.
ə stands for a in about, e in taken,
i in pencil, o in lemon, and u in circus.

flag A piece of cloth having different colours and designs on it. Flags are used as symbols of countries or of organizations. Flags are also sometimes used for giving signals. *Noun.*
—To stop or signal. She *flagged* a taxicab by waving her hand. *Verb.*
flag (flag) *noun, plural* **flags;** *verb,* **flagged, flagging.**

Canadian Flag

flair A natural talent. Monty has a *flair* for acting. ▲ Another word that sounds like this is **flare.**
flair (fler) *noun, plural* **flairs.**

flake 1. A small, thin flat piece. Large *flakes* of snow covered the window sill. 2. *Canadian.* A platform for drying fish; a fish flake. *Noun.*
—To chip or peel off in flakes. The painter *flaked* the old paint off the wall. *Verb.*
flake (flāk) *noun, plural* **flakes;** *verb,* **flaked, flaking.**

flame 1. One of the tongues of light given off by a fire. 2. Gas or vapour that has been set on fire to give off light or heat. She lowered the *flame* under the frying pan on the stove. 3. The condition of burning. The house burst into *flame. Noun.*
—1. To burn with flames; blaze. The fire *flamed* for hours. 2. To light up or glow. His face *flamed* with anger at her rudeness. *Verb.*
flame (flām) *noun, plural* **flames;** *verb,* **flamed, flaming.**

flamingo A pink or red bird that has a long thin neck and legs, and webbed feet. Flamingos live near shallow lakes and lagoons in tropical areas throughout the world.
fla·min·go (flə ming′gō) *noun, plural* **flamingos** or **flamingoes.**

flammable Able to be set on fire easily. Some gases are very *flammable.*
flam·ma·ble (flam′ə bəl) *adjective.*

flank The part between the ribs and the hip on either side of the body of a person or an animal. *Noun.*

Flamingo

—1. To be at the side of. Two statues of lions *flanked* the entrance to the library. 2. To attack or move around the side of. Our ships *flanked* the enemy fleet. *Verb.*
flank (flangk) *noun, plural* **flanks;** *verb,* **flanked, flanking.**

flannel A soft cotton or woollen material. Flannel is used for such things as nightgowns, babies' clothes, and shirts.
flan·nel (flan′əl) *noun, plural* **flannels.**

flap 1. To move up and down. The bird *flapped* its wings. 2. To swing or wave loosely and with noise. The curtain *flapped* in the breeze. *Verb.*
—1. The motion or the noise made by something when it flaps. We could hear the *flap* of the shutters against the house. 2. Something that is attached at only one edge so that it may move. The cover over the opening of a pocket is called a flap. The part of an envelope that is folded down in closing it is a flap. *Noun.*
flap (flap) *verb,* **flapped, flapping;** *noun, plural* **flaps.**

flare 1. To burn with a sudden, very bright light. The match *flared* in the darkness and went out. 2. To break out with sudden or violent feeling. Her temper *flared* at the insulting remark he made. 3. To open or spread outward. Mary's new skirt *flares* from the waist. *Verb.*
—1. A sudden bright light. A flare usually lasts only a short time. 2. A fire or burst of light used as a signal or to give light. The captain of the ship in trouble sent up *flares* as a signal for help. *Noun.* ▲ Another word that sounds like this is **flair.**
flare (fler) *verb,* **flared, flaring;** *noun, plural* **flares.**

flash 1. A sudden, short burst of light or flame. The *flash* of lightning scared the puppy. 2. A very short period of time; instant. The fire engines were at the scene of the fire in a *flash. Noun.*
—1. To burst out in sudden light or fire. Lightning *flashed* in the sky. 2. To show suddenly and for a short time. Her eyes *flashed* with anger. 3. To come or move suddenly or quickly. The ambulance *flashed* by. The answer to the riddle *flashed* into his mind. *Verb.*
flash (flash) *noun, plural* **flashes;** *verb,* **flashed, flashing.**

flashlight An electric light that is powered by batteries and is small enough to be carried around.
flash·light (flash′līt′) *noun, plural* **flashlights.**

flask A small bottle that is used to hold liquids.
flask (flask) *noun,* *plural* **flasks.**

flat¹ **1.** Smooth or even; level. It is easy to ride a bicycle on a *flat* road. The field is *flat* in some parts. **2.** Lying, placed, or stretched at full length; spread out. He was still *flat* on his back. **3.** Not very deep or thick; shallow. The food was served on a large *flat* tray. **4.** That cannot

Flask

be changed. The bus charges a *flat* rate for the trip. **5.** Without much interest or energy; dull. The singer gave a *flat* performance. **6.** Containing little or no air. We got a *flat* tire riding over the broken glass. *Adjective.*
—**1.** A flat part or surface. He hit the table with the *flat* of his hand. **2.** A tire that has little or no air. **3.** In music, a tone or note that is one half note below its natural pitch. **4.** A symbol (♭) that shows this tone or note. *Noun.*
—**1.** In a flat manner. The cat lay *flat* on the ground. **2.** Exactly; precisely. He ran the race in four minutes *flat.* **3.** Below the true pitch in music. She sang *flat. Adverb.*
flat (flat) *adjective,* **flatter, flattest;** *noun,* *plural* **flats;** *adverb.*

flat² An apartment or set of rooms on one floor of a building.
flat (flat) *noun, plural* **flats.**

flatcar A railway car that has a floor but no roof or sides. It is used for carrying freight.
flat·car (flat′kär′) *noun, plural* **flatcars.**

flatfish A fish that has a flattened body. A flatfish has both eyes on the upper side of the body. Flounder, sole, and halibut are flatfish.
flat·fish (flat′fish′) *noun, plural* **flatfish** or **flatfishes.**

Flatfish

flatten To make or become flat or flatter.
flat·ten (flat′ən) *verb,* **flattened, flattening.**

flatter **1.** To praise too much or insincerely. He *flattered* her by saying that she was the most beautiful girl in the world. **2.** To show as more attractive than is actually true. That picture *flatters* him.
flat·ter (flat′ər) *verb,* **flattered, flattering.**

flavour **1.** A particular taste. Adding pepper to the stew will give it a spicy *flavour.* **2.** A special or main quality. The speaker's personal experiences as a policeman added *flavour* to the lecture. *Noun.*
—To give flavour or taste to. Mother *flavoured* the apple pie with cinnamon. *Verb.*
This word is also spelled **flavor.**
fla·vour (flā′vər) *noun, plural* **flavours;** *verb,* **flavoured, flavouring.**

flavouring Something added to food or drink to give flavour. This word is also spelled **flavoring.**
fla·vour·ing (flā′vər ing) *noun, plural* **flavourings.**

flaw A scratch, crack, or other defect. There is a *flaw* in that glass vase. That young man's selfishness is a *flaw* in his character.
flaw (flä) *noun, plural* **flaws.**

flax **1.** A kind of plant. **2.** A fibre that comes from the stem of this plant. This fibre is spun into thread, and the thread is used to make linen cloth, ropes, and rugs.
flax (flaks) *noun.*

flea An insect without wings. Fleas feed on the blood of human beings, dogs, cats, and other animals. A flea can sometimes carry disease by giving it to the person or animal it is living on. ▲ Another word that sounds like this is **flee.**
flea (flē) *noun, plural* **fleas.**

Flax

fled The thief stole the jewellery and *fled* from the house.
fled (fled) *verb.*

at; āpe; cär; end; mē; it; īce; hot; ōld;
wood; fōōl; oil; out; up; turn; sing;
thin; this; hw in white; zh in treasure.
ə stands for a in about, e in taken,
i in pencil, o in lemon, and u in circus.

flee   1. To run away. The family tried to *flee* from the burning house. 2. To move or pass away quickly. The days of my vacation *fled* by. ▲ Another word that sounds like this is **flea**.

fleece   The coat of wool covering a sheep. *Noun.*
—To cut the fleece from. The farm hand used a pair of clippers to *fleece* the sheep. *Verb.*
fleece (flēs) *noun; verb,* **fleeced, fleecing.**

fleet¹   1. A group of warships under one command. The admiral ordered the *fleet* to sail. 2. Any group of ships, airplanes, or cars. My uncle owns a *fleet* of taxicabs.
fleet (flēt) *noun, plural* **fleets.**

fleet²   Fast. The deer is a *fleet* animal.
fleet (flēt) *adjective,* **fleeter, fleetest.**

fleeting   Passing very quickly; very brief. The woman had only a *fleeting* look at the car because it drove by her so fast.
fleet·ing (flēt′ing) *adjective.*

flesh   1. The soft part of the body that covers the bones and is covered by skin. 2. The soft part of fruit or vegetables that can be eaten.
flesh (flesh) *noun.*

fleshy   Plump; fat. We eat the *fleshy* part of a banana.
flesh·y (flesh′ē) *adjective,* **fleshier, fleshiest.**

fleur-de-lis   1. The flower of the iris plant. 2. A design that looks like an iris. It is the royal emblem of France. It is also used as an emblem of Quebec.
fleur-de-lis (flur′də lē′) *noun, plural* **fleurs-de-lis.**

flew   The bird *flew* away as soon as it saw the cat creeping up on it. Look up **fly** for more information. ▲ Other words that sound like this are **flu** and **flue.**
flew (floo) *verb.*

flex   To bend. The baseball pitcher *flexed* his throwing arm often to keep it loose.
flex (fleks) *verb,* **flexed, flexing.**

flexible   Able to bend without breaking; not stiff. Rubber is a *flexible* material.
flex·i·ble (flek′sə bəl) *adjective.*

flick   A light, quick snap. Jim turned the lock on the door with a *flick* of the wrist. *Noun.*
—1. To hit or remove with a quick, light snap. She *flicked* the crumbs off the table before serving the dessert. 2. To make a light, quick movement. Bob *flicked* a string in front of the cat to get her to chase it. *Verb.*
flick (flik) *noun, plural* **flicks;** *verb,* **flicked, flicking.**

flicker¹   1. To burn with an unsteady or wavering light. The candles *flickered* in the breeze from the open window. 2. To move back and forth with a quick, unsteady movement. Shadows from the leaves of the trees *flickered* on the barn door. *Verb.*
—1. An unsteady or wavering light. The *flicker* of the firelight made strange shadows on the wall. 2. A quick, unsteady movement. We watched the *flicker* of the snake's tongue. *Noun.*
flick·er (flik′ər) *verb,* **flickered, flickering;** *noun, plural* **flickers.**

flicker²   A North American woodpecker. It has yellow markings on its wings and tail.
flick·er (flik′ər) *noun, plural* **flickers.**

Flicker

flied   The batter *flied* to left field. Look up **fly** for more information.
flied (flīd) *verb.*

flier   A person or thing that flies. The eagle is a powerful *flier.* This word is also spelled **flyer.**
fli·er (flī′ər) *noun, plural* **fliers.**

flies   More than one fly. Look up **fly** for more information.
flies (flīz) *noun plural.*

flight¹   1. Movement through the air with the use of wings; flying. We watched the graceful *flight* of the gull. 2. The distance or course travelled by something flying. It is a short airplane *flight* from Calgary to Edmonton. 3. A group of things flying through the air together. We saw a *flight* of birds heading south for the winter. 4. A trip in an airplane. The senator has a ticket on the night *flight* to Ottawa. 5. A set of stairs or steps between floors or landings of a building. Bryn climbed two *flights* of stairs to get to her room.
flight (flīt) *noun, plural* **flights.**

flight²   The act of running away; escape. Our shouts put the robber to *flight.*
flight (flīt) *noun, plural* **flights.**

flight attendant   A person who serves passengers on an airplane.

flimsy   Without strength; light and thin; frail. Helen felt cold in the cool night air because she had on a *flimsy* summer blouse. Zoë's parents didn't believe her *flimsy* excuse for being late.
flim·sy (flim′zē) *adjective,* **flimsier, flimsiest.**

flinch To draw back from something that is painful, dangerous, or unpleasant. Charlie *flinched* when the doctor gave him the flu shot.
flinch (flinch) *verb,* **flinched, flinching.**

fling To throw or move suddenly and with force. Jack always *flings* his books and coat on his bed. *Verb.*
—**1.** A throw. The boy gave the pebble a *fling* and it landed in the pond. **2.** A time of doing exactly what one pleases. After graduating from university, Mary went to Europe and had a *fling* before looking for a job. *Noun.*
fling (fling) *verb,* **flung, flinging;** *noun, plural* **flings.**

flint A very hard, grey stone that makes sparks when struck against steel. Before the invention of matches, flint was used to light fires.
flint (flint) *noun, plural* **flints.**

flintlock An old-fashioned gun. In a flintlock, flint is struck against steel to make sparks that set the gunpowder on fire.
flint·lock (flint′lok′) *noun, plural* **flintlocks.**

Flintlock

flip To toss or move with a quick, jerking motion. Tom and Nat decided to *flip* a coin to see who would go first. Ed *flipped* the pages of the book until he came to the part he was looking for. *Verb.*
—A toss. The argument between the boys was decided by a *flip* of a coin. *Noun.*
flip (flip) *verb,* **flipped, flipping;** *noun, plural* **flips.**

flipper **1.** A broad, flat limb on a seal, turtle, penguin, or other animal. Flippers are used for swimming and moving along on land. Many Newfoundlanders like seal flippers. **2.** One of a pair of rubber shoes shaped like a duck's feet. Flippers are worn to make swimming or skin diving easier.
flip·per (flip′ər) *noun, plural* **flippers.**

flirt To act romantic in a playful way. The pretty girl liked to *flirt* with every boy she met.
flirt (flurt) *verb,* **flirted, flirting.**

flit **1.** To move quickly and lightly. We watched the butterflies *flit* among the flowers. **2.** To pass lightly and swiftly. Thoughts about summer *flitted* through her mind as she stood at the window and watched the falling snow.
flit (flit) *verb,* **flitted, flitting.**

float **1.** To rest on top of water or other liquid. In swimming class Lucy learned how to *float* on her back. Sailboats *floated* on the lake. The cork *floated.* **2.** To move along slowly in the air or on water. The children *floated* gently down the river on a raft. **3.** To drift or be carried along in the air. Large clouds *floated* across the prairie sky. Leaves *floated* down from the trees and fell into the quiet waters of Grenadier Pond. *Verb.*
—**1.** Anything that rests on top of water. A raft anchored on the edge of the swimming area in a lake is a float. Jane and Sue dived into the lake to see who could get to the *float* first. **2.** A low, flat platform on wheels that carries an exhibit in a parade. My sister and I thought that the *floats* we saw in last year's Grey Cup parade were the best we had ever seen. **3.** A hollow metal ball or other device that floats on a body of liquid. **4.** A drink that has ice cream in it. At the restaurant we ordered two pineapple *floats* and two hamburgers. *Noun.*
float (flōt) *verb,* **floated, floating;** *noun, plural* **floats.**

flock **1.** A group of animals of one kind that is herded or gathered together. The farmer tends his *flock* of sheep. We saw a *flock* of geese flying south. **2.** A large number or group. A *flock* of newspaper reporters crowded around the prime minister after he gave his speech. The minister gave a sermon every Sunday morning to the faithful members of his *flock. Noun.*
—To move or gather as a group. People always *flock* to the beaches during the hot summer weather. *Verb.*
flock (flok) *noun, plural* **flocks;** *verb,* **flocked, flocking.**

at; āpe; cär; end; mē; it; īce; hot; ōld;
wood; fōōl; oil; out; up; turn; sing;
thin; this; hw in white; zh in treasure.
ə stands for a in about, e in taken,
i in pencil, o in lemon, and u in circus.

floe A mass or sheet of floating ice. ▲ Another word that sounds like this is **flow**.
floe (flō) *noun, plural* **floes.**

Floe

flood 1. A great flow of water over dry land. The people who lived in the river valley feared a *flood* because there was a lot of heavy rain. 2. A great flow of anything. The girl told all her problems to her friend in a *flood* of words mixed with tears. 3. *Canadian.* The breaking up of the ice on the lakes and rivers in the spring. This word is most common in Quebec where the breaking up and melting of the ice on the St. Lawrence River is usually accompanied by dangerous flooding. *Noun.*
—1. To cover with water. The town was *flooded* when the dam broke. 2. To fill or overwhelm. The baseball field was *flooded* with light for the night game. 3. To build up an ice rink by spraying water on the surface and allowing it to freeze. The ice is made thicker by applying water again and again. We had a good ice rink last winter because we *flooded* it every night. *Verb.*
flood (flud) *noun, plural* **floods;** *verb,* **flooded, flooding.**

floor 1. The part of a room that a person walks or stands on. The kitchen *floor* is covered with tiles. 2. Any surface that is like a floor. The ship sank to the ocean *floor.* 3. The storey of a building. Mother's office is on the second *floor* of the building. *Noun.*
—1. To cover with a floor. Dad decided to *floor* the basement with cement. 2. To knock down. The boxer *floored* the other fighter in the sixth round. *Verb.*
floor (flōr) *noun, plural* **floors;** *verb,* **floored, flooring.**

flop 1. To drop or fall heavily. John was so tired he couldn't wait to get home and *flop* into bed. 2. To move around or flap loosely. The dog's ears *flopped* when it ran. 3. To fail completely. The new restaurant *flopped* after being open for only a month. *Verb.*
—1. The act or sound of dropping or falling heavily. The seal jumped into the water with a *flop.* 2. A complete failure. The new play was such a *flop* it closed after the first performance. *Noun.*
flop (flop) *verb,* **flopped, flopping;** *noun, plural* **flops.**

floral Relating to flowers.
flo·ral (flōr′əl) *adjective.*

florist A person who sells flowers.
flo·rist (flōr′ist) *noun, plural* **florists.**

flounder¹ To struggle or stumble about. Henry and his friends went hiking and had to *flounder* about in mud that came way above their ankles.
floun·der (floun′dər) *verb,* **floundered, floundering.**

flounder² A flatfish that lives in salt water. It is eaten as food.
floun·der (floun′dər) *noun, plural* **flounders** or **flounder.**

flour A fine meal that is made by grinding and sifting wheat, rye, or other grains. Flour is used to make bread and cake.
flour (flour) *noun, plural* **flours.**

flourish 1. To grow or develop strongly and with vigour. Tomatoes will *flourish* in a very sunny garden if they are given lots of water. A highly developed civilization *flourished* in Greece thousands of years ago. 2. To wave in the air boldly. The guard *flourished* a gun at the escaping prisoners. *Verb.*
—A showy or bold action or sound. The leading actor walked on stage with a *flourish.* The trumpets announced the coming of the king with a *flourish. Noun.*
flour·ish (flur′ish) *verb,* **flourished, flourishing;** *noun, plural* **flourishes.**

flow 1. To move along steadily in a stream. A stream *flows* past the back of our house. Electricity *flows* through wires. The crowd *flowed* out of the football stadium when the game was over. 2. To hang or fall loosely. Mary's long hair *flowed* to her waist. *Verb.*
—1. The act of flowing. The *flow* of a river can be controlled by building a dam. 2. Something that flows. Every morning the highways going into the city are filled with a steady *flow* of cars. *Noun.* ▲ Another word that sounds like this is **floe.**
flow (flō) *verb,* **flowed, flowing;** *noun, plural* **flows.**

flower 1. The part of a plant that has coloured petals; blossom. The flower contains seeds that are able to produce new plants. 2. The finest part or time. The adventures of King Arthur and his knights took place when knighthood was in *flower. Noun.*
—To produce flowers; blossom. Cherry trees *flower* in the early spring. *Verb.*
flow·er (flou′ər) *noun, plural* **flowers;** *verb,* **flowered, flowering.**

flown The bird had *flown* out of the cage. Look up **fly** for more information.
flown (flōn) *verb.*

flu A disease that is like a very bad cold. It is caused by a virus and can easily spread from one person to another. This word is a short form of **influenza,** which is the full name for this disease. ▲ Other words that sound like this are **flew** and **flue.**
flu (flōō) *noun, plural* **flus.**

flue A passage in a chimney that draws the smoke from a fireplace out of the room and into the outside air. ▲ Other words that sound like this are **flew** and **flu.**
flue (flōō) *noun, plural* **flues.**

fluff A soft, light material. The baby's hair is just like *fluff. Noun.*
—To pat or puff into a soft, light mass. Alice *fluffed* up the cushions on the couch before the guests arrived. *Verb.*
fluff (fluf) *noun; verb,* **fluffed, fluffing.**

fluffy Covered with or like fluff. Dad took us to the farm to see the *fluffy* baby chicks.
fluff·y (fluf′ē) *adjective,* **fluffier, fluffiest.**

fluid A gas or liquid. Fluids can flow easily. Air and water are fluids. *Noun.*
—Flowing; not solid. Water is *fluid. Adjective.*
flu·id (flōō′id) *noun, plural* **fluids;** *adjective.*

flung Peter *flung* the glass against the wall in anger. Look up **fling** for more information.
flung (flung) *verb.*

flurry A sudden outburst or stir. There is always a *flurry* of excitement on Christmas morning when the children come down to open their presents. Today's weather report calls for snow *flurries.*
flur·ry (flur′ē) *noun, plural* **flurries.**

flush¹ 1. To turn red or cause to turn red; blush. The woman's face *flushed* when she could not remember her guest's last name. 2. To flow or rush suddenly. Water *flushed* through the pipes. 3. To empty or wash with a sudden rush of water. The city sent some workmen to *flush* out the drain on the corner that was clogged with leaves and litter. *Verb.*
—1. A reddish colour or glow. Ruth came in from skiing with a healthy *flush* on her cheeks. 2. A sudden rush or flow. Ted turned on the water for the garden hose and a *flush* of water poured all over the walk. *Noun.*
flush (flush) *verb,* **flushed, flushing;** *noun, plural* **flushes.**

flush² Even or level. The orange juice was *flush* with the rim of the glass. We tried to hang the second picture on the wall *flush* with the first one.
flush (flush) *adjective; adverb.*

fluster To make embarrassed or nervous; confuse. It *flustered* Tim and Sarah to be the only couple on the dance floor. *Verb.*
—Nervous confusion. The bridegroom was in a *fluster* the morning of the wedding. *Noun.*
flus·ter (flus′tər) *verb,* **flustered, flustering;** *noun.*

flute A long, thin musical instrument. A person plays a flute by holding it out to one side and blowing across a hole at one end. The player makes different notes by covering the holes with his fingers or by pushing down keys that cover the holes.
flute (flōōt) *noun, plural* **flutes.**

Flute

flutter To move or fly with quick, light movements. The flag *fluttered* in the breeze. Butterflies *fluttered* among the flowers. *Verb.*
—1. A quick, light movement. We heard a *flutter* of wings and hoped it might be the wild geese returning to their nests. 2. A state of excitement or confusion. The appearance of the movie star caused a *flutter* among his fans. *Noun.*
flut·ter (flut′ər) *verb,* **fluttered, fluttering;** *noun, plural* **flutters.**

at; āpe; cär; end; mē; it; īce; hot; ōld;
wood; fōōl; oil; out; up; turn; sing;
thin; this; hw in white; zh in treasure.
ə stands for a in about, e in taken,
i in pencil, o in lemon, and u in circus.

fly¹ One of a large group of insects that have two wings. Houseflies, mosquitoes, and gnats are flies.

fly (flī) *noun, plural* **flies.**

fly² **1.** To move through the air with wings. Some birds that live in cold areas *fly* south for the winter. **2.** To pilot or travel in an aircraft. My uncle *flew* a bomber during the war. Arthur *flew* to Vancouver last night to visit his grandmother. **3.** To move or float in the air. The ocean spray *flew* into our faces. The boy went to the park to *fly* his kite. A flag *flew* from the ship's mast. **4.** To go swiftly. The mother *flew* up the stairs when she heard her baby crying. **5.** To hit a ball high into the air in baseball. The batter *flied* to left field. *Verb.*
—**1.** A flap of material that covers buttons or a zipper on a piece of clothing. Men's trousers have a *fly* in front. **2.** A baseball hit high into the air. The batter hit a *fly* to centre field. *Noun.*

fly (flī) *verb,* **flew, flown, flying** (*for definitions 1–4*) or **flied, flying** (*for definition 5*); *noun, plural* **flies.**

flycatcher A bird that flies after insects and catches them for food.

fly·catch·er (flī′-kach′ər) *noun, plural* **flycatchers.**

flyer A person or thing that flies. This word is usually spelled **flier.** Look up **flier** for more information.

Flycatcher

flying fish A saltwater fish that has fins like wings. The flying fish uses its fins to leap into the air and glide above the surface of the water.

Flying Fish

flying saucer An unidentified flying object that is in the shape of a saucer. Some people think that flying saucers come from outer space.

flywheel A heavy wheel that keeps an engine running at an even speed.

fly·wheel (flī′wēl′ *or* flī′hwēl′) *noun, plural* **flywheels.**

foal A young horse, donkey, zebra, or similar animal.

foal (fōl) *noun, plural* **foals.**

foam A mass of bubbles. *Foam* forms on waves as they break against the shore. *Noun.*
—To form or flow in a mass of bubbles. The beer *foamed* when it was poured into the glass. *Verb.*

foam (fōm) *noun; verb,* **foamed, foaming.**

foam rubber A firm, spongy rubber that is used for seats, mattresses, and pillows.

focus **1.** The point at which light rays meet after being bent by a lens. **2.** The distance from the lens to the point where the rays meet. The eye of a farsighted person has a longer *focus* than the eye of a person with normal eyesight. **3.** A centre of activity or interest. The speaker was the *focus* of attention for the audience. *Noun.*
—**1.** To bring to a meeting point or focus. A magnifying glass can be used to *focus* the sun's rays on a piece of paper and start a fire. **2.** To bring into focus so as to make a clear image. The photographer *focussed* the camera before taking the picture. **3.** To fix or direct. The wedding guests *focussed* all their attention on the bride and groom. *Verb.*

fo·cus (fō′kəs) *noun, plural* **focuses;** *verb,* **focussed, focussing** or **focused, focusing.**

fodder Food for horses, cows, and other farm animals. Hay and cornstalks are fodder.

fod·der (fod′ər) *noun, plural* **fodders.**

foe An enemy. The knight said to the stranger, "Are you friend or *foe?*"

foe (fō) *noun, plural* **foes.**

fog **1.** A cloud of small drops of water close to the earth's surface. The thick *fog* made driving dangerous. **2.** A state of confusion. Before Father has his coffee in the morning, he walks around the house in a *fog. Noun.*
—To cover or become covered with fog. We had trouble driving home because the heavy mist had *fogged* the road. *Verb.*

fog (fog) *noun, plural* **fogs;** *verb,* **fogged, fogging.**

foggy **1.** Full of or hidden by fog; misty. It was such a *foggy* evening we could not see the tops of the tallest buildings. **2.** Confused or unclear. John had only a *foggy* idea of what was wrong with his car.

fog·gy (fog′ē) *adjective,* **foggier, foggiest.**

foghorn A horn that is sounded to give a warning to ships when it is foggy.
fog·horn (fog′hôrn′) *noun, plural* **foghorns.**

foil[1] To stop from being successful. The police were able to *foil* the bank robbery because they had been told about it ahead of time.
foil (foil) *verb,* **foiled, foiling.**

foil[2] Metal that is rolled into very thin sheets. Dick's mother wrapped his sandwich and cookies in aluminum *foil* to keep them fresh until lunch.
foil (foil) *noun, plural* **foils.**

foil[3] A long sword used in fencing. The tip of a foil is covered to prevent injury.
foil (foil) *noun, plural* **foils.**

fold[1] **1.** To bend or double over on itself. *Fold* the letter and put it in the envelope. **2.** To bring together close to the body. The girl *folded* her hands in her lap and waited patiently. The bird *folded* its wings and went to sleep. *Verb.*
—A part that is bent or doubled over on itself. Susan's dress hung in graceful *folds.* Cut the paper along the *fold. Noun.*
fold (fōld) *verb,* **folded, folding;** *noun, plural* **folds.**

fold[2] A pen or other closed-in area for sheep. The farmer herded his sheep into the *fold* for the night.
fold (fōld) *noun, plural* **folds.**

folder **1.** A holder for loose papers. A folder is often a folded sheet of light cardboard. **2.** A booklet made up of folded sheets of paper. When we took our trip to Europe, we got travel *folders* on all the places we were going to see.
fold·er (fōl′dər) *noun, plural* **folders.**

foliage The leaves on a tree or other plant.
fo·li·age (fō′lē ij) *noun.*

folk **1.** People. City *folk* like to take their vacations in the country. If you talk to the old *folks* who live here, you can learn a lot about the town's history. **2.** Family or relatives. During the Christmas holidays, Linda is going to visit her *folks.*
folk (fōk) *noun, plural* **folk** or **folks.**

folk dance **1.** A dance coming from the common people. **2.** The music for this kind of dance.

folk music The music of the common people of a region or country.

folk song A song of a region or country that has been handed down among the common people.

folk tale A story that has been handed down among the common people.

follow **1.** To go or come after. The boy trained his dog not to *follow* him across the busy street. Spring *follows* winter. **2.** To go along. *Follow* this road down the hill and turn left at the stop sign. **3.** To act according to; obey. *Follow* the instructions on the package. **4.** To watch or listen closely. The students *followed* the story with interest. **5.** To understand. Do you *follow* the solution to this arithmetic problem?
fol·low (fol′ō) *verb,* **followed, following.**

follower A person or thing that follows. That boy is a leader, not a *follower.*
fol·low·er (fol′ō ər) *noun, plural* **followers.**

following That comes after in order or time. Jim and Susan are going to pack on Thursday evening and start on their trip the *following* morning. *Adjective.*
—A group of followers. That author has a large *following. Noun.*
fol·low·ing (fol′ō ing) *adjective; noun, plural* **followings.**

folly A lack of good sense; foolishness. It is *folly* to think that you can drive anywhere in this thick fog.
fol·ly (fol′ē) *noun, plural* **follies.**

fond Liking or loving. Susie is very *fond* of animals.
fond (fond) *adjective,* **fonder, fondest.**

fondle To pat or touch lovingly. Dick *fondled* his dog's ears.
fon·dle (fon′dəl) *verb,* **fondled, fondling.**

font A basin used to hold water for baptism.
font (font) *noun, plural* **fonts.**

food Something that is eaten or taken in by people, animals, or plants that keeps them alive and helps them grow.
food (food) *noun, plural* **foods.**

fool **1.** A person who does not have good sense. My brother is a *fool* to think that he can drive all day and all night without any sleep. **2.** A person who used to be kept by a king or lord to entertain people. *Noun.*
—**1.** To trick. The prisoner's plan to escape did not *fool* the guards. **2.** To be silly; joke; tease. Don't be angry; I was only *fooling. Verb.*
fool (fool) *noun, plural* **fools;** *verb,* **fooled, fooling.**

at; āpe; cär; end; mē; it; īce; hot; ōld;
wood; fool; oil; out; up; turn; sing;
thin; this; hw in white; zh in treasure.
ə stands for a in about, e in taken,
i in pencil, o in lemon, and u in circus.

foolish Without good sense; unwise. It is *foolish* to dive into a lake without knowing how deep it is.

    fool·ish (fŏŏl′ish) *adjective.*

foot **1.** The end part of the leg that man and other animals walk on or stand on. **2.** The lowest or supporting part. It took all day to hike down to the *foot* of the mountain. Would you hold the *foot* of the ladder steady while I climb up? **3.** The part opposite the head. Joan put an extra blanket at the *foot* of the bed in case she got cold during the night. **4.** A measure of length in the Imperial System of Measure equal to twelve inches. One foot is about one-third of a metre. *Noun.*

—To pay a bill. Father *foots* the bill whenever we eat out in a restaurant. *Verb.*

    foot (fŏŏt) *noun, plural* **feet;** *verb,* **footed, footing.**

football **1.** A game played by two teams of twelve players each on a large field with goals at each end. Each team tries to score by carrying or kicking the ball across the other team's goal. **2.** The ball used in this game.

    foot·ball (fŏŏt′bäl′) *noun, plural* **footballs.**

Football

footing **1.** The safe or firm placing of the feet. You can easily lose your *footing* on those wet, slippery rocks. **2.** A safe place or support for the feet. The icy ledge provided no *footing* for the mountain climbers. **3.** A position or relationship. We started off on a bad *footing* with our neighbours because we trampled on their flower beds.

    foot·ing (fŏŏt′ing) *noun, plural* **footings.**

footlights The row of lights along the front of a stage in a theatre.

    foot·lights (fŏŏt′līts′) *noun plural.*

footnote A note or explanation at the bottom of a page.

    foot·note (fŏŏt′nōt′) *noun, plural* **footnotes.**

footprint A mark made by a foot or shoe. My dirty feet made *footprints* on the floor.

    foot·print (fŏŏt′print′) *noun, plural* **footprints.**

footstep **1.** A step of the foot. We all watched with delight as the baby took its first *footsteps.* **2.** The sound made by a step. Joan knew her father was home because she heard his *footsteps* in the hall.

    foot·step (fŏŏt′step′) *noun, plural* **footsteps.**

footstool A low stool you can rest your feet on while you are sitting down.

    foot·stool (fŏŏt′stŏŏl′) *noun, plural* **footstools.**

Footstool

for We worked *for* two hours cleaning up the house. The boys hiked *for* five kilometres. This closet is *for* dishes and glasses. The teacher praised him *for* his good work. We went *for* a bicycle ride Sunday afternoon. We should go, *for* it is late. ▲ Other words that sound like this are **fore** and **four.**

    for (fōr *or* fər) *preposition; conjunction.*

forage Hay, grain, or other food for cows, horses, and other animals. *Noun.*

—To look for or get food or supplies. We *foraged* about in the refrigerator for a snack after school. *Verb.*

    for·age (fōr′əj) *noun; verb,* **foraged, foraging.**

forbade The teacher *forbade* us to talk during the fire drill.

    for·bade (fər bad′ *or* fər bād′) *verb.*

forbid To order not to do something; prohibit. The school *forbids* smoking.

    for·bid (fər bid′) *verb,* **forbade, forbidden, forbidding.**

force **1.** Power or strength. The batter hit the ball with great *force.* The *force* of the explosion broke windows in nearby buildings. **2.** The use of power or strength against a person or thing. The policeman dragged the thief off by *force.* Ruth had to use *force* to open the jar. **3.** A group of people who work together. The police *force* in this city is one of

the best in the country. **4.** Something that moves a body or stops or changes its motion. The *force* of gravity causes things to fall when they are dropped. *Noun.*
—**1.** To make do something. The robber *forced* the banker to open the safe and give him the money. **2.** To break open. Jim *forced* the lock on his suitcase because he had lost the key. *Verb.*
  force (fōrs) *noun, plural* **forces;** *verb,* **forced, forcing.**

forceps A small tool for gripping and holding things. Forceps are used by doctors and dentists in operations.
  for·ceps (fōr′seps) *noun, plural* **forceps.**

ford A shallow place where a river or other body of water may be crossed. *Noun.*
—To cross at a shallow place. The riders *forded* the river. *Verb.*
  ford (fōrd) *noun, plural* **fords;** *verb,* **forded, fording.**

fore At or toward the front. He stood at the *fore* part of the ship. Look up the word **aft** for a picture of this. ▲ Other words that sound like this are **for** and **four.**
  fore (fōr) *adjective.*

forearm The part of the arm between the elbow and the wrist.
  fore·arm (fōr′ärm′) *noun, plural* **forearms.**

forecast To tell what will or may happen; predict. The gypsy said that she had the power to *forecast* the future. *Verb.*
—A statement that tells what will or may happen; prediction. Let's listen to the weather *forecast* to find out if it's going to rain tomorrow. *Noun.*
  fore·cast (fōr′kast′) *verb,* **forecast** or **forecasted, forecasting;** *noun, plural* **forecasts.**

forecheck To get in the way of the hockey player with the puck while he is still in his own territory. This makes it harder for the other team to organize an attack.
  fore·check (fōr′chek′) *verb,* **forechecked, forechecking.**

forefather An ancestor. His *forefathers* came to this country before Confederation.
  fore·fa·ther (fōr′fä′<u>th</u>ər) *noun, plural* **forefathers.**

forefinger The finger next to the thumb.
  fore·fin·ger (fōr′fing′gər) *noun, plural* **forefingers.**

forefoot One of the front feet of an animal that has four feet.
  fore·foot (fōr′foot′) *noun, plural* **forefeet.**

foregone Known or decided ahead of time. Carl's election as captain of the basketball team was a *foregone* conclusion.

fore·gone (fōr′gon) *adjective.*

foreground The part of a picture or view nearest to a person's eye. That painting shows a small village in the *foreground* and snow-covered mountains in the background.
  fore·ground (fōr′ground′) *noun, plural* **foregrounds.**

The boy is in the **foreground** and the buildings are in the background.

forehead The part of the face above the eyes.
  fore·head (fōr′hed′) *noun, plural* **foreheads.**

foreign **1.** Of or from another country. My neighbour from France speaks English with a *foreign* accent. **2.** Outside a person's own country. Have you ever visited any *foreign* countries? **3.** Having to do with other countries. The prime minister has many people to advise him on what the country's *foreign* policy should be.
  for·eign (fōr′ən) *adjective.*

foreigner A person who is from another country.
  for·eign·er (fōr′ə nər) *noun, plural* **foreigners.**

foreleg One of the front legs of an animal that has four legs.
  fore·leg (fōr′leg′) *noun, plural* **forelegs.**

foreman **1.** A workman who is in charge of a group of workers. Ron is the *foreman* at the factory. **2.** The chairman of a jury. The *foreman* announced the verdict of the jury.
  fore·man (fōr′mən) *noun, plural* **foremen.**

foremost First in position or importance. The mayor was considered the *foremost* citizen of the town.
  fore·most (fōr′mōst′) *adjective.*

---

at; āpe; cär; end; mē; it; īce; hot; ōld;
wood; fōōl; oil; out; up; turn; sing;
thin; <u>th</u>is; hw in white; zh in treasure;
ə stands for a in about, e in taken,
i in pencil, o in lemon, and u in circus.

forerunner A person or thing that comes before. A brisk wind and a dark sky are often *forerunners* of a storm.
fore·run·ner (fōr′run′ər) *noun, plural* fore-runners.

foresaw We *foresaw* the difficulty of climbing the mountain.
fore·saw (fōr sä′) *verb.*

foresee To know or see ahead of time. No one can really *foresee* what the world will be like one hundred years from now.
fore·see (fōr sē′) *verb,* foresaw, foreseen, foreseeing.

foreseen We should have *foreseen* that we did not have enough gasoline for the trip.
fore·seen (fōr sēn′) *verb.*

foresight Care or thought for the future. Emily showed *foresight* in bringing along an umbrella.
fore·sight (fōr′sīt′) *noun.*

forest Many trees and plants covering a large area of land; woods.
for·est (fōr′əst) *noun, plural* forests.

foretell To tell ahead of time; predict. The old woman said she could *foretell* a person's future by looking at the stars.
fore·tell (fōr tel′) *verb,* foretold, foretelling.

foretold The prophet *foretold* the king's death.
fore·told (fōr tōld′) *verb.*

forever 1. Throughout all time; without ever coming to an end. No one can expect to live *forever.* 2. Without letting up; always; constantly. That girl is *forever* complaining about something.
for·ev·er (fər ev′ər) *adverb.*

forfeit To lose or have to give up because of some fault or mistake. Jane *forfeited* the tennis match because she was sick and couldn't play. *Verb.*
—Something lost because of some fault or mistake. *Noun.*
for·feit (fōr′fit) *verb,* forfeited, forfeiting; *noun, plural* forfeits.

forgave Tom's grandmother *forgave* him for accidentally breaking her vase.
for·gave (fər gāv′) *verb.*

forge¹ A furnace or hearth in which metal is heated. The fire softens the metal so that it can be hammered into shape. A blacksmith uses a forge to make horseshoes. *Noun.*
—1. To heat in a forge until very hot and then hammer into shape. Blacksmiths used to *forge* iron into tools as well as horseshoes. 2. To make or form. The United Nations *forged* a peace agreement between the two

countries that were at war. 3. To copy in order to trick or cheat. The police caught the man trying to *forge* someone else's signature on the check. *Verb.*
forge (fōrj) *noun, plural* forges; *verb,* forged, forging.

Forge

forge² To move forward slowly but steadily. The ferry *forged* through the rough waters of the bay.
forge (fōrj) *verb,* forged, forging.

forget 1. To not be able to remember. Harry wrote down Joan's telephone number so he would not *forget* it. 2. To fail to think of or do. I *forgot* to tell my parents that I would be late for dinner.
for·get (fər get′) *verb,* forgot, forgotten or forgot, forgetting.

forgetful Likely to forget; having a poor memory. Tom is so *forgetful* that he can never remember where he has left his glasses.
for·get·ful (fər get′fəl) *adjective.*

forget-me-not A small blue or white flower. The forget-me-not grows in clusters on a low plant.
for·get-me-not (fər-get′mē not′) *noun, plural* forget-me-nots.

forgive To stop blaming or feeling anger toward; pardon or excuse. John knew his father would *forgive* him for breaking the window. After Kate apologized, her mother *forgave* her rude remark.
for·give (fər giv′) *verb,* forgave, forgiven, forgiving.

Forget-me-not

forgiven Margaret has *forgiven* her brother for tearing her sweater.
for·giv·en (fər giv′ən) *verb.*

forgot Phyllis was late for school because she *forgot* to set the alarm clock to wake her up. Look up **forget** for more information.
for·got (fər got′) *verb.*

forgotten Ruth realized that she had *forgotten* her keys. Look up **forget** for more information.
for·got·ten (fər got′ən) *verb.*

fork 1. A tool with a handle at one end and two or more thin pointed parts at the other. One kind of fork is used for eating food. Another very large fork is used for pitching hay. 2. The place where something divides. Turn left at the *fork* in the road. *Noun.*
—1. To lift or pitch with a fork. The farmer *forked* hay into the wagon. 2. To divide into branches. The river *forks* two miles upstream. *Verb.*
fork (fōrk) *noun, plural* **forks;** *verb,* **forked, forking.**

form 1. The outside of something; shape. Ed could see the dim *form* of the bridge through the fog. 2. Kind or type. The tree is one *form* of plant. 3. A way of behaving or of doing something. Dick worked to improve his *form* in diving. 4. A sheet of paper with blanks that are to be filled in. The man who was applying for a job filled out a *form. Noun.*
—1. To make or shape. The artist *formed* a woman's head out of clay. The robbers *formed* a plan to rob the bank. 2. To take shape. The water dripping from the roof *formed* into icicles. 3. To make up. Students *formed* the biggest part of the crowd waiting to get into the concert. *Verb.*
form (fōrm) *noun, plural* **forms;** *verb,* **formed, forming.**

formal 1. Very stiff and proper. The teacher's manner was so *formal* that the students were a little afraid of him. 2. Following strict custom or ceremony. The queen gave the prime minister a *formal* welcome. 3. Done or made with authority; official. A lawyer had to write a *formal* contract when we bought our house. *Adjective.*
—A formal dress or a formal dance or other event. *Noun.*
for·mal (fōr′məl) *adjective; noun, plural* **formals.**

formation 1. The process of forming or making. The *formation* of ice from water requires a temperature of less than zero degrees. 2. Something formed or made.

Scientists agree that some rock *formations* are billions of years old. 3. The way something is formed. The school band was told to line up in parade *formation.*
for·ma·tion (fōr mā′shən) *noun, plural* **formations.**

former 1. The first of two. Jack and Bill are both on the hockey team; the *former* (Jack) is a forward and the latter (Bill) is a goalie. 2. Belonging to or happening in the past; earlier. In *former* times, people used fireplaces to heat their houses.
for·mer (fōr′mər) *adjective.*

formerly In time past; once. Trains were *formerly* pulled by steam locomotives.
for·mer·ly (fōr′mər lē) *adverb.*

formula 1. A set method of doing something. There is no real *formula* for making friends. 2. A set order of letters, symbols, or numbers that is used to express a rule or principle. H_2O is the *formula* for water.
for·mu·la (fōr′myə lə) *noun, plural* **formulas.**

forsake To give up or leave. He has decided to *forsake* the city and live on a farm.
for·sake (fōr sāk′) *verb,* **forsook, forsaken, forsaking.**

forsaken Bob took in a stray puppy whose owners had *forsaken* it.
for·sak·en (fōr sā′kən) *verb.*

forsook Jill's friends *forsook* her just when she needed them most.
for·sook (fōr sook′) *verb.*

forsythia A shrub that has yellow flowers shaped like little bells. The flowers grow in clusters along the stem and bloom in the early spring.
for·syth·i·a (fōr sith′ē ə) *noun, plural* **forsythias.**

fort A strong building or area that can be defended against an enemy.
fort (fōrt) *noun, plural* **forts.**

forth 1. Forward. From that day *forth,* the man was never lonely again. 2. Out into view. The buds on our rosebush burst

Forsythia

---

at; āpe; cär; end; mē; it; īce; hot; ōld;
wood; fo͞ol; oil; out; up; turn; sing;
thin; this; hw in white; zh in treasure.
ə stands for a in about, e in taken,
i in pencil, o in lemon, and u in circus.

257

forth all at once. ▲ Another word that sounds like this is **fourth.**
forth (fōrth) *adverb.*

fortieth 1. Next after the thirty-ninth. 2. One of forty equal parts; ¹/₄₀.
for·ti·eth (fōr′tē ith) *adjective; noun, plural* **fortieths.**

fortify 1. To protect. Two thousand years ago the Chinese built a wall on their northern border to *fortify* themselves against invaders. 2. To make strong or stronger. This breakfast cereal is *fortified* with vitamins and iron.
for·ti·fy (fōr′tə fī′) *verb,* **fortified, fortifying.**

fortress A strong place that can be defended against attack; fort.
for·tress (fōr′trəs) *noun, plural* **fortresses.**

fortunate Lucky. Sarah is very *fortunate* to have won first prize in the contest.
for·tu·nate (fōr′chə nət) *adjective.*

fortune 1. Something either good or bad that will happen to a person. The gypsy in the circus said she could tell my *fortune.* 2. Luck. It was Donna's good *fortune* to find a summer job she liked at the first place she looked. 3. Great wealth; riches. The queen has a *fortune* in jewels.
for·tune (fōr′chən) *noun, plural* **fortunes.**

fortuneteller A person who claims to be able to tell another person's fortune.
for·tune·tell·er (fôr′chən tel′ər) *noun, plural* **fortunetellers.**

forty Four times ten; 40.
for·ty (fōr′tē) *noun, plural* **forties;** *adjective.*

forum 1. The public square of an ancient Roman city. All business and other important activities took place in the forum. 2. A meeting to discuss issues or questions of public interest. An open *forum* was held at the school to discuss the plans for the new library.
fo·rum (fōr′əm) *noun, plural* **forums.**

forward Toward what is in front or ahead. The soldier stepped *forward* to receive the medal. We are looking *forward* to our holidays. This word is also spelled **forwards.** *Adverb.*
—1. At or toward the front. John had a *forward* seat on the plane. The quarterback completed a *forward* pass. 2. Bold or rude. Linda is a *forward* girl who talks back to her teacher. *Adjective.*
—To send ahead to a new address. Jane's parents *forwarded* the mail she got during the summer to her address at camp. *Verb.*
—A player whose position is near the front lines in certain games. Dave played *forward* on the basketball team. *Noun.*

for·ward (fōr′wərd) *adverb; adjective; verb,* **forwarded, forwarding;** *noun, plural* **forwards.**

fossil The remains or traces of an animal or plant that lived long ago. The boys found *fossils* of ancient sea animals in some rocks.
fos·sil (fos′əl) *noun, plural* **fossils.**

Fossil

foster To help the growth or development of. Tom's parents tried to *foster* his interest in music by giving him piano lessons. *Verb.*
—Giving or receiving care in a family without being related by birth or adoption. The city has a special department that tries to find *foster* parents for children who have no homes of their own. *Adjective.*
fos·ter (fos′tər) *verb,* **fostered, fostering;** *adjective.*

fought Bob *fought* in a boxing match. Look up **fight** for more information.
fought (fot) *verb.*

foul 1. Very unpleasant or dirty. There was a *foul* odour in the air when the sewer pipes broke. I would never go swimming in that river because the water is *foul.* 2. Cloudy, rainy, or stormy. *Foul* weather delayed the ship. 3. Very bad; evil. The police are investigating a *foul* crime that occurred in our neighbourhood last night. 4. Breaking the rules; unfair. An umpire or referee is used in sports to apply the rules and prevent any *foul* play. 5. Outside the foul line in a baseball game. The batter hit a *foul* ball. *Adjective.*
—1. A breaking of rules. The basketball player committed a *foul* by knocking down another player. 2. A baseball that is hit outside the foul line. *Noun.*
—1. To make dirty. The factory *fouled* the lake by pumping all its garbage and waste into it. 2. To tangle or become tangled. The boy *fouled* the fishing line in the bushes along the shore. 3. To hit a foul ball in baseball. The batter *fouled* the ball to the right of first base. *Verb.* ▲ Another word that sounds like this is **fowl.**
foul (foul) *adjective,* **fouler, foulest;** *noun, plural* **fouls;** *verb,* **fouled, fouling.**

foul line Either of the two lines in baseball that go from home plate through first or third base to the limits of the playing field.

found¹ Janet *found* the watch she thought she had lost. Look up **find** for more information.

found (found) *verb.*

found² To start or bring into being; establish. The students worked together to *found* a science club.

found (found) *verb*, **founded, founding.**

foundation Something that serves as a base or support. The *foundation* of the old house was made of brick.

foun·da·tion (foun dā′shən) *noun, plural* **foundations.**

foundry A place where metal is melted and formed into different shapes.

found·ry (foun′drē) *noun, plural* **foundries.**

fountain 1. A stream of water that is made to shoot up. Some fountains are used to drink from, and others are used only as decoration. 2. The source of anything. That teacher is a real *fountain* of knowledge about Canadian history.

foun·tain (foun′tən) *noun, plural* **fountains.**

Fountain

fountain pen A pen that has a little tube inside to hold and feed ink to the writing point.

four One more than three; 4. ▲ Another word that sounds like this is **for.**

four (fōr) *noun, plural* **fours;** *adjective.*

Four-H clubs A group of organizations for young people. It teaches skill in farming and homemaking.

Four-H clubs (fōr′āch′).

fourteen Four more than ten; 14.

four·teen (fōr′tēn′) *noun, plural* **fourteens;** *adjective.*

fourteenth 1. Next after the thirteenth. 2. One of fourteen equal parts; ¹/₁₄.

four·teenth (fōr′tēnth′) *adjective; noun, plural* **fourteenths.**

fourth 1. Next after the third. 2. One of four equal parts; ¹/₄. ▲ Another word that sounds like this is **forth.**

fourth (fōrth) *adjective; noun, plural* **fourths.**

fowl 1. One of a group of birds that are used for food. The chicken, turkey, and duck are kinds of fowl. 2. Any bird. Andy likes to hunt pheasant and other wild *fowl*. ▲ Another word that sounds like this is **foul.**

fowl (foul) *noun, plural* **fowl** or **fowls.**

fox A wild animal that is something like a dog. A fox has a pointed nose and ears, a bushy tail, and thick fur.

fox (foks) *noun, plural* **foxes.**

Fox

foxhound A hound with a very sharp sense of smell. It is trained to hunt foxes.

fox·hound (foks′hound′) *noun, plural* **foxhounds.**

fraction 1. A part of a whole; small part. Only a *fraction* of the people watching the football game left before it was over. 2. A number that is one or more of the equal parts of a whole. A fraction shows the division of one number by a second number. ²/₃, ³/₄, and ¹/₁₆ are fractions.

frac·tion (frak′shən) *noun, plural* **fractions.**

fracture To crack or break. Steve *fractured* his ankle playing hockey. *Verb.*

—A crack or break. Mary's *fracture* kept her in the hospital for two weeks. *Noun.*

frac·ture (frak′chər) *verb*, **fractured, fracturing;** *noun, plural* **fractures.**

fragile Easily broken; delicate. That china cup is very *fragile*.

frag·ile (fraj′əl *or* fraj′īl) *adjective.*

fragment A small part that is broken off. We found some arrowhead *fragments*.

frag·ment (frag′mənt) *noun, plural* **fragments.**

fragrance A sweet or pleasing smell. Roses

at; āpe; cär; end; mē; it; īce; hot; ōld;
wood; fōōl; oil; out; up; turn; sing;
thin; <u>th</u>is; hw in white; zh in treasure.
ə stands for a in about, e in taken,
i in pencil, o in lemon, and u in circus.

259

have a beautiful *fragrance.*

fra·grance (frā′grəns) *noun, plural* **fra-grances.**

fragrant Having a sweet or pleasing smell. Ann was wearing a *fragrant* perfume.

fra·grant (frā′grənt) *adjective.*

frail 1. Lacking in strength; weak. The child was too *frail* to take part in gym classes. 2. Easily broken or torn; delicate. That lace is very old and *frail.*

frail (frāl) *adjective,* **frailer, frailest.**

frame 1. A structure that borders or supports something. The window *frame* needs painting. 2. The way a person's body is formed. Joe has such a big *frame* he has trouble finding clothes to fit him. *Noun.*
—1. To set in a border. The painter *framed* his picture and sold it at an art show. 2. To draw up or make. The teacher *framed* his questions so that the pupils could easily understand them. *Verb.*

frame (frām) *noun, plural* **frames;** *verb,* **framed, framing.**

framework A structure that gives shape or support to something. The *framework* of the building is steel.

frame·work (frām′wurk′) *noun, plural* **frameworks.**

franc A coin of France, Belgium, Switzerland, and some other countries. ▲ Another word that sounds like this is **frank.**

franc (frangk) *noun, plural* **francs.**

France A country in western Europe. Its capital is Paris.

France (frans) *noun.*

Francophone *Canadian.* A person who speaks French in a country where the French language is one of two or more main languages.

Franc·o·phone (frangk′ə fōn′) *noun, plural* **Francophones.**

frank Honest and open in expressing one's real thoughts and feelings. Let me be *frank* with you and tell you what I really think. ▲ Another word that sounds like this is **franc.**

frank (frangk) *adjective,* **franker, frankest.**

frankfurter A reddish sausage made of beef or beef and pork. It is often served on a long roll with mustard and relish.

frank·furt·er (frangk′fər tər) *noun, plural* **frankfurters.**

▲ The word **frankfurter** comes from a German word that means "of or from Frankfurt." Frankfurt is a city in Germany, and it is possible that this kind of sausage was first made in Frankfurt.

frantic Wildly excited by worry or fear. The mother was *frantic* when she lost her child in the crowded department store.

fran·tic (fran′tik) *adjective.*

fraternity A social organization or club for men or boys. Some students at the university pay dues to belong to a *fraternity.*

fra·ter·ni·ty (frə tur′nə tē) *noun, plural* **fraternities.**

fraud 1. A tricking of someone in order to cheat him. The salesman tried to sell fake diamonds and was arrested for *fraud.* 2. A person or thing that tricks or cheats. A man is a *fraud* if he practises medicine when he really isn't a doctor.

fraud (fräd) *noun, plural* **frauds.**

fray To separate into loose threads. Years of wear had *frayed* the cuffs of Sam's coat.

fray (frā) *verb,* **frayed, fraying.**

freak 1. A person, animal, or plant that has not developed normally. A mouse with two tails would be a *freak.* 2. Anything odd or unusual. Heavy rain in a desert would be a real *freak.*

freak (frēk) *noun, plural* **freaks.**

freckle A small brownish spot on the skin. Helen has bright red hair and *freckles.*

freck·le (frek′əl) *noun, plural* **freckles.**

free 1. Having one's liberty; not under another's control. Canada is a *free* country where every adult citizen has a right to vote. 2. Not held back or confined. You are *free* to come and go as you like in the library. 3. Not troubled by something. My aunt lives a life *free* from care or worry. 4. Without cost. We got *free* tickets to the show. *Adjective.*
—Without cost. *Adverb.*
—To make or set free. The child *freed* the trapped animal. *Verb.*

free (frē) *adjective,* **freer, freest;** *adverb;* *verb,* **freed, freeing.**

freedom 1. The condition of being free; liberty. 2. The condition of being able to move or act without being held back. Our dog has complete *freedom* of the house.

free·dom (frē′dəm) *noun, plural* **freedoms.**

Freedomite A member of the Sons of Freedom, a radical branch of the Doukhobors.

Free·dom·ite (frē′dəm īt′) *noun, plural* **Freedomites.**

freeway A highway with more than two lanes. A freeway is used for fast and direct driving.

free·way (frē′wā′) *noun, plural* **freeways.**

freeze 1. To harden because of the cold. When water *freezes,* it becomes ice. 2. To cover or become covered with ice; block with ice. The cold weather *froze* the pipes in our house while we were away. **3.** To make or become very cold. I almost *froze* waiting for the bus. **4.** To become fixed or motionless. Jack *froze* when he saw the snake. **5.** To damage or be damaged by cold or frost. The strawberry crop in southern Ontario *froze* last spring.

freeze (frēz) *verb,* **froze, frozen, freezing.**

freezer An appliance used to freeze food quickly or to store frozen food.

freez·er (frēz′ər) *noun, plural* **freezers.**

freeze-up *Canadian.* The time of year when lakes and rivers freeze over.

freeze-up (frēz′up′) *noun, plural* **freeze-ups.**

freight **1.** The carrying of goods by land, air, or water. **2.** The goods carried in this way; cargo.

freight (frāt) *noun.*

freighter A ship used for carrying cargo.

freight·er (frāt′ər) *noun, plural* **freighters.**

French **1.** The people of France. **2.** The language of France. *Noun.*
—Having to do with France, its people, or their language. *Adjective.*

French (french) *noun; adjective.*

French Canada **1.** All the people in Canada who speak French. **2.** The part of Canada where the majority of people speak French.

French Canadian **1.** A Canadian who speaks French. **2.** A Canadian whose ancestors came from France. *Noun.*
—Of French Canada or French Canadians. *Adjective.*

French fries Potatoes that are cut into thin strips and fried in deep fat.

French horn A brass musical instrument with a long, coiled tube that widens into the shape of a bell.

Frenchman A person who was born or is living in France. The word **Frenchwoman** is also used.

French·man (french′mən) *noun, plural* **Frenchmen.**

frenzy Wild excitement. Margot was in a *frenzy* to escape from the bees.

fren·zy (fren′zē) *noun, plural* **frenzies.**

French Horn

frequency **1.** A repeated happening. The people were afraid to go out at night because of the *frequency* of robberies on the streets. **2.** The number of times something happens or

takes place during a period of time. The *frequency* of a person's heartbeat is between sixty and ninety beats a minute.

fre·quen·cy (frē′kwən sē) *noun, plural* **frequencies.**

frequent Happening often; taking place again and again. There are *frequent* thunderstorms in this area every summer. The campers made *frequent* visits to town to shop.

fre·quent (frē′kwənt) *adjective.*

fresh **1.** Newly done, made, or gathered. We put on a *fresh* coat of paint in the kitchen. **2.** New; another. Don came to Canada to get a *fresh* start in life. **3.** Clean or refreshing. It was very stuffy in the room so we stepped outside for a breath of *fresh* air. **4.** Not salty. A lake has *fresh* water. **5.** Rude; impudent. She was kept after school for being *fresh* to the teacher.

fresh (fresh) *adjective,* **fresher, freshest.**

freshman A student in first year university.

fresh·man (fresh′mən) *noun, plural* **freshmen.**

freshwater Living in fresh water. The trout is a *freshwater* fish.

fresh·wa·ter (fresh′wä′tər) *adjective.*

friar A man who belongs to a religious order of the Roman Catholic Church.

fri·ar (frī′ər) *noun, plural* **friars.**

friction **1.** The rubbing of one thing against another. The *friction* of the rope in Mike's hand gave him a burn. **2.** A force that resists movement between two surfaces that are touching one another. The *friction* between two parts of a machine can be reduced by oiling them. **3.** Anger or ill will. There was much *friction* between the two nations.

fric·tion (frik′shən) *noun.*

Friday The sixth day of the week.

Fri·day (frī′dē *or* frī′dā) *noun, plural* **Fridays.**

▲ **Friday** comes from an earlier English word that meant "Frigg's day." People who lived in England long ago believed that Frigg was the queen of the gods of the sky.

fried I *fried* an egg for my breakfast this morning. Look up **fry** for more information.

fried (frīd) *verb.*

at; āpe; cär; end; mē; it; īce; hot; ōld; wood; fo͞ol; oil; out; up; turn; sing; thin; this; hw in white; zh in treasure. ə stands for a in about, e in taken, i in pencil, o in lemon, and u in circus.

friend A person one knows and likes.
friend (frend) *noun, plural* **friends.**

friendly 1. Like a friend; showing friendship. The teacher was always ready to give her students *friendly* advice whenever they needed it. 2. Not angry or fighting; not hostile.
friend·ly (frend′lē) *adjective,* **friendlier, friendliest.**

friendship The warm feeling between friends. The two boys' *friendship* started when they used to go to school together.
friend·ship (frend′ship′) *noun, plural* **friendships.**

fright 1. A sudden fear or alarm. The people in the burning building were seized with *fright.* 2. A person or thing that is ugly or shocking. That witch costume you wore on Hallowe'en made you look a *fright.*
fright (frīt) *noun, plural* **frights.**

frighten 1. To make or become suddenly afraid or alarmed. The loud explosion *frightened* everyone. 2. To drive away by scaring. The dog *frightened* away the squirrels.
fright·en (frīt′ən) *verb,* **frightened, frightening.**

frigid 1. Very cold. The Inuit know how to live in a *frigid* climate. 2. Cold in feeling; unfriendly. The political candidate gave his opponent a *frigid* greeting when they met.
frig·id (frij′id) *adjective.*

fringe 1. A border of hanging threads or cord. The bedspread has a *fringe* around the edge. 2. Anything like a fringe. A *fringe* of bushes lined the driveway. *Noun.*
fringe (frinj) *noun, plural* **fringes.**

Fringe

Frisbee A trademark for a plastic disk that players throw back and forth in a game.
Fris·bee (friz′bē) *noun, plural* **Frisbees.**

frivolous Lacking seriousness or sense; silly. That girl is so *frivolous* that she can't seem to keep her mind on anything for very long.
friv·o·lous (friv′ə ləs) *adjective.*

frog A small animal with webbed feet and no tail, that lives in or near water. A frog has strong back legs that it uses for hopping.
frog (frog) *noun, plural* **frogs.**

Frog

frogman A swimmer who is specially trained and equipped to work underwater.
frog·man (frog′man′) *noun, plural* **frogmen.**

frog run The second flow of sap from a maple tree in the spring. This sap is not as good as that from the first flow called the **robin run.** It is better than the sap coming from the third flow called the **bud run.**

frolic To play about happily and gaily. We liked to watch the colts *frolic* in the field.
frol·ic (frol′ik) *verb,* **frolicked, frolicking.**

from We flew *from* Halifax to Montreal. I go to school *from* nine o'clock to three. Two *from* five leaves three. Bob shivered *from* the cold. It's easy to tell lions *from* tigers.
from (from, frum *or* frəm) *preposition.*

frond The leaf of a fern.
frond (frond) *noun, plural* **fronds.**

front 1. The part that faces forward or comes first. Jane sits in *front* of me in history class. 2. The land that lies along a street or body of water. We rented a cabin on the lake *front* for the summer. 3. A place where fighting is going on between two enemy forces. 4. The boundary line between two air masses of different temperatures. We will have a drop in temperature tonight as a cold *front* moves in. *Noun.*
—On or near the front. The important news stories are printed on the *front* page of the newspaper. *Adjective.*
—To face toward. Our house *fronts* on a busy street. *Verb.*
front (frunt) *noun, plural* **fronts;** *adjective; verb,* **fronted, fronting.**

frontier 1. The last settled area of a country before the part that is not settled or developed begins. 2. The border between two countries. We crossed the *frontier* between Canada and the United States on our automobile trip. 3. Any new area. Doctors are constantly exploring the *frontiers* of medicine.
fron·tier (fron′tēr′) *noun, plural* **frontiers.**

frost 1. Tiny crystals that form on a surface when the temperature is below freezing. Frost is formed by the freezing of water vapour in the air. There was *frost* on the windowpanes this morning. 2. Very cold weather. *Frost* destroyed the apple crop in southern British Columbia this year. *Noun.*
—To cover with frost or something like frost. Ruth *frosted* the birthday cake with chocolate icing. *Verb.*
frost (frost) *noun, plural* **frosts;** *verb,* **frosted, frosting.**

frostbite The freezing of some part of the body caused by exposure to extreme cold. *Noun.*
—To injure by exposure to extreme cold. The explorer's fingers and toes were *frostbitten* by the cold. *Verb.*
frost·bite (frost'bīt') *noun; verb,* **frostbit, frostbitten, frostbiting.**

frosting A mixture of sugar, butter, and flavouring used to cover a cake or cookies; icing.
frost·ing (fros'ting) *noun, plural* **frostings.**

frosty Cold enough for frost; freezing. Our family loves to take walks on crisp, *frosty* evenings.
frost·y (fros'tē) *adjective,* **frostier, frostiest.**

froth A mass of bubbles formed in or on a liquid; foam. The *froth* on top of the ice cream soda tickled Janet's nose when she drank it. *Noun.*
—To form froth. The tired horse *frothed* at the mouth. *Verb.*
froth (froth) *noun, plural* **froths;** *verb,* **frothed, frothing.**

frown A wrinkling of the forehead. A person makes a frown because he is thinking hard or is angry or worried about something. A *frown* came to Linda's face when she tried to think of an answer to the riddle. *Noun.*
—1. To wrinkle the forehead in thought, anger, or worry. Mike *frowned* when his father made him stay home on Saturday to do his homework. 2. To look with anger or disapproval. Louise's parents *frown* on her staying out late at night. *Verb.*
frown (froun) *noun, plural* **frowns;** *verb,* **frowned, frowning.**

froze The lake *froze* last night, so we went ice-skating today. Look up **freeze** for more information.
froze (frōz) *verb.*

frozen The water dripping from the roof had *frozen* and formed icicles. Look up **freeze** for more information.
fro·zen (frō'zən) *verb.*

frugal 1. Not wasteful; saving. A person who is frugal is very careful not to spend money on things that are not needed. 2. Costing little. I ate a *frugal* meal of beans.
fru·gal (froo'gəl) *adjective.*

fruit The part of a plant that contains the seeds. Pears, apples, and nuts are fruits that can be eaten.
fruit (froot) *noun, plural* **fruit** or **fruits.**

frustrate To discourage or prevent. Joe was *frustrated* by his bad luck in trying to find a summer job. The rainy weather threatened to *frustrate* our plans for a camping trip.
frus·trate (frus'trāt) *verb,* **frustrated, frustrating.**

fry To cook in hot fat. Andy *fried* bacon and eggs for his breakfast.
fry (frī) *verb,* **fried, frying.**

fudge A soft candy made out of sugar, milk, butter, and flavouring.
fudge (fuj) *noun, plural* **fudges.**

fuel Something that is burned to provide heat or power. Coal, wood, and oil are fuels.
fu·el (fyoo'əl) *noun, plural* **fuels.**

fugitive A person who runs away or tries to escape. A person who runs away from the police is a fugitive from the law.
fu·gi·tive (fyoo'jə tiv) *noun, plural* **fugitives.**

fulcrum The support on which a lever turns when it is moving or lifting something. The farmer used a rock as a *fulcrum* to move the heavy boulder.
ful·crum (fool'krəm) *noun, plural* **fulcrums.**

fulfil 1. To carry out or finish. Jim quickly *fulfilled* his chores for the day and went home early. 2. To meet or satisfy. Jack was not hired for the job because he did not *fulfil* all the requirements. This word is also spelled **fulfill.**
ful·fil (fool fil') *verb,* **fulfilled, fulfilling.**

full 1. Holding as much or as many as possible. Henry poured himself a *full* glass of milk. Janet's parents had a house *full* of guests for the party. 2. Complete; entire. Each of these soup bowls holds a *full* cup. We have a *full* two weeks of vacation. 3. Having a rounded outline; plump. That girl has a *full*, round face. 4. Having a lot of cloth. The dress has a *full* skirt. *Adjective.*

at; āpe; cär; end; mē; it; īce; hot; ōld;
wood; fōol; oil; out; up; turn; sing;
thin; this; hw in white; zh in treasure.
ə stands for a in about, e in taken,
i in pencil, o in lemon, and u in circus.

—Completely; entirely. He filled the pitcher *full* with lemonade. *Adverb.*
full (fool) *adjective,* **fuller, fullest;** *adverb.*

fullback **1.** A football player who stands farthest behind the front line. **2.** A soccer player who plays closest to his goal.
full·back (fool′bak′) *noun, plural* **fullbacks.**

full moon The moon when all of the side that faces the earth is shining.

fully **1.** Completely; entirely. I don't *fully* understand that arithmetic problem. **2.** At least; not less than. The train was *fully* an hour late.
ful·ly (fool′ē) *adverb.*

fumble **1.** To look for in a clumsy way. Jill *fumbled* around in her purse looking for her keys. **2.** To handle clumsily or drop. Bob *fumbled* the football and made it possible for the other team to score. *Verb.*
—The act of fumbling. The quarterback's *fumble* helped the other team to get a touchdown. *Noun.*
fum·ble (fum′bəl) *verb,* **fumbled, fumbling;** *noun, plural* **fumbles.**

fume A smoke or gas that is harmful or has a bad smell. The *fumes* from automobiles make the city's air harmful to breathe. *Noun.*
—To be filled with anger or irritation. The driver *fumed* as he waited in the heavy traffic jam. *Verb.*
fume (fyoom) *noun, plural* **fumes;** *verb,* **fumed, fuming.**

fun Enjoyment or playfulness. We had *fun* riding our sleds down the hill. Harry is always full of *fun.*
fun (fun) *noun.*
to make fun of. To laugh at; ridicule. Jane *made fun of* her brother when he tried to cook breakfast.

function **1.** Use or purpose. What is Susan's *function* in the club? The *function* of the heart is to pump blood through the body. **2.** A formal gathering. All the supporters of the art museum went to a *function* to celebrate its fiftieth anniversary. *Noun.*
—To work or serve. A motor *functions* best when it is kept well oiled. *Verb.*
func·tion (fungk′shən) *noun, plural* **functions;** *verb,* **functioned, functioning.**

fund **1.** A sum of money set aside for a specific purpose. Mrs. Black set up a *fund* for her children's university education. **2.** A supply. This book has a *fund* of information on North American Indians. **3. funds.** Money that is ready for use. The province does not have the *funds* to repair the highway.
fund (fund) *noun, plural* **funds.**

fundamental Serving as a basis; essential; basic. Learning the rules is a *fundamental* part of any game. *Adjective.*
—An essential part. Addition is one of the *fundamentals* of arithmetic. *Noun.*
fun·da·men·tal (fun′də ment′əl) *adjective; noun, plural* **fundamentals.**

funeral The ceremony and services held before the burial of a dead person. A funeral is often held in a church or temple.
fu·ner·al (fyoo′nər əl) *noun, plural* **funerals.**

fungi More than one fungus.
fun·gi (fun′jī) *noun plural.*

fungus One of a large group of plants that does not have flowers or leaves. Fungi do not have green colouring matter and therefore must live on other plants. Mushrooms, mildews, and moulds are fungi.
fun·gus (fung′gəs) *noun, plural* **fungi** or **funguses.**

Fungus

funnel **1.** A utensil that has a wide cone at one end and a thin tube at the other. When a funnel is used, something can be poured into a container with a small opening without spilling. **2.** A round chimney or smokestack on a steamship or steam engine.
fun·nel (fun′əl) *noun, plural* **funnels.**

funny **1.** Causing laughter. **2.** Strange; odd. It seems *funny* that he never told us his name.
fun·ny (fun′ē) *adjective,* **funnier, funniest.**

fur **1.** The soft, thick, hairy coat of certain animals. **2.** The skin of an animal that has fur. Fur is used in making clothing, rugs, and many other things. ▲ Another word that sounds like this is **fir.**
fur (fur) *noun, plural* **furs.**

fur brigade *Canadian.* A number of canoes or dog sleds that carried furs and other goods to and from trading posts.

furious **1.** Very angry. Father was *furious* when he missed the train by one minute. **2.** Violent; fierce. Summer is often a time of *furious* thunderstorms.
fu·ri·ous (fyoor′ē əs) *adjective.*

furlong A measure of distance in the Imperial System of Measure equal to one-eighth of a mile. A furlong is about two hundred metres.

fur·long (fur′lon̊g) *noun, plural* **furlongs.**

furnace An enclosed place where heat is produced. We use a furnace to heat a house or other building.

fur·nace (fur′nəs) *noun, plural* **furnaces.**

furnish 1. To supply with furniture. Debbie's parents *furnished* a playroom in their basement. 2. To supply or provide. The book *furnished* us with facts about Confederation.

fur·nish (fur′nish) *verb,* **furnished, furnishing.**

furniture Tables, chairs, beds, and other movable articles used in a home or office.

fur·ni·ture (fur′ni chər) *noun.*

furrow A long, narrow groove. Farmers plant seeds in the *furrows* they dig. The cars made *furrows* in the dusty road.

fur·row (fur′ō) *noun, plural* **furrows.**

Furrows

furry Like fur or covered with fur. The new rug in the living room is soft and *furry.* A hamster is a *furry* little animal that many children have as pets.

fur·ry (fur′ē) *adjective,* **furrier, furriest.**

further The student went to the encyclopaedia for *further* information on the subject of space travel. Look up **far** for more information. *Adjective, Adverb.*
—To help forward; support. The United Nations was formed to *further* the cause of peace. *Verb.*

fur·ther (fur′thər) *adjective; adverb; verb,* **furthered, furthering.**

furthermore In addition; moreover; besides. I don't want to go to bed yet, and *furthermore* I have some homework to do.

fur·ther·more (fur′thər mōr′) *adverb.*

furthest John threw the ball *furthest* of all the players. Going to Mexico for a visit is the *furthest* distance Carol has ever been from home. Look up **far** for more information.

fur·thest (fur′thəst) *adverb; adjective.*

fury 1. Violent anger; rage. The man flew into a *fury* when his store was robbed. 2. Violence; fierceness. The *fury* of the storm raged all night.

fu·ry (fyoor′ē) *noun, plural* **furies.**

fuse[1] 1. A strip of metal in an electric circuit. The fuse melts and breaks the circuit if the current becomes too strong. Fuses are used to prevent fire that can result from overloaded wires. 2. A piece of cord that can burn. A fuse is used to set off a bomb or other explosive.

fuse (fyo͞oz) *noun, plural* **fuses.**

fuse[2] 1. To melt by heating. He *fused* the metal by intense heat. 2. To blend or unite. Because gold is such a soft metal, it is *fused* with silver or copper to harden it.

fuse (fyo͞oz) *verb,* **fused, fusing.**

fuselage The main body of an airplane that holds the passengers, cargo, and crew.

fu·se·lage (fyo͞o′sə läzh′ *or* fyo͞o′sə ləj) *noun, plural* **fuselages.**

fuss An unnecessary stir or bother over small or unimportant things. Ralph's mother always makes a *fuss* over him when he comes home from summer camp. There was a big *fuss* among the premiers over who would give the welcome speech. *Noun.*
—To make an unnecessary stir or bother over small or unimportant things. Father *fussed* because his necktie had a stain on it. *Verb.*

fuss (fus) *noun, plural* **fusses;** *verb,* **fussed, fussing.**

future That will be or will happen; coming. Jim's teacher said she hoped that his *future* work would be better. *Adjective.*
—The time that is to come. In the *future,* please call if you are going to be late for dinner. *Noun.*

fu·ture (fyo͞o′chər) *adjective; noun.*

fuzz Fine, loose fibres or hair. A peach is covered with *fuzz.*

fuzz (fuz) *noun.*

fuzzy 1. Covered with or like fuzz. Caterpillars are *fuzzy.* The blanket was soft and *fuzzy.* 2. Not clear; blurred. That would be a good photograph except that it's too *fuzzy.*

fuzz·y (fuz′ē) *adjective,* **fuzzier, fuzziest.**

at; āpe; cär; end; mē; it; īce; hot; ōld;
wood; fo͞ol; oil; out; up; turn; sing;
thin; this; hw in white; zh in treasure.
ə stands for a in about, e in taken,
i in pencil, o in lemon, and u in circus.

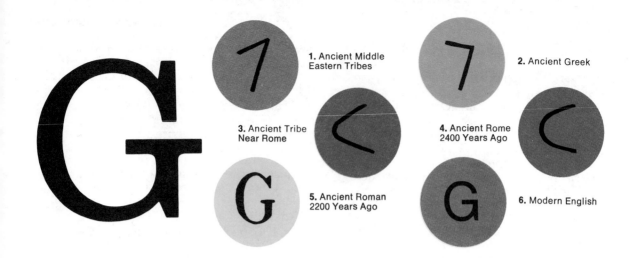

1. Ancient Middle Eastern Tribes
2. Ancient Greek
3. Ancient Tribe Near Rome
4. Ancient Rome 2400 Years Ago
5. Ancient Roman 2200 Years Ago
6. Modern English

G is the seventh letter of the alphabet. Although the modern letter **G** was invented by the Romans, its history goes back to the earliest alphabets. The oldest form of the letter **G** was the third letter of the alphabet used by several ancient tribes (**1**) in the Middle East. The Greeks (**2**) borrowed this letter about 3000 years ago. It was pronounced as a hard *g,* such as the *g* in *game.* This letter was then borrowed by an ancient tribe (**3**) that settled north of Rome about 2800 years ago. These people made no distinction between the hard *g* sound and the *k* sound, such as the *k* in *king.* Because of this, they began to use the letter to stand for both sounds. The Romans (**4**) borrowed the letter from them and also used it to stand for both the hard *g* and *k* sounds. The *k* sound was used more often than the hard *g* sound in the language of the Romans. So this letter, which had once been used for only the hard *g* sound, came to be used for only the *k* sound. About 2200 years ago, the Romans (**5**) invented a new letter to stand for the hard *g* sound. This letter, which was made by adding a short line to the letter **C,** was written in almost the same way that we write the capital letter **G** today (**6**).

g, G   The seventh letter of the alphabet.
  g, G (jē) *noun, plural* **g's, G's.**

g   Gram or grams.

gable   The end of a sloping roof, along with the part between the sides of the roof.
  ga·ble (gā′bəl) *noun, plural* **gables.**

gadget   A small, unusual tool or device. A bottle opener with a penknife at one end is a *gadget.*
  gadg·et (gaj′ət) *noun, plural* **gadgets.**

gag   **1.** Something put in the mouth to keep a person from talking or shouting. **2.** A joke. The comedian told many *gags. Noun.*
  —**1.** To keep someone from talking or shouting by using a gag. The robbers tied up and *gagged* the shopkeeper. **2.** To choke. The boy always *gags* when he takes that bitter medicine. *Verb.*
  gag (gag) *noun, plural* **gags;** *verb,* **gagged, gagging.**

gaiety   Joy and fun; being merry; cheerfulness. She loves the *gaiety* of Christmas. The *gaiety* of the clown made us smile.
  gai·e·ty (gā′ə tē) *noun, plural* **gaieties.**

gaily   In a gay manner; happily; cheerfully. The campers sang *gaily* around the campfire.
  gai·ly (gā′lē) *adverb.*

gain   To get or win. Our team *gained* control of the ball. Ann will *gain* experience by working at the store. The army *gained* a victory. The car *gained* speed as it moved down the hill. *Verb.*
  —Something gained. The football player made a *gain* of three points. Eating too much food can cause a *gain* in weight. *Noun.*
  gain (gān) *verb,* **gained, gaining;** *noun, plural* **gains.**

gait   A way of moving on foot. The boy walked with a slow *gait.* ▲ Another word that sounds like this is **gate.**
  gait (gāt) *noun, plural* **gaits.**

galaxy   A very large group of stars. There are many galaxies in the universe. The Milky Way is a galaxy.
  gal·ax·y (gal′ək sē) *noun, plural* **galaxies.**

gale   **1.** A very strong wind. The *gale* drove the ship against the rocks. **2.** A sudden, loud bursting out or bursting forth. The clown's funny tricks sent the children into *gales* of laughter.
  gale (gāl) *noun, plural* **gales.**

gallant   Good and brave. The *gallant* knight died for his king.
  gal·lant (gal′ənt) *adjective.*

gallery **1.** The highest balcony of a theatre or large hall. **2.** A room or building where paintings and statues are shown or sold.
gal·ler·y (gal′ər ē) *noun, plural* **galleries.**

galley **1.** A long, low ship used in early times. A galley had sails and oars. **2.** The kitchen of a ship or airplane.
gal·ley (gal′ē) *noun, plural* **galleys.**

gallon A unit of measure for liquids in the Imperial System of Measure. A gallon equals four quarts. It is slightly more than four litres.
gal·lon (gal′ən) *noun, plural* **gallons.**

gallop The fastest gait of a horse or other four-footed animal. *Noun.*
—To move or ride at a gallop. The racehorses *galloped* to the finish line. *Verb.*
gal·lop (gal′əp) *noun, plural* **gallops;** *verb,* **galloped, galloping.**

gallows A frame from which criminals are hanged.
gal·lows (gal′ōz) *noun, plural* **gallows** or **gallowses.**

galoshes Overshoes made of rubber or plastic. Galoshes are worn in snowy or rainy weather.
ga·losh·es (gə losh′əz) *noun plural.*

gamble **1.** To play a game for money; bet. The men *gambled* with dice. He *gambled* his money on the horse race. **2.** To take a chance. The coach *gambled* when he used the new player in an important game. *Verb.*
—A risk. Buying a used car without trying it out is a big *gamble. Noun.*
gam·ble (gam′bəl) *verb,* **gambled, gambling;** *noun, plural* **gambles.**

Galoshes

game **1.** A way of playing. Let's play a *game* of ball. **2.** A sport or contest with certain rules. Are you going to the football *game?* Jeff likes the *game* of checkers. **3.** Wild animals, birds, or fish hunted or caught for sport or food. *Noun.*
—Full of spirit and courage. Are you *game* for a swim in the cold water? *Adjective.*
game (gām) *noun, plural* **games;** *adjective,* **gamer, gamest.**

gander A grown male goose.

gan·der (gan′dər) *noun, plural* **ganders.**

gang A group of people who do things together. Hank went fishing with a *gang* of his friends. The men on the road *gang* are building a new highway. A *gang* of thieves robbed the bank.
gang (gang) *noun, plural* **gangs.**

gangplank A movable board or bridge used for getting on and off a boat or ship.
gang·plank (gang′plangk′) *noun, plural* **gangplanks.**

Gangplank

gangster A member of a gang of criminals.
gang·ster (gang′stər) *noun, plural* **gangsters.**

gangway A passageway on either side of a ship's deck.
gang·way (gang′wā′) *noun, plural* **gangways.**

gap A break, crack, or opening. Our dog got out of the yard through a *gap* in the fence.
gap (gap) *noun, plural* **gaps.**

garage A building where cars and trucks are parked or repaired.
ga·rage (gə räzh′ *or* gə räj′) *noun, plural* **garages.**

garbage Food and other things that are thrown out from a kitchen.
gar·bage (gär′bəj) *noun.*

The word **garbage** first meant "the insides of an animal used as food." These were usually eaten only by people who could not afford to eat more expensive meat, and other people threw them out. So the word *garbage* came to mean "food that is thrown out."

---

at; āpe; cär; end; mē; it; īce; hot; ōld;
wood; fool; oil; out; up; turn; sing;
thin; this; hw in white; zh in treasure.
ə stands for **a** in about, **e** in taken,
i in pencil, **o** in lemon, and **u** in circus.

garden A piece of ground where flowers or vegetables are grown. Mother planted a rose *garden* in the yard. The farmer grows peas, tomatoes, and beets in his *garden. Noun.*
—To work in a garden. Mr. Edwards *gardens* every day after work. *Verb.*
gar·den (gär′dən) *noun, plural* **gardens;** *verb,* **gardened, gardening.**

gardenia A yellow or white flower with waxy petals. Gardenias have a sweet smell.
gar·de·nia (gär dēn′yə) *noun, plural* **gardenias.**

Gardenia

gargoyle A spout in the form of an odd or ugly person or animal. Gargoyles stick out from the roof of a building and carry off rain water.
gar·goyle (gär′goil) *noun, plural* **gargoyles.**

Gargoyle

garlic A plant that is related to the onion. The bulb of the plant is used for flavouring in cooking.
gar·lic (gär′lik) *noun, plural* **garlics.**

garment A piece of clothing. A coat, a sweater, or a shirt are garments.
gar·ment (gär′mənt) *noun, plural* **garments.**

garnet A deep-red gem that is used in jewellery.
gar·net (gär′nət) *noun, plural* **garnets.**

garnish To decorate. The cook *garnished* the fish with slices of lemon.
gar·nish (gär′nish) *verb,* **garnished, garnishing.**

garrison A place where soldiers are stationed. A *garrison* protected the town from enemy troops.
gar·ri·son (gar′ə sən) *noun, plural* **garrisons.**

garter A strap or band that holds up a stocking or sock. A garter is usually made of elastic.
gar·ter (gär′tər) *noun, plural* **garters.**

garter snake A snake that is green or brown with yellow stripes. It is harmless to people.

gas **1.** A form of matter that is not solid or liquid. Gas can move about freely and does not have a definite shape. The air we breathe is made of gases. Some kinds of gases burn and are used for heating or cooking. **2.** Gasoline. We filled the car's tank with *gas.* Look up **gasoline** for more information.
gas (gas) *noun, plural* **gases.**

gaseous In the form of gas; like gas. The air we breathe is *gaseous.*
gas·e·ous (gas′ē əs *or* gash′əs) *adjective.*

gas mask A mask worn over the nose and mouth. It has a filter that keeps a person from breathing poisonous gases and other harmful substances.

gasoline A liquid that burns easily. It is made mostly from petroleum. Gasoline is used as a fuel to make cars, trucks, and airplanes go.
gas·o·line (gas′ə lēn′ *or* gas′ə lēn′) *noun, plural* **gasolines.**

gasp To draw in air suddenly or with effort. She *gasped* for breath after running in the race. *Verb.*
—The act or sound of gasping. We heard a *gasp* from the frightened man. *Noun.*
gasp (gasp) *verb,* **gasped, gasping;** *noun, plural* **gasps.**

gate A movable part like a door that is put in an opening in a fence or wall. ▲ Another word that sounds like this is **gait.**
gate (gāt) *noun, plural* **gates.**

gateway **1.** An open place in a fence or wall where a gate is put. **2.** The way to get someplace or do something. A good education is one *gateway* to success.
gate·way (gāt′wā′) *noun, plural* **gateways.**

gather **1.** To come or bring together. Billy *gathered* his books off the table and put them away. The bird *gathered* twigs for its nest. A crowd *gathered* at the scene of the accident. **2.** To reach an opinion; conclude. We *gathered* from the dark clouds that a storm was coming. **3.** To bring cloth together in folds. She *gathered* the skirt at the waist.

gath·er (ga<u>th</u>′ər) *verb*, **gathered, gathering.**

gaudy Too bright and showy. The yellow and pink coat with green buttons looked *gaudy.*

gaud·y (gä′dē) *adjective,* **gaudier, gaudiest.**

gauge **1.** A standard of measurement. There is a *gauge* for measuring the barrel of a shotgun. There is also a *gauge* for measuring the distance between two rails on a railway track. **2.** An instrument for measuring. A barometer is a *gauge* that measures the pressure of the atmosphere. *Noun.*
—To measure. Scientists can *gauge* the exact amount of rain that falls during a storm. *Verb.*

gauge (gāj) *noun, plural* **gauges;** *verb,* **gauged, gauging.**

gaunt Very thin. The man was *gaunt* and bony from hunger.

gaunt (gänt) *adjective,* **gaunter, gauntest.**

gauze A very thin cloth that you can see through. It is used mostly for making bandages.

gauze (gäz) *noun.*

gave Nancy *gave* her boyfriend a gift. Look up **give** for more information.

gave (gāv) *verb.*

gavel A small wooden hammer. It is used by the person in charge of a meeting or trial to call for order or attention.

gav·el (gav′əl) *noun, plural* **gavels.**

gay Full of joy and fun; merry; cheerful. The children were *gay* at the birthday party. Ruth wore a *gay* dress with many pink ribbons.

gay (gā) *adjective,* **gayer, gayest.**

Gavel

gaze To look at something a long time without looking away. Ken *gazed* at the beautiful sunset. *Verb.*
—A long, steady look. Her *gaze* rested on her friend's new bicycle. *Noun.*

gaze (gāz) *verb,* **gazed, gazing;** *noun, plural* **gazes.**

gazelle A graceful animal that can run very fast. It is found in Africa and Asia.

ga·zelle (gə zel′) *noun, plural* **gazelles** or **gazelle.**

Gazelle

gear **1.** A wheel with teeth on the edge. The teeth are made to fit in between the teeth of another gear, so that one gear can cause the other to turn. **2.** Equipment for a particular purpose. My hiking *gear* includes a knapsack, sleeping bag, and cooking kit. *Noun.*
—To fit. The school was *geared* to meet the needs of bright students. *Verb.*

gear (gēr) *noun, plural* **gears;** *verb,* **geared, gearing.**

gearshift A part that joins a set of gears to a motor. An automobile has a gearshift.

gear·shift (gēr′shift′) *noun, plural* **gearshifts.**

geese More than one goose. Look up **goose** for more information.

geese (gēs) *noun plural.*

Geiger counter A device used to discover and measure the strength of rays from a radio-active substance.

Gei·ger counter (gī′gər).

▲ The **Geiger counter** was named after Hans *Geiger.* He was a German scientist who helped invent this device.

at; āpe; cär; end; mē; it; īce; hot; ōld; wood; fōōl; oil; out; up; turn; sing; thin; <u>th</u>is; hw in white; zh in treasure. ə stands for **a** in about, **e** in taken, **i** in pencil, **o** in lemon, and **u** in circus.

gelatin A substance like jelly. It is made from the skin, bones, and other parts of animals. Gelatin is used in jellies and desserts and in making glue.
gel·a·tin (jel′ə tən) *noun.*

gem A precious stone that has been cut and polished; jewel. The queen wore rubies, diamonds, and other *gems.*
gem (jem) *noun, plural* **gems.**

Kinds of Gems

Sapphire
Jade
Ruby
Turquoise
Diamond
Topaz
Emerald
Opal

gene One of the tiny units of a cell of an animal or plant that determines the characteristics that an offspring inherits from its parent or parents.
gene (jēn) *noun, plural* **genes.**

general 1. For all; for the whole. A *general* meeting of the club was held to discuss the new rules. That exhibit is open to the *general* public. 2. By all or many. There was a *general* panic during the earthquake. *Adjective.*
—In the Canadian Armed Forces, an officer of the highest rank in the land or air force. The four ranks of general are **general, lieutenant general, major general,** and **brigadier general.** *Noun.*
gen·er·al (jen′ər əl) *adjective; noun, plural* **generals.**

general election 1. A election in which all the voters of a country can vote. 2. An election for the federal parliament or for a provincial legislative assembly.

generally 1. Usually. I *generally* walk to school. 2. Without going into detail. *Generally* speaking, the book was good.
gen·er·al·ly (jen′ər ə lē) *adverb.*

generate To bring about or produce. That machine *generates* electricity.
gen·er·ate (jen′ə rāt′) *verb,* **generated, generating.**

generation 1. A group of persons born around the same time. My parents call me and my friends the younger *generation.*

2. One step in the line of descent of a family. A grandmother, father, and daughter make up three *generations.*
gen·er·a·tion (jen′ər ā′shən) *noun, plural* **generations.**

generator A machine that produces electricity, steam, or other energy.
gen·er·a·tor (jen′ər ā′tər) *noun, plural* **generators.**

generous 1. Unselfish. A generous person is willing and happy to share with others. Bill is *generous* with his new bicycle and lets his friends ride it. 2. Large; abundant. She gave him a *generous* helping of cake.
gen·er·ous (jen′ər əs) *adjective.*

genie A spirit with magic powers in Arab fairy tales.
ge·nie (jē′nē) *noun, plural* **genies.**

genius 1. Great ability to think, invent, or create things. The artist who painted those great paintings in the gallery was a person of *genius.* 2. A person who has this ability. A great scientist, musician, or artist is a *genius.*
gen·ius (jēn′yəs) *noun, plural* **geniuses.**

gentle 1. Mild and kindly. She gave the baby a *gentle* hug. 2. Soft or low. We heard the *gentle* tapping of the rain on the window. She spoke in a *gentle* voice. 3. Gradual; not steep. The children slid down the *gentle* slope on their sleds.
gen·tle (jent′əl) *adjective,* **gentler, gentlest.**

▲ The word **gentle** was used first to mean "noble" or "born of a good family." Being kind was thought of as a quality of people of noble birth. So we began to use *gentle* to mean "kind and friendly."

gentleman 1. A man who is polite, kind, and honourable. The judge was a real *gentleman* and was admired by all the people in town. 2. A man of high social position. 3. Any man. "A *gentleman* is at the door to see you," Bill said. The word **gentlewoman** is also used.
gen·tle·man (jent′əl mən) *noun, plural* **gentlemen.**

gently In a gentle way. The snow fell *gently.* He petted the kitten *gently.*
gen·tly (jent′lē) *adverb.*

genuine 1. Real. This belt is made of *genuine* leather. 2. Sincere; honest. She made a *genuine* effort to help us.
gen·u·ine (jen′yo͞o ən) *adjective.*

geographical Having to do with geography.
ge·o·graph·i·cal (jē′ə graf′ə kəl) *adjective.*

geography The study of the surface of the earth and the plant, animal, and human life on it. When you study geography, you learn about the earth's countries and people, and about its climate, oceans and rivers, mountains, and natural resources.
ge·og·ra·phy (jē og′rə fē) *noun, plural* **geographies.**

geological Having to do with geology.
ge·o·log·i·cal (jē′ə loj′ə kəl) *adjective.*

geology The study of the history of the earth. When you study geology, you study rocks and minerals to find out what the earth is made of and what changes have taken place on the earth's surface.
ge·ol·o·gy (jē ol′ə jē) *noun, plural* **geologies.**

geometric Having to do with geometry. A triangle is a *geometric* form. The rug has a *geometric* design of circles and squares.
ge·o·met·ric (jē′ə met′rik) *adjective.*

geometry The part of mathematics that has to do with the measurement and comparison of points, lines, angles, plane figures, and solids.
ge·om·e·try (jē om′ə trē) *noun.*

geranium A plant with bright red, pink, or white flowers.
ge·ra·ni·um (jə rā′nē əm) *noun, plural* **geraniums.**

germ A tiny plant or animal. Germs are so small that they can be seen only through a microscope. Many germs cause disease.
germ (jurm) *noun, plural* **germs.**

Geraniums

German **1.** A person who was born or is living in Germany. **2.** The language of Germany. *Noun.* —Having to do with Germany, its people, or their language. *Adjective.*
Ger·man (jur′mən) *noun, plural* **Germans;** *adjective.*

Germany A country in north-central Europe. It is divided into **West Germany** and **East Germany.**
Ger·ma·ny (jur′mə nē) *noun.*

gesture **1.** A movement of the hands, head, or other part of the body that shows what a person is thinking or feeling. Holding out your hand with the palm up is a *gesture* that you want something. **2.** Something done to express a feeling or for effect. Going to visit her sick classmate was a kind *gesture. Noun.* —To make or use gestures. The policeman

gestured for the driver to stop. *Verb.*
ges·ture (jes′chər) *noun, plural* **gestures;** *verb,* **gestured, gesturing.**

get **1.** To receive or take as one's own; gain; earn. Alice hopes to *get* a new bicycle for Christmas. Stephen thinks he will *get* an A on the test. **2.** To cause to do, be, or become; bring about or happen. He will *get* lunch ready. When will we *get* home? I'm afraid I'll *get* a cold. The boys may *get* lost in the woods. I *get* up at seven o'clock. Hold the dog or he will *get* away.
get (get) *verb,* **got, got** or **gotten, getting.**

get out. *Canadian.* To send a radio signal from somewhere in the far North to a more settled place in the South. During bad weather in remote parts of the Yukon, a radio operator may be unable to *get out* for days.

Geyser

geyser A hot spring from which steam and hot water shoot into the air.
gey·ser (gī′zər) *noun, plural* **geysers.**

ghastly Terrible; horrible. The story was a *ghastly* tale of murder.
ghast·ly (gast′lē) *adjective,* **ghastlier, ghastliest.**

at; āpe; cär; end; mē; it; īce; hot; ōld;
wood; fōol; oil; out; up; turn; sing;
thin; this; hw in white; zh in treasure.
ə stands for a in about, e in taken,
i in pencil, o in lemon, and u in circus.

ghetto 1. A place in a city where Jews were forced to live because they were discriminated against. Ghettos were often crowded with old, run-down buildings. 2. A part of a city where members of a certain race or religion live.

ghet·to (get′ō) *noun, plural* **ghettos** or **ghettoes.**

ghost The supposed spirit of a dead person.
ghost (gōst) *noun, plural* **ghosts.**

ghostly Of a ghost; like a ghost. He thought he heard *ghostly* sounds coming from the old house.

ghost·ly (gōst′lē) *adjective,* **ghostlier, ghostliest.**

giant 1. An imaginary creature like a huge man. A giant has great strength. 2. A person or thing that is very large, powerful, or important. That man is a *giant* in the field of medicine. That company is a *giant* in the manufacturing industry. *Noun.*
—Very large. The scientist looked through a *giant* telescope. *Adjective.*

gi·ant (jī′ənt) *noun, plural* **giants;** *adjective.*

gibbon A small animal that lives in trees. A gibbon has long arms and no tail. It is a kind of ape.

gib·bon (gib′ən) *noun, plural* **gibbons.**

giddy 1. Having a spinning feeling in the head; dizzy. Nancy felt *giddy* after swinging high on the swing. 2. Playful; silly. That *giddy* girl spends most of her time going to dances and parties.

gid·dy (gid′ē) *adjective,* **giddier, giddiest.**

Gibbon

gift 1. Something given; present. Jean could hardly wait to open her birthday *gifts.* 2. Talent; ability. He has a *gift* for music.
gift (gift) *noun, plural* **gifts.**

gigantic Like a giant; huge and powerful. A *gigantic* whale swam under the ship.
gi·gan·tic (jī gan′tik) *adjective.*

giggle To laugh in a high, silly way. The boy *giggled* at the funny joke. *Verb.*
—A high, silly laugh. The girl gave a *giggle* when she saw the clown. *Noun.*
gig·gle (gig′əl) *verb,* **giggled, giggling;** *noun, plural* **giggles.**

gild To cover with a thin layer of gold or golden colour. The artist *gilded* the picture frame. ▲ Another word that sounds like this is **guild.**
gild (gild) *verb,* **gilded, gilding.**

gill The part of a fish and most other water animals used for breathing. A gill takes in oxygen from the water.
gill (gil) *noun, plural* **gills.**

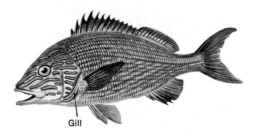

Gill

gin¹ A colourless alcoholic drink that is flavoured with juniper berries.
gin (jin) *noun, plural* **gins.**

gin² A machine for separating cotton from its seeds.
gin (jin) *noun, plural* **gins.**

ginger A hot spice that comes from the root of a tropical plant. Ginger is used in food and medicine.
gin·ger (jin′jər) *noun, plural* **gingers.**

gingerbread A dark, sweet cake or cookie flavoured with ginger.
gin·ger·bread (jin′jər bred′) *noun, plural* **gingerbreads.**

gingham A strong cotton fabric. It usually has a pattern of checks, stripes, or plaid.
ging·ham (ging′-əm) *noun, plural* **ginghams.**

giraffe A large animal that lives in Africa. The giraffe has a very long neck, long, thin legs, and a coat with brown patches. Giraffes are the tallest living animals.
gi·raffe (jə raf′) *noun, plural* **giraffes.**

Giraffe

girder A large, heavy beam. Girders are used to support floors and the frameworks of buildings and bridges.
gird·er (gur′dər) *noun, plural* **girders.**

girl A female child from birth to the time she is a young woman.
girl (gurl) *noun, plural* **girls.**

△ The word **girl** used to mean "a child or young person." The word was used for both boys and girls, and boys were sometimes called "knave girls." Later people began to use *girl* for female children only.

Girl Guide A member of the Girl Guides.

Girl Guides An organization for girls. It helps girls to develop character and physical fitness.

give 1. To hand over or grant to another or others. Ellen's parents will *give* her a bicycle for Christmas. *Give* the kitten a bowl of milk. Mr. Smith will *give* Frank three dollars for mowing the lawn. The teacher *gave* them permission to leave the room. The thief *gave* himself up to the police. 2. To make or do; bring about; cause. Tim *gave* a shout when he found the cave. The puppy will not *give* you any trouble. The noise *gives* me a headache. 3. To break down; yield. If the dam *gives*, the town will be flooded. She would not *give* in and admit she was wrong.
give (giv) *verb,* **gave, given, giving.**

given Ann has *given* her brother a present.
giv·en (giv′ən) *verb.*

glacier A large mass of ice. A glacier is formed by snow that does not melt. It moves slowly across land or down a valley. Long ago, glaciers covered much of North America, Europe, and Russia.
gla·cier (glā′shər) *noun, plural* **glaciers.**

Glacier

glad Happy; pleased. Alan is *glad* to be home. I am *glad* to meet you.
glad (glad) *adjective,* **gladder, gladdest.**

△ The word **glad** used to mean "bright and shining." For example, someone might have said, "This gold is *glad*." Often when people are happy, their faces are bright. So the word *glad* came to mean "very happy."

gladiator In ancient Rome, a man who fought another man for public entertainment.
glad·i·a·tor (glad′ē ā′tər) *noun, plural* **gladiators.**

gladiolus A flower shaped like a funnel that grows in clusters along a long stem.
glad·i·o·lus (glad′ē ō′-ləs) *noun, plural* **gladioli** or **gladioluses.**

glance A quick look. She gave me an angry *glance* over her shoulder. *Noun.*
—**1.** To take a quick look. He *glanced* in the mirror. **2.** To hit something and move off at a slant. The sword *glanced* off the knight's armor. *Verb.*
glance (glans) *noun, plural* **glances;** *verb,* **glanced, glancing.**

Gladiolus

gland A part inside the body that makes a substance that the body uses or gives off. Glands near the eyes make tears. Another kind of gland makes a substance that helps control the growth of the body.
gland (gland) *noun, plural* **glands.**

glare 1. A strong, unpleasant light. The *glare* of the car's headlights hurt my eyes. 2. An angry look or stare. Sue gave Jack a *glare* when he stepped on her foot. *Noun.*
—**1.** To shine with a strong, unpleasant light. The sunlight *glared* on the sand of the beach. **2.** To give an angry look. The old man *glared* at the noisy children. *Verb.*
glare (gler) *noun, plural* **glares;** *verb,* **glared, glaring.**

at; āpe; cär; end; mē; it; īce; hot; ōld; wood; fōōl; oil; out; up; turn; sing; thin; this; hw in white; zh in treasure. ə stands for a in about, e in taken, i in pencil, o in lemon, and u in circus.

glare ice *Canadian.* Smooth, shiny ice that is very slippery.

glass 1. A hard material that breaks easily. Glass can be seen through. 2. A container made of glass that is used for drinking. He drank three *glasses* of water. 3. **glasses.** A pair of lenses made of glass, used to help a person see better; eyeglasses.
  glass (glas) *noun, plural* **glasses.**

gleam A flash or beam of bright light. I could see the *gleam* of a flashlight. The polished silver has a nice *gleam. Noun.*
  —To shine; glow. The new car *gleamed* in the sunlight. *Verb.*
  gleam (glēm) *noun, plural* **gleams;** *verb,* **gleamed, gleaming.**

glee Joy or delight. The little boy laughed with *glee* when he opened his presents.
  glee (glē) *noun.*

glen A small, narrow valley. The hikers rested in a *glen* between the hills.
  glen (glen) *noun, plural* **glens.**

glide To move smoothly along without any effort. The skater *glided* across the ice.
  glide (glīd) *verb,* **glided, gliding.**

glider An aircraft that flies without a motor. Rising air currents keep a glider in the air.
  glid·er (glī′dər) *noun, plural* **gliders.**

glimmer 1. A dim, unsteady light. We could see the *glimmer* of a distant star. 2. A weak sign; hint. There was not even a *glimmer* of hope that we would find the lost dog. *Noun.*
  —To shine with a dim, unsteady light; flicker. The lights on the airplane *glimmered* in the night sky. *Verb.*
  glim·mer (glim′ər) *noun, plural* **glimmers;** *verb,* **glimmered, glimmering.**

glimpse A quick look; glance. He caught a *glimpse* of his friend in the crowd. *Noun.*
  —To look quickly; see for a moment. I *glimpsed* the famous actor as he drove by. *Verb.*
  glimpse (glimps) *noun, plural* **glimpses;** *verb,* **glimpsed, glimpsing.**

glisten To shine with bright flashes; sparkle. The snow *glistened* in the sun. Tears *glistened* on the little boy's cheeks.
  glis·ten (glis′ən) *verb,* **glistened, glistening.**

glitter To shine with bright flashes; sparkle. The gold ring *glittered* on her finger. Stars *glittered* in the sky.
  glit·ter (glit′ər) *verb,* **glittered, glittering.**

gloat To look at or think about something with great satisfaction. The gambler *gloated* over all the money he had won.
  gloat (glōt) *verb,* **gloated, gloating.**

globe 1. The world. Fred travelled around the *globe* and saw many new and interesting things. 2. A round ball with a map of the world on it. We studied the oceans and continents on a *globe* in our classroom. 3. Anything shaped like a ball. Mother placed a glass *globe* over the light bulb in the hall.
  globe (glōb) *noun, plural* **globes.**

Globe

gloom 1. Dim light or darkness. She could not see anything in the *gloom* of the forest at night. 2. Low spirits; sorrow; sadness. He was filled with *gloom* when his best friend moved away.
  gloom (glōōm) *noun.*

gloomy 1. Sad. Joan felt *gloomy* because she couldn't go to the party. 2. Dim; dark. He was scared to go into the *gloomy* hallway. It was a *gloomy*, rainy day.
  gloom·y (glōō′mē) *adjective,* **gloomier, gloomiest.**

glorify To praise or worship. The people will *glorify* the great hero.
  glo·ri·fy (glôr′ə fī′) *verb,* **glorified, glorifying.**

glorious Full of glory; grand; magnificent. A *glorious* sunset filled the sky.
  glo·ri·ous (glôr′ē əs) *adjective.*

glory 1. Great praise; honour; fame. John did all the work, but his brother got the *glory*. 2. Great beauty; splendour; magnificence. The sun shone in all its *glory.*
  glo·ry (glôr′ē) *noun, plural* **glories.**

gloss A smooth, bright look; shine; lustre. Stephen waxed the floor to give it a nice *gloss.*
  gloss (glos) *noun, plural* **glosses.**

glossary A list of hard words and their meanings. The words in a glossary are in alphabetical order. Some books have a glossary at the end.
  glos·sa·ry (glos′ə rē) *noun, plural* **glossaries.**

glossy Having a smooth, bright look; shiny. The photograph has a *glossy* surface. My cat has *glossy* fur.
  gloss·y (glo′sē) *adjective,* **glossier, glossiest.**

glove A covering for the hand. Most gloves have separate parts for each of the four fingers and for the thumb. However, boxing gloves and some baseball gloves hold the four fingers together in one part.
  glove (gluv) *noun, plural* **gloves.**

glow A light or shine. At sunrise, the sky has an orange *glow*. A firefly gives off a *glow*. Her face has the *glow* of good health. *Noun.*
—To shine. The light bulb *glows* brightly. Karen's face *glowed* with health. *Verb.*
　glow (glō) *noun, plural* **glows;** *verb,* **glowed, glowing.**

glue A substance for sticking things together. *Noun.*
—**1.** To stick things together with glue. Jack *glued* the broken vase together. **2.** To fasten or hold tightly. She *glued* her eyes to the television screen. *Verb.*
　glue (gloo) *noun, plural* **glues;** *verb,* **glued, gluing.**

gnarled Having a rough, twisted look. There is a *gnarled* old oak tree beside our house. The old sailor has *gnarled* hands.
　gnarled (närld) *adjective.*

gnat A small fly. Some gnats bite and suck blood from people and animals. Others feed on plants.
　gnat (nat) *noun, plural* **gnats.**

gnaw To bite again and again so as to wear away little by little. The dog *gnawed* the bone. A rat had *gnawed* a hole through the fence.
　gnaw (nä) *verb,* **gnawed, gnawing.**

gnome A kind of dwarf in fairy tales.
　gnome (nōm) *noun, plural* **gnomes.**

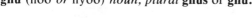

▲ The word **gnome** is said to go back to the Greek word for "intelligence." People used to believe that gnomes knew all about the minerals and riches that could be found under the ground.

gnu A large animal that lives in Africa. A gnu is a kind of antelope. ▲ Other words that sound like this are **knew** and **new.**
　gnu (noo *or* nyoo) *noun, plural* **gnus** or **gnu.**

Gnu

go **1.** To move from one place to another; move along, ahead, or away. They plan to *go* to the beach today. I have to *go* now, or I'll be late. **2.** To pass. Time *goes* quickly when you're busy. **3.** To reach; lead. The road *goes* east from here. The lamp cord isn't long enough to *go* from the wall to the table. **4.** To be, become, or continue. Ellen always *goes* to sleep early on school nights. **5.** To work; run. Our car won't *go*. **6.** To have as a result; turn out. The game didn't *go* well for our team. **7.** To be given. First prize *goes* to Holly. **8.** To have a place; belong. That chair *goes* in the kitchen.
　go (gō) *verb,* **went, gone, going.**

goal **1.** Something that a person wants and tries to get or become; aim; purpose. Gail's *goal* in life is to become a doctor. **2.** A place in certain games where players must get the ball or puck in order to score. The hockey player shot the puck into the *goal*.
　goal (gōl) *noun, plural* **goals.**

goaler A goalie.
　goal·er (gōl′ər) *noun, plural* **goalers.**

goalie A player who guards the goal to stop the other team from scoring.
　goal·ie (gōl′ē) *noun, plural* **goalies.**

goalkeeper A goalie.
　goal·keep·er (gōl′kēp′ər) *noun, plural* **goalkeepers.**

goal tender A goalie.

goat An animal that is related to the sheep. Goats have short horns and a tuft of hair under their chins that looks like a beard. They are raised in many parts of the world for their milk, hair, meat, and skin.
　goat (gōt) *noun, plural* **goats** or **goat.**

Goat

goatee A small pointed beard. It is only large enough to cover the chin and ends in a point just below the chin.
　goat·ee (gō tē′) *noun, plural* **goatees.**

at; āpe; cär; end; mē; it; īce; hot; ōld;
wood; fool; oil; out; up; turn; sing;
thin; this; hw in white; zh in treasure.
ə stands for a in about, e in taken,
i in pencil, o in lemon, and u in circus.

gobble¹   To eat something quickly and in large chunks. The boys *gobbled* their food and then ran out to play.
   gob·ble (gob′əl) *verb,* **gobbled, gobbling.**

gobble²   To make the sound that a turkey makes. *Verb.*
   —The sound that a turkey makes. *Noun.*
   gob·ble (gob′əl) *verb,* **gobbled, gobbling;** *noun, plural* **gobbles.**

goblet   A kind of drinking glass. A goblet is tall and is set on a long stem.
   gob·let (gob′lət) *noun, plural* **goblets.**

God   The being that people worship as the maker and ruler of the world.
   God (god) *noun.*

god   A being who is supposed to have special powers over the lives and doings of people. The myths of ancient Greece and Rome tell stories about *gods* and goddesses.
   god (god) *noun, plural* **gods.**

goddess   A female god. Gods and *goddesses* ruled the world in Greek myths.
   god·dess (god′əs) *noun, plural* **goddesses.**

goelette   *Canadian.* A boat with a flat bottom used for carrying freight on the St. Lawrence River.
   go·el·ette (gōl′et′) *noun, plural* **goelettes.**

goes   Tom *goes* to school.
   goes (gōz) *verb.*

gold   **1.** A heavy yellow metal used to make jewellery and coins. Gold is a chemical element. **2.** The yellow colour of this metal. *Noun.*
   —Having the colour gold. The leaves are red and *gold* in the fall. *Adjective.*
   gold (gōld) *noun, plural* **golds;** *adjective.*

golden   **1.** Made of or containing gold. Susan owns a pair of *golden* earrings that once belonged to her grandmother. **2.** Having the colour or shine of gold; bright or shining. The field of *golden* wheat swayed in the wind. **3.** Very good or valuable; excellent. If he takes that job, it will be a *golden* opportunity for him to become successful.
   gold·en (gōld′ən) *adjective.*

goldenrod   A tall plant that has long stalks of yellow flowers.

Goldenrod

   gold·en·rod (gōld′ən rod′) *noun, plural* **goldenrods.**

goldeye   *Canadian.* A common Canadian freshwater fish. Goldeye is prepared by smoking.

gold·eye (gōld′ī′) *noun, plural* **goldeye** or **goldeyes.**

goldfinch   A North American songbird that is yellow with black markings.
   gold·finch (gōld′finch′) *noun, plural* **goldfinches.**

Goldfinch

goldfish   A small fish that is usually orange-gold in colour.
   gold·fish (gōld′fish′) *noun, plural* **goldfish** or **goldfishes.**

Golf

golf   A game played outdoors on a special course of carefully kept grass. It is played with a small, hard ball and a set of long, thin clubs with iron or wooden heads. The object of the game is to hit the ball into each of a series of holes with as few strokes at the ball as possible. *Noun.*
   —To play the game of golf. *Verb.*
   golf (golf) *noun; verb,* **golfed, golfing.**

gondola   **1.** A long, narrow boat with a high peak at each end. It is rowed at its stern by one person with an oar or pole. Gondolas are used to carry passengers along the canals of Venice, Italy. **2.** A compartment under a dirigible or large balloon. It is used to carry passengers and equipment. **3.** *Canadian.* A booth built near the roof of an arena for announcers to broadcast hockey games.

gon·do·la (gon′də lə) *noun, plural* **gondolas.**

Gondola

gone Stan had already *gone* home when we arrived. Look up **go** for more information. *Verb.*
—Used up or spent. The cake is all *gone. Adjective.*
gone (gon) *verb; adjective.*

gong A piece of metal shaped like a plate that is used as a musical instrument. It is played with a stick that looks like a small hammer. A gong makes a deep sound when it is struck.
gong (gong) *noun, plural* **gongs.**

good Of high quality; not bad or poor. The food at this restaurant is *good.* I thought the movie was very *good.* Paul is a *good* swimmer. Her health has always been *good.* It's a *good* day for a picnic. We had a *good* time at the party. The children were *good* all afternoon. *Adjective.*
—**1.** Benefit; advantage. I'm telling you this for your own *good.* **2.** Kindness or honesty. She feels there is some *good* in everybody. *Noun.*
good (good) *adjective,* **better, best;** *noun.*
for good. Forever; permanently. Joan said she was leaving *for good.*

good-bye Farewell. "*Good-bye!*" she called, as we drove down the driveway. After saying our *good-byes,* we left the party. This word is also spelled **good-by.**
good-bye (good′bī′) *interjection; noun, plural* **good-byes.**

Good Friday The Friday before Easter. It is set aside as the anniversary of the day Jesus died.

good-natured Pleasant, kindly, and cheerful toward others. She's very *good-natured* and never minds when people drop in without being invited.
good-na·tured (good′nā′chərd) *adjective.*

goodness A being good; kindness or generosity. He helped us out of the *goodness* of his heart. *Noun.*
—A word used to express surprise. My *goodness,* I never thought she'd say such a thing! *Interjection.*
good·ness (good′nəs) *noun, interjection.*

goods **1.** Things that are sold; merchandise. All of the store's *goods* are on sale. **2.** Things that belong to someone; belongings. The family lost all their household *goods* in the fire.
goods (goodz) *noun plural.*

goose **1.** A bird that looks like a duck but is larger and has a longer neck. Geese can swim and they have webbed feet. Many kinds of geese are wild, but others are tame and are raised for food. **2.** A female goose. A male goose is called a gander.
goose (go͞os) *noun, plural* **geese.**

gopher A small animal that looks like a chipmunk but is larger. Gophers have large pouches in their cheeks. They burrow under the ground to build long tunnels in which they live. Gophers are found throughout North America.
go·pher (gō′fər) *noun, plural* **gophers.**

Gopher

gorge A deep, narrow valley or canyon that has steep, rocky walls. *Noun.*
—To eat a very large amount of food; stuff with food. She *gorged* herself with four helpings of spaghetti. *Verb.*
gorge (gōrj) *noun, plural* **gorges;** *verb,* **gorged, gorging.**

gorgeous Very beautiful to look at. We took a drive in the country and saw the *gorgeous* colours of the autumn leaves.
gor·geous (gōr′jəs) *adjective.*

at; āpe; cär; end; mē; it; īce; hot; ōld;
wood; fo͞ol; oil; out; up; turn; sing;
thin; <u>th</u>is; hw in white; zh in treasure.
ə stands for a in about, e in taken,
i in pencil, o in lemon, and u in circus.

gorilla   A large, very strong animal that is a kind of monkey. Gorillas have big, heavy bodies, short legs, and long arms. They live in Africa. ▲ Another word that sounds like this is **guerrilla**.
go·ril·la (gə ril′ə) *noun, plural* **gorillas.**

▲ The word **gorilla** comes from a Greek word that means "wild, hairy person." Some early explorers in Africa thought that the gorillas were wild people instead of animals.

Gorilla

gospel   **1.** The teachings of Jesus and the Apostles. **2. Gospel.** In the Bible, any one of the first four books of the New Testament. They are about the life and teachings of Jesus. **3.** Anything believed as absolutely true. The old woman took her doctor's advice as *gospel.*
gos·pel (gos′pəl) *noun, plural* **gospels.**

gossip   **1.** Talk or rumours about other people. Gossip is talk that is often untrue and unkind. There's a lot of *gossip* going around about why he is leaving town. **2.** A person who repeats rumours to others and who enjoys talking about other people. She's nothing but a *gossip,* and I'd never trust her to keep a secret. *Noun.*
—To repeat what one knows or is told about other people; spread gossip. My uncle likes to *gossip* about his neighbours. *Verb.*
gos·sip (gos′ip) *noun, plural* **gossips;** *verb,* **gossiped, gossiping.**

got   I *got* a new jacket last week. Look up **get** for more information.
got (got) *verb.*

gotten   We had already *gotten* a letter from her when she called. Look up **get** for more information.
got·ten (got′ən) *verb.*

gouge   **1.** A tool with a curved, hollow blade. A gouge is used for making holes or grooves in wood. **2.** A hole, groove, or cut. Ben got a long *gouge* in his hand when he fell against the nail. *Noun.*
—To cut or scoop out. The carpenter *gouged* the wood for the shelves. *Verb.*
gouge (gouj) *noun, plural* **gouges;** *verb,* **gouged, gouging.**

Gourds

gourd   A rounded fruit related to the pumpkin or squash. Gourds grow on vines and have a hard outer rind. They are used to make bowls, jugs, and dippers.
gourd (gōrd) *noun, plural* **gourds.**

gourmet   A person who loves fine food and knows a great deal about it. My uncle is a *gourmet* who has written a cookbook, and he does most of the cooking for his family.
gour·met (goor mā′ *or* goor′mā) *noun, plural* **gourmets.**

gout   A disease that causes painful swellings of the joints in the body. Gout usually affects the joints in the big toe.
gout (gout) *noun.*

govern   To rule, control, or manage. The prime minister and the cabinet *govern* the nation. The man's actions were *governed* by his desire to make money.
gov·ern (guv′ərn) *verb,* **governed, governing.**

government   **1.** The group of people in charge of ruling or managing a country, province, city, or other place. In this country the *government* is elected by the people. **2.** A way of ruling or governing. Canada has a democratic *government.*
gov·ern·ment (guv′ərn mənt *or* guv′ər mənt) *noun, plural* **governments.**

Government House   **1.** The official residence of the Governor General of Canada. **2.** The official residence of the Lieutenant-Governor of a province.

governor   **1.** A person who rules or governs. **2.** The person elected to be the head of government of a state in the United States.

3. A device that controls the speed of an engine.

gov·er·nor (guv′ər nər) *noun, plural* **governors.**

Governor General   The representative of the Crown in Canada and in other countries of the Commonwealth.

gown   **1.** A woman's dress. Gowns are usually worn to parties and other special occasions. **2.** A long, loose robe. Students at graduation ceremonies wear gowns.

gown (goun) *noun, plural* **gowns.**

grab   To take hold of suddenly; seize, snatch. Danny had to *grab* his jacket and run to get the bus because he was late. The painter *grabbed* at the window sill as the ladder began to sway. *Verb.*
—A sudden, snatching movement. The goalie made a *grab* for the puck, but it flew over his head. *Noun.*

grab (grab) *verb,* **grabbed, grabbing;** *noun, plural* **grabs.**

grace   **1.** Smooth, beautiful motion or action. The ballerina danced with *grace.* **2.** A short prayer said before or after a meal. **3.** Kindness and courtesy to others; manners. He had the *grace* to apologize for being so rude. *Noun.*
—To add honour or beauty to. A bouquet of roses *graced* the table. The queen *graced* the dinner with her presence. *Verb.*

grace (grās) *noun, plural* **graces;** *verb,* **graced, gracing.**

graceful   Smooth and beautiful in motion or action. The dancer made a *graceful* bow to the audience.

grace·ful (grās′fəl) *adjective.*

gracious   Showing kindness and courtesy; full of grace and charm. The man was a *gracious* host who made his guests feel welcome.

gra·cious (grā′shəs) *adjective.*

grackle   A kind of blackbird. It has a long tail and shiny black feathers.

grack·le (grak′əl) *noun, plural* **grackles.**

Grackle

grade   **1.** A year or level of work in school. My brother is in the Grade 1. **2.** A number or letter showing how well a student has done in work at school; mark. Barbara's *grade* on her geography paper was A. **3.** A degree or step in value, quality, or rank. This beef is of the highest *grade.* **4.** The slope of a road or a railroad track. There was a steep *grade* on the road that went up the side of the mountain. *Noun.*
—**1.** To place or arrange in grades; sort. The farmer *graded* the eggs by size and colour. **2.** To give a grade to; mark. The teacher *graded* the spelling tests. **3.** To make ground more level; make less steep. The bulldozer *graded* the new road. *Verb.*

grade (grād) *noun, plural* **grades;** *verb,* **graded, grading.**

grade school   A school for children from the ages of about six to twelve or fourteen. This school is often called an **elementary school,** a **public school,** or a **separate school.**

gradual   Happening little by little; moving or changing slowly. Tom watched the *gradual* growth of the seeds into plants in his vegetable garden.

grad·u·al (graj′ōō əl) *adjective.*

graduate   **1.** To finish studying at a school or college and be given a diploma. My sister Vivian *graduated* from high school last year. **2.** To mark off in equal spaces for measuring. This thermometer is *graduated* in degrees. *Verb.*
—A person who has finished studying at a school or university and has been given a diploma. *Noun.*

grad·u·ate (graj′ōō āt′ *for verb;* graj′ōō ət *for noun*) *verb,* **graduated, graduating;** *noun, plural* **graduates.**

graduation   **1.** The act of graduating. Certain subjects must be taken for *graduation* from Grade 12. **2.** The ceremony of graduating from a school or university. Susan's whole family went to her *graduation.*

grad·u·a·tion (graj′ōō ā′shən) *noun, plural* **graduations.**

graft   **1.** To put a shoot, bud, or branch from one plant into a cut or slit in another plant so that the two pieces will grow together and form one plant. **2.** To transfer a piece of skin

at; āpe; cär; end; mē; it; īce; hot; ōld; wood; fōōl; oil; out; up; turn; sing; thin; this; hw in white; zh in treasure. ə stands for a in about, e in taken, i in pencil, o in lemon, and u in circus.

or bone from one part of the body to another, or from one person to another. The doctors *grafted* skin from the patient's leg onto his burned arm. *Verb.*

—Something that has been grafted. *Noun.*

graft (graft) *verb,* **grafted, grafting;** *noun, plural* **grafts.**

grain **1.** The seed of wheat, corn, rice, oats, and other cereal plants. That breakfast cereal is made from *grains* of rice. **2.** A tiny, hard piece of something. *Grains* of sand ran through Jesse's fingers as he dug a hole near the shore. **3.** The lines and other marks that run through wood, stone, and other things.

grain (grān) *noun, plural* **grains.**

gram A unit for measuring mass. There are one thousand grams in a kilogram. This word is also spelled **gramme.**

gram (gram) *noun, plural* **grams.**

grammar **1.** A system of arranging words in sentences so that the meaning of what is said is clearly communicated. Grammar is based on a series of rules. Most of these rules come naturally to us as we use our language or as we hear it used by other people. **2.** The use of words in a way that is thought of as correct. Many people think that the word "ain't" is bad *grammar.*

gram·mar (gram′ər) *noun.*

grammatical **1.** Following the rules of grammar. The sentence "Bought I a shirt white" is not *grammatical,* while "I bought a white shirt" is. **2.** Having to do with grammar. His book report has several *grammatical* errors.

gram·mat·i·cal (grə mat′i kəl) *adjective.*

grand **1.** Large and splendid. King Louis XIV lived in a *grand* palace at Versailles. **2.** Including everything; complete. The *grand* total of his winnings in the contest was five thousand dollars. **3.** Most important; main. The dance was held in the *grand* ballroom of the new hotel. **4.** Very good or excellent. We all had a *grand* time at Jennifer's birthday party.

grand (grand) *adjective,* **grander, grandest.**

Grand Banks A shallow area in the Atlantic, southeast of Newfoundland. The Grand Banks are famous fishing grounds.

grandchild The child of one's son or daughter.

grand·child (grand′chīld′) *noun, plural* **grandchildren.**

granddaughter The daughter of one's son or daughter.

grand·daugh·ter (gran′dä′tər) *noun, plural* **granddaughters.**

grandfather The father of one's mother or father.

grand·fa·ther (grand′fä′thər *or* gran′fä′thər) *noun, plural* **grandfathers.**

grandfather clock A clock that is in a tall, narrow cabinet that stands on the floor.

grandmother The mother of one's mother or father.

grand·moth·er (grand′muth′ər *or* gran′-muth′ər) *noun, plural* **grandmothers.**

grandparent The parent of one's mother or father. A grandparent is either a grandmother or a grandfather.

grand·par·ent (grand′par′ənt *or* gran′par′-ənt) *noun, plural* **grandparents.**

grandson The son of one's son or daughter.

grand·son (grand′sun′ *or* gran′sun′) *noun, plural* **grandsons.**

grandstand The place where people sit when watching a parade or sports event. It is made up of raised rows of seats that are sometimes covered by a roof.

grand·stand (grand′stand′) *noun, plural* **grandstands.**

Grandstand

granite A hard kind of rock. Granite is used to build monuments and buildings.

gran·ite (gran′it) *noun.*

grannie **1.** A grandmother. **2.** An old woman. This word is also spelled **granny.**

gran·nie (gran′ē) *noun, plural* **grannies.**

grant **1.** To give or allow. The teacher *granted* him permission to go home early. **2.** To admit to be true. I'll *grant* that your argument makes sense. *Verb.*

—Something that is granted; a gift. She got a *grant* of land from the king. *Noun.*

grant (grant) *verb,* **granted, granting;** *noun, plural* **grants.**

to take for granted. To suppose something to be true without question. We *took it for granted* that you wanted to sleep late this morning, so we turned off the alarm clock.

grape A small, juicy, round fruit that grows in bunches on vines. Grapes have a smooth, thin skin that is usually green or purple in colour. They are eaten raw or used to make raisins, jelly, jam, and wine.
grape (grāp) *noun, plural* grapes.

Grapes

grapefruit A round, pale-yellow fruit. It is like an orange, but larger and more sour.
grape·fruit (grāp′frōōt′) *noun, plural* grape-fruits.

▲ This fruit is called **grapefruit** because it grows in bunches the way grapes do.

grapevine 1. A vine that grapes grow on. 2. A secret or informal way of spreading news or rumours from person to person. We heard it through the *grapevine* that he asked her to the dance weeks ago.
grape·vine (grāp′vīn′) *noun, plural* grape-vines.

graph A drawing that shows the relationship between changing things. The class drew a *graph* to show how the population of Canada has grown over the past one hundred years.
graph (graf) *noun, plural* graphs.

graphite A soft, black mineral that is a form of the element carbon. It is used as the writing lead in pencils.
graph·ite (graf′īt) *noun.*

▲ The word **graphite** goes back to the Greek word "to write" because graphite is used for lead in pencils.

grasp 1. To take hold of firmly with the hand. Chuck *grasped* the handle of the bat tightly and swung at the ball. 2. To see the meaning of; understand. I had a hard time *grasping* the meaning of that poem. *Verb.*
—1. The act of grasping. His *grasp* on the railing slipped, and he fell down the stairs. 2. Knowledge; understanding. Julie has a good *grasp* of the problem. *Noun.*
grasp (grasp) *verb,* grasped, grasping; *noun, plural* grasps.

grass Any of a large number of plants that have narrow leaves called blades. Grasses grow in lawns, fields, and pastures. Horses, cows, and sheep eat grass. Wheat, rye, oats, corn, rice, and bamboo are grasses.
grass (gras) *noun, plural* grasses.

grass hockey Field hockey. Look up **field hockey** for more information.

grasshopper An insect that has long, powerful legs which it uses for jumping. It also has wings. Grasshoppers make a chirping sound.
grass·hop·per (gras′hop′ər) *noun, plural* grasshoppers.

Grasshopper

grassland Land that is covered mainly with grass and has few trees on it. It is often used as pasture for animals.
grass·land (gras′land′) *noun, plural* grass-lands.

grassy Covered with grass. They had a picnic in the *grassy* meadow.
grass·y (gras′ē) *adjective,* grassier, grassiest.

grate¹ 1. A frame of iron bars set over a window or other opening. It is used as a cover, guard, or screen. 2. A frame of iron bars for holding burning fuel in a fireplace or furnace. ▲ Another word that sounds like this is **great.**
grate (grāt) *noun, plural* grates.

grate² 1. To make into small pieces or shreds by rubbing against a rough surface. Karen *grated* some cheese to sprinkle on top of the spaghetti. 2. To rub or scrape with a harsh, grinding noise. The chalk *grated* on the blackboard. 3. To be annoying, irritating, or unpleasant. Her shrill laugh really *grates* on my nerves. ▲ Another word that sounds like this is **great.**
grate (grāt) *verb,* grated, grating.

grateful Full of thanks or warm feelings for a favour that one has received or for something that makes one happy. We were *grateful* to be inside on such a cold night.
grate·ful (grāt′fəl) *adjective.*

gratify To give pleasure or satisfaction to; please. Sally was *gratified* when her teacher praised her report.
grat·i·fy (grat′ə fī′) *verb,* gratified, gratifying.

at; āpe; cär; end; mē; it; īce; hot; ōld; wood; fōōl; oil; out; up; turn; sing; thin; this; hw in white; zh in treasure. ə stands for a in about, e in taken, i in pencil, o in lemon, and u in circus.

grating¹ A frame of iron bars set over a window or other opening. It is used as a cover, guard, or screen. Some banks and post offices have windows with gratings over them.
grat·ing (grāt′ing) *noun*, *plural* gratings.

Grating

grating² 1. Making a harsh, grinding sound. There was a loud *grating* noise as we pulled the rusty lid open. 2. Not pleasant; annoying. I find his habit of cracking his knuckles very *grating*.
grat·ing (grāt′ing) *adjective*.

gratitude A feeling of thanks for a favour one has received or for something that makes one happy. She was full of *gratitude* for the help that we gave her.
grat·i·tude (grat′ə tōōd′ *or* grat′ə tyōōd′) *noun*.

grave¹ A hole dug in the ground where a dead body is buried.
grave (grāv) *noun*, *plural* graves.

grave² 1. Thoughtful and solemn; serious. The doctor's face was *grave* as he described the child's operation to her family. 2. Very important. The general had to make *grave* decisions when the war broke out.
grave (grāv) *adjective*, graver, gravest.

gravel Pebbles and small pieces of rock. It is used for making driveways and roads. *Noun.*
—To cover with gravel. *Verb.*
grav·el (grav′əl) *noun*, *plural* gravels; *verb*, gravelled, gravelling or graveled, graveling.

graveyard A place where people are buried; cemetery.
grave·yard (grāv′yärd′) *noun*, *plural* graveyards.

gravitation The force or pull that draws all the bodies in the universe toward one another. Gravitation is the force that keeps the planets in their orbit around the sun. It also keeps objects on the surface of the earth.
grav·i·ta·tion (grav′ə tā′shən) *noun*.

gravity 1. The force that pulls things toward the centre of the earth. Gravity is the force that causes objects to fall when they are dropped. It also pulls them back to earth when they are thrown upward. Gravity also causes objects to have weight. 2. Serious nature. Because of the *gravity* of the situation, troops were sent to guard the fort.
grav·i·ty (grav′ə tē) *noun*, *plural* gravities.

gravy A sauce made from the juices that come from meat during cooking.
gra·vy (grā′vē) *noun*, *plural* gravies.

gray A colour made by mixing black and white. This word is usually spelled **grey**. Look up **grey** for more information.

graze¹ To feed on growing grass. The flock of sheep *grazed* on the hillside.
graze (grāz) *verb*, grazed, grazing.

graze² To scrape lightly. He *grazed* his knee when he fell.
graze (grāz) *verb*, grazed, grazing.

grease 1. Melted animal fat. Bacon *grease* can be used in cooking. 2. A thick oil. *Grease* is put on the parts of an automobile engine that move against one another. *Noun.*
—To rub or put grease on. *Grease* the baking pan so that the cake won't stick. *Verb.*
grease (grēs) *noun*, *plural* greases; *verb*, greased, greasing.

greasy 1. Soiled with grease. The mechanic's overalls were *greasy* after he repaired the car. 2. Containing much grease or fat. This fried chicken is *greasy*.
greas·y (grē′sē) *adjective*, greasier, greasiest.

great 1. Very large in size, number, or amount. A *great* crowd gathered to welcome the astronauts to the city. 2. Very important, excellent, or remarkable. William Shakespeare was a *great* writer. 3. More than is usual; much. We'll never forget her *great* kindness to us when our mother was ill.
▲ Another word that sounds like this is **grate**.
great (grāt) *adjective*, greater, greatest.

Great Dane A large, powerful dog. It has a smooth, short coat.
Great Dane (dān).

Great Divide The crust of the Rocky Mountains from which rivers flow west to the Pacific Ocean or east and north to Hudson's Bay and the Arctic Ocean.

Great Lakes The five freshwater lakes that are included in the St. Lawrence waterway. The Great Lakes are Lake Superior, Lake Huron, Lake Michigan, Lake Erie, and Lake Ontario.

greatly Very much; highly. We *greatly* appreciated the beautiful gift you gave us.
great·ly (grāt′lē) *adverb*.

Greece A country in southeastern Europe.
Greece (grēs) *noun*.

greed A very great and selfish desire for more than one's share of something. Because of his *greed* for money, the grocer tried to cheat everyone who came into his store.
greed (grēd) *noun, plural* **greeds.**

greedy Having a great and selfish desire for more than one's share of something. The king was *greedy* for power, and he was eager to go to war to get more land.
greed·y (grē′dē) *adjective,* **greedier, greedi-est.**

Greek Having to do with ancient or modern Greece, its people, or their language or culture. *Adjective.*
—**1.** A person who was born or is living in Greece. **2.** A person who lived in ancient Greece. **3.** The language of Greece. *Noun.*
Greek (grēk) *adjective; noun, plural* **Greeks.**

green **1.** The colour of growing grass and of leaves in the spring and summer. It is made by mixing blue and yellow. **2.** Ground covered with grass. The meeting took place near the village *green.* **3.** On a golf course, the area around the hole for the ball. **4. greens.** Green leaves and stems of plants that are used for food. *Noun.*
—**1.** Having the colour green. Mother bought a *green* coat. **2.** Covered with growing plants, grass, or leaves. The cows grazed over *green* pastures. **3.** Not full-grown; not ripe. I won't eat those *green* tomatoes. **4.** Having little or no training or experience. Mark was *green* compared to the other boys on the team. *Adjective.*
green (grēn) *noun, plural* **greens;** *adjective,* **greener, greenest.**

greenhouse A building for growing plants.
green·house (grēn′hous′) *noun, plural* **green-houses.**

greet **1.** To speak to or welcome in a friendly or polite way. Sharon *greeted* her guests at the door. **2.** To respond to; meet; receive. The news that school would end early was *greeted* with cheers by the students.
greet (grēt) *verb,* **greeted, greeting.**

greeting **1.** The act or words of a person who greets others. His *greeting* to us was a wave of his hand. **2. greetings.** A friendly message that is sent by someone. My friend sent me *greetings* on my birthday.
greet·ing (grēt′ing) *noun, plural* **greetings.**

grenade A small bomb that can be thrown by hand.
gre·nade (grə nād′) *noun, plural* **grenades.**

grew He *grew* tomatoes on his farm. Look up **grow** for more information.
grew (grōo) *verb.*

grey A colour made by mixing black and white. *Noun.*
—Having the colour grey. Jean has *grey* eyes. *Adjective.*
This word is also spelled **gray.**
grey (grā) *noun, plural* **greys;** *adjective,* **grey-er, greyest.**

greyhound A slender dog with a smooth coat and a long nose. It can run very fast.
grey·hound (grā′hound′) *noun, plural* **grey-hounds.**

Greyhound

griddle A heavy, flat metal plate with a handle. It is like a frying pan and is used for cooking pancakes and other food.
grid·dle (grid′əl) *noun, plural* **griddles.**

grief Very great sadness or pain. His *grief* at the death of his grandfather was great.
grief (grēf) *noun, plural* **griefs.**

at; āpe; cär; end; mē; it; īce; hot; ōld; wood; fool; oil; out; up; turn; sing; thin; this; hw in white; zh in treasure. ə stands for a in about, e in taken, i in pencil, o in lemon, and u in circus.

Greenhouse

grieve 1. To feel grief; mourn. The entire nation *grieved* at the death of the Governor General. 2. To make someone feel grief or sorrow. His unkind words *grieved* his parents.
grieve (grēv) *verb*, **grieved, grieving.**

Grill

grill A framework of metal bars for broiling meat or other food over an open fire. My father broiled hot dogs on the *grill* in the backyard. *Noun.*
—1. To broil on a grill. The campers *grilled* hamburgers for supper. 2. To question closely, harshly, and for a long time. The police *grilled* the bank robber until he told them where he had hidden the money. *Verb.*
grill (gril) *noun, plural* **grills;** *verb,* **grilled, grilling.**

grim 1. Stern, frightening, and harsh. Her face had a cold, *grim* expression. 2. Refusing to give up; very stubborn. The wrestlers fought with *grim* determination.
grim (grim) *adjective,* **grimmer, grimmest.**

grimace A twisting of the face. People often make a grimace when they are not comfortable, pleased, or happy about something. *Noun.*
—To make a grimace. Eileen *grimaced* when she tasted the bitter medicine. *Verb.*
gri·mace (grim′əs *or* gri mās′) *noun, plural* **grimaces;** *verb,* **grimaced, grimacing.**

grime Dirt that is covering or rubbed into a surface. The windows were covered with *grime.*
grime (grīm) *noun.*

grin To smile very broadly and happily. Jack *grinned* when his father gave him his birthday present. *Verb.*
—A very broad, happy smile. Judy had a big *grin* on her face as she accepted first prize in the spelling contest. *Noun.*
grin (grin) *verb,* **grinned, grinning;** *noun, plural* **grins.**

grind 1. To crush or chop into small pieces or into a fine powder. We watched the butcher *grind* the meat. 2. To make something smooth or sharp by rubbing it against something rough. The farmer *ground* his axe on the grindstone. 3. To rub or press down in a harsh or noisy way. She *grinds* her teeth whenever she gets very angry.
grind (grīnd) *verb,* **ground, grinding.**

grindstone A round, flat stone that is set in a frame. By turning it around and around, a person can use it to sharpen knives, axes, and other tools or to polish or smooth things.
grind·stone (grīnd′stōn′) *noun, plural* **grindstones.**

Grindstone

grip 1. A firm hold; tight grasp. I kept a good *grip* on the dog's collar when he tried to run after the cat. 2. Firm control or power. The city was in the *grip* of a heavy snowstorm. *Noun.*
—To take hold of firmly and tightly. Mickey *gripped* his stick and shot the puck as hard as he could. *Verb.*
grip (grip) *noun, plural* **grips;** *verb,* **gripped, gripping.**

grit 1. Very small bits of sand or stone. The strong wind at the beach blew *grit* in my eyes and my hair. 2. Bravery; courage. Jennifer showed real *grit* when she found her way back to camp after dark. *Noun.*
—To press together hard. Doug *gritted* his teeth and then held out his arm for the doctor to give him the flu shot. *Verb.*
grit (grit) *noun; verb,* **gritted, gritting.**

Grit A member of the Liberal Party. *Noun.*
—Having to do with the Liberal Party. *Adjective.*
Grit (grit) *noun, plural* **Grits;** *adjective.*

grizzled Grey or mixed with grey. The old man had a *grizzled* beard.

griz·zled (griz′əld) *adjective.*

grizzly bear A very large, powerful bear. It has long claws and usually brown or grey fur. Grizzly bears live in western North America.

griz·zly bear (griz′lē).

Grizzly Bear

groan A deep, sad sound that people sometimes make when they are unhappy, annoyed, or in pain. *Noun.*
—To make a deep, sad sound. Michael *groaned* when he twisted his ankle. *Verb.*
▲ Another word that sounds like this is **grown.**

groan (grōn) *noun, plural* **groans;** *verb,* **groaned, groaning.**

grocer A person who sells food and household supplies.

gro·cer (grō′sər) *noun, plural* **grocers.**

grocery **1.** A store that sells food and household supplies. **2. groceries.** Food and other things sold by a grocer. Mother sent Sam out to buy some *groceries.*

gro·cer·y (grō′sər ē) *noun, plural* **groceries.**

gronker *Canadian.* Another name for the Canada goose. Look up **Canada goose** for more information.

gronk·er (grongk′ər) *noun, plural* **gronkers.**

groom **1.** A man who has just been married. **2.** A person whose work is taking care of horses. *Noun.*
—**1.** To wash, brush, and take care of horses. Ted learned to *groom* horses on a farm. **2.** To make neat and pleasant in appearance. She *groomed* her hair for the party. *Verb.*

groom (groom) *noun, plural* **grooms;** *verb,* **groomed, grooming.**

groove A long, narrow cut or dent. The wheels of the car made *grooves* in the dirt road. A phonograph record has *grooves* in it

for the needle of the record player. *Noun.*
—To make a groove or grooves in. The carpenter *grooved* the sides of the bookcase so that the shelves would fit into place. *Verb.*

groove (groov) *noun, plural* **grooves;** *verb,* **grooved, grooving.**

grope **1.** To feel about with the hands. As he entered the dark room, Jerry *groped* for the light switch. **2.** To search about in the mind for something. He *groped* for the right answer as everyone waited for him to speak. **3.** To find one's way by feeling about with the hands. The audience *groped* its way to the door as the theatre filled with smoke.

grope (grōp) *verb,* **groped, groping.**

gross **1.** With nothing taken out; total; entire. A person's *gross* income is all the money he or she earns before taxes. **2.** Very bad or wrong; terrible. It is a *gross* injustice to send this innocent man to jail. **3.** Coarse; vulgar. His *gross* jokes annoyed us. *Adjective.*
—**1.** The total amount. The company's *gross* for the year was five million dollars. **2.** Twelve dozen; 144. The tennis coach ordered a *gross* of balls. *Noun.*

gross (grōs) *adjective,* **grosser, grossest;** *noun, plural* **grosses** (*for definition 1*) or **gross** (*for definition 2*).

grotesque Strange, ugly, or not natural.

gro·tesque (grō tesk′) *adjective.*

▲ The word that **grotesque** comes from was first used for paintings of strange beings that were part man and part animal. These paintings were found in caves in Italy hundreds of years ago, and the word for them came from the word for "cave." Now it is used for anything that is strange and ugly.

---

grouch A person who is cross and bad-tempered.

grouch (grouch) *noun, plural* **grouches.**

ground[1] **1.** The part of the earth that is solid; soil; land. The *ground* was covered with snow. **2. grounds.** The land around a house or other building. The school *grounds* were planted with trees and flowers. **3.** An area or piece of land used for some special purpose. A brook runs through the picnic *grounds.* **4.** The cause for something said,

at; āpe; cär; end; mē; it; īce; hot; ōld;
wood; fōōl; oil; out; up; turn; sing;
thin; this; hw in white; zh in treasure.
ə stands for a in about, e in taken,
i in pencil, o in lemon, and u in circus.

done, or thought; a reason. What *grounds* do the police have for thinking that he is the thief? **5.** grounds. The bits of coffee that settle at the bottom of a cup or that are left over in the coffee pot. *Noun.*
—**1.** To force or stay on the ground or to come down to the ground. The airport *grounded* the plane for three hours because of bad weather. **2.** To cause to hit the bottom of a river or other body of water. The captain *grounded* his ship on the sand bar. **3.** To hit a baseball so that it rolls or bounces along the ground. The batter *grounded* to the first baseman. **4.** To fix or base firmly. You must *ground* an argument in fact. **5.** To connect with the ground. These electric wires are dangerous if they aren't *grounded. Verb.*
  ground (ground) *noun, plural* **grounds;** *verb,* **grounded, grounding.**

ground² The wheat was *ground* into flour. Look up **grind** for more information.
  ground (ground) *verb.*

groundhog A stout animal with short legs and coarse, brown fur. Groundhogs live underground. This animal is also called a **woodchuck.**
  ground·hog (ground′hog′) *noun, plural* **groundhogs.**

Groundhog

Groundhog Day February 2, the day the groundhog is supposed to come out of its hole to see if the sun is shining. If the groundhog sees its shadow, it returns to its hole for six more weeks of winter.

group **1.** A number of persons or things together. A *group* of people gathered on the corner to watch the firemen put out the fire. **2.** A number of persons or things that belong together or that are put together. The teacher divided the class into *groups* who would read different stories. *Noun.*
—To form into a group. Our camp counsellor *grouped* us by age. The girls *grouped* around the famous movie star. *Verb.*
  group (groop) *noun, plural* **groups;** *verb,* **grouped, grouping.**

grouse A bird that looks like a plump chicken. Grouse have brown, black, or grey feathers and are hunted as game.
  grouse (grous) *noun, plural* **grouse** or **grouses.**

grove A group of trees standing together. Peaches grow in *groves.*
  grove (grōv) *noun, plural* **groves.**

grow **1.** To become bigger; increase. That plant will *grow* quickly. Joan *grew* two centimetres last year. **2.** To come into being and live; exist. Cactuses don't *grow* in this part of the country. **3.** To cause to grow. That farmer *grows* corn. **4.** To become. It *grew* cold as the sun went down. He *grew* rich as his business became successful.
  grow (grō) *verb,* **grew, grown, growing.**
  to grow up. To become an adult. Susan said she wants to become a lawyer when she *grows up.*

growl To make a deep, harsh, rumbling sound in the throat. Dogs and other animals often growl when they are angry. The bear *growled* when we got too close to its cage. *Verb.*
—A deep, harsh, rumbling sound made in the throat. He greeted us with a *growl* when he had to get out of the shower to open the door for us. *Noun.*
  growl (groul) *verb,* **growled, growling;** *noun, plural* **growls.**

grown Sandra has *grown* very pretty. These trees have *grown* very tall. Look up **grow** for more information. ▲ Another word that sounds like this is **groan.**
  grown (grōn) *verb.*

grown-up **1.** Having come to full growth; adult. He's a *grown-up* person now. **2.** Of or like an adult. Maria's *grown-up* manners make you think she's older than she is. *Adjective.*
—A person who has come to full growth; an adult. The *grown-ups* watched as the children swam in the pool. *Noun.*
  grown-up (grōn′up′ *for adjective;* grōn′up′ *for noun*) *adjective; noun, plural* **grown-ups.**

growth **1.** The process of growing. Jim planted some seeds in his back yard and then watched their *growth.* The *growth* of Mr. Jackson's business has been very rapid. **2.** Something that has grown. A thick *growth* of weeds covered the path leading to the old house.

Grouse

growth (grōth) *noun, plural* **growths.**

grub A beetle or other insect in an early stage of growth, when it looks like a worm. *Noun.*
—To dig in the ground; dig up from the ground. Pigs *grub* for food with their hooves and snouts. *Verb.*
  grub (grub) *noun, plural* **grubs;** *verb,* **grubbed, grubbing.**

grudge Dislike or anger that has been felt for a long time. He's held a *grudge* against her ever since she ran against him for class president. *Noun.*
—To be unwilling to give or allow. Even though you don't like her, don't *grudge* her first prize if she deserves it. *Verb.*
  grudge (gruj) *noun, plural* **grudges;** *verb,* **grudged, grudging.**

gruelling Very difficult or exhausting. The cross-country bicycle race was *gruelling.* This word is also spelled **grueling.**
  gru·ell·ing (grooˈling) *adjective.*

gruesome Causing disgust or fear; horrible. When we walked past the cemetery, we remembered all those *gruesome* stories about ghosts.
  grue·some (grooˈsəm) *adjective.*

gruff 1. Deep and rough-sounding. The guard asked us in a *gruff* voice what we were doing in the building so late. 2. Not friendly, warm, or polite. His manner is *gruff,* but he's really very kind.
  gruff (gruf) *adjective,* **gruffer, gruffest.**

grumble To complain in a low voice; mutter in an unhappy way. Ted got out of bed and *grumbled* about having to wake up so early. *Verb.*
—1. Unhappy complaining or muttering. She answered with a *grumble* that she was tired of having to walk the dog and that it was Larry's turn. 2. A low, rumbling sound. We could hear the *grumble* of thunder in the distance. *Noun.*
  grum·ble (grumˈbəl) *verb,* **grumbled, grumbling;** *noun, plural* **grumbles.**

grumpy In a bad mood; cross or grouchy. He's often *grumpy* when his older brother teases him.
  grump·y (grumˈpē) *adjective,* **grumpier, grumpiest.**

grunt A short, deep sound. The hog finished eating and lay down with a *grunt.* *Noun.*
—To make a short, deep sound. The man *grunted* in pain as the woman's umbrella poked him in the ribs. *Verb.*
  grunt (grunt) *noun, plural* **grunts;** *verb,* **grunted, grunting.**

guarantee A promise to repair or replace something or to give back the money for it, if anything goes wrong with it before a certain time has passed. This toaster comes with a *guarantee* of one year. *Noun.*
—1. To give a guarantee for. The company *guarantees* this dishwasher for one year. 2. To make sure or certain. Having that singer perform will *guarantee* that the dance will be a success. 3. To promise something. The plumber *guaranteed* the work would be finished on time. *Verb.*
  guar·an·tee (garˈən tēˈ) *noun, plural* **guarantees;** *verb,* **guaranteed, guaranteeing.**

guard 1. To keep safe from harm or danger; protect. The dog *guarded* the house. 2. To watch over or control. The policeman *guarded* the prisoner. 3. To try to prevent a player on another team from scoring. Jack *guarded* the other team's star player during the game. *Verb.*
—1. A person or group of persons that guards. The museum *guard* collected our tickets at the door. 2. A close watch. A sentry kept *guard* at the army camp. 3. Something that protects. Patrick's chin *guard* slipped during the football game, and he got cut in the mouth. 4. A player at either side of the centre in football. 5. In basketball, either of two players whose position is toward the back of the court. *Noun.*
  guard (gärd) *verb,* **guarded, guarding;** *noun, plural* **guards.**
  guard against. To prevent by being careful. She wore galoshes to *guard against* the snow and slush.
  on guard. Ready to protect. The dog stood *on guard* at the front door of the luxurious mansion.

guardian A person chosen by law to take care of someone who is young or who is not able to care for himself. After the baby's parents died, her uncle became her *guardian.*
  guard·i·an (gärˈdē ən) *noun, plural* **guardians.**

guerrilla A member of a small band of soldiers. Guerrillas are not part of the regular army of a country. They often fight the enemy by making quick, surprise attacks. ▲ Another

at; āpe; cär; end; mē; it; īce; hot; ōld; wood; fool; oil; out; up; turn; sing; thin; this; hw in white; zh in treasure. ə stands for a in about, e in taken, i in pencil, o in lemon, and u in circus.

word that sounds like this is **gorilla**.

guer·ril·la (gə ril′ə) *noun, plural* **guerrillas**.

guess **1.** To form an opinion without having enough knowledge or facts to be sure. Without a watch, he could only *guess* what time it was. **2.** To get the correct answer by guessing. I *guessed* the end of the mystery story. **3.** To think; believe; suppose. I *guess* he forgot her birthday because he didn't send her a card. *Verb.*
—An opinion formed without having enough knowledge or facts to be sure. His *guess* is that Ellen will be home by now. *Noun.*

guess (ges) *verb,* **guessed, guessing;** *noun, plural* **guesses.**

guest **1.** A person who is at another's house for a meal or a visit. We are having *guests* for dinner tonight. **2.** A customer in a restaurant, hotel, or similar place. This motel has room for fifty *guests*.

guest (gest) *noun, plural* **guests.**

guide To show the way; direct. The Boy Scout *guided* the other campers through the woods. *Verb.*
—A person or thing that shows the way or directs. When my aunt and uncle were up North, a guide took them through the bush. *Noun.*

guide (gīd) *verb,* **guided, guiding;** *noun, plural* **guides.**

guided missile A missile that is guided along a certain course throughout its flight. It is guided by an automatic control inside it or by radio signals that it receives from the ground.

guide word One of the words that appear at the top of a page in dictionaries and some other books. Guide words show the first and last things that appear on a page. The guide words on this page of your dictionary are **guess** and **gulf**.

guild **1.** In the Middle Ages, a group of people in the same trade or craft who joined together. Guilds were set up to see that the quality of work done was good and to look out for the interests of their members. **2.** An organization of people with the same interests or aims. The women's *guild* of our church is holding a cake sale to raise money.
▲ Another word that sounds like this is **gild**.

guild (gild) *noun, plural* **guilds.**

guillotine A machine for executing a person by cutting off his head. It is made of a heavy blade that is dropped between two posts.

guil·lo·tine (gil′ə tēn′) *noun, plural* **guillotines.**

▲ The **guillotine** was named after Joseph I. *Guillotin*. He was a French doctor who is supposed to have urged the use of this machine as a fast and less painful way of executing people.

guilt **1.** The state or fact of having done wrong or broken the law. The lawyer said that the new evidence proved the man's *guilt* in the robbery. **2.** A feeling of having done something wrong; regret; shame. He felt a good deal of *guilt* after he'd been rude to the old woman.

guilt (gilt) *noun, plural* **guilts.**

guilty **1.** Having done wrong; deserving to be blamed or punished. The jury found him *guilty* of armed robbery. We're all *guilty* of losing our temper sometimes.
2. Feeling or showing guilt or shame. She had a *guilty* conscience for days after she told the lie.

guilt·y (gil′tē) *adjective,* **guiltier, guiltiest.**

Guinea Fowl

guinea fowl A bird that has dark-grey feathers with small, white spots. It comes from Africa. Guinea fowl are raised as food in many parts of the world. A guinea fowl is sometimes also called a **guinea hen**.

guin·ea fowl (gin′ē).

guinea pig A small, plump animal with short ears, short legs, and no tail. It is often used in scientific experiments. Guinea pigs are very gentle and are often kept as pets.

Guinea Pig

guitar A musical instrument with a long neck and six or more strings. It is played by plucking or strumming the strings. Some kinds of guitars use electricity to make their sound louder.

gui·tar (gi tär′) *noun, plural* **guitars.**

gulf A part of an ocean or sea that is partly enclosed by land. A gulf is usually larger and deeper than a bay.

gulf (gulf) *noun, plural* **gulfs.**

gull A bird with grey and white feathers. It lives on or near bodies of water. It has long wings and a thick, slightly hooked beak. It is also called a **sea gull**.
gull (gul) *noun, plural* **gulls.**

Gull

gullible Believing or trusting in almost anything; easily fooled, tricked, or cheated. Everyone plays jokes on him because he's *gullible* enough to believe any story you tell him.
gul·li·ble (gul'ə bəl) *adjective.*

gully A narrow ditch. After the rainstorm, there were *gullies* along the sides of the road.
gul·ly (gul'ē) *noun, plural* **gullies.**

gulp **1.** To swallow quickly, greedily, or in large amounts. Robin *gulped* a glass of milk and ran out to catch the bus. **2.** To draw in or swallow air; gasp. When her father asked her who had broken the window, Joyce *gulped* and said nothing. *Verb.*
—The act of gulping. Frank finished the lemonade in two *gulps. Noun.*
gulp (gulp) *verb,* **gulped, gulping;** *noun, plural* **gulps.**

gum¹ **1.** A thick, sticky juice that comes from various trees and plants. Gum hardens when it is dry. It is used for sticking paper and other things together. **2.** Gum that is made sweet and thick for chewing.
gum (gum) *noun, plural* **gums.**

gum² The pink, tough flesh around the teeth.
gum (gum) *noun, plural* **gums.**

gumdrop A small piece of candy that is like jelly coated with sugar.
gum·drop (gum'drop') *noun, plural* **gumdrops.**

gun **1.** A weapon made up of a metal tube through which a bullet or something similar is shot. Pistols, rifles, and cannons are guns. **2.** Something that is like a gun in shape or use. Keith used a spray *gun* to paint the bookcase. *Noun.*

—To shoot or hunt with a gun. The outlaw in the movie tried to *gun* down the sheriff. *Verb.*
gun (gun) *noun, plural* **guns;** *verb,* **gunned, gunning.**

▲ The word **gun** is probably a short form of the name *Gunnhildr. Gunnhildr* was a common name for women in an old Scandinavian language. Men often gave women's names to their weapons, and the name *Gunnhildr* may have been chosen for a weapon because it was made up of two words that meant "war" and "battle."

gunner A soldier or other person in the armed forces who handles and fires cannons and other large guns.
gun·ner (gun'ər) *noun, plural* **gunners.**

gunpowder A powder that burns and explodes when set on fire. It is used in guns, fireworks, and blasting.
gun·pow·der (gun'pou'dər) *noun, plural* **gunpowders.**

gunwale The upper edge of the side of a ship or boat.
gun·wale (gun'əl) *noun, plural* **gunwales.**

guppy A very small fish. The male is brightly coloured. The guppy is often kept as a pet.
gup·py (gup'ē) *noun, plural* **guppies.**

Guppies

▲ The word **guppy** comes from the name of R. J. L. *Guppy.* He was a British minister who knew a great deal about these fish and gave samples of them to a museum.

at; āpe; cär; end; mē; it; īce; hot; ōld;
wood; fōol; oil; out; up; turn; sing;
thin; this; hw in white; zh in treasure.
ə stands for a in about, e in taken,
i in pencil, o in lemon, and u in circus.

gurgle **1.** To flow or run with a bubbling sound. The stream *gurgled* around the rocks. **2.** To make a sound like this. The baby *gurgled* in her crib.
gur·gle (gur′gəl) *verb,* **gurgled, gurgling.**

gush **1.** To pour out suddenly and in large amounts. Water *gushed* from the broken pipe. His cut finger *gushed* blood until it was bandaged. **2.** To talk with so much feeling and eagerness that it seems silly. Our neighbour is always *gushing* about how smart her grandchildren are. *Verb.*
—A sudden, heavy flow. Oil poured out of the well in a *gush. Noun.*
gush (gush) *verb,* **gushed, gushing;** *noun, plural* **gushes.**

gust **1.** A sudden, strong rush of wind or air. A *gust* of wind lifted Paul's cap off his head and carried it across the street. **2.** A short or sudden bursting out of feeling. *Gusts* of laughter greeted the comedian as he danced out on stage.
gust (gust) *noun, plural* **gusts.**

gutter **1.** A channel or ditch along the side of a street or road to carry off water. Julie's ball rolled off the sidewalk into the *gutter.* **2.** A pipe or trough along the lower edge of a roof. It carries off rain water.
gut·ter (gut′ər) *noun, plural* **gutters.**

guy[1] A rope, chain, or wire used to steady or fasten something. Guys are used to steady a tent.
guy (gī) *noun, plural* **guys.**

guy[2] A boy or man; fellow. Marty is a very nice *guy.* ▲ This word is used only in everyday conversation.
guy (gī) *noun, plural* **guys.**

gym **1.** A room or building that is used for physical exercise; gymnasium. The school basketball team practises in the *gym* almost every day after classes. **2.** A course in physical education that is given in a school or university.
gym (jim) *noun, plural* **gyms.**

gymnasium A room or building with equipment for physical exercise or training and for indoor sports.
gym·na·si·um (jim nā′zē əm) *noun, plural* **gymnasiums.**

gymnastics Exercises done to develop the body.
gym·nas·tics (jim nas′tiks) *noun plural.*

Gymnastics

Gypsy A person belonging to a group of people who came to Europe from India long ago. Gypsies are a wandering people and they now live scattered throughout the world.
Gyp·sy (jip′sē) *noun, plural* **Gypsies.**

▲ The word **Gypsy** is short for "Egyptian." People used to think that Gypsies came from Egypt.

gyroscope A wheel that is mounted so that its axis can point in any direction. A gyroscope is used as a compass and to keep airplanes and ships steady.
gy·ro·scope (jī′rə skōp′) *noun, plural* **gyroscopes.**

---

at; āpe; cär; end; mē; it; īce; hot; ōld;
wood; fōōl; oil; out; up; turn; sing;
thin; this; hw in white; zh in treasure.
ə stands for **a** in about, **e** in taken,
i in pencil, **o** in lemon, and **u** in circus.

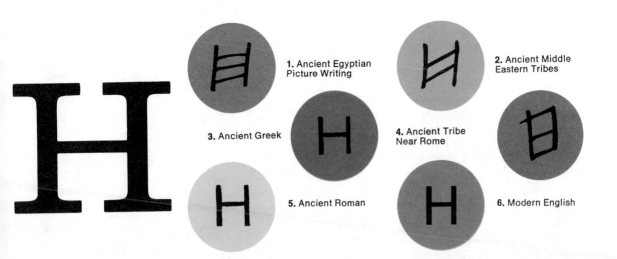

1. Ancient Egyptian Picture Writing
2. Ancient Middle Eastern Tribes
3. Ancient Greek
4. Ancient Tribe Near Rome
5. Ancient Roman
6. Modern English

H is the eighth letter of the alphabet. The oldest form of the letter **H** was probably a drawing that the ancient Egyptians (**1**) used in their picture writing more than 5000 years ago. This drawing, which meant "fence," was borrowed by several ancient tribes (**2**) in the Middle East. They used this letter to stand for an *h* sound made at the back of the throat. When the ancient Greeks (**3**) borrowed this letter they wrote it, at first, in the shape of two squares, one on top of the other. Later, the Greeks gave the letter its modern form of two tall lines connected by a short bar. The earlier form of **H** was borrowed by a tribe (**4**) that settled north of Rome about 2800 years ago. But the Romans (**5**) used the later Greek form of the letter. By about 2400 years ago, the Romans were writing this letter in almost the same way that we write the capital letter **H** today (**6**).

h, H The eighth letter of the alphabet.
h, H (āch) *noun, plural* **h's, H's.**

ha **1.** A word used to show surprise, joy, or victory. "*Ha!* I've found the treasure!" cried the pirate. **2.** A word used to express laughter. "*Ha, ha, ha,*" laughed the boys at the funny joke.
ha (hä) *interjection.*

habit **1.** An action that you do so often or for so long that you do it without thinking. A habit is hard to stop or control. He has the bad *habit* of biting his fingernails. It is my dad's *habit* to read the paper at breakfast. **2.** A certain kind of dress. The nun's *habit* was black.
hab·it (hab′it) *noun, plural* **habits.**

Habit

habitant *Canadian.* **1.** A French Canadian farmer. **2. the Habitants.** The Montreal Canadiens hockey team. *Noun.*
—Having to do with French Canada, especially life in the country. Did you eat *habitant* food in Quebec City? *Adjective.*

hab·i·tant (hab′ə tänt′) *noun, plural* **habitants;** *adjective.*

habitat The place where an animal or plant naturally lives and grows. The Arctic is the *habitat* of the polar bear.
hab·i·tat (hab′ə tat′) *noun, plural* **habitats.**

hack **1.** To cut or chop unevenly with heavy blows. This is often done with a hatchet or cleaver. The explorers *hacked* their way through the thick forest. **2.** To cough with short, harsh sounds.
hack (hak) *verb,* **hacked, hacking.**

had He *had* fun at the party. Look up **have** for more information.
had (had *or* həd *or* əd) *verb.*

hadn't I *hadn't* met her until yesterday.
had·n't (had′ənt) contraction for "had not."

hail¹ To greet or attract the attention of by calling or shouting. She *hailed* a taxi by waving her arm. *Verb.*
—A motion or call used as a greeting or to attract attention. *Noun.*
hail (hāl) *verb,* **hailed, hailing;** *noun, plural* **hails.**
to hail from. To come from. He *hails* from Nova Scotia.

hail² **1.** Small roundish pieces of ice that fall in a shower like rain. The *hail* came down so hard that it crushed many of the flowers in the garden. **2.** A heavy shower of anything.

291

The married couple ran off in a *hail* of rice thrown by the guests. *Noun.*
—To pour down like hail. The bully *hailed* punches on the smaller boy. *Verb.*
hail (hāl) *noun; verb,* **hailed, hailing.**

hair **1.** A very thin, threadlike growth on the skin of people and animals. **2.** A mass of such growths. The girl's *hair* is brown and wavy. **3.** A very thin, threadlike growth on the outer layer of plants. ▲ Another word that sounds like this is **hare.**
hair (her) *noun, plural* **hairs.**

haircut The act or style of cutting the hair.
hair·cut (her′kut′) *noun, plural* **haircuts.**

hairy Covered with hair; having a lot of hair. An ape is a *hairy* animal.
hair·y (her′ē) *adjective,* **hairier, hairiest.**

half **1.** One of two equal parts of something. Two is *half* of four. We ate *half* the pie. She will be away at camp for a month and a *half.* **2.** Either of two time periods in certain sports. A football game or a basketball game is divided into two *halves. Noun.*
—Being one of two equal parts. We bought a *half* litre of ice cream. *Adjective.*
—Not completely; partly. I was *half* asleep by the time the movie ended. *Adverb.*
half (haf) *noun, plural* **halves;** *adjective; adverb.*

half-mast The position of a flag when it is halfway down from the top of a pole. It is used as a sign of mourning for someone who has died or as a signal of distress.
half-mast (haf′mast′) *noun.*

halfway **1.** Half the distance; midway. We climbed *halfway* up the mountain. **2.** Not completely; partly. The movie is *halfway* over. *Adverb.*
—**1.** Half the way between two points. Ann was winning the sailboat race as her boat reached the *halfway* mark. **2.** Not finished; incomplete. *Halfway* measures will not solve the problem of pollution. *Adjective.*
half·way (haf′wā′) *adverb; adjective.*

halibut A large fish with a flat body. It may have a mass of several hundred kilograms. This fish is found in the northern waters of the Atlantic and Pacific Oceans.
hal·i·but (hal′ə bət) *noun, plural* **halibut** or **halibuts.**

▲ The word **halibut** comes from two earlier English words that meant "holy" and "flatfish." This fish was called "holy" because it was eaten on holy days when Christians were not allowed to eat meat.

hall **1.** A passageway onto which rooms open in a house or other building. The students lined up in the *hall* before they went into the auditorium. **2.** A room at the entrance to a building; lobby. We left our wet umbrellas in the *hall.* **3.** A building or room used for a particular purpose. We went to the concert *hall.* The dining *hall* of our school is in the basement. ▲ Another word that sounds like this is **haul.**
hall (häl) *noun, plural* **halls.**

Hallowe'en The evening of October 31. Hallowe'en is celebrated by dressing up in costumes and playing tricks. This word is also spelled **Halloween.**
Hal·low·e'en (hal′ə wēn′ *or* hal′ō ēn′) *noun, plural* **Hallowe'ens.**

hallway A hall or passageway.
hall·way (häl′wā′) *noun, plural* **hallways.**

halo **1.** A ring of light painted by an artist around the head of a saint or angel. **2.** A circle of light that seems to surround the sun, the moon, or another heavenly body. The planet Saturn has two *halos.*
ha·lo (hā′lō) *noun, plural* **halos** or **haloes.**

halt A stop for a short time. The car came to a *halt* at the red light. *Noun.*
—To stop. The troops will *halt* when the sergeant gives the order. *Verb.*
halt (hält) *noun, plural* **halts;** *verb,* **halted, halting.**

halter A rope or strap used for leading or tying an animal. It fits over the animal's nose and over or behind its ears.
hal·ter (häl′tər) *noun, plural* **halters.**

Halter

halve **1.** To divide into two equal parts. I *halved* an apple so that I could share it with my sister. **2.** To make less by half. Susan *halved* the recipe so there would be enough for two instead of four. ▲ Another word that sounds like this is **have.**
halve (hav) *verb,* **halved, halving.**

halves More than one half. Look up **half** for more information.
halves (havz) *noun plural.*

ham **1.** The meat from the back leg or shoulder of a hog. It is usually salted or smoked. **2.** An amateur radio operator.
ham (ham) *noun, plural* **hams.**

hamburger **1.** Ground beef. The recipe calls for a kilogram of *hamburger*. **2.** A flat cake of ground beef. It is broiled or fried and usually served on a bun or roll.

ham·burg·er (ham′bur′gər) *noun, plural* **hamburgers.**

▲ The word **hamburger** comes from *Hamburger steak* or *Hamburg steak*. These names were first used in the beginning of the 1900s and came from the city of Hamburg, Germany. No one knows exactly why it is that hamburgers came to be named after this German city.

hammer **1.** A tool with a heavy metal head on a long handle. A hammer is used for driving nails and for beating or shaping metals. **2.** Anything that is like a hammer in shape or use. The *hammer* of a gun causes it to fire when the trigger is pulled. *Noun.*
—**1.** To strike again and again; pound. He *hammered* nails into the wall. The angry man *hammered* at the door with his fist. **2.** To pound into shape with a hammer. We learned to *hammer* a bowl out of copper. *Verb.*

ham·mer (ham′ər) *noun, plural* **hammers;** *verb,* **hammered, hammering.**

hammock A swinging bed that is hung between two trees or poles. It is made from a long piece of canvas or netting.

ham·mock (ham′ək) *noun, plural* **hammocks.**

Hammock

hamper[1] To get in the way of action or progress. Stalled cars *hampered* efforts to remove the snow from the streets.

ham·per (ham′pər) *verb,* **hampered, hampering.**

hamper[2] A large basket or container with a cover. There are food *hampers* for picnics and clothes *hampers* for dirty laundry.

ham·per (ham′pər) *noun, plural* **hampers.**

hamster An animal that is like a mouse. It has a plump body, a short tail, and large cheek pouches. A hamster is a rodent.

ham·ster (ham′stər) *noun, plural* **hamsters.**

Hamster

hand **1.** The end part of the arm from the wrist down. It is made up of the palm, four fingers, and a thumb. We use our hands to pick up and hold onto things. **2.** Anything like a hand in shape or use. The *hands* of the clock pointed to three o'clock. **3. hands.** Control or possession. The town is in enemy *hands*. The decision is in your *hands*. **4.** A member of a group or crew; workman. The *hands* on the farm get up early to start their work. **5.** A way of doing something. Richard has such a quick *hand* at doing magic tricks that he always fools us. **6.** A part in something; share; role. Each student had a *hand* in planning the class dance. **7.** Help; aid. Ann gave me a *hand* in cleaning the blackboard. **8.** A round of applause; clapping. The audience gave the actors a big *hand*. **9.** One round of a card game. **10.** The cards a player holds in one round of a card game. **11.** A measurement of about ten centimetres used to tell the height of a horse. *Noun.*
—To give or pass with the hand. He *handed* the book to the librarian. Please *hand* me the salt. *Verb.*

hand (hand) *noun, plural* **hands;** *verb,* **handed, handing.**

on hand. Ready or available for use. We always keep canned foods *on hand*.

on the other hand. From another point of view. That player is not very fast, but *on the other hand* he is very strong.

to hand down. To pass along. That gold watch was *handed down* to my father from his grandfather.

at; āpe; cär; end; mē; it; īce; hot; ōld; wood; fōol; oil; out; up; turn; sing; thin; this; hw in white; zh in treasure. ə stands for a in about, e in taken, i in pencil, o in lemon, and u in circus.

handbag A bag or case used by women; pocketbook. Women carry a wallet, keys, or cosmetics in it.

   hand·bag (hand′bag′) *noun, plural* **handbags.**

handball **1.** A game in which players take turns hitting a small rubber ball against a wall with the hand. **2.** The ball that is used in this game.

   hand·ball (hand′bäl′) *noun, plural* **handballs.**

handbook A book that has information or instructions about a subject. We bought a *handbook* about Vancouver when we went there for a visit.

   hand·book (hand′book′) *noun, plural* **handbooks.**

handcuff One of two metal rings joined by a chain. Handcuffs are locked around the wrists of a prisoner to keep him from using his hands. *Noun.*
—To put handcuffs on. The policeman *handcuffed* the suspected thief and led him away. *Verb.*

   hand·cuff (hand′kuf′) *noun, plural* **handcuffs;** *verb,* **handcuffed, handcuffing.**

handful **1.** The amount the hand can hold at one time. She took a *handful* of peanuts from the jar. **2.** A small amount or amount. Only a *handful* of people showed up for the club meeting.

   hand·ful (hand′fool′) *noun, plural* **handfuls.**

handicap Anything that makes it harder for a person to do well or get ahead. Being short can be a *handicap* in playing basketball. *Noun.*
—To put at a disadvantage; hinder. His poor eyesight *handicaps* him in his work. *Verb.*

   hand·i·cap (han′dē kap′) *noun, plural* **handicaps;** *verb,* **handicapped, handicapping.**

handicraft A trade, work, or art in which skill with the hands is needed. Making pottery and weaving are handicrafts.

   hand·i·craft (han′dē kraft′) *noun, plural* **handicrafts.**

handkerchief A square, soft piece of cloth. It is usually used to wipe the nose or face.

   hand·ker·chief (hang′kər chif) *noun, plural* **handkerchiefs.**

handle The part of an object that is made to be grasped by the hands. A frying pan, a suitcase, a tennis racket, a knife, and a broom have handles. *Noun.*
—**1.** To touch or hold with the hand. Please *handle* the glass carefully so that it won't fall and break. **2.** To manage, control, or deal with. She knows how to *handle* dogs so they will obey her. Tom *handled* the problem well. *Verb.*

handle (han′dəl) *noun, plural* **handles;** *verb,* **handled, handling.**

handlebars The curved bar on the front of a bicycle or motorcycle. The rider grips the ends of the bars and uses them to steer.

   han·dle·bars (han′dəl bärz′) *noun plural.*

handsome **1.** Having a pleasing appearance; good-looking. He is a *handsome* man. That old desk is very *handsome*. **2.** Fairly large or generous. The family gave Sue a *handsome* reward for finding their pet dog.

   hand·some (han′səm) *adjective,* **handsomer, handsomest.**

handspring A leap in which you spring onto your hands with your feet over your head and then land back on your feet again.

   hand·spring (hand′spring′) *noun, plural* **handsprings.**

Handspring

handwriting Writing done by hand. It is writing done with a pen or pencil, not with a machine. Her *handwriting* is hard to read.

   hand·writ·ing (hand′rī′ting) *noun, plural* **handwritings.**

handy **1.** Within reach; nearby. Bob always keeps a handkerchief *handy*. **2.** Working well with one's hands; skilful. Mike is *handy* with tools. **3.** Easy to use or handle. My parents bought me a *handy* carrying case for all my school books.

   hand·y (han′dē) *adjective,* **handier, handiest.**

hang **1.** To fasten something from above only, without support from below. We will *hang* our wet bathing suits on the line. Please *hang* the pictures on that empty wall. **2.** To attach something so it moves freely back and forth. We *hung* the gate on hinges. **3.** To put a person to death by hanging by a rope tied around the neck. *Verb.*
—**1.** The way something hangs or falls. Kathy did not like the *hang* of her new dress. **2.** A way of doing something. It takes a while to get the *hang* of riding a bicycle. *Noun.*

   hang (hang) *verb,* **hung** *(for definitions 1 and 2)* or **hanged** *(for definition 3),* **hanging;** *noun.*

hangar A building or shed to keep airplanes in. ▲ Another word that sounds like this is **hanger**.
han·gar (hang′ər) *noun, plural* **hangars**.

hanger A device on which something is hung. I hung my coat on a *hanger*. ▲ Another word that sounds like this is **hangar**.
hang·er (hang′ər) *noun, plural* **hangers**.

hangnail A piece of skin that hangs loosely at the side or bottom of a fingernail.
hang·nail (hang′nāl′) *noun, plural* **hangnails**.

happen 1. To take place; occur. The accident *happened* last week. 2. To take place without plan or reason; occur by chance. Her birthday just *happens* to be the same day as mine. 3. To come or go by chance. A policeman *happened* along just after the robbery. 4. To be done. Something must have *happened* to the telephone, because it isn't working.
hap·pen (hap′ən) *verb,* **happened, happening.**

happening Something that happens; event. George told us about some of the *happenings* in the neighbourhood while we were away in Winnipeg.
hap·pen·ing (hap′ə ning) *noun, plural* **happenings**.

happily 1. With pleasure or gladness. After the teacher praised her work, Ann walked *happily* home. 2. Luckily. *Happily,* no one was hurt in the fire.
hap·pi·ly (hap′ə lē) *adverb.*

happiness The state of being glad or content. Their vacation on the farm was full of *happiness*.
hap·pi·ness (hap′ē nəs) *noun.*

happy Feeling or showing pleasure or gladness. The children were *happy* when they got a new dog.
hap·py (hap′ē) *adjective,* **happier, happiest.**

harass To bother or annoy again and again. The bully *harassed* the younger children by teasing them.
har·ass (har′əs *or* hə ras′) *verb,* **harassed, harassing.**

harbour A sheltered place along a coast. Ships and boats often anchor in a harbour. *Noun.*
—1. To give protection or shelter to. It is against the law to *harbour* a criminal in your house. 2. To keep in one's mind. Paul *harboured* a grudge against the boy who had been rude to him. *Verb.*
This word is also spelled **harbor.**
har·bour (här′bər) *noun, plural* **harbours;** *verb,* **harboured, harbouring.**

hard 1. Solid and firm to the touch; not soft. Rocks are *hard*. 2. Needing or using much effort. Chopping wood is a *hard* job. This is a *hard* arithmetic problem. Bob is a *hard* worker. 3. Full of sorrow, pain, or worry. Life was *hard* for the man after he lost his job. 4. Having great force or strength. The fighter hit his opponent with a *hard* blow. *Adjective.*
—1. With effort or energy. Alan works *hard* on his farm. 2. With force or strength. It rained so *hard* yesterday that the roads were flooded. 3. With difficulty. The runner breathed *hard* after he had finished the race. *Adverb.*
hard (härd) *adjective,* **harder, hardest;** *adverb.*

hard-boiled Boiled until hard. A *hard-boiled* egg is boiled until its yolk and white are solid.
hard-boiled (härd′boild′) *adjective.*

harden To make or become hard. Joan made a clay bowl and put it in the sun to *harden*.
hard·en (härd′ən) *verb,* **hardened, hardening.**

hardly 1. Just about; barely. We could *hardly* see the path in the dim light. 2. Not likely; not quite. Since she is sick in bed, she will *hardly* be able to come to the party tonight.
hard·ly (härd′lē) *adverb.*

hardship Something that causes difficulty, pain, or suffering. The flood was a great *hardship* to the people of the town.
hard·ship (härd′ship′) *noun, plural* **hardships**.

hardware Metal articles used for making and fixing things. Tools, nails, and screws are hardware.
hard·ware (härd′wer′) *noun.*

hardwood The strong, heavy wood of certain trees. Oaks, beeches, and maples are hardwoods. Hardwood is used for furniture, floors, and sports equipment.
hard·wood (härd′wood′) *noun, plural* **hardwoods**.

hardy Strong and healthy. Henry is a *hardy* boy who loves being outdoors. Ivy is a *hardy* plant.
har·dy (här′dē) *adjective,* **hardier, hardiest.**

at; āpe; cär; end; mē; it; īce; hot; ōld;
wood; fōōl; oil; out; up; turn; sing;
thin; this; hw in white; zh in treasure.
ə stands for a in about, e in taken,
i in pencil, o in lemon, and u in circus.

hare An animal that is like a rabbit, but larger. It has very long ears, strong back legs and feet, and a short tail. ▲ Another word that sounds like this is **hair.**
hare (her) *noun, plural* **hares** or **hare.**

Hare

harm 1. Injury or hurt. To make sure no *harm* would come to the children, their mother made them wear life jackets when they went sailing. 2. An evil; wrong. The child saw no *harm* in taking the small lost kitten home. *Noun.*
—To do damage to; hurt. The dog looks fierce, but it will not *harm* you. *Verb.*
harm (härm) *noun, plural* **harms;** *verb,* **harmed, harming.**

harmful Causing harm; damaging. A poor diet is *harmful* to your health.
harm·ful (härm′fəl) *adjective.*

harmless Not able to cause harm; not damaging. That snake is *harmless.* They played a *harmless* joke on their friend.
harm·less (härm′ləs) *adjective.*

harmonica A musical instrument. It is a small case with slots that contain a series of metal reeds. It is played by blowing in and out through the slots.
har·mon·i·ca (här mon′i kə) *noun, plural* **harmonicas.**

Harmonica

harmonize 1. To arrange, sing, or play in harmony. The voices of the church choir *harmonized* in song. 2. To go together in a pleasing way. The colours of the curtains and the rug *harmonize* well. 3. To add notes to a melody to form chords in music.
har·mo·nize (här′mə nīz′) *verb,* **harmonized, harmonizing.**

harmony 1. A combination of musical notes to form chords. 2. A going well together. The *harmony* of the colours of the rainbow is very beautiful.
har·mo·ny (här′mə nē) *noun, plural* **harmonies.**

harness The straps, bands, and other fastenings used to attach a work animal to a cart, plow, or wagon. *Noun.*
—1. To put a harness on. The farmer *harnessed* his horses. 2. To control and make use of. At that dam water power is *harnessed* to generate electricity. *Verb.*
har·ness (här′nəs) *noun, plural* **harnesses;** *verb,* **harnessed, harnessing.**

harp A large, stringed musical instrument. The strings are set in an upright, triangle-shaped frame with a curved top. It is played by plucking the strings with the fingers.
harp (härp) *noun, plural* **harps.**

harpoon A weapon similar to a spear with a rope attached. A harpoon is used to kill or capture whales and other sea animals. It is shot from a gun or thrown by hand. *Noun.*
—To strike, catch, or kill with a harpoon. The sailors *harpooned* the whale after a long chase. *Verb.*
har·poon (här poͦn′) *noun, plural* **harpoons;** *verb,* **harpooned, harpooning.**

Harp

harpsichord A stringed musical instrument with a keyboard. It looks like a piano.
harp·si·chord (härp′sə kord′) *noun, plural* **harpsichords.**

harrow A heavy frame with upright disks or teeth. It is used to break up and level ploughed land.
har·row (har′ō) *noun, plural* **harrows.**

harsh 1. Rough or unpleasant to the ear, eye, taste, or touch. The towel felt *harsh* against my sunburned skin. 2. Very cruel.

The prisoners got *harsh* treatment from the guards if they did not obey.

harsh (härsh) *adjective,* **harsher, harshest.**

harvest **1.** The gathering in of a crop when it is ripe. The men soon finished the *harvest* of the wheat. **2.** The crop that is gathered. The farmer has a large *harvest* of potatoes. *Noun.*
—To gather in a crop. We have to *harvest* the fruit now that it is ripe. *Verb.*

har·vest (här′vəst) *noun, plural* **harvests;** *verb,* **harvested, harvesting.**

has Betty *has* a new bicycle.

has (haz) *verb.*

hash **1.** A cooked mixture of chopped meat, potatoes, and other vegetables. **2.** A mess; jumble. He made such a *hash* of the model airplane that it had to be done over.

hash (hash) *noun, plural* **hashes.**

hasn't She *hasn't* done any work at all.

has·n't (haz′ənt) contraction for "has not."

haste Quickness in moving or in acting; speed; hurry. Ruth left the house in great *haste* so she wouldn't miss the bus.

haste (hāst) *noun.*

hasten To move quickly; speed up; hurry. The medicine *hastened* the recovery of the sick boy.

has·ten (hās′ən) *verb,* **hastened, hastening.**

hasty **1.** Quick; hurried. We ate a *hasty* breakfast because we were already late for school. **2.** Too quick; careless or reckless. Alice made a *hasty* decision that she was sorry for later.

hast·y (hās′tē) *adjective,* **hastier, hastiest.**

hat A covering for the head. It often has a brim and crown.

hat (hat) *noun, plural* **hats.**

hatch¹ **1.** To cause young to come from an egg. The mother robin *hatched* her eggs. **2.** To come from an egg. The chicks *hatched* by pecking through their shells.

hatch (hach) *verb,* **hatched, hatching.**

hatch² **1.** An opening in the deck of a ship. It leads to lower decks. **2.** A cover or trap door for such an opening.

hatch (hach) *noun, plural* **hatches.**

hatchery **1.** A place where the eggs of fish are hatched. We went to see the salmon *hatchery* at Capilano on our trip to British Columbia. **2.** A place where the eggs of chickens are hatched.

hatch·er·y (hach′ər ē) *noun, plural* **hatcheries.**

hatchet A small axe with a short handle. It is made to be used with one hand.

hatch·et (hach′ət) *noun, plural* **hatchets.**

hate To have very strong feelings against; dislike very much. She *hates* people who treat animals cruelly. I *hate* to clean the house.

hate (hāt) *verb,* **hated, hating.**

hatred A strong feeling against a person or thing. The people felt *hatred* toward the cruel dictator.

ha·tred (hā′trəd) *noun, plural* **hatreds.**

hat trick The scoring of three goals in one game of hockey by the same player.

haughty Having or showing too much pride in oneself. The *haughty* queen thought she was the most beautiful person in all the kingdom.

haugh·ty (hä′tē) *adjective,* **haughtier, haughtiest.**

haul **1.** To pull or move with force; drag. It took three of us to *haul* the heavy trunk up the stairs. **2.** To carry; transport. Railways *haul* freight from one end of the country to the other. *Verb.*
—**1.** The act of hauling. Give the rope a *haul.* **2.** Something that is gotten by catching or winning. The fishermen came home with a big *haul* of fish. **3.** The distance something is hauled. It's a long *haul* from our farm to the town. *Noun.* ▲ Another word that sounds like this is **hall.**

haul (häl) *verb,* **hauled, hauling;** *noun, plural* **hauls.**

haunch A part of the body of an animal around its hind leg. The lion sat on its *haunches* and roared.

haunch (hänch) *noun, plural* **haunches.**

haunt To visit or live in. People say that ghosts *haunt* the old house at the corner of Stanley and Sherbrooke.

haunt (hänt) *verb,* **haunted, haunting.**

have **1.** They *have* a house in the country. Do you *have* any questions? I hope to *have* a good time at Lucy's party. My brother might *have* the chicken pox. Mother told me I *have* to clean my room before I can play. My cat will *have* kittens in about a week. **2.** *Have* is also used as a helping verb. It shows that the action of the main verb is finished. We *have* done the work. They *have* written a story about an Inuit girl. ▲ Another word that

at; āpe; cär; end; mē; it; īce; hot; ōld;
wood; fōōl; oil; out; up; turn; sing;
thin; this; hw in white; zh in treasure.
ə stands for a in about, e in taken,
i in pencil, o in lemon, and u in circus.

sounds like this is **halve**.
    have (hav) *verb*, **had, having**.

haven A place of safety or shelter. The cool woods were a *haven* for the hot and tired hikers. A harbour is a *haven* for boats.
    ha·ven (hā′vən) *noun, plural* **havens**.

haven't I *haven't* gone shopping yet.
    have·n't (hav′ənt) contraction for "have not."

hawk[1] A bird of prey. It has a sharp, hooked beak, strong claws, and short rounded wings.
    hawk (häk) *noun, plural* **hawks**.

hawk[2] To offer goods for sale by calling out. The peddler *hawked* fruit in the street.
    hawk (häk) *verb*, **hawked, hawking**.

hawthorn A thorny shrub or tree. It is similar to the rose. The hawthorn has small red, yellow, or black berries.
    haw·thorn (hä′thôrn′) *noun, plural* **hawthorns**.

Hawk

hay Grass, alfalfa, or clover. Hay is cut and dried for use as feed for livestock. ▲ Another word that sounds like this is **hey**.
    hay (hā) *noun, plural* **hays**.

hay fever A condition that causes a stuffy nose, itching eyes, and sneezing. Hay fever is an allergy that is caused by breathing the pollen of plants.

haystack A pile of hay stacked outdoors.
    hay·stack (hā′stak′) *noun, plural* **haystacks**.

hazard Something that can cause harm or injury; risk; danger. Icy roads are a *hazard* to drivers in winter.
    haz·ard (haz′ərd) *noun, plural* **hazards**.

haze Mist, smoke, or dust in the air. The morning *haze* hid the bridge from us.
    haze (hāz) *noun, plural* **hazes**.

hazel 1. A tree or shrub that has light-brown nuts that can be eaten. 2. A light-brown colour like the colour of this nut. *Noun.*
—Having the colour hazel; light-brown. Nancy has beautiful *hazel* eyes. *Adjective.*
    ha·zel (hā′zəl) *noun, plural* **hazels**; *adjective*.

hazy Not clear; blurred or confused. On a *hazy* day, we can see only a dim outline of the mountains. Bob's understanding of how a computer works is *hazy*.
    ha·zy (hā′zē) *adjective*, **hazier, haziest**.

H-bomb A powerful bomb. It is also called a **hydrogen bomb**. Look up **hydrogen bomb** for more information.
    H-bomb (āch′bom′) *noun, plural* **H-bombs**.

he Bob promised that *he* would be on time. Is your puppy a *he* or a she?
    he (hē) *pronoun; noun, plural* **he's**.

head 1. The top part of a person's body. The head is where the eyes, ears, nose, and mouth are. The brain is inside the head. 2. The part of any other animal that is like a human head. Dogs, fish, and birds have heads. 3. Anything that is like a head in shape or position. I walked up to the *head* of the stairs. Hit the nail on the *head*. Please buy a *head* of lettuce. Billy was at the *head* of the class. 4. A person who is above the others; chief. The Queen is the *head* of our country's government. 2. A single person or animal. The cowboys rounded up forty *head* of cattle. *Noun.*
—Top, chief, or front. Ed is the *head* lifeguard at the pool. *Adjective.*
—1. To be or go to the top or front of. The scout leader *headed* his troop in the parade. 2. To be in charge of. Frank *heads* the school newspaper. 3. To direct or move in a direction. The captain *headed* the ship northward. Dan *heads* for the lake on hot days. *Verb.*
    head (hed) *noun, plural* **heads** *(for definitions 1-4)* or **head** *(for definition 5); adjective; verb*, **headed, heading**.

headache A pain in the head.
    head·ache (hed′āk′) *noun, plural* **headaches**.

headdress A covering or decoration for the head. The Indian wore a *headdress* of feathers.
    head·dress (hed′dres′) *noun, plural* **headdresses**.

headfirst With the head going in front. He dove *headfirst* into the water.
    head·first (hed′furst′) *adverb*.

heading A title for a page or chapter.
    head·ing (hed′ing) *noun, plural* **headings**.

Headdress

headland A point of land that sticks out into the water; cape.
    head·land (hed′lənd) *noun, plural* **headlands**.

headlight A bright light on the front of an automobile or other vehicle. It got dark during the drive home, so Mother put on the car's *headlights*.
    head·light (hed′līt′) *noun, plural* **headlights**.

headline A line printed at the top of a newspaper or magazine article. A headline tells what the article is about. It is printed in large or heavy type. *Noun.*
—To be the main attraction of a show. A magic act *headlined* the show. *Verb.*
　head·line (hed′līn′) *noun, plural* **headlines**; *verb*, **headlined, headlining.**

headlong 1. With the head first. He ran *headlong* into the kitchen door in the darkness. 2. In a reckless way; rashly. He rushed *headlong* into buying the used bicycle without noticing that it was damaged. *Adverb.*
—With the head first. She made a *headlong* dive into the lake. *Adjective.*
　head·long (hed′long′) *adverb; adjective.*

head-on With the head or front end first. The car hit the pole *head-on*. The two cars were in a *head-on* crash.
　head-on (hed′on′) *adverb; adjective.*

headphone A radio or telephone receiver held against the ear. It is held in place by a band that fits over the head.
　head·phone (hed′fōn′) *noun, plural* **head-phones.**

headquarters Any centre of operations or business. The general issued orders from his *headquarters*. That company's *headquarters* are in Winnipeg.
　head·quar·ters (hed′kwōr′tərz) *noun, plural* **headquarters.**

headstone A stone set at the head of a grave; tombstone.
　head·stone (hed′stōn′) *noun, plural* **head-stones.**

headwaters The small streams at the beginning of a river. They all come together to form the river.
　head·wa·ters (hed′wä′tərz) *noun plural.*

headway Forward movement or progress. It was hard for the small ship to make any *headway* through the high waves. I can't make much *headway* with this problem in arithmetic.
　head·way (hed′wā′) *noun.*

heal To make or become well. The doctor *healed* the sick child with medicine. Her sprained ankle *healed* quickly, and she was soon skiing again. ▲ Other words that sound like this are **heel** and **he'll.**
　heal (hēl) *verb*, **healed, healing.**

health 1. Freedom from illness. You will lose your *health* if you don't eat the proper foods. 2. The condition of the body or mind. The doctor told Claire that she was in very good *health*.
　health (helth) *noun.*

healthful Helping one have good health. Exercise is *healthful*.
　health·ful (helth′fəl) *adjective.*

healthy Having, showing, or giving good health. The young farm boy had a *healthy* look. Walking is a *healthy* exercise.
　health·y (hel′thē) *adjective*, **healthier, health-iest.**

heap A collection of things piled together. Lisa left a *heap* of books lying in the middle of her bed. *Noun.*
—1. To make into a pile. We *heaped* the fallen leaves. 2. To give in large amounts. Mother *heaped* my plate with mashed potatoes. *Verb.*
　heap (hēp) *noun, plural* **heaps**; *verb*, **heaped, heaping.**

hear 1. To receive sound through the ears. I *hear* someone calling my name. My grandfather can't *hear* very well, so please speak loudly. 2. To listen to. Dad will *hear* both sides of our quarrel. 3. To get information about. The winner of the contest will *hear* the good news soon. Have you *heard* from Dick lately? ▲ Another word that sounds like this is **here.**
　hear (hēr) *verb*, **heard, hearing.**

heard I *heard* my brother coming home late last night. ▲ Another word that sounds like this is **herd.**
　heard (hurd) *verb.*

hearing 1. The ability to hear. Tina has very good *hearing*. 2. The act of listening or getting information. *Hearing* that her sister had won the contest made Ann very happy. 3. The chance to be heard. The mayor gave both sides a fair *hearing* before making a decision.
　hear·ing (hēr′ing) *noun, plural* **hearings.**

hearing aid A small device that makes sounds louder. It is worn in or near the ear to make poor hearing better.

heart 1. The part of the body that pumps blood. 2. The heart thought of as the centre of a person's feelings. The happy boy spoke from his *heart* when he thanked us for finding his puppy. 3. Spirit; courage. The team lost *heart* after their defeat. 4. The centre or middle of anything. We got lost in the *heart*

---

at; āpe; cär; end; mē; it; īce; hot; ōld;
wood; fōol; oil; out; up; turn; sing;
thin; this; hw in white; zh in treasure.
ə stands for a in about, e in taken,
i in pencil, o in lemon, and u in circus.

of the forest. Let's get to the *heart* of the problem. **5.** A playing card marked with one or more red figures like this: (♥). **6.** Anything shaped like a heart. The children cut out paper *hearts* to make Valentine's Day cards.
    heart (härt) *noun, plural* **hearts.**
    by heart. From or by memory. Susan learned her lines for the play *by heart.*

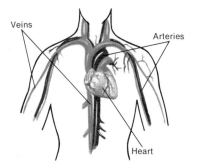

Veins   Arteries   Heart

heartbroken Filled with sorrow or grief. She was *heartbroken* when her dog died.
    heart·bro·ken (härt′brō′kən) *adjective.*

hearth The floor of a fireplace.
    hearth (härth) *noun, plural* **hearths.**

hearty **1.** Full of warmth, kindness, or enthusiasm. My uncle gave us a *hearty* welcome. **2.** Big and satisfying. Thanksgiving dinner is a *hearty* meal at our house.
    heart·y (här′tē) *adjective,* **heartier, heartiest.**

heat **1.** The state of being hot; high temperature; warmth. Heat is a form of energy. The sun gives off *heat.* The *heat* of the fire warmed the whole room. **2.** Strong feeling; excitement. He slammed the door in the *heat* of anger. *Noun.*
    —To make or become hot or warm. Mom *heated* the milk before giving it to my baby sister. *Verb.*
    heat (hēt) *noun; verb,* **heated, heating.**

heater A device that gives heat. A radiator or a furnace is a kind of heater. We put an electric *heater* in the cold room.
    heat·er (hēt′ər) *noun, plural* **heaters.**

heath A flat, open piece of land. It is covered with heather or low bushes.
    heath (hēth) *noun, plural* **heaths.**

heathen A person who does not believe in the God of the Christians, Jews, or Muslims. *Noun.*
    —Having to do with heathens. Ancient *heathen* tribes worshipped many gods. *Adjective.*
    hea·then (hē′thən) *noun, plural* **heathens** or **heathen;** *adjective.*

▲ The word **heathen** comes from an Old English word that meant "a person who lives on the heath." *On the heath* meant "in the country." Most people who lived in the country at that time were not Christians. So calling someone a *heathen,* or country person, was the same as saying that he was not a Christian.

heather A low shrub that has purple and pink flowers. It grows wild in Scotland and England.
    heath·er (heth′ər) *noun, plural* **heathers.**

heave **1.** To lift, raise, or throw using force or effort. The men *heaved* bales of hay onto the truck. Jack *heaved* a rock across the stream. **2.** To give out with much force. Joey *heaved* a sigh of relief when he saw that his brother was not hurt. **3.** To rise and fall. The runner's chest *heaved* after the race.
    heave (hēv) *verb,* **heaved, heaving.**

Heather

heaven **1.** In the Christian religion, the place where God and the angels live. **2. heavens.** The sky. You can see many stars in the *heavens* on a clear, dark night.
    heav·en (hev′ən) *noun, plural* **heavens.**

heavenly **1.** Having to do with heaven; divine. Angels are *heavenly* beings. **2.** Having to do with the sky. The sun, the moon, and the stars are *heavenly* bodies. **3.** Happy, pleasing, or beautiful. This quiet, shaded place is a *heavenly* spot for a picnic.
    heav·en·ly (hev′ən lē) *adjective.*

heavily In a heavy way. The snow fell *heavily* on the ground during the blizzard.
    heav·i·ly (hev′əl ē) *adverb.*

heavy **1.** Having great weight; hard to lift or move. The desk was too *heavy* for Brad to move by himself. **2.** Having more than the usual weight. It's so cold that I need a *heavy* blanket to keep me warm. **3.** Large in size or amount. We were late because we got stuck in *heavy* traffic. We had a *heavy* rainfall last night.
    heav·y (hev′ē) *adjective,* **heavier, heaviest.**

Hebrew **1.** A member of one of the Jewish tribes of ancient times. **2.** The language spoken by the ancient Jews. The people living in

Israel speak a form of this language.

He·brew (hē′brōō) *noun, plural* **Hebrews.**

hectare A unit of measurement equal to about 10 000 square metres.

hec·tare (hek′tär′ *or* hek′ter′) *noun, plural* **hectares.**

he'd *He'd* better hurry. ▲ Another word that sounds like this is **heed.**

he'd (hēd) contraction for "he had" and "he would."

Hedge

hedge A row of shrubs or small trees planted close together. *Noun.*
—1. To surround, close in, or separate with a hedge. 2. To avoid answering a question directly. Johnny *hedged* the teacher's question because he hadn't done his homework. *Verb.*

hedge (hej) *noun, plural* **hedges;** *verb,* **hedged, hedging.**

hedgehog An animal that eats insects. It has a pointed snout and sharp, hard spines on its back and sides. When it is frightened or attacked, it rolls up into a ball with only its spines showing.

Hedgehog

hedge·hog (hej′-hog′) *noun, plural* **hedgehogs.**

heed To pay careful attention to; listen or mind. *Heed* my advice. ▲ Another word that sounds like this is **he'd.**

heed (hēd) *verb,* **heeded, heeding.**

heel¹ 1. The rounded back part of the human foot below the ankle. 2. Anything like a heel in shape, use, or position. The heel of the hand is the part of the palm near the wrist. *Noun.*
—To follow closely. The dog was taught to *heel* at its trainer's side. *Verb.* ▲ Other words that sound like this are **heal** and **he'll.**

heel (hēl) *noun, plural* **heels;** *verb,* **heeled, heeling.**

heel² To lean to one side. The strong winds forced the small sailboat to *heel* to the left.

▲ Other words that sound like this are **heal** and **he'll.**

heel (hēl) *verb,* **heeled, heeling.**

heifer A young cow.

heif·er (hef′ər) *noun, plural* **heifers.**

height 1. The distance from bottom to top. The mountain stands at a *height* of one kilometre above sea level. 2. A high place. I am afraid of *heights* and will never climb a tree. 3. The highest point. The singer retired at the *height* of his career.

height (hīt) *noun, plural* **heights.**

heighten To make or become high or higher. The carpenter *heightened* the house by adding a third story to it.

height·en (hīt′ən) *verb,* **heightened, heightening.**

height of land *Canadian.* A region of high ground which forms a watershed. The most famous height of land is at the northwest end of Lake Superior.

heir A person who has the right to the money or property of a person after that person is dead. ▲ Other words that sound like this are **air** and **ere.**

heir (er) *noun, plural* **heirs.**

held She *held* the ball in her hand. Look up **hold** for more information.

held (held) *verb.*

helicopter An aircraft that is kept in the air by blades that rotate above the craft.

hel·i·cop·ter (hel′ə kop′tər) *noun, plural* **helicopters.**

Helicopter

at; āpe; cär; end; mē; it; īce; hot; ōld;
wood; fōol; oil; out; up; turn; sing;
thin; this; hw in white; zh in treasure.
ə stands for a in about, e in taken,
i in pencil, o in lemon, and u in circus.

helium A light gas that has no colour or odor. Helium is a chemical element.
he·li·um (hē′lē əm) *noun.*

▲ The word **helium** comes from the Greek word for "sun." Helium was first discovered by people who were studying the rays of light that come from the sun.

hell In the Christian religion, the place where Satan lives and where wicked people will be punished after death.
hell (hel) *noun.*

he'll *He'll* come to see us when he has time. *He'll* clean his room if I have anything to say about it! ▲ Other words that sound like this are **heal** and **heel**.
he'll (hēl) contraction for "he will" and "he shall."

hello A word used as a greeting. *"Hello,"* he called, when he met us on the street. They gave us a warm *hello* when we arrived.
hel·lo (he lō′ or hə lō′) *interjection; noun, plural* **hellos.**

helm The part of a ship used for steering. It is usually a wheel or tiller.
helm (helm) *noun, plural* **helms.**

helmet A covering for the head that is worn for protection. Soldiers, firefighters, football players, and astronauts wear helmets.
hel·met (hel′mət) *noun, plural* **helmets.**

Helmet

help 1. To give or do something that is useful, wanted, or needed; aid; assist. Barbara *helped* the blind woman across the street. Rick *helped* his brother paint the room. The coach's advice *helped* the team to win. Please *help* yourself to more potatoes. 2. To stop or avoid. I couldn't *help* laughing when I heard the story. *Verb.*
—1. The act of helping. Do you need *help?* 2. A person or thing that helps. Ruth is a big *help* to her mother around the house. *Noun.*
help (help) *verb,* **helped, helping;** *noun, plural* **helps.**

helpful Giving help; useful. A dictionary is *helpful* in spelling words correctly.
help·ful (help′fəl) *adjective.*

helping A serving of food for one person. Would you like a second *helping* of turkey?
help·ing (help′ing) *noun, plural* **helpings.**

helpless Not able to take care of oneself. He was made almost *helpless* by his broken ankle. A newborn kitten is *helpless*.
help·less (help′ləs) *adjective.*

hem The border of a garment or piece of cloth. It is made by folding over the edge and sewing it down. Dresses, pillowcases, and curtains have hems. *Noun.*
—To fold over the edge of a piece of cloth and sew it down. Mother *hemmed* the dress. *Verb.*
hem (hem) *noun, plural* **hems;** *verb,* **hemmed, hemming.**
to hem in. To close in; surround. John felt *hemmed in* by the crowd of people who were watching the parade.

hemisphere One-half of the earth. The equator divides the earth into the Northern Hemisphere and the Southern Hemisphere. The earth is also divided into the Eastern Hemisphere and the Western Hemisphere. Europe, Africa, and Asia are in the Eastern Hemisphere. North and South America are in the Western Hemisphere.
hem·i·sphere (hem′is fēr′) *noun, plural* **hemispheres.**

hemlock 1. A tall evergreen tree similar to the pine. It has reddish bark and flat needles. 2. A poisonous plant that has spotted, hollow stems and clusters of white flowers.
hem·lock (hem′lok′) *noun, plural* **hemlocks.**

Needles

Cone

Hemlock Tree

hemp A strong, tough fibre made from the stem of a tall plant. It is used to make rope.
hemp (hemp) *noun, plural* **hemps.**

hen 1. The adult female of fowl on farms. 2. The female of various other birds.
hen (hen) *noun, plural* **hens.**

hence **1.** As a result; therefore. Joan lived with a family in Spain last summer and *hence* learned to speak Spanish quite well. **2.** From this time or place. The friends agreed to meet two weeks *hence* at the same place.
hence (hens) *adverb*.

her I gave *her* the book. *Her* coat is on the chair.
her (hur) *pronoun; adjective*.

herb **1.** Any plant whose leaves, stems, seeds, or roots are used in cooking for flavouring or in medicines. Mint and parsley are herbs. **2.** Any flowering plant that dies at the end of one growing season and does not form a woody stem.
herb (urb *or* hurb) *noun, plural* **herbs**.

herbivorous Feeding mainly on plants. A cow is a *herbivorous* animal.
her·biv·o·rous (hur biv′ər əs) *adjective*.

herd A group of animals. A *herd* of cattle grazed in the pasture. *Noun.*
—To group or lead in a herd. The cowboys *herded* the cattle and drove them to market. Our tour guide *herded* us into the bus. *Verb.*
▲ Another word that sounds like this is **heard**.
herd (hurd) *noun, plural* **herds**; *verb*, **herded**, **herding**.

here At, in, or to this place. I have been waiting *here* for an hour. Bring the book *here* and I'll read it to you. *Adverb.*
—This place. Can you show me how to get home from *here? Noun.*
—A word used in answering a roll call, calling an animal, or attracting attention. *Interjection.* ▲ Another word that sounds like this is **hear**.
here (hēr) *adverb; noun; interjection*.

hereditary Passed on or able to be passed on from an animal or plant to its offspring. Blue eyes are *hereditary*.
he·red·i·tar·y (hə red′ə ter′ē) *adjective*.

heredity The passing on of characteristics from an animal or plant to its offspring.
he·red·i·ty (hə red′ə tē) *noun, plural* **heredities**.

here's *Here's* the book I was telling you about.
here's (hērz) contraction for "here is."

heritage Something that is handed down from earlier generations or from the past; tradition. Canadians think of the right to vote as part of their *heritage*.
her·it·age (her′ə təj) *noun, plural* **heritages**.

hermit A person who lives alone and away from other people. A hermit often lives like this for religious reasons.
her·mit (hur′mit) *noun, plural* **hermits**.

hero **1.** A man or boy who is looked up to by others because he has done something brave or outstanding. The man who saved the boy from drowning was a *hero*. **2.** The main male character in a play, story, poem, or film. The *hero* in the story killed the evil dragon.
he·ro (hēr′ō) *noun, plural* **heroes**.

heroic Having to do with a hero. The firefighter made a *heroic* attempt to save the child.
he·ro·ic (hē rō′ik) *adjective*.

heroin A powerful, habit-forming drug. The *heroin* addict was rushed to the hospital.
her·o·in (her′ō in) *noun*.

heroine **1.** A woman or girl who is looked up to by others because she has done something brave or outstanding. Nellie McClung is my *heroine*, because I want to be a politician like her some day. **2.** The main female character in a play, story, poem, or film.
her·o·ine (her′ō in *or* hēr′ō in) *noun, plural* **heroines**.

heron A bird with a long slender neck, a long pointed bill, and long thin legs.
her·on (her′ən) *noun, plural* **herons**.

herring A bony, saltwater fish of the northern Atlantic Ocean. It is used as food.
her·ring (her′ing) *noun, plural* **herring** or **herrings**.

hers This is my coat and that is *hers*.
hers (hurz) *pronoun*.

herself She *herself* knitted the sweater. Mary cut *herself*. Betty has not been *herself* lately.
her·self (hur self′) *pronoun*.

he's *He's* going to come with us. *He's* seen that movie three times.
he's (hēz) contraction for "he is" and "he has."

Heron

at; āpe; cär; end; mē; it; īce; hot; ōld;
wood; fōōl; oil; out; up; turn; sing;
thin; this; hw in white; zh in treasure.
ə stands for a in about, e in taken,
i in pencil, o in lemon, and u in circus.

hesitant Doubtful; uncertain. Beth was *hesitant* about jumping into the cold lake.
hes·i·tant (hez′ət ənt) *adjective.*

hesitate 1. To wait or stop a moment. The speaker *hesitated* and then went on with her speech. 2. To fail to do because of doubt or fear. Tom *hesitated* to ask Doris to the dance because he was afraid that she'd say no.
hes·i·tate (hez′ə tāt′) *verb,* **hesitated, hesitating.**

hesitation The act of hesitating. Wendy accepted the job of class president without *hesitation.*
hes·i·ta·tion (hez′ə tā′shən) *noun, plural* **hesitations.**

hey A word used to attract attention or to show surprise or pleasure. "*Hey!* Watch where you're going! ▲ Another word that sounds like this is **hay.**
hey (hā) *interjection.*

hi A word used to say "hello." ▲ Another word that sounds like this is **high.**
hi (hī) *interjection.*

hibernate To spend the winter sleeping. Bears and squirrels hibernate.
hi·ber·nate (hī′bər nāt′) *verb,* **hibernated, hibernating.**

hiccup 1. A quick catching of the breath that one cannot control. 2. **hiccups.** The condition of having one hiccup after another. You'll get the *hiccups* if you drink your milk too fast. *Noun.*
—To have hiccups. *Verb.*
This word is sometimes spelled **hiccough.**
hic·cup (hik′up) *noun, plural* **hiccups;** *verb,* **hiccupped, hiccupping.**

hickory A tall tree of North America. The hickory has nuts that are good to eat and strong, hard wood.
hick·o·ry (hik′ər ē) *noun, plural* **hickories.**

hid The squirrel *hid* the acorns in a tree.
hid (hid) *verb.*

hidden The dog has *hidden* his bone.
hid·den (hid′ən) *verb.*

hide¹ 1. To put or keep out of sight. Maria *hides* the money she saves in her dresser drawer. Jack tried to *hide* behind a tree, but the others found him. The heavy snowfall *hid* the deer's tracks. 2. To keep secret. The lost little boy tried to *hide* his fears.
hide (hīd) *verb,* **hid, hidden** or **hid, hiding.**

hide² The skin of an animal. Leather shoes are made from hides.
hide (hīd) *noun, plural* **hides.**

hide-and-seek A children's game in which one player has to find all of the other players who are hiding.
hide-and-seek (hīd′ən sēk′) *noun.*

hideous Very ugly; horrible. Tom dressed up as a *hideous* monster for Hallowe'en.
hid·e·ous (hid′ē əs) *adjective.*

hideout A place where one can hide. The thieves used a cave as their *hideout* from the police.
hide·out (hīd′out′) *noun, plural* **hideouts.**

hieroglyphic A picture or symbol that stands for a word, sound, or idea. The ancient Egyptians used hieroglyphics in their writing.
hi·er·o·glyph·ic (hī′ər ə glif′ik) *noun, plural* **hieroglyphics.**

Hieroglyphics

high 1. Tall. That mountain is very *high.* The building is forty storeys *high.* 2. At a great distance from the ground. The bird was *high* in the sky. 3. Above or more important than others. He had a *high* rank in the army. 4. Greater than others. *High* winds swept the snow into drifts. The racing car was going at a *high* speed. She is trying to sell her bicycle for a *high* price. 5. Shrill; sharp. The soprano sang a *high* note. *Adjective.*
—At or to a high place. He climbed *high* up the hill. *Adverb.*
—A high place or point. The temperature today reached a new *high* for the year. *Noun.*

Leaves

Hickory Tree

▲ Another word that sounds like this is **hi.**
high (hī) *adjective,* **higher, highest;** *adverb;*
noun, plural **highs.**

High Commissioner The person who represents one Commonwealth country in another.

high jump A contest in which you jump as high as you can over a bar set between two upright poles.

High Jump

highland A part of a country that is high or hilly.
high·land (hī′lənd) *noun, plural* **highlands.**

highly 1. Very much; very. A cool swim in the ocean is *highly* pleasant on a hot summer day. 2. With much praise or approval. The students think *highly* of their teacher. 3. At a high price. Tom was not *highly* paid for mowing his neighbour's lawn.
high·ly (hī′lē) *adverb.*

Highness A title of respect used when speaking to or about a member of a royal family. A king is spoken of as "His *Highness,*" and a queen is spoken of as "Her *Highness.*"
High·ness (hī′nəs) *noun, plural* **Highnesses.**

high-rise An apartment building which has many storeys. They live in a *high-rise* in Halifax.
high-rise (hī′rīz′) *noun, plural* **high-rises.**

high school A school attended after elementary school or junior high school.

high-sticking An illegal check in hockey made by blocking a player or hitting the puck with the stick held above the shoulders.
high-sticking (hī′stik′ing) *noun.*

highway A main road. The province has built a new *highway* between the two cities.
high·way (hī′wā′) *noun, plural* **highways.**

highwayman A robber who holds up travellers on a road.
high·way·man (hī′wā′mən) *noun, plural* **highwaymen.**

hijack To take by force. Two armed men *hijacked* the airplane.
hi·jack (hī′jak′) *verb,* **hijacked, hijacking.**

hike To take a long walk. The Boy Scout troop *hiked* to their camp by the lake. *Verb.*
—A long walk. We took a long *hike* in the woods. *Noun.*
hike (hīk) *verb,* **hiked, hiking;** *noun, plural* **hikes.**

hilarious Very funny or gay. Jack told a *hilarious* story that made us all laugh.
hi·lar·i·ous (hi ler′ē əs) *adjective.*

hill 1. A raised, rounded part of the earth's surface. A hill is not as high as a mountain. 2. A small heap or mound. Ants have made a *hill* in our backyard.
hill (hil) *noun, plural* **hills.**

hillside The side or slope of a hill. Cattle grazed on the *hillside* near the farm.
hill·side (hil′sīd′) *noun, plural* **hillsides.**

hilltop The top of a hill. We climbed to the *hilltop* to find a place for our picnic.
hill·top (hil′top′) *noun, plural* **hilltops.**

hilly Having many hills. He lives in a *hilly* part of town.
hill·y (hil′ē) *adjective,* **hillier, hilliest.**

hilt The handle of a sword or dagger.
hilt (hilt) *noun, plural* **hilts.**

him We saw *him* yesterday at the game. I lent my bicycle to *him.* ▲ Another word that sounds like this is **hymn.**
him (him *or* im) *pronoun.*

himself My father *himself* could not solve my arithmetic problem. That man has the habit of talking to *himself.* Tom has not been *himself* since he caught that bad cold.
him·self (him self′) *pronoun.*

hind At the back; rear. Our dog hurt one of his *hind* legs.
hind (hīnd) *adjective.*

hinder To hold back. The snowstorm *hindered* the search for the missing child. Mary's rudeness *hinders* her friendships with people.
hin·der (hin′dər) *verb,* **hindered, hindering.**

at; āpe; cär; end; mē; it; īce; hot; ōld;
wood; fōōl; oil; out; up; turn; sing;
thin; <u>th</u>is; hw in white; zh in treasure.
ə stands for **a** in about, **e** in taken,
i in pencil, **o** in lemon, and **u** in circus.

hinge A jointed piece on which a door, gate, or lid moves back and forth or up and down. The *hinges* on the old gate squeak when you open or close it. *Noun.*
—**1.** To put hinges on; attach by hinges. The carpenter *hinged* the cupboard doors. **2.** To depend. The team's chances of winning the championship *hinge* on next week's game. *Verb.*
hinge (hinj) *noun, plural* **hinges;** *verb,* **hinged, hinging.**

hint A slight sign or suggestion. If you can't guess the answer to the riddle, I'll give you a *hint.* There is a *hint* of spring in the air this morning. *Noun.*
—To give a slight sign or suggestion. Mother *hinted* that I might be getting a bicycle for my birthday. *Verb.*
hint (hint) *noun, plural* **hints;** *verb,* **hinted, hinting.**

hip The bony part that sticks out on each side of the body just below the waist.
hip (hip) *noun, plural* **hips.**

hippopotamus A very large, heavy animal that eats plants. It lives in and near rivers and lakes in Africa. Hippopotamuses have short legs and thick skin with no hair.
hip·po·pot·a·mus (hip′ə pot′ə məs) *noun, plural* **hippopotamuses.**

Hippopotamus

▲ The word **hippopotamus** comes from the Greek name for this animal. The Greek name meant "river horse."

---

hire To pay for the work of a person or for the use of a thing. My mother *hired* a new secretary today. Ronnie's sister *hired* a car to drive to Moncton. *Verb.*
—The act of hiring. That man has fishing boats for *hire. Noun.*
hire (hīr) *verb,* **hired, hiring;** *noun.*

his This is my book and that one is *his. His* dog has floppy ears.
his (hiz) *pronoun; adjective.*

hiss **1.** To make a sound like a long *s.* An angry cat *hisses.* **2.** To make this sound to show disapproval. The fans *hissed* when the referee called a penalty. *Verb.*
—A sound like a long *s.* We heard the *hiss* of steam from the radiator. *Noun.*
hiss (his) *verb,* **hissed, hissing;** *noun, plural* **hisses.**

historian A person who knows a great deal about history. Historians write history books.
his·to·ri·an (his tōr′ē ən) *noun, plural* **historians.**

historic Important in history. The committee tried to preserve all the *historic* old houses in town.
his·tor·ic (his tōr′ik) *adjective.*

historical Having to do with history. I am reading a *historical* book.
his·tor·i·cal (his tōr′i kəl) *adjective.*

history The story or record of what has happened in the past. The *history* of Canada as a nation can be thought of as beginning with Confederation.
his·to·ry (his′tər ē) *noun, plural* **histories.**

hit **1.** To give a blow to; strike. Jerry *hit* his brother. Lou *hit* the ball over the fence. **2.** To come against. The ball *hit* the fence. **3.** To come to; reach. The car *hit* 120 kilometres per hour. We finally *hit* upon the answer. **4.** To have a bad effect on. The unhappy news *hit* her hard. *Verb.*
—**1.** A blow or strike. The *hit* on her head stunned her. **2.** A person or thing that is successful or popular. His guitar playing was the *hit* of the party. The new movie is a big *hit.* **3.** The hitting of a baseball by the batter in a way that allows him to get on base. *Noun.*
hit (hit) *verb,* **hit, hitting;** *noun, plural* **hits.**

hitch **1.** To fasten with a rope, strap, or hook. The farmer *hitched* the horse to the wagon. **2.** To move or lift with a jerk. The boy *hitched* up his trousers. *Verb.*
—**1.** A fastening. The *hitch* between the car and the trailer broke. **2.** An unexpected delay or problem. A sudden storm put a *hitch* in their plans to leave that day. **3.** A quick, jerky movement. He straightened his tie and gave his trousers a *hitch.* **4.** A kind of knot used to attach things together temporarily. *Noun.*
hitch (hich) *verb,* **hitched, hitching;** *noun, plural* **hitches.**

hitchhike To travel by walking along a road and getting free rides from cars or trucks that are passing by.
hitch·hike (hich′hīk′) *verb,* **hitchhiked, hitchhiking.**

hive **1.** A box or house for bees to live in. **2.** All the bees that live together in the same hive.

hive (hīv) *noun, plural* **hives.**

hives An itchy rash on the skin.

hives (hīvz) *noun plural.*

HM His or Her Majesty.

HMCS **1.** Her Majesty's Canadian Ship. **2.** Her Majesty's Canadian Service.

hoard To save and store or hide away. Jack *hoarded* his allowance until he had enough money to buy a camera. *Verb.*
—Something that is stored or hidden away. Susan had a *hoard* of candy bars in her desk drawer. *Noun.* ▲ Another word that sounds like this is **horde.**

hoard (hōrd) *verb,* **hoarded, hoarding;** *noun, plural* **hoards.**

hoarse **1.** Having a harsh, deep sound. Alice's voice was *hoarse* because of her bad cold. **2.** Having a harsh voice. Bill was *hoarse* after all the shouting he did at the game. ▲ Another word that sounds like this is **horse.**

hoarse (hōrs) *adjective,* **hoarser, hoarsest.**

hoax A trick meant to fool people. The report that a sea monster was seen in the bay was a *hoax.*

hoax (hōks) *noun, plural* **hoaxes.**

hobble **1.** To move or walk awkwardly with a limp. Judy *hobbled* around with a sprained ankle for two weeks.

Hobble

2. To keep from moving easily or freely. You *hobble* a horse by tying its front or back legs together. *Verb.*
—A rope, strap, or other thing used to hobble a horse or other animal. *Noun.*

hob·ble (hob′əl) *verb,* **hobbled, hobbling;** *noun, plural* **hobbles.**

hobby Something that a person does regularly in his spare time because he enjoys it. Raising tropical fish is my *hobby.*

hob·by (hob′ē) *noun, plural* **hobbies.**

▲ The word **hobby** comes from an earlier English word that once meant "toy horse." People used this word for a grown person's pastime because they thought that having a hobby was like playing with a toy horse.

hockey **1.** A game played on ice by two teams of six players each. The players wear ice skates and hit a rubber disk, called a puck, with curved sticks. Each team tries to get the puck into the other team's goal. Outside of Canada this game is usually called **ice hockey.** **2.** A game played on a field by two teams of eleven players each. Curved sticks are used to hit a ball along the ground into the other team's goal; field hockey.

hock·ey (hok′ē) *noun.*

Hockey

hoe A tool with a wide, thin blade set across the end of a long handle. Hoes are used to loosen the soil around plants. *Noun.*
—To dig with a hoe. We *hoe* the garden once a week to keep the soil loose. *Verb.*

hoe (hō) *noun, plural* **hoes;** *verb,* **hoed, hoeing.**

hog **1.** A full-grown pig. Hogs are raised for their meat. **2.** A greedy or dirty person. *Noun.*
—To take more than one's share. She *hogged* all the food at the party. *Verb.*

hog (hog) *noun, plural* **hogs;** *verb,* **hogged, hogging.**

Hog

at; āpe; cär; end; mē; it; īce; hot; ōld; wood; fool; oil; out; up; turn; sing; thin; this; hw in white; zh in treasure. ə stands for a in about, e in taken, i in pencil, o in lemon, and u in circus.

hogan A house made of stones or logs with a roof of branches covered with earth. Some Navaho Indians live in hogans.
ho·gan (hō′gän) *noun, plural* **hogans.**

Hogan

hoist To lift or pull up. The sailors *hoisted* the cargo onto the ship's deck with a crane. We *hoisted* the flag up the pole. *Verb.*
—**1.** A device used to lift or pull up something heavy. He put the car on a *hoist* to raise it. **2.** A lift. Tom gave me a *hoist* up the tree. *Noun.*
hoist (hoist) *verb,* **hoisted, hoisting;** *noun, plural* **hoists.**

hold[1] **1.** To take and keep in the hands or arms; grasp; grip. If you will *hold* the packages, I will unlock the door. She had to *hold* tightly to the railing as she came down the steep stairs. **2.** To keep in a certain place or position. The little boy would not *hold* still. The dam *held* back the flooding river. A good book *holds* your attention. **3.** To contain. This bottle *holds* two litres. The bus will *hold* fifty people. **4.** To take part in; carry on. The club will *hold* its next meeting on Saturday. **5.** To believe to be; think. The judge *held* him responsible for the accident. *Verb.*
—**1.** A grasp; grip. He didn't have a good *hold* on the heavy lamp, and he dropped it. **2.** Something that can be gripped. The boys couldn't find enough *holds* to climb the side of the cliff. **3.** A mark or symbol in music that shows a pause. *Noun.*
hold (hōld) *verb,* **held, holding;** *noun, plural* **holds.**

hold[2] A space in a ship or airplane where cargo is stored.
hold (hōld) *noun, plural* **holds.**

holding An illegal act in hockey or lacrosse in which a player grabs an opponent or his stick in order to hamper his movements.
hold·ing (hōld′ing) *noun, plural* **holdings.**

holdup **1.** A robbery by someone who is armed. There was a *holdup* in the jewellery store last week. **2.** A stopping or delay. There was a *holdup* of traffic because of the storm.
hold·up (hōld′up′) *noun, plural* **holdups.**

hole **1.** A hollow place in something solid. There was a big *hole* in the street after the heavy rain. The dog dug a *hole* in the ground to hide his bone. **2.** An opening through something. I wore a *hole* in the elbow of my old sweater. **3.** A small hollow place on the green of a golf course. The ball is hit into the hole. ▲ Another word that sounds like this is **whole.**
hole (hōl) *noun, plural* **holes.**

holiday **1.** A day or days on which most people do not work. Canada Day is a national *holiday.* **2.** A vacation. Last year we went down East to Prince Edward Island for our summer *holidays.*
hol·i·day (hol′ə dā′) *noun, plural* **holidays.**

▲ The word **holiday** comes from an Old English word that meant "holy day." In England long ago, the only days when people did not work were ones that were set aside as special religious feast days.

hollow **1.** Having a hole or an empty space inside; not solid. A water pipe is *hollow.* **2.** Curved in like a cup or bowl; sunken. The thin woman had *hollow* cheeks. **3.** Deep and dull. The miners' footsteps made a *hollow* sound as they walked through the empty tunnel. *Adjective.*
—**1.** A hole or empty space. The car bounced over a *hollow* in the dirt road. **2.** A valley. The farm nestled in the hollow between the hills. *Noun.*
—To make an empty space inside. The rabbits *hollowed* out a burrow in the ground. *Verb.*
hol·low (hol′ō) *adjective,* **hollower, hollowest;** *noun, plural* **hollows;** *verb,* **hollowed, hollowing.**

holly An evergreen tree. Holly has very shiny leaves with sharp, pointed edges and bright red berries. Its leaves

Holly

and berries are often used as Christmas decorations.
hol·ly (hol′ē) *noun, plural* **hollies.**

hollyhock A tall plant that has stalks of large, brightly coloured flowers. It grows on a tall plant that has wrinkled leaves.
hol·ly·hock (hol′ē hok′) *noun, plural* **hollyhocks.**

holster A leather case for carrying a gun. Holsters for pistols are worn on a belt around a person's waist.
hol·ster (hōl′stər) *noun, plural* **holsters.**

Holster

holy 1. Belonging to God; sacred. The priest stood at the *holy* altar. 2. Free from sin; like a saint. The nuns led a *holy* life. ▲ Another word that sounds like this is **wholly.**
ho·ly (hō′lē) *adjective,* **holier, holiest.**

home 1. The place in which a person lives. Steve's *home* is in an apartment building. Betty's *home* is that house up the road. 2. A person's family. Tommy, his sister Paula, and their parents have a happy *home.* 3. The place that a person comes from. Calgary has always been my *home.* 4. The goal or place of safety in some sports and games. 5. A place for the care of persons unable to care for themselves. *Noun.*
—1. At or to the place a person lives. My brother will come *home* for Christmas. 2. To the place or mark aimed at. She aimed at the tree and the arrow hit *home. Adverb.*
home (hōm) *noun, plural* **homes;** *adverb.*

homebrew 1. Beer that is made at home. 2. *Canadian.* A professional athlete who plays in the country of his or her birth.
home·brew (hōm′brōō′) *noun, plural* **homebrews.**

homeland A country where a person was born or has his home. His *homeland* is Sweden, although he is now living in Dawson.
home·land (hōm′land′) *noun, plural* **homelands.**

homely 1. Having a plain appearance; not good-looking. Our dog is *homely,* but we love it. 2. Simple and for every day; not fancy. The campers gave us a good, *homely* meal.
home·ly (hōm′lē) *adjective,* **homelier, homeliest.**

homemade Made at home in a person's own kitchen or by hand. Mother bakes *homemade* bread on Saturdays. We have a *homemade* swing on a tree in the yard.
home·made (hōm′mād′) *adjective.*

home plate The place where a baseball player stands to hit a pitched ball. A runner must touch home plate after rounding the bases in order to score a run.

homer A hit that scores a run. Look up **home run** for more information.
hom·er (hōm′ər) *noun, plural* **homers.**

homeroom A classroom to which all the pupils in a class go in the mornings. Attendance is checked and special announcements are made there.
home·room (hōm′rōōm′) *noun, plural* **homerooms.**

home run A hit made by a baseball player that lets him go around all the bases to home plate and score a run.

homesick Sad or sick because of being away from one's home or family. The soldier was *homesick* during his first few months in the army.
home·sick (hōm′sik′) *adjective.*

homespun A cloth that is woven by hand at home, instead of in a factory by big machines.
home·spun (hōm′spun′) *noun.*

homestead 1. A farm with its house and other buildings. 2. A piece of land that was given by the federal government to a settler in western Canada. The land was to be used for farming.
home·stead (hōm′sted′) *noun, plural* **homesteads.**

homeward Toward home. The hikers turned *homeward* for the walk back.
home·ward (hōm′wərd) *adverb; adjective.*

homework A school lesson that is meant to be done at home, not in the classroom.
home·work (hōm′wurk′) *noun.*

homogenized milk Milk in which the cream has been spread evenly throughout and will not separate and rise to the top.
ho·mog·e·nized milk (hə moj′ə nīzd′).

homograph A word with the same spelling as another, but with a different origin and meaning and, sometimes, a different pronunciation. *Bow* meaning "to bend forward" and *bow* meaning "a weapon for shooting arrows" are homographs.
hom·o·graph (hom′ə graf′) *noun, plural* **homographs.**

homonym A word with the same pronunciation as another, but with a different meaning and, often, a different spelling. *Lean* meaning

at; āpe; cär; end; mē; it; īce; hot; ōld;
wood; fōōl; oil; out; up; turn; sing;
thin; this; hw in white; zh in treasure.
ə stands for **a** in about, **e** in taken,
i in pencil, **o** in lemon, and **u** in circus.

"to bend" and *lean* meaning "thin" are homonyms.

> **hom·o·nym** (hom′ə nim′) *noun, plural* **homonyms.**

homophone A word with the same pronunciation as another, but with a different meaning and spelling. *Know* and *no* are homophones.

> **hom·o·phone** (hom′ə fōn′) *noun, plural* **homophones.**

honest Truthful, fair, or trustworthy. An honest person does not cheat, lie, or steal. That farmer earns an *honest* living.

> **hon·est** (on′əst) *adjective.*

honesty The quality of being honest; truthfulness; fairness. He answered all the questions with *honesty.*

> **hon·es·ty** (on′əs tē) *noun.*

honey 1. A thick, sweet liquid made by bees. Bees collect nectar from flowers and make honey, which they store in honeycombs. 2. A person or thing that is very dear and sweet; darling.

> **hon·ey** (hun′ē) *noun, plural* **honeys.**

honeybee A bee that makes and stores honey.

> **hon·ey·bee** (hun′ē bē′) *noun, plural* **honeybees.**

honeycomb 1. A wax structure made by bees to store their honey in. A honeycomb is made up of layers of six-sided cells. 2. Something that looks like a bee's honeycomb. There was a *honeycomb* of subway tunnels under the city. *Noun.*
—To make full of tunnels or cells like a bee's honeycomb. Secret passages *honeycombed* the castle. *Verb.*

> **hon·ey·comb** (hun′ē kōm′) *noun, plural* **honeycombs;** *verb,* **honeycombed, honeycombing.**

honeymoon A vacation taken by a man and a woman who have just been married. *Noun.*
—To be or go on a honeymoon. *Verb.*

> **hon·ey·moon** (hun′ē mōōn′) *noun, plural* **honeymoons;** *verb,* **honeymooned, honeymooning.**

▲ There was an old custom of having newly married people drink wine with honey in it for the first month of their marriage. A month was sometimes called a *moon,* and this early part of a marriage became known as the "honey month" or "honey moon." Now the word **honeymoon** is used for the trip that people take at the beginning of their marriage.

---

honeysuckle A climbing plant that has many small, sweet-smelling flowers.

> **hon·ey·suck·le** (hun′ē-suk′əl) *noun, plural* **honeysuckles.**

honk 1. The cry of a goose. 2. Any sound like the cry of a goose. The *honk* of the automobile horn scared the deer. *Noun.*
—To make the cry of a goose or any sound like it. We heard the geese *honk* as they flew overhead. *Verb.*

> **honk** (hongk) *noun, plural* **honks;** *verb,* **honked, honking.**

Honeysuckle

honour 1. A sense of what is right or honest. A man of *honour,* Ray did not cheat on tests. 2. A good name or reputation. When the bully called him a coward, Jack felt his *honour* was at stake. 3. A cause of respect, pride, or glory. It was a great *honour* for her to receive the scholarship award. 4. **Honour.** A title of respect used in speaking to or of a judge, mayor, or other official. *Noun.*
—To show great respect. *Verb.*
This word is also spelled **honor.**

> **hon·our** (on′ər) *noun, plural* **honours;** *verb,* **honoured, honouring.**

honourable 1. Having or showing a sense of what is right or honest. The judge is an *honourable* man. 2. Worthy of or bringing honour or respect. Winning a prize at the science fair was an *honourable* achievement. This word is also spelled **honorable.** 3. **the Honourable** A title of respect for certain public officials such as judges of a supreme court, members of a cabinet, and the Speaker of the House of Commons.

> **hon·our·a·ble** (on′ər ə bəl) *adjective.*

hood 1. A covering for the head and neck. A hood is often attached to the collar of a coat. 2. The metal cover that is over the engine of an automobile. 3. Something that looks like a hood or is used as a cover. There is a metal *hood* over our stove.

> **hood** (hood) *noun, plural* **hoods.**

Hood

hoodlum A rough and nasty person who causes trouble for other people. Several teen-age *hoodlums* were caught stealing lunch money from the younger children in the school.

hood·lum (hŏŏd′ləm) *noun, plural* **hoodlums.**

hoof The hard covering on the feet of horses, cattle, deer, and other animals.

hoof (hoof *or* hŏŏf) *noun, plural* **hoofs** or **hooves.**

hook 1. A bent piece of metal, wood, or other strong material that is used to hold or fasten something. There is a row of coat *hooks* in the closet in our classroom. My dress has a *hook* on the collar. 2. Anything bent or shaped like a hook. A curved piece of wire with a barb at one end used for catching fish is a hook. *Noun.*
—1. To hang, fasten, or attach with a hook. We *hooked* the wire picture hanger over the nail. 2. To catch with or on a hook. The fisherman *hooked* three fish. 3. To have or make into the shape of a hook. Bob *hooked* his leg over the arm of the chair. *Verb.*

hook (hook) *noun, plural* **hooks;** *verb,* **hooked, hooking.**

hoop A ring made of wood, metal, or other material. Metal *hoops* hold together the staves of a barrel. Plastic *hoops* are a toy that can be spun around your body. Lions leap through flaming *hoops* in the circus. ▲ Another word that sounds like this is **whoop.**

hoop (hŏŏp) *noun, plural* **hoops.**

hoot 1. The sound that an owl makes. 2. A sound like the cry of an owl. People make a hoot when they do not like or do not believe some-

Hoop

thing. John's friends gave a *hoot* when he said he saw a ghost in the old house. *Noun.*
—To make the sound of an owl or any sound like this. The fans *hooted* when the other team made an error. *Verb.*

hoot (hŏŏt) *noun, plural* **hoots;** *verb,* **hooted, hooting.**

hooves More than one hoof. Look up **hoof** for more information.

hooves (hoovz *or* hŏŏvz) *noun plural.*

hop¹ 1. To make a short jump on one foot. When you play hopscotch, you have to *hop* from one square to another. 2. To move by jumping on both feet or all feet at once. Rabbits and frogs *hop*. 3. To jump over. We *hopped* the fence instead of walking around to the gate. *Verb.*
—A short jump or leap. She went down the street with a *hop* and a skip. *Noun.*

hop (hop) *verb,* **hopped, hopping;** *noun, plural* **hops.**

hop² A greenish-yellow fruit shaped like a cone that grows on a vine. Hops are used to flavour beer.

hop (hop) *noun, plural* **hops.**

hope To want or wish for something very much. I *hope* Susan will feel better soon. The girls *hoped* for a sunny day so that they could go to the beach. *Verb.*
—1. A strong wish and belief that a thing will happen. Alex is full of *hope* that he will go to university. 2. Something that is wished for. His *hope* is that he will be elected captain of the team. *Noun.*

hope (hōp) *verb,* **hoped, hoping;** *noun, plural* **hopes.**

hopeful 1. Having or showing hope. She was *hopeful* that they would be able to get tickets for the movie. 2. Giving promise that what is wished for will happen. Ginny thought that her mother's smile was a *hopeful* sign that she could go to the party.

hope·ful (hōp′fəl) *adjective.*

hopeless Having or giving no hope. When he failed the test after studying so hard, he felt *hopeless.*

hope·less (hōp′ləs) *adjective.*

hopper 1. A person or an animal that hops. Grasshoppers and kangaroos are hoppers. 2. A holder for grain, coal, or other things. Hoppers are wide open at the top with a small opening at the bottom. They are used to empty something into a container.

hop·per (hop′ər) *noun, plural* **hoppers.**

hopscotch A children's game on numbered squares that are drawn on the ground. The players hop into the squares in a certain order and try to pick up a stone or other object that has been tossed into one of the squares.

hop·scotch (hop′skoch′) *noun.*

horde A very large group. A *horde* of ants came out of the anthill. A *horde* of people

at; āpe; cär; end; mē; it; īce; hot; ōld;
wood; fŏŏl; oil; out; up; turn; sing;
thin; this; hw in white; zh in treasure.
ə stands for a in about, e in taken,
i in pencil, o in lemon, and u in circus.

311

pushed their way into the stadium. ▲ Another word that sounds like this is **hoard.**

horde (hōrd) *noun, plural* **hordes.**

horizon 1. The line where the sky and the ground or the sea seem to meet. We could see a huge ship on the *horizon.* 2. The limit of a person's knowledge, interests, or experience. He widened his *horizons* by reading many books.

ho·ri·zon (hə rī′zən) *noun, plural* **horizons.**

horizontal Flat and straight across; parallel to the horizon. The workmen put the *horizontal* beams of the house in place.

hor·i·zon·tal (hōr′ə zont′əl) *adjective.*

The road is **horizontal.** The trees are vertical.

hormone A substance made in the body that helps it grow or stay healthy. Hormones are made in certain glands and enter into the bloodstream. The blood carries them to the parts of the body where they are needed.

hor·mone (hōr′mōn) *noun, plural* **hormones.**

horn 1. A hard, pointed growth on the head of some animals. Deer, sheep, and rhinoceroses have horns. 2. Something that looks like the horn of an animal. Some owls have tufts of feathers on their heads called horns. 3. A brass musical instrument. Horns have a narrow end that you blow into to play them. 4. A device used to make a warning signal. The bus driver honked his *horn* at the children in the street.

Horns

horn (hōrn) *noun, plural* **horns.**

horned toad A lizard that has spiny horns on its head and scales on its body. Horned toads live in dry areas in North America.

horned toad (hōrnd).

Horned Toad

hornet A large wasp that can give a very painful sting.

hor·net (hōr′nət) *noun, plural* **hornets.**

horny Made of horn or something that is hard like a horn. A deer's antlers are a *horny* growth.

horn·y (hōr′nē) *adjective,* **hornier, horniest.**

horrible 1. Causing great fear or shock. It was *horrible* to see the house burn to the ground. Murder is a *horrible* crime. 2. Very bad, ugly, or unpleasant. There was a *horrible* smell by the garbage heap.

hor·ri·ble (hōr′ə bəl) *adjective.*

horrid 1. Causing great fear or shock; horrible. She thought the monster movie was so *horrid* that she left before it was over. 2. Very bad, ugly, or unpleasant. My brother thinks spinach tastes *horrid,* but I like it more than any other vegetable.

hor·rid (hōr′id) *adjective.*

horrify To cause great fear or shock. Seeing the two cars crash *horrified* him.

hor·ri·fy (hōr′ə fī′) *verb,* **horrified, horrifying.**

horror 1. A feeling of great fear and dread. They watched with *horror* as the ship burned and sank. He has a *horror* of being alone in the dark. 2. A strong feeling of dislike or shock. She looked around the dirty old house with *horror.* 3. A person or thing that causes great fear, shock, or dislike. They all felt that war was a *horror.*

hor·ror (hōr′ər) *noun, plural* **horrors.**

horse 1. A large animal with four legs with hoofs and a long, flowing mane and tail. Horses are used for riding and pulling heavy loads. 2. A frame with legs. Some horses have soft, leather pads on top and are used in gym for doing exercises. Others are plain and are used with a board across them as work tables. ▲ Another word that sounds like this is **hoarse.**

 horse (hōrs) *noun, plural* **horses.**

horseback On the back of a horse. Don and Linda are going to ride *horseback* to the campsite.

 horse·back (hōrs′bak′) *adverb.*

horsefly A large fly with a fat body. The female gives a painful bite to horses and other animals and to people.

 horse·fly (hōrs′flī′) *noun, plural* **horseflies.**

horseman 1. A person who rides on a horse. 2. A person who is skilled in riding or handling horses. Her uncle is a fine *horseman.* The word **horsewoman** is also used.

 horse·man (hōrs′mən) *noun, plural* **horsemen.**

horsepower A unit for measuring the power of an engine in the Imperial System of Measure.

 horse·pow·er (hōrs′pou′ər) *noun.*

horseshoe 1. A U-shaped piece of metal curved to fit the shape of a horse's hoof. A horseshoe is nailed onto the hoof to protect it. 2. **horseshoes.** A game played by throwing a U-shaped piece toward a post so that it will land around the post.

 horse·shoe (hōrs′shoō′) *noun, plural* **horseshoes.**

hose 1. A tube of rubber or other material that will bend easily. Hoses are used to carry water or other fluids from one place to another. The boy watered the garden with a *hose.* Gasoline is pumped through a *hose* into a car. 2. Stockings or socks. *Noun.*
—To wash or water with a hose. We *hosed* down the car before we waxed it. *Verb.*

 hose (hōz) *noun, plural* **hoses** *(for definition 1)* or **hose** *(for definition 2); verb,* **hosed, hosing.**

Hose

hospitable Making a guest or visitor feel welcome and comfortable; friendly. The lady who owned the small hotel was very *hospitable,* even though we arrived late at night.

 hos·pi·ta·ble (hos′pi tə bəl *or* hos pit′ə bəl) *adjective.*

hospital A place where doctors and nurses take care of people who are sick or hurt.

 hos·pi·tal (hos′pi təl) *noun, plural* **hospitals.**

▲ The first meaning of **hospital** was "a place where travellers can find rest and food." These places often took care of poor people who could not pay to stay at other places, and eventually the word *hospital* was used for any place that took care of poor sick people. This last use of *hospital* led to our meaning, "a place for the care of sick people."

hospitality A friendly welcome and treatment of guests or visitors. We thanked our friends for their *hospitality* to us last weekend.

 hos·pi·tal·i·ty (hos′pə tal′ə tē) *noun, plural* **hospitalities.**

hospitalize To put a person in a hospital so that he will get the care he needs. The skier was *hospitalized* for weeks with a broken leg.

 hos·pi·tal·ize (hos′pit əl īz′) *verb,* **hospitalized, hospitalizing.**

host¹ A man who invites people to come to his home as his guests. We thanked our *host* for a wonderful party.

 host (hōst) *noun, plural* **hosts.**

host² A large number. On a clear night, you can see a *host* of stars in the sky.

 host (hōst) *noun, plural* **hosts.**

hostage A person who is held as a prisoner by someone until money is paid or promises are kept. The passengers and crew of the hijacked plane were held as *hostages* until a ransom was paid.

 hos·tage (hos′təj) *noun, plural* **hostages.**

hostel A place that gives cheap lodging to young people on bicycle tours or hikes.

 hos·tel (host′əl) *noun, plural* **hostels.**

hostess 1. A woman who invites people to come to her home as her guests. Mrs. Davis was the *hostess* at a large dinner party for the

at; āpe; cär; end; mē; it; īce; hot; ōld;
wood; foōl; oil; out; up; turn; sing;
thin; this; hw in white; zh in treasure.
ə stands for a in about, e in taken,
i in pencil, o in lemon, and u in circus.

Governor General. **2.** A woman who serves food and greets people in a restaurant or on an airplane.

host·ess (hōs′təs) *noun, plural* **hostesses.**

hostile Feeling or showing hatred or dislike. After their fight, the boys wouldn't talk to each other for a week, and just gave each other *hostile* looks.

hos·tile (hos′tīl′) *adjective.*

hot **1.** Having a high temperature. I burned my hand when I touched the *hot* iron. We were *hot* after sitting in the sun for an hour. **2.** Having a burning, sharp taste. We put *hot* mustard on our hamburgers. **3.** Violent; raging. Jack has a *hot* temper. **4.** Following very closely. The police were in *hot* pursuit of the robbers.

hot (hot) *adjective,* **hotter, hottest.**

hot dog A long, thin sausage; frankfurter. It is often served on a long roll with mustard and relish.

hotel A building with many rooms that people pay to sleep in. Most hotels serve meals.

ho·tel (hō tel′) *noun, plural* **hotels.**

hothouse A heated building made mainly of glass where plants are grown; greenhouse. Some people grow exotic flowers and plants in hothouses.

hot·house (hot′hous′) *noun, plural* **hothouses.**

Houseboat

hound A dog that has been raised and trained to hunt. Beagles and bloodhounds are two kinds of hounds. *Noun.*

—To keep urging; pester. Father *hounded* me all last week about cleaning up my room. *Verb.*

hound (hound) *noun, plural* **hounds;** *verb,* **hounded, hounding.**

hour **1.** A unit of time equal to sixty minutes. There are twenty-four hours in a day. We waited for one *hour,* from four o'clock to five o'clock, for Tom to meet us. **2.** A time of the day that is shown on a clock or watch. At what *hour* should we leave for the station? **3.** The time for anything. The doctor's office *hours* are from nine o'clock to four o'clock. Our lunch *hour* starts at twelve o'clock. ▲ Another word that sounds like this is **our.**

hour (our) *noun, plural* **hours.**

hourglass A device for measuring time. It is a glass tube with a narrow middle. A quantity of sand runs from the top part to the bottom part in exactly one hour.

hour·glass (our′glas′) *noun, plural* **hourglasses.**

hourly Done or happening every hour. There are *hourly* bus trips from the airport to the centre of the city. *Adjective.*

—Every hour. The weather is reported *hourly* on the radio. *Adverb.*

hour·ly (our′lē) *adjective; adverb.*

Hourglass

house **1.** A building in which people live; home. Dave asked us to come to his *house* for dinner. **2.** The people who live in a house. Our whole *house* was awakened when the fire engines went by. **3.** Any building used for a special purpose. The town has a new movie *house.* **4. the House.** The House of Commons. The Canadian Parliament is made up of the House of Commons, which is the Lower *House,* and the Senate, which is the Upper *House.* **5.** An audience. There was a full *house* for the opening of the new show. *Noun.*

—To give someone a place to live. We *housed* our friends for a month until their new home was ready. *Verb.*

house (hous *for noun;* houz *for verb*) *noun, plural* **houses** (houz′əz); *verb,* **housed, housing.**

houseboat A big boat that people can live on.

house·boat (hous′bōt′) *noun, plural* **houseboats.**

housefly A fly that lives in and near people's houses. It eats food and garbage.

house·fly (hous′flī′) *noun, plural* **houseflies.**

household All the people who live in a house. Our *household* was very busy the week before Christmas. *Noun.*

—Having to do with a household. On Saturday, we all helped with cleaning, ironing, and other *household* chores. *Adjective.*

house·hold (hous′hōld′) *noun, plural* **households;** *adjective.*

housekeeper A person whose job is to take care of a house. A housekeeper is responsible for housework and sometimes child care.
house·keep·er (hous′kē′pər) *noun, plural* **housekeepers.**

House of Assembly The provincial legislature of Newfoundland and Labrador.

House of Commons 1. The Lower House of the Canadian Parliament. The members of the House of Commons are elected. 2. The chamber in Ottawa where the Members of Parliament meet.

House of Lords The upper house of the British Parliament.

housewife A woman who takes care of a house and the needs of a family.
house·wife (hous′wīf′) *noun, plural* **housewives.**

housework Washing, ironing, cleaning, cooking, and other work that has to be done in taking care of a house and a family.
house·work (hous′wurk′) *noun.*

housing 1. A number of houses. There is a lot of new *housing* being built in our town. 2. A covering for the moving parts of a machine. The *housing* on Dad's drill gets very hot when the drill is used for a long time.
hous·ing (houz′ing) *noun, plural* **housings.**

hover To stay in the air, flying right above one place. The bird *hovered* over its nest.
hov·er (huv′ər *or* hov′ər) *verb,* **hovered, hovering.**

how *How* will we get home from school today? *How* cold is it outside? *How* did you like the movie? *How* tall is he? *How* are you today? *How* did he happen to be so late?
how (hou) *adverb.*

however It is the middle of winter; *however,* it is very warm outside. *However* did you get such a bad cut on your arm?
how·ev·er (hou ev′ər) *conjunction; adverb.*

howl To make a loud, wailing cry. A dog and a wolf both howl. The wind howls when it blows hard. Jack *howled* when he hurt his toe. We *howled* with laughter. *Verb.*
—A loud, wailing cry. We heard the *howl* of the wind in the rafters of the barn. *Noun.*
howl (houl) *verb,* **howled, howling;** *noun, plural* **howls.**

hub 1. The middle part of a wheel. A round cap covers the *hub* of a car wheel. 2. A centre of interest or movement. The gym was the *hub* of activity during the game.
hub (hub) *noun, plural* **hubs.**

huckleberry A small, shiny, dark-blue berry. Huckleberries grow on small, low shrubs. They are like blueberries but are smaller and darker.
huck·le·ber·ry (huk′əlber′ē) *noun, plural* **huckleberries.**

Huckleberries

huddle To gather close together in a bunch. The boys and girls *huddled* around the fire. *Verb.*
—A group of people or animals gathered close together. *Noun.*
hud·dle (hud′əl) *verb,* **huddled, huddling;** *noun, plural* **huddles.**

Hudson's Bay Company A company established in 1670 to carry on the fur trade with North American Indians.

▲ At first called "The Company of Adventurers of England Trading into Hudson's Bay," The **Hudson's Bay Company** developed much of northwestern Canada.

hue A colour or a shade of a colour.
hue (hyōō) *noun, plural* **hues.**

hug 1. To put the arms around a person or thing and hold close and tightly. 2. To keep close to. He *hugged* the curb as he rode along the busy street. *Verb.*
—A close, tight clasp with the arms. *Noun.*
hug (hug) *verb,* **hugged, hugging;** *noun, plural* **hugs.**

huge Very big; enormous. An elephant is a *huge* animal.
huge (hyōōj) *adjective,* **huger, hugest.**

hull 1. The outer covering of a nut, grain, or other seed. 2. The small leaves around the stem of a strawberry and certain other fruits. 3. The sides and bottom of a boat or ship. *Noun.*
—To remove the hull from a seed or fruit. I *hulled* the strawberries. *Verb.*
hull (hul) *noun, plural* **hulls;** *verb,* **hulled, hulling.**

Hull

at; āpe; cär; end; mē; it; īce; hot; ōld;
wood; fōōl; oil; out; up; turn; sing;
thin; <u>th</u>is; hw in white; zh in treasure.
ə stands for a in about, e in taken,
i in pencil, o in lemon, and u in circus.

the lights *hushed* the audience. **2.** To keep secret. They all agreed to *hush* up about the party so they could surprise her. *Verb.*
—Be quiet. "*Hush*," their mother said, "or you will wake the baby." *Interjection.*
  hush (hush) *noun, plural* **hushes;** *verb,* **hushed, hushing;** *interjection.*

husk The dry, outside covering of some vegetables and fruits. We take the *husk* off corn before we cook it. *Noun.*
—To take off the husk from. If you *husk* the corn, I will peel the potatoes. *Verb.*
  husk (husk) *noun, plural* **husks;** *verb,* **husked, husking.**

husky[1] **1.** Big and strong. The tennis player was a *husky* boy. **2.** Rough and deep in sound. His voice was *husky* when he had a cold.
  husk·y (hus′kē) *adjective,* **huskier, huskiest.**

husky[2] A strong dog with a thick coat of hair and a bushy tail. Huskies are used in the North for pulling sleds. A husky is sometimes called an **Eskimo dog.**
  husk·y (hus′kē) *noun, plural* **huskies.**

hustle To move or do something very quickly and with energy. We had to *hustle* to finish all our work in an hour.
  hus·tle (hus′əl) *verb,* **hustled, hustling.**

hut A small, roughly built house or shelter. There is a *hut* on the beach that we use to keep our fishing equipment in.
  hut (hut) *noun, plural* **huts.**

hutch A house for rabbits or other small animals.
  hutch (huch) *noun, plural* **hutches.**

hyacinth A sweet-smelling flower that has a thick stem with small flowers growing up and down it. Hyacinths grow from bulbs and have long leaves that grow up from the ground.
  hy·a·cinth (hī′ə sinth′) *noun, plural* **hyacinths.**

Hyacinth

hybrid A plant or animal that is a mixture of two different kinds of plants or animals. A mule is a hybrid because its father is a donkey and its mother is a horse. *Noun.*
—Having to do with or being a hybrid. Dad raises *hybrid* roses. *Adjective.*
  hy·brid (hī′brid) *noun, plural* **hybrids;** *adjective.*

hydrant A wide, covered pipe that sticks out of the ground and is attached to a water main. Fire hoses are attached to hydrants to get water to put out fires.
  hy·drant (hī′drənt) *noun, plural* **hydrants.**

hydro *Canadian.* Hydro-electric power. The *hydro* was shut off to repair the overhead wires.
  hyd·ro (hī′drō) *noun.*

hydro-electric Having to do with electricity developed from water power. Niagara Falls is one of the greatest sources of hydro-electric power.
  hyd·ro·e·lec·tric (hī′drō ə lek′trik) *adjective.*

hydrogen A gas that burns very easily. It has no colour, taste, or odour. Hydrogen is a chemical element.
  hy·dro·gen (hī′drə jən) *noun.*

hydrogen bomb A very powerful bomb that explodes with great force. The fusion of atoms of hydrogen to form atoms of helium causes the explosion. The hydrogen bomb is more powerful than the atomic bomb.

hyena An animal that looks like a wolf. A hyena has a large head and front legs that are longer than the back legs. Hyenas live in Africa and Asia and hunt other animals for food.
  hy·e·na (hī ē′nə) *noun, plural* **hyenas.**

hygiene Things that must be done to keep people and places healthy and clean. Washing yourself and brushing your teeth are part of your personal *hygiene.*
  hy·giene (hī′jēn) *noun.*

hymn A song of praise to God. ▲ Another word that sounds like this is **him.**
  hymn (him) *noun, plural* **hymns.**

hyphen A mark (-) used to connect two or more parts of a word or two or more words. The word "merry-go-round" has two *hyphens* in it.
  hy·phen (hī′fən) *noun, plural* **hyphens.**

hyphenate To put a hyphen or hyphens in a word. In the definition of *hygiene* on this page, the word *washing* is hyphenated.
  hy·phen·ate (hī′fə nāt′) *verb,* **hyphenated, hyphenating.**

hypnotize To put someone in a trance that is like sleep. Someone who has been hypnotized can hear what the person who has hypnotized him says, and does what he is told to do by that person.
  hyp·no·tize (hip′nə tīz′) *verb,* **hypnotized, hypnotizing.**

hysterical Caused by a very strong fear or sorrow. She burst into *hysterical* crying when she heard that her house had burned.
  hys·ter·i·cal (his ter′i kəl) *adjective.*

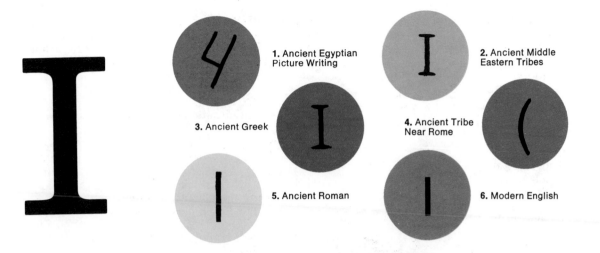

1. Ancient Egyptian Picture Writing
2. Ancient Middle Eastern Tribes
3. Ancient Greek
4. Ancient Tribe Near Rome
5. Ancient Roman
6. Modern English

I is the ninth letter of the alphabet. The oldest form of the letter I was a drawing that the ancient Egyptians (1) used in their picture writing nearly 5000 years ago. This drawing was borrowed by several ancient tribes (2) in the Middle East. They gave the letter its modern shape, writing it as a tall line with a short bar at the top and bottom. The ancient Greeks (3) borrowed this letter without changing its shape. The letter was then borrowed by an ancient tribe (4) that settled north of Rome about 2800 years ago. They changed its shape by not writing the short line at the top and bottom of the letter. The Romans (5) borrowed this form of I from them. Our modern capital letter I (6) looks very much like the ancient Greek letter.

i, I The ninth letter of the alphabet.
  i, I (ī) *noun, plural* **i's, I's.**

I *I* have a dog and a cat. ▲ Other words that sound like this are **aye** and **eye.**
  I (ī) *pronoun.*

ice **1.** Water that has been made solid by cold; frozen water. The fisherman cut a hole through the *ice* on the lake. **2.** A frozen dessert made with sweetened water and fruit flavours. It was such a hot day that I bought a strawberry *ice* to cool me off. *Noun.*
  —**1.** To become covered with ice. The lake *ices* over in the winter. **2.** To keep or make cold. We *iced* the lemonade before we drank it. **3.** To decorate with icing. *Verb.*
  ice (īs) *noun, plural* **ices;** *verb,* **iced, icing.**

iceberg A very large piece of floating ice. It comes from a glacier. The ship was damaged when it hit an *iceberg* in the stormy seas.
  ice·berg (īs′burg′) *noun, plural* **icebergs.**

icebox **1.** A box or chest cooled with blocks of ice. It is used for storing food and drinks. **2.** A refrigerator.
  ice·box (īs′boks′) *noun, plural* **iceboxes.**

icebreaker A ship that is built to cut through ice. Icebreakers clear the way for the first ships up the St. Lawrence River in the spring.
  ice·break·er (īs′brāk′ər) *noun, plural* **icebreakers.**

icecap A sheet of ice with a high centre. It covers an area of land and moves out from the centre in all directions as it becomes larger.
  ice·cap (īs′kap′) *noun, plural* **icecaps.**

ice cream A frozen dessert. It is made from milk products, sweeteners, and flavouring.

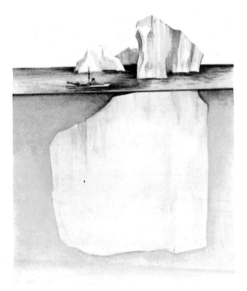

Iceberg

319

ice-skate To skate on ice.
  ice-skate (īs′skāt′) *verb*, **ice-skated, ice-skating.**

ice skate A boot with a metal blade on the bottom. It is used for ice-skating.

icicle A pointed, hanging piece of ice. It is formed by water that freezes as it drips.
  i·ci·cle (ī′si kəl) *noun, plural* **icicles.**

icing 1. A mixture of sugar, eggs, butter, and flavouring. Icing is used to cover or decorate cakes or other baked goods. 2. The shooting of the puck in hockey from one's own end into the other team's end. Unless one's team is serving a penalty at the time, icing the puck causes play to be stopped, and the puck is brought back to the end it was shot from for a face-off.
  ic·ing (ī′sing) *noun, plural* **icings.**

Icicles

icy 1. Made of or covered with ice. Lynn slipped on the *icy* sidewalk. 2. Very cold. When the *icy* winds blew, it grew cold in the house. 3. Cold and unfriendly. Jane gave me an *icy* stare the next time I saw her after our big argument.
  i·cy (ī′sē) *adjective*, **icier, iciest.**

I'd She asked if *I'd* borrowed her book. *I'd* think you would enjoy that movie.
  I'd (īd) contraction for "I had," "I would," and "I should."

idea 1. A thought, belief, or opinion formed in the mind. The author had an *idea* for a new novel. John has some very good *ideas* for the party decorations. 2. The purpose of something. The *idea* of the game of soccer is to score goals for your team.
  i·de·a (ī dē′ə) *noun, plural* **ideas.**

ideal A person or thing thought of as perfect. The famous hockey player was the *ideal* of many boys. *Noun.*
  —Being exactly what one would hope for; perfect. The breeze makes it an *ideal* day for going sailing. *Adjective.*
  i·de·al (ī dē′əl) *noun, plural* **ideals;** *adjective.*

identical 1. The very same. Her birthday is on the *identical* day as mine. 2. Exactly alike. The twins always wore *identical* clothes.
  i·den·ti·cal (ī den′ti kəl) *adjective.*

identification 1. The act of identifying. The woman's *identification* of the robber was needed before the police could arrest him. 2. Something used to prove who a person is. John's father carried his passport for *identification* when he travelled because it had his picture in it.
  i·den·ti·fi·ca·tion (ī den′tə fi kā′shən) *noun, plural* **identifications.**

identify 1. To show or prove that a person or thing is who or what you say it is. Mrs. Jones *identified* the robber by the scar on his face. 2. To think of or treat as the same. Randy is always *identified* with his twin brother Ralph because no one can tell them apart.
  i·den·ti·fy (ī den′tə fī′) *verb*, **identified, identifying.**

identity 1. What or who a person or thing is. His driver's licence gave his *identity* as Mr. Brown. The famous actress tried to hide her *identity* by wearing a wig. 2. The condition of being exactly the same. The *identity* of the twins made it hard for their friends to tell them apart.
  i·den·ti·ty (ī den′tə tē) *noun, plural* **identities.**

idiom A phrase or expression whose meaning cannot be understood from the ordinary meanings of the separate words in it. "To pull a person's leg" is an idiom that means "to trick or tease."
  id·i·om (id′ē əm) *noun, plural* **idioms.**

▲ Because **idioms** are a part of our everyday speaking and writing, we don't often think of the fact that they don't make sense according to the meanings of their separate words. It is only because we learn to speak our own language naturally as young children that the idioms in English don't seem strange or foolish to us. Try to imagine what a foreign boy learning English would think the first time he heard someone say, "I don't believe your story about the purple dragon; you're just pulling my leg!"

idiot 1. A person who has little ability to learn. 2. A very silly or foolish person. I was an *idiot* for not remembering that today was your birthday!
  id·i·ot (id′ē ət) *noun, plural* **idiots.**

idle 1. Not working or being used; not busy. The piano in our house is *idle* because two keys are broken and it can't be played. 2. Lazy. She is an *idle* person who never does her share of work around the house. 3. Having little worth or usefulness. Gossip is just *idle* talk. *Adjective.*

—**1.** To spend time doing nothing. He *idled* around the house all evening and did not do his homework. **2.** To run slowly and out of gear. When a machine *idles*, it does not produce any power. He left the car *idling* in the driveway while we went back into the house. **3.** To waste. He *idled* away the morning lying in bed. *Verb.* ▲ Another word that sounds like this is **idol.**
　i·dle (ī′dəl) *adjective,* **idler, idlest;** *verb,* **idled, idling.**

idol **1.** Something that is worshipped as a god. An idol is often a statue of a god. **2.** A person who is greatly loved or admired. Mrs. Sterling was an *idol* to many of her students. ▲ Another word that sounds like this is **idle.**
　i·dol (ī′dəl) *noun, plural* **idols.**

if *If* I hurt your feelings, I'm sorry. Even *if* it rains, the game will still be played. I will go *if* you do. I don't know *if* he will be there.
　if (if) *conjunction.*

igloo A dome-shaped hut used by Inuit to live in. It is usually built from blocks of hardened snow.
　ig·loo (ig′lōō) *noun, plural* **igloos.**

▲ **Igloo** comes from an Inuit word *iglu.* This word means "a place to live in." Since Inuit, years ago, did not have a written language like ours, our word *igloo* is the closest in sound that English speakers could come to the original Inuit word.

Igloo

igneous Produced with great heat or by a volcano. An *igneous* rock is formed when lava from a volcano hardens.
　ig·ne·ous (ig′nē əs) *adjective.*

ignite **1.** To burn or set on fire. We *ignited* the dead leaves with a match. **2.** To begin to burn; catch on fire. You must be careful with oily rags because they *ignite* easily.
　ig·nite (ig nīt′) *verb,* **ignited, igniting.**

ignition **1.** The act of igniting. The *ignition* of the rockets sent the spacecraft into orbit.

2. A system for starting a car, a boat, or some other vehicle. The ignition starts the fuel and air burning in the engine.
　ig·ni·tion (ig nish′ən) *noun, plural* **ignitions.**

ignorance A lack of knowledge; being ignorant. He hurt his leg skiing because of his *ignorance* of how to turn on the slopes.
　ig·no·rance (ig′nər əns) *noun.*

ignorant Having or showing a lack of education or knowledge. He made the *ignorant* remark that all people who have brown eyes are smart.
　ig·no·rant (ig′nər ənt) *adjective.*

ignore To pay no attention to. Ann was angry with Jerry, so she *ignored* him when he spoke to her.
　ig·nore (ig nōr′) *verb,* **ignored, ignoring.**

▲ The first meaning of **ignore** was "not to know." Long ago someone could have said, "The young maiden *ignored* (did not know) how to thank the knight for saving her." If a person refuses to look at or will not talk to another person, he pretends he does not know the other person is there. So *ignore* came to mean "to refuse to pay attention to."

---

iguana A large greenish-brown lizard. It is found in the very warm parts of North and South America. The iguana lives in trees.
　i·gua·na (i gwä′nə) *noun, plural* **iguanas.**

Iguana

ill **1.** Not healthy or well. He is absent from school because he is *ill* with a cold. **2.** Bad or evil. There is an old saying that says "An ill wind does no one any good." *Adjective.*
—Unkindly; badly. Don't speak *ill* of my friend Jacques because he really is a nice boy. *Adverb.*
—**1.** Trouble, evil, or misfortune. War is one of the *ills* of mankind. **2.** A sickness. Chicken

---

at; āpe; cär; end; mē; it; īce; hot; ōld;
wood; fōōl; oil; out; up; turn; sing;
thin; <u>th</u>is; hw in white; zh in treasure.
ə stands for a in about, e in taken,
i in pencil, o in lemon, and u in circus.

pox is a common *ill* among children. *Noun.*
ill (il) *adjective,* **worse, worst;** *adverb; noun, plural* **ills.**
ill at ease. Uncomfortable. The shy girl was *ill at ease* among strangers.

I'll *I'll* win the contest no matter what it takes. *I'll* go if you will. ▲ Other words that sound like this are **aisle** and **isle.**
I'll (īl) contraction for "I will" and "I shall."

illegal Not legal; against laws or rules. It is *illegal* to shoot off fireworks in that town. He made an *illegal* check in the hockey game and a penalty was called.
il·le·gal (i lē′gəl) *adjective.*

illiterate Not able to read or write; lacking education. The young boy was *illiterate* because he had never gone to school.
il·lit·er·ate (i lit′ər ət) *adjective.*

illness A sickness or disease. Many illnesses can be cured by taking the right medicine.
ill·ness (il′nəs) *noun, plural* **illnesses.**

illuminate To light up; give light to. A lamp *illuminated* one corner of the dark room.
il·lu·mi·nate (i loo′mə nāt′) *verb,* **illuminated, illuminating.**

illusion A false idea or belief; misleading idea. If you put a straw in a glass of water, you have the *illusion* that the part in the water is larger than the part out of the water, though they're really the same size. We were under the *illusion* that the party was on Friday and not Saturday.
il·lu·sion (i loo′zhən) *noun, plural* **illusions.**

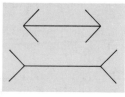
This **illusion** makes the bottom line seem longer.

illustrate **1.** To make clear or explain. The teacher *illustrated* how the human eye works by comparing it to a camera, which works in a similar way. **2.** To draw a picture or diagram to explain or decorate something written. The famous artist *illustrated* a book about tropical birds.
il·lus·trate (il′əs trāt′ *or* i lus′trāt′) *verb,* **illustrated, illustrating.**

illustration **1.** Something used to make clear or explain. The teacher showed us how to solve the arithmetic problem as an *illustration* of how to do other problems of the same kind. **2.** A picture or diagram used to explain or decorate something written. The *illustrations* in this dictionary help to explain words that have been defined.

il·lus·tra·tion (il′əs trā′shən) *noun, plural* **illustrations.**

ill will Unfriendly feeling. After the fight, the two boys felt *ill will* toward each other.

I'm *I'm* going to the zoo today.
I'm (īm) contraction for "I am."

im- A *prefix* that means "not." *Imperfect* means "not perfect." *Impractical* means "not practical."

image **1.** A picture, idea, or likeness of a person or thing. A penny has an *image* of Queen Elizabeth on one side of it. Christopher is the *image* of his father. **2.** A typical example; picture. That athlete is the *image* of good health.
im·age (im′əj) *noun, plural* **images.**

imaginary Existing only in the mind; unreal. Most people believe that ghosts are *imaginary.*
i·mag·i·nar·y (i maj′ə ner′ē) *adjective.*

imagination **1.** The forming of pictures in the mind of things that are not really there. She pictured her summer vacation over and over in her *imagination* because it had been such fun. **2.** The ability or power to create or form new images or ideas. It took great *imagination* to write such a clever story.
i·mag·i·na·tion (i maj′ə nā′shən) *noun, plural* **imaginations.**

imaginative **1.** Having a good imagination. The *imaginative* child made up stories to tell the younger children. **2.** Showing imagination. Bill wrote an *imaginative* story about a boy who could turn into anything he wanted to be.
i·mag·i·na·tive (i maj′ə nə tiv) *adjective.*

imagine **1.** To picture a person or thing in the mind. Nancy tried to *imagine* life on the moon. The ending of the book was different from what I had *imagined.* **2.** To suppose; guess. I don't *imagine* we will go on a picnic if it rains.
i·mag·ine (i maj′in) *verb,* **imagined, imagining.**

imitate **1.** To try to act or behave like another person does; copy. Joan *imitates* her older sister by dressing like her. Tony *imitated* the popular singer for his friends. **2.** To look like; resemble. The wooden floors were painted to *imitate* marble.
im·i·tate (im′ə tāt′) *verb,* **imitated, imitating.**

imitation **1.** The act of copying. Russ does a great *imitation* of his teacher's voice. **2.** Something that is a copy of something else. We bought an *imitation* of a famous painting to hang in the den. *Noun.*
—Made to look like something real; not real.

My sister bought an *imitation* diamond ring that was really made of glass. *Adjective.*

im·i·ta·tion (im′ə tā′shən) *noun, plural* **imitations;** *adjective.*

immature Not having reached full growth; not mature. *Immature* corn is not ready to pick and eat.

im·ma·ture (im′ə choor′ *or* im′ə toor′ *or* im′ə tyoor′) *adjective.*

immediate 1. Done or happening right away; without delay. When he asks his teacher a question, David gets an *immediate* answer. 2. Close in time or space; near. Paul's parents said they won't get him a dog in the *immediate* future, but he may get one when he is older. He has no *immediate* plans for after graduation.

im·me·di·ate (i mē′dē ət) *adjective.*

immediately Right away; now. If we leave *immediately,* we can get to the movie in time.

im·me·di·ate·ly (i mē′dē ət lē) *adverb.*

immense Of great size; very large; huge. The whale is an *immense* animal that can grow as long as twenty metres.

im·mense (i mens′) *adjective.*

immigrant A person who comes to live in a country in which he or she was not born. My grandfather was an *immigrant* to Canada from Italy.

im·mi·grant (im′ə grənt) *noun, plural* **immigrants.**

immigrate To go to live in a country in which one was not born. My grandparents *immigrated* to Canada from Poland.

im·mi·grate (im′ə grāt′) *verb,* **immigrated, immigrating.**

immoral Wicked; evil; not moral. Lying about his friend was an *immoral* thing to do.

im·mor·al (i môr′əl) *adjective.*

immortal Living, lasting, or remembered forever. The ancient Greeks believed that their gods were *immortal.*

im·mor·tal (i môrt′əl) *adjective.*

immune Protected from a disease. The doctor gave me a vaccination that made me *immune* to smallpox.

im·mune (i myo͞on′) *adjective.*

impact The action of one object striking against another. The *impact* of the car crashing into the pole smashed the front fender of the car.

im·pact (im′pakt) *noun, plural* **impacts.**

impair To weaken; lessen the quality or strength of. The heavy fog *impaired* the driver's vision.

im·pair (im per′) *verb,* **impaired, impairing.**

impala A small, slender African antelope. It has a reddish or golden-brown coat. The impala can leap great distances.

im·pal·a (im pal′ə) *noun, plural* **impalas.**

impartial Not favouring one more than others; fair; just. A judge must be *impartial.*

im·par·tial (im-pär′shəl) *adjective.*

impatience A not being able to put up with delay or opposition calmly

Impala

and without anger. Dad's *impatience* with George was caused by George's not keeping his room clean. Mother could sense the children's *impatience* for summer holidays.

im·pa·tience (im pā′shəns) *noun.*

impatient Not able to put up with delay or opposition calmly and without anger. Joan became *impatient* when people were late for her party.

im·pa·tient (im pā′shənt) *adjective.*

impeach To bring formal charges of wrong conduct against a public official. The judge was *impeached* for taking a bribe from the criminal.

im·peach (im pēch′) *verb,* **impeached, impeaching.**

imperial 1. Having to do with an empire or an emperor or empress. The *imperial* palace was the home of the emperor of the country. 2. Having to do with one country's control over another or others. Canada started out as a colony under the *imperial* rule of Britain.

im·pe·ri·al (im pēr′ē əl) *adjective.*

Imperial System of Measure A system of measurement used in Britain. It uses the yard for length, the pound for weight, and the gallon for volume. It was used in Canada until the metric system was adopted.

impersonate To copy the appearance and actions of. The man was arrested for *imper-*

---

at; āpe; cär; end; mē; it; īce; hot; ōld;
wood; fo͞ol; oil; out; up; turn; sing;
thin; <u>th</u>is; hw in white; zh in treasure.
ə stands for a in about, e in taken,
i in pencil, o in lemon, and u in circus.

steep *inclination* of the hill makes it great for sledding.

in·cli·na·tion (in′klə nā′shən) *noun, plural* **inclinations.**

incline To slope or slant. The road is hard to walk on because it *inclines* upward. *Verb.*
—A surface that slopes. The ball rolled down the *incline* to the bottom of the hill. *Noun.*

in·cline (in klīn′ *for verb;* in′klīn′ *or* in klīn′ *for noun*) *verb,* **inclined, inclining;** *noun, plural* **inclines.**

Incline

include **1.** To have as part of the whole; contain. You don't have to buy batteries with that toy because they are already *included* in the box. **2.** To put in a group. Besides his own friends, he *included* some of his sister's friends in the list of people he would invite to the party.

in·clude (in klo͞od′) *verb,* **included, including.**

income Money received for work or from property or other things that are owned.

in·come (in′kum′) *noun, plural* **incomes.**

income tax A tax on a person's income.

incomplete Not complete; not finished. The boy's picture was *incomplete* because he ran out of paint.

in·com·plete (in′kəm plēt′) *adjective.*

incorporate To include something as part of something else. Let's *incorporate* her idea into our plan for the camping trip.

in·cor·po·rate (in kôr′pə rāt′) *verb,* **incorporated, incorporating.**

incorrect Not right or correct; not proper. You must do this problem in arithmetic over because your answer is *incorrect.*

in·cor·rect (in′kə rekt′) *adjective.*

increase To make or become greater in number or size. The library has *increased* its collection of mystery books. The number of students trying out for the band has *increased* this year. *Verb.*
—The amount by which something is increased. He got an *increase* of fifty cents in his allowance. *Noun.*

in·crease (in krēs′ *for verb;* in′krēs′ *for noun*) *verb,* **increased, increasing;** *noun, plural* **increases.**

increasingly More and more. As the day wore on it became *increasingly* hotter.

in·creas·ing·ly (in krēs′ing lē) *adverb.*

incredible Hard or impossible to believe. Do you think Bob's *incredible* story of helping to stop a bank robbery is true?

in·cred·i·ble (in kred′ə bəl) *adjective.*

incredulous Not able to believe something. Many people were *incredulous* when the men said they had found gold in the mountains.

in·cred·u·lous (in krej′ə ləs) *adjective.*

incubate To sit on eggs and keep them warm for hatching. A hen *incubates* her eggs.

in·cu·bate (ing′kyə bāt′) *verb,* **incubated, incubating.**

incubator A heated container. Some incubators are used for babies who are born too early. Others are used to hatch eggs.

in·cu·ba·tor (ing′kyə bā′tər) *noun, plural* **incubators.**

indeed Really; truly. He was *indeed* grateful to her for helping him.

in·deed (in dēd′) *adverb.*

indefinite **1.** Not clear, set, or exact; vague. His plans for the summer are still *indefinite.* **2.** Having no limits; not fixed. Jack will be away for an *indefinite* number of days.

in·def·i·nite (in def′ə nit) *adjective.*

indefinite article The indefinite article is *a* or *an*. *A* or *an* is used to show that the noun before which it comes is not a particular person or thing. *A* boy ran across the street. Is there *an* apple in the box?

indent To start a written line farther in than the other lines. We always *indent* the first sentence of a paragraph.

in·dent (in dent′) *verb,* **indented, indenting.**

independence Freedom from the control of another or others. In 1867 Canada gained her *independence* from Britain.

in·de·pend·ence (in′di pen′dəns) *noun.*

independent Free from the control or rule of another or others; separate. The United States fought with Britain to become an *independent* country. Jane moved out of town because she wanted to be *independent* of her family. He does what he wants, *independent* of anyone's wishes.

in·de·pend·ent (in′dē pen′dənt) *adjective.*